FORENSIC EVIDENCE: SCIENCE AND THE CRIMINAL LAW

SECOND EDITION

FORENSIC EVIDENCE: SCIENCE AND THE CRIMINAL LAW

SECOND EDITION

Terrence F. Kiely

Taylor & Francis
Taylor & Francis Group

Boca Raton   London   New York

A CRC title, part of the Taylor & Francis imprint, a member of the
Taylor & Francis Group, the academic division of T&F Informa plc.

Published in 2006 by
CRC Press
Taylor & Francis Group
6000 Broken Sound Parkway NW, Suite 300
Boca Raton, FL 33487-2742

International Standard Book Number-10: 0-8493-2858-6 (Hardcover)
International Standard Book Number-13: 978-0-8493-2858-9 (Hardcover)
Library of Congress Card Number 2005050625

Library of Congress Cataloging-in-Publication Data

Kiely, Terrence F.
   Forensic evidence : science and the criminal law / Terrence F. Kiely.-- 2nd ed.
      p. cm.
   Includes index.
   ISBN 0-8493-2858-6
   1. Evidence, Expert--United States. 2. Forensic sciences--United States. I. Title.

KF8961.K54 2005
345.73'067--dc22
                                               2005050625

Dedication

This book is dedicated to the loving memory of my mother, Elizabeth Wolfe, and my step-father, John Wolfe.

Preface

In investigations of every kind it is essential that a correct estimate be made, of the kind and degree of assurance of which the subject admits.

In the subjects of moral science, the want of appropriate words, and the occasional application of the same word to denote different things, have given occasion to much obscurity and confusion both of idea and expression; of which a remarkable exemplification is presented in the words probability and certainty.

William Wills: An Essay on the Principles
of Circumstantial Evidence (1838)

Forensic Evidence: Science and the Criminal Law (Second Edition), is intended to serve as an introduction and guide to the appreciation and understanding of the significant historic, contemporary, and future relationship between the world of the forensic sciences and the criminal justice system. This book is not intended to be a close study of forensic science, nor was it ever conceived as becoming one. It is devoted to a study of *the judicial response to uses of forensic science* in the investigation, prosecution, and defense of a crime. The audience to which this study is directed are those intimately or potentially involved in that relationship: police, forensic scientists, prosecutors, defense lawyers, and professors and students of the criminal law. It is meant to stand on its own but also to complement the growing number of excellent treatises and studies in the forensic sciences proper, many of which are published in the CRC Press series in the area of forensic sciences.

The book will focus on those cases questioning the legal acceptability under a *Frye* or *Daubert* standard of the methodological basis of the forensic science at issue. However, equally, if not more important, will be the discussions of the numerous cases where the courts, assuming the acceptability of the underlying methodology, have scrutinized and accepted or rejected a wide variety of *investigative uses* of the science under discussion, offered as proof of one or more material facts in a criminal prosecution. This latter area of study is of equal, if not more central importance in understanding the place of forensic science in the criminal justice system of the 21st century.

It is time for another close look at both the body of claims and actual expert opinions supplied to the criminal justice system as we enter the first decade of the new century. The totally justified attention given rapid DNA developments should not overshadow the ongoing judicial acceptance and use of the more traditional body of forensic sciences such as hair, fiber, ballistics, or fingerprints, most of which have never been fully challenged. The contributions of forensic science to the criminal justice system have been, and remain, significant.

This book is divided into 12 chapters, most of which, with the exceptions of Chapters 1, Science, Forensic Science, and Evidence and Chapter 2, Science and the Criminal Law, address the legal profile of a specific forensic science.

Chapter 1, Science, Forensic Science, and Evidence, briefly analyses the historical and contemporary context in which legal arguments directed to the adequacy of the findings of forensic science are conducted. This is a necessary precursor to the more criminally focused discussion that constitutes the bulk of this volume. The framework of the *Frye* and *Daubert* standards for the introduction of scientific opinion will be discussed here as well as the significant differences that exist when the legal challenge comes in a civil as opposed to a criminal law forum.

Chapter 2, Science and the Criminal Law provides an overview of the entire subject of the uses of forensic sciences in the investigation, prosecution, and defense of criminal cases in American courts. Central topics addressed there are the historical and contemporary relationship between forensic science and proof of crime, the fundamentals of the application of forensic science disciplines to the investigation and prosecution of a criminal case, the function of probabilistic to that process and an extended discussion of the legal aspects of the modern crime scene. A brief listing of those chapters follows:

Chapter 3, Hair Analysis, will discuss the court's response to both class and individual opinions as respects attempts to connect one or more hairs found at a crime scene to an individual suspect. This controversial subject will set the analytical framework for the discussions to follow on a wide range of forensic science applications.

Chapter 4, Fiber Analysis, will discuss the identification and use of a wide variety of fiber materials from crime scenes and the processes used to link any such materials to a suspect.

Chapter 5, Ballistics and Toolmarks, will address the subjects of firearms and projectile identification, the matching of bullets to a weapon, gunshot residue and toolmark identification and attempts to match crime scene striations to a tool associated with a suspect.

Chapter 6, Soil, Glass, and Paint, discusses the nature of soil and glass shard particle identification and the attempt to connect such materials with an individual suspect.

Chapter 7, Footwear and Tire Impressions, addresses the identification, photographing, and or casting of footwear and tire impressions found at a crime scene to those associated with a suspect.

Chapter 8, Fingerprints, discusses the subject of fingerprint identification procedures and the recent Automated Fingerprint Identification System (AFIS).

Chapter 9, Blood Spatter Analysis, analyses cases involving the subject of presumptive testing for blood products as well as the subject of blood stain pattern analysis and its importance in many key aspects of crime scene reconstruction efforts.

Chapter 10, DNA Analysis, will analyze the court's scientific conditions for the acceptance of identification testimony arising from RFLP, PCR, STR DNA and mitochondrial (MtDNA) analyses, in addition to the small but growing number of cases and articles addressing nonhuman DNA testing, in particular, dog, cat, and plant DNA testimony.

Chapter 11, Forensic Anthropology and Entomology will briefly examine those decisions that utilize the methodologies and findings of these fields as aides to the investigation and identification of human remains and providing time of death estimates.

Chapter 12, Epilogue, will provide a brief summary note on the subjects not covered in this book and the major points sought to be made in the entire work.

The Author

Terrence F. Kiely is a professor of law and the director of the DePaul University College of Law's Center for Law and Science.

Professor Kiely graduated from Loyola University in Chicago (B.S., humanities) in 1964, DePaul University College of Law (Juris Doctor) in 1967 and also received an LL.M (foreign and comparative law) from New York University School of Law in 1970. Professor Kiely is an expert in the area of the interaction between science and the civil and criminal law. He is the author of five previous books:

Preparing Products Liability Cases (John Wiley & Sons, 1987)
Using Litigation Databases (John Wiley & Sons, 1989)
Modern Tort Litigation (John Wiley & Sons, 1990)
Forensic Evidence: Science and the Criminal Law (CRC Press, 2001)
Science and Litigation: Products Liability in Theory and Practice (CRC Press, 2002)

Professor Kiely has been a full time member of the DePaul University College of Law faculty since 1972. He teaches in the areas of torts, products liability, criminal law, evidence and forensic evidence. During the academic years 1995–1996 he was the Robert A. Clifford Professor of Tort Law and Public Policy. His work with the Center for Law and Science involves the maintenance of a comprehensive law and science Web site and organizing and participating in forensic science and evidence seminars at the College of Law.

Contents

Science and the Criminal Law

1

We have also houses of deceits of the senses, where we represent all manner of feats of juggling, false apparitions, impostures and illusions, and their fallacies. And surely you will easily believe that we, that have so many things truly natural which induce admiration, could in a world of particulars deceive the senses if we would disguise those things, and labor to make them more miraculous. But we do hate all impostures and lies, insomuch as we have severely forbidden it to all our fellows, under pain of ignominy and fines, that they do not show any natural work or thing adorned or swelling, but only pure as it is, and without all affectation of strangeness.

Francis Bacon: The New Atlantis (1626)

I. Science and the Legal Process

The term science in the discussions that follow has little or no connection to the use and understanding of that term as it is uniformly thought of by the international scientific community. John Horgan, former editor of *Scientific American*, in his excellent book *The End of Science: Facing the Limits of Knowledge in the Twilight of the Scientific Age*,[1] sought out the world's leading philosophers of science — theoretical physicists, evolutionary biologists, mathematicians, astronomers, and chaos theorists — to get their perspectives on whether "science" was at a close, with nothing significant left to be discovered. This book is a superb survey of modern scientific thinking across a very wide variety of fields. The contemporary legal question regarding the adequacy of a scientific methodology to support an expert opinion is light years away from the type of scientific inquiry discussed by the scholars Horgan interviewed. Horgan notes the criticism by Nobel prize-winning chemist Professor Stanley Miller of scientific papers culled from other published papers where no hard-won finding has resulted from extensive laboratory work. Professor Miller referred to such works as "paper chemistry." In the hard-fought, science-based civil cases, such as the breast-implant actions or the polychlorinated biphenyl (PCB) and cancer litigation, we can borrow the idea and refer to the use of previously published articles, by extrapolation in such cases, to claim or deny causation as "paper science," a charge that may be made in part only about forensic science-based testimony in criminal cases.[2]

The attempts to formulate an overarching answer to the question of "What is science?" in the world of scientific endeavor and the American legal system are clearly distinct in overall goals, methodology, and practical applications. When the question is restricted to the area of law, the use of science in civil tort cases and in criminal prosecutions is also based on significantly different goals, methods, and practical effects. The issues of whether long-term exposure to phencyclidine (PCP) can cause cancer in a products liability lawsuit are quite different from the forensic issue of whether hair or fiber expert testimony can be used to link a defendant to a crime scene in a homicide prosecution. It is also important to understand the differences between civil and criminal cases with respect to the performance of laboratory work pursued to answer key factual issues in the cases. Forensic scientists in white lab coats are routinely involved in criminal prosecutions. Their work is used to shed light on the physical dynamics that created the crime scene, to add significant information linking a defendant to a crime scene, and to move toward the identification of the perpetrator. Forensic scientists are rarely involved in answering the essential scientific causation issues at the center of modern products liability litigation.

II. Forensic Science Questions

Examining a set of rhetorical questions that revolve around our core inquiry about the nature and value of forensic science can help to clarify the discussions that follow.

- What facts or assumptions or surmises can be obtained from the examination of one or more physical items gathered at a crime scene?
- What is the likely basis for such assumptions or projections, or guesses?

- What value can be assigned to any factual estimation in a criminal justice system where life and liberty and justice to a victim all play a part?
- What is the meaning of statements that report one or more fibers or hairs or footprints, are or are not consistent with, or not dissimilar or substantially similar to, another fiber, hair, or footprint?
- What is the basis for such statements and what value can be allocated to them if one set of exemplars was taken from a crime scene and the other exemplars belong to a suspected perpetrator?
- What are the implications of such statements in the context of long-held requirements that the elements of a crime must be proven beyond a reasonable doubt? How does circumstantial evidence fit into prosecutorial efforts designed to meet such a high bar of proof in a case partially supported by hair or fiber evidence?
- How dependent is the power of forensic evidence on the traditional observation by eyewitnesses?
- How much of forensic analysis and comparison testimony have to do with scientific theory or recognized scientific methodology?
- What science, if any, has been traditionally associated with hair, fiber, paint, or glass analysis; and how has that science changed as we enter the 21st century?
- Is forensic analysis, aside from microscopy, scientific because of the theoretical underpinnings of the discipline, or because of its use of microscopy and other processes that aid its essentially observational nature?
- What is the difference if the bulk of the forensic science analyses are simply a combination of experience and modern microscopy? What else, from a forensic scientist standpoint, can be said about fiber, hair, footprints, fingerprints, or ballistics and their examinations and the factual assumptions that result? Can more be found to give such disciplines as great or greater credibility than fingerprint impression, ballistics, tool marks, or deoxyribonucleic acid (DNA)?

The repetition of these recurring questions across the range of the forensic sciences discussed in this book indicates the great similarity of trace-evidence analysis, in both a class characteristic and especially in individualistic statements, that seeks to link a particular suspect to a crime scene. In hair analysis; footwear and tire impressions; glass, paint, and soil analyses; bite-mark impressions, and most other, forensic science settings, we seek to discover what general nonsuspect-related categories of information can be gleaned from the analysis of a datum, for example, fiber obtained at a crime scene.

These class statements begin the sketch of the person or persons who were present and are essential investigative links in the chain of circumstantial evidence pointing toward a particular suspect. The success of such efforts, of course, is directly related to the integrity of the crime-scene preservation. The sad results in the recent Jon Benet Ramsey murder investigation testify to that simple fact.

When speaking of law and science matters, there are two distinct areas of legal practice involved. On the civil side, science-related issues are typically involved in the area of product liability and its subset of chemical-based injuries, often referred to as "toxic torts." A wide range of business-related legal issues may involve scientific matters, from contracts, to patent infringement, to antitrust, and so on. On the criminal-law side, the science-based issues cover considerable ground, ranging from proof offerings in the areas of hair and fiber analyses; soil, glass, and paint identification; and a host of facts related to forensic pathology, toxicology, blood products, as well as the area of ballistics and tool marks. In these kinds of criminal cases, some science is accomplished to generate material facts, such as DNA identifications or bullet or shell-casing matching, in the case at hand. This use of science is different from civil, product-liability-type cases that are centered in issues of causation, where not only no science is performed for the immediate case, but where published scientific articles, usually not precisely descriptive of the science at issue, are used through extrapolation analyses.[3]

Forensic scientists "in white lab coats" are routinely involved in forensic evidence-focused criminal prosecutions. Their work is used to shed light on the physical dynamics that created the crime scene and to add significant linking information as to the identity of the perpetrator. They are rarely involved in answering the dispositive "scientific"-causation issues at the center of modern product-liability litigation, such as "Does migrating silicone from a ruptured breast implant cause autoimmune system damage?" These types of issues are the focus of recent and ongoing United States Supreme Court decisions that seek to finalize a "one-size-fits-all" definition of "science."[4]

Forensic evidence involves the efficacy of information that has been scientifically generated for a particular case, the validity of which is grounded in past experiences in similar cases as evidenced in the forensic literature. Forensic evidence is a much more-real scientific application to the case at hand. Tort cases, on the other hand, present a radically different situation. True "science" questions are rarely central issues even in the most complex tort products-liability cases. A clear cause-in-fact or causal-relation problem — seldom the central issue in these cases — the questions revolve almost exclusively around the issue of "science as business." Most product liability cases do not deal with "science" understood in the sense discussed in the world of international science, at least not in any sense of the term as research scientists understand it. More often the focus is on one of the ways a manufacturing corporation, utilizing complex but practical science to develop and market products, designs it, or often publishes communications with regard to the risks customers are exposed to by using such products.[5]

The historical hallmark of crime-scene investigation has always included close observation, well-paid attention, and the application of common sense and logic to solving the crime being observed. These characteristic actions were associated with crime scenes well before the current preoccupation of the courts and legal scholars with the precise relationship of law and science, especially in areas of tort causation in the civil law and the forensic sciences in the criminal law. The law brings little to the table with respect to developing acceptable scientific methodologies, theories, and opinions. What it has pursued, especially at the very end of 20th century, is to craft legal doctrine designed to ensure that proffered scientific explanations and opinions comport with the most credible scientific thinking about methods and conclusions based on such, in instances where expert opinion is offered in a civil or criminal case.

Recourse has always been to the scientific community involved for guidance. This guidance was viewed, however reluctantly, as an inevitable necessity in some form, from the earliest days of the common law. In Spencer Cowper's Trial,[6] held in England in 1699, the ongoing skirmish between courts and expert witnesses can be seen in the following exchange:

Dr. Crell: "Now, my lord, I will give you the opinion of several ancient authors."

Baron Hatsell: "Pray, doctor, tell us your own observations."

Dr. Crell: "My lord, it must be reading, as well as a man's own experience, that will make anyone a physician, for without the reading of books of that art, the art itself cannot be attained to. Besides, my lord, I conceive that in such a difficult case as this, we ought to have a great deference for the reports and opinions of learned men. Neither do I see why I should not quote the fathers of my profession in this case as well as you gentlemen of the long robe quote Coke upon Littleton in others."

Baron Hatsell's understandable reluctance to allow "testimony" of authors not subject to cross-examination notwithstanding, the common law's dependence on the world of science and its experts remains.

Modern criminal courts, post-Daubert, are feeling the increasing need to comply with defense demands to delve into the scientific bases of the whole body of the forensic sciences, not the least of which are the trace evidence staples of hair, fiber, soil, and finger and footwear impressions. What is coming to the surface in these recent challenges are basic observational disciplines aided by modern microscopy, without the existence of the minimal type of comparative statistical databases available in more science-based disciplines such as DNA typing and population predictability. The primarily observational base of a significant amount of forensic sciences' contribution to the criminal law may seem alarming, but close observation has always been the case. This reality does not detract from the increasingly modern scientific environment in which so much forensic work is achieved and its factual offerings input into modern criminal trials.[7]

III. Forensic Science and Circumstantial Evidence

Circumstantial evidence, specifically, the subjects — traditional modes of observation and examining forensic practices and probability analyses — are separate but intimately related aspects of historical and contemporary attempts at truth seeking and truth finding in the criminal trial process. Contemporary forensic-evidence conferences and the forensic literature exhibit considerable enthusiasm for the power and potential of twenty-first-century scientific advances for the investigation and solution of crimes, such as DNA research and developments in laser-based technology. It is often forgotten or overlooked, however, that the greater number of the traditionally employed forensic sciences are, in effect, based on and centered in close observation, aided by modern microscopy, and do not employ any additional statistics-based projections as to the potential accuracy of the laboratory "match."[8] The term forensic is a very old word, always cast in terms of the presentation of arguments in public forums.[9] In the face of ongoing criticism that forensic or rhetorical arguments merely taught methods for embellishing the truth, the rejoinder, from Plato's day, has, on the contrary, been that forensic argument is designed to "make the truth sound like the truth."[10]

An examination of American criminal cases from the earliest days of the republic reveals several interesting observations about expert assistance in establishing material facts in a prosecution for crime. Initially, it is of value to note just how few such cases there are that address the issue in any significant way. Additionally, it is clear — as in the numerous science-based patent cases — that courts were generally willing to listen, even gratefully, to qualified experts, but given the basic observational and logical foundation for forensic-based testimony, were generally much more skeptical and, at times, demanding.

The beginnings of the legal response to information, based on studied observation, logic, and common sense, are to be found in the late 18th century and the second half of the 19th century. The real history of forensic evidence and the criminal law does not begin with the increasingly impressive applications of science since the 1920s and 1930s. Until that modern period, there were a series of reported decisions employing what might be referred to as *forensic evidence before forensic science*. If the assumption is that forensic science is basically and historically centered in observation and if extrapolation is accurate, its history runs much deeper than currently considered.[11]

A long common-law history of attempts to solve crimes and successfully prosecute the offender goes back well into the 18th, 19th, and early 20th centuries. The early evidence treatises by Jeremy Bentham,[12] S. M. Phillipps,[13] William Wills,[14] Simon Greenleaf,[15] Alexander Burrill,[16] and John Henry Wigmore[17] are filled with analyses of crimes solved by close attention to the items of evidence left at a crime scene. Books relating the tales of murder most foul solved by close observation and common sense were extremely popular and remain so today.[18] This era of forensics before forensic science is not only interesting reading, but also demonstrates that a great amount of today's forensic science has as much in common with inferential, circumstantial evidence theory as it does with modern scientific theory. The proving power of the tug of circumstance lies in the fact that the discussion of forensics is had in the context of crime-scene items linked to the defendant in hand.

IV. Forensic Science, Forensic Evidence, and the Modern Crime Scene

The basic methodologies of the vast majority of the forensic sciences have received guarded acceptance in most state courts. Many, however, have never really been subjected to a close Frye or Daubert preliminary scrutiny. Until very recent years, forensic sciences, such as hair and fiber analysis, have simply been routinely accepted without objection.

A good recent example is the Indiana Supreme Court's 1997 opinion in *McGrew v. State*,[19] a rape case involving testimony "matching" a pubic hair found in the car where the victim was allegedly attacked and a pubic hair exemplar from the defendant. Prior to releasing the state's expert hair analyst, the court directed a telling series of questions to him:

COURT: (I)n regard to the examination. It is simply a physical, visual examination of the hair?

ANALYST: Yes, sir.

COURT: You simply say that one hair looks like another one or it doesn't look like another one?

ANALYST: I say it's sufficiently similar to have come from that person or it is dissimilar.

COURT: And if you say that it … (is) similar to come from that person … that doesn't mean that it comes from that person.

ANALYST: It just simply means that it could have come from that person.

COURT: And you do not know the statistical percentages of how many people would have similar hair?

ANALYST: There are no statistics. It's hard to say.[20]

Modern case reports are increasingly filled with lengthy discussions of forensic expertise.[21] Whether use of claims of incompetence of counsel or the trial court's failure to supply indigents with adequate funding to hire their own experts, courts are increasingly engaging in wide-ranging forensic science discussions. A striking fact about such recent cases is that in most states before the post-Daubert era, the bulk of the contemporary claims of scientific inadequacy were either not raised at all or given short shrift by the courts. Today, prosecutors, citing the years' long use by police of these sciences, argue for their unchallenged acceptance. Defense counsels are increasingly seeking to challenge the bases for forensic science, especially in the trace-evidence area. Admissions by the Federal Bureau of Investigation (FBI) of major mistakes in the area of fingerprint examination and recent major disagreements between traditional hair analysts and mitochondrial DNA (mtDNA) hair experts are indications of the change in the unchallenged nature of forensic science testimony. Nonetheless, recent examination of cases seems to indicate that a serious post-Daubert challenge to the scientific validity of the body of forensic sciences may be inadequate.[22]

V. Scientific Foundations and the Courts

In civil as well as criminal cases, the parties seek to prove or disprove a sufficiently strong connection between defendant's act or omission and the death or injury in suit. However, the "science" at issue in civil cases, often centered on questions of causation, normally consists of scientific peer-reviewed studies that may only be probative of any such connection by extrapolation. Can this pharmaceutical cause cancer or birth defects? Such testimony, often by the use of inferential statistical analyses of epidemiological studies, does not provide the individualizing expert testimony typically given by forensic scientists in criminal litigation. In the criminal case, the use of forensic science means that some form of laboratory work has been performed to resolve factual matters in the case itself.[23]

While there are repetitive areas of scientific focus in civil cases, such as chemistry and pharmaceuticals, or biological, mechanical, or electrical engineering, much less opportunity exists to discuss the general outlines of acceptable methodology. The forensic sciences, traditionally associated with the prosecution of crime, such as fiber comparisons, allow such broad methodological reviews and accordingly are required to varying degrees by criminal courts. Nonetheless, the legal concerns are basically the same. The evidence part of the concept of forensic evidence refers to a distinct set of procedures unique to the litigation process, separate and distinct from the processes of any particular forensic science that is the basis for the decision to admit or not to admit evidence.

It is important to recall the fundamentally different reasons for the introduction of scientifically generated information in the civil and criminal litigation systems. The use of the term litigation is important here because it is in the process of litigation that the issues discussed are brought out. Distinct from other contexts, the nature or acceptability of scientific methodologies or opinions is at the center of the inquiry, such as grant requests, patents, contractual disputes, or publication in a scientific, peer-reviewed publication.

Forensic information generated by one or more of the forensic sciences comes to the law in one or both of two forms of expert witness opinion. The first is referred to as a class characteristic statement that speaks generally to some aspect of the crime scene under examination. Testimony that the pubic hairs found on a rape-homicide victim came from a Caucasian male or that shell casings found at the scene came from a certain make and model of firearm are two typical examples of this type of statement. The second type of potential testimony generated by a forensic science is known as individual or matching statements, i.e., that serve to link some data found at the crime scene to a particular defendant. Testimony finding that court-ordered pubic hair exemplars obtained from the defendant is consistent in all respects to the hair located on the victim, or that fibers found on the victim's clothing are consistent with fibers from the defendant's jacket, will serve as examples.[24] This idea of class characteristic statements refers to the reality that many confident general conclusions about the dynamics of a crime scene may be made under the auspices of an individual forensic discipline.[25]

The context in which the science-based questions addressed in this book arise is in the proffer of expert testimony in civil or criminal cases, where one side, at a pretrial hearing or at trial, seeks to challenge the propriety of the other side's experts testifying at all, or more frequently, to challenge the reliability or general acceptability of the methodology used by the expert in forming an opinion. For example, a lawyer in a civil product liability case wants his expert to testify that long-term exposure to PCBs caused cancer in his client. The company lawyers have their own experts, who will deny the carcinogenic potential of PCBs. In a criminal prosecution for sexual assault and murder, the state wishes to present complex DNA, hair, and fiber testimony to place the defendant at the crime scene.[26]

According to tried and true evidence law theory, any such witness may be challenged on four basic grounds. First, the case may simply not call for expertise at all and the jury may decide the disputed fact without the need for lengthy (and often highly prejudicial) testimony. Second, a particular expert witness may be challenged on basic qualifications to give any opinion in the field at issue because of insufficient background in education or experience to have anything of value to offer on the fact at issue. Third, either the methodology utilized by the expert to support an opinion is not in fact scientifically sound, thereby not capable of supporting the proffered opinion, or the methodology is sufficiently scientifically sound to support an opinion, but this witness' opinion based on such method is not sufficiently derived from such scientific methodology.[27] The third and fourth process-based objections are the key objections at the center of the current state and federal controversy over the utilization of scientific opinion in America's courts.

VI. Science and the Courts

You cannot separate, for trial purposes, forensic evidence from the testimony of forensic experts. Based upon this reality, many legal issues result, not the least of which is a minimal understanding of the rules of criminal discovery and the overarching rules of evidence themselves, which control the entirety of the information flow in any trial, not just a trial for the prosecution of a criminal act. Many important dispositive questions arise from the necessary presence of forensic experts in criminal trials: What is science? Who qualifies as an expert? Who must pay for these experts? How does criminal discovery provide for the exchange of scientific information between the prosecution and defense?

The first question is "What are the appropriate standards of 'forensic' science that can support a proffer of fact that can be used to establish a material fact in a case?" It cannot be overlooked that the term forensic science implies the use of a scientific theory or methodology to generate facts in the investigation and prosecution of a crime. The Daubert question is a preliminary question as to whether it is a reliable and fair way to generate a material fact, let alone a particular fact that may be used in any particular prosecution.

State and federal courts in both civil and criminal cases are increasingly occupied with cases centered on the need for an encompassing and practice-oriented definition of science and scientific method as an essential precursor to the admissibility of opinions of experts based upon that science. In the past decade, the subject of the propriety and extent of expert testimony in civil and criminal cases has been attacked from both sides in an ongoing battle as to what is a legally acceptable scientific foundation for the proffering of expert opinion. The following section examines the key federal cases that set the current parameters for the introduction of science-based expert opinion in the nation's courts.

VII. *Frye v. United States*

The Frye test had its origin in *Frye v. United States*,[28] a short and citation-free 1923 United States Court of Appeals decision concerning the admissibility of evidence derived from a systolic blood-pressure deception test, a crude precursor to the polygraph machine. In Frye, the defendant was convicted of the crime of murder in the second degree. In the course of the trial, defense counsel proffered an expert to testify to the results of a "deception test" made upon the defendant. The test was characterized as a "systolic blood-pressure deception test." It was claimed that changes in blood pressure would be caused by changes in the emotions of the witness, and systolic blood-pressure rises were brought about by nervous impulses sent to the autonomic nervous system. Scientific experiments, the defendant asserted, confirmed that fear, rage, and pain routinely produced an elevation of systolic blood pressure, and that conscious deception or falsehood, concealment of facts, or guilt of crime, accompanied by fear of detection when the person is under examination, raised the systolic blood pressure in a curve, which corresponds exactly to the struggle going on in the subject's mind, between fear and attempted control of that fear, as the examination touches the vital points about which he was attempting to deceive the examiner.[29]

The proffer was objected to by the government, and the court sustained the objection. Counsel for defendant then offered to have the proffered witness conduct a test in the presence of the jury, which was also denied.

The defendant's counsel agreed that no cases directly in point had been found. The broad ground, however, upon which they based the case, was that the rule stated that the opinions of experts or skilled witnesses were routinely admissible in cases where the matter of inquiry is such that inexperienced persons were likely to be incapable of forming a correct judgment upon the matter, due to its subject being a matter of art or science with which they would be unfamiliar. When the question involved did not lie within the range of common experience or knowledge, but required special experience or knowledge, the opinions of witnesses skilled in that particular science, art, or trade to which the question related were admissible in evidence.[30]

Here, rather than questioning the expertise of defendant's expert, the government challenged the basic foundation for the methodology of any such machine. Thus the court was required to construct a rule that would assist it and future courts in determining the sufficient level of confidence that should be reposed in a scientific methodology supporting any proffered opinion based upon it. Such analysis was to be had as a precursor to the admissibility of an opinion based upon it.

The court, speaking through Judge Van Orsdel, noted that the issue of exactly when a scientific principle or discovery crosses the line between the experimental and demonstrable stages was difficult to define:

Somewhere in this twilight zone, the court continued, the evidential force of the principle must be recognized, and while courts will go a long way in admitting expert testimony deduced from a well-recognized scientific principle or discovery, the thing from which the deduction is made must be sufficiently established to have gained general acceptance in the particular field in which it belongs. We think the systolic blood-pressure deception test has not yet gained such standing and scientific recognition among physiological and psychological authorities as would justify the courts in admitting expert testimony deduced from the discovery, development, and experiments thus far made.[31]

Thus the court, realizing that legal doctrine had nothing to supplant the views of the scientists, took the position that if the methodology at issue was generally accepted by the relevant scientific community that would be acceptable to the law.

The general acceptability rule was thus born and continued to be the rule for the next 70 years, until the decision by the United States Supreme Court in the famous case of *Daubert v. Merrell Dow Pharmaceuticals*,[32] in 1993. The period of 1923 to1993 saw the gradual development and eventual explosion of product liability law in the 1960s and 1970s.

The major work of the nation's courts in the products field was the creation and refinement of the mass of principles involved in forming the law of strict liability for products.[33] It was not until 1993, when defendant Merrell Dow Pharmaceuticals challenged the methodology of plaintiff's expert in determining that the body of epidemiological studies established, according to his unique methodology, that the ingestion of the drug Bendectin was the cause of fetal malformations, that the sea change occurred.

VIII. *Daubert v. Merrell Dow Pharmaceuticals*

In the Daubert decision, petitioners were minor children born with serious birth defects, alleged to have been caused by their mothers' ingestion of Bendectin, a prescription antinausea drug marketed by defendant Merrell Dow Pharmaceuticals. The plaintiffs in Daubert were children and their parents who claimed the children's birth defects were caused by their mothers' ingestion of Bendectin, a drug prescribed to combat nausea during pregnancy.

Merrell Dow, the marketer of Bendectin, moved for summary judgment, supporting its motion with the affidavit of an expert who stated that no published study of patients had found Bendectin to cause malformations in fetuses. The plaintiffs responded with the testimony of eight experts who concluded that Bendectin can cause birth defects, basing their conclusions upon animal-cell and live-animal studies, pharmacological studies, and reanalyses of previously published epidemiological studies.[34] After considerable discovery, Merrell Dow moved for summary judgment, contending that Bendectin does not cause birth defects in humans and that petitioners would be unable to come forward with any admissible evidence that it did. In support of its motion, Dow filed the affidavit of Dr. Steven H. Lamm, a physician and epidemiologist, who was an experienced and solidly supported expert on the risks from exposure to various chemical substances. Lamm said that he had reviewed all 30 published studies on both Bendectin and human birth defects, involving more than 130,000 patients, and stated that none had found Bendectin to be a substance capable of causing malformed fetuses. Doctor Lamm concluded that maternal use of Bendectin during the first trimester of pregnancy had not been proven to be a risk factor for human birth defects.[35]

Plaintiffs did not contest this portrayal of the birth defect literature, but countered with the testimony of eight experts of their own, each of whom concluded that Bendectin can cause birth defects. Their conclusions were based upon in vitro (test tube) and in vivo (live) animal studies that found a link between Bendectin and malformations; pharmacological studies of the chemical structure of Bendectin that purported to show similarities between the structure of the drug and that of other substances known to cause birth defects; and the "reanalysis" of previously published epidemiological (human statistical) studies.[36]

The district court granted respondent's motion for summary judgment, where, citing Frye, the court stated that scientific evidence was admissible only if the principle upon which it is based was sufficiently established to have general acceptance in the field to which it belonged, concluding that petitioners' evidence did not meet this standard. The court held expert opinion that was not based on epidemiological evidence was not admissible to establish causation.[37] The animal-cell studies, live-animal studies, and chemical-structure analyses on which petitioners had relied could not, alone, establish a reasonably disputable jury issue regarding causation. Petitioners' epidemiological analyses, based as they were on recalculations of data in previously published studies that had found no causal link between the drug and birth defects, were ruled to be inadmissible because they had not been published or subjected to peer review.[38]

The United States Court of Appeals for the Ninth Circuit affirmed,[39] holding that expert opinion based on a scientific technique was unacceptable unless the technique was "generally accepted" as reliable in the relevant scientific community. The court held that expert opinion based on a methodology that significantly deviated from the procedures accepted by recognized authorities in the field could not be established to be generally accepted as a reliable technique.[40]

The court stressed that other courts of appeals that had addressed the alleged dangers of Bendectin had declined to accept reanalyses of epidemiological studies that had not been published nor subjected to peer review.[41] Those courts had indeed adjudged unpublished reanalyses exceptionally problematic in light of the great import of the original published studies supporting Merrell Dow's, all of which studies had been subject to close review by the scientific community.

The United States Supreme Court, speaking through Justice Blackmun, noted that in the 70 years since its formulation in the Frye case, the "general acceptance" test has been the dominant standard for determining the admissibility of novel scientific evidence at trial, and that, while under increasing criticism, nonetheless continued to be followed by a majority of courts,[42] including the Ninth Circuit. Justice Blackmun observed that the merits of the Frye test had been much debated, and that the scholarship on its proper scope had continued to grow at an ever increasing pace.[43] Here the court agreed with Merrell Dow that the proper focus of such discussions should henceforth be the provisions of the Federal Rules of Evidence, not the 70-year-old Frye decision. The court was required to interpret the legislatively enacted Federal Rules of Evidence as they would any statute, and that Rule 401 and 402 provided the baseline theory.[44] These two rules of relevancy were to be used in these cases in conjunction with Rule 702, setting forth the basic principle regarding the admissibility of expert testimony.[45]

The court observed that nothing in the language of Rule 702 or the Rules as a whole ingrain general acceptance as an absolute prerequisite to admissibility and, indeed, would be at odds with the liberal thrust of the Federal Rules of Evidence.

Having concluded that the Frye test was replaced by the Rules of Evidence, however, did not mean that there were no checks on the admissibility of purportedly scientific evidence, and a trial judge was not disabled from screening such evidence. Under the Federal Rules of Evidence, the trial judge was required to warrant that any and all scientific testimony or evidence admitted was not only relevant, but reliable.[46] The primary locus for this obligation was Federal Rule of Evidence 702.

When presented an offer of expert scientific testimony, a trial judge must determine at the outset whether the expert was proposing to testify to scientific knowledge that would assist the trier of fact to understand or determine a fact in issue. If so, a preliminary assessment was required of whether the reasoning or methodology underlying the testimony was scientifically valid and of whether that reasoning or methodology properly could be applied to the facts at issue.[47]

Several observations can help clarify with respect to the ruling in Daubert. A summary of the requirements for the admissibility of scientific expert witness opinion under Frye and Daubert is included here. Under either decision, and regardless of what facts or factors are agreed to in a particular case, courts could examine only a limited number of questions:

1. Are there any published peer-reviewed books or articles?
2. Is this methodology taught in universities or discussed in professional scientific meetings or colloquia?
3. Can this methodology be tested for accuracy? Does it have a known error rate?
4. Is this methodology generally accepted in the relevant scientific community where similar concepts are studied and used?

No other significant questions can be asked and the same questions are basically asked under either Frye or Daubert. In Daubert, in rejecting the Frye rule, the court essentially wrapped the above balancing criterion in a Federal Rules of Evidence package, with a stated preference to treat general acceptability as only one, but not the essential, factor to receive attention. Hence the relevant and reliable standard of Daubert, rather than the general acceptability rule of Frye, is functionally the same as far as its implementation is concerned. The Daubert relevancy standard simply means that the scientific information that a party seeks to introduce into evidence has the ability to make some fact that is of consequence to the action more probable or less probable than it would be without it.[48]

The Daubert decision has yet to be formally accepted by all state courts, many of which adhere to a Frye standard. However, the greatest number of states has accepted Daubert's more liberal, open analysis approach, making the real differences between the two models increasingly difficult to see. The Daubert case prompted another four years of decisions applying what was perceived as its requirements in an extensive variety of scientific methodologies.[49] The important question of the extent to which the Daubert gatekeeper could make a pretrial judgment about the opinion of an expert, arguably based on relevant and reliable methods, was not addressed in Daubert.

This important point was resolved in the affirmative in the 1997 decision of the U.S. Supreme Court in the case of *General Electric v. Joiner*,[50] involving the question of whether long-term exposure to PCBs could cause cancer. The case also provides an extended discussion of the Daubert criterion, especially with regard to the importance of the presence or absence of peer-reviewed scientific articles on the questioned methodology.

This section and others present a series of key product-liability decisions of the past decade. All such cases involve common-law actions for damages grounded in products liability theory. Otherwise, Daubert applies with full force to the numerous and extremely important science decisions made by federal regulatory agencies in the enforcement mission.[51]

IX. *General Electric v. Joiner*

Robert Joiner began work as an electrician in the Water and Light Department of Thomasville, Georgia (City) in 1973. Joiner's job required him to work with and around the City's electrical transformers, which used a mineral-based dielectric fluid as a coolant. Joiner often had to stick his hands and arms into the fluid to make repairs and the fluid would sometimes splash onto him, occasionally getting into his eyes and mouth. In 1983 the City discovered that the fluid in some of the transformers was contaminated with PCBs. PCBs are widely considered to be hazardous to human health. Congress, with limited exceptions, banned the production and sale of PCBs in 1978.[52]

Joiner's theory of liability was that his exposure to PCBs and their derivatives "promoted" the cultivation of his lung cancer. In support of that theory, he proffered the deposition testimony of a number of expert witnesses. Defendants argued that Joiner's experts' testimonies regarding causation were nothing more than unscientific speculation, stressing the absence of any peer-reviewed epidemiological studies and that their testimony was based exclusively on disconnected studies of laboratory animals. The trial court agreed with petitioners that the animal studies did not support Joiner's position that exposure to PCBs had caused or significantly contributed to his cancer. The trial court also ruled that the four epidemiological studies on which Joiner's experts had relied were not a sufficient basis for their opinions on causation.[53]

In an important concurring opinion, Justice Breyer addressed the perceived problem of the difficulty of the district court gatekeepers getting high-level, objective, expert support for its pretrial function in these cases. He noted that the trial judges would sometimes be required to make subtle and sophisticated determinations about scientific methodology and its relation to the conclusions an expert witness sought to offer.[54] This would be particularly so in cases where the involved area of science was tentative or uncertain, or where epidemiological or laboratory testing was offered to prove individual causation. Amici had reminded the court of the dangers existent due to judge's lack of scientific expertise and lack of opportunities for meaningful training.[55] Justice Breyer was particularly impressed with the amici brief filed by *The New England Journal of Medicine* and its editor-in-chief, Marcia Angell, M.D., in which the *Journal* writes: (A) judge could better fulfill this gatekeeper function if he or she had help from scientists. Judges should be strongly encouraged to make greater use of their inherent authority ... to appoint experts .... Reputable experts could be recommended to courts by established scientific organizations, such as the National Academy of Sciences or the American Association for the Advancement of Science.[56] Justice Breyer concluded by stating his view that given this kind of offer of cooperative effort, from the scientific to the legal community, and given the various Rules-authorized methods for facilitating the court's task, Daubert's gatekeeping function would not prove overly arduous to achieve.[57]

The Joiner decision thus expands the prerogative of the trial court gate-keeper to include rejecting an expert's opinion, although admittedly based on acceptable or reliable methodology, if the court is of the view that such opinion was not rationale supported by such methodology.[58]

The most recent major Supreme Court decision in the Frye-Daubert line, decided on March 23, 1999, is *Kumho Tire v. Carmichael*,[59] addressing the important question of whether the Daubert guidelines apply to all expert witnesses or exclude experts in applied technology or other forms of expe-rience-based expertise, thus depriving corporate defendants of pretrial opportunity to challenge expert witnesses.

X. *Kumho Tire v. Carmichael*

This case arose from the explosion of a minivan tire resulting in death and injuries. Plaintiff expert Carlson concluded that the tire at issue was defective in design, which defect led to the fatal explosion. Carlson's conclusion was based upon a number of factors, including his personal examination of the tire carcass. Carlson concluded that the tire did not bear at least two of the four "overdeflection symptoms," nor was there any less obvious cause of separation; and because neither overdeflection nor the punctures caused the blowout, he surmised that either a manufacturing or design defect caused the separation.[60]

Defendant Kumho Tire moved the district court to bar Carlson's testi-mony on the basis that his methodology for defect analysis was not reliable under a Daubert standard. Justice Breyer, speaking for the court, held that the primary issue here was whether the gatekeeping obligation imposed on federal trial courts applied only to scientific testimony or to expert testimony of all types, cutting edge or familiar. Justice Breyer and the court ruled that the Daubert factors analysis was available to test all manner and forms of expert testimony, not just opinions arising out of cutting-edge science. The court stated that it would prove difficult, if not impossible, for judges to administer evidentiary rules under which a gatekeeping obligation depended upon a distinction between "scientific" knowledge and "technical" or "other specialized" knowledge. There is no bright line that divides the one discipline from another. Engineering rested solidly on scientific knowledge, and so-called pure scientific theory itself often hinged for its emergence and evolution upon observation and properly engineered machinery. The court observed that conceptual efforts to distinguish the two were unlikely to produce clear legal lines capable of application in any particular case.[61]

In addition, Justice Breyer continued, there was no perceived need to carve out any such demarcations between science and engineering: Neither is there a convincing need to make such distinctions:

Experts of all kinds tie observations to conclusions through the use of what Judge Learned Hand called "general truths derived from … specialized experience." (Citations omitted.) And whether the specific expert testimony focuses upon specialized observations, the specialized translation of those observations into theory, a specialized theory itself, or the application of such a theory in a particular case, the expert's testimony often will rest "upon an experience confessedly foreign in kind to (the jury's) own." … The trial judge's effort to assure that the specialized testimony is reliable and relevant can help the jury evaluate that foreign experience, whether the testimony reflects scientific, technical, or other specialized knowledge.[62]

The court answered in the affirmative when asked by the petitioners if trial courts may consider the several specific reliability factors that Daubert said could bear on a gatekeeping determination:

The petitioners asked specifically whether a trial judge determining the admissibility of an engineering expert's testimony may consider several more specific factors that Daubert said might "bear on" a judge's gatekeeping determination. Those factors include: (1) whether a theory or technique can be (and has been) tested; (2) whether it has been subjected to peer review and publication; (3) whether, in respect to a particular technique, there is a high known or potential rate of error, and whether there are standards controlling the technique's operation; and (4) whether the theory or technique enjoys general acceptance within a relevant scientific community.[63]

The court, after emphasizing the elastic nature of the Daubert Rule 702 criterion, observed that those factors did not all necessarily apply in a particular case and that one or more could serve as the deciding factor or factors in a particular instance.

The court concluded that expert Carlson's testimony here was not reliable under the Daubert criteria, and would be barred. There was no indication in the record that other experts in the industry used Carlson's two-factor test or that tire experts such as he generally made the fragile distinctions about the symmetry of shoulder tread wear that were necessary, if based upon Carlson's own theory, to support his conclusions. The court also emphasized that there was an absence of any peer-reviewed articles or papers that confirmed the reliability of Carlson's method.[64] Indeed, Justice Breyer continued, no one had argued that Carlson himself, were he still working for Michelin, would have concluded in a report to his employer that a similar tire was similarly defective on grounds identical to those upon which he rested his conclusion here.

In sum, the court concluded, Rule 702 grants the district judge the discretionary authority, reviewable for its abuse, to determine reliability in light of the particular facts and circumstances of the particular case.

XI. *People v. Sutherland*: A Case Study

Before investigating the individual forensic sciences and how they have been responded to by prosecutors, defense counsel and the courts, consider a complex case study arising from the rape and murder of a 10-year-old child in a rural Illinois community. It demonstrates the complexity of a modern crime-scene investigation in a case involving kidnapping, sexual assault, and homicide. The Sutherland case is essentially a circumstantial evidence case, that is, one without any direct evidence of the defendant's participation in the crime. The case study is appropriate to our discussion here because virtually all the facts pointing toward defendant's guilt was generated by expert testimony based on several of the traditional forensic sciences. This case study is an excellent, current example of the process of using forensic sciences to generate forensic evidence for use at trial. It sets the stage for the detailed analyses of the various forensic sciences in later chapters. The forensic sciences at the center of the state's proof here are hair analysis, mitochondrial DNA (Mt DNA) hair analysis, fiber analysis, footwear impressions, and tire-tread impressions. Nuclear DNA evidence was not tested given the fact that at the time of the murder, which occurred in 1987, DNA testimony was not used in Illinois courts. There were no witnesses to this horrible crime and the sole evidence linking the defendant Cecil Sutherland to it was the testimony of a small number of forensic scientists. The defendant's conviction was affirmed by the Illinois Supreme Court in 1993. In 2000, the same court granted the defendant a new trial, based on incompetency of counsel in his first trial, as the result of a new appeal by new counsel. The Sutherland case was scheduled for a retrial in downstate Illinois in April or May 2004, 17 years after the date of the murder of Amy Schultz.

In *People v. Sutherland*,[65] decided by the Illinois Supreme Court in 1993, the defendant had been convicted of aggravated kidnapping, aggravated criminal sexual assault, and murder. This conviction was based solely on circumstantial evidence, most of which was generated by forensic science. In 2001 the Illinois Supreme court reversed the conviction, based on a finding of incompetence of counsel.[66] The Sutherland cases are excellent examples of the interaction of forensic science with the preexisting and overriding body of considerations that constitute the legal process.

An oil field worker discovered the nude body of 10-year-old Amy Schultz. Her clothes — her shirt, shorts, underpants, shoes, and socks — were found strewn along the oil lease road. Due to the lack of any eyewitnesses, the trial was centered on the presentation of forensic evidence in the areas of forensic pathology, hair and fiber analysis, and tire-tread casting impression comparisons. The Sutherland case study is a clear example of the ongoing interrelationship between the world of forensic science and the investigation and proof of crime. Significant questions about justice are at the heart of prosecutions, such as Sutherland, that are grounded in facts generated by one or more of the forensic sciences discussed in this book.

The Sutherland Case Facts

At 9 a.m. on July 2, 1987, an oil field worker discovered the nude body of 10-year-old Amy Schultz of Kell, Illinois. The body was found lying on its stomach covered with dirt approximately 100 feet from an oil lease access road in rural Jefferson County. There were shoeprints on her back and several hairs were found stuck in her rectal area. In addition, a large open wound on the right side of Amy's neck exposed her spinal cord area. A pool of blood around Amy's head indicated that the murderer had killed her where she lay.[67]

Amy Schultz's shirt, shorts, underpants, shoes, and socks were found scattered along the oil lease road. Seventeen feet from the body, automobile tire impressions were found, and near the tire impressions, a shoeprint impression similar in design to that on the body was found. The police took casts of the tire and shoeprint impressions.

Dr. Steven Neurenberger performed an autopsy on July 3, 1987, wherein he observed a 14.5 centimeter wound, running from the middle of Amy's throat to behind her right ear lobe, which cut through the neck muscles, severing the carotid artery and jugular vein, and cutting into the cartilage between the neck and vertebrae. Amy's right eye was hemorrhaged and there was a small abrasion near her left eyebrow; her ear was torn off the skin at the base of the ear and both her lips were lacerated from being compressed against the underlying teeth; there were also linear abrasions to the outer lips of the vagina which demonstrated that force had been applied to the back, forcing the vagina against the ground.

His search for internal injuries found three hemorrhages inside the skull, a fractured rib, a torn liver and tearing of the rectal mucosa. Amy's vocal cords were hemorrhaged and her esophagus was bruised. Dr. Neurenberger deduced from these injuries that the killer had strangled Amy to unconsciousness or death, anally penetrated her, slit her throat, and stepped on her body to force exsanguination. Dr. Neurenberger placed the time of death between 9:30 and 11 p.m. on July 1, 1987, based on the contents of her stomach.[68]

The Prosecution's Forensic Evidence: The Tire Tracks

Several months after the discovery of Amy's body, the police at Glacier National Park in Montana, notified Illinois authorities about Sutherland's abandoned car, a 1977 Plymouth Fury. At the time of the murder, Sutherland had been living in Dix, Illinois, in Jefferson County, on the county line between Dix and Kell. Illinois police authorities ascertained that defendant's car had a Cooper "Falls Persuader" tire on the right front wheel. Deputies and David Brundage, a criminalist, then traveled to Montana where they made an ink impression of the right front wheel of Sutherland's car. Illinois State Police Forensic Scientist David Brundage evaluated the plaster casts of the tire print impressions made at the scene of the crime and testified that the tire impressions left at the scene were consistent in all class characteristics with only two models of tires manufactured in North America, the Cooper "Falls Persuader," and the Cooper "Dean Polaris."[69] After comparing the plaster casts of the tire impression at the scene with the inked impression of the tire from Sutherland's car, Brundage concluded that the tire impression at the scene corresponded with Sutherland's tire and could have been made by that tire. Brundage, however, was unable to exclude all other tires as having made the impressions due to the lack of comparative individual characteristics, such as nicks, cuts, or gouges.[70]

Mark Thomas, the manager of mold operations at the Cooper Tire Company, determined "mal" wear similarity, and hence Sutherland's tire could have made the impression found at the crime scene. Thomas also compared blueprints of Cooper tires with the plaster casts of the tire impressions and determined that the "probability" was "pretty great" that a size P2175/B15 tire — the same size as Sutherland's Falls Persuader tire — had made the impression preserved in the casts. He admitted that there were a great number of such tires on the roads of America.[71]

The Prosecution's Forensic Evidence: The Hair Evidence

Criminalist Kenneth Knight compared the two pubic hairs recovered from Amy Schulz's rectal area with Sutherland's pubic hair. He also made comparisons with pubic hairs from members of Amy's family as well as pubic hairs from 24 prior offenders, concluding that the pubic hairs found on Amy did not originate from her family or the 24 suspects, but "could have originated" from Sutherland.

Knight also examined 34 dog hairs found on Amy's clothing and concluded that the dog hairs were consistent with and could have originated from Sutherland's black Labrador, Babe. Knight also testified that the dog hairs on Amy's clothes were dissimilar from her family's three dogs, her grandparents' dog, and dogs of three neighbor families. Tina Sutherland, Sutherland's sister-in-law, testified that Sutherland usually carried Babe in his car, making it virtually impossible to be in the car without getting covered with dog hair. Multiple dog hairs found in Sutherland's car were found to be consistent with the hairs from Babe.[72]

The Prosecution's Forensic Evidence: The Fiber Evidence

Knight also examined Amy's clothing for foreign fibers, finding a total of 29 gold fibers in her socks, shoes, underwear, shorts, and shirt. Knight testified that all but one of the gold fibers found on Amy's clothes "could have originated" from defendant's auto carpet, but could not exclude all other auto carpets as possible sources. He also testified that the one remaining gold fiber found on Amy's clothes could have originated from defendant's car upholstery.

Knight also examined and compared 12 cotton fibers and 4 polyester fibers found on the front passenger-side floor of Sutherland's automobile with cotton and polyester fibers from Amy's shirt, concluding that the fibers from the car displayed the same size, shape, and color of the fibers from the shirt and thus could have originated from the shirt. He also compared three polyester fibers found on the front passenger seat and floor with fibers from Amy's shorts and found them consistent in diameter, color, shape, and optical properties and opined that the fibers from the car could have originated from the shorts.[73]

The forensic defense expert Richard Bibbing, agreed with the state's experts' conclusions on all the comparison evidence, except as to the cotton fibers found in defendant's car. He did not agree that the cotton fibers were consistent, due to what he determined were differences in size and color.[74]

Prior to an examination of the Illinois Supreme Court's analyses in the two decisions in the Sutherland case, we will raise a series of questions to consider on the relationship of forensic evidence and justice. These questions are a summary of concerns that are continually raised in basic forensic-evidence-influenced criminal trials.

What facts or assumptions or surmises may be obtained from the examination of one or more hairs or fibers gathered at a crime scene? What could serve as the basis for any such assumptions or projections, or simply guesses? What value should be assigned to any such factual estimation in our criminal justice system where life and liberty and justice to a victim are all in play? What does it mean to say that one or more hairs or fibers or tire tracks are or are not consistent or not dissimilar or substantially similar with another? What would be the basis for any such statements and what value should be allocated to them if one set of exemplars was taken from a crime scene and the others from a suspected perpetrator?

What does in mean in terms of long held requirements that the elements of a crime must be proven beyond a reasonable doubt? How does forensically generated circumstantial fact fit in prosecutorial efforts designed to meet such a high bar of proof in a case partially supported by hair or fiber evidence? How much does hair, fiber or tire tread evidence depend for its force upon other more traditional observation by eyewitnesses?

How much of all of this in the area of hair or fiber analysis and comparison testimony has to do with scientific theory or recognized scientific methodology? What science, if any, has been traditionally associated with hair, fiber or tire tread analyses and how has that changed as we entered the 21st century? Is hair, fiber or tire-tread comparison scientific with respect to the theoretical underpinnings of those who are devoted to its functioning in a criminal investigation and trial, or because of its use of microscopy, business, or other processes that aid its essentially observational nature?

Should it make any difference if they are simply a combination of experience and modern microscopy? What else, from a forensic scientist's standpoint, is there to say about hair, fiber, or tire tread analyses and the factual assumptions that follow? Is there more there to give hair, fiber, or tire-tread analysis as great or greater claim to belief than fingerprint, impression, ballistics, tool marks, or DNA?

In the "trace areas" of hair, fiber, soil, paint, and glass, the predictive capabilities will vary widely, with something less or much less than individual identification of a sample exemplar with crime scene data. So, for each separate discipline discussed the courts need to ask what this science can say and what it cannot say. What are the basic methodologies used in this field in its practitioner's efforts to bring forth "identifying" evidence? How many accepted modes are there to compare hair, fiber, tire casts, soil samples, DNA, bullets and shell casings, etc.? How have the courts responded to these various techniques and their exclusionary or inclusionary claims? It is also very important to note the definitive exclusionary capability of these "trace" sciences. The trick here is trying to figure out how strong is the inclusion.

The Court's Analysis: The Hairs and Fibers

Defendant argued that the prosecution's circumstantial hair, fiber, and tire-print comparison evidence was insufficient to prove guilt beyond a reasonable doubt, contending that the probative value of the state's forensic evidence lay merely in establishing that defendant could not be excluded as the possible offender, not that he must be found by a jury to actually be the offender.[75]

The court ruled that the evidence here, when viewed in the light most favorable to the prosecution, established that defendant was proved guilty beyond a reasonable doubt. The overwhelming and overlapping nature of the circumstantial evidence supported the jury finding that defendant kidnapped, sexually assaulted, and murdered 10-year-old Amy Schulz.[76]

The court also rejected defendant's claim that the prosecutor had overstepped the bounds in arguing that the forensic testimony here had established a series of fiber "matches" when the actual testimony was couched in terms of consistency. The state argued in its closing that:

...In every single case the fibers found on Amy's socks, shoes, and underpants, and shorts, and shirt were consistent with the fibers from the defendant's car carpeting and dissimilar to all the carpets in her home environment, and in her grandparents' house and the vehicles that they drove, and in the business where her father works, so there can be no doubt that she got them from there. They came from one place. Those fibers on her clothing came from the defendant's car.

......The red shorts are a very big part of this case ... Mr. Bibbing (defense expert witness) didn't examine the shorts at all, and we know from Ken Knight's testimony that fibers from the shorts were found in the passenger side of the car.

* * *

...This evidence doesn't stand alone. It can be considered together with the carpet fibers on Amy's clothing, the seat-fabric fiber on her shirt, the dog hair all over her clothes, the foam rubber on her clothing, the defendant's tire impressions being the — same as that found near Amy, and the clothing fibers from Amy's shirt and shorts, which were deposited in the front passenger-side area of the car.

* * *

You know, with regard to the evidence in the car that Amy was in there, you know what's uncontradicted in this case? The evidence that the red polyester fibers from her shorts were found in the passenger-side area of the defendant's car. That is fibers just like them, uncontradicted because the defense expert didn't look at them.[77]

Defendant argued that these alleged misstatements constituted reversible error, citing the important case of *People v. Linscott*,[78] decided in 1991. In Linscott, the state's evidence established that hairs found in the victim's apartment were consistent with the defendant's hairs. As in this case, the State's expert could not conclusively identify the hairs as originating from the defendant. Despite the expert witness's testimony to such effect, the prosecutor argued to the jury that "the rug in the area where Karen was laying (sic) was ripped out sometime later, rolled up, and shipped to the laboratory. And that another group of hairs was obtained. The head hairs of Steven Linscott."

The Linscott court found such overreaching to be reversible error.

The Sutherland Case: The Court's Analyses

In the Sutherland case the court was also of the opinion that the prosecutor's overstatement of the fiber-comparison evidence was improper. Prosecutorial misconduct in closing argument, the court ruled, warranted reversal and a new trial, however, only if the improper remarks resulted in substantial prejudice to the defendant. In other words, the comments must have constituted a material factor in the conviction, circumstances absent in Sutherland's case:

We do not find that the remarks in this case substantially prejudiced the defendant. Unlike Linscott ... the evidence in this case was not closely balanced. The State presented an overwhelming volume of circumstantial evidence: the tire print found by the crime scene was consistent with defendant's car's tire; the dog hair on the victim's clothing was consistent in all respects to the defendant's dog's hair and the dog hair found in his car; the foreign fibers found on the victim's clothing were consistent with the carpeting and upholstery in defendant's car; the clothing fibers found in the defendant's car were consistent with the fibers in the victim's clothing; finally, the pubic hair found on the victim were consistent with the pubic hair standards obtained from the defendant. Given the amount of evidence, it is implausible to think that the prosecutor's remarks could have been a material factor in the conviction. In this case, the jury would not have reached a different result, even if the prosecutor had not made the remarks. (citations omitted) Accordingly, defendant was not denied a fair trial and we will not disturb the conviction.[79]

Sutherland II Case

Seven years later, in 2001, the Illinois Supreme Court reversed Sutherland's conviction and granted him a new trial,[80] not on the basis of any perceived weaknesses in the specifics of the forensic case, but on the basis of the incompetence of his counsel at trial. Defendant, after his conviction, filed a post-conviction petition in the circuit court raising a variety of claims. The court dismissed most of the claims in the petition, but granted an evidentiary hearing on the following allegations: (1) that defendant's trial counsel was ineffective in failing to discover and present evidence that defendant's purchase of "Texas Steer" boots[81] and installation of the Cooper "Falls Persuader" tire on his car both occurred after the date of the crime; (2) that the conviction of Amy's step-grandfather for sexual abuse subsequent to her death constituted evidence of defendant's actual innocence.

A mental health counselor and sex-offender treatment provider then testified that, based on her research, pedophiles attracted to prepubescent females show a 22% crossover in also molesting males, and those attracted to males show a 62% crossover in also molesting females. She testified that she had reviewed William Willis' medical and psychological evaluations and had spoken with him briefly. In her opinion, there was a high probability that Willis would cross over from sexually abusing young boys to abusing young girls. She also testified that Willis was prone to outbursts of anger and that when a victim resisted, he used more violent physical force, escalating from fondling to anal rape.[82]

Ronald Lawrence, a friend of defendant, testified that he had changed all of the tires on defendant's car two separate times after Amy Schultz's death and before defendant left for Montana. Lawrence explained that he and defendant had to change tires frequently because the rock road leading to Lawrence's house contained metal particles and railroad spikes. Lawrence testified that he told police and the public defender after defendant's arrest that he had changed the tires on defendant's car after the date of Amy Schultz's murder.[83]

This additional evidence, insufficiently addressed by Sutherland's original counsel, was found to be of great importance by the Illinois Supreme Court:

Testimony presented at the post-conviction hearing indicated that, prior to defendant's trial, defense counsel was aware of evidence that defendant did not own a pair of Texas Steer boots at the time of Amy Schultz's murder. Specifically, trial counsel testified at the evidentiary hearing that defendant informed him prior to trial that defendant had purchased his Texas Steer boots two months after the crime occurred. Counsel also testified that he was aware that defendant's mother had the boots in her possession at the time of trial, but that he did not request to examine them. Additionally, defendant's mother testified that at the time of the murder, defendant typically wore a different kind of boots.[84]

The testimony at the post-conviction hearing also indicated that defendant's trial counsel was aware prior to trial of evidence that defendant claimed that he had changed the tires on his car after the time of Amy Schultz's death but before defendant drove to Montana. Specifically, there was substantial testimony presented at the hearing that counsel learned of this information from three different sources: defendant, defendant's mother, and a friend of defendant's, one Ronald Lawrence. Counsel himself acknowledged at the hearing that he was aware of such evidence, but failed to investigate it or present it at trial.

The court found this combination of mishaps adequate to reverse defendant's conviction on grounds of incompetence of counsel:

We hold that trial counsel was ineffective in failing to investigate and present evidence concerning the boots and tire. Because the state's evidence at trial consisted primarily of a variety of items introduced to associate defendant with the crime scene, an attack on the suggested links between defendant and the boots and tire could have played a prominent role in the defense:

Trial counsel testified at the evidentiary hearing that his main trial strategy was to discredit the expert testimony purportedly tying defendant to the crime. In light of this strategy, it was incumbent on counsel to use available means of casting doubt on the physical evidence which the state relied upon. Although counsel sought to convince the jury that the hair and fiber evidence introduced by the state was not conclusive proof of defendant's guilt, he failed to present the jury with evidence discrediting two of the most salient and significant items in the state's case. Counsel's performance thus fell below a reasonable level of assistance.

We also find that counsel's ineffective performance caused substantial prejudice to defendant. Although the state presented numerous items of evidence associating defendant with the crime, none of them was singularly compelling. If counsel had succeeded in raising questions as to whether the boots and tires owned by defendant played any role in the crime committed against Amy Schultz, there is a reasonable probability that the jury also would have doubted at least some of the other physical evidence which the State attempted to link to the crime, and hence quite possibly may have acquitted defendant.[85]

The shifting nature of inferences during the trial process is exemplified by the Sutherland case. The seemingly solid forensic case was reversed by a second look at the available evidence without questioning the findings of the forensic experts who testified at trial. The possibility of inferences establishing innocence may always trump seemingly irrefutable forensic evidence. The two Sutherland cases, with a third yet to be tried, illustrate the tremendous impact but lack of absolute certainty in the area of forensically generated circumstantial evidence.

The new trial, taking place in the summer of 2004, focused on the same forensic evidence as in the first trial, but added some significant new forensic offerings, resulting in Sutherland's reconviction. Former FBI Agent William Bodziak, the nation's premier shoeprint expert, testified that the boot mark found on the child victim's back was close to the size of defendant's same brand boot. Mt DNA Analyst Terry Melton opined that the pubic hair found in the child's anus was left by the defendant or someone in his matrilineal line. Finally, Dr. Joy Halverson linked the numerous dog hairs found on the victim to defendant's black Labrador Babe. Sutherland again received the death penalty.

Sutherland Conclusion

The Sutherland case study is an example of all of the points discussed in this chapter, which has attempted to provide an overview of the subject of forensic evidence. A great deal remains to be said about the court's response to forensic testimony admitted in a host of discrete areas, such as blood spatter analysis, DNA, forensic anthropology, odontology, entomology and fingerprint analysis. The new century will bring rapid and amazing new developments in this vital area of criminal law and science. It is more important than ever before for lawyers and courts to increase efforts to both understand and responsibly use the awesome potential of the world of forensic science in our criminal justice system. It is not the absolute truth of the theory being utilized that is the essential goal of the use of forensic science in the trial of crimes, but rather the basic rightness and common sense

APPENDIX: Daubert Progeny

The most recent Frye-Daubert cases address the appropriateness of forensic-science expert opinion in criminal cases. Because the majority of the forensic sciences have garnered court approval, it is not surprising that the most interesting recent cases have come from what is referred to as the soft sciences, in particular, psychiatry and psychology.[86] A representative sampling of that category of cases is demonstrated by the following brief listing.

State v. Swinton, 268 Conn.781, 847 A. 2d 921 (2004) (Enhanced photographs and computer-generated overlays of bite marks.) Enhanced photographs and computer-generated overlays of bite marks in murder case were demonstrative evidence rather than merely illustrative evidence and thus could not be admitted based on trial court opinion that they would assist the jury in understanding expert testimony, but rather required proper foundation.

Goddard v. State, 144 S.W.3d 848 (Missouri, 2004) (Use of actuarial instrument theory as predictor of sexual violence recidivism.) Testimony of a physician regarding risk prediction of sexually deviant behavior that was based on results of actuarial instruments was admissible expert testimony in commitment case under Sexually Violent Predator Act. Testimony and exhibits demonstrated wide use of the actuarial instruments in the relevant scientific community and their general acceptance. This was supported by two textbooks demonstrating the scientific validity of actuarial instruments, as well as testimony that actuarial instruments were subject of peer review and publication, and there was an additional showing to demonstrate the scientific validity of the instruments via a peer-reviewed research article. See also, *Roeling v. State*, 880 So. 2d 1234 (Fl 2004) to the same effect.

People v. Smith, 2 Misc.3d 1007(A), 784 N.Y.S.2d 923(2004): (Eyewitness Testimony Expertise.) Defendant made a motion to be permitted to present testimony at trial of an expert in eyewitness identification.

Defendant initially advised that such expert would testify in various areas: (1) the effect of weapon focus on identification; (2) effect of stress on identification; (3) the suggestiveness of photo array and lineup; (4) the occurrence of post-trauma amnesia in victims; (5) relation back of subsequent identification to the initial identification; (6) lack of correlation between confidence and accuracy in eyewitness identification; (7) the effect of post event information on identification; (8) effect of exposure duration on identification; (9) effect of color perception on identification; (10) double-blind lineups; (11) cross-racial identifications; and (12) psychological factors affecting perception and memory. After hearing arguments from the parties, this court denied the motion as to many of the proffered areas of expertise and ordered a Frye hearing as to the remaining six: weapon focus, stress, post-event information, unconscious transference, confidence and accuracy noncorrelation, and confidence malleability.

Excluding the proffered areas of expert testimony does not preclude the defense from using all of the issues raised in cross-examination. Indeed, they may have expert assistance in that endeavor. That is a different proposition, however, from altering the time-honored method by which juries assess the validity and strength of eyewitness testimony, their own life experience and cognitive powers. The court of appeals has ruled that expert testimony in these area may be appropriate. Indeed, although not before this court, the area of cross racial identification may indeed be ripe for expert testimony. But that is not before this court today. The issues before the court are not yet appropriate areas for expert testimony.

State v. Medrano, 127 S.W. 3d 781 (Texas 2004): (Admission of hypnotically induced testimony.)

The factors previously adopted for the admission of hypnotically induced testimony adopted in were the level of training in the clinical uses and forensic applications of hypnosis by the person performing the hypnosis; the hypnotist's independence from law enforcement investigators, prosecution, and defense; the existence of a record of any information given or known by the hypnotist concerning the case prior to the hypnosis session; the existence of a written or recorded account of the facts as the hypnosis subject remembers them prior to undergoing hypnosis; the creation of recordings of all contacts between the hypnotist and the subject; the presence of persons other than the hypnotist and the subject during any phase of the hypnosis session, as well as the location of the session; the appropriateness of the induction and memory retrieval techniques used; the appropriateness of using hypnosis for the kind of memory loss involved; and the existence of any evidence to corroborate the hypnotically-enhanced testimony.

The court ruled that this standard provided the Texas trial courts with an appropriate framework to protect against the four-prong dangers of hypnosis. These four dangers, hypersuggestibility, loss of critical judgment, confabulation, and memory cementing, are dangers that directly undercut the reliability of a witness' hypnotically enhanced testimony. To adopt a broader standard that was created without hypnotically enhanced testimony in mind in place of a narrowly defined standard specifically designed to ensure the reliability of hypnotically enhanced testimony would be imprudent. The decision of the court of appeals was affirmed

State v. Torregano. 875 So. 2d 842 (La. 2004): (Expertise on area of victim delayed disclosure in prosecution for sexual battery.)

Trial court did not abuse its discretion in finding medical doctor was competent to testify as expert on area of delayed disclosure in prosecution for sexual battery of a juvenile; witness was employed as director of pediatric forensic medicine for children at risk evaluation center, witness had attended several continuing medical training conferences at the national, state, and local level that pertained to the evaluation of children who are suspected of being abused and/or neglected, witness had written papers in such areas that had been published, and witness testified that he was very familiar with the phenomenon of delayed disclosure in child sexual abuse cases. The validity of the phenomenon of delayed disclosure in child sexual abuse cases was not raised in the trial court.

Dotson v. State, 2004 WL 1103596 (Texas App. 2004): (Expertise regarding delayed outcries by sexual assault victims.)

Social worker was qualified to testify as an expert regarding delayed outcries by sexual assault victims, in prosecution for aggravated sexual assault of a child under the age of 14; she was qualified by her experience and her education, and her testimony regarding delayed outcries was specialized knowledge that was helpful to jury in understanding delay by victim in reporting sexual abuse. In a Daubert hearing, the witness established that she was the clinical director at the Dallas Children's Advocacy Center, that she had treated about 800 children, that she was experienced in the relevant field, that she had read many studies with respect to child abuse, and that she was a licensed social worker and clinical practitioner. Based upon the literature and her experience, the witness asserted that delayed outcries by child victims of sexual abuse were common. The trial court overruled appellant's Daubert objection and allowed Alexander to testify before the jury. During direct examination by the prosecutor, Alexander testified about her qualifications and about the phenomenon of delayed outcry in general. Affirmed.

People v. Albertson, 2004 WL 1842552 (Ca 2004) (Parafilia testimony in sexual violence recidivism commitment hearings.)

State expert testimony that appellant met all the SVP criteria and suffered from paraphilia not otherwise specified (NOS), substance abuse, and anti-social personality disorder was scientifically acceptable. The doctor stated that most rapists do not suffer from a mental disorder within the meaning of the SVP Act. The distinguishing factor for an SVP is that the offender is predisposed to commit sexually violent acts and, because of a mental disorder, lacks the emotional or volitional capacity to resist the urge to engage in sexually violent predatory behavior. With respect to the likelihood of reoffending, the witness considered appellant's criminal and clinical history, literature on criminal recidivism, and a Static 99 test that calculated the risk of reoffending. Although appellant's age (47) indicated a low risk of reoffending, there were other high-risk factors, such as appellant's long term mental disorder, failure to acknowledge the mental disorder or seek treatment, appellant's substance and alcohol abuse, and appellant's social history that included sexually violent offenses, 14 to 20 burglaries, the use of drugs and alcohol, an undesirable discharge from the Army for going AWOL, and two reprimands in prison for fighting. The witness opined that appellant was likely to reoffend if released. The judgment (SVP commitment) was affirmed.

State v. Demeniuk, 888 So.2d 655 (Florida App. 2004) (Modern antidepressants known as selective serotonin reuptake inhibitors [SSRIs] as basis of an insanity defense.)

The defendant noted that she intended to rely on the defense of insanity. The court concluded that the trial court erred in making a determination that the antidepressant testimony proposed by the defendant was exempt from Frye testing as pure opinion. Accordingly, the court granted the state's petition, with instructions to conduct a full Frye hearing, at which both the defendant and the state are permitted to present evidence and to cross-examine on all issues associated with the introduction of new and novel scientific evidence.

State v. Vandermark, 2004 WL 2746157 (Del 2004) (Shaken Baby Syndrome.)

Dr. Christian, the expert, was a pediatrician, professor, lecturer, and author. She is a director of a child abuse program and had given expert testimony in trials involving child abuse. From her background, training, and experience, she was thus well qualified to speak about child physical abuse, shaken baby impact syndrome, and inflicted head trauma. Among her achievements, she had played significant organizing roles in scientific meetings regarding child abuse questions relevant to this case. She has authored textbook materials on the subject and written over eighty papers. Twenty involved research in this area, and her publications have been peer reviewed.

One of her articles, which she coauthored, was titled "Non-Accidental Head Injury in Infants — The Shaken-Baby Syndrome." It appeared in the New England Journal of Medicine in the June 18, 1998 issue. According to Dr. Christian, it was generally accepted in the scientific community in the field of pediatrics that shaking, blunt force, or a combination injure children. A classic constellation of findings includes subdural and retinal hemorrhages. Children manifesting these injuries were virtually all under 3 years of age. The appearance of retinal hemorrhage suggests a diagnosis of Shaken Baby Impact Syndrome or Inflicted Head Trauma together with a history of a child's prior good health, bleeding in the brain, and trauma to other parts of the body.

State v. Armstrong, 2004 WL 2376467 (Ohio, 2004) (Dog Tracking Handler's Testimony.)

The foundational prerequisites which are required before a dog-handler's testimony will be admitted, act as a sufficient gatekeeper to exclude unreliable dog-tracking evidence. Before evidence of dog trailing may be admitted, the training and reliability of the dog, the qualifications of the person handling the dog, and the circumstances surrounding the trailing by the dog must be shown. If the foregoing foundational requirements are demonstrated by the dog-handler, the dog-tracking evidence may be properly admitted. Here, the handler gave a substantial amount of testimony regarding his qualifications as a dog-handler, and the training and reliability of the tracking dog Skyler, described the circumstances surrounding Skyler's track, and testified that he checked for contamination of the crime scene and initiated Skyler's search near the back passenger seat and rear of the subject vehicle.

This summary review of several recent Frye-Daubert decisions demonstrates both the wide range of current Frye-Daubert challenges and the posture of general acceptability of most state-sponsored offers of expertise in criminal cases. For an excellent recent overview of the issues raised as a result of federal regulatory agency encounters with Daubert issues, see, D. Hiep Truong, Daubert and Judicial Review: How Does an Administrative Agency Distinguish Valid Science from Junk Science?, 33 *Akron L. Rev.* 365 (2000). As noted by the author:

In regulating the nation's health, regulatory agencies must often make risk assessments based on scientific paradigms that are incomplete at best and questionable at worst. Substantive review of agency decision making is the only assurance that agencies are basing their decisions on valid and legitimate scientific evidence. The rebuttal to this argument is that although regulatory agencies make educated predictions based on the best available scientific resources and evidence, these predictions are naturally going to be incomplete as agencies are given general grants of authority to fulfill their broad statutory mandates.

...The agencies' mandate to assess risk has greatly expanded the available sources of evidence from which administrators could base their decision making and with which they could characterize as dangerous, or presenting a level of risk that is unacceptable. These sources of evidence, however, may either be from scientific or nonscientific sources. Ibid. at 365-366.

Also see, Cass R. Sunstein, Health-Health Tradeoffs, 63 *U.Chi.L.Rev.* 1533 (1996); Cass R. Sunstein, On the Costs and Benefits of Aggressive Judicial Review of Agency Action, 1989, *Duke L.J.* 522; Peter H. Schuck & E. Donald Elliott, To the Chevron Station: An Empirical Study of Federal Administrative Law, 1990, *Duke L.J.* 984; Richard J. Pierce, Jr., Two Problems in Administrative Law: Political Polarity on the District of Columbia Circuit and Judicial Deterrence of Agency Rulemaking, 1988, *Duke L.J.* 300; Peter L. Strauss, Considering Political Alternatives to "Hard Look" Review, 1989, *Duke L.J.* 538. Also see, R. Melnick, Regulation And The Courts: The Case Of The Clean Air Act (1983); M. Shapiro, Who Guards The Guardians? Judicial Control Of Administration (1988); Andrew Trask, Daubert and the EPA: An Evidentiary Approach to Reviewing Agency Determinations of Risk, 1997, *U.Chi.Legal.F.* 569. [Cited in Trong, at n.13].

The idea of *soft* science is meant to communicate the absence of forensic laboratory-based observational disciplines or those forensic sciences grounded in medicine, anatomy, or chemistry.

Endnotes

1. John Horgan: *The End of Science: Facing the Limits of Knowledge in the Twilight of the Scientific Age* (Addison-Wesley 1996). See also, John Maddox: *What Remains to be Discovered: Mapping the Secrets of the Universe, the Origins of Life and the Future of the Human Race.* (Free Press, 1998).

2. Horgan, at 139.

3. See the discussion of peer review and the difficulties of determining causal relation in Marcia Angell's comprehensive, if flawed, analysis of the breast implant controversy in *Science on Trial* (Norton, 1997).

4. See discussion of the Daubert, Frye, Joiner, and Kumho Tire cases infra.

5. See, generally, Keeton, Dobbs, Keeton and Owen: *Product Liability* (West Publishing, 1999); Owen, Montgomery, Keeton and Dobbs: *Products Liability and Safety, Cases and Materials* (3rd ed. West Publishing, 1998); *Phillips' Products Liability In A Nutshell* (West Publishing, 4th ed.).

6. Spencer Cowper's Trial, 13 How. St.Tr. 1106, 1163 (1699). The Spencer Cowper case is cited as one of the earliest instances of the legal issues raised by attempts to utilize authoritative treatises to establish a fact or, alternatively, to effect impeachment of an expert under the strictures of the hearsay rule.

7. See, Saferstein: *Criminalistics: An Introduction to Forensic Science* (6th ed. Prentice Hall (1998), at pp. 1–26.

8. This observation would arguably apply to the analysis of hair, fiber, soil, footprints, fingerprints, tire impressions, forensic anthropology and archeology, entomology, limnology, and bite mark identification techniques.

9. (F)orensic 1. Pertaining to or used in courts of law or in public debate. 2. Adapted or suited to argumentation. Random House, Webster's College Dictionary (1995). It was applied in ancient times to the law arguments in the Athenian democracy and taught until the late 19th century as a mainstay of the English public school curriculum. It has always been used in tandem or even interchangeably with the idea of classical rhetoric. The term *Forensics* is still used today to reference secondary school programs of instruction and competition in speech, dramatic oratory, and legislative argument.

10. See, Carol G. Thomas and Edward Kent Webb, From orality to rhetoric: an intellectual transformation, in *Persuasion: Greek Rhetoric In Action* (Ian Worthington, ed. Routledge, 1994).

11. A full-blown history of forensic science and the criminal law awaits being written. See, Saferstein: *Criminalistics,* supra. Chapter 1, for a general overview. Also see, Wilson: *Clues! A History of Forensic Detection* (Warner Books, 1989).

12. Benthan: *A Treatise on Judicial Evidence* (London, 1825) [Rothman Reprint 1981].

13. Phillipps: *The Theory of Presumptive Truth* (Gould, New York, 1816); Phillipps: *Famous Cases of Circumstantial Evidence* (Rothman reprint, 1979).

14. Wills: *Essay on the Principles of Circumstantial Evidence* (London, 1838) [Rothman reprint, 1981].

15. Greenleaf: *Greenleaf on Evidence* (Cambridge, 1842).

16. Burrill: *Burrill On Circumstantial Evidence* (New York, 1856).

17. Wigmore: *The Principles of Judicial Proof* (Boston, 1913). *Wigmore on Evidence,* his 10-volume evidence treatise, is still the most often cited evidence source and contains a wealth of case summaries in the era of *forensic evidence before forensic science.*

18. See, e.g., Roughead: *The Trial of Doctor Pritchard* (Edinburgh and Glasgow, 1906) [Famous poisoning case from the mid-18th century]; Roughead: *Trial of Mary Blandy* (Edinburgh and London, 1914) [another Victorian poisoning case]; Smith: *Mostly Murder* (New York, 1959) [Famous forensic pathologist Sir Sidney Smith]; Williams: *Suddenly at the Priory* (1957) [Victorian poisoning *cause celebre*]; Hartman: *Victorian Murderesses* (London, 1985) [Victorian murderesses]. The trend continues with a series of volumes on the Charles Manson, O.J. Simpson, Jon Benet Ramsey, and Scott Peterson murder trials.]

19. 85. 682 N.E.2d 1289 (Indiana Sp. Ct. 1997).

20. *McGrew v. State*, 682 N.E.2d 1289, 1292. See Chapter 3, Hair Analysis, for an extended discussion of the McGrew appellate and Supreme Court decisions.

21. See, e.g., Mealey's Daubert Reports available on Westlaw, Lexis, and in most law school libraries. Also see, Giannelli and Imwinkelried: *Scientific Evidence* (2d ed. The Michie Company, 1993, plus supplements).

22. See the discussion of recent decisions in the chapters to follow addressing individual forensic sciences.

23. In both civil and criminal cases the information provided from scientific sources must be relevant to one of the issues in the case. In civil cases this typically involves the question of whether some commercial application of some scientific formulation "caused" the plaintiff's death or injury.

24. This division of the information supplied to the criminal justice system into *class* and *individual* is of the utmost importance for both forensic scientists and the criminal bar and will receive extensive examination in each of the chapters in this book.

25. See, generally, Saferstein, *Criminalistics: An Introduction to Forensic Science* (6th ed. Prentice Hall, 1998); Eckert: *Introduction to Forensic Sciences* (2d ed. CRC Press, 1997); Fisher: *Techniques of Crime Scene Investigation* (5th ed. CRC Press, 1993); Bodziak: *Footware Impression Evidence* (CRC Press, 1995); Geberth: *Practical Homicide Investigation* (3d ed. CRC Press, 1996); DiMaio and DiMaio: *Forensic Pathology* (CRC Press, 1993); Pickering and Bachman: *The Use of Forensic Anthropology* (CRC Press, 1997); Janes (ed.): *Scientific and Legal Applications of Bloodstain Pattern Interpretation* (CRC Press, 1999); Ogle and Fox: *Atlas of Human Hair: Microscopic Characteristics* (CRC Press, 1999). Also see, Cyril H. Wecht (ed.) *Forensic Sciences.* (Matthew Bender Co., New York, 1997) [a five-volume, 90-chapter loose-leaf collection of a wide variety of forensic science subjects, both traditional and contemporary.]

26. See, Saferstein: *Criminalistics: An Introduction to Forensic Science* (Prentice Hall, 7th ed., 2000).

27. See, Giannelli: *Understanding Evidence* (LexisNexis, 2003) [Excellent recent treatise]; Lilly: *An Introduction to the Law of Evidence* (West, 1996), at 554; Graham: *Federal Rules of Evidence In A Nutshell* (West, 2001), at 310.

28. *Frye v. United States*, 54 App.D.C. 46, 293 F. 1013 (1923).

29. *Frye v. United States* at 47, 1014.

30. Ibid.

31. Ibid.

32. 509 U.S. 579,113 S.Ct. 2786 (1993).

33. See, generally, Owen: *Products Liability and Safety* (Foundation Press, 3rd ed. 1996); Henderson and Twerski: *Product Liability, Problems and Process* (Aspen Law & Business, 2000); David Owen, *Products Liability Restated*, 49 S.C. L.Rev. 273 (1998).

34. Daubert, at 583.

35. Daubert, at 582. Doctor Steven H. Lamm, a physician and an epidemiologist, testified that he had "reviewed all the literature on Bendectin and human birth defects — more than 30 published studies involving over 130,000 patients. No study had found Bendectin to be a human teratogen (i.e., a substance capable of causing malformations in fetuses). On the basis of this review, Doctor Lamm concluded that maternal use of Bendectin during the first trimester of pregnancy has not been shown to be a risk factor for human birth defects." Id.

36. *Daubert v. Richardson Merrell Pharmaceutical*, at 2792

37. *Daubert v. Richardson Merrell Pharmaceutical* [trial Court], 727 F.Supp., at 575.

38. Id.

39. 951 F.2d 1128 (1991).

40. Id., at 1130, quoting *United States v. Solomon*, 753 F.2d 1522, 1526 (CA9 1985).

41. 951 F.2d at 1130–1131.

42. Daubert, supra, n. 4, at 2793. For a comprehensive listing of the many cases on either side of this controversy, see P. Giannelli & E. Imwinkelried, *Scientific Evidence* (2d. Edition, 1998 Supp. Vol. I §§' 1-10-1-10(H).

43. Justice Blackmun cited as examples, Green, Expert Witnesses and Sufficiency of Evidence in Toxic Substances Litigation: The Legacy of Agent Orange and Bendectin Litigation, 86 *Nw.U.L.Rev.* 643 (1992) (hereinafter Green); Becker & Orenstein, The Federal Rules of Evidence After Sixteen Years — the Effect of "Plain Meaning" Jurisprudence, the Need for an Advisory Committee on the Rules of Evidence, and Suggestions for Selective Revision of the Rules, 60 *Geo.Wash.L.Rev.* 857, 876-885 (1992); Hanson, James Alphonzo, Frye is Sixty-Five Years Old; Should He Retire?," 16 *West.St.U.L.Rev.* 357 (1989); Black, A Unified Theory of Scientific Evidence, 56 *Ford.L.Rev.* 595 (1988); Imwinkelried, The "Bases" of Expert Testimony: The Syllogistic Structure of Scientific Testimony, 67 *N.C.L.Rev.* 1 (1988); Proposals for a Model Rule on the Admissibility of Scientific Evidence, 26 *Jurimetrics J.* 235 (1986); Giannelli, The Admissibility of Novel Scientific Evidence: *Frye v. United States*, a Half-Century Later, 80 *Colum.L.Rev.* 1197 (1980); The Supreme Court, 1986 Term, 101 *Harv.L.Rev.* 7, 119, 125-127 (1987).

44. Rule 402 provides: All relevant evidence is admissible, except as otherwise provided by the Constitution of the United States, by Act of Congress, by these rules, or by other rules prescribed by the Supreme Court pursuant to statutory authority. Evidence which is not relevant is not admissible. Rule 401 provides: Relevant evidence is defined as that which has "any tendency to make the existence of any fact that is of consequence to the determination of the action more probable or less probable than it would be without the evidence."

45. Rule 702 provides: If scientific, technical, or other specialized knowledge will assist the trier of fact to understand the evidence or to determine a fact in issue, a witness qualified as an expert by knowledge, skill, experience, training, or education, may testify thereto in the form of an opinion or otherwise.

46. Justice Blackmun cited as examples, Green, Expert Witnesses and Sufficiency of Evidence in Toxic Substances Litigation: The Legacy of Agent Orange and Bendectin Litigation, 86 *Nw.U.L.Rev.* 643 (1992) (hereinafter Green); Becker & Orenstein, The Federal Rules of Evidence After Sixteen Years — the Effect of "Plain Meaning" Jurisprudence, the Need for an Advisory Committee on the Rules of Evidence, and Suggestions for Selective Revision of the Rules, 60 *Geo.Wash.L.Rev.* 857, 876-885 (1992); Hanson, James Alphonzo, Frye is Sixty-Five Years Old; Should He Retire?," 16 *West.St.U.L.Rev.* 357 (1989); Black, A Unified Theory of Scientific Evidence, 56 *Ford.L.Rev.* 595 (1988); Imwinkelried, The "Bases" of Expert Testimony: The Syllogistic Structure of Scientific Testimony, 67 *N.C.L.Rev.* 1 (1988); Proposals for a Model Rule on the Admissibility of Scientific Evidence, 26 *Jurimetrics J.* 235 (1986); Giannelli, The Admissibility of Novel Scientific Evidence: *Frye v. United States*, a Half-Century Later, 80 *Colum.L.Rev.* 1197 (1980); The Supreme Court, 1986 Term, 101 *Harv.L.Rev.* 7, 119, 125-127 (1987).

47. Rule 402 provides: All relevant evidence is admissible, except as otherwise provided by the Constitution of the United States, by Act determine a fact in issue, a witness qualified as an expert by knowledge, skill, experience, training, or education, may testify thereto in the form of an opinion or otherwise.

48. Daubert, supra, note 24, at 2795.

49. 509 U. S. at 593.

50. Federal Rules of Evidence Rule 401.

51. For an excellent discussion of Daubert and its considerable progeny, see, Michael H. Graham, "The Daubert Dilemma: At Last a Viable Solution," 179 F.R.D. 1 (1998)

52. *General Electric v. Joiner*, 118 S. Ct. 512 (1997).

53. See 90 Stat.2020, 15 U.S.C. 2605(e)(2)(A).

54. In concluding, the court held that abuse of discretion was the proper standard by which to review a district court's decision to admit or exclude scientific evidence, and because it was within the district court's discretion to conclude that the studies upon which the experts relied were not sufficient, whether individually or in combination, to support their conclusions that Joiner's exposure to PCBs contributed to his cancer, the district court did not abuse its discretion in excluding their testimony. *General Electric v. Joiner*, at 519.

55. Joiner, at 520.

56. See, e.g., Brief for Trial Lawyers for Public Justice as Amicus Curiae 15; Brief for *The New England Journal of Medicine* et al. as Amici Curiae 2 ("Judges … are generally not trained scientists ").

57. Brief for *The New England Journal of Medicine* 18-19; cf. Fed. Rule Evid. 706. The Joiner case drew an extraordinary number of amici briefs from business interests seeking to support the decision to bar the testimony of plaintiff's experts. The one that made the most impression was that supplied by Marcia Angell, editor-in-chief of *The New England Journal of Medicine*. Also see, Angell: *Science on Trial: The Clash of Medical Evidence and the Law in the Breast Implant Case* (W.W. Norton 1996).

58. Justice Breyer has followed through on his enthusiasm for the idea of cooperation of scientists and courts in the legal task of analyzing the solidity of scientific methodologies and opinions based on them. See, Breyer, "The Interdependence of Science and Law," 1998 AAAS Meeting, February 16, 1998, advocating the now implemented program whereby the American Association for the Advancement of Science would facilitate the cooperation of members with federal trial courts in a selection of cases involving complex gatekeeper pretrial hearings. This experimental program is called Court Appointed Scientific Experts (CASE).

59. See *Hall v. Baxter Healthcare Corp.*, 947 F. Supp. 1387, 1392 (D. Or. 1996) (stating that "in an effort to effectively discharge my role as 'gatekeeper' under Daubert I, I invoked my inherent authority as a federal district court judge to appoint independent advisors to the court.") Based upon a subsequent report by his experts, the district court dismissed a large block of breast-implant cases.

60. 119 S.Ct. 1167 (1999). Two excellent Texas cases, decided just prior to Kumho Tire, addressed the issue of what types of expertise are covered by Daubert and whether all of the Daubert criteria needed to be addressed for a reliability finding. See, *Gammil v. Jack Williams Chevrolet*, 972 S.W.2d 713 (Sp. Ct. Texas 1998) and *Ford Motor Company v. Aguiniga*, 9 S.W.3d 252 (Ct. App. Texas 1999).

61. Id. at 1172.

62. Id. at 1174.

63. Kumho Tire, at 1175.

64. Id.

65. Kumho Tire, at 1178.

66. 155 Ill.2d 1, 610 N.E.2d 1 (1993). The defendant in this case is currently awaiting a retrial of his case. See discussion infra.

67. *People v. Sutherland*, 194 Ill.2d 289, 742 N.E.2d 306 (2001)

68. Id.

69. Ibid. At the time of defendant's indictment in connection with Amy Schulz's death, he was serving a 15-year sentence in a federal prison after pleading guilty to shooting at employees of the National Park Service at Glacier National Park, in Montana. Prior to the trial, the defense filed a motion-in-limine to exclude from evidence knives found in his possession at the time of his arrest in Glacier National Park. The trial court denied the motion,

ruling that the knives had "some slight probative value" and would not substantially prejudice the defendant by their introduction.

70. Id.

71. Id.

72. Sutherland, supra n. 20, at 9.

73. Id. at 10.

74. Id.

75. Id. at 11.

76. *People v. Sutherland*, at 17.

77. Id.

78. Sutherland, supra, note 20, at 11.

79. 142 Ill.2d 22, 566 N.E.2d 1355 (1991). Also see, *People v. Giangrande*, 101 Ill.App.3d 397, 56 Ill.Dec. 911, 428 N.E.2d 503 (1981).

80. Sutherland, supra, note 20, at 12.

81. *People v. Sutherland*, 194 Ill. 2d 289, 742 N.E. 2d 306 (2001).

82. The issue of the boot print was not addressed during the original trial and not investigated adequately by original defense counsel.

83. *People v. Sutherland*, 194 Ill. 2d at 295.

84. Id.

85. Ibid. at 298.

86. *People v. Sutherland*, 194 Ill. 2d 289, 311-312.

Science, Forensic Science, and Evidence

We have three that bend themselves, looking into the experiments of their fellows, and cast about how to draw out of them things of use and practice for man's life and knowledge, as well for works as for plain demonstration of causes, means of natural divinations, and the easy and clear discovery of the virtues and parts of bodies. These we call dowry-men or benefactors.

Then after divers meetings and consults of our whole number, to consider of the former labors and collections, we have three that take care out of them to direct new experiments, of a higher light, more penetrating into nature than the former. These we call lamps.

We have three others that do execute the experiments so directed, and report them. These we call inoculators.

Lastly, we have three that raise the former discoveries by experiments into greater observations, axioms, and aphorisms. These we call interpreters of nature.

Francis Bacon, The New Atlantis (1627)

I. Introduction

Shakespeare's Sir John Falstaff's impassioned narrative in Henry IV, Part I, of the circumstances of his skirmish with a group of vicious highwaymen, actually the very friends to whom he was relating the tale, has been declaimed for almost 500 years:

I am a rogue if I were not at half sword with a dozen of them two
hours together. I have scaped by miracle. I am eight times thrust
through the doublet, four through the hose, my buckler cut —
through and through, my sword hacked like a handsaw — ecce
signum! (Behold the proof!)[1]

Falstaff's spirited request to Prince Hal and companions to simply behold
the proof, as observationally convincing as it might have been, fell on deaf
ears in Mistress Quickly's Inn. Alas, the inferences were there, but the truth
was known to be otherwise. Police, lawyers, and judges unfortunately do not
have the benefit of knowledge of truth like Shakespeare's boon companions
having a great time at Falstaff's expense. Appearances are often all they have.
Often those appearances are only there as a result of hard-won advances in
the theoretical bases and laboratory tools of modern forensic science.[2]

This book presents the general framework of the ongoing use of forensic
science to produce forensic evidence in the criminal justice system. Forensic
evidence, simply stated, is a body of factual material generated by the application of a wide variety of the forensic sciences, to serve as evidence in
criminal prosecutions. Due to the scientific and specialized processes used to
generate any such testimony by forensic experts, each of the forensic sciences
must continue to justify the basis for any forensically grounded linkage
testimony proffered in a case.[3] The areas of forensic science addressed here
at length — hair, fiber, ballistics and toolmarks, soil, glass and paint, footwear
and tire impressions, fingerprints, blood spatter, DNA, and forensic anthropology and entomology — are staple fare of appellate tribunals in state and
federal courts. It must be stressed at the outset, however, that the vast majority
of the forensic sciences referenced daily in American courts are routinely
accepted as reliable bases for an expert's opinion in a particular case, without
any effort by defense counsel to challenge them. For that reason, and because
of their central importance in the daily work of the criminal justice system,
the numerous cases addressing various aspects of the introduction of forensic
evidence are the meat of this book. The examination of the pattern of use of
these scientific and observational tools to produce forensic evidence in modern trials is most important for prosecutors, defense lawyers, and judges. This
book provides these patterns for each of the major forensic sciences through
discussions of recent cases, supplemented by detailed references to current
books, articles, and Web sites.

The goal of this present volume, as of its predecessor, is to provide a
comprehensive, concise, single volume, setting out the general lines of the
judicial perspective on the use of forensic science in American courts. The
number of appellate decisions, not to mention statutory measures addressing
the forensic sciences analyzed here, are representative of an equal or greater
volume of new decisions that will need to be found, analyzed, and classified.

It is the purpose of this second edition to address and integrate the most important of these new materials generated since the original publication of the book in 2001.

The increasing interest in forensic science and forensic evidence has resulted in an explosion of cases, articles, books, and Internet sites. Prosecutors justifiably complain about the Crime Scene Investigation (CSI) Effect, arguably causing jurors to have increasingly high and often unrealizable expectations of the scientific efforts to be presented in contemporary criminal trials.[4] This current second edition attempts to fill the gaps created by the increased issuance of new materials for another several years.

The author recognizes that an equal amount of attention could be given to vast areas of highly specialized areas of forensic science, such as forensic pathology, forensic toxicology, or forensic odontology. There is also room for lengthy studies of the development of laser technology, image digitalization processes, voice analysis technology, handwriting and computer-generated document analysis, and a host of subjects that will be the main concern of the future. Entire areas, often referred to as the *soft sciences*, have also been omitted. Many of these essential disciplines, such as forensic psychiatry, forensic psychology, serial-killer profiling techniques, witness-credibility assessment expertise, coerced confessions expertise, and a number of other mind-science disciplines, merit extended attention.[5]

In November of 2004, at Lyon, France, Interpol sponsored the 14th International Forensic Science Symposium [IFSS].[6] Interpol brings together executives and senior scientists from crime laboratories and forensic services throughout the world, to evaluate on a regular basis progress made within the past three-year period. The various forensic science areas in the 2004 symposium were grouped into seven major areas:

- *Scenes of Crime Evidence* (that included tool marks and impressions, firearms, fibers, paint and glass, and forensic geology)
- *Individual Identification Evidence* (biological evidence, mainly DNA)
- *Questioned Documents* (handwriting)
- *Forensic Acoustics and Imaging*
- *Chemical and Material Analysis Evidence* (drugs, toxicology, fire cause, and fire
- Debris Analysis, Explosives, and Environmental Crime
- *Media Evidence* with Image Analysis, Questioned Documents (other than handwriting), and Digital Evidence

The Interpol Web site's continuing focus on the establishment of international standards for forensics and their close tracking of the world's forensic science literature, justifies frequent perusal by lawyers involved in the criminal justice system.[7] The observations of the 2004 Interpol 14th Annual

Forensic Science Symposium will be referenced for each of the discreet forensic science areas visited in this new second edition.

The importance of forensic science to criminal law lies in its potential to supply vital information about how a crime was committed and who committed it. The information may survive the screening function of the rules of Evidence and be accepted as evidence of a material fact in the ensuing trial. Evidence is simply court-approved information that the trier of fact, typically a jury, is allowed to consider when determining a defendant's guilt or innocence. The admissibility or inadmissibility of trial information, whether eyewitness testimony, photographs, physical objects, or scientifically-generated information, such as DNA, is determined by the trial court's application of the rules of Evidence. This set of evidentiary rules are basically exclusionary in nature, that is, they filter out information presented by either side that may be irrelevant to the factual and legal issues at hand, or that violate long-standing prohibitions such as those against the admissibility of hearsay or substantially prejudicial information.

II. Forensic Science and Evidence

The system of rules that constitutes the law of Evidence controlling the flow of information in civil and criminal litigation is exclusionary, that is, it is the basis for keeping evidence away from jury scrutiny if its potential for the truth is jeopardized by either the nature or source of the information being offered or its probative value would be substantially outweighed by prejudice, confusion of the issues, or characterization as the needless presentation of cumulative evidence.[8]

The basic circumstantial evidence inference-based argument used in modern trials, whether aimed toward proving a scientific result or a more routine establishment of an important fact, has served the law as the primary method for proof of a past event, such as the commission of a crime and identification of a perpetrator. All trials are attempts to establish a version of history that relates to a past event, such as a sexual assault, robbery, burglary, or homicide. The state has its version of what happened and the defendant has another. The trial is an effort to convince a jury of the correctness of one or the other versions of the past event at issue, the facts leading up to it, and the identity of important participants.

As noted by the famous American historian Carl Becker:

> Let us admit that there are two histories: the actual series of events that once occurred, and the ideal series that we affirm and hold in memory. The first is absolute and unchanged — it was what it was whatever we do or say about it; the second is relative, always

changing in response to the increase or refinement of knowledge. The two series correspond more or less; it is our aim to make the correspondence as exact as possible; but the actual series of events exists for us only in terms of the ideal series we affirm and hold in memory. This is why I am forced to identify history with knowledge of history. For all practical purposes history is, for us and for the time being, what we know it to be.[9]

Becker's observation can apply to any factual search in litigation, including efforts to establish scientific facts that will determine the central issues in environmental, products liability, medical malpractice, and criminal cases.

The ultimate goal of litigation is not to find absolute truth. Any system that allows a jury to reach a verdict of guilty or not guilty in such important matters would appear to have something else in mind. The hope of the American litigation system is to provide the best, the fairest, and the most optimal context for a jury to find the truth that the evidence allows them to find. This goal of providing the best opportunity for a jury to find its version of the truth is especially important to understand before we discuss the court's current preoccupation with forensic and a host of other science questions.

Litigation involving questions of science or the nature of the validity of modes of scientific inquiry has been part of the legal system since the start of our nation, beginning with patent cases in the 18th century. In examining the background of the current preoccupation of legal scholars and courts regarding the meaning and application of science in civil and criminal cases, one is struck by the absence of argument on that point until fairly recent times.[10]

The real-life context from which the science-based questions addressed in this book arise are based on the proffer of expert testimony in criminal cases. One side, at a pretrial hearing, may seek to challenge the propriety of testimony by the opposing side's experts or, more commonly, may challenge the reliability or acceptability of the methodology used by the expert in forming an opinion. According to established evidence law theory, any witness may be challenged on several grounds. A case may not require his or her expertise. A jury may decide the disputed fact without the need for lengthy and potentially prejudicial testimony. An expert witness may be challenged on his or her basic qualifications and ability to give an opinion in the field at issue. The expert may have insufficient education or experience to have anything of value to offer. The methodology utilized by an expert to support his or her opinion may not be scientifically sound or capable of supporting the proffered opinion. The methodology may be sufficiently scientifically sound to support an opinion, but the opinion based on the method is not sufficiently derived from that scientific methodology. These process-based objections are key factors in the current state and federal controversy over the use of expert scientific opinion in America's courts.

Becker's observation on writing history applies with equal force to the investigation and prosecution of a civil case:

> I ought first of all to explain what I mean when I use the term history. I mean knowledge of history. No doubt throughout all past time there actually occurred a series of events which, whether we know what it was or not, constitutes history in some ultimate sense. Nevertheless, much the greater part of these events we can know nothing about, not even that they occurred; many of them we can know only imperfectly; and even the few events that we think we know for sure we can never be absolutely certain of, since we can never revive them, never observe or test them directly. The event itself once occurred, but as an actual event it has disappeared; so that in dealing with it the only objective reality we can observe or test is some material trace which the event has left...[11]

Forensic evidence, along with all other evidence, is used to reconstruct the historical event that encompasses the crime being prosecuted. Given speedy trial rules and other constitutional protections, not the least of which are the rules of evidence, such recreations are often a formidable task for prosecutors and defense counsel. Increasingly, in the early 21st century criminal trial, this circumstantial proof often comes in the form of forensic evidence. The long history of proof of crime has always depended more on the experience of jurors' lives than any startling analysis developed in a laboratory. Logic and common sense have always had and will continue to have as great, if not greater force than probabilistically based forensic facts.[12]

This is an old idea, recognized by ancient, Renaissance, and modern advocates.[13] The word *forensic* itself originates in the idea of the study of argumentation in public forums. Any reference to a scientific conclusion, as opposed to argument, is of fairly recent vintage.[14]

In 81 B.C., the famous advocate and orator Marcus Tullius Cicero, then the leading defense lawyer in Rome, represented Sextus Roscius of Ameria, accused of murdering his father to get possession of the patrimonial estates in the country. In the absence of forensic science assistance, Cicero relied on the juror's sense of community mores, experience, common sense, and logic:

> Well, what sort of a person is he then? Obviously he must be some degenerate youth, who has been corrupted by men of evil character. On the contrary: he is over forty years old. Well, then, he must be a veteran cut-throat, a ferocious individual thoroughly accustomed to committing murders. But the prosecutor has never even begun to suggest anything of the kind. So I suppose he must

have been driven to his criminal act by extravagant habits, or huge debts, or ungovernable passions. As regards extravagant living, Erucius himself has already cleared him of that when he indicated that Sextus hardly ever even attended a party. Debts? He never had any. Passions? Not much scope for these in a man, who, as the prosecutor himself critically remarked, has always lived in the country, devoting his time to the cultivation of his land.[15]

In response to an assertion that the defendant may have simply hired paid assassins, Cicero countered with more logic and common sense:

...I won't even ask you why Sextus Roscius killed his father. I only ask how he killed him... How did he kill his father then? Did he strike the blow himself, or get others to do the job? If you are trying to maintain that he did it himself, let me remind you that he wasn't even in Rome. If you say he got others to do it, then who were they? Were they slaves or free men? If they were free men, identify them. Did they come from Ameria, or were they some of our Roman assassins?... If they were from Rome, on the other hand, how had Roscius got to know them? For after all he himself had not been to Rome for many years, and had never on any occasion stayed there for more than three days at a time. So where did he meet them? How did he get into conversation with them? What methods did he use to persuade them? He gave them a bribe. Who did he give it to? Who was his intermediary? Where did he get the money from, and how much was it?[16]

This steady logical marshaling of facts comporting with the life experience of triers of fact still remains the bedrock of any criminal justice system. Forensic science, as we will see, draws on the same experiential resources, by producing facts to which the jury can apply their common sense and judgment.

The highly publicized O. J. Simpson, Jon Benet Ramsey, and Scott Peterson murder cases are recent modern examples of this inherent difficulty in the history-finding function of the American justice system. Similar difficulties are experienced daily in American civil trials, as evidenced by the ongoing judicial debates on causation in the breast implant cases and a wide variety of chemical- or pharmacological-centered litigation. Both sides to the investigation of a case have their respective versions of "what happened that day." The proof of facts in litigation is the proof of a relevant history, within which individual or corporate responsibility may be determined.

The importance of getting our theories straight in determining past fact is essential in litigation. It is not simply some unimportant academic exercise that can be bandied about by law professors. As noted by Professor Steven Shaplin and Professor Simon Schaffer in their excellent study of the search for scientific fact, *Leviathan and the Air Pump*:

> A discarded theory remains a theory. There are good theories and bad theories — theories currently regarded as true by everyone and theories that no one any longer believes to be true. However, when we reject a matter of fact, we take away its entitlement to the description: It never was a matter of fact at all.[17]

III. Forensic Evidence and History

Any trial, in any area of law, from the simplest to the most complex, is in essence an exercise in establishing a version of history. In a criminal case, such as murder, sexual assault, or robbery, the historical period of interest is typically a fairly restricted one, amounting in some cases to as little as several minutes. However, in a protracted patent infringement, contract, anti-trust, or more particularly here, a complex products liability or toxic tort case, the relevant historical period can reach back decades, and involve the scrutiny of thousands of pieces of scientific scholarship and in-house corporate documents.

If a case has proceeded to trial, the existence or exact nature of one or more material facts are still in question and thus must be determined by the jury as case *historians*, in their function as the triers of fact. Once the jury has determined the basic facts, the court can instruct it as to the law on any facts as found by it to have occurred. The history of Anglo-American common law trials is testimony to the great and ongoing difficulty in determining the factual basis of a case.[18]

In the 1997 science-fiction film Gattaca, directed by New Zealand director Andrew M. Nicol, a genetically engineered society of the very near future has perfected its use of DNA and hair analysis to the point where they serve as common identification methods as we would use a driver license or social security number today. The plot elements, involving forensic science, mixed identities, and murder are chillingly close to the 21st-century world of forensic science we will soon experience.[19] In a recent editorial in the British forensic science journal *Science and Justice*, entitled *Where will all the forensic scientists go?*,[20] Professor Brian Caddy ponders the possibility of police authorities having forensic scientists as part of the initial police response to notice of a crime, noting the current ability to do an online computer search of a fingerprint from the crime scene. He observes that recent improvements in DNA profiling, by the gradual elimination of gel-based DNA profiling in favor of microchip as a medium for DNA strand analyses, will facilitate a major change in crime scene processing:

From these small beginnings, we shall see handheld microchip-based devices placed in the hands of the crime scene officer who will have the capability of relaying the scene DNA profile to the data bank for comparison. The data bank then becomes a primary function of the forensic science laboratory, but as robotization advances this role will be managed by a small number of technicians.[21]

Similar advances, such as the Automated Fingerprint Identification System (AFIS) or the recently created and rapidly expanding CODIS system, linking American state and federal DNA data banks, prove the point.[22] It is essential to make a clear distinction between 21st century methods for recognizing, storing, and testing potentially important crime scene data and the conceptual apparatus used to interpret it in a court of law. As we enter the new century, it is time to look back on the relationship between the law and the world of forensic science that has developed up to this point. This book intends to provide this analytical retrospective by discussing the legal context within which the claims and offerings of the forensic sciences are articulated as we leave the century where forensic science and forensic evidence were born and developed.

In the quotation that precedes this chapter, Francis Bacon warns of the dangers inherent in exaggerated, misleading, or simply absurd claims made about the results of scientific theory and experimentation.[23] The historian Carl Becker points out the elusive nature of the proof of historical events and the near impossibility of recreating them in later times. This is the central problem encountered in litigation, especially in the American criminal justice system, where more often than not proof statements are couched in terms of probabilities. The economist John Maynard Keynes, among a host of others, alerts us to the continuing problem of society (herein especially in litigation), of carelessly accepting a certain level of proof of a probability that certain facts are true as proof that they are true:

It has been pointed out already that no knowledge of probabilities, less in degree than certainty, helps us to know what conclusions are true, and that there is no direct relation between the truth of a proposition and its probability. Probability begins and ends with probability.[24]

Probability, as will be noted throughout this book, is the central and controlling idea in the utilization of forensic science in the modern criminal trial.[25]

Proof of fact in significant late 20th and early 21st century litigation has increasingly focused on inferences flowing from the application of the findings in one or more of the natural sciences. The methodologies change as science progresses. The legal system has survived many such changes and will survive yet more as the 21st century rushes into our national life. The important aspect of this increasing dependence of scientific method as a basis for determining dispositive facts, as far as the litigants are concerned, is the fact generated, not the method used to produce it. The existence or nonexistence of a matter of fact depends in large part on the theory of fact-finding being used by the fact seekers.

IV. Forensic Evidence and the Crime Scene

Discussions of the use of science in the criminal law typically revolve around the subject of forensic evidence. *Forensic evidence* refers to facts or opinions proffered in a criminal case that have been generated or supported by the use of one, typically more than one, of the corpus of forensic sciences routinely used in criminal prosecutions. There is an extensive list of such disciplines, the legal ramifications of which receive extended attention in subsequent chapters. The more important of these forensic sciences are:

- Hair Analysis
- Fiber Analysis
- Glass Fragments
- Paint Chips Analyses
- Soil Analysis
- Ballistics
- Toolmarks
- Bitemarks
- Fingerprints
- Footwear
- Tire Impressions
- Blood Spatter Analysis
- DNA Analysis
- Forensic Anthropology
- Forensic Archeology
- Forensic Entomology
- Forensic Palynology
- Forensic Pathology
- Forensic Odontology
- Questioned Document Analysis
- Forensic Psychiatry and Psychology (Soft Sciences)
- Statistics (Soft Sciences)[26]

The central concept in the utilization of the findings of forensic science is *the crime scene*. While a crime scene can consist of the basement of a counterfeiter or the jimmied back door lock of a super mart, usually the term refers to the scene of a violent crime, such as a sexual assault or a homicide. The use of the crime scene paradigm is not only a familiar focus for the training of forensic scientists, it is also the central source and reference point for analysis of the many legal issues that are involved directly or indirectly in the field of forensic evidence. What types of materials are normally or often found at a crime scene that may, through close examination by forensic scientists, yield valuable information leading to an arrest and successful prosecution of the perpetrator or the equally important elimination or exclusion of a putative suspect?

A brief listing of the data and the accompanying forensic sciences follows:

- Blood, Semen, and Saliva (DNA matching and typing; blood-spatter analysis)
- Nonhuman DNA (dog, cat, deer, whales)
- Drugs (drug identification, forensic pathology)
- Explosives (bomb and arson identifications and source traces)
- Fibers (fiber typing, source identification, and matching)
- Hair (hair typing and matching)
- Fingerprints (fingerprint matching, AFIS, etc.)
- Bones (gender and age typing; identification of remains; weapon identification)
- Wound analysis (weapon typing; physical movement patterning)
- Firearms and ammunition (ballistics and tool-mark identification)
- Powder residues (shootings, suicides)
- Glass (glass typing and matching)
- Foot, tire, and fabric impressions (impression typing and matching)
- Paint (paint typing and matching in automobile collisions, hit and run)
- Petroleum products (product typing and matching)
- Plastic bags (typing and matching; garbage bags as suffocation device or when used in transports)
- Soils and minerals (mineral typing and matching; forensic geology)
- Tool marks (tool identification and matching; homicides, burglary, home invasions, etc.)
- Wood and vegetative matter (plant typing and matching; plant DNA)
- RAPD matching; limnology, Forest Service Lab
- Insects, larvae, maggots; forensic entomology; time of death; location analyses)

- Dentition and bite marks (identification of victim; matching bite marks to defendant)
- Tobacco and related smoking materials
- Documents (typewriter, printer, and handwriting analyses)[27]

V. Forensic Evidence Basics

The term *forensic evidence* encompasses two distinct ideas and processes. The forensic part refers to the laboratory and observational processes utilized in the forensic science at issue through which facts are generated. The manner in which DNA is extracted, tested, and subjected to population analyses is a primary example. The methodology of hair, fiber, and fingerprint examination are other illustrations. The area of forensic science encompasses a fairly discrete number of well-known disciplines, whereas the "science" addressed in products liability and environmental civil cases does not lend itself to such finite boundaries. While there are repetitive areas of scientific focus in civil cases, such as chemistry and pharmaceuticals or biological, mechanical, or electrical engineering, there is much less of an opportunity to discuss the general outlines of acceptable methodology in such cases. The forensic sciences, traditionally associated with the prosecution of crime, do allow for such broad methodological reviews, and accordingly, are required to varying degrees by criminal courts. Nonetheless, the legal concerns are basically the same.

It is important to remember the fundamentally different reasons for the introduction of scientifically generated information in the civil and criminal litigation systems. The use of the term *litigation* is important here because it is in the process of litigation that the issues discussed are focused on. This focus is quite distinct from other contexts where the nature or acceptability of scientific methodologies or opinions is at the center of the inquiry, such as grant requests, patent applications, contractual disputes, or publication in a scientific peer-reviewed publication. The legal issues most involved in the science debates of the past decade are questions of the relation between scientific and legal standards to determine causation in civil cases. As the century closes, similar questions are being directed to the information claims of the forensic sciences.

The evidence part of the concept of *forensic evidence* refers to a distinct set of procedures unique to the litigation process, separate and distinct from the processes of any forensic science or sciences that are the basis for the proffer of facts in a criminal case. At this point a discussion of the basic components of what may be referred to as the forensic science process, across individual disciplines, is necessary to further understanding of the broad judicial support given the evidentiary contributions made to the criminal justice system in the form of factual assertions and opinions from the forensic community.

In civil as well as in criminal cases, the parties are seeking to prove or disprove a sufficiently strong connection between defendant's act or omission and the death or injury in suit. However, the science at issue usually consists of studies that may only be probative of any such connection through *extrapolation*, without the individualizing expert testimony typically provided by forensic scientists.[28] Forensic evidence deals with scenarios far different from those in a civil law tort case, wherein no real science is carried out to serve the theoretical need to prove causation. In the criminal case, the use of forensic science means that some form of laboratory work is performed to resolve factual matters in the case itself. In both civil and criminal cases, the information provided from scientific sources must be relevant to one of the issues in the case.[29]

The value of forensic evidence for police and prosecutors lies in its ability to interpret multiple physiological aspects of a crime scene and to link a particular suspect to it. In this respect, it is of central importance to recognize that in any criminal case there are actually four crime scenes involved, each with its own set of rules and guiding principles:

- The physical crime scene created and left by the perpetrator
- The crime scene material collected by the crime scene personnel
- The crime scene material capable of being tested by the crime lab, and the results of any such tests
- The crime scene information allowed into evidence by the trial court according to the case issues and the rules of Evidence

The relative importance and focus of each of these successive crime scenes thus depend upon a solid understanding of four major factors that are the basis for all aspects of the forensic sciences:

- Recognition — the ability to understand what could be present at the scene
- Collection procedures — understanding and utilizing the most current thinking on the subject of collection procedures
- Testing procedures — understanding and utilizing the most current thinking on the subject of forensic laboratory testing protocols
- Trial evidence requirements — witness and exhibit foundation requirements and the applicability of relevancy under the rules of Evidence

The value of information generated by the techniques and methods of forensic science, as far as the law is concerned, initially rests upon the police authorities at the scene of a crime recognizing an item as having potential value and properly collecting and storing it prior to lab analysis. If the material is not seen and collected the forensic evidence analysis is nullified. This reality underscores the need for increased training, especially in the smaller communities across America in the basic and advanced procedures for crime scene analysis.[30] In a post-O. J. Simpson legal environment, the collection process itself has become fair game for defense lawyers eager to stop the forensic evidence process from reaching its evidentiary conclusion.[31]

In many ways the O.J. Simpson trial was a timely catalyst for the current renewed focus by trial counsel, judges, and the public on the rights and wrongs of crime scene investigation and testing, from alleged failure to conduct an adequate crime scene investigation, contamination of samples, deficient testing processes, and a host of other crime scene related issues. Law school and post-graduate legal training has recently begun reemphasizing the importance of forensic evidence instruction as well as the more familiar tools of criminal law, such as constitutional criminal procedure, criminal law theory, and the law of Evidence.

The importance of forensic science to the criminal law lies in its potential to supply vital information about how a crime was committed and who committed it, which information can survive the screening function of the rules of Evidence and be accepted as evidence of a material fact in the ensuing trial.

In broadest terms the "matching" process utilized by forensic scientists involves demonstrating the manner in which a physical item from a crime scene or other data may be analyzed so as to provide a purported link between the defendant and the crime scene involved in the prosecution. Each of the datum recovered from a crime scene, whether hair, fiber, soil, glass particles, blood products, foot or tire prints, or firearms, may be broken down into a series of subcomponents for analysis and comparison. It is important that prosecutors and defense counsel make a detailed study of these separate disciplines, along with the analytical processes and the criminal justice system response to them (discussed in detail later).[32]

It is most important to recall that the greatest number of the forensic sciences routinely used in criminal cases are basically observational, experience-based disciplines, centered in the employment of the latest microscope technology such as the comparison microscope. In today's judicial climate, especially as seen in the string of recent United States Supreme Court "science" cases, the designation of forensic science as science has come under pretrial scrutiny with respect to the relevant methodologies that a forensic scientist routinely relies upon. The gradual legal protections against the so-called "coerced" confessions and illegally seized evidence by way of Fourth and Fifth Amendments case-law sanctions[33] has gradually increased the simple need to prove a crime by way of *circumstantial evidence*. This typically comes in the form of inference "packaging" from physical data retrieved from a crime scene, analyzed in a forensic lab, and presented to a court and jury to meet one or more of the essential facts required by criminal law theory. While the development of federal criminal procedural rights has indeed thrown prosecutorial units back onto the more traditional proof processes, it has always been the case, throughout the history of common law trials, to center proof in inferences generated from a wide variety of circumstantial evidence.

VI. Forensic Evidence and Circumstantial Evidence

In the early twenty-first century criminal trial, circumstantial proof often came and continues to come in the form of forensic evidence. While this book concentrates on the subject of contemporary forensic evidence, it is important to note that the long history of proof of crime has always depended more on the inferences gained through the experience of juror's lives than any startling analysis developed in a laboratory. Logic and common sense have always had and will continue to have as great, if not greater influence than probabilistically based forensic facts.[34]

A history of forensic proof might as well be referred to as a history of close observation or paying attention. Doctor Watson observed of Holmes:

> …Tells at a glance different soils from each other. After walks has shown me splashes upon his trousers, and told me by their colour and consistence in what part of London he had received them.[35]

Holmes' observation in that famous case, that the most mysterious crime scene is the most common one, still rings true in the early years of the 21st century:

> *It is a mistake to confound strangeness with mystery. The most commonplace crime is often the most mysterious, because it presents no new or special features from which deductions may be drawn.*[36] Inspector Lestrade's caution to the world's greatest detective, that *(it's) all very well for you to laugh, Mr. Sherlock Holmes. You may be very smart and clever, but the old hound is the best, when all is said and done,*[37] is a longstanding concern that lies at the heart of many modern arguments as to the validity of forensic pronouncements in modern trials.[38]

The history of the forensic sciences is a fascinating study,[39] primarily centered on the work of individual scientific pioneers, rather than any truly systematized, publicly funded entities designed and intended to aid government prosecutors as at present.[40] The aspect of the forensic sciences that is of interest to practitioners in the criminal justice system is the potential for the production of forensic evidence, that is, facts, which, when typically combined with probability assessments geared toward defendant's participation in a crime, aid in establishing one or more essential elements of the crime such as intent.

Police and prosecutors can use a wide variety of aids as investigative tools, including experience, hunches, and informers, but their later use of physical data recovered from a crime scene is determined by the "evidentiary" care shown towards the entire crime scene investigation process, not the least of which is the seizing, collecting, and protection shown to the physical evidence before and after laboratory analysis. *If the authorities do not recognize it at all or do not collect, store, and transfer it properly, it may very well be useless information.*

Forensic evidence, along with all other evidence, is used circumstantially to reconstruct the historical event that gives rise to the crime being prosecuted. Given speedy trial rules and other constitutional protections, not the least of which are the rules of Evidence, such re-creations are often a formidable task for prosecutors and defense counsel. The O. J. Simpson, the Jon Benet Ramsey, and the Scott Peterson cases establish this point.[41]

Any trial, in any area of law, from the simplest to the most complex, is in essence an exercise in establishing a version of history. If a case has proceeded to trial then one or more material facts are in question and thus must be determined by the trier of fact. Once the jury has determined the basic facts, the court can instruct it as to the law on any facts as found by it to have occurred. Both sides to the investigation of a case have their respective versions of "what happened that day." The rules of Evidence that channel the information flow in a trial, as we know and use them, are primarily *exclusionary* rules, which determine what historical facts — or on occasion, opinions — the jury will get to hear. In its simplest terms, evidence is legally approved information.

The search for past fact by a court or jury is a form of historical research, but with significant differences. First, the facts presented are proffered by interested parties in an adversary encounter, unaccompanied by the objective search allegedly hopefully utilized by academic historians. Second, the rules of Evidence do not open the inquiry to any and all facts that may appear logically relevant to the search, but rather, hedge the presentation of facts in a context ruled by numerous areas of policy that do not bind professional historians.[42]

Historians do not have as strong a prejudice against hearsay as the law nor require the rigorous foundation requirements for admission as is needed in common law trials. Historians have little time constraints as to when the task is completed, whereas civil and, especially, criminal litigants are under a number of time constraints, such as statutes of limitations, 120 speedy trial rules within which the state must try an arrestee, discovery deadlines, and the disfavor that long trials receive by today's judiciary. Finally, while historians have set high standards to determine the validity of historical conclusions[43] they are not formally operating under a *beyond a reasonable doubt or preponderance of the evidence* standard as are lawyers in criminal and civil cases. The historian's standard is necessarily more fluid.[44] Nonetheless, the history-seeking function of common law trials suffers from the same infirmity as efforts by historians to reproduce the past event.

Historian Carl Becker's observation on historical method, noted earlier, could equally apply to any factual search in litigation, not the least of which are efforts to establish scientific facts that will be determinative of the central issues in contemporary environmental, products liability, medical malpractice, and criminal prosecutions. (The subject of inference, probabilistics-, statistics-, and extrapolation-based testimony are discussed later in this book.) In the extensive areas of causation theory and forensic science and forensic evidence, the history question continues to be a major component in any analysis of proof of scientific fact.[45]

VII. Forensic Science, Probability, and the Law

Robert Hooke, the early seventeenth-century inventor of the microscope and an associate of the great experimentalist Sir Robert Boyle, along with Francis Bacon, recognized the difficulty of finding adequate systems for the testing of scientific claims and productions, especially in cases of attempts to fashion one uniform set of constructs for any such task:

> ...for the limits to which our thoughts are confined, are small in respect of the vast extent of Nature itself; some parts of it are too large to be comprehended, and some too little to be perceived, and from thence it must follow that not having a full sensation of the object, we must be very lame and imperfect in our conceptions about it, and in all the propositions which we build upon it; hence we often take the shadow of things for the substance, small appearances for good similitudes, similitudes for definitions; and even many of those, which we think to be the most solid definitions are rather expressions of our misguided apprehension than of the true nature of the things themselves...[46]

The danger of seeing more than there is to see in the results of experimental processes continues to be a focus of attention in countless criminal appeals involving forensic evidence issues. It is an old worry that has been with us from the birth of modern scientific method.

Professor Steven Shaplin and Professor Simon Schaffer in their book *Leviathan and the Air Pump* provide a fascinating study of the struggle between theorists and those who considered themselves experimentalist pioneers in the study of nature. They observe:

> The English experimentalists of the mid-seventeenth century and afterwards increasingly took the view that all that could be expected of physical knowledge was 'probability,' thus breaking down the radical distinction between 'knowledge,' and 'opinion.' Physical hypotheses were provisional and revisable; assent to them was not obligatory, as it was to mathematical demonstrations: and physical science was, to varying degrees, removed from the realm of the demonstrative. The probabilistic conception of physical knowledge was not regarded by its proponents as a regrettable retreat from more ambitious goals; it was celebrated as a wise rejection of a failed project. By the adoption of a probabilistic view of knowledge, one could attain to an approximate certainty and aim to secure legitimate assent to knowledge-claims. The quest for necessary and universal assent to physical propositions was seen as inappropriate and illegitimate. It belonged to a 'dogmatic' enterprise, and dogmatism was seen not only as a failure but as dangerous to genuine knowledge.[47]

This perceptive observation applies with equal force to contemporary discussions of the place of probability in the forensic sciences and the use of probability theory to the investigation and trial of criminal cases.

Beginning with the famous decision by the California Supreme Court in *People v. Collins*, in 1968, there has been steady stream of law review articles and symposia that come and go, arguing for or against the development of a mathematically centered system for the weighing of evidence in criminal cases and the devising of a juror system for both weighing and compounding such values into a verdict. The rapid disintegration of all such proposals into mathematical symbols that would befuddle the most conscientious judge and jury has considerably diminished the attractiveness of the ideas for the practicing forensic scientists and trial lawyers.[48] Nonetheless, there is still considerable respectable academic interest in and support for such systems of evidence evaluation.[49]

In a recent article in the *Jurimetrics Journal* entitled *Forerunners of Bayesianism in Early Forensic Science*,[50] authors F. Taroni, C. Champod, and P. Margot observe that in many areas of forensic science, such as those involving hair, fiber, fingerprints, tool marks, shoe prints, paint, and document examination, the Bayesian approach remains formally ignored or untrusted. The article argues that it is time for Bayesian probabilistic methods of evaluating evidence to be generalized to all transfer traces including shoeprints and fingerprints. Such a broad use of the Bayesian perspective, the authors contend, not only follows from the recent achievements of statistical argument in forensic science, but also from the history of its earlier and productive use, at the turn of the century, in a number of disparate of trace evidence cases and contexts.[51]

As noted by Taroni et al:

> Scientific evidence, though used in court for centuries, did not achieve real prominence until the end of the 19th century, when new scientific techniques (such as anthropometry and fingerprinting) became increasingly common in police inquiries. Alphons Bertillon provided solutions to the problem of identification of habitual offenders. His most famous innovation was the application of anthropometry in the context of criminal law, following the techniques employed at the time by Quetelet, Topinard, or Broca. Bertillon proposed to use somatic measurements (nine, and later twelve, measures taken with utmost precision at particularly invariable adult body locations) as discriminating characteristics for the identification of habitual offenders.[52]

Edmond Locard was perhaps the most famous forensic scientist of the 19th century, renowned for his "Locard Principle," i.e., all close physical contacts usually result in an exchange of trace amounts of matter, typically hairs, fibers, soils, and other trace-evidence, physical specimens. He taught that the physical certainty provided by scientific evidence rested upon evidential values of different orders, which were measurable and could be expressed numerically:

> Hence the expert knows and argues that he knows the truth, but only within the limits of the risks of error inherent to the technique. This numbering of adverse probabilities should be explicitly indicated by the expert. The expert is not the judge: he should not be influenced by facts of a moral sort. His duty is to ignore the trial. It is the judge's duty to evaluate whether or not a single negative evidence, against a sextillion of probabilities, can prevent him from acting. And finally it is the duty of the judge to decide if the evidence is, in that case, proof of guilt... These guidelines remain pertinent to scientists or lawyers even today, eighty years later.[53]

Taroni, Champod, and Margot indicate in their footnote materials a somewhat blasé acceptance of the reality that to date, there are no statistics available for the greatest number of forensic sciences, such as hair, fiber, soil, footprints, and tire impressions, etc:

> Currently, probabilities of error are not provided with most scientific evidence. While DNA evidence is necessarily accompanied by some statistics, other forensic fields, such as those involving fingerprints, shoe prints, tool marks, or document examinations, do not appear to lend themselves to a statistical approach.... Moreover, even if probabilities are common in biological evidence, a large span of error estimations (in laboratory errors, for example) is systematically ignored.[54]

An editorial in *Science and Justice*, the leading British forensic journal, entitled, "Does Justice Require Less Precision Than Chemistry?",[55] takes issue with the latest, and perhaps most successful, brief for a Bayesian approach to the evaluation of criminal evidence, *Interpreting Evidence*,[56] by Robertson and Vignaux. The editorial cites recent DNA rulings in England holding that the use of statistics based on Bayes' theory by a jury trespassed on an area particularly within the province of the jury's traditional prerogatives. The English Appeal Court has held that the use of defense-sponsored mathematical formulas for the weighing of evidence was inappropriate and might be impractical should different jurors apply different values to particular items of evidence, commenting that jurors evaluate evidence by the joint application of individual common sense and knowledge of the world to the material before them.[57] The editorial writer, Alistair R. Brownie, concludes:

> This appears to signal a fairly comprehensive rejection of the use of probability calculations in English criminal law and a dashing of the hope expressed by Robertson and Vignaux that logic, probability, and inference would provide the language of which lawyers and scientists would communicate with each other ... justice in the United Kingdom does not require or welcome the precision of the chemist. Or at least at present it does not encourage the amateur to dabble.[58]

The combination of logic, experience and common sense remains the tool of judges, prosecutors, defense lawyers, and jurors as it has since the earliest days of English and American criminal jurisprudence. The use of probability analysis in nonforensic criminal settings illustrates its ongoing validity, if not necessity, in a criminal justice system centered in the balancing of conflicting bodies of circumstantial evidence. Indeed, given the historical necessity for the gathering and arguing of inferences from circumstantial evidence and the concomitant use of formal or informal probability analyses, we must always remind ourselves that our system of criminal justice resides in a world of probability.

The use of inferences is at the center of many, if not most of our fact-finding experience. As observed by the historian Robin Winks:

> We all make inferences daily, and we all collect, sift, evaluate, and then act upon evidence. Our alarm clocks, the toothpaste tube without a cap, warm milk on the breakfast table, and the bus that is ten minutes late provide us with evidence from which we infer certain unforeseen actions. The historian must reconstruct events often hundreds of years in the past, on the basis of equally homely although presumably more significant data, when the full evidence will never be recoverable and, for that portion of it recovered, when it may have meanings other than we would attach to similar evidence today. Thus the historian has evolved his standards of inquiry, of thoroughness, and of judgment to provide him with a modus operandi.[59]

Given the fragility of criminal litigation's version of reconstructing an historical event due to the consistent absence of direct proof on central issues, how do we accept and shape our uses of probability and what does its centrality say about our theoretical insistence on proof beyond a reasonable doubt?

> The standing of probability analyses in our criminal justice system is still of the greatest concern with respect to basic justice in our criminal justice trial system. This is especially the case in the area of forensic science and its outgrowth in the form of forensic evidence. Not the least of the probability analyses question marks is the absence of a statistical base in most of the forensic sciences, with which to determine the chances of any proffered "match" occurring in the general population.[60]

VIII. Forensic Science and the Courts: Frye, Daubert, and Beyond

A basic requirement toward the admissibility of trial information is the pre-requisite of a solid supportive *foundation*, for any offer of evidence, especially in instances of scientifically-generated data such as ballistics, fingerprints, fiber, or hair analyses. A foundation consists of sufficiently supportive information presented to a judge to convince her that the proposed witness or item of information has the potential to be true and hence a jury could reasonably determine that it is or is not true.

A simple example of a nonscientific foundation is in a fatal automobile crash, where the plaintiff offers a witness who wishes to testify as to the speed of the defendant's vehicle. The foundation here might consist of preliminary testimony that the witness was in an opportune position to see the accident and was a licensed and experienced driver capable of estimating the relative speeds of two automobiles. In instances of forensic or scientifically generated information, such as toxicology or forensic pathology, the required foundation is usually much more complex to allow an expert to offer an opinion in a case.

Information generated by the forensic sciences is referred to as *forensic evidence* simply to distinguish it from nonscientifically generated information, such as witness statements and other circumstantial data, addressing the period preceding, during, and following a crime. The importance of the forensic sciences to the criminal justice system is the ability to supply inferential facts. Once established, such facts, i.e., defendant's presence at the crime scene, are evidence to be weighed by the jury along with all other facts. Prior to allowing a forensic scientist or crime scene technician to render an opinion linking a defendant to a crime scene, a court will require a showing by the offering party that the scientific basis underlying the proffered opinion is generally accepted in the scientific community out of which it arises, or, under a federal Daubert standard, it is *relevant and reliable.*[61]

Once the information produced and testified to by expert witnesses successfully survives the evidence rules and foundational process, it becomes circumstantial evidence, along with other inference-based information available for jury consideration. The aspect of the forensic sciences that is of interest to practitioners in the criminal justice system is its potential for the production of forensic evidence, that is, facts, which when typically combined with nonformal, common-sense-based probability assessments geared toward defendant's participation in a crime, aid in establishing one or more essential elements of the crime. It is those elements, such as *actus reus* (affirmative act), intent, and causation that must be proved beyond a reasonable doubt.

How does forensic evidence differ from other evidence? Well, it does and it doesn't. Forensic science involves the application of scientific theory accompanied by laboratory techniques, some of which involve a wide variety of the traditional academic natural sciences, such as anthropology, DNA analysis, and geology. Some disciplines associated with forensics are nonacademic in nature, such as footwear impressions, fingerprints, and hair analysis (often

centered around the use of the comparison microscope and other developments in the field of microscopy), which are routinely used with very telling
results in the investigation and prosecution of crime. Remembering that the
reason for using the forensic sciences is to generate forensic evidence — the
forensic part — the whole point is to get to the evidence part. All of this
carefully gathered information is generated to accomplish the goal of establishing a material fact or facts at or before trial, not to demonstrate the latest
technological advance or the most recent forensic science methodology.[62]

Discussions of the use of science in criminal law normally revolve around
the subject of forensic evidence — facts or opinions generated or supported
by the use of one (or typically more than one) of the forensic sciences
routinely used in criminal prosecutions. The list of such disciplines is extensive and their legal ramifications receive extended attention in this book,
despite its devotion to the description and analysis of the legal importance
of individual forensic sciences.

Direct evidence is information that establishes directly, without the need
for further inference, the fact for which the information is offered. A clear
example is eyewitness testimony that the defendant fired the fatal shot in a
murder prosecution. All forensic evidence is primarily offered as *circumstantial evidence* of a material fact required for a conviction. Forensic anthropology, forensic entomology, forensic geology, DNA, fingerprints, hair, fiber, and
footwear and tire impressions evidence, and numerous other types of information generated by the body of forensic sciences, all serve the vital function
of bringing to light important inculpatory or exculpatory facts.

Forensic evidence is subsumed under the general Evidence category of
circumstantial evidence. Circumstantial evidence, which includes the larger
portion of evidentiary offerings in American courts, allows the trier of fact
to accept as proven a fact for which direct evidence is unavailable, by inference
from a fact which has been directly proven. Examples are the connecting of
crime scene DNA, hairs, fibers, glass, footprints, fingerprints, or bullets or
shell casings in some fashion to the defendant, which is offered to infer the
defendant's presence at the crime scene and thus inferentially connect him
to that crime scene.

In many ways, the O. J. Simpson murder trial was a timely catalyst for
the current renewed interest in the subject of forensic science. The success
of the crime scene investigation (CSI) and its numerous progenies, and
related fictional and nonfictional televised police dramas, speak to the strong
public interest in the area of crime and science. More to the point here, there
has been a noticeable increase in the attention paid by trial counsel and judges
to the rights and wrongs of crime scene investigation and testing, including
alleged failures by police to conduct an adequate forensic investigation, contamination of crime scene samples, deficient or fraudulent testing, and a host

of other crime scene-related issues. Law schools and postgraduate legal training courses have recently begun reemphasizing the importance of forensic evidence courses along with the more familiar tools of criminal law, such as criminal procedure and federal courts.

The scientific nature of information generated by one or more forensic sciences, such as hair or fiber evidence, may require a preliminary determination of whether the scientific methodology on which a forensic expert's testimony is based is either generally accepted in the scientific community, or, under the federal Daubert standard, is relevant and reliable. If information produced and testified to by expert witnesses successfully survives the Evidence rules and foundational processes, it and other items of inference-based information become available for jury consumption.

All this carefully gathered information is generated to meet the goal of establishing material facts at or before trial, not to demonstrate the latest technological advances or most recent methodologies.

IX.   Basic Questions Related to Forensic Science and Forensic Evidence

Listed here are some of the more important general issues from a series of questions that courts, prosecutors, and defense counsel need to address as they approach the use of forensic science in the prosecution or defense of a crime.

- What is the relevant scientific world I need to know? Is it toxicology, pathology, chemistry, microscopy, biology, or ballistics?
- Where can I locate the scientific literature that I must master to effectively use forensic science to generate evidence to prosecute or defend a crime or to counter any such evidence presented?
- What are the key scientific treatises on the general subjects of criminalistics and the individual forensic sciences, such as DNA, hair, glass, or fibers?
- What are the key practice texts for both the theoretical and practical application of each of the discrete forensic disciplines such as forensic anthropology, DNA analysis, or crime scene blood-stain interpretation?
- What are the basics of the individual forensic science involved in a case?
- What are the leading forensic science journals that reflect both tried-and-true as well as cutting-edge thinking about forensic science theory and applications? What is the latest thinking by the experts?
- Who are the leading experts in each field? How is that determined? What are the professional associations that certify any such experts?

- What are the testing protocols used by experts in the field, for example, the interpretation of blood spatters at a crime scene?
- What, if any, ethical protocols are required in the various disciplines, such as fingerprint analyses?
- What are the emerging theories in the world of forensic science? Where are the upcoming conferences to be held, what papers will be presented, and how are they accessible?[63]

Class and Individual Characteristics

Forensic evidence comes into court in two basic forms: (1) class characteristic evidence that does not reference a particular suspect; and (2) individual characteristics that do, inferentially, associate a particular individual with the commission of a crime. Testimony that the pubic hairs found on a rape and homicide victim came from a Caucasian male or that shell casings found at the scene came from a certain make and model of firearm are two typical examples of class characteristics statements.

The second type of potential testimony generated by a forensic science is the individual characteristic or *matching* statement that serves to link data found at the crime scene to a particular defendant. Testimony finding that court-ordered pubic hair exemplars obtained from the defendant are consistent in all respects to the hair found on the victim or that fibers found on a victim's clothing are consistent with fibers from a defendant's jacket are typical examples.[64] DNA "matching" is another obvious example of an individual or matching statement.

Class characteristic statements garnered from forensic analyses illustrate the great value in a criminal investigation of statements drawing contextual lines for subsequent attempts to link a particular suspect to a crime scene, especially by excluding other potential categories' suspects, such as male or female, Caucasian or Asian perpetrators. The ultimate goal of all forensic science is the linking of a potential offender to a crime scene through testimony as to individual characteristics, by connecting a physical sample obtained from the suspect with a similar sample from the crime scene.

The *exclusionary* potential of class or individual forensic findings is equally important as it can eliminate a suspect or void a conviction based on lack of or adequate forensic investigation and testing.[65]

On the other hand, according to Barry Sheck and Peter Neufeld of the Cardozo School of Law, the Innocence Project post-conviction DNA analyses have resulted in the release of over 150 prisoners.

The ultimate goal of all forensic science is the linking of a potential offender to the crime scene through testimony as to individual characteristics, connecting some physical sample obtained from the suspect like datum from the crime scene. It is equally important, in class or individual forms, for its exclusionary potential, thus eliminating a suspect or, as recently, resulting in the voiding of convictions based on sloppy or no forensic evidence.[66] Increasingly, a portion of modern, reported decisions in the criminal law discuss where and how such linkages have been successfully testified to by forensic experts.

X. Laboratory Matches and Courtroom Rules of Evidence

A very limited number of occasions exist where an expert is allowed to make any absolute claims of any *match*. Many forensic sciences, including DNA, do not support any such claims and the courts have consistently refused to allow this testimony or similar prosecutorial glosses in closing arguments.[67] Francis Bacon's fear in the early period of the development of scientific method that scientists may give out *a dream of their imagination for a pattern of the world,*[68] is still a major concern of criminal defense lawyers in cases involving the contributions of forensic science experts. According to the defense bar, statements of forensic scientists wrapped in impressive credentials and complex foundational testimony have always put a shine on prosecution witnesses' testimony and glazed the entire case with an aura of certainty that it may not possess. This is especially the case, they argue, where defendant's lack needed forensic support because financial support for indigent's forensic requirements is typically not forthcoming.

Terms allowed by courts to support the "identification" of a crime scene item, such as hair, for example, with a sample taken from defendant, include the following:

- Match (reversible error in most states) usually limited to fingerprint and ballistics testimony
- Compatible with
- Consistent with
- Similar in all respects
- Not dissimilar
- Same general characteristics
- Identical characteristics
- Could have originated from
- Cannot be excluded

These conclusory linkage pronouncements and variations on them are the meat of forensic testimony in a wide variety of crimes and forensic disciplines.

However, a less-than-certain opinion nonetheless has a powerful effect on a jury. These linkage discussions do not occur in general or universal terms, but are grounded in some significant relationship between the items found at the actual crime scene and the defendant in the case. The guilt-oriented inferences rising from such less-than-certain testimony is strong evidence in any case, requiring defense counsel to provide alternative inferences or to challenge the credentials or opinion base of the testifying expert or experts. This point was demonstrated in the extensive discussion of the Sutherland Case Study in Chapter 1, Science and the Criminal Law.

This type of testimony is frequently directed to support the basic common sense of the jury, used by ordinary people in connecting facts to events. It might even be seen as a scientific contribution to the venerable *who-is-kidding-whom* test known to all jurors. It is up to the defense counsel to achieve a sufficient knowledge of the expertise at issue to be able to effectively cross-examine the expert on what he or she bases that conclusion on, and to elicit what characteristics exactly are the basis of the opinion at issue.

The traditional antagonism between forensic scientists, courts, and trial counsel can be encapsulated in two questions. How far can forensic scientists go in making definitive statements about crime scenes or linking suspect to them because they have microscope? How far do we let them go because we have a Constitution? The importance of these questions lies in the recognition of how far and on what empirical basis such statements can be made at all, and the impact they may have on a jury in causing such match testimony, albeit given in a qualified manner, to be taken as true by a jury. The concern has always been that a scientist's testimony that a hair or fiber obtained from a suspect was consistent in all respects or not dissimilar will be internalized by jurors as statement of a definite match. With the possible exception of fingerprint and ballistics testimony, the opinions of most forensic experts are routinely couched in such qualified terms.

The matching process utilized by forensic scientists involves demonstrating the manner in which a physical item from a crime scene or other data may be analyzed so as to provide a purported link between the defendant and the crime scene. Each datum recovered from a crime scene, whether hair, fiber, soil, glass particles, blood products, foot or tire prints, or bullets or shell casings, may be broken into a series of subcomponents for analysis and comparison. (These analytical processes and the responses of the criminal justice system were discussed in Chapter 1.) It is important that prosecutors and defense counsel make a detailed study of the separate disciplines. In both the civil and criminal cases, the parties seek to prove or disprove a sufficiently strong connection between defendant's act or omission and the death or injury in suit. However, the science at issue in civil cases, often centered on questions of causation, typically consists of studies that may only be probative of any such connection by way of extrapolation. Such testimony does not provide the individualizing expert facts typically provided by forensic scientists in criminal trials. In criminal cases, the use of forensic science means that some form of laboratory work is performed to resolve factual matters in the case.

Whether the importance of the testimony of a forensic scientist lies in general or class characteristic statements about units of crime scene data or an opinion linking the defendant to the crime scene through an individual or "match" opinion, the scientific foundation for such testimony, as in civil cases, is of the utmost concern to the law. The term forensic evidence encompasses two distinct ideas and processes. Forensic, as in science, refers to the processes utilized in the forensic science at issue through which linking facts are generated. The manner in which DNA is extracted, tested, and subjected to analysis serves as a major example. The methods of hair, fiber, and fingerprint examination are other illustrations. Forensic science encompasses a fairly discrete number of well-known disciplines, whereas the "science" addressed in products liability and environmental civil cases does not lend itself to such finite topical boundaries.

The evidence part of the concept of forensic evidence refers to a distinct set of procedures unique to the litigation process and is distinct from the scientific processes that are the bases for opinions provided by forensic expert witnesses. It is important to recall the fundamentally different reasons for the introduction of scientifically generated information in the civil and criminal litigation systems. The use of the term *litigation* is important here because the process of litigation brings the issues discussed to the fore. This is quite distinct from other noncriminal contexts where the nature or acceptability of scientific methodologies or opinions is at the center of issues, such as grant requests, patent applications, contractual disputes, or publication in a peer-reviewed scientific journal.

Proof of fact in significant early 21st century litigation is increasingly focused on inferences flowing from the application of the findings in one or more of the natural sciences. The methodologies change as science progresses. The legal system has survived many such changes and will survive more as the 21st century rushes into our national life. The important aspect of this increasing dependence on scientific method as a basis for determining dispositive facts, as far as the litigants are concerned, is the fact generated, not the method used to do it. The existence or nonexistence of a matter of fact depends in large part on the theory of fact finding being used by the fact seekers.

The importance of this question lies in the recognition of exactly how far and on what empirical basis any such statements can be made at all, and the impact that any such statements may have on a jury in causing any such match testimony, albeit given in a qualified manner, to be taken as true by a jury. The concern there has always been, that a criminalist's testimony that a hair or fiber obtained from a suspect was *consistent in all respects or not dissimilar or cannot be eliminated*, will be internalized by jurors as statement of a definite match. Other than the possible exception of fingerprint and ballistics testimony, the opinion of most forensic experts is routinely permitted to be couched only in such qualified terms.

In broadest terms, the "matching" process utilized by forensic scientists involves the offering party demonstrating the manner in which a physical item from a crime scene or other data may be analyzed to provide a purported link between the defendant and the crime scene involved in the prosecution. Each of the datum recovered from a crime scene, whether hair, fiber, soil, glass particles, blood products, foot or tire prints, or firearms, may be broken down into a series of subcomponents for purposes of analysis and comparison. These analytical processes and the response of the criminal justice system to them will be discussed in the subsequent the chapters of this book.

XI. Conclusion

Theories come and go. The criminal justice system's need to fairly and responsibly search for facts continues into the 21st century. It remains to be seen how the nation's courts will respond to the forensic science of the 21st century. As noted by author John Horgan, in his insightful study of the end of 20th century science:

> Science's success stems in large part from its conservatism, its insistence on high standards of effectiveness. Quantum mechanics and general relativity were as new, as surprising, as anyone could ask for. But they were believed ultimately not because they imparted an intellectual thrill, but because they were effective: They accurately predicted the outcome of experiments. Old theories are old for a good reason. They are robust, flexible. They have an uncanny correspondence to reality. They may even be true.

The literature reviews in each of the major areas of forensic science were published in a 585-page document, which may be downloaded free at http://www.interpol.int/Public/Forensic/IFSS/meeting14/abstracts.asp.

This is a fact quite distinct from whether these forensic sciences themselves have been sufficiently challenged on their basic assumptions, to justify *any* opinion being given. See, Michael J. Saks, *Merlin and Solomon: Lessons from the Law's Formative Encounters with Forensic Identification Science,* 49 Hastings L.J. 1069, 1081 (1998), for an analysis of the heretofore unquestioning acceptance by the courts of most forensic sciences, in particular, the much debated discipline of handwriting analysis.

Endnotes

1. William Shakespeare, Henry IV, Act II, Scene IV.

2. A portion of this chapter will appear as Chapter 31, Forensic Science and the Law, of *Forensic Science: An Introduction to Scientific and Investigative Techniques* (Stuart James and Jon J. Nordby, Eds. CRC Press, 2005)

3. The challenge to the claims of the forensic sciences as evidenced by the recent rejection of ear print evidence and the ready acceptance of lip print testimony, discussed in Chapter 8, continues unabated.

4. See, *'CSI effect'* has juries wanting more evidence, Richard Willing, USA TODAY, 8/5/2004. *In Belleville, Ill., [in the Cecil Sutherland murder case] last spring, prosecutor Gary Duncan called on seven nationally recognized experts to testify about scientific evidence against a man accused of raping and murdering a 10-year-old girl. The witnesses included specialists in human and animal DNA, shoe-print evidence, population statistics and human mitochondrial DNA, genetic material that is inherited only from one's mother and that seldom is used in criminal cases… "I wanted to be certain the jury was clear on the evidence and its meaning," he says. "These days, juries demand that." Duncan won a conviction.* See the extensive discussion of the Sutherland case, infra, Chapter 2.

5. See ForensicNetBase, http:/www.forensicnetbase.com for a comprehensive fulltext listing of numerous new books addressing a wide variety of forensic psychiatry, psychology and other soft science topics. This relatively inexpensive service is provided by CRC Press, the publisher of a large number of the leading texts in those fields. Also see the offerings of the Academic Press, located at http://www.academicpress.com.

6. Forensic science has an established place within Interpol, in the operational police support directorate. Interpol provides ongoing database support in forensic key areas such as DNA, fingerprints, counterfeiting of travel documents, or credit card fraud.

7. See Federal Rule of Evidence §402: "Relevant evidence" means evidence having any tendency to make the existence of any fact that is of consequence to the determination of the action more probable or less probable than it would be without the evidence.

8. Carl Becker, *Everyman His Own Historian*, American Historical Review, XXVII (January, 1932), quoted in Winks, *The Historian as Detective* (Harper Torchbooks, 1968) at 6. Also see, David Hackett Fischer, *Historians' Fallacies: Toward a Logic of Historical Fact* (Harper Torchbooks, 1970).

9. See, Kiely: *Science and Litigation: Products Liability in Theory and Practice* (CRC Press, 2002) at 18 et. seq.

10. Carl Becker, *Everyman His Own Historian*, American Historical Review, XXVII (January, 1932), quoted in Winks, The Historian as Detective (Harper Torchbooks, 1968) at 6.

11. The famous French mathematician Pierre Laplace observed in 1820 that *[t]he theory of probabilities is at bottom nothing but common sense reduced to calculus.* See, Pierre Simon de Laplace, *Theorie Analytique des Probabilities, Introduction* (1820): W. H. Auden and L. Kronenberger, *The Viking Book of Aphorisms* (New York, 1966)

12. See, Hacking: *The Emergence of Probability* (Cambridge, 1975).

13. Id.

14. Cicero: *Murder Trials*, Michael Grant, trans. (Penguin Books, 1990), at 50.

15. Cicero: *Murder Trials*, Michael Grant, trans. (Penguin Books, 1990), at 67.

16. Steven Shaplin & Simon Schaffer: *Leviathan and the Air Pump* (1985), at 23.

17. For very current and fascinating discussions of this historically vexing problem, see, *Burnett: A Trial by Jury* (Knopf, 2001) and Scheck, Neufeld and Dwyer: *Actual Innocence* (Doubleday, 2000). Also see, *Wigmore: the Principles of Judicial Proof* (Little, Brown, and Company 1913; Robertson and Vignaux: *Interpreting Evidence: Evaluating Science in the Courtroom* (John Wiley & Sons 1995) for additional attempts to theorize the fact-finding process.

18. The FBI has joined forces with the Society of Police Futurists International (PFI) to study the nature of criminal dection in the distant future. In 2000 they held their first joint conference, entitled Futurists and Law Enforcement — The Millenium Conference. The Futures Working Group (FWG) is a collaboration between the FBI and the Society of Police Futurists International (PFI). Its purpose is to develop and encourage others to develop forecasts and strategies to ethically maximize the effectiveness of local, state, federal, and international law enforcement bodies as they strive to maintain peace and security in the 21st century. See, http://www.fbi.gov/hq//td/fwg/workhome. htm, for an FBI sponsored Web site addressed to this joint effort.

19. *Science & Justice*, Volume 37, No. 4 1997, at 223 (1997).

20. The routine use of forensic scientists is not the norm in most countries, especially in civil law legal systems. This underutilization may well be the result of limited resources, but can also be attributed to a lack of sophistication about the advantages of a rigorous forensic science component in routine police crime scene work. See, P.R. De Forest, Editorial, *Proactive forensic science, Science & Justice*, Volume 38, No. 1, at 1 (1998). For the utilization of forensic sciences in civil law systems, see, generally, Pierre Margot, Editorial, *The role of the forensic scientist in an inquisitorial system of justice, Science & Justice*, Volume 38, No.2, at 71 (1998). For an examination of the effort to achieve international standards for the gathering, testing, and use of crime scene data, see generally, Janet Thompson, Editorial, *International forensic*

science, Editorial, *Science & Justice,* Volume 38, No. 3, at 141 (1998). For a detailed study of the developments in international forensic science standards and methodologies, see, Editors, Richard S. Frank and Harold W. Peel, *Proceedings of the 12th Interpol Forensic Science Symposium* (The Forensic Sciences Foundation Press, 1998).

21. Professor Caddy further notes that with the advent of microcolumns being etched onto microchips, the miniaturization of gas chromatographic and capiary electrophoretic systems seems to be assured as crime scene instruments, especially when new detector systems for drugs, fire accelerants, and explosives have been developed. Id.

22. The desire to develop a paradigm for the validation of scientific discoveries and methodology has been a constant struggle since the very early period of modern scientific thinking in 17th century England. Sir Francis Bacon, Lord Chancellor and one of the fathers of modern scientific thinking, wrote a work called *The New Atlantis,* wherein he created a mythical institution called Saloman's House or the College of the Six Days Work, where the inhabitants were devoted to a serious and widespread search for the identification of scientific discoveries and developing rigorous standards for testing their credibility.

23. John Maynard Keynes, *Treatise on Probability* (MacMillan, 1948 reprint of 1921 ed.), at 322.

24. The use of probability theory, along with its cousins inferential statistics and extrapolation theory, is also at the heart of causation debates in products liability, toxic tort, and environmental litigation. See, Kiely: *Science and Litigation: Products Liability in Theory and Practice* (CRC Press 2002)

25. See, *Reference Manual on Scientific Evidence* (Federal Judicial Center 2d Ed 2000).

26. Also note that while the greatest amount of the forensic evidence issues arise from a crime scene, there are many crimes involving forensics where there is no crime scene in a traditional sense. Examples would be the movement of a body, forgery and mail fraud, and other questioned documents settings and many cases where there simply is only little or no forensic evidence to be had.

27. See *Duran v. Cullinan,* 286 Ill.App.3d 1005, 677 N.E.2d 999 (1997).

28. In civil cases this typically involves the question of whether some commercial application of some scientific formulation "caused" the plaintiff's death or injury.

29. See, Fischer, *Techniques of Crime Scene Investigation* (CRC Press, 5th ed., 1993); Geberth: *Practical Homicide Investigation: Tactics, Procedures and Forensic Techniques* (CRC Press, 4th ed., 1998); Eckert: *Introduction to Forensic Sciences* (CRC Press, 2d ed., 1995); Eckert: *Interpretation of Bloodstain Evidence at Crime Scenes* (CRC Press, 1989); Saferstein: *Criminalistics: An Introduction to Forensic Science* (Prentice-Hall, 6th ed., 1998); Brenner: *Forensic Science Glossary,* CRC Press (2000).

30. See generally, Geberth: *Practical Homicide Investigation* (CRC Press, 3rd ed., 1996); Fisher: *Techniques of Crime Scene Investigation* (CRC Press, 5th ed.,

1993); Saferstein: *Criminalistics: An Introduction to Forensic Science* (Prentice-Hall, 6th ed., 1998); Eckert: *Introduction to Forensic Sciences* (CRC Press, 2d ed., 1997). Also see the trial transcript testimony of Dr. Henry Lee in the O.J. Simpson murder trial, available on Westlaw.

31. Ibid.

32. See, Decker, *Revolution to the Right: Criminal Procedure Jurisprudence during the Burger-Rehnquist Court Era*, (Garland Series, 1992), for a history and concern over retrenchments in this area.

33. 4. The famous French mathematician Pierre Laplace observed in 1820 that *[t]he theory of probabilities is at bottom nothing but common sense reduced to calculus.* Pierre Simon de Laplace, *Theorie Analytique des Probabilities, Intro-duction* (1820) W. H. Auden and L. Kronenberger, *The Viking Book of Aph-orisms* (New York, 1966)

34. A considerable number of the modern forensic sciences were presaged in the first Sherlock Holmes story, *A Study in Scarlet (1887)*, where Holmes, to the amazement of Doctor Watson, arrives at important clues by rudimentary deductions utilizing blood, soil, anatomical and footwear analyses. Arthur Conan Doyle, *A Study in Scarlet*, at 13.

35. Ibid. at 64.

36. Ibid. at 30.

37. In 1889, in Chicago, the famous trial of William Coughlin and others for the murder of Doctor Phillip Patrick Cronin, which was the longest criminal trial in American history to that point, involved no forensic proof. In fact, a noteworthy point of contention among expert witnesses was whether a dif-ference could be determined between animal and human blood. See, *Coughlin v. People*, 144 Ill. 140, 33 N.E. 1 (Sp. Ct. Ill. (1889).

38. See, *Colin Wilson: Clues: A History of Forensic Detection* (Warner Books, 1989). Also see Jurgen Thorvald: *Century of the Detective* (Harcourt, Brace and World, 1965); Crime and Science (Harcourt, Brace and World, 1966).

39. See, generally, Saferstein: *Criminalistics: An Introduction to Forensic Science* (Prentice-Hall, 7th ed., 2000). The Saferstein text is the standard text in the field and should be in the library of anyone interested in the forensic sciences. The following summary is adapted from his introductory pages. Mathieu Orfila (1787-1853), often referred to as the father of forensic toxicology, was a Spaniard who became a famous French professor of medicine and wrote the first major work on the detection of poisons and their effect on animals; Alphonse Bertillon (1853-1914) developed a system of measurement of the facial features of criminals to identify criminals from witness statements. (See discussion infra, re Bayesianism); Francis Galton (1822-1911) made the first serious study of the possibility of a fingerprint identification theory and system. His seminal work *Fingerprints* was published in 1892. The statistical study therein serves as the basis for today's system; Leon Lattes (1887-1956) and Dr. Karl Landsteiner (1901) developed blood typing [A, B, AB, O]. Lattes

developed a system for determining the typing for a dried bloodstain.; Calvin Goddard (1891-1955) pioneered ballistics identifications through his work with the comparison microscope, still the basic laboratory tool of contemporary firearms examiners; Albert Osborn (1858-1946) authored the standard text *Questioned Documents*, establishing the discipline of examining questioned documents;. Hans Gross (1847-1915) was the author of *Criminal Investigation*, the first book to systematically analyze the many applications of the natural sciences to the investigation of crime. This was the "bible" in the area of criminal investigations for many years and is still quoted, although most recently by feminist legal scholars for his dubious references to women as morally unsuitable witnesses. Edmond Locard (1877–1966) is famous for his theories and experiments regarding what today is referred to as "trace evidence" (fiber, glass shards, soil, metal traces on clothes and tools, etc., and the famous "Locard Principle" — i.e., something is always left and always taken away as a predictable result of close contact of two persons; August Vollmer and Paul Leland Kirk (1920's–1950's) were architects of the first major, professional crime labs in California. See Saferstein, at 3-7.

40. See, Carl Becker, *Everyman His Own Historian*, American Historical Review, XXVII (January, 1932), quoted in Winks, *The Historian as Detective* (Harper Torchbooks, 1968) at 6. Also see, David Hackett Fischer, *Historians' Fallacies: Toward a Logic of Historical Fault* (Harper Torchbooks, 1970).

41. See. e.g., Federal Rules of Evidence provisions barring prejudicial evidence, character evidence, and hearsay.

42. On this subject, see, generally, David Hackett Fischer: *Historians' Fallacies: Toward a Logic of Historical Thought* (Harper Torchbook, 1970); E.H. Carr: *What is History* (New York, 1962); *The Historian as Detective: Essays on Evidence* (Robin W. Winks, Ed., Harper Torchbooks, 1968).

43. As noted by historian Robin Weeks: *Evidence means different things to different people, of course. The historian tends to think mainly in terms of documents. A lawyer will mean something rather different by the word, as will a sociologist, or a physicist, or a geologist, or a police officer at the moment of making an arrest. For certain problems evidence must be 'hard," while for others it may be 'soft." Even if no acceptable or agreed-upon definitions of evidence may be given, most of us recognize intuitively what we mean when we use the word. The Historian as Detective: Essays on Evidence* (Robin W. Winks, Ed., Harper Torchbooks, 1968), at xv.

44. See generally, Kiely: *Science and Litigation: Products Liability in Theory and Practice* (CRC Press, 2002).

45. Robert Hooke: *Micrographia, or Some Physiological Descriptions of Minute Bodies Made by Magnifying Glasses with Observations and Inquiries Thereon* (1667), at Preface, 2.

46. Steven Shaplin & Simon Schaffer: *Leviathan and the Air Pump* (1985), at 24.

47. 438 P.2d 33 (Cal. 1968). This case refused to allow a professor's probability analysis of whether defendants were at the crime scene and resulted in years

of law review articles on the wisdom, or lack of it, of using formal Bayesian analyses to the trial of criminal evidence. See Tribe, Trial by Mathematics: Precision and Ritual in the Legal Process, 84 *Harvard L. Rev.* 1329 (1971) for a review and refutation of the professorial Bayesian movement in criminal trials.

48. See, e.g., Richard Lempert, *Some Caveats Concerning DNA As Criminal Identification Evidence: With Thanks to the Reverend Bayes*, 13 *Cardozo L. Rev.* 303 (1991); Ordway Hilton, *The Relationship of Mathematical Probability to the Handwriting Identification Problem*, 1 *Int. J. Forensic Document Examiners* 224 (1995); James McGivney and Robert Barsley, A Method For Mathematically Documenting Bitemarks, 44 *J. For. Sci.*, No.1, 45 (1999); F. Taroni and C.G.G. Aitken, *Probabilistic Reasoning in the Law: Part I: assessment of probabilities and explanation of the value of trace evidence other than DNA evidence*, 38 *Sci & Just*, no.3, at 179 (1998); J.M. Curran, C.M. Triggs, J.S. Buckelton, K.A.J. Walsh and T. Hicks, *Assessing transfer probabilities in a Bayesian interpretation of forensic glass evidence*, 38 *Sci & Just*, No. 1 (1998); Frederick Schauer and Richard Zeckhauser, *On The Degree Of Confidence For Adverse Decisions*, 25 *J. Legal Stud.* 27 (1996); Richard Lempert, *The New Evidence Scholarship: Analyzing the Process of Proof*, 66 *B.U. L. Rev.* 439 (1986); Symposium, *Decision and Inference in Litigation*, 13 *Cardozo L. Rev.* 253 (1991); Frederick Mosteller & Cleo Youtz, *Quantifying Probabilistic Assessments*, 5 *Statistical Sci.* 2 (1990); Edward J. Imwinkelried, *The Use of Evidence of an Accused's Uncharged Misconduct to Prove Mens Rea: The Doctrines Which Threaten to Engulf the Character Evidence Prohibition*, 51 *Ohio St. L.J.* 575, 586-93 (1990). Also see generally, Ian Hacking, *The Emergence of Probability* (Cambridge University Press, 1975).

49. 38 *Jurimetrics J.* 183 (1998). This is an excellent review of the earliest Bayesian type applications of probabilities in the investigation of crime. It should be examined by anyone interested in this central problem in criminal justice and legal studies.

50. Id. at 188-189.

51. The classification of the anthropometric forms (one per individual) was based on a division of measurements into three classes (small, medium, and large), defined arbitrarily by such fixed intervals as would apportion an average set of measurements into three approximately equal divisions. In practice, data were classified according to the following procedure. When an arrested individual refused to provide his identity after an inquiry, his anthropometric measurements were taken. If a match with previously collected data could be found, taking into account the table of tolerance values established by Bertillon, the identification was completed by the examination of accompanying file photographs and physical marks (such as tattoos, scars, etc.). Faced with the evidence, the suspect generally admitted his identity. Id. at 184-185.

52. Taroni et al., at 187.

53. Id. at footnote 13, citing Taroni, et al., *Statistics: A Future in Tool Marks Comparisons?*, 28 *J. Ass'n Firearms & Toolmarks Examiners* 222 (1996) and

Jonathan J. Koehler et al., *The Random Match Probability in DNA Evidence: Irrelevant and Prejudicial?*, 35 *Jurimetrics J.* 201 (1995); Frederick Schauer and Richard Zeckhauser, *On The Degree Of Confidence For Adverse Decisions*, 25 *J. Legal Stud.* 27 (1996) for an interesting article quantifying levels of proof in non-criminal processes for allocating guilt.

54. 37 *Sci & Just.*, No.2 at 73-74 (1997). The title originates with a famous question posed by Jeremy Bentham in his classic work on evidence, *A Treatise on Judicial Evidence* (1825)

55. B. Robertson and G.A. Vignaux, *Interpreting Evidence: Evaluating Forensic Evidence in the Courtroom* (John Wiley & Sons, 1995).

56. See, *Denis Adams* [1996] 2 Cr. App. R. 467.

57. 37 *Sci & Just*, No. 2, at 73-74 (1997).

58. Robin W. Winks: *The Historian as Detective: Essays on Evidence* (1969), p. xvi.

59. 84. See, Frederick Schauer and Richard Zeckhauser, *On The Degree Of Confidence For Adverse Decisions*, 25 *J. Legal Stud.* 27 (1996) for an interesting article quantifying levels of proof in non-criminal processes for allocating guilt.

60. For a more detailed discussion in non-criminal cases, see, Kiely: *Science and Litigation: Products Liability in Theory and Practice* (CRC Press, 2002), Chapter 2, Science, Products Liability and the Courts; Judge Harry Brown, *Eight Gates for Expert Witnesses*, 36 *Houston L. Rev.* 743 (1999); Judge Harry Brown, *Procedural Issues Under Daubert*, 36 *Houston L. Rev.* 1133 (1999); Michael H. Graham, *The Expert Witness Predicament: Determining "Reliable" under the Gatekeeping Test of Daubert, Kumho, and Proposed Amended Rule of the Federal Rules of Evidence*, 54 U. Miami L. Rev. 317 (2000).

61. While proof at trial is the primary purpose of generating forensically-based facts, such facts are also routinely used to generate investigative leads and to provide factual support for search warrants and charging instruments, such as indictments and criminal complaints.

62. A host of additional questions will arise when court and counsel are deep into admissibility arguments as regards the factual offspring of the application of a particular forensic science. Questions of that nature for each discipline covered will be isolated and addressed in the remainder of this book.

63. This division of the information supplied to the criminal justice system into *class* and *individual* is of the utmost importance for both forensic scientists and the criminal bar and has received extensive examination in each of the chapters above. This chapter focuses on the legal acceptance or rejection of these specific offerings by experts in the forensic sciences.

64. See the discussion of the Mark Reid case, infra, Chapter 3, Hair Analysis, where defendant was excluded as a suspect by Mt DNA hair analysis, after being convicted of rape based on traditional microscopic hair analyses.

65. See, Scheck, Neufeld & Dwyer: *Actual Innocence* (Doubleday (2000) for an absorbing and in-depth look at the phenomenon of wrongly convicted prisoners freed by the application of contemporary applications of post-trial forensic science. Also see the Innocence Project website at http://www.innocenceproject.org/ for current information on the ongoing work of the Project.

66. See, e.g., *People v. Sutherland*, 155 Ill. 2d 1, 610 N.E. 2d 1 (1993); *McGrew v. State*, 682 N.E. 2d 1289 (Ind. Sp. Ct. 1997); *People v. Linscott*, 142 Ill. 2d 22, 566 N.E. 2d 1355 (1991).

67. Sir Francis Bacon: *Novum Organum: Aphorisms on the Interpretation of Nature and the Empire of Man.* (1620) [Peter Urbach and John Gibson, trans. Open Court, 1994], at 29-30.

68. John Horgan: *The End of Science* (1996) at p. 136.

Hair Analyses

3

And all depends on keeping the mind's eye fixed on things themselves, so that their images are received exactly as they are. For God forbid that we should give out a dream of our imagination for a pattern of the world.

Sir Francis Bacon: Novum Organum: Aphorisms on the Interpretation of Nature and the Empire of Man. (1620)

I. Introduction

The forensic discipline of hair analysis is still largely centered in microscopy — the close examination of a hair sample using modern microscope technology. However, recent advances in the mitochondrial DNA (mtDNA) analysis of human hair has required laboratories to rethink their heavy reliance on microscopy in this important member of the forensic science disciplines.[1] While it may be and is used to determine the kind and category of a hair sample, i.e., whether human, animal, or even a hair at all, the principal goal in hair analysis is to establish a common origin between known and recovered samples linked to a suspect in a criminal case. Recently, in addition to visually-oriented examinations, impressive work on identification has been investigated using DNA methodology in instances of the presence of adequate hair root cells.[2] More often than not, however, such material is not available so the new DNA methods are unavailable as a tool.

Great strides have been and continue to be made in the use of mtDNA to compare hair samples. While mtDNA currently lacks the inclusive features of nuclear DNA, it is a telling exclusionary tool and is used increasingly as a backup to traditional microscopy in forensic hair analysis. Hair analysis is also used extensively in criminal prosecutions to garner investigative leads and material facts for use at trial.[3] International focus on mtDNA as a primary tool in crime scene investigation is seen in recent Interpol papers reviewing world literature on this subject.

The ongoing general utility of hair analysis was noted in the *Proceedings of the 12th Interpol Forensic Science Symposium* in 1998:

> It is therefore not possible to dispense with the microscopic examination of hairs. Such a situation could only be envisaged if DNA profiling became so simplified that all hairs which were found could be analyzed with little effort and with the certainty that the analysis would have evidentiary value.[4]

The literature review summary of the 13th Interpol Forensic Science Symposium[5] agreed, while increasing its focus on the use of mtDNA as an important adjunct to traditional microscope-centered hair analysis:

> The second use of mtDNA is the analysis of hair shafts (Higuchi et al., 1988).

> Although it is not problematical to extract genomic DNA from the hair root, this is usually not an option unless the hairs have been physically plucked. Hairs which are shed naturally, because they are in the telogen phase, are usually devoid of roots and the shaft itself is almost devoid of genomic DNA. MtDNA can be routinely analyzed however...[6]

Noting that mtDNA is inherited through the maternal line (i.e., the mother passes her mtDNA to all offspring and will share the same mtDNA with her grandmother, great-grandmother, and so on) the reviewers gave the following caveat:

> Consequently, it is not uncommon for differences to be observed in the DNA sequence when comparing close maternal relatives (such as mother and son) (Parsons et al., 1997). Somatic mutation has also been observed, especially in hairs, and this means that differences may be observed between different hairs and tissues within an individual (Wilson et al., 1997; Sullivan et al., 1997). Consequently, if there are apparent mismatches between the questioned and known samples, this does not automatically exclude the questioned sample, although the strength of the evidence must be diminished. It is well established that the mitochondrial mutation

rate is substantially higher than that encountered with genomic DNA.[7]

The Interpol 14th Annual Forensic Science Symposium Review, published in 2004,[8] observed that interest in the forensic examination of hairs during the last three years had remained high, although not yet reflected in the number of published papers. The report stressed that the goal of establishing hair examination on a foundation more reliable than presently entertained was at the center of interested hair-analysis groups. This was especially so, given the increased use of and potential conflict with mitochondrial DNA analyses.[9]

The 2004 *Interpol Review* authors concluded that *hairs, and in particular human hairs, will remain an important trace material for the future if for no other reason than it is a physical reality in routine case work. As humans lose 100 or more hairs each day, hairs will always be present as potential evidence.... Microscopic examination will remain a core technique but debate will continue regarding its value and reliability. ...DNA analysis will continue to be a very important adjunct to hair examination.*[10]

The *Review*, while recognizing the importance of recent mtDNA advances in hair analysis, concluded that it was unlikely that the situation will greatly improve in the next three years due to availability and cost. Nevertheless, it was clear that the literature about mtDNA and hair analysis over the past three years led to the conclusion that the traditional grounding of hair analyses in microscopy needs a second look:

> What should change through DNA testing, particularly mtDNA, is that, *where this is available*, the hair examiner should change thinking from exclusion to avoid a wrong inclusion, to acceptance of more hairs for testing using mtDNA as the ultimate exclusion or inclusion tool. This acceptance will require an understanding by users that the apparent "fail rate" for microscopic examination should increase.[11]

II. Hair Analysis Basics

What is there to compare in hair analyses? The new *Atlas of Human Hair: Microscopic Characteristics*, by Robert Ogle, Jr. and Michelle J. Fox,[12] posits and presents photographic plates referencing 24 microscopic characteristics of human hair. The primary purpose of this new text, according to the authors, is to present photographic archetypes that can provide a uniform basis for the generation of data on study populations, so that data from different researchers or examiners can be combined to form a larger database of characteristic variate frequencies.[13] This laudable goal is necessary, the authors maintain, if hair analysis as currently engaged in by criminalists is to gain the respect afforded other observation-based forensic disciplines, such as fingerprints and ballistics, or is to rise to the respectability currently afforded to disparate DNA methodologies and population frequency databases projections.

All forensic sciences function in a context of providing information in one of two modes: class characteristics or individual characteristics. Class characteristics provide a valuable number of facts about a crime scene sample that do not reference any particular suspect. These class characteristics put discussions of individualized investigative efforts in a context. In the area of hair analysis, class characteristic information may include a great amount of exclusory information in this broad contextual analysis. In these areas, we can expect very solid evidence of exclusion of a suspect's sample from participation in the crime, but cannot achieve unqualified identification as is claimed for fingerprints or DNA[14] or the very solid identifications provided by ballistics.

In the so-called trace areas of hair, fiber, soil, paint, and glass, the predictive capabilities will vary widely, with something less or much less than individual identification of a sample exemplar with crime scene data. So, for each separate discipline studied henceforth (as with our non-DNA blood spatter discussions to follow), we need to ask what this science can say and what it cannot say. What are the basic methodologies used in this field in its practitioner's efforts to bring forth "identifying" evidence? How many accepted modes are available to compare hair, soil samples, DNA, bullets, and shell casings, etc.? How have the courts responded to these various techniques and their exclusionary or inclusionary claims? Always remember that the exclusionary capability of these "trace" sciences is very strong.

In the area of hair analysis, a number of class characteristic observations may be confirmed with a fairly high confidence level.

- Is the examined item actually hair or a fiber?
- Is it a human hair or an animal hair? If it is an animal hair, what kind of animal is it?
- Is it male or female hair?
- Is it infant or mature adult hair? Is the hair source a human of Caucasian, African, or Asiatic ethnicity?
- Does the hair appear to have been forcibly removed? If so, is there sufficient root tissue to perform new DNA testing?
- What part of the body was its apparent source, i.e., was it a head or pubic hair?

- Does the hair contain traces of drugs or other chemical content, such as cocaine, heroin, methamphetamine, alcohol, or prescription drugs?
- Does is the hair indicate the presence and type of a shampoo product?
- Is there an indication of some identifiable illness that may be gleaned from hair analysis methods?

This sampling of potential contributions in the form of class characteristic statements garnered from modern hair analyses[15] illustrates the great value in a criminal investigation of statements drawing the contextual lines for subsequent attempts to link a particular suspect to the crime scene, especially in the exclusion of one or a body of potential suspects.[16] The ultimate goal of all forensic science is the linking of a potential offender to the crime scene by way of testimony as to individual characteristics, connecting some physical sample obtained from the suspect to like datum from the crime scene. A considerable portion of this book is will be devoted to the examination of reported decisions where such linkages have been testified to by forensic experts.

III. Discovery Issues

Court and counsel must understand the scope and importance of pretrial forensic evidence discovery. Just as in science-centered civil cases, such as products liability, the lawyers must know what there is to discover. The party seeking discovery needs a good sense of the nature, flow, and documentary information typically present, but also must know how to read these materials for accuracy and completeness. In inherently complex forensic areas, such as DNA discovery, some states have drafted new Supreme Court Rules to reflect such complexity which will be amended as the technology and accompanying documentation change.[17] However, most states have only general criminal discovery provisions. This situation puts the burden on the party seeking discovery [usually the defendant] to know what is there to discover, how it is documented, and what steps to use over the course of the case in bringing the questioned testing to its conclusion.

Relying on the continuing obligation for the prosecution to update its discovery responses is illusory at best. The recent Florida case of *Hoffman v. State*[18] addresses this very point.

In Hoffman, a Florida murder case, the state Supreme Court held that the prosecution was required to disclose to defendant all exculpatory results of scientific hair analysis and that the state's failure to do so was prejudicial to defense requiring a reversal. The state contended that in its response to a discovery request, it disclosed the existence of a hair analysis to defense counsel. This disclosure, the state asserts, should have placed Hoffman's attorney on notice of any other evidence flowing therefrom and put the burden on him to forward another detailed request.

Evidence presented at the evidentiary hearing indicated that a long, brown hair was found in the right hand of the female victim, and that hairs were found in the clutch of her left hand. Evaluation by the state lab showed that these hairs were Caucasian male head and pubic hairs that did not match that of the defendant. Additionally, the head hair did not match that of the male victim. The hair was also excluded as belonging to the female victim. There was no indication that the state ever disclosed this report to the defense, and the state did not argue that this report was disclosed. Instead, the state essentially argued that defense counsel should have inquired further once told of the existence of other hair analyses.

The Florida Supreme Court held that the state was required to disclose to the murder defendant all results of scientific hair analysis performed upon strands of hair found in one victim's hands, rather than mere existence of a hair analysis, where the test results, obtained after the state answered defendant's discovery demands, excluded defendant, his codefendant, and both victims as possible sources of the hairs. In an important ruling, the court found that defense counsel was not obligated to make continuing inquiries once generally informed of existence of hair analyses, and a state serologist's trial testimony indicating that hairs had been recovered from murder scene was not equivalent of proper disclosure.

IV. Matching Statements

A forensic expert is permitted to make any absolute claims of a match between a crime scene item and the defendant in a very limited number of occasions. A majority of the forensic sciences, including DNA, does not support any such claims, and the courts have consistently refused to allow any such testimony or prosecutorial glosses of this type in closing arguments. Fingerprint and ballistics, two forensic science areas where absolute identifications are permitted, have been questioned in an increasing number of cases. The recent FBI Brandon Mayfield fisaco[19] has raised a red flag about the genuineness of any absolute fingerprint accuracy. Francis Bacon's fear that scientists may give out a dream of our imagination for a pattern of the world,[20] is still a major concern of criminal defense lawyers in cases involving some contribution of forensic science experts. Statements of forensic scientists, wrapped in impressive credentials, and complex foundational testimony, have always put a shine on prosecution witnesses' testimonies and glazed an entire case with an aura of certainty that it may not possess. This white coat and resumé problem is especially acute where adequate forensic financial support for indigents is typically not forthcoming.

Terms allowed by courts to support the "identification" of a crime scene hair, for example, with a sample taken from defendant, have included the following:

- Match (Reversible error in most states)
- Compatible with
- Consistent with
- Similar in all respects
- Not dissimilar
- Same general characteristics
- Identical characteristics
- Could have originated from
- Cannot be eliminated

These conclusory linkage pronouncements and variations on them are the meat of forensic testimony in a wide variety of crimes and forensic disciplines. Not that such testimony is grossly unfair and a fraud on the court. It is quite the contrary. This something-less-than-certain opinion has a powerful effect on a jury. It may essentially be deemed to support the basic common sense of the jury as to its understanding of the culture and the historical connection between and among events. This kind of opinion might even be seen as the scientific contribution to the venerable who-is-kidding-who test known to all jurors from the earliest years. The Cecil Sutherland case discussed in Chapter 2 is illustrative of this phenomenon.

This important issue was recently discussed by the U.S. Seventh Circuit Court of Appeals in the case of *Buie v. McAdory*,[21] an important 2003 Seventh Circuit Court of Appeals decision. In Buie, the court addressed the central issue of the constitutional propriety of an expert's opinion couched in terms of consistent in all respects and reasonable degree of scientific certainty. After the affirmance[21] of his state conviction for murder, and exhaustion of state remedies, defendant filed a petition for federal habeas relief. The U.S. District Court for the Northern District of Illinois denied the petition but granted a certificate of appealability. The court of appeals held that the trial court's admission of a prosecution expert witness' testimony that allegedly overstated the degree of confidence of a laboratory match made between hair strands by use of the phrase "reasonable degree of scientific certainty" did not violate due process.

Buie's principal argument was that the trial judge violated the due process clause by permitting an expert witness to overstate the strength of her conclusion. Police found some strands of hair on victim Ervin's clothing and among shards of glass on the basement floor. (Ervin had been beaten with a bottle as well as a hammer.) Maria Pulling, who Buie acknowledged to be a legitimate expert in hair analysis, testified that the hair "exhibited characteristics that were the same as Joel Buie's head hair standards." After detailing for the jury the respects in which the hairs matched, Pulling testified that "Within a reasonable degree of scientific certainty, I would say that the hair came from Joel Buie." She told the jury that her methodology did not exclude the possibility that the hairs came from someone else, but that she thought this probability low. She repeated these limitations on cross-examination. Buie presented a hair expert of his own, who testified that Pulling had overstated the degree of confidence allowed by tests available at the time. He did not, however, examine the hairs himself, conclude that they came from someone other than Buie, or even opine that the set of potential donors for these strands was particularly large.[23]

Defendant petitioner argued that the Constitution forbids any expert witness to misstate scientific conclusions in a criminal prosecution. The Court observed that it was far from clear that Pulling did this:

> ...she and the defense expert debated the accuracy of hair analysis, and Buie does not cite any scientific literature establishing that Pulling was in the wrong. "Reasonable degree of scientific certainty" is a plastic phrase. Let us assume, however, that Buie's expert had the better of the argument. Still, to obtain collateral relief, Buie must show that the state's decision "was contrary to, or involved an unreasonable application of, clearly established federal law, as determined by the Supreme Court of the United States" (citations omitted.) No decision of the Supreme Court "clearly establishes" that experts (or any other witnesses) must be right; the constitutional rule is that the defendant is entitled to a trial that will enable jurors to determine where the truth lies. That a witness may give false or mistaken testimony therefore is not an independent Constitutional violation. What the Constitution provides is assurance that evidence may be tested by cross-examination and by contrary proofs. Whether a given expert witness overstated her conclusion is meat for cross-examination, and no one impaired Buie's ability to elicit from her how likely (or unlikely) a "reasonable degree of scientific certainty" was in her vocabulary.[24]

The court also noted that the state paid for an expert witness to evaluate the issue and testify on behalf of the defense.

The court concluded that although the Federal Constitution may be offended when probative exculpatory evidence is pointlessly excluded, no comparable rule condemns the admission of evidence that the defendant deems untrustworthy, as long as the state affords the defendant the means to demonstrate its weaknesses (and its use does not violate the confrontation clause):

> Informants may be lying, eyewitnesses may be tricked by their own memories, and experts may produce flawed analyses. The tools of the adversary process supply the means to expose these testimonial shortcomings. The Constitution does not impose Fed. R.Evid. 702 on the states, let alone require that federal courts scrutinize line by line the state-court testimony of experts conceded to be competent.[25]

Hair is class evidence and thus it is not possible to determine that a questioned hair sample came from a particular individual to the exclusion of all others. However, as long as a match is not claimed, and there is a sufficient number of variants compared and found consistent, or not dissimilar, etc., such particular transactional facts can often resolve a factual dispute in the eyes of a jury. The specific case analyses that follow, especially in the Moore and Williams prosecutions, illustrate this central point.

While macroscopic and microscopic characteristic variates used by the forensic examiner in the comparison of hairs can be used to distinguish between hairs from different individuals, no systematic attempt to develop data on the frequency of those characteristic variates in study populations has been made as there has in DNA analyses.[26] The lack of such population databases that would be useful in determining the chances of any such "match" occurring in the general population here, as in most of the forensic sciences, is of major concern to students of the criminal justice system.[27]

V. Recent Case Discussions: Qualifications

The qualifications of a forensic expert are a key component in the acceptance or rejection of the expert's opinion and supporting methodology by a jury. It is important to keep track of all such cases in an attempt to gauge the level of expertise that will suffice in the nation's criminal trials. Currently no standard is used in each of the disciplines that has gained acceptance in the courts. Efforts are underway by distinct disciplines to achieve this, but no agreed-upon level of education, training, and experience.[28]

In *Wentz v. State*,[29] a proffered hair analyst testified on *voir dire* that she was employed by the Indiana State Police as a forensic serologist and hair analyst, that she held an associate in arts degree and a bachelor of science degree, that she attended an eighteen-week state police training program for hair analysis, that she had passed the required proficiency tests, that she had attended the FBI Academy of Hairs and Fibers, and that she belonged to the Midwestern Association of Forensic Scientists, which was sufficient to qualify her as an expert. The court found no violation of Indiana Evidence Rule 702, and concluded that had defendant's counsel objected to her qualifications, the result would have been the same. This unimpressive background would no doubt pass muster in most states.

In the case of *State v. Duncan*,[30] a murder case, defendant appealed, in part, questioning the qualifications of a hair analyst with regard to dog hairs from defendant's dogs found in the victim's home. The trial court was found to have acted within its discretion in admitting expert testimony that several hairs found in victim's home were consistent with a sample of hairs obtained from defendant's dogs.

The state called Bill Gartside, a criminologist in the DNA serology section of the Nebraska State Patrol laboratory, who had examined a number of hairs from victim Bennett's home and found that several were consistent with a reference sample of hairs collected from Duncan's dogs. Duncan objected to Gartside's qualifications as an expert in hair analysis and made a motion *in limine* to preclude Gartside from offering any testimony regarding hair analysis. It was Garside's position that the dog hairs were carried into the victim's home on the defendant's clothing or shoes, and were left as he moved through the defendant's residence.

The Nebraska Supreme Court ruled that the trial court acted within its discretion in determining that criminologist was qualified to testify as an expert witness in the field of hair analysis, where the criminologist testified that he worked in the DNA serology section of State Patrol laboratory, where he examined evidence for blood, body fluids, and hairs; had received specialized training in his field, and had authored published articles and papers related to his work. He also described the procedures used to examine hair and estimated that he had probably looked at "thousands" of hairs in his career. The trial court acted within its discretion in admitting expert testimony that several hairs found in murder victim's home were consistent with a sample of hairs obtained from defendant's dogs and that expert testimony could have assisted jury in determining if defendant was guilty of victim's murder.[31]

The discussion of the response to the claims of forensic hair analysis by contemporary courts begins with a detailed examination of two important decisions by Indiana's appellate court and Supreme Court in the case of *McGrew v. State*.[32] These two opinions merit close attention because they address the very foundations of forensic hair analysis, focus on the key concerns of lawyers, and provide a clear example of the potential conflict between the methodology of observation-based forensic sciences and the constitutional requirement of proof beyond a reasonable doubt.

In the McGrew case, the defendant was charged with deviate sexual assault. The state alleged that McGrew struck up a conversation with the victim, whom he had met before, in a local tavern. They traveled to several other bars to continue their conversations. On their way to a final destination, they drove in defendant's automobile, until the defendant pulled onto a dead-end road to urinate. The victim testified that when he returned he entered on the passenger side, instructing her to move behind the steering wheel. After a brief period of talking and kissing, McGrew forced her to perform oral sex on him.[33] McGrew was indicted on a charge of criminal deviate conduct.

Two weeks after the incident, several hairs were recovered from an area near the center of the front seat, and were compared with head and pubic hair samples obtained from both the victim and the defendant McGrew. Upon defense motion, a hearing was held outside the presence of the jury to determine the admissibility of proffered testimony by Carl Sobieralski, a state police DNA analyst, who was also trained in hair analysis and did the comparisons of the hairs taken from McGrew's automobile. McGrew moved to exclude Sobieralski's testimony, asserting that microscopic hair analysis had never been empirically tested and that, accordingly, any findings by an expert such as Sobieralski, were too uncertain to be scientifically reliable. The trial court denied the motion, observing that expert testimony focused on microscopic hair analysis had recently been allowed in Indiana courts. Therefore, any issues regarding the reliability of the results went to the weight, and not the admissibility, of Sobieralski's testimony. The trial judge acknowledged that microscopic hair analysis was not a traditional scientific evaluation, but rather, was simply a person's observations under a microscope, much like an expert in handwriting analysis comparing handwriting exemplars.[34]

Sobieralski then testified, over McGrew's objection, that examination of the hairs retrieved from his car revealed a hair dissimilar to McGrew's head hair sample, but sufficiently similar to the victim's head hair sample to be of common origin, thus evidencing her presence in that area of his car. However, the opposite result was obtained when Sobieralski compared a pubic hair recovered from the car with McGrew's pubic hair sample. Sobieralski acknowledged that he was not testifying the hairs found in the car were from the victim's head and McGrew's pubic region, only that they were sufficiently similar to her head hair and McGrew's pubic hair.[35]

The Indiana Court of Appeals observed that while Indiana had previously used the spirit of the general acceptability standard of the Frye case, the Indiana Supreme Court had made it clear that expert scientific testimony was no longer admissible unless the court was satisfied that the scientific principles upon which the testimony rests were reliable, a precondition to be imposed on all scientific evidence, regardless of whether the underlying principles were based on novel science or were rooted in established principles.[36] Once the court has determined that the particular scientific technique is capable of producing reliable results, however, any questions regarding the reliability of a specific testing procedure, or the results of a specific test, go to the weight of the scientific testimony and not its admissibility.[37]

In this case, the court noted, the trial court did not expressly take judicial notice of the reliability of the scientific principles supporting microscopic hair analysis. In fact, it was apparent that the trial judge did not consider hair analysis to be a "traditional" type of scientific evaluation requiring the proponent to lay a foundation of reliability. The court observed that while a colorable argument could possibly be made to support this view, neither party had argued that microscopic hair analysis was non-scientific testimony exempt from the foundational requirement imposed by Evid.R. 702(b).[38] It seemed clear that in the McGrew case the court was dealing with more than just a visual observation of a hair under a microscope. In that sense, the court ruled, there were therefore "scientific principles" intimately and necessarily involved in the process that led to the expert testimony.[39]

The appellate court carefully noted that the "scientific" principles at work in this case were far from sophisticated assurances of reliability and of probative value:

> As noted, the conclusion of microscopic hair comparison is usually couched in terms merely of "similarity," "might be," or "could be." Such testimony does not lend itself to categorization as evidence of meaningful probative value. This deficiency has prompted a good deal of the debate concerning admissibility of hair analysis by comparison microscope. Early on, at least one commentator noted that hair analysis by microscope was primitive even in 1982 and not the best technological device to produce meaningful hair analysis evidence. The author proposed that hair analysis evidence was underemployed because of the valid criticism of less conclusive methods such as by comparison microscope, and that "the modern hair analyst has tools more powerful than the microscope ... and that the analyst can make many findings more specific than a general conclusion that two hair samples appear similar."[40]

The appellate court made it clear that it was not concerned whether hair analysis could be made more meaningful to a criminal jury or whether it could be made meaningful at all, but assuming that hair analysis could aid the jury in its deliberations and might be relevant, the task is simply to determine whether an appropriate and adequate foundation preceded the admission of the expert opinion.[41]

During trial, the expert Sobieralski explained that microscopic hair analysis consisted of visually examining the hair samples side by side under a comparison microscope, looking at a number of different physical characteristics, such as the cortex, cuticle, root, tip, cortical fusi, ovoid bodies, pigment and pigment dispersal, cuticle thickness, gaping, and whether the hair had been dyed or specially treated. If, upon comparison, the hairs were found to be sufficiently similar, he would make a determination that they could have come from the same person. He defined "sufficiently similar" in the context of microscopic hair analysis with the following example:

> (I)f I took that pubic hair and dropped it into a pile of standards that was pulled from [the victim, J.W.], I'd be able to tell the difference. But when I dropped [the pubic hair recovered from the car] into a pile of standards of (McGrew), I could not tell the difference between them.[42]

The Court of Appeals, while noting that microscopic hair analysis has been routinely admitted by state and federal courts for many years with little skepticism,[43] found here that the state witnesses' bald assertions totally failed to present any evidence to satisfy the first three prongs of Daubert:

> Upon questioning by McGrew's counsel and the trial court, Sobieralski acknowledged that he was not aware of any error ratio for the technique, nor was he aware of any articles or journals disputing the methodology. He also admitted that he did not know the statistical percentages of certain hair characteristics in the general population or the probability of a particular hair sample coming from persons other than McGrew or J.W. The court emphasized that expert Sobieralski did make the bald assertion that microscopic hair analysis was accepted in the scientific community, but did not describe which scientific community nor expound upon the degree of acceptance.[44]

Here, the appellate court ruled that the trial court erred in admitting Sobieralski's testimony. The court emphasized that it was not establishing a *per se* rule of unreliability and hence inadmissibility for microscopic hair analysis. It was obvious, from the cited sources in the area, that the methodology had been to a degree tested and peer-reviewed, and that an expert could conceivably come to court prepared with sufficient information in the form of data, studies, and scholarly articles to meet at least three of the

Daubert prongs. Here, however, the state mistakenly believed that a Daubert reliability foundation was only required for novel scientific techniques, and thus did not even attempt to lay a requisite foundation.[45]

The evidence that hair found in McGrew's car "probably" came from the victim's head was merely cumulative of McGrew's admission that J.W. was in his car. The same could not be said, however, of Sobieralski's testimony that a pubic hair found on the front seat was substantially similar to McGrew's. In this case, the court noted, the conviction rested in large part upon the victim's credibility. The pubic hair comparison was the only physical evidence corroborating her claim that McGrew removed his pants. Defendant had not admitted to disrobing in his car and there was no medical evidence that an act of sexual deviate conduct had occurred.[46] The pubic hair testimony would most likely have had a considerable influence upon the mind of the average juror because it was the only evidence implying that McGrew exposed his genitals:

> This impact was heightened by the special aura of trustworthiness surrounding expert testimony, and the fact that, in the case of microscopic hair analysis, jurors do not generally have the opportunity for direct evaluation... We conclude that the erroneous admission of the pubic hair evidence constitutes reversible error because, reviewing the record as a whole, there is a substantial likelihood that this evidence contributed to the conviction.[47]

In the Indiana Supreme Court's decision in *McGrew v. State*,[48] the court, with misgivings, reversed the appellate court's decision and reinstated McGrew's conviction, noting that the court of appeals found that the trial court erroneously admitted the expert testimony on hair comparison analysis and reversed the defendant's conviction. At the trial, the court observed, immediately prior to the hair analyst's testimony during the trial, the defendant challenged the admissibility of the hair comparison analysis under Indiana Evidence Rule 702(b). In a hearing outside the presence of the jury, the defendant called the Indiana State Police analyst to the stand.

When asked by the defendant what scientific principle is used to base the reliability of hair sample technique, the analyst testified, *Scientific principle? It's just simply a physical comparison of one hair directly to another one.* He testified that he used a microscope to make a physical comparison of one hair to another, looking at several different physical characteristics. Specifically, he testified that he compares the medulla, cortex, cuticle, root, tip, cortical fusi, ovoid bodies, pigment, thickness, gaping, the condition of hair, whether the hair had been cut with a razor or scissors, and whether it had been dyed or specially treated. He testified that these characteristics were physically observed through a microscope.[49]

The court observed that when the defendant questioned the analyst about the statistical error ratio for hair comparison as compared to the statistical error ratio for blood or DNA typing, the analyst testified that, while blood or DNA typing had statistical error ratios, he was not aware of any statistics with regard to the probability of a hair sample belonging to someone else. This lack of information, the expert continued, was simply due to the nature of hair comparison. The defendant had asked whether there was no other way to determine this information scientifically, except from his or your own physical observations. The analyst answered yes and testified that this was accepted in the scientific community, and that there were absolutely no articles or journals that [he was] aware of that dispute this method.[50] On cross-examination, the state elicited testimony that microscopes were generally accepted in the scientific community, that, as far as he knew, no state disallowed hair comparisons, and that he was an expert in the use of microscopes.[51]

Prior to dismissing the expert, the trial court directed several questions to him:

> Court: [I]n regard to the examination. It is simply a physical, visual examination of the hair?
>
> Analyst: Yes, sir.
>
> Court: You simply say that one hair looks like another one or it doesn't look like another one.
>
> Analyst: I say it's sufficiently similar to have come from that person or it is dissimilar.
>
> Court: And if you say that it … [is] similar to come from that person … that doesn't mean that it comes from that person.
>
> Analyst: It just simply means that it could have come from that person.
>
> Court: And you do not know the statistical percentages of how many people would have similar hair?
>
> Analyst: There are no statistics. It's hard to say.[52]

In finding the evidence to be admissible, the trial court had concluded:

> As I see it, what we're talking about is not the traditional scientific evaluation. We are talking about simply a person's observations

under a microscope, which is a magnification to compare some hairs to one another, much as an expert in handwriting analysis compares handwriting. They can't tell you how many people out there have the same ... handwriting. They just say whether it's sufficiently similar. I believe that it has been accepted in the state. Although I don't know of any ... specific cases. I know that it has been utilized here before.... It seems to me as though it goes to the weight of the evidence and it is, of course, highly subject to the questions about [the] statistical comparisons and, apparently, there are none .... but it can say that this hair looks like the other hair....7 So what (the analyst) has observed through the microscope will be admissible.[53]

In the present case, the Indiana Supreme Court concluded that the trial court, contrary to the ruling of the Court of Appeals, had indeed exercised appropriate discretion as to the reliability of the proffered hair comparison analysis:

The analyst testified that the hair comparison he performed was a comparison of physical characteristics, as seen under a microscope. Inherent in any reliability analysis is the understanding that, as the scientific principles become more advanced and complex, the foundation required to establish reliability will necessarily become more advanced and complex as well. The converse is just as applicable, as demonstrated by the trial court's conclusion that "what we're talking about is not the traditional scientific evaluation. We are talking about simply a person's observations under a microscope." This conclusion is not unlike our recent statement that the evidence at issue was more a "matter of the observations of persons with specialized knowledge" than "a matter of 'scientific principles' governed by Indiana Evidence Rule 702(b)."[54]

The judgment of the trial court against defendant McGrew was affirmed.

The status of hair analysis as an observational discipline utilizing modern microscopes as opposed to a novel scientific technique requiring an extensive Daubert reliability hearing was raised again in the recent 1999 Montana Supreme Court decision in *State v. Southern*.[55] There, the defendant was convicted of kidnapping, burglary, theft, and sexual intercourse without consent. The victims were all older women who were sexually assaulted in the same limited geographical area — either in their homes in Helena, Montana; at a rural location west of Helena;, or both. The perpetrator covered each victim's face with an article of clothing and demanded money. All assaults occurred within a time span of two and one-half years (April 25, 1994 to November 2, 1996).[56]

Among a host of alleged errors claimed by defendant, he cited the denial of his motion-*in-limine* regarding the state's proposed offer of microscopic hair analysis. Southern filed a motion *in limine* to exclude the testimony of a forensic scientist at the Montana State Crime Lab, who eventually testified at the trial that she microscopically compared Southern's hair sample to hairs from the rape scenes and that the hair from the rape scenes was either similar to or consistent with the defendant's sample. Southern objected to this testimony, maintaining that her testimony was inadmissible because it did not satisfy the factors for the reliability of expert testimony that the United States Supreme Court set out in *Daubert v. Merrell Dow Pharmaceuticals, Inc.*[57]

The State responded that, because microscopic hair comparison was not considered novel scientific evidence, the defendant's reliance on Daubert was misplaced. The Montana Supreme Court took note of the recent United States Supreme Court ruling in *Kumho Tire Co. v. Carmichael*,[58] that the trial court's gatekeeping obligation under Federal rule of Evidence Rule 702 applied not only to testimony based on scientific knowledge but also to testimony based on technical and other specialized knowledge. Regardless of *Kumho Tire*, the Montana Supreme Court emphasized that the test of reliability was flexible and that Daubert's factors neither necessarily nor exclusively apply to all experts or in every case.[59]

In the instant case, the court ruled that microscopic hair comparison was not novel scientific evidence, its research having indicated that the court had considered and so found on at least five cases since 1978 where a witness had testified on microscopic hair comparison.[60] Moreover, the court noted, here the expert had testified that comparing hair samples with a microscope had been done for decades. Therefore, because microscopic hair comparison was not considered novel scientific evidence, the District Court was not in error in refusing to conduct a Daubert reliability hearing to test its reliability.[61]

The above discussion of the McGrew and Southern cases clearly demonstrates the general acceptability or reliability of microscopic hair analysis by recent decisions of American courts. It remains to be seen if this basic pattern of acceptance is of sufficient substance to place this issue legally to rest, or if it simply reflects momentary resignation in the face of the ubiquitous use of hair analysis and its recent disfavor in comparison to mtDNA advances in the area of hair analysis.[62]

Prosecutorial Characterizations of Hair Testimony

The extent to which forensic scientists can make linking statements, given the nature of microscopic hair analysis and the other trace evidence disciplines, is a question that has been the subject of a number of appellate cases and is one of the areas of clear difference between practitioners of the forensic sciences and those of the criminal law. This issue can be examined from the standpoints of investigation of crime and its prosecution. Investigators quite properly are less insistent on the legally precise linking terminology than courts, choosing to take an expert's statement of a match for hair, fiber, soils, etc., as solid leads In the legal world, this difference in language query can be understood simply by asking two questions. What can the expert legally say? What can the prosecutor say the expert said?

In the 1991 Illinois Supreme Court decision in *People v. Linscott*,[63] the court extensively addressed the pitfalls of statistical evidence in relation to hair analysis as well as the linguistic range of permissible "match" statements by expert witnesses and prosecutors. Karen Ann Phillips, the victim, was found dead in her apartment in Oak Park, Illinois. Police found the victim's body face down and naked, except for a nightgown pushed up around her neck and shoulders. An autopsy revealed that her death was caused by several blows to her head and strangulation. Hairs were found clasped in the victim's hands, in her pubic region, and in a carpet on the floor of her apartment. These hairs were removed and tests were conducted on them as part of the investigation.[64]

Three expert witnesses testified on the subject of hair comparisons. Mark Stolorow, the coordinator of serology for the Illinois Department of Law Enforcement, testified for the State concerning the procedures for hair comparison testing that were employed by the department, explaining that through the employment of a comparison microscope, a simultaneous visual comparison is made of the characteristics of hair samples from two different sources. He testified that this methodology excluded classes of individuals from consideration as suspects in an investigation and was conclusive, if at all, only to negate identity.[65]

A second state expert, Mohammad Tahir, a forensic scientist for the Illinois Department of Law Enforcement, testified regarding hair comparisons he performed on the hair samples taken from the victim and from the defendant, explaining that he looked at approximately 7 to 12 characteristics.[66] Based upon those comparisons, Tahir concluded that certain of the hairs found in the victim's apartment were consistent with the samples provided by defendant. Tahir defined consistent as no dissimilarity. Tahir testified that defendant's hair samples were consistent with those hairs found in the victim's right hand, hairs found on the carpet, and two pubic hairs that were combed from the victim's pubic region. On cross-examination, however, Tahir conceded that a person cannot be identified by the hairs he leaves behind:

Defense: And you sure can't determine from whose head that hair came from, can you?

Tahir: You cannot positively say.

*   *   *

Q. Okay, you couldn't even say that if you had two pieces of hair from the same head, could you?

A. *My answer is the same, what I told you* (is) that you cannot say that this hair came from this individual, only could say that it is consistent with (sic).[67]

Despite this testimony, the prosecutor argued that hairs found in the victim's apartment and on the victim's body were in fact defendant's hairs. In closing argument, the prosecutor told the jury that:

...the rug in the area where Karen was laying (sic) was ripped out sometime later, rolled up, and shipped to the laboratory. And that another group of hairs (was) obtained — the head hairs of Steven Linscott.

*   *   *

...he (defendant)] left eight to ten hairs of his in that apartment; his (defendant's) pubic hairs [were found] in her crotch; and his (defendant's) hairs are found in the most private parts of the woman's body.[68]

The court ruled that the prosecutor improperly argued, by these statements, that the hairs removed from the victim's apartment were conclusively identified as coming from defendant Linscott's head and pubic region, when there simply was no testimony at trial to support such assertions. In fact, the court continued, both state experts, as well as defendant's, had all testified that no such identification was possible. The prosecutor's misrepresentation of the hair-comparison evidence was compounded, the court observed, by his argument that the mathematical probabilities that the hairs found on the victim's body and in her apartment came from anyone other than defendant were minuscule. The prosecutor relied on hair-comparison studies published by the forensic scientist Barry Gaudette for the statistics he used. The only testimony heard on these numerical arguments was elicited from defendant's expert on cross-examination.

Because of the importance of this subject and the scarcity of judicial discussion of it, the entire text of the cross-examination follows:

> Prosecutor: You are aware of a forensic scientist by the name of Barry Gaudette, are you not?
>
> Siegesmund: Gaudette is one of the proponents of x-ray analysis.
>
> Q. Mr. Gaudette performed a study in the early to middle 70s, did he not, with regard to the percentages and probabilities of hair comparisons?
>
> A. Absolutely.
>
> Q. And his technique that he used was with a comparison microscope, was it not, sir?
>
> A. He used comparison. And he also used other microscopes.
>
> Q. But he used a comparison microscope. The one microscope you did not use, is that correct?
>
> A. Yes, he did use that, also.
>
> Q. And his probabilities came to the substance that a match between head hairs is likely in one out of every 4,500 cases, is that correct.
>
> A. Well, can I explain that?
>
> Q. I'll rephrase the question. Did he not come up with a figure that, (in) any two individuals, the probability they would have matching head hairs is a likelihood in one out of 4,500?
>
> A. It depends on how many hairs you are talking about.
>
> Q. Would you say, the more hairs you have to compare, the closer to that figure you get?
>
> A. The higher the probability, that is correct.

Q. So, in this case, if we had but one hair that Mr. Tahir linked to Mr. Linscott, that would have that much meaning, is that correct?

A. Yes. Using the conventional techniques that Gaudette used, yes.

Q. That Gaudette used, that's correct?

A. Yes.

Q. If you have two to three hairs, your information is a little better, is that correct?

A. Yes. Only if you do the forty tests he recommends.

Q. Fine, if you had, approximately, seven or eight hairs, you have more information to base it on?

A. According to Gaudette, that would give you a higher probability. If you did the forty tests.[69]

Based on the evidence at trial, the court ruled that the mathematical probabilities from Gaudette's study should not have been considered by the jury. Siegesmund had made it clear in his testimony that Gaudette's findings in his work were based on the completion of 40 tests, not simply the 7 to 12 comparison tests performed by state expert Tahir. Because no evidence was available that "forty tests" were ever performed in this case, no foundation for the thesis that Gaudette's mathematical statistics were applicable here existed. In addition, the prosecutor in closing argument commented that the defendant's hair had been found at the crime scene. The Linscott court found that the prosecutor's comment was improper because the evidence merely showed that the defendant was in a class of possible donors of the hair and not that the hair conclusively belonged to the defendant. Because the evidence in Linscott was so closely balanced, this court concluded that the improper comment amounted to plain error.[70]

In most published opinions involving hair evidence, the underlying methodology has gone unchallenged or is deemed reliable by a court to its allegedly venerable past acceptance by courts across the nation. It bears repeating that the existence of adequately founded expert witness testimony has very considerable impact on a jury that may be unable or unwilling to separate less-than-certain conclusions from the scientific patina given the testimony by the establishing of the expert's credentials and her description of the laboratory procedures used in the case at hand. Again, this is not to criticize the experts, but simply to recognize the cleansing effect that such tentative but microscopically based forensic disciplines can have on the more traditional types of evidence presented in criminal cases, such as eyewitness testimony. In the past several decades, more than 200 reported decisions have been made passing reference to the propriety of using microscopic hair analysis in prosecutions. The following cases highlight some of the numerous uses of microscopic hair analysis testimony made in a wide variety of fact settings.

In the case of *People v. Moore*,[71] defendant was charged with first-degree murder, home invasion, residential burglary, aggravated criminal sexual assault, robbery, and arson. Defendant had previously worked at the victim's home as a house painter, and the victim was alone at her home when the defendant returned. The victim was bound with duct tape, tied to the back of a car, and set on fire.[72] Having compared hairs found on the floor mat of defendant's car to known standards, a forensic scientist testified that two hairs were consistent with the victim's head hairs, and that one hair was consistent with the defendant's head hairs and showed signs of extreme heat damage.[73]

Defendant argued that the prosecutor in rebuttal also overstated the evidence when he said, Judy Zeman didn't know that that burnt hair was in her car that came off his [defendant's] head…, [because] a forensic scientist had only testified [that]the burnt hair was consistent with his hair, not that the burnt hair was conclusively defendant's. Defendant argued that the prosecutor's burnt-hair statement constituted reversible error. Here, as in Linscott, the court ruled the prosecutor's comment that the burnt hair in the car came from the defendant's head had indeed overstated the evidence. However, unlike the evidence in Linscott, the evidence here was not closely balanced, and the court concluded that the burnt-hair statement did not deprive the defendant of a fair trial.[74]

Microscopic hair testimony involving the age of the victim was presented in the case of *State v. Williams*,[75] where the defendant was charged with aggravated child abuse. The victim, the defendant's stepdaughter, was thirteen months old when she suffered the very serious injuries in question. Defendant claimed that the child had fallen from its crib when he was out of the room.

The left side of the child's head was bruised and swollen to such an extent that her left ear extended perpendicular to her head. X-rays disclosed a hematoma and fracture on the left side and back of the child's head. A child-abuse investigator searched the defendant's home and in the process found that the distance between the crib and a twin bed in the same room was thirty and one-half inches. The investigator testified if the crib railing was lowered, the distance to the floor was thirty-two and one half inches, estimating that the distance with the railing raised would be approximately forty-four and one-half inches. During the course of the search, the investigator noticed a louvered door that was broken and off its track and contained a blonde hair in a broken slat found on the kitchen table. A hair sample of the victim was obtained and subsequently sent to the Federal Bureau of Investigation Crime Lab for comparison with the hair found on the broken slat.[76]

Dr. Donald Lewis, a pediatrician at Holston Valley Hospital, testified that his examination of the child victim revealed a hematoma to the left side of the child's head and a fracture to the right back portion of the child's skull. He testified that this was not the type of injury that could conceivably result from a thirty-two-and-one-half-inch fall to a carpeted surface. He also testified that the injuries were the result of more than one impact. Because the skull of a thirteen-month-old infant was considerably more pliant than that of an adult, it would take significantly more force to cause trauma to a child's skull. In his view, a fall onto a tiled surface would cause less significant injuries than those suffered by the victim, and that these injuries were consistent with the child being struck with a cornered or edged object and that swinging the child into a louvered door would be one possible scenario as to how these severe injuries occurred.

Clealand Blake, an anatomic pathologist with twenty-eight years' experience, who had examined more than one hundred children, many of whom were victims of head injuries, examined the child victim here and observed an enlarged lymph node near the fracture, which was consistent with the body's reaction to injury. The child's left eyelid and left ear still showed some residual bruising and, based upon the pictures taken at the hospital, the injuries seemed to be approximately thirty-six hours old. Dr. Blake was of the opinion that the child's injuries could not conceivably have occurred as a result of falling two feet, two and one-half feet, or three feet off a bed onto a carpeted floor or even a vinyl floor, commenting that it takes a fall from above a third-story window onto a hard surface for a child to experience such a major head injury. He also opined that there were at least two major injuries to the head of the victim in the case.[77]

Wayne Oakes, a supervisory special agent with the FBI crime laboratory, testified that the blonde hair found in the slat had been forcibly removed and showed no microscopic differences from the hair taken from the child's head during her examination by Dr. Blake. While conceding that microscopic hair analysis did not provide an absolute personal identification, based upon his experience, the hair found on the slat came from a very young child and contained no bleach or dyes.[78]

In the Arkansas Supreme Court decision in *Suggs v. State*,[79] a first-degree murder case, the defendant was accused of murdering his girlfriend, Debbie McKenzie. Defendant challenged the opinion of State Criminalist Don Smith, who testified that he was given hair samples from Debbie McKenzie's body and from Suggs, and he compared those samples with hair found on a tennis shoe belonging to the defendant, concluding that the hair found on Suggs' shoe was McKenzie's. However, defendant noted that expert Smith agreed with the statement that the scientific field of microscopic hair analysis cannot prove the hair came from a certain individual to the exclusion of any other person, thus rendering his testimony in error.[80]

Here, the appeals court held, the trial court correctly qualified Smith as an expert concerning the field of trace evidence. Smith testified that, as a criminalist, he dealt with scientific evidence and trace evidence or residues recovered at a crime scene, which includes such things as hair. His training was in specialized areas of hair analysis, including experience with the FBI lab and St. Louis Metropolitan Police lab. The court observed that after having been qualified as an expert, Smith went into considerable detail concerning the analysis performed on Suggs' and McKenzie's hair samples and how those samples were analyzed and compared with the hair found on Suggs' tennis shoe. Suggs' counsel then took the opportunity to thoroughly cross-examine Smith concerning his qualifications and whether he could actually prove the hair on Suggs' shoe belonged to McKenzie. The court concluded that both sides did a more than adequate job of airing the hair analysis issues and that the weight to be given his testimony was for the jury. In sum, the trial court did not err in allowing Smith's testimony.[81]

Many interesting and illustrative cases that address various aspects of the use of microscopic hair analysis can be found in American criminal trials. These cases are deserving of brief attention in this chapter.

In the case of *Pruitt v. State*,[82] decided by the Georgia Supreme Court in 1999, defendant was accused of the rape and murder of a 10-year-old female victim who lived in a trailer next door to his ex-wife's trailer, where he was staying the night. The police became suspicious of Pruitt due to the description of his movements during the last few hours before the estimated time of death. The police noticed that he had scratches and cuts on his hands and found bloodstains on the clothes Pruitt had been wearing the previous night. Given the strength of the Locard Principle, discussed in Chapter 2, that close physical encounters inevitably result in trace transfers of hair and fiber, and the reality of the considerable physical interaction in rape-homicide settings, it is rare that any such cases will depend solely upon hair analysis. Here, inside the victim's bedroom, hairs consistent with Pruitt's head hair were found on the bedroom floor, a bedsheet, a pillow, and the victim's body, panties, socks, and shirt. Hairs consistent with Pruitt's pubic hair were also found on the bedsheet and the bedroom floor. Considerable other forensic evidence was found at the scene and testified to at trial.[83]

The defendant was convicted of murder in the first degree of his wife in the 1999 case of *Commonwealth v. Snell*.[84] Here, the victim had obtained a protective order and an arrest warrant against the defendant. The next day, when the victim's children were unable to reach her, police were called and located the victim's body in the family home. The medical examiner concluded that the victim had died as a result of asphyxia due to smothering, and recorded seventeen injuries on the victim's body that were inflicted contemporaneously or within minutes of the time of her death.[85]

In attacking the entirety of the crime-scene investigation, defendant argued that the police had not sufficiently investigated the case, in particular, by failing to gather evidence that might have exculpated him. Specifically, defendant argued that the court erred in failing to continue the case to permit further DNA testing on hairs found on the blanket used to cover the victim's body. Testing had previously determined that some hairs recovered from the blanket were consistent with the victim's hair, and that seminal fluid on the blanket probably came from the defendant. The trial court ruled that the onus was on the defendant to explain the delay and to establish a need for further testing. The court determined that there was no basis seen in the testimony of the defendant's chemist, or elsewhere, to indicate that further testing of hairs found on the blanket might furnish exculpatory evidence. Hence, the trial judge properly ruled that further delay was unwarranted. Obtaining sufficient, or any, funding for purposes of conducting forensic testing for the defense is directly related to the quality of the demonstration of what could be potentially exculpatory. The Massachusetts Supreme Court made an interesting observation with respect to such requests:

> The defendant's expert removed approximately 300 hairs from the blanket. Some were animal hairs and some were human hairs. The expert testified that examination for trace evidence was important, if there was nothing else. He did not say that failing to look for trace evidence might show something wrong with the investigation. He indicated that it was the decision of the investigators, based on what they felt was necessary at the time. The expert testified to the presence of five separate categories of hair found on the blanket, but did not suggest the hair had come from different people. It may have come from only two people. The defendant lived with the victim in the marital home.[86]

The initial lack of adequate funding in most jurisdictions illustrates the "Catch 22" nature of any such motions.

In *State v. Ware*,[87] a 1999 Tennessee appellate court decision, defendant Paul Ware was indicted in 1994 for felony murder and multiple counts of rape of a child. Defendant was staying with the victim's mother and according to the state, sexually assaulted the child after the mother and friends left the residence to go to a tavern. Significant issues in this case involved certain hairs found on and inside the child's body. During the autopsy, a "reddish hair" was found that was stuck to the victim's lip, a dark-brown body hair that was "partly touching … the mucosa of the rectum and partly touching the skin of the anus," and a reddish pubic hair from the victim's pharynx. The defendant had hair coloring that was deemed red or auburn. In a horrifying rendition of the autopsy findings, the pathologist testified that with regard to the dark-brown hair, "it would take direct contact and a little pressure applied to get that hair to stick to the mucosal lining in the rectum.... Any handling of the body, moving of the body from one place to another, examination of the body by a person or persons could potentially be sources of contamination to supply loose hair...." Furthermore, he testified that the pubic hair found in the victim's pharynx was highly unusual. He explained that a normal, breathing, living person would not be expected to tolerate a hair in this location because any intrusion into this area would trigger a cough reflex.[88]

Special Agent Chris Hopkins of the FBI Hair and Fibers Unit characterized the hair that was found in the victim's pharynx as a "red Caucasian pubic hair," which had been "naturally shed." He also discussed "at least ten red Caucasian pubic hairs" that were taken from the sheet on the bed where defendant admitted he had placed the sleeping victim. He testified that pubic hairs were naturally shed from putting on and off your underwear, changing clothes, or taking a shower. He also stated that pubic hairs may be naturally shed when one person rubs against another. Agent Hopkins explained that the hairs on the sheet were very significant:

(W)hen hair or fibers fall on a piece of evidence, they tend not to stay there very long.... (I)f there is no activity in (a) bed, then you would expect the hairs to stay there because there is no reason for them to move around, but if someone is using that bed on a regular basis, … you wouldn't expect those hairs to stay there.

He also stated, "I would not expect to find that many pubic hairs in [a] bed that has just been slept in."[89]

Hopkins opined that all hairs, the hair from the victim's pharynx and those from the sheet, were consistent with originating from the [d]efendant. As in all other cases, when pressed, he testified that hair comparison was "not capable of individual identification and thus he was unable to state conclusively whether the hairs belonged to the defendant. However, he did conclude that Carl Sanders, Danny Gaddis, and Paul Crum, the other men in the home at that period, were each eliminated as being potential sources of the pubic hairs.[90]

Agent Hopkins also concluded that the hair found on the victim's lip was red in color and was likely a chest hair. He stated that the hair removed from the victim's anus was a brown Caucasian body hair and therefore was "not suitable for comparison," explaining:

> The only two regions, the only two types of hairs that are suitable for comparison purposes are... head hairs and pubic hairs.... Hairs, other hairs than head hairs and pubic hairs, these body area hairs or hairs on your arms or your legs, they tend to look like other people's hair, so there's not a significant association that can *be made when comparing those hairs.*[91]

Despite some evidence suggesting that the defendant may not have committed the crime, there was clearly substantial evidence presented at trial in addition to the crucial hair testimony indicating that the defendant did commit the crime. As noted above, sufficiently clear and well-presented trace evidence, such as microscopic hair analysis, can lend significant support to the credibility of nonscientific evidence, which typically constitutes the greater part of the state's proof.[92]

In *Manning v. State,*[93] a 1998 Mississippi Supreme Court decision involving numerous aspects of forensic science, the defendant was charged with the double homicide and armed robbery of two college students. The State called Chester Blythe, a special agent with the FBI, to testify as an expert in the field of hair analysis. He testified that he could microscopically determine if the hairs looked alike and determine with some degree of certainty, although not absolutely, if hairs, for example, found in vacuum sweepings from an automobile, originated from a particularly named individual. He also testified that in the two specimens he had, which were collected from victim Tiffany Miller's car, he was able to determine that hairs found in these specimens exhibited characteristics associated with the black race.[94]

Defendant argued that hair analysis was "latter-day voodoo." The court, disagreeing, stated that hair-analysis expert testimony was admissible, finding it to be a very useful tool in criminal investigation. Here, the expert did not claim that the hair matched that of the defendant, but only that the hair came from a member of the black race. He also admitted that his expertise could not produce absolute certainty. This did not invade the province of the jury, the court stated, but left the matter to it to decide if these were Manning's hairs or not.[95]

In another case involving child victims, *State v. Butler,*[96] a 1998 Missouri ruling, the defendant was convicted of one count of sodomy, one count of felonious restraint, and two counts of armed criminal action, arising out of the sexual assaults upon two minor males. The victims described the man as about five feet, seven or eight inches tall, 170 lbs., with brown curly hair that came down from under a dark baseball cap, wearing a dark tee shirt, shorts, and tennis shoes. The defendant, who lived in the same mobile-home park, became a suspect, and head and pubic hair samples were taken from him. The major point on appeal concerned the state's expert testimony with regard to an unknown head hair recovered from victim J.L.'s shirt, and the unknown pubic hair recovered from J.L.'s underwear.

The state expert forensic chemist testified the unknown hair came from the same person. She admitted that microscopic hair analysis was unable to positively identify individuals based on hair comparison. She testified that there were not as many distinguishing characteristics in hair as in DNA samples or fingerprints, so that a criminalist could not tell what percent of the population could have contributed that hair, and the opinion would be subjective but based on experience. As to the head hair samples, she stated: I feel there is a very strong probability that those two hairs came from the defendant.[97] Her opinion was based in part on an unusual spot on a certain part of the hair found on the victim, which also appeared in the same spot on Butler's hair. The witness testified that she could, within a reasonable degree of certainty, testify that the unknown hairs were in fact from the defendant.

Defendant argued that the circumstantial evidence of the match between his head and pubic hair with those taken from the victim's clothing was insufficient, and without other evidence of the defendant's involvement, the state's case was insufficient. The court noted that the issue raised here did not depend upon the admissibility of hair testimony, but rather, the lack of certainty inherent in the discipline of hair examination and the inability of an expert to quote statistical support as in DNA contexts:

> This court is mindful of Butler's contention the only thing linking him to this crime is the opinion evidence of the state's forensic expert, but, ... that evidence is sufficient to sustain the verdict reached by the jury. The jury here was free to reject Butler's assertion he had been at the park's swimming pool the afternoon in question and the hairs could have been picked up by the victim during the afternoon when he may have been swimming at the same pool. The expert's testimony was admitted into evidence, and was sufficient to allow the jury to find that the head and pubic hairs found on the victim which contained the same characteristics and unusual mark as those of Butler, were Butler's hairs, and conclude that Butler was the assailant.[98]

VI. Mitochondrial DNA [mtDNA] and Hair Analysis

The most recent important development in the forensic examination of hair is the increasing use of mitochondrial DNA (mtDNA) testing of hairs as a backup or replacement for the traditional microscopic examination and comparison of hair samples from the crime scene and those associated with the defendant.[99] The overwhelming number of forensic microscopic hair examinations have been and continue to be core methodology for forensic hair examinations. That situation is rapidly changing as a series of new cases address and approve the use of mtDNA analysis in these cases. Because mtDNA analysis is certainly the future for forensic hair analysis, the following sections turn to analysis of several of the most important mtDNA cases in both state and federal courts, considering the leading case of *State v. Pappas*,[100] a 2001 Connecticut Supreme Court decision where defendant was convicted of bank robbery, in part, by hair expertise linking to the crimes by the use of mitochondrial DNA analysis. The clarity and detail of this central mtDNA opinion warrants extensive examination here.

During their investigation, the police recovered two head hairs from a sweatshirt (questioned sample) that had been recovered following the robbery. The FBI performed an mtDNA analysis of the questioned sample and the defendant's head hair (known sample), compared the results and concluded that the defendant could not be excluded as the source of the questioned sample. Before trial, the defendant moved to exclude all evidence regarding mtDNA testing and analysis and, pursuant, requested a hearing as to the reliability of mtDNA testing and analysis. During the hearing, the trial court heard testimony from the state's expert, FBI Special Agent Mark Wilson, and the defendant's expert, William Shields, a professor of biology.

Wilson testified about DNA generally, the mtDNA extraction process, and the statistical significance of a match of mtDNA types.[101] He testified that DNA was located in two places in humans, the vast majority of which is stored within the nucleus of a human cell and is known as nuclear DNA. Nuclear DNA consists of approximately three billion base pairs, and the particular sequence of the base pairs in nuclear DNA makes each individual unique and accounts for our genetic traits. Wilson explained that mitochondrial DNA, or mtDNA, differs from nuclear DNA with respect to its location within a cell, its uniqueness among individuals, sequence length, and its mode of inheritance.

First, mtDNA is found within mitochondria, which are circular structures surrounding the cellular nucleus that provide a cell with energy. Second, mtDNA, unlike nuclear DNA, cannot be used to establish positive identification because mtDNA consists of but a single marker that is approximately 16,569 base pairs in length. By comparison, nuclear DNA consists of approximately three billion base pairs and many discrete markers, or loci, that can be compared to establish a positive match between DNA samples.[102] Wilson explained that, because mtDNA has only one marker, the probability of a random match is much higher between mtDNA samples than between nuclear DNA samples. Thus, according to Wilson, mtDNA is significantly less probative of identity than is nuclear DNA. Third, whereas nuclear DNA is inherited from both parents, mtDNA is inherited maternally.

The trial court, in its oral decision, extensively summarized that process as follows:

> The first step in an mtDNA analysis of a hair sample is to perform microscopic analysis. If the hairs appear microscopically similar, the mtDNA analysis is performed to determine on a molecular level whether or not the hair is consistent with (hair) originating from a particular person.[103]

> The next step is a washing step to remove any contaminating materials surrounding or coating the evidentiary sample. The next step is DNA extraction where the homogenate obtained by placing the hair sample in a solution and (while) grinding and shearing it is exposed to a mixture of organic chemicals which separate the DNA from other biological molecules such as proteins. The organic mixture is spun in a centrifuge, and the DNA is soluble in the top, water-based layer, while the rest of the cellular components are soluble in the bottom, organic layer, or in the interface between the two (layers). The top layer is then removed and filtered for further separation from the other cellular materials.

> The next step is amplification by Polymerase Chain Reaction (PCR). PCR is a technique which takes a small amount of DNA and copies it in a process known as amplification. The two strands of the DNA helix are separated from one another, which is accomplished by heating the sample. At this point, the original DNA molecules in the extract, called the templates, separate into their component strands. A new DNA strand is made by using an enzyme that copies the existing DNA molecule. This copying process is repeated a number of times and, during each repetitive cycle, the amount of DNA in the reaction is doubled. At the end of this process, many more copies of the original DNA in the extract are present.

> The next step is known as post-amplification purification and quantification. This is to determine how much product was generated by PCR. This step is completed with a capillary electrophoresis machine. Blank samples, which contain no DNA, and known control samples are used to assess the amplification of the

samples (to ensure that a sufficient number of copies have been made).

The next step is sequencing. The method of DNA sequencing is known as Sanger's method. This technique uses the process of DNA synthesis to accomplish the determination of the sequence of bases in an individual's mtDNA. The sequencing process differs from PCR in that another set of the A, G, C, and T bases, with slight chemical differences, is added to the reaction mix. These bases differ from the normal bases in that they lack a chemical group that would normally allow the enzyme to place another base after them. These altered bases also carry a fluorescent dye which is readily detected by an automated machine. As they become incorporated into the growing DNA strand, the process of synthesis ends due to the inabilities of the enzyme to add another base to the altered fluorescent one. The sequencing reaction is subjected to thermal cycling, just as in PCR. The normal bases compete with the altered bases for incorporation into the new strand and what results is a collection of DNA products which, when pooled, have altered bases inserted at every possible position in the area to be sequenced.

The next step is sequence determination. The many products resulting from the sequence reaction are separated based on their length through gel migration. The size of the pores in the gel matrix regulates the distance that each DNA product travels. These products all begin from the same starting point on a gel and the fluorescence detector from the sequencing machine reads off the bases as they occur from the bottom of the gel back up to the top. The identity of each was revealed by the fluorescent tag on the altered base. The machine will generate a chromatogram, or colored graph, depicting the wavelength of the dye that it reads one base at a time. The sequence of the DNA is determined from a series of these sequencing reactions.[104]

Agent Wilson also testified about the FBI procedures utilized to prevent and detect contamination of samples. He stated that mtDNA analysis was a sensitive process and that, because contamination could affect the result, the FBI laboratory procedures seek to eliminate contamination.[105] Wilson stated that contamination could reach 20 to 25% without compromising the typing results, but under the FBI protocol, if contamination exceeds 10 percent, that sample is discarded and the process is performed again. Wilson testified that if contamination did occur, it would not cause a false positive (a false inclusion) but, rather, would result in a false negative (a false exclusion).

Finally, Wilson testified that the FBI laboratory undergoes semi-annual external proficiency tests. The test provider sends samples to the FBI lab and the lab technicians analyze those samples as if they are evidence from a case. The test provider then compares the FBI lab results to the known sequences. Wilson testified that the FBI lab always has successfully completed these tests.

Wilson stated that extraction, PCR amplification, capillary electrophoresis, and the use of an automated sequencing machine to generate a chromatograph all are generally accepted within the scientific community.[106] He stated that all of the techniques used in mtDNA analysis were developed for nonforensic uses, that he was not aware of any peer-reviewed articles that suggested that the FBI's mtDNA process or analysis were not scientifically valid, and that the results were objectively verifiable.[107]

Wilson testified that, after the sequencing of the mtDNA, the next step compares the sequence in the questioned sample to the sequence in the known sample to determine whether they share a common base at every position along the 610 base pairs in HV1 and HV2. The FBI requires that two examiners independently examine the sequences in the case of sequence concordance; if both examiners conclude that the known and questioned samples share a common base at every position, there is a match, which means that the questioned sample cannot be excluded as deriving from the same maternal lineage from which the donor's sample is derived.

Wilson cautioned that the examiner cannot positively establish identity on the basis of mtDNA because all those having a common maternal lineage, absent mutation, share the same mtDNA.[108] The final step in mtDNA analysis, the court noted, compares the mtDNA sequence of the questioned sample to the FBI database of mtDNA sequences to determine the relative prevalence of that mtDNA sequence.[109]

Wilson testified that the FBI had analyzed the mtDNA evidence in the Pappas case prior to the defendant's trial; they sequenced the mtDNA taken from the hair from the submitted sweatshirt and from the defendant's hair, compared them, and concluded that those samples shared a common base at every position. Thereafter, Wilson compared that sequence with those in the FBI database and found that the sequence previously had not been observed. Relying on that comparison, Wilson concluded that approximately 99.75 percent of the Caucasian population could be excluded as the source of the mtDNA in the sample.[110]

After setting out his credentials, the defendant's expert, Professor William Shields, testified that the analysis[111] and use of mtDNA as evidence of identity was problematic for three reasons. First, Shields stated that the FBI does not adequately address the potential for heteroplasmy — the presence of different sequences of mtDNA within one person. He stated that, until recently, most geneticists had assumed that an individual's mtDNA sequence would be identical within that individual and would be the same as the mtDNA sequence of that individual's mother. Shields testified that recent studies indicate that point heteroplasmy, a difference at one base pair in a sequence from samples of the same individual, occurs in between 10 to 20 percent of all people, and may occur in hair samples in 100 percent of the population. Shields testified that, because of the possibility of heteroplasmy, the FBI changed their matching criteria as to when two samples may be said to match, that is, when the donor of the known sample cannot be excluded as the source of the questioned sample. Shields concluded that, while the new matching criteria reduce the probability of false negatives, they increase the likelihood of false positives, i.e., incorrectly including a known sample as a source of the questioned sample. Shields also testified that the FBI had not performed validation studies concerning the extent of contamination by the DNA of others resulting from their handling of mtDNA.[112]

After their exhaustive examination of the mtDNA testimony presented at the trial, the Connecticut Supreme Court concluded:

We agree with the trial court's conclusion that the procedures used to extract and chart the chemical bases of mtDNA — extraction,

PCR amplification, capillary electrophoresis, and the use of an automated sequencing machine to generate a chromatograph — are scientifically valid and generally accepted in the scientific community.[113] The trial court had properly concluded that issues regarding contamination are important and may bear on the weight of mtDNA evidence in a particular case, but that those issues did not undermine the admissibility of the results of the mtDNA sequencing process used in this case.

The court continued:

"We reject the defendant's argument that, given Shields' testimony regarding heteroplasmy and the FBI match criteria, the trial court should not have admitted the mtDNA analysis presented at his trial. First, there was no evidence of heteroplasmy in either the known or questioned samples in this case. The defendant's known mtDNA sequence not only shared a common base at every position with the questioned sample, but also had exactly the same pattern at every position as that sample. Second, heteroplasmy, to the extent that it is present, would result in false exclusions, not false inclusions."[114]

The trial court had carefully considered all of the evidence and concluded that the proffered testimony of Wilson was statistically sound and that it was likely to be helpful to the jury in assessing the probative value of the mtDNA evidence. The trial court did not abuse its discretion in concluding that the statistical statements met the threshold standard for admissibility.[115] The Pappas case has spawned a series of law review articles and approving case law and remains the leading case in the new territory of mtDNA and hair analysis.[116]

In *United States v. Beverly*,[117] a well-written and comprehensive 2004 Sixth Circuit Court of Appeals decision, Noah Beverly, Douglas A. Turns, and Johnny P. Crockett were indicted for multiple bank robberies. Beverly appealed the introduction of mtDNA evidence against him at trial, arguing that the evidence was not scientifically reliable. The Circuit Court of Appeals found that the district court did not abuse its discretion in admitting expert testimony that less than 1% of population would be expected to have mtDNA pattern of hair found at crime scene. This was so, even assuming that mtDNA was not as precise an identifier as nuclear DNA. Any objections in that regard or as to issues going to the conduct of tests were fully developed and subject to cross-examination in the instant case. The court concluded that foundation presented was sufficiently reliable, and the mathematical basis for the evidentiary power of mtDNA evidence was carefully explained.[118]

Beverly also argued that mtDNA testing was not scientifically reliable because the laboratory that did the testing in this case was not certified by an external agency, the procedures used by the laboratory sometimes yielded results that were contaminated, and that the particular tests performed in this case were contaminated. In addition, Beverly argued that even if the mtDNA evidence was determined to be sufficiently reliable, its probative value was substantially outweighed by its prejudicial effect. In this part of his argument, Beverly focused on the statistical analysis presented, which he claims artificially enhanced the probative value of the mtDNA evidence. According to Beverly, Dr. Terry Melton, the government's expert, should only have been allowed to testify that Beverly could not be excluded as the source of the sample in question.[119]

The court, as in the Pappas case, provided a very useful overview concerning mtDNA analysis:

> Generally speaking, every cell contains two types of DNA: nuclear DNA, which is found in the nucleus of the cell, and mitochondrial DNA, which is found outside the nucleus in the mitochondrion. The use of nuclear DNA analysis as a forensic tool has been found to be scientifically reliable by the scientific community for more than a decade. The use of mtDNA analysis is also on the rise, and it has been used extensively for some time in FBI labs, as well as state and private crime labs.[120] This technique, which generally looks at the differences between people's mitochondrial DNA, has some advantages over nuclear DNA analysis in certain situations. For example, while any given cell contains only one nucleus, there are a vast number of mitochondria. As a result, a significantly greater amount of mtDNA exists in a cell from which a sample can be extracted by a lab technician, as compared *to nuclear DNA. Thus, this technique was very useful for minute samples or ancient and degraded samples.*[121]

The court took note of the fact that mitochondrial DNA could be obtained from some sources that nuclear DNA cannot, for example, mtDNA can be found in shafts of hair, which do not have a nucleus, but do have plenty of mitochondria, whereas nuclear DNA can only be retrieved from the living root of the hair where the nucleus resides.[122] On the other hand, the court also noted, mtDNA was not as precise an identifier as nuclear DNA. In the case of nuclear DNA, half was inherited from the mother and half from the father, and each individual, with the exception of identical twins, almost certainly has a unique profile. MtDNA, by contrast, was inherited only from the mother and thus all maternal relatives will share the same mtDNA profile, unless a mutation has occurred. Because it is not possible to achieve the extremely high level of certainty of identity provided by nuclear DNA, mtDNA typing has been said to be a test of exclusion, rather than one of identification.[123] The entire mtDNA sequence, the court noted, about sixteen thousand base pairs, was considerably shorter than nuclear DNA, which had approximately three billion pairs.[124]

In its decision here, the Sixth Circuit court first addressed and dismissed the defendant's argument that the lack of external certification of the mtDNA expert's laboratory, disqualified her opinion:

This point had been raised in the pretrial hearing, and although there is no legal requirement that Dr. Melton's lab be so certified, the district court did question Dr. Melton on this point. Laboratories doing DNA forensic work are accredited through the American Society of Crime Laboratory Directors. However, Dr. Melton's lab, having only been actively engaged in case work for about 11 months at the time of the trial, was not yet able to apply for the accreditation, but was expected to go through the process the following spring. Furthermore, Dr. Melton's own credentials are considerable. Not only has she been working with mtDNA since 1991, she has a PhD from Pennsylvania State University in genetics; her thesis investigated mitochondrial DNA as it would apply to forensic applications. In addition, Dr. Melton has published a significant amount of work in this field.[125]

Beverly further argued that Dr. Melton's procedures would sometimes yield results that were contaminated, and that, furthermore, the sample analyzed in this particular case was contaminated. However, the court noted, Dr. Melton was confident that no contamination of the sample itself had occurred. The reagent blank in the test of the sample itself did not show any indication of contamination, in contrast to a separate reagent blank, used in a different test tube, which was a control in the experiment. Therefore, the actual data relied upon in this case, obtained from the sequencing machine, and did not indicate any presence of a contaminant.

As to the defendant's argument that the probative value of the evidence would be substantially outweighed by prejudice, the court noted that the district court carefully considered during the pretrial hearing the question of whether the relevance of this evidence outweighed its probative value:

In particular, Beverly argued that the jury would associate mitochondrial DNA analysis with nuclear DNA analysis and give it the same value, in terms of its ability to "fingerprint" a suspect. The district court, however, decided that this issue was more appropriately dealt with through a vigorous cross-examination, and in fact that was exactly what occurred at trial. Moreover, the court noted the important probative value that this evidence added to the trial.

Finally, the court separately considered the scientific reliability of the statistical analysis offered by the government, concluding that:

> The predictive effect of the statistical analysis is based upon a formula which is apparently recognized in the scientific community and used in a variety of scientific contexts, and it has been used specifically here in the analysis of mitochondrial DNA results. The court concludes that it's an accepted and reliable estimate of probability, and in this case, it led to results, interpreted results, which substantially increase the probability that the hair sample is the hair of the defendant in this case.[126]

Based on the record compiled in the district court's careful and extensive hearing on this issue, the court found no abuse of discretion in admitting the mtDNA testing results. The mathematical basis for the evidentiary power of the mtDNA evidence was carefully explained, and was not more prejudicial than probative:[127]

> It was made clear to the jury that this type of evidence could not identify individuals with the precision of conventional DNA analysis. Nevertheless, any particular mtDNA pattern is sufficiently rare, especially when there is no contention that the real culprit might have been a matrilineal relative of the defendant, that it certainly meets the standard for probative evidence: "any tendency to make the existence of any fact that is of consequence to the determination of the action more probable or less probable than it would be without the evidence."[128]

This chapter concludes with an extensive analysis of the 2004 case of *Reid v. State*, an important case decided by a Superior Court in Connecticut. The case, although not yet reviewed by a higher appellate tribunal, is extremely useful as a thorough examination of the potential clash between practitioners of the traditional microscopy approach to hair analysis and the increasingly sophisticated employment of mtDNA technology in hair cases. The Reid cases is centered in such a clash and raises troublesome questions about the traditional consistent-in-all-respects basis of contemporary hair analysts.

In *Reid v. State*,[129] a sexual assault and kidnapping case, a petition for a new trial was filed alleging that mitochondrial DNA (mtDNA) evidence, relating to hair specimens, was newly discovered, could not have been discovered earlier by the exercise of due diligence, was material, not merely cumulative, and likely to produce a different result upon retrial. The trial court, after a careful consideration of the extensive information submitted on the MtDNA evidence, granted the defendant's petition.[130]

The victim had been grabbed in a park and violently assaulted. The perpetrator was picked out of a photo array and a lineup by the victim. In addition to the victim's identification, two pubic hairs were located on the victim and subjected to microscopic hair analysis by a criminalist from the Connecticut State Police Forensic Laboratory.[131] The defendant is an African-American male. The victim was a Caucasian female.

The court having denied the motion to exclude hair analysis evidence, Mr. Settachatgul, a criminalist from the Connecticut State Crime Laboratory, testified before the jury. He noted that hair comparison analysis procedures had been employed for many decades (for perhaps over one-hundred years), that such comparison testimony had been accepted in all fifty states, in numerous other countries, and was generally accepted as reliable within the field of forensic science.[132] His opinion, as summarized by the court, is set out here in full:

> Before the jury, Settachatgul testified that he had examined the clothes that the victim was wearing on the night of the attack and recovered three pubic hairs that did not come from the victim. Then, through a process known as microscopic hair analysis, Settachatgul compared these unknown [pubic] hairs to [pubic] hairs provided by the defendant. Settachatgul found that the characteristics of the known hairs from the defendant were similar to the characteristics of those recovered from the victim's clothing...
>
> During his testimony, Settachatgul displayed an enlarged photograph of one of the defendant's hairs and one of the hairs recovered from the victim's clothing as they appeared side by side under the comparison microscope. Settachatgul explained to the jurors how the hairs were similar and what particular features of the hairs were visible. He also drew a diagram of a hair on a courtroom blackboard for the jurors. The jurors were free to make their own determinations as to the weight they would accord the expert's testimony in the light of the photograph and their own powers of observation and comparison.
>
> Mr. Settachatgul testified that the three hairs recovered from the victim's clothing were pubic hairs. These hairs were rootless, indicating that they were shed, not plucked; one was found on the victim's jeans, another on a sock, and another on her lower undergarment (panty). According to Mr. Settachatgul, the pubic hairs

were recovered from the aforesaid items of clothing by a standard process of combing or scraping down the clothing surface. The rootless hair specimens so recovered were then microscopically compared with the pulled or plucked pubic hairs contributed by the defendant. Based on the microscopic analysis, Mr. Settachatgul's conclusion was that the three rootless hairs recovered from M.'s (the victim's) clothing were Negroid pubic hairs which had similar characteristics to the pubic hairs supplied by petitioner. The witness indicated that he could state, "to a reasonable degree of scientific certainty," that the pubic hairs found on the victim's clothing were microscopically similar to those pubic hair samples taken from Mark Reid.[133]

Most importantly, Mr. Settachatgul emphasized that all he could determine from his microscopic analysis was that the hairs recovered from the clothing were pubic hairs, that they were negroid pubic hairs, and that they were similar to the pubic hairs obtained from defendant; that is, the pubic hairs recovered from the victim's clothing (sock, jeans, and panty) had characteristics similar to those pubic hairs supplied by defendant. Mr. Settachatgul clearly stated that the microscopic comparative analysis procedure would not, and could not, permit him to conclude that the clothing pubic hairs were identical to the samples provided by defendant.[134]

With regard to the hair analysis evidence, the assistant state's attorney argued in his summation:

The victim's clothes that were taken from her [at the hospital] are sent to the lab and they are processed for hair. Hairs from the defendant are also sent to the lab for comparison. Three Negroid pubic hairs are found on the victim's clothing and are compared with the defendant's pubic hairs. The examiner's opinion is that the hairs are microscopically similar. Hair comparison analysis does not allow you to state that it is an exact match. So, the conclusion that is drawn by the examiner is that they are microscopically similar.[135]

Concerning the hair analysis evidence, the defense attorney argued to the jury, as follows:

The hair evidence, I will just talk about briefly. I'd ask you to recall the demeanor of the witness on the stand. Yes, he's been doing it by eyeballing it and not measuring anything. And the reason why I put in that *forensic handbook, which he seems to think is no big deal, is the one important thing that it talks about is how important it is to measure...*

This is a witness who guesses. He guesses at the amount of hair analysis he's done. You know, can we credit anything that he says with his regard to his work? He appeared to be a little bit defensive. I don't think he wanted to be questioned or challenged at all with regard to his work.

He didn't follow his own procedure, which indicates that you should put in your reports that this procedure is not something by which you can identify someone. There's no way you can identify someone by hair analysis. You can't even say whether the hair came from a man or woman.[136]

The assistant state's attorney, in her rebutting comments, argued to the jury that although the hair comparison evidence was not conclusive, the Negroid origin of the unknown pubic hairs, and their similarity with defendant's pubic hairs, were significant with respect to establishing defendant's involvement in this crime. She told the jury:

... keep in mind that these were the only three Negroid hairs found on the victim's clothes. And, remember, she testified she did not come in contact with any other black individuals on that evening. And that her jeans were clean when she put them on that night ...

Mr. Settachatgul testified that these are hairs that fell out. They did not have their root attached. Is it not a reasonable inference that, when her attacker was on top of her, and his pubic hairs fell out, that they landed on the nearest surface, the surface that he was sitting on? The victim, and the victim's jeans, and the victim's underwear. You are allowed to draw reasonable inferences, ladies and gentlemen. The judge will tell you that.

And is it also not a reasonable inference that, when she stood up and he was helping her do her pants, or trying to do her pants, and she did her pants, that one of those hairs went down the leg of her jeans and ended up in her socks? Ask yourself if that's not also a reasonable inference.

...And think about it, ladies and gentlemen. This was three Negroid pubic hairs, all similar to the defendant's on three separate items of clothing. It's not a case where one was similar and two were not. They are all hairs that are consistent with the defendant's. And these are the only Negroid hairs on her clothing …

…And two of the items the hairs were found on were covered by her jeans. Her underpants and her socks … So, I submit to you it's far less likely that those [pubic] hairs ended up on her by chance …

…And, with regard to the photo of the hair [State's Exhibit # 11], you don't have to be an expert hair examiner with twenty-three years' experience to look at those two hairs and know that those two hairs are similar. You can recognize the similarities yourself. Just like the victim, in looking at this photo, was able to recognize that this is the defendant's face, the face of her attacker.[137]

VII. The Evidence on the Petition for New Trial

At the trial on his petition, petitioner presented no testimony but instead offered two three-page reports of Mitotyping Technologies, LLC regarding separate mtDNA analyses, dated May 9, 2002, and June 3, 2002.[138] Important terstimony was presented by Dr. Terry Melton, president and CEO of Mitotyping Technologies, the expert in the Beverly case discussed above, who presented an overview of mtDNA technology prior to discussing her findings as to the hairs submitted to her for analysis. Dr. Melton testified that mtDNA testing is a form of analysis that is often applied to specimens such as skeletal remains and rootless hair samples, which are not susceptible to standard nuclear DNA testing. Such testing was used to exclude individuals as the contributors of samples because it is possible to obtain a DNA type; it is a mitochondrial DNA profile, which is a DNA sequence. Thus, she continued, this method of analysis can eliminate an individual as the contributor of samples. Its primary difference from nuclear DNA testing is that mtDNA is not a unique identifier. Unlike nuclear DNA which is found at the center of the human cell, and which is inherited from both parents, only maternal lineage exhibits the same mitochondrial profile.[139]

In her brief testimony, Dr. Melton testified, consistent with the 5/9/02 report, entered in evidence as petitioner's Exhibit #1, that her laboratory was requested to develop mtDNA profiles from the three questioned hairs in evidence at the criminal trial and to compare them to the mtDNA profile of petitioner to determine if Mark Reid could be excluded as the contributor of those hairs. The mtDNA sequences for the three unknown or questioned hairs did match one another, but did not match the sequence of 2212K1 (Mark Reid). Therefore, petitioner was excluded as the contributor of the three questioned hairs, all of which could have come from the same unknown individual.[140]

Dr. Melton stated that while microscopic hair analysis and mtDNA testing were "complementary" or "used in conjunction," mtDNA testing was "more discriminating." Microscopic hair analysis looks at the visual physical characteristics of the sample, while mtDNA testing considers its genetic characteristics.

The court had no difficulty in accepting the exclusion of Mark Reid as a contributor to any of the sample pubic hairs, which appeared to actually have belonged to the victim in the case:

> From all of the aforesaid, it seems that petitioner is excluded as the contributor of the three pubic hairs recovered from M.'s clothing, and admitted into evidence at the criminal trial; further, that based on this evidence, it would appear likely that the three pubic hairs were those of the victim. On cross-examination, however, Dr. Melton stated that neither the gender nor the race of a possible contributor could be determined by mtDNA testing.[141]

The court reviewed the testimony of Dr. Melton at the civil trial, as well as the reports of Mitotyping Technologies which were admitted in evidence as petitioner's exhibits, and could find no basis for concluding that the testing methodology employed was deficient, or that the professional opinion of Dr. Melton excluding the petitioner as a source of the unknown pubic hairs was unsound:

> The state had never suggested that the new mtDNA evidence was unreliable or not credible and both parties relied on the mtDNA testing: petitioner to exclude himself as a depositor of the questioned hairs, and respondent to establish that the mtDNA from the questioned hairs was consistent with the victim's mtDNA obtained from the buccal swab. The new mtDNA evidence satisfies the initial, required threshold on credibility; if a new trial were granted, this expert testimony would, likely, be before the second jury, with the usual instruction on expert testimony, permitting the jury to accord it whatever weight, if any, that jury felt it merited.[142]

The court concluded with a comment on the implications of the clash between traditional microscopic hair analysis and the new mtDNA typing methodologies:

This is a close, difficult case. The new mtDNA evidence merely excludes petitioner as the depositor of the unknown hairs; it *clearly does not exonerate him.*

Simply put, at the criminal trial, the identification by the victim was presented to the jury along with strong circumstantial evidence provided by the Settachatgul expert testimony which, if accepted, furnished powerful support for the victim's identification; guilty verdicts resulted. At a retrial, the victim's identification would not have the support of such circumstantial evidence in view of the new mtDNA evidence excluding petitioner as the source of the pubic hairs. That I may consider the victim's identification reliable is of limited significance; the ultimate determination as to its credibility rests with a jury. Although the former jury had to have accepted the victim's identification to convict, it did so in a proceeding where it was presented with expert testimony circumstantially supporting that identification. At a retrial, any such circumstantial support for the identification, even if present in the state's case, would be undercut by the new mtDNA evidence; that is, the credibility of the identification would have to be assessed absent microscopic hair comparison evidence, and possibly (depending on how a new trial unfolded), in light of the new mtDNA evidence showing that pubic hairs found on the victim's garments were not petitioner's.[143]

Increasing interest in mtDNA and hair analysis has been expressed by the last two Interpol's Forensic Science Symposia, a growing number of articles on the subject in the Journal of Forensic Science, and important cases, such as Pappas, Beverly, and Reid, discussed earlier. While mtDNA hair analysis has by no means supplanted the physical visual microscopic examinations of hairs, prosecutors, defense lawyers, and judges must be aware of these developments in this most often utilized of the corpus of the forensic sciences.

VIII. Conclusion

The foregoing discussion of microscopic hair analysis and mitochondrial DNA (mtDNA) analyses, may serve to set the tone for most of the subjects yet to be covered. The reality of the greatest number of the forensic sciences is their grounding in close observations and comparisons of characteristics of the type of crime scene datum under review, by use of the latest microscopic aids. Fiber, soil, glass and paint, ballistics, tool marks, and footwear and fingerprint analyses are all observational disciplines where current and future value hinges in large part on developments in modern microscopy. These investigative disciplines work within a culture of proof guided by probability analyses to provide assistance in the investigation and trial of criminal cases. The tremendous effect of recent use of mtDNA in hair analysis is a potent example of the rush of developments revolving around the interjection of DNA science into the criminal justice process. Chapter 10, DNA Analysis, addresses many of these developments.

Endnotes

1. See the Interpol Forensic Science Symposium selections, infra.

2. W. Bruschweiler and M.C. Grieve, *State of the Art In the Field of Hair and Textile Fibre Examinations*, Proceedings of the 12th Interpol Forensic Science Symposium (1998), at 179–180.

3. See, Deedrick, Hairs, Fibers, Crime, and Evidence, Part 1: Hair Evidence. Forensic Science Communications, Vol. 2, No. 3 (2000) (FBI at http://www. fbi.gov/hq/lab/fsc/backissu/july/deedric1.htm.)

4. See, Interpol Proceedings 13th Annual Forensic Science Symposium, at http:\\www.interpol.org, at the Forensic section.

5. Held in Lyon, France, October 16–19 2001. The extensive lterature review summary may be downloaded from the Interpol site, under Forensics, at http:\\www.interpol.org.

6. Ibid.

7. Ibid.

8. The Interpol 14th Annual Forensic Science Symposium Review, Lyon, France November (2004), Biological Evidence Hair, James Robertson, PhD, Australian National Police, at 148–155. The extensive 585 page literature review summary and bibliography may be downloaded from the Interpol site, under Forensics, at http:\\www.interpol.org.

9. Ibid.

10. Considerable interest in the past three years for mtDNA in hairs has involved debate regarding the level of heteroplasmy in hairs See, Melton, Dimick, Higgins, Lindstrom, and Nelson, Forensic Mitochondrial DNA Analysis of 691 Casework Hairs, 50, JFS at 1 (2005). Also see the extensive discussion of the Mark Reid case, infra.

11. 14th Annual Forensic Science Symposium, supra, n. 8 at 153.

12. Id.

13. Ogle and Fox: *Atlas of Human Hair: Microscopic Characteristics* (CRC Press, 1999) at 5.

14. The authors of this important new study offer a numerical scoring system permitting the hair type to be presented as an array of alphanumerical scores, with the goal of simplifying the development of the database noted above. Id.

15. See, Houck, Statistics and Trace Evidence: The Tyranny of Numbers, *Forensic Science Communications,* Vol. 1 No. 3 (Oct. 1999), where an FBI trace analyist argues for examiner experience as equivalent to statistics in the trace evidence field.

16. See, generally, Saferstein, *Criminalistics: An Introduction to Forensic Science* (6th ed., Prentice Hall, 1998); Eckert: *Introduction to Forensic Sciences* (2d ed., CRC Press, 1997); Fisher: *Techniques of Crime Scene Investigation* (5th ed., CRC Press, 1993); Bodziak: *Footwear Impression Evidence* (CRC Press, 1995); Geberth: *Practical Homicide Investigation* (3d ed., CRC Press, 1996); DiMaio and DiMaio: *Forensic Pathology* (CRC Press, 1993); Pickering and Bachman: *The Use of Forensic Anthropology* (CRC Press, 1997); Janes (ed.): *Scientific and Legal Applications of Bloodstain Pattern Interpretation* (CRC Press, 1999); Ogle and Fox: *Atlas of Human Hair: Microscopic Characteristics* (CRC Press, 1999).

17. See the discussion of the Sutherland case study in Chapter 2, Science and the Criminal Law, as to exclusions of suspects by class characteristic statements.

18. See, for example **Illinois Supreme Court Rule 417. DNA Evidence: (a) Statement of Purpose**. This rule is promulgated to produce uniformly sufficient information to allow a proper, well-informed determination of the admissibility of DNA evidence and to ensure that such evidence is presented competently and intelligibly. The rule is designed to provide a minimum standard for compliance concerning DNA evidence, and is not intended to limit the production and discovery of material information. **(b) Obligation to Produce.** In all felony prosecutions, post-trial and post-conviction proceedings, the proponent of the DNA evidence, whether prosecution or defense, shall provide or otherwise make available to the adverse party all relevant materials, including, but not limited to the following: (i) Copies of the case file including all reports, memoranda, notes, phone logs, contamination records, and data relating to the testing performed in the case. (ii) Copies of any autoradiographs, lumigraphs, DQ Alpha Polymarker strips, PCR gel photographs and electropherograms, tabular data, electronic files, and other data needed for full evaluation of DNA profiles produced and an opportunity to examine the originals, if requested. (iii) Copies of any records reflecting compliance with quality control guidelines or standards employed during the testing process utilized in the case. (iv) Copies of DNA laboratory procedure manuals, DNA testing protocols, DNA quality assurance guidelines or standards, and DNA validation studies. (v) Proficiency testing results, proof of continuing professional education, current curriculum vitae and job description for examiners, or analysts and technicians involved in the testing and analysis of DNA evidence in the case. (vi) Reports explaining any discrepancies in the testing, observed defects or laboratory errors in the particular case, as well as the reasons for those and the effects thereof. (vii) Copies of all chain of custody

documents for each item of evidence subjected to DNA testing. (viii) A statement by the testing laboratory setting forth the method used to calculate the statistical probabilities in the case. (ix) Copies of the allele frequencies or database for each locus examined. (x) A list of all commercial or in-house software programs used in the DNA testing, including the name of the software program, manufacturer, and version used in the case. (xi) Copies of all DNA laboratory audits relating to the laboratory performing the particular tests.

19. 800 So.2d 174 (2001) Also see, *Allen v. State*, 854 So. 2d v1255 (2003) (Although the undisclosed hair analysis excluded Allen, it did not exclude the victim and no other testing could be done.)

20. See Chapter 8, Fingerprints, for a discussion of the Mayfield inquiry.

21. *Buie v. McAdory*, 341 F. 3d 625 (7th. Cir. 2003)

22. Ibid.

23. 238 Ill.App.3d 260, 179 Ill.Dec. 447, 606 N.E.2d 279 (1993).

24. Buie, at 625.

25. *Herrera v. Collins*, 506 U.S. 390, 398-405, 113 S.Ct. 853, 122 L.Ed.2d 203 (1993).

26. Buie, at 341 F. 3d 625, 626.

27. Id.

28. But see, Houck, *The Tyranny of Numbers*, Forensic Science Communications Archive, http:\\www.fbi.gov, arguing against the idea that the absence of trace element statistics or databases diminishes the strength of an expert's opinion.

29. However, see the *FBI Handbook of Forensic Services* for an extensive discussion of basic evidence examination techniques. This is available free of charge and is routinelyu updated. It is used as a resource by a large number of police units in state and local law enforcement. See, http://www.fbi.gov. to download a copy.

30. 766 N.E.2d 351 (2002).

31. 265 Neb. 406, 657 N.W.2d 620 (2003).

32. Also see, Halverson and Basten, A PCR Multiplex and Database for Forensic DNA Identification of Dogs, 50 (2) *J. Forensic Science* (2005).

33. *McGrew v. State*, 673 N.E.2d 787 (Ct. App. Indiana 1997).; 682 N.E.2d 1289 (Ind. Sp. Ct. 1997).

34. *McGrew v. State*, 673 N.E. 2d at 791.

35. Id. at 796.

36. Id.

37. *McGrew v. State*, at 797. See, *Harrison v. State*, 644 N.E.2d 1243 (Indiana Sp. Ct. 1995).

38. See, *Hopkins v. State*, 579 N.E.2d 1297, 1305 (1991).

39. Under both the Indiana and the federal rules, the general test for the admission of expert testimony regarding "scientific, technical, or other specialized knowledge" was that it must assist the trier of fact to understand the evidence or determine a fact in issue. Evid.R. 702(a). Federal courts are still split, however, as to whether additional requirements imposed by Daubert should apply to nonscientific testimony. See the discussion of *Kumho Tire v. Carmichael,* in Chapter 1, Science, Forensic Science and Evidence. Also see, *United States v. Quinn* (1994) 9th Cir., 18 F.3d 1461, 1464-65, cert. denied, 512 U.S. 1242, 114 S.Ct. 2755, 129 L.Ed.2d 871 ("photogrammetry," in which the varying heights of known objects in a photograph are used to calculate the height of other objects in the photograph, does not require analysis under Daubert); *United States v. Velasquez* (1995) 3d Cir., 64 F.3d 844, 850, reh'g denied (questioning whether Daubert standard should be applied to handwriting analysis); *Iacobelli Const. v. County of Monroe* (1994) 2d Cir., 32 F.3d 19, 25 (determining that affidavits from geotechnical consultant and underground construction consultant are not the type of "junk science" targeted by Daubert); *United States v. Starzecpyzel* (1995) S.D.N.Y., 880 F.Supp. 1027, 1040–41 (Daubert not applicable to nonscientific field of forensic document examination.) But see *Frymire-Brinati v. KPMG Peat-Marwick* (1993) 7th Cir., 2 F.3d 183, 186 (Daubert analysis applied to decision to admit accountant's testimony).

40. *McGrew,* at 798–799.

41. *McGrew* at 799. See, Edward J. Imwinkelried, *Forensic Hair Analysis: The Case Against the Underemployment of Scientific Evidence* (1982) 39 *Wash. & Lee L.Rev.* 41. (1982). Also see, Clive A. Stafford Smith & Patrick D. Goodman, *Forensic Hair Comparison Analysis: Nineteenth Century Science or Twentieth Century Snake Oil?, 27 Colum. Hum. Rts. L.Rev.* 227, 231 (1996).

42. *McGrew* at 799.

43. Id.

44. *King v. State* (1988) Ind., 531 N.E.2d 1154; *Bivins v. State* (1982) Ind., 433 N.E.2d 387; *Fultz v. State* (1976) 265 Ind. 626, 358 N.E.2d 123; see generally Clive A. Stafford Smith & Patrick D. Goodman, *Forensic Hair Comparison Analysis: Nineteenth Century Science or Twentieth Century Snake Oil?, 27 Colum. Hum. Rts. L.Rev.* 227, 231 (1996). Whether microscopic hair analysis rested upon reliable scientific principles was an issue of first impression for Indiana courts.

45. *McGrew,* 673 N.E.2d 787, 800 (Ct. App. Indiana 1997). The court recognized that Daubert reliability assessments did not formally require, although it did permit, precise identification of a relevant scientific community and an explicit finding of a particular degree of acceptance within any such identified community.

46. Id. at 802.

47. Id. The court also observed that the State's own medical expert admitted that the defendant suffered from a severe case of Peyronie's disease, making it extremely painful for him to achieve sexual arousal. *McGrew* at 803.

48. On appeal, the United States Court of Appeals for the Tenth Circuit affirmed the district court's decision based on petitioner's ineffective assistance of counsel claim. *Williamson v. Ward*, 110 F.3d 1508, 1510 (10th Cir.1997). However, the Tenth Circuit specifically reversed the district court's ruling on the admissibility of hair analysis evidence because the district court had applied the wrong standard. Id. at 1522–23. 682 N.E.2d 1289 (Ind. Sp. Ct. 1997).

49. The expert testified that the microscope used was a "centrical light type microscope that allows various different magnifications," unlike an electron microscope. The court noted that, although the terms used sounded *technical and scientific*, the meanings were quite simple, citing, 6 James G. Zimmerly, M.D., J.D., M.P.H., *Lawyers Medical Cyclopedia* 45.2, at 768 (3rd Ed. 1991). See, Robert R. Ogle, Jr. and Michelle J. Fox: *Atlas of Human Hair: Microscopic Characteristics* (CRC Press, 1999), listing 24 characteristics for hair analysis. This small but excellent study should be in the library of all prosecution and defense offices.

50. *McGrew*, at 1291.

51. 682 N.E.2d 1289 (Ind. Sp. Ct. 1997), at 1290–1291.

52. Id. at 1292.

53. 682 N.E.2d 1289, 1290–1291.

54. Id. See, *Jervis v. State*, 679 N.E.2d 875, 881 n. 9 (Ind.1997).

55. 980 P.2d 3 (Mont. Sp. Ct. 1999).

56. Id. at 10.

57. 509 U.S. 579, 113 S.Ct. 2786 (1993). Also see, *State v. Moore*, 268 Mont. 20, 885 P.2d 457 (1994). Also see Chapter 1, Science, Forensic Science and Evidence for a discussion of the Daubert case and its progeny.

58. 119 S.Ct. 1167, 1175 (1999).

59. *Kumho Tire v. Carmichael*, 119 S.Ct. at 1175.

60. See *State v. Bromgard* (1993), 261 Mont. 291, 293-94, 862 P.2d 1140, 1141; *State v. Kordonowy*, 251 Mont. 44, 47, 823 P.2d 854, 856 (1991); *Coleman v. State*, 194 Mont. 428, 447, 633 P.2d 624, 636 (1981); *State v. Higley*, 190 Mont. 412, 428, 621 P.2d 1043, 1053 (1980); and *State v. Coleman*, 177 Mont. 1, 26–27, 579 P.2d 732, 747 (1978). See also Gregory G. Sarno, *Annotation, Admissibility and Weight, in Criminal Case, of Expert or Scientific Evidence Respecting Characteristics and Identification of Human Hair*, 23 A.L.R.4th 1199 (1983).

61. The court, in this regard, found that a proper foundation for the witness to qualify as an expert was established. She had been working with trace evidence (such as hair, fibers, glass, and paint) for four and one-half years at the

Montana State Crime Lab, spent about ninety per cent of her time examining trace evidence, had taken several training courses at the FBI Academy that dealt with trace evidence, as well as several other courses on forensic microscopy. She was a member of two forensic scientist groups, was involved with writing guidelines for trace evidence examination for one of the groups, and had been found qualified to testify in other cases regarding her examinations of trace evidence. *Southern*, at 17. Also see, *State v. Fukusaku*, 85 Hawai'i 462, 946 P.2d 32 (1997), where the Hawaii Supreme Court also placed microscopic hair analysis outside of the Daubert reliability requirements.

62. See the discussion of the Mark Reid case, infra.

63. 142 Ill.2d 22, 566 N.E.2d 1355 (1991).

64. Id. at 26.

65. Id.

66. See, Ogle, Jr. and Fox, *Atlas of Human Hair: Microscopic Characteristics* (CRC Press 1999), setting out 24 characteristic capable of comparison.

67. Linscott, supra, at 1359.

68. Id.

69. Id.

70. Linscott, 142 Ill.2d at 28-34, 153 Ill.Dec. 249, 566 N.E.2d 1355. Similarly, in *People v. Giangrande*, 101 Ill.App.3d 397, 56 Ill.Dec. 911, 428 N.E.2d 503 (1981), the court held that a prosecutor overstated the evidence arguing that defendant's hair had been found at the crime scene, when the State's expert testified only that hairs from the crime scene could have originated from the defendant. (Giangrande, 101 Ill. App.3d at 402-03, 56 Ill.Dec. 911, 428 N.E.2d 503.) The appellate court found such arguments improper and reversed the conviction stating that it could not conclude "that the closing argument comments of the prosecutor *25 did not result in substantial prejudice to defendant." Giangrande, 101 Ill.App.3d at 403, 56 Ill.Dec. 911, 428 N.E.2d 503.

But see, *People v. Gomez*, 215 Ill.App.3d 208, 574 N.E.2d 822 (1991), where the court reversed a first-degree murder conviction because there was insufficient circumstantial evidence to establish the defendant's guilt beyond a reasonable doubt. There was evidence of the defendant's fingerprint at the murder scene, a place where he paid his monthly rent, as well as samples of blood and paint taken from murder scene and the defendant's home. The state also introduced, as part of its case in chief, hairs found on the victim's body that shared some similarity with the defendant's hair. The court held that hair samples "do not possess the necessary unique qualities of fingerprints to allow positive identification." Id. at 828, 158 Ill.Dec. at 715. "The mere physical probabilities inferred from ... hair ... samples alone are insufficient to sustain a conviction beyond a reasonable doubt." Id. Also see *People v. Brown*, 122 Ill.App.3d 452, 77 Ill.Dec. 684, 687, 461 N.E.2d 71, 74 (Ill.App.1984). (Because the court found that the circumstantial evidence was insufficient to prove guilt, the court reversed the defendant's conviction.)

71. 171 Ill.2d 74, 662 N.E.2d 1215 (1996).

72. A forensic scientist testified that two fingerprints on the adhesive side of the duct tape removed from the victim's hair and one fingerprint on a key tag found in the victim's abandoned car were identified as defendant's. Another forensic scientist testified that seminal material taken from the victim's vaginal swab was consistent with defendant's blood type. See Chapter 8, Fingerprints, and Chapter 10, DNA Analysis.

73. *People v. Moore*, at 92.

74. Id.at 100.

75. 1995 WL 324021 (Tenn.Crim.App. 1995).

76. Id. at *1.

77. Id. at *2.

78. *Williams*, supra, n.62, at *2.

79. 322 Ark. 40, 907 S.W.2d 124 (1995).

80. Id. at 126.

81. *Suggs*, at 322 Ark at 44.

82. 270 Ga. 745, 514 S.E.2d 639 (1999).

83. A broken window screen at the Gottschalk trailer indicated the assailant's entry point, and beneath the window inside the trailer was a vinyl chair containing a partial shoe print. A State expert determined that this shoe print matched Pruitt's Reeboks. Gottschalk testified that Pruitt had never been a guest in her home; the only time she had ever seen him in her trailer was the brief time he felt for the victim's pulse on the morning of April 10, 1992. Semen was discovered in the victim's anus and DNA extracted from the semen matched Pruitt. The state's DNA expert testified that the frequency of this DNA profile among Caucasians is one in seven billion. Type O blood was found on the jeans and shirt that Pruitt had been wearing the night of the murder, and on the steering wheel cover in his car. At the Gottschalk trailer, type A blood was found on the porch light bulb, the screen door latch, and near the entry window. Pruitt is type A and the victim was type O. Id. at 644.

84. 428 Mass. 766, 705 N.E.2d 236 (1999).

85. Id. at 239.

86. *Snell*, at 705 N.E.2d 772.

87. (Tenn.Crim.App)

88. Id. at *6.

89. Id. at *8.

90. Id.

91. Id.

92. Also see, *State v. Montgomery*, 341 N.C. 553, 461 S.E.2d 732, 735 (1995), where defendant was convicted of first-degree murder, for the rape-murder

of a college coed after wrongfully entering her apartment. Five pubic hairs, which were consistent with those of defendant, were found in front of and on the sofa and love seat. The police later found the missing butcher knife in a parking lot located between Piccolo's apartment and the house owned by defendant's sister; defendant was staying in this house with his sister at the time of the murder. Blood and fibers consistent with fibers from Piccolo's sweatshirt were on the knife.

93. 726 So.2d 1152 (Miss. Sp. Ct. 1998).

94. Id. at 1180.

95. Id. Also see, *Mason v. State*, 1998 WL 96608 (Ala.Crim.App.1998), where the defendant was convicted of murder committed during the course of a robbery and sentenced to death. (A Negroid pubic hair, *consistent with a known pubic hair from the appellant*, was found in the combings from the victim's pubic hair.)

96. 1998 WL 141993 (Mo.App. W.D.).

97. Id. at *1.

98. *Butler* at *2.

99. Bisla, *It all came down to a single hair: the probability of exclusion vs. the probability of guilt through the use of mitochondrial DNA evidence in State v. Pappas*, 26 WTLR 263 (2004). Also see, *U.S. v. Coleman*, 202 F. Supp. 2d 962 (2002) [[Approval of mtDNA sequencing testimony].

100. 256 Conn. 854, 776 A. 2d 1091 (2001).

101. Pappas, at 867 et seq.

102. Ibid at 868.

103. Ibid at 869.

104. Ibid at 870.

105. Ibid at 871. He stated that the known and questioned samples are tested separately; the questioned sample is sequenced before the known sample is unsealed and processed. The lab areas, machines, and pipettes used to process the DNA material are cleaned using a bleach solution or ultraviolet light. Wilson testified that the FBI lab uses several controls to monitor possible contamination: a reagent blank, a negative control, a positive control, and a sequencing base control. The reagent blank is used throughout the process starting at the extraction step and it allows monitoring of the amount of DNA at each step of the process. The negative control is introduced at the PCR step, and it would indicate contamination in the reagents. The positive control is a known DNA sequence that is introduced to ensure that the amplification reaction was successful and to assess the quality of the sequencing process.

106. Pappas, at 872.

107. Id.

108. Wilson also testified about heteroplasmy, which is the presence of two or more mtDNA sequences in an individual. He stated that heteroplasmy is

observed in approximately 5 to 10 percent of cases, and that the presence of heteroplasmy would not lead to a false inclusion because, in order to match, the sequences would still have to share a common base at every position. Wilson testified that there was no evidence of heteroplasmy in the present case.

109. Pappas, at 873. At the time the defendant's hair was analyzed, the FBI database contained 1657 known sequences of mtDNA, 916 of which were Caucasian sequences. Using a statistical technique, the FBI estimates the rarity or prevalence of a given mtDNA sequence based upon whether the sequence has been observed in the database and, if so, how often it has been observed. Wilson explained that this method is not used to establish positive identification; rather, it allows the FBI to estimate, on the basis of its database, the probability that a given mtDNA profile would be expected to occur in the general population. He also stated that, although the most common mtDNA type probably has a population frequency of 4%, the database was not yet large enough to know the population frequency of rare types, that is, types that have not been seen in the database.

110. Wilson stressed that this figure was based upon the database, so that as the database grew, the estimate would change. Wilson aso testified that all Caucasians have the same distribution of mtDNA types and thus additional subgroupings of Caucasians were not necessary.

111. Ibid. at 874.

112. Shields stated that, even if it is assumed that heteroplasmy or contamination were not at issue, the statistical calculations used by Wilson are incorrect because of the way that the FBI determines a "failure to exclude" between two mtDNA samples. Shields stated that, because the FBI would not exclude as a match two samples that differed by one chemical base, other samples in the database that differ by one such base should be included in the estimated mtDNA type frequency. Shields concluded that, if one took into account samples in the FBI database that differed by one such base, the frequency of the mtDNA sequence observed from the defendant's sample in this case would be doubled. Thus, instead of a frequency of approximately 0.3 percent, which would mean that 99.7 percent of the Caucasian population could be excluded, Shields calculated that type frequency would be approximately 0.7 percent, which would exclude 99.3 percent of the Caucasian population. Pappas, at 875.

113. Citing, M. Holland & T. Parsons, "Mitochondrial DNA Sequence Analysis — Validation and Use for Forensic Casework," 11 *Forensic Sci. Rev.* 22, 35 (1999) (citing articles as to validity of DNA extraction, PCR amplification and sequencing); M. Wilson et al., "Extraction, PCR Amplification and Sequencing of Mitochondrial DNA from Human Hair Shafts," 18 *Biotechniques* 662 (1995). Pappas, at 881.

114. Pappas, at 882.

115. Pappas, at 886.

116. See, *Reid v. State*, 2003 WL 21235422, (Conn.Super. May 14, 2003) discussed below and Chapter 10, DNA for additional recent cases on MtDNA. Also see, Bisla, It All Came Down to a Single Hair: The Probability of Exclusion vs. the Probability of Guilt through the Use of Mitochondrial DNA Evidence In *State v. Pappas*, 26 *Whittier Law Rev.* 263 (2004); Walker, 43 *Jurimetrics J.* 427 (2003); DNA Evidence: Changing the Face of Criminal Justice, *Criminal Practice Guide* (July/August 2004). Also see, Houck and Budowle, Correlation of Microscopic and Mitochondrail DNA Hair Comparisons, *Journal of Forensic Science*, 47(5), 964–967 (2002).

117. 369 F. 3d 516 (U.S. Ct. App. 6th Cir 2004).

118. Beverly, at 523.

119. Beverly, at 528.

120. Citing, Micah A. Luftig & Stephen Richey, *Symposium: Serenity Now or Insanity Later?: The Impact of Post-Conviction DNA Testing on the Criminal Justice System: Panel One: The Power of DNA*, 35 New Eng. L.Rev. 609, 611 (2001). Beverly at 529.

121. Beverly, at 530.

122. Citing, *United States v. Coleman, 202 F.Supp.2d 962, 965 (E.D.Mo.2002)* (accepting expert testimony by Dr. Melton, the expert in this case, and admitting evidence based on mtDNA testing).

123. *United States v. Coleman*, at 966.

124. *United States v. Beverly*, at 530.

125. Also see, *People v. Mason*, 2004 WL 2951972 (Ct. App. Mich 2004): Dr. Terry Melton, the president and CEO of Mitotyping Technologies, a company that specializes in mitochondrial DNA (mtDNA) testing, testified that defendant's mtDNA profile matched that of the foreign hair found on the decedent's body and that 99.93% of the population of North America would not match this profile.

126. Beverly at 531.

127. Beverly at 531. See, Erica Beecher-Monas, *The Heuristics of Intellectual Due Process: A Primer for Triers of Science, 75 N.Y.U.L.Rev. 1563, 1655 n. 535 (2000).*

128. *Fed.R.Evid. 401.* "The statistical evidence at trial showed that, at most, less than 1% of the population would be expected to have this mtDNA pattern. Even an article critical of mtDNA stated the most frequent pattern applies in no more than 3% of the population. It would be unlikely to find a match between Beverly's hair and the hair of a random individual. The testimony was that, with a high degree of confidence, less than one percent of the population could be expected to have the same pattern as that of the hair recovered from the bank robbery site, and that Beverly did have the same pattern, and thus could not be excluded as the source of the hair. Finding Beverly's mtDNA at the crime scene is essentially equivalent to finding that the last two digits of a license plate of a car owned by defendant matched the

last two numbers of a license plate of a getaway car. It would be some evidence — not conclusive, but certainly admissible. We find the same here." Beverly at 531.

129. 2003 WL 21235422 (2004).

130. The court observed that petitioner was tried to a jury, before this court, on a two-count information charging Sexual Assault in the First Degree, *General Statutes Section 53a-70(a)(1)*, and Kidnapping in the First Degree, *General Statutes Section 53a-92(a)(2)(A)*. Evidence commenced on October 29, 1997, and on November 10, 1997, the jury returned verdicts of guilty on both counts. The convictions were affirmed by the Connecticut Supreme Court on September 5, 2000. *[FN2] State v. Reid, 254 Conn. 540 (2000)*.

131. The trial court conducted a Daubert type hearing on the defense motion to exclude any hair analysis evidence. Two witnesses testified at the hearing, Mr. Kiti Settachatgul, lead criminologist, and Ms. Deborah Messina, supervising criminologist, both from the Connecticut State Police Forensic Laboratory. Mr. Settachatgul testified that he was a criminalist in the Trace Evidence Section of the State Laboratory, that he performed the hair analysis or comparison in this case, that he has been doing such analyses and comparisons since 1974, that he has been qualified to testify as a hair analysis expert in the courts of various jurisdictions over one hundred times, and in Connecticut on more than thirty occasions. Mr. Settachatgul also testified to his education, training, and experience in forensic science. Ms. Messina testified that Criminalistics includes the Trace Section, which performs analyses of hair, fibers, solids, and glass. In addition, the State Forensic Laboratory has an Instrumentation Unit, which takes care of gunshot residue and instrumental analyses, an Arson and Explosives Unit, which is part of the Chemistry Section, and a Forensic Biology Unit, which takes up standard serology and DNA analysis. Ms. Messina supervises all of the aforesaid sections or units. She testified that the standard and most widely used method for hair analysis is the microscopic comparison method employed in this case. *1

132. He stated that the basic and primary tool used in hair analysis was the comparison or bridge microscope; this device permits the microscopic viewing of two specimens, the known and the unknown, side by side, in order to determine similar or dissimilar characteristics. Hair specimens are composed of various components, and based on the size, shape, distribution, and density of certain of those components, as observed microscopically, conclusions can be drawn by a trained and experienced examiner concerning the species or origin (human or animal) of the specimens, racial origin (Caucasian, Asian, or Negroid), and somatic origin (scalp, pubic, beard, etc.). Thus, when the known and unknown specimens are examined by means of the bridge microscope, the expert can determine the origins of the unknown specimen (human or animal, racial, and somatic), and formulate an opinion regarding the similarities or dissimilarities between the visible characteristics of the two specimens. The witness explained that other methods of hair analysis exist,

but that the above-described methodology has been widely used because it is not destructive of the evidence and the slides can be preserved, allowing the specimens to be viewed by another examiner (or anyone else) in the future.

133. Reid, at *4–5.

134. Mr. Settachatgul explained to the jury the microscopically visible similarities using State's Exhibit # 11, a photograph depicting a "hundred magnification" of two strands of pubic hair, each on a slide, as they would appear to a viewer through the comparison microscope (on the left-hand slide was a pubic hair recovered from the victim's clothing; on the right slide was the pubic hair contributed by Mark Reid) In explaining the use of the bridge microscope, and the viewing of the components of a strand of hair, the witness drew on the blackboard, for the jury, a diagram of a hair strand showing, essentially, what components would be visible for making the comparison. It was abundantly clear, as confirmed by the language in the Supreme Court decision, that Mr. Settachatgul was testifying only to the very "narrow opinion" that the three pubic hairs recovered from the victim's clothing were *similar* to the samples obtained from the defendant, and, that he, Settachatgul could *not* say that the questioned specimens were the pubic hairs of petitioner/defendant. Cf. 254 Conn. at p. 551.

135. Reid, at *7.

136. Reid, at 9–10*.

137. Reid, at 9–10*.

138. Exhibits # 3 through # 7 are transcripts of the entire trial (*voir dire* through acceptance of verdicts, including the court's charge and the *Porter* hearing). The court also took judicial notice of the official court file in the criminal case.

139. Reid, at 11*.

140. Dr. Melton further testified, consistent with the 6/3/02 report, petitioner's Exhibit # 2, that Mitotyping Technologies received from the Connecticut Forensic Science Lab buccal sample swabs taken from the victim, M., which sample was designated 2212K2. Mitotyping was requested to develop an mtDNA profile from the known buccal swab(s) to ascertain if M. could be excluded as the contributor of the unknown hairs. Dr. Melton testified her lab could not exclude the unknown hairs as coming from the victim. As explained in Exhibit # 2, the mtDNA sequences of 2212Q1, 2212Q2, and 2212Q3, the questioned pubic hairs, match the sequence of 2212K2, the known swab, and accordingly, M. cannot be excluded as the contributor of the three questioned hairs. That is, the mtDNA sequence that Mitotyping observed in the three questioned or unknown hairs that were tested as set forth in the May 9, 2002 report (Exhibit # 1) was "a match to or exactly the same" as the mtDNA sequence in 2212K2, the saliva sample (swab) from M., as set forth in Exhibit # 2.

Exhibit 2, Dr. Melton's 6/3/02 report, states that a search was made of the SWCDAM database of human mtDNA sequences, which database is maintained by the FBI (DNA Unit II — mtDNA unit), for the sequence observed in 2212Q1, Q2, and Q3 and 2212K2. It was determined that the sequence had never been seen in the database, which at the time of the search contained 4,839 human mtDNA sequences of North American forensic significance. In other words, M.'s DNA type, Dr. Melton explained, has not previously been observed in the database; therefore, upon engaging in "a very simple statistical calculation, which is based on some sampling theory," Dr. Melton concluded that 99.94% of North Americans would not be expected to have this profile." Or, conversely, "no more than six one-hundredths of one percent of North Americans would be expected to have this type." Therefore, 99.94% of the population of North America would be excluded as the source of this particular DNA sequence. Reid, at 12*.

141. Reid, at 12*.

142. Reid, at 18*. The court stressed that the newly discovered mtDNA evidence must be considered, not just in the context of the victim's identification, but also in the context of the entire evidence, including the Settachatgul testimony, and, various other portions of M.'s testimony. As petitioner points out, Mr. Settachatgul's expert testimony was the only forensic evidence tending to connect petitioner to the commission of this crime. At this point, the probative value of microscopically visible similarities between the known and unknown hair samples is substantially diminished by the results of the mtDNA testing excluding Mark Reid as a source of the unknown hairs. Left is Mr. Settachatgul's conclusion that the unknown hair samples are Negroid pubic hairs, which conclusion is not placed in question by Mitotyping testing covered by the May 9, 2002 report. The Settachatgul conclusion as to Negroid origin, however, is placed in question by the report of June 3, 2003 indicating that the victim (white) cannot be excluded as the contributor of the questioned hairs; although Dr. Melton made clear the mtDNA testing could not distinguish race or gender, she also testified that "no more than six one-hundredths of one percent of North Americans would be expected to have" the same mtDNA profile found in both M's buccal swab and the three questioned hairs. (FN34) As to the three unknown samples being pubic hair, there was no apparent reason to reject Mr. Settachatgul's conclusion regarding somatic origin. Reid, at 19*.

143. Reid, at 20*–21*.

Fiber Analysis

4

(F)or the limits to which our thoughts are confined, are small in respect of the vast extent of Nature it self; some parts of it are too large to be comprehended, and some too little to be perceived, and from thence it must follow, that not having a full sensation of the object, we must be very lame and imperfect in our conceptions about it, and in all the propositions which we build upon it; hence we often take the Shadow of things for the substance, small appearances for good similitudes, similitudes for definitions; and even many of those, which we think to be the most solid definitions, are rather expressions of our misguided apprehensions than of the true nature of the things themselves.

Robert Hooke, Micrographia (1665)

I. Introduction

The 2004 14th Interpol Forensic Science Symposium Review paper[1] on fiber (fibre) covers advances in scientific methods applied to the forensic examination of fibres reported since the 13th Interpol Forensic Science Symposium in October 2001. A literature review was conducted covering articles published in the principal forensic science journals, supplemented by an extensive search of Internet sources, for articles related to forensic fibre examination.[2] The authors took note that the scientific working groups (SWGs) in Europe and North America had been active in attempting to coordinate training, research efforts, and the development of protocols for forensic fibre examination, including laboratory analysis and determination of the evidential value of any such analyses.[3] The European Fibres Group (EFG) also published in late 2001 the *Manual of Best Practice for the Forensic Examination of Fibres*. This document is credited with significantly raising the standard of forensic fibre examination on a world basis.[4]

The *Fibres Report* noted that contamination was found to be a major issue, stressing that careful consideration should also be given as to whether legitimate contact could have occurred prior to an offence being committed. According to Wiggins and Grieves, leading authors in the forensic hair area, the efficiency of the examination should be improved and the evidential value of the findings should be expressed in a clearer way. Areas where particular progress could be made were listed as:

- Improved communication and exchange of information between the investigator and the scientist
- Streamlining analysis by using the latest equipment, effective case management
- Better use of existing data pertaining to fibre frequencies, accumulating new data by using the resources of working groups, and improving training procedures especially in the area of evidence interpretation.[5]

Efficient and correct fiber recovery is, as with all crime scene collection, a crucial step for any forensic fiber examination. The *Fibres Report* analyzes recent literature addressing manual recovery with tweezers, tape lifting, scraping, and vacuuming, noting differences between European and American practices. The report notes the increased risk of contamination when the scraping method[6] is used because of an increased number of loose fibers transferred onto the examiner's clothing and fibers when exiting the search room. The paper concludes that it is unlikely that a completely clean search room could be obtained, but concluded, with proper precautions, that it is possible to minimize and monitor the contaminant fiber sample population.[7] The *Report* notes the absence of any truly new techniques for fiber analysis and considers current practices as to fiber materials and dye lots[8] adequate.

The *Report* emphasized that the interpretation of fiber evidence had been consistently recognized as the most challenging topic related to the forensic examination of fibers. The authors noted that much modeling and empirical research has occurred in the last 15 years, with the last three years being no different, and many studies reported:

> The question of commonality in fibre evidence is often posed to the expert, suggesting that the acquired evidence is not significant. Knowledge of the frequency of occurrence of fibre types in a given population and of the chance of a random nondiscrimination is therefore required to assess the evidential value of finding fibres

that could not be differentiated from a suspect source. This information becomes increasingly important when a Bayesian model is applied to the interpretation of fibre evidence.[9]

The Report authors examined a series of studies about attempts to identify factors in large samples that might show the specificity and value of transferred fibres in providing forensic evidence.[10] Recent studies of the transfer and persistence of fibers were considered of prime importance in the fiber area, especially the cross-transfer of fibers and the dependencies that could exist between the number of fibers transferred in one direction and the number of fibers transferred in the other direction.[11]

The *Fibre Report* stressed the ongoing importance of general background knowledge in recent textile technology (UV absorbers, new finishing agents, etc.) The *Report* provides a long list of Web sites containing a wide variety of current fiber industry information, from manufacture listings, dye companies, and a host of expert fiber groups.[12] The Report ended on an optimistic note:

Significant progress has been made in the last three years in placing the forensic examination of fibres on a sound basis. The work of peak bodies, such as the European Network of Forensic Science Institutes (ENFSI), European Fibres Group (EFG) and the Fiber subgroup of FBI Scientific Working Group on Materials Analysis (SWGMAT) has been central, resulting in a manual of best practice and a comprehensive training manual.[13]

The *Fibre Report* contains discussions or references to 78 of the significant papers published between 2001 and May 2004. The 14th Interpol Forensic Science Symposium Review paper is well worth downloading and examining. The fiber section, as all other sections, provides an excellent current synopsis and bibliography of world forensic science literature. It is available free of charge at the Interpol site at http\\www.interpol.org/forensic.

II. Fiber Evidence in the Courtroom

What can a simple fiber tell us from a class characteristic standpoint? To what degree should police and defense counsel be concerned with weather, temperature, terrain, wildlife, and other nonfiber elements invariably present in many crime scene scenarios that may effect the legitimacy of any opinions regarding fiber datum?[14] What are potential fiber sources in each crime scene?

What is there to compare in fiber analyses?[15] What are the comparison points to look at in attempts to connect fibers found at the crime scene to fibers associated with the defendant in the case at hand? Initially, it is important to identify the broadest categories of fibers and then work down to the fiber characteristics actually used in making fiber comparisons and accompanying pronouncements by forensic specialists. The FBI has substantially upgraded the offerings on its Web site, one of which is the Forensic Fiber Examination Guidelines, published by the FBISWGMAT. This is an extensive release of technical papers about fiber analysis, including materials on the general background to this discipline, fiber analysis and modern microscopy, visible spectroscopy, thin-layer chromatography of nonreactive dyes in textile fibers, pyrolysis gas chromatography of textile fibers, infrared analysis of textile fibers, and fabrics and cordage.[16] Despite recent criticisms of practices at the FBI laboratory, the forensic collection practices, trace evidence, impression and DNA databases and testing protocols, and standards remain the primary judicial reference for forensic science standards. These standards are not foolproof, as evidenced by the recent FBI misidentification of the fingerprints in the Brian Mayfield Spanish train-bombing scandal.[17] However, courts are not likely to dismiss lightly the recommendations of the Federal Bureau of Investigation.[18]

Fibers fall into two broad categories, natural and manmade.[19] Both types are used in the manufacture of commercial products of a wide variety, ranging from all types of apparel, automobile seat covers, and home, office, and automobile coverings. All commercial applications have an immense variety of styles and colors to choose from. Most of such fiber and the commercial processes used to produce the fiber and its applications are patented and collected in massive proprietary databases maintained by manufacturers.[20]

Natural fibers are broken down into three categories of animal, vegetable, and mineral. Animal fibers used in commercial production, led by wool, are wool, silk, camel hair, and a wide variety of furs, such as mink, raccoon, chinchilla, and alpaca. The vegetable category contains such fibers as cotton, linen, hemp, sisal, and jute. Cotton is the primary fiber used in commercial applications.[21] Fiber materials, classified under the term mineral, include asbestos, glass wool, and fiberglass.

Synthetic fibers are extensive in category and subcategory, but may be readily identified due to the massive commercial and FBI database collections used for proprietary and investigative purposes. Synthetic fiber categories include acetates, acrylics, aramid, modacrylic, nylon, olefin, polyester, PBI, PBF, rayon, spandex, Sulfar, and Vinyon.[22]

Many synthetic fiber categories exist, with an extensive listing of brand names under each heading.[23] Those listed represent a general sampling. With the available databases, the chance of identifying the generic type, origin, and a typical commercial source of fibers found at a crime scene is excellent. The question remains how many others in the general population have clothing, carpeting, etc., that would yield similar consistent-in-all-respects forensic conclusions. The class characteristic statements in the fiber area are significant aids to getting an investigation focused and moving toward a suspect.

In Chapter 2, Science, Forensic Science, and Evidence, a discussion relating to fiber evidence was initiated during the course of the case study analysis of the case of *People v. Sutherland*.[24] That case involved considerable fiber transfers from the seats and floor covering of defendant's car to the body of the child victim and of the victim's shorts to the defendant's car. This chapter concentrates on fiber cases only, introducing a significant problem for defendants, as in hair cases, of an absence of databases to determine the presence in the general population of fibers of a similar laboratory match. Fiber testimony is subject to the same linguistic limitations of all other trace evidence categories, i.e., conclusions may only be couched in less than certain or absolute terms.

In *State v. Dawkins*,[25] a routine fiber setting, defendant was convicted of first-degree murder. Significant fiber evidence was introduced against him at trial.

Responding to the defendant's first argument that there was not sufficient evidence that defendant was the perpetrator of the crime, the court noted that fibers found in the victim's hair and the towel and blanket in which she was wrapped were consistent with the carpet found in defendant's house in the master bedroom. There was no sign of forcible entry into defendant's house. Luminol testing revealed the presence of blood not belonging to defendant on his master bedroom carpet around the bed and toward the entrance of the bedroom. Red and black acrylic fibers, consistent with the blanket in which the victim's body was wrapped, were found in the defendant's boat.[26]

The testimonial qualifications for a forensic hair expert remain fairly minimal, as recently demonstrated in a 2004 Georgia case, *Fox v. State*.[27] Here, defendant was convicted of rape and aggravated sodomy. Fiber evidence was presented against him and he objected to the state's expert due to her minimal qualifications. The appellate court ruled that the trial court did not abuse its discretion in qualifying the state's witness as expert in fiber analysis, even though she had never testified as a fiber expert before. The court noted that a witness may be qualified as expert based on knowledge gained through study or experience and, to qualify as expert, generally all that was required is that the person be knowledgeable in a particular matter and that any such special knowledge may be derived from experience, as well as study, and formal education in the subject was not requisite for expert status:

> Here, the State's expert fiber analyst had worked at the Georgia Bureau of Investigation (GBI) for two years as a microanalyst in the Forensic Sciences Division, and had a bachelor of science

degree in Forensic Science. She also completed a nine-month training course in the hair and fiber fields, and "completed several oral and written tests." Her duties included analyzing, comparing, and evaluating physical evidence, such as hairs, fibers, and shoe-prints. She had worked on approximately 50 cases while she was employed at the GBI. Previously, she had testified as an expert in hair analysis and physical evidence, but not as a fiber expert.[28]

A typical "consistent with" opinion was recently addressed in the Tennessee case of *State v. Rogers*,[29] where the defendant was convicted of first-degree murder and kidnapping. FBI Scientist Max Houck testified that he took fiber samples vacuumed from the defendant's car and the defendant's carpet at his residence and compared them with fibers taken from the victim's shorts. He identified light-yellow carpet fibers in the samples taken from the defendant's car and residence that "exhibited the same microscopic characteristics and optical properties" as fibers taken from the victim's shorts. Although he could not identify the source of the fibers, the fibers appeared to have the same properties and characteristics as samples taken from the living-room carpet in the defendant's residence. Agent Houck testified that either the victim's shorts had been in the defendant's living room, or the fibers had been transferred to the shorts through contact. He explained that the fibers could have been transferred to the defendant's car via the defendant's shoes or clothing and then transferred to the victim's shorts if she came into contact with the defendant's car. Additionally, FBI Chemist Ronald Menold tested the fibers forwarded to him by Agent Houck. He found the fibers from the victim's shorts and the vacuumings of the defendant's car and residence to be consistent in polymeric composition.[30] Once again, database examination of the frequency of any such match was not provided. Agent Houck is the author of an important paper published by the FBI supporting the opinions of trace evidence experts even with any support from population databases with respect to the trace evidence at issue.[31]

III. Discovery

Broeckel v. State[32] was a case addressing discovery issues in a routine microscopic fiber analysis setting. Here, defendant was convicted of first-degree sexual assault. Defendant assaulted the adult victim at his home during the course of a social visit. The state submitted a number of items to the state crime lab for testing, including the defendant's bathrobe and items of the victim's clothing that had been collected in the investigation. The victim's clothing was examined to see if there were fibers that matched those from

Broeckel's robe. The court set out its basic understanding of the fiber examination process:

> Fibers that compose a garment have identifying characteristics such as the color, shape, and origin of the material from which they are made. When one garment comes in contact with another, small fibers can transfer. Fibers can be collected from a garment, as by the lab here, with a tapelift, which is essentially similar to a sizable piece of adhesive tape that can be applied to successive areas of the garment causing loose fibers to stick to it. The tape is then examined under magnification in an attempt to locate fibers that could have originated from another garment.[33]

> In the laboratory's original examination, fibers with the same color, composition, and shape as those from Broeckel's robe were found on the victim's pants, pantyhose, bra, and blouse.

A discovery violation was alleged by defendant based upon his investigator's subsequent interview with lab personnel. Broeckel's investigator spoke to state criminalist Janeice Fair about her report, when she allegedly stated that she had found fibers that matched fibers from Broeckel's bathrobe on every item of victim A.D.'s clothing, but she did not find any on the inside of A.D.'s pants. Soon after, Fair reexamined the tapelifts originally taken from the victim's clothing and, upon such reexamination, she concluded that some of the fibers that matched fibers from Broeckel's robe on the tapelift originally were taken from inside the victim's body, having apparently having been overlooked during her original internal examination. The first the defense knew about this was when Fair testified at trial that she had found fibers that matched fibers from Broeckel's robe inside the pants.

Broeckel argued that his case had been irretrievably prejudiced because his opening statement and his cross-examination of prosecution witnesses had been carried out in the expectation that Fair would testify that no fibers were found inside A.D.'s pants.[34]

In affirming defendant's conviction, the court ruled the impact of discovery violations based on a mistake in the criminalist's reports as to the absence of fibers on certain clothing of the victim and the expert's subsequent change in testimony did not warrant a reversal. The court concluded that the absence of matching fibers inside the victim's pants would not have ruled out the assault:

> Although Broeckel and his counsel were surprised by the discovery violation, they had not promised the jury that they would present any evidence regarding the presence or absence of fibers. Whether

or not Fair originally found fibers on the tapelift taken from the inside of A.D.'s pants that matched fibers from Broeckel's robe, Broeckel knew before trial that Fair had found matching fibers on tapelifts taken from all of the other items of A.D.'s clothing and on the tapelift from the outside of A.D.'s pants. Also, the prosecutor did not argue that the fibers inside the pants had any greater significance than the presence of fibers on A.D.'s other articles of clothing. The absence of matching fibers inside A.D.'s pants would not have ruled out the assault. The matching fiber evidence only supports the conclusion that Broeckel's robe was likely to have come in contact with A.D.'s clothing. Even if there had been no matching fibers on the inside of A.D.'s pants, the absence of those fibers would not have undermined the state's case in the manner argued by Broeckel, because the testing found fibers on every item of A.D.'s clothing including A.D.'s pantyhose.

The matching fiber evidence only supported the conclusion that defendant's robe was likely to have come in contact with the victim's clothing.[35]

Fiber cases differ from hair cases in that the initial determination of its basic character is significantly more complex than determining if a human hair was male, female, Caucasian, Negroid, or Asian and from what portion of the body it came. These crucial matters are revisited in the discussions of the Wayne Williams Atlanta murders case discussed next.

The best-known, if not the best-reasoned fiber case in American legal history involving fiber evidence issues is the Wayne Williams trial growing out of the famous Atlanta murders of twelve young African-American males in 1979–1980.[36] The Williams case involved all of the subjects still in controversy as we enter the world of forensic science and forensic evidence in the 21st century. How do we gain sufficient knowledge of fiber manufacture, dyes, commercial applications, and differences among them, to make any intelligent class characteristic or individual-linking statements in a criminal case? What are the primary characteristics of fibers per se or fiber types that allow for a comparative examination? How does the absence of meaningful fiber match databases from which to engage in population frequency analyses affect our confidence in the meaningfulness of fiber testimony? How do probability analyses work here? Are these analyses better, worse, or the same as in any other trace evidence exercise attempting to link a suspect to a crime scene?

In *Williams v. State*,[37] defendant was charged and convicted of two of the twelve murders actually involved. Given the centrality of the Williams case in fiber analysis literature and judicial authorities, a detailed recitation of the central facts and forensic analyses is warranted. In a case of such complexity, it is essential to always place whatever forensic claims that are made squarely in the midst of the nonforensic context where they arose. Probabilistically based forensic facts originate from real-world contexts that support or deter from belief in the fact for which it is offered. The crime scene facts are the thread weaving all forensic claims and give them meaning and credibility. The central issues raised by Williams on appeal focused on the collection, testing, and testimony as regards certain fibers located in Williams' home and automobiles and linked by experts to similar fibers found on a number of the murder victims.

IV. Wayne Williams Case

Initially the court set out a recital of facts the jury would have been authorized to find from the evidence presented on the homicides of Jimmy Ray Payne and Nathaniel Carter, the two crimes with which appellant was charged. Over a 22-month period beginning in July 1979, more than thirty African-American children and young men were reported as missing in the Atlanta, Georgia area. Williams was charged with the murder of two of the victims, Nathaniel Carter, aged 28, and Jimmy Payne, aged 21. The murders of ten other victims were linked to Williams in support of the identity element, by way of complex fiber analysis testimony. Some victims were found floating in the Chattahoochee River, while others were discovered on or near rural roads or abandoned buildings in the Atlanta area.[38]

Victim Payne was 21 years of age, unemployed, and had no automobile or driver's license. A product of a broken home, he lived with his mother, sister, and girlfriend. The late morning of April 21, 1981, was the last time Payne was seen by any member of his household. It was then he told his mother he was on his way to the Omni. The following day a witness saw Williams and Payne standing by a taxi cab that was stopped on Highway 78 approximately one mile from the Chattahoochee River. The witness saw Williams and Payne talking to the driver of the taxicab, and he also saw a white station wagon parked on the opposite side of the street from the cab.

Payne's body was discovered clad only in red shorts in the Chattahoochee River on April 27, 1981. The medical examination and autopsy resulted in opinion evidence that the cause of death was asphyxia by an undetermined method.[39]

The state presented the testimony of seven fiber and hair associations between Wayne Williams and Jimmy Ray Payne. Larry Peterson testified: 1) that two pale-violet acetate fibers removed from Payne were consistent with violet acetate fibers present in the bedspread of Williams, except that they were lighter in color; 2) that three green Wellman-type fibers removed from Payne's shorts were similar to and could have originated from appellant's bedroom carpet, again, except that they were lighter in color; 3) that a blue-green or blue-gray rayon fiber removed from Payne was consistent with the rayon fibers comprising the carpet of the 1970 station wagon; 4) that several light-yellow rayon fibers and a light-yellow acrylic fiber found on Payne were consistent with fibers composing the yellow blanket found in appellant's bedroom, except that they were lighter in color; and 5) that a blue acrylic fiber removed from Payne was consistent with the blue acrylic fibers that composed the blue throw rug found in appellant's bathroom. Harold Deadman testified: 1) that a blue rayon fiber removed from Payne was consistent with blue rayon fibers, for which no source was known, found in various fibrous debris removed from the Williams home, and 2) that the approximately seven animal hairs removed from Payne could have originated from appellant's German Shepherd dog. There was evidence that the fibers found on Payne that were lighter in color than their supposed counterparts from the Williams environment were lighter because of their exposure to river water.[40]

Nathaniel Carter was 28 years old, lived at the Falcon Hotel in downtown Atlanta, and did not own an automobile. Robert Henry, a friend of Carter, saw Carter holding hands with Wayne Williams outside the Rialto Theatre about 9:00 to 9:15 p.m. on May 21, 1981. About 3:00 a.m., May 22, 1981, a member of a police surveillance team stationed at the Jackson Parkway Bridge heard a loud splash in the Chattahoochee River and saw a circle of waves form on the water. An automobile was then observed starting up and crossing the bridge. When the car was stopped, it was found to be a white Chevrolet station wagon and Wayne Williams was the driver. Carter's body was discovered in the Chattahoochee River on Sunday, May 24, 1981. It was located about 200 yards downstream from Interstate Highway 285 (the body was found only a short distance from the location at which the Payne body was found). The medical examination and autopsy of the body revealed Carter weighed about 146 pounds and that his death was caused by asphyxia due to some kind of choke hold formed with a broad, soft surface such as a forearm.

Carter's body was nude; therefore, only his pubic and head hair regions were capable of holding fiber or hair evidence.[41] Even so, several fibers and hairs were recovered. Larry Peterson testified: 1) that two pale-violet acetate fibers removed from the head hair of Carter had the same characteristics as the violet acetate fibers present in Williams's bedspread, except that they were lighter in color; 2) that a green nylon fiber removed from Carter's head hair had similar characteristics and properties as the fibers that composed the carpet in appellant's bedroom, except that it was lighter in color; 3) that a green polypropylene fiber taken from Carter's pubic hair had the same microscopic and optical characteristics as the fibers that composed the carpet in the workroom in the Williams home; 4) that a melted nylon fiber removed from Carter's head hair was consistent with nylon fibers found in the fibrous debris vacuumed from appellant's 1970 station wagon; 5) that a yellow rayon fiber removed from Carter's hair was consistent with the properties of the fibers present in the yellow blanket found in appellant's bedroom, except that it was lighter in color; and 6) that four animal hairs recovered from Carter were consistent with the characteristics of the hair of Williams' dog. There was evidence that the fibers found on Carter that were lighter in color than their supposed counterparts in the Williams environment were lighter because of their exposure to river water.[42]

The court next set out the evidence pertaining to connections between Williams and the other ten murder victims. The circumstantial evidence linking the defendant and each of these ten other victims was a combination of the range of similarity in the victims' lack of a strong family base, some sightings of the victim with Wayne Williams, and most importantly evidence of fiber found on each that experts testified was linked to his home or automobiles. The fiber testimony was presented as to each victim by Agent Harold Deadman of the Federal Bureau of Investigation's lab. The actual comparisons were conducted by three state's experts: FBI Microanalyst Harold Deadman, GBI employee Larry Peterson, and Royal Canadian Mounted Police employee Barry Gaudette.[43]

The types of fibers and hairs that Agent Deadman testified were taken from appellant and his environment, along with the items from which they were taken, are as follows:

1. Violet acetate and green cotton fibers representing the composition of a bedspread found in Williams' bedroom
2. Green and yellow nylon fibers used to fabricate the carpet found in Williams' bedroom
3. Dog hairs removed from Williams' German Shepherd
4. Yellow rayon and acrylic fibers used to fabricate a yellow blanket found in Williams' bedroom
5. Rayon and nylon fibers used to fabricate the carpet of a white 1970 Chevrolet station wagon to which Williams had access during part of the period over which the crimes occurred
6. Blue acrylic fibers used to fabricate a blue throw rug found in the porch or garage area of Williams' home
7. Polypropylene fibers used to fabricate a carpet located in a workroom in the back of Williams' home that was adjacent to his bedroom

8. Yellow nylon, blue rayon, white polyester, and pigmented polypropylene fibers, for which no source from Williams' environment was identified, but which were recovered from vacuum sweepings made by the state of defendant's 1970 station wagon
9. Fibrous debris removed from a vacuum cleaner found in Williams' home
10. White polypropylene fibers used to fabricate the trunk liner of a 1978 Plymouth Fury to which Williams had access during part of the period over which the crimes in question occurred
11. White acrylic and secondary acetate fibers used to fabricate the trunk liner and red tri-lobal nylon fibers used to fabricate the interior carpet of a burgundy colored 1979 Ford LTD to which Williams had access during part of the period over which the crimes in question occurred
12. Blue secondary acetate fibers representing the composition of a bedspread taken from the porch or garage area of Williams' home
13. Brown woolen and rayon fibers that composed the lining of a leather jacket owned by Williams
14. Gray acrylic fibers used to fabricate a gray glove that was found in the glove compartment of Williams' 1970 station wagon
15. Yellow nylon fibers that were used to fabricate a toilet seat cover taken from the Williams home and that were found in the fibrous debris vacuumed from the 1970 station wagon
16. Yellow acrylic fibers used to fabricate a carpet that was found in the kitchen of Williams' home[44]

Significant amounts of fiber evidence was presented by Deadman and supported by expert Larry Peterson, allegedly linking Wayne Williams to ten other young victims in addition to the two for whose murder he was on trial.

The state offered expert testimony of four fiber and hair associations between Williams and victim Alfred Evans, aged 15. FBI Agent Harold Deadman testified that two violet acetate fibers removed from Evans exhibited the same microscopic and optical properties as violet acetate fibers removed from the bedspread of appellant; that a fiber removed from Evans exhibited the same microscopic and optical properties as the Wellman fibers present in the carpet in Williams' bedroom and could have originated from that carpet; that six polypropylene fibers found on Evans could have originated from the trunk liner of Williams' 1978 Plymouth Fury; and that animal hairs removed from Evans could have originated from defendant's dog.[45]

The linking fiber evidence as to Eric Middlebrook, aged 14, consisted of testimony by Agent Deadman that four violet acetate fibers removed from Middlebrook were consistent with having originated from Williams' bedspread; that 32 red nylon fibers that were found in a clump on one of his shoes could have originated from the interior carpet of the 1979 Ford LTD; that two white acrylic and two secondary acetate fibers found on Middlebrook could have originated from the trunk liner of the 1979 Ford; that one yellow nylon fiber found on Middlebrook could have originated from either the toilet cover in the Williams home or from the same source (unidentified) that produced the loose yellow nylon fibers that were found in the debris vacuumed from the 1970 Chevrolet station wagon; and finally, that one animal hair removed from Middlebrook could have originated from Williams' dog.[46]

The body of Charles Stephens, aged 12, was also found to contain similar fiber samples. Agent Deadman testified that it contained thirty-five violet acetate and a number of green cotton fibers that could have originated from the bedspread found on Williams' bed; that three yellow nylon fibers removed from Stephens could have originated from the carpet found in Williams' bedroom; that two polypropylene fibers found on Stephens could have originated from the workroom in the back of the Williams home; that about thirty undyed synthetic and about 20 secondary acetate fibers recovered from Stephens were consistent with having originated from the trunk liner of the 1979 Ford LTD; that nine blue rayon fibers found on Stephens were similar to blue rayon fibers, the source of which was unknown, found in debris vacuumed from the 1970 station wagon, debris removed from the sweeper found in the Williams home, and debris removed from the bedspread found in Williams' bedroom; that one yellow nylon fiber taken from Stephens could have originated from the toilet cover found in the Williams home, or from the same source, which was unknown, that produced the yellow nylon fibers found on some of Williams' clothing in the debris removed from the 1970 station wagon; that five coarse white polyester fibers removed from Stephens could have originated from the same source (unknown) that produced the white polyester fibers removed from a white rug found in Williams' 1970 station wagon; and finally that the approximately seventeen animal hairs found on Stephens could have originated from Williams' dog.[47]

Regarding victim Terry Pue, aged 15, Deadman testified that over one hundred violet acetate and a number of green cotton fibers found on Pue were all consistent with having originated from the bedspread found in Williams' bedroom; that three yellow nylon fibers found on Pue could have originated from the carpet located in Williams' bedroom; that two pale green polypropylene fibers removed from Pue could have originated from the carpet located in the workroom in the back of the Williams home; that one coarse white polyester fiber recovered from Pue had the same properties as white polyester fibers, the source of which was unknown, vacuumed from the rug and interior of Williams' 1970 station wagon; and that approximately seventeen animal hairs found on Pue could have originated from Williams' dog.[48]

Deadman testified regarding victim Lubie Geter, aged 14, that several violet acetate fibers found on Geter were consistent with having originated from the bedspread found in Williams' bedroom; that five yellow nylon carpet fibers removed from Geter had the same characteristics as the fibers present in the carpet located in Williams' bedroom; that one yellow acrylic fiber discovered on Geter could have originated from a carpet found in the kitchen of the Williams home; that a green rayon fiber found on Geter could have originated from the carpet of Williams' 1970 station wagon; and that ten animal hairs removed from the body could have come from Williams' dog.[49]

The body of Patrick Baltazar, aged 11, was found by Deadmen to contain violet acetate and green cotton fibers consistent with having originated from Williams' bedspread; that seven yellow nylon Wellman-type fibers removed from Baltazar exhibited the same characteristics and properties as fibers present in the carpet located in Williams' bedroom and could have originated from that carpet; that four yellow rayon fibers removed from Baltazar's jacket could have come from the yellow blanket found in Williams' bedroom; that four deteriorated rayon fibers, ranging in color from green to yellow, could have originated from the carpet of Williams' 1970 station wagon; that two woolen fibers and one rayon fiber found on Baltazar's remains exhibited the same characteristics as woolen and rayon fibers taken from the cloth waistband of Williams' leather jacket; that thirteen gray acrylic fibers removed from the tee shirt, jacket, and shirt of Baltazar could have originated from the gray glove that was found in the glove compartment of Williams' 1970 station wagon; that a light-yellow nylon fiber, a coarse white polyester fiber, and a pigmented polypropylene fiber had the same properties as fibers present in the debris vacuumed from the 1970 station wagon, and could have originated from the same sources (unknown) that produced the fibers discovered in the debris; that the approximately twenty animal hairs found on the clothing of Baltazar could have come from Williams' dog; and that two scalp hairs removed from Baltazar were inconsistent with Baltazar's own scalp hair, but were consistent with scalp hairs taken from Williams, and could have originated from appellant.[50]

With respect to the body of 18-year-old Larry Rogers, Deadman testified that it was found to contain thirteen violet acetate fibers consistent with the violet acetate fibers taken from Williams' bedspread; that three yellow-green nylon fibers removed from Rogers were similar to the Wellman fibers found in Williams' bedroom carpet; that eight yellow rayon fibers discovered on Rogers could have originated from the yellow blanket found in Williams' bedroom; that one yellow-brown to green fiber taken from Rogers could have come from the carpet of the 1970 station wagon; that two secondary acetate fibers removed from the deceased's shorts could have originated from the bedspread that was found in Williams' garage; and that a light-yellow nylon fiber removed from the head hair of Rogers exhibited the same characteristics as yellow nylon fibers removed from the toilet cover found in Williams' home, from the sweepings made of the 1970 station wagon, and from several items of clothing of appellant.[51]

The fully clothed body of twenty-eight-year-old John Porter was found by Deadman and the other experts to contain violet acetate and green cotton fibers that could have originated from Williams' bedspread; that one yellow-green nylon fiber removed from the sheet used to carry Porter exhibited the same characteristics as the Wellman fibers making up Williams' bedroom carpet and could have originated from that carpet; that three yellow rayon fibers removed from Porter matched the yellow rayon fibers removed from the blanket found in Williams' bedroom; that several green rayon fibers removed from Porter could have originated from the carpet of the 1970 station wagon; that two secondary acetate fibers removed from Porter could have originated from the bedspread found in the carport of the Williams home; that a blue rayon fiber found on Porter could have come from the same source (unknown) that produced the blue rayon fibers found in the debris removed from the 1970 station wagon and in the debris removed from the vacuum cleaner found in Williams' home; and that the approximately seven animal hairs removed from Porter were consistent with having originated from Williams' dog.[52]

The remains of Joseph Bell, aged 15, contained five blue rayon fibers that were similar to rayon fibers recovered from debris collected from the 1970 station wagon and from debris collected from Williams' bedspread; and two pale-violet acetate fibers that were consistent with the fibers present in the bedspread of Williams, with the exception that they were considerably lighter in color.[53]

Agent Deadman testified that with respect to the body of William Barrett, aged 16, it contained many violet acetate and green cotton fibers that could have originated from Williams' bedspread; that five yellow-green nylon fibers recovered from Barrett could have originated from Williams' bedroom carpet; that seven yellow rayon fibers removed from Barrett could have originated from the blanket found under Williams' bed; that a blue rayon fiber recovered from Barrett had the same characteristics as blue rayon fibers recovered from the debris removed from the station wagon, from the vacuum cleaner found in Williams' home, and from his bedspread; that approximately thirty gray acrylic fibers recovered from Barrett could have originated from the glove recovered from the glove compartment of defendant's 1970 station wagon; that three fibers removed from Barrett could have originated from the carpet of the 1970 station wagon; and that the approximately thirteen animal hairs recovered from Barrett could have come from Williams' dog.[54]

Although there was significant fiber evidence, as set forth above, the court recognized that the principal support for the state's fiber evidence case was expert testimony concerning the alleged uniqueness of two types of carpet fibers recovered and analyzed by the state's experts: the green nylon carpet in Williams' bedroom, and the green-black rayon floorboard carpet of the 1970 Chevrolet station wagon Williams was driving the night he was discovered near the Jackson Parkway bridge.[55]

The carpet found in Williams' bedroom was central to the forensic fiber testimony in the case, being referenced as unique in its textile makeup and in its pattern of commercial manufacture, sale, and subsequent distribution. The director of technical services for Wellman, Incorporated, a Boston, Massachusetts manufacturer of synthetic textile fibers, testified that he had begun working for Wellman in 1967, and that one of the first things he was asked to do was to assist in the development of a synthetic fiber known as the 181-b. According to the director, this fiber had an unusual shape, trilobal with two long lobes and one short lobe, which was designed to avoid infringing upon a patented DuPont equilateral trilobal shape. The witness was shown state's exhibit #616, which was identified as a scanning electron microscope photograph of a fiber from the green carpet in Williams' bedroom, and he said it appeared to be a Wellman 181-b fiber. Gene Baggett, an employee of West Point Pepperell, a Dalton, Georgia carpet manufacturing company, testified that his company had purchased the Wellman fibers in 1970 and 1971 and used the Wellman 181-b fiber to manufacture several lines of carpet, including lines known as Luxaire and Dreamer, both of which, he testified, had been colored with a dye formulation dubbed English Olive. He testified that while he was not a chemist, and was not qualified to perform microscopic analysis and identification of single fibers, based upon his visual inspection of such aggregate physical characteristics as height of pile, weight of carpet, and type of backing, the company sample appeared to be similar to a similar fiber taken from defendant's home.[56]

Harold Deadman testified that the FBI had obtained the latter exhibit from West Point Pepperell, which had identified it as a piece of Luxaire and that based on his examination of the gross physical characteristics of the two exhibits, he could find no significant differences in their construction, and concluded that "in all probability they were manufactured by the same company. They certainly could have come from the same source."[57]

Harold Deadman compared the gross physical characteristics of the commercial carpet sample with a piece of the Williams bedroom carpet and concluded that there were no significant differences in construction and that hence they were probably manufactured by the same company. Deadman relied on Luxaire and Dreamer sales records of West Point Pepperell, information orally supplied him by Baggett, housing statistics provided by the

Atlanta Regional Commission, and according to the dissent, a number of wholly speculative assumptions (chief of which was that the Williams carpet was in fact a West Point Luxaire or Dreamer English Olive carpet), Deadman attempted to use the calculus of compound probabilities to perform a series of calculations to establish the rarity of that type of carpet in the Atlanta metropolitan area.[58]

Deadman concluded that there was a one in 7792 chance of randomly selecting a home in the Atlanta area and finding a room containing carpet similar to the Williams bedroom carpet. Regarding the green-black 1970 Chevrolet carpet, both Deadman and his fellow expert Peterson testified that they had information indicating that in the Atlanta area only 620 out of over two million cars had that type of carpet. Deadman explained that this data had been supplied by the General Motors Corporation.[59]

Williams argued that in addition to the substantial error in allowing evidence as to ten murders for which he was never charged, the court erred in permitting Deadman to discuss mathematical probabilities concerning the fiber evidence and in permitting the prosecutor to argue mathematical probabilities to the jury. The majority, in a surprisingly terse ruling, held that neither of those contentions had merit, as experts were permitted to give their opinions, based upon their knowledge, including mathematical computations. Counsel is given wide latitude in closing argument, the court opined, and is not prohibited from suggesting to the jury inferences that might be drawn from the evidence. Such suggestions may include those based upon mathematical probabilities.[60]

The sole dissent, Justice Smith, noted that during closing arguments the district attorney summarized this testimony and then proceeded to embellish his summary with his personal attempt to quantify the probative force of the fiber evidence:

> Accordingly, he rounded off the figures for the 181-b bedroom carpet and the green-black floorboard carpet and multiplied them together calculate the chances "that there is another house in Atlanta that has the same kind of carpet as the Williams house and that the people who live in that house have the same type station wagon as the Williamses do ...", arriving at a probability of one in forty million. Adjusting this figure to account for an additional assumption of his own, the prosecutor argued that the appropriate figure was actually one in an astounding one hundred fifty million.[61]

Taken at face value, Justice Smith continued, the testimony establishing the rarity of the two fiber types would appear to provide substantial support for the critical opinions of the experts that the fibers of those types found on the bodies were probably transferred from the Williams home or car. Examining the majority opinion's factual review of the Payne and Carter murders, Justice Smith continued, and the ten uncharged offenses, one was indeed struck by a number of similarities among the twelve crimes. Each of the victims was a low-income black male, slightly built, who was often seen alone in the streets of Atlanta. Payne, Carter, and five of the ten other crime victims were seen with Williams sometime prior to their death. All but two of the victims, Porter and Middlebrook, were killed by some form of asphyxiation.[62]

However, those similarities were outweighed by the significant dissimilarities between the two charged offenses and the ten extrinsic crimes:

Payne and Carter, age 21 and 28, respectively, were adults; the ages of the victims of the uncharged crimes ranged from 11 years to 28 years and averaged only 15.7 years. With the exception of 28-year-old John Porter, the extrinsic offense victims were essentially children. Another striking dissimilarity between the Payne and Carter killings, on the one hand, and the ten extrinsic offenses, on the other, is that while the bodies of Payne and Carter were both apparently thrown into the Chattahoochee River near the I-285 overpass, only one of the ten extrinsic offense victims' bodies, that of Joseph Bell, was found in a river.[63]

Justice Smith observed that victim Bell's body was discovered in the South River near Rockdale County, miles from where Payne and Carter were found and that the remaining nine were deposited on land. Although there was evidence tending to show that the Carter killing was sexually motivated, there was a total absence of medical evidence showing sexual abuse of any of the other victims:

In addition, it is critical to note that the state's fiber evidence allegedly linking Williams to all twelve victims, while slightly probative on the issue of whether Williams actually perpetrated the ten other crimes, ... has no relevance to the modus operandi issue, for the simple reason that the fiber evidence in this case provides no information as to the murderer's technique in killing or disposing of his victims. The state's own experts testified that they could not determine the exact mechanism of the alleged transfer of fibers from Williams to the victims. Thus, the sole implication of this type of trace evidence is that each of the victims possibly was in contact with Williams, his house, or his car sometime before his death. Although this inference may be probative of the identity of the killer of the ten extrinsic victims, it does not establish a unique modus operandi, because it would be possible for the murderer to apprehend, kill, and dispose of his twelve victims in dissimilar ways, yet transfer fibers to them in each case ... Thus the presence or absence of fiber evidence has no relevance in the case before us to the narrow issue of modus operandi.[64]

The dissent by Justice Smith is well worth reading for its trenchant criticism of the majority's legitimization of microscopic hair analysis, and especially the probabilistic extensions made from such comparisons in this case. Nonetheless the conviction was affirmed. The Wayne Williams case still fascinates the American media and public and efforts to get Williams a new trial continue.[65]

V. Additional Fiber Cases

Microscopic fiber evidence is used routinely in police work across the world and has consistently been discussed in appellate decisions.[66] The ubiquity of fiber transfers in close-encounter crime scenes has always had a significant circumstantial power to convict. The 1996 Illinois case of *People v. Miller* may serve as an example of this point.

In *People v. Miller*,[67] defendant was convicted of first-degree murder. In September 1993, the nude bodies of three women were found in rural Peoria County. The body of Marcia Logue was found in a drainage ditch in the 500 block of South Cameron Lane on September 18, with a pillow case stuck in her mouth. The body of Helen Dorrance was found 50 feet from Logue's body on the same date. The body of Sandra Csesznegi was found in a drainage ditch near Christ Church Road on September 26. Csesznegi's body was in a state of advanced decomposition. All three women were known prostitutes in the Peoria area.

On September 29, 1993, the authorities went to the defendant's Peoria apartment to question him about crimes in the Peoria area, where a search of defendant's apartment uncovered two robes, female underwear, a broken miniblind rod and a brown and white cloth covered with what appeared to be dried blood. The police also recovered pillows and a mattress, which contained reddish-brown stains. Blood splatters were also found on a wall of the bedroom and the bed's headboard. A subsequent search uncovered a glove, a throw rug, and more women's underwear. During the second search, the police collected hair and fibers.[68]

Glenn Schubert, a forensic scientist, testified regarding the hair and fibers recovered from the defendant's apartment, Logue's body, and the maroon automobile, reporting that debris from the pillow case found in Logue's mouth was consistent with the defendant's pubic hair, that fibers on the pillow case matched fibers taken from a throw rug located in the defendant's apartment, and fibers collected from the defendant's living-room floor. Several fibers taken from Logue's body also matched fibers taken from the living-room floor of defendant's apartment. Also, several acrylic-like fibers from the car were consistent with the fibers found on defendant's floor.[69]

The discussion that follows focuses on the use of fiber evidence in several of the more important of the cases published since the first edition of this book in 2000.

Two recent decisions address the important issue of whether defense lawyers' failure to call their own forensic fiber experts rises to the Strickland[70] level for ineffective counsel. This issue is increasingly raised today, especially when legislatures and courts are providing increased funding for expert support. As defense counsel become more educated in the world of forensics and thus better able to conduct solid cross-examinations, courts are less interested in ineffectiveness claims where the record shows a solid competence on the part of defense counsel.

In *Crawford v. Head*,[71] an 11th Circuit Court opinion, defendant, convicted of felony murder, filed for a writ of habeas corpus, arguing, among other points, the ineffectiveness of counsel for failure to call a forensic fiber analyst. Considerable hair and fiber evidence was found on the victim, including three hairs on the victim's pajama top that were consistent with Crawford's head hair, and some fibers that were consistent with fibers from Crawford's car. Also, the police recovered the tee-shirt worn by Crawford on the night of the murder, which they found stuffed behind a dresser in the house in which Crawford slept on the night of the murder. The shirt had blood on it, although the blood could not be typed conclusively. In addition, a pillow case, mattress pad, and bedsheet were recovered on the edge of the road not far from the body of the victim, and Crawford's wife identified these items as coming from their trailer. This bedding also had hairs consistent with Crawford and the victim, as well as fibers consistent with the carpet in Crawford's car. Type O blood, the type shared by the victim and Crawford, was found on the bedsheet.[72]

The prosecution presented witnesses from the Georgia Bureau of Investigation Crime Lab to testify concerning the evidence in the case. Larry Peterson testified concerning the types of analysis performed on hair and fiber evidence that was recovered. He stated that he tested known head, pubic, and arm hair samples taken from Crawford, as well as hair samples from Leslie English. He also stated that he tested fiber samples taken from Crawford's car. Given these samples, Peterson testified that he was able to determine that several hairs taken from the victim's body and pajama top were consistent with the head and pubic hair of Crawford, and that fiber samples taken from the same sources were consistent with Crawford's car. Peterson further testified that the bedding which was recovered from beside the road contained hairs that were consistent with the victim's hair as well as Crawford's head and pubic hair. The mattress cover additionally had a fiber consistent with Crawford's car. He also stated that the socks that Crawford's wife saw him take out of his car and dispose of had hairs consistent with Crawford's head and pubic hair and with fibers from his car. Finally, Peterson testified that a hair consistent with Crawford's arm hair was found inside the victim's vaginal cavity, although this particular evidence was later excluded after Siemon established a chain-of-custody problem.

The court noted that defense counsel's cross-examination of Peterson largely focused on the limitations on hair and fiber testing, and on the fact that this testing only permitted conclusions that certain hairs or fibers were consistent, but not whether they actually came from the same source. Peterson also testified that hairs and fibers could be transferred from one place to another, and that it was not possible to determine when various hairs or fibers were picked. Therefore, Siemon got Peterson to admit that the hair and fiber evidence could only establish that the victim had some contact with "the car or person of Eddie Crawford."[73]

The record further revealed that defense counsel was well aware of the limitations of the scientific evidence on which the prosecution relied, and that he was able to point out those limitations to the jury. As he testified during the state habeas proceedings, he was very familiar with such evidence as a result of a previous case that he had handled. Moreover, through a chain-of-evidence argument, Siemon was able to get one of the most damning pieces of hair and fiber evidence excluded from the trial. Given these factors, the court rejected defendant's claim of ineffective counsel under Strickland.

In *Jenkins v. State*,[74] a 2004 Alabama case, the defendant was convicted of capital murder and filed a petition for post-conviction relief. The court held that defense counsel's failure to use funds that had been approved to hire a forensic fiber expert did not constitute ineffective assistance of counsel. While the state used fiber evidence to establish defendant's identity, the record demonstrated that defense counsel spent considerable time and effort learning about fiber analysis, interviewed the state's fiber expert, and thoroughly cross-examined the state's fiber expert on known problems with fiber analysis.

During the evidentiary hearing in the post-conviction case, Scofield was questioned about his preparation for the state's forensics fiber expert — Steve Drexler, trace-evidence examiner with the Alabama Department of Forensic Sciences. This exchange merits extended attention here:

"Q [Assistant attorney general]: How did you prepare for the anticipated fiber analysis testimony?

"A [Scofield]: In talking to Mr. Drexler, [the State's forensics expert], I think it was a telephone conversation I may have had with him. I asked him whether or not there were any treatises that might assist me in that preparation. He told me there was a doctor in Auburn — Dr. Hall or something like that — that had written a book on fiber analysis. I could probably get him. I contacted Dr. Hall and got a copy of his book. I bought a copy of his book on fiber analysis and identification.

"Q: Did you use that book?

"A: Yes, I did.

"Q: How much time did you spend preparing through the use of the book and talking to Mr. Drexler?

"A: It is hard to ballpark. I spent considerable time. I went through his book. I tried to learn as much as I could about fiber analysis. I did not specifically discuss the facts or issues with Dr. Hall. In other words, I didn't call him and say, 'Could you tell me about this?' I pretty much said, 'I understand you have a book. How much is it? Could you mail it to me?' He mailed me a copy of the book. I spent a lot of time on that. Drexler, I met with him on one occasion. He corresponded with me on another occasion when it turned out there was some other evidence that he learned or some information he learned that he supplied to me. I may have talked to him on the phone one time. In terms of overall time, I really don't know. It was pretty considerable. I did a good bit of preparation on the fiber analysis stuff.

"Q: Were you surprised in any way by the testimony he offered?

"A: No. It was precisely what he said it would be. He didn't pull any punches.

"Q: Did you come to a conclusion after all your preparation that Drexler would have testified to anything different?

A: I can't say that. I came to the conclusion that I was satisfied about what Drexler would say. I also felt pretty satisfied that

Drexler was going to confirm that fiber analysis was not an exact science. You can't really match this fiber and say this fiber came from here or here, like a fingerprint. I felt like, given the state of testimony of what Drexler was going to say, that would be the best I could hope for. I did not go get another expert to say or follow up on whether Drexler did his comparisons correctly. I was satisfied that Drexler — his testimony was going to hurt but it could be minimized by the mere nature of fiber analysis."[75]

(R. 375-77.)

When addressing this issue in its order the circuit court stated:

(O)n cross-examination by the state, Mr. Scofield testified concerning his preparation for the forensic evidence presented at trial by the State. The court finds that Mr. Scofield's preparation was both extensive and significant. Mr. Scofield stated that he was in no way surprised by any of the forensic evidence presented at trial. He effectively cross-examined all of the state's forensic experts, pointing out discrepancies and shortcomings which supported the chosen theory of defense. Trial counsel's actions, in relation to this claim, were not outside 'the wide range of reasonable professional assistance.'[76] In presenting no forensic expert testimony at the Rule 32 hearing, Jenkins has shown no reasonable probability that, had a particular forensic expert been retained by the defense, the result of the trial would have been different. Id. at 694, 104 S.Ct. 2052."

The appellate court agreed and held that Jenkins had failed to satisfy the Strickland test requirements for inadequacy of counsel.

In *Ross v. State*,[77] the defendant was convicted of two counts of rape, two counts of kidnapping, two counts of aggravated sodomy, two counts of armed robbery, violation of the Georgia Controlled Substances Act, and possession of a firearm by a convicted felon. Defendant and a friend stopped two women in a car, entered, demanded their jewelry and money, and then forced the women to disrobe and repeatedly raped them. The women were also threatened throughout the night-long ordeal with guns and were tortured by being burned with cigarette lighters and candle wax.[78]

Defendant alleged ineffective counsel requiring a new trial. While some DNA evidence was used at the trial, fingerprint, fiber, and hair analyses were not because they failed to connect the defendant to the crime. The defendant argued that his counsel was ineffective because of his failure to secure the testimony of an expert in the field of microscopic fiber analysis to testify that none of the fibers taken from the apartment where the victims were held were found on defendant's clothing and that none of the fibers from defendant's clothing were found at the crime scene. The court noted that the record clearly indicated that the jury was aware that fiber samples were taken and that the tests of the samples did not indicate defendant as a match, through the testimony of state experts.

The jury was free to make its own decision based upon the information, and the failure of the defendant's counsel to present an expert to speak about the lack of match regarding fiber samples did not likely have an influence on the outcome of the case. Without a proffer as to what the testimony of this microscopic fiber expert would have been at trial, Ross could not show there was a reasonable probability that, but for trial counsel's failure to call this expert as a witness, the trial's result would have been different.[79]

VI. Fiber Persistence

In some instances, the fiber issue involves the distribution path of the fibers and their persistence in remaining on various surfaces.[80] In *Barfield v. State*,[81] a 2004 Florida murder case, it was held that the trial court abused its discretion in excluding the proffered testimony of defendant's expert as to how a truck accident occurred, how fibers consistent with defendant's pants were released, and how the fibers could have been distributed by the accident. The court determined that such testimony could have assisted the jury in determining the significance of the fiber distribution in a truck in light of contested issue of whether defendant was driving the truck. Defendant testified that he was only a passenger in the truck and had exited via driver's door after the accident. Eyewitness testimony established that another person was also in the truck. The testimony of state's expert, as to locations and numbers of fibers, was intended to convince the jury that defendant was sole driver.

The undisputed facts established that a pickup truck was stolen from a Shell gas station while the truck's owner was inside the station. When he saw his pickup being driven away he raced out and leaped into the bed. The driver accelerated to a high speed and began swerving, apparently attempting to throw the victim out. Many witnesses saw the victim being tossed around in the truck bed and heard him crying for help. The stolen truck eventually hit another vehicle, causing the driver of the truck to lose control and crash. The victim died a short time later from injuries sustained in the accident. A witness who lived near the accident scene saw a man leave the truck and flee into a swampy area next to the witness's home. Employing a tracking dog, the police found Barfield in a wooded area about a mile and half away.

Barfield told the jurors his version of the day's events., testifying that he said he went to the Shell station to call his mother from the pay phone and ask for a ride home. But he saw a friend, an Hispanic youth named Vega, backing up in a pickup truck. Vega opened the passenger door and told Barfield to get in. Just after he climbed into the truck, Barfield heard a man beating on the back window. Vega began driving very fast, swerving and trying to throw the man out of the truck bed. Barfield was scared and crouched on the passenger side floorboard. He begged Vega to stop, but Vega refused. Eventually, Vega lost control of the truck and it crashed. Barfield was knocked unconscious. He remembered feeling dizzy when he came to, and leaving the truck through the driver's side door, which was open. He did not see Vega but he saw the victim walking around. Barfield was scared and ran into the wooded area because he was a convicted felon and was in possession of marijuana. As he ran, he discarded the marijuana in a lake. A police dog eventually found him and the canine officer arrested him.[82] Several witnesses corroborated Barfield's story. On rebuttal, however, the state called several witnesses who testified that Vega did not know how to drive. Vega and his girlfriend's father testified he was at her home during the relevant time.

The state also presented the testimony of a fiber analyst from the Florida Department of Law Enforcement who found 77 fibers consistent with Barfield's pants on a towel kept on the driver's seat of the truck. She also found four fibers on the ceiling of the cab and six fibers on the passenger's seat and floorboard, but she did not find any fibers on the driver's floorboard. To rebut the implication of this evidence, Barfield sought to introduce the opinion testimony of an accident reconstructionist and forensic scientist concerning how the accident happened, how the fibers were released, and how they could be distributed as a result of the accident. The expert would have opined that tears in the knee and back hip pocket of Barfield's pants were the result of a rollover accident and were consistent with his being a passenger who was tossed around the cab. The fibers would have been released when Barfield's pants tore. The fibers discovered on the ceiling of the cab were consistent with a rollover. Barfield's expert also believed that the many fibers found on the towel in the driver's seat and the absence of fibers on the driver's floorboard demonstrated that Barfield had crawled on his hands and knees from the passenger seat to the driver's seat after the rollover accident.

The state moved to exclude the expert's opinion about the fiber evidence. It argued that the opinion did not require any specialized knowledge or experience, that it was within the common experience of an ordinary person, and that the jurors had the ability to understand the evidence. The trial court agreed and excluded the expert's testimony.

The appellate court, noting the centrality of the issue of whether Barfield was driving the truck, and that the state's fiber evidence was intended to convince the jurors that Barfield was the driver, found that the defense expert's testimony would have explained why that evidence could lead to a different conclusion:

> Injuries and their causes, in automobile accidents or otherwise, are subjects within most people's common knowledge. How fibers are released from clothing, and the possible significance of the presence or absence of fibers in a particular part of an automobile after an accident, are not (citation omitted). The expert opinion in this case could have assisted the jury in determining the significance of this physical evidence. The trial court abused its discretion in excluding the testimony of Barfield's expert. We reverse and remand for a new trial.

A unique fiber setting is reported in the 2004 California case of *People v. Ewell*,[83] where defendants Dana James Ewell and Joel Patrick Radovcich were convicted of murder, with special death penalty circumstances of multiple murder for financial gain. During the search of the home of Radovcich's mother, a container of drill bits (called a drill bit index) was seized from the garage. In the drill bit index, police found particulate matter which included larger white particles, drill turnings, and small pieces of what appeared to be steel wool. He also found a lot of particulate matter on the clothes Glee was wearing when she was killed, including small metallic particles, particles of what appeared to be a dark, rubbery-type substance, and fluorescing yellow fibers that were consistent with the nap on tennis balls.

Police concluded that tennis ball particles, such as those found on victim Glee's clothing and in the piece of carpet that had been under Glee's body, would have been ejected had a bullet been fired through a sound suppressor made with tennis balls; and that steel wool particles, again such as those found on Glee's clothing, would also have been ejected from a homemade sound suppressor. Boudreau also determined that the piece of carpet contained particles of chrome molybdenum steel, of like composition to drilled metal specimens from Green Mountain barrels.[84]

Lucien Haag, a criminalist with his own consulting firm who is an expert in firearms with a special emphasis on reconstruction, also examined the evidence. He confirmed that one gun — possibly an AT-9 — had fired all six bullets; that the gun's barrel had been ported in a crude attempt to make a silenced weapon; and that a homemade silencer had, in fact, been used. He also determined that a metal particle recovered from Glee's clothing was comparable in composition to the barrel recovered from Ponce. However, a portion of that barrel was corroded from being in the ground. Because of the effect of this corrosion on test-fired bullets, Haag was able to conclude only that the barrel was "'entirely consistent'" with having fired the bullets recovered from the scene and autopsy.

The basic circumstantial strength of forensic fiber evidence is the linkage of fibers associated with the victim or defendant's actual clothing to each other. Such linkage raises serious inferences toward guilt that defense counsel must vigorously rebut. Explaining away the type of connections established in the Sutherland and Wayne Williams cases is a considerable undertaking, more often than not fatal to a defendant's forensic defense. This is not to maintain that a strong defense is unavailable. Several more cases illustrate the point.

In *Trawick v. State*,[85] the defendant was convicted of murder and kidnapping. On October 10, 1992, the partially nude body of victim Stephanie Gash was found on the side of a road. Her mouth and nose were covered with duct tape and a medical examiner testified that she died as a result of both a three-inch knife wound that entered her heart and asphyxiation caused by strangulation.

Steven Drexler, of the Alabama Department of Forensic Sciences, testified that two fibers found on the victim's sweater, which was recovered from the crime scene, were consistent with fibers from the carpet of the defendant's Toyota van. Also, fibers found on the duct tape that covered the victim's mouth were the same as the fibers from the carpet of the Toyota van.

The appellant gave a detailed statement to the police in which he confessed to having murdered Stephanie Gash. The appellant's confession was corroborated by the following facts. The Toyota van was towed to the police station where police discovered a piece of carpet, a tarpaulin, ball-peen hammer, and a plastic bucket that contained an 11-inch knife. Using luminol spray, police discovered blood traces on the tarpaulin, the piece of carpet, the ball-peen hammer, the tailgate of the van, and on the knife. A Ford station wagon that the appellant was known to drive was also impounded. A toy gun was found in the passenger's floorboard of that vehicle.

In *State v. Smith*,[86] defendant was convicted of aggravated kidnapping, rape of a child, and sodomy on a child. Information given by the victim led the authorities to defendant. Physical evidence, consisting, among others, of microscopic fiber analyses findings, confirmed the victim's rendition of her attack.

Fibers on the victim's clothing matched fibers from Smith's shirt and in the carpet of his car. Pubic hair matching defendant's was found on the victim, and head hairs consistent with the victim's were found in defendant's back seat. Fibers matching the fibers in Smith's shirt and in the carpet of his car were found on the victim's clothing.[87]

In *State v. Blanton*,[88] the defendant, James Blanton, was convicted by a jury of two counts of first-degree premeditated murder, four counts of grand larceny, and three counts of first-degree burglary.

Eight escaped convicts, including the defendant, committed a series of robberies, burglaries, and the murder and home invasion involved in this case. The victims' residence had one entryway, which was through a screen door located at the side of the house opposite the victims' bedrooms. A cloth glove was on the ground by the concrete block. Following the discovery of the victim's bodies at the Vester residence, the sheriff's deputies began checking cabins in the surrounding area, and learned that the Crawford residence, less than a quarter of a mile from the murder victim's home, had been burglarized. One of the gloves found at the Crawfords' trailer matched a glove found outside the Vesters' front bedroom window. A fiber analysis of the two gloves indicated that it was likely that they were originally sold together as a pair.

State v. Higgenbotham,[89] a murder and kidnapping case, established that defendant sought out a prostitute, "hog tied," gagged, and killed her and then dumped the body in a ditch. In affirming the kidnapping conviction, the Kansas Supreme Court accepted fiber evidence to establish that the defendant had satisfied the elements of the crime of kidnapping. The victim Jodi's body was face-down in the dirt. A white sweater and bra were on one side, a pair of panties on the other. Jodi's shirt was pulled down to her waist. Her hands and feet were bound together (hog-tied) behind her back with black plastic pull ties. A yellow rope secured the pull ties. A separate piece of yellow rope was around one of her wrists. Green duct tape was wrapped around her nose and mouth. A bandanna that had been used as a gag was found under the duct tape over her mouth.[90]

Defendant's wife led police to a storage rented by her husband's friend, Chuck Peters, who allowed defendant (real name Murphy) to use the locker to work on cars. The wife spoke to the victim who was sitting in the car. The police began an investigation of defendant and were led to the storage unit, wherein a search turned up black nylon wire ties, rolls of duct tape, and yellow rope. Wadded-up duct tape was found in the back of a Chevette that was inside the unit and a button was located on the floor as well as a used condom found in a cardboard box. A crime scene investigator collected hairs and fibers from the Chrysler vehicle parked in the locker area. The defendant's friend testified that the black plastic ties that were found in his storage shed did not belong to him.[91]

The FBI lab's hair and fiber analysis found evidence of hair transfer between Higgenbotham's items and the deceased's. However, the FBI examiner reported that red fibers found on Jodi's socks were consistent with a carpet sample from the defendant's Chrysler. Also, blue olefin fibers that were found on all of the items of Jodi's clothing, and on the rope on her body, were consistent with fibers from the deck area of the Chevette, causing the examiner to believe Jodi had been in both of those vehicles. A similar blue fiber was also found in Higgenbotham's Plymouth. He also compared the thread from the button in the shed with the thread in a button from Jodi's shirt and found they were consistent, however, the rope on the body was not the same rope from the storage shed. Finally, head hairs on the duct tape in the Chevette, while not consistent with Jodi's, were consistent with Higgenbotham's.[92]

Tests performed by a microanalyst from the Bureau of Criminal Apprehension and a private analytic forensic microscopist were discussed in *State v. Profit*,[93] a 1999 Minnesota homicide case. The defendant was convicted of two counts of first-degree murder and one count of intentional second-degree murder for the May 1996 killing of one Renee Bell, whose nude body was found floating in Basset Creek in Theodore Wirth Park in Golden Valley, Minnesota. An elastic waistband from an article of clothing had been wrapped around Bell's neck and was secured in a knot and one end looped through Bell's mouth and under her tongue in a gag-like manner. An autopsy report concluded that the victim had been strangled with the ligature and that Bell had been dead from one day to one week. Police discovered defendant's wallet a few feet from where Bell's body had been discovered.[94]

Bell's body was just the first of several bodies to be found in or near Theodore Wirth Park during the summer of 1996.[95]

After defendant's brother-in-law, who had lent a vehicle and clothing to him, stated that defendant had implicated himself in the murder and burning of Keooudorn Phothisane, a male transvestite, the police executed search warrants for Profit's home and the various vehicles driven by him or his family. While searching a 1990 Pontiac Grand Am known to have been driven by Profit, investigators found threads and fibers similar to threads and fibers found on the ligature used to strangle Bell. Tests performed by a microanalyst from the Bureau of Criminal Apprehension and a private analytic forensic microscopist revealed that the threads and fibers from the trunk were chemically and physically indistinguishable from the threads and fibers from the ligature.[96]

In *Floudiotis v. State*,[97] defendants were convicted in the Superior Court, New Castle County in Delaware, of second- and third-degree assault and second-degree conspiracy arising from beating of a couple in the parking lot of a tavern. Both sustained broken jaws, cuts, and bruises, and Mark also sustained a broken collarbone.[98] Police observed the same pickup truck described by witnesses to the assault and followed it on suspicion of drunken driving. Police pulled the pickup truck over and arrested the four occupants, one of whom was the defendant Eaton. Subsequent to an interview and photo session, Detective Johnson seized the footwear of all four suspects because he had reason to believe that all four were involved in the assault at the Deer Park and that the footwear might contain hairs or fibers that would implicate them. Through subsequent forensic tests, the state discovered fibers on defendant Eaton's shoes that were consistent with the same source of the fibers taken from the tank top victim Kimberly Butler wore the night of the incident.[99]

Eaton contends that the trial court erred in admitting evidence recovered from his combat boots. He argues that, because Detective Johnson illegally seized his boots at the police station, they are the fruit of this unlawful warrantless search, and the fibers consistent with Kimberly Butler's tank top that the police found on his boots should not have been admitted by the trial court.[100] The fiber evidence went unchallenged here as is so often the case in recent decisions.

In *State v. Young*,[101] defendant was convicted of aggravated murder from the killing of 14-year-old Heidi Bazar, whom he had been dating until a breakup occurred. At the conclusion of a dance, a friend accompanied Heidi to the store and overheard her telephoning defendant to come and pick her up there. The friend heard the deceased arguing with defendant on the phone. Heidi disappeared and her body was found at the bottom of a remote "lover's lane" location. The police arrested defendant. Defendant stated that after exiting his truck, they began to fight and he pushed Heidi after she slapped him a second time, that she was apparently too close to the cliff's edge, and fell backwards down the side of the cliff. He claimed that Heidi fell off the cliff after he instinctively pushed her when she slapped him.

The autopsy, however, indicated that the victim suffered more than 30 wounds, including a fractured jaw, a broken nose, a liver severed almost in half, a tooth knocked out of her braces and strangulation, which were clearly indicative of an intentional, not accidental killing:

The coroner and pathologist testified that the wounds that caused the death could not have resulted from a 13-foot fall off a cliff or from an accident, and most likely were caused by multiple blunt force to her face and neck. (Tr. pp. 230–231; 247; 285; 290; 314.) From the number and severity of the wounds suffered by Heidi, any reasonable trier of fact could find that there existed an intent to kill by appellant.[102]

While defendant denied striking the deceased in any manner with any object, and testified that he never struck or beat Heidi in any manner or with any object, including his hands, except for pushing at her, the court noted that a large brick, an 18-pound chunk of concrete, and a board were found near the location of Heidi's body and contained Heidi's blood:

The board contained fibers from Heidi's blue jeans and the chunk of concrete had been thrown away from Heidi's body. (Tr. p. 441). Appellant's testimony that he only pushed Heidi and she fell over the cliff to her death is inconsistent with the testimony of the coroner, the pathologist conducting the autopsy, and the forensic pathologist. These experts testified that Heidi's fatal injuries resulted from a deliberate and intentional infliction of blunt force impacts to her head and trunk and did not result from a thirteen-foot fall or an accident...[103]

From this scientific testimony, the court concluded, the jury could have reasonably inferred that Heidi was beaten to an extent that caused her to bleed and then beaten again on already exposed blood sources. Additionally, the testimony of the coroner and pathologist established that Heidi sustained approximately thirty-five wounds, many that were inconsistent with a fall, including a severed liver, a fractured jaw, a tooth missing from her braces, a fractured eye socket, and manual strangulation.

In *Woodward v. United States*,[104] defendant was convicted of second-degree murder. James Butler went out the back door of his house and saw what he believed to be a body lying on top of some brush. After his neighbor and a nearby woman confirmed that it was a body, the police were called. The body was that of a woman wearing dark-colored sweatpants and a blue and grey sweatshirt with no shoes. On November 24, 1992, police officers entered a building at 924 Ingraham Street where the body was found at the rear of the building. Defendant had recently vacated an apartment in the structure. The police discovered blood on the side of a dresser inside the room and found in the basement a large light-blue plastic trash can that had dried blood on it and contained a blanket with a very large blood stain on one end. The door to the basement opened out of the rear of the house into the Ingraham alley where the victim's body was found.[105]

An FBI special agent assigned to the Hairs and Fibers Unit testified that the carpet fibers found on the deceased's sweatshirt matched those in Woodard's second-floor bedroom. He also testified that the dog hairs found on the victim's sweatpants and on the victim's transport sheet matched the dog hairs in Woodard's home.

In *State v. Timmendequas*,[106] defendant was convicted of capital murder. The victim, Megan Kanka, aged 7, lived diagonally across the street from the defendant, who, upon questioning stated that he had killed the young victim and put her body in a nearby park. In his statement defendant said that victim came to his house while his roommates were out, wanting to see defendant's puppy. He then forced her into his bedroom and attacked and killed her. Testimony by a forensic chemist and a criminalist indicated that the fragments of the victim's shorts found in the garbage of defendant's home contained fibers chemically and physically consistent with fibers found on defendant's bedroom rug, the sleeping bag, and in the lint trap of defendant's dryer. Fibers were also found on defendant's sweatpants that matched those taken from Megan's blouse.[107]

Finally, the famous Locard Principle,[108] whereby all close physical contacts allegedly result in hair or fiber transfers, was discussed in the case of *State v. Goney*,[109] where the defendant was convicted of rape and raises incompetency of counsel in his post-conviction filing.[110] A forensic examination of hair and fibers from the couch where the rape was alleged to have occurred was negative when compared to defendant Goney. Defendant argued that Detective Menke, the trace evidence examiner, should have been called to testify. The crime lab report indicated that a small envelope labeled "Hair and Fibers from Love Seat" had been tested, showing Caucasian head hairs similar to that of the victim, Caucasian body hair not suitable for comparison, and fibers of various colors. Defendant argued that based on this report, his lawyer should have called the examiner to proffer an "expert" opinion that a rape could not have taken place on the couch in the absence of such physical evidence.

The court soundly rejected this Locard-type argument, both from an analysis of the relative positions of the defendant and victim at the couch and the simple lack of relevance of the basic argument based on the supposed inevitability of trace material transfers in sexual assault settings:

> ...we fail to see the relevance of this point. Clearly, sexual intercourse and ejaculation did take place without the defendant leaving apparent fiber or hair evidence. In fact, the lab technician who testified at trial said she did not perform any hair analysis based on Goney's hair samples because no foreign hairs were obtained from a nightgown Canton was wearing or from the sexual assault kit (which included pubic hair combing). Given the absence of hair in these areas where it could be expected, the lack of hair or fibers on the couch where the rape allegedly occurred is not surprising. Furthermore, we have serious doubt (and Goney has not convinced us otherwise) that a police deputy — or indeed, any "expert" — could competently conclude from the absence of fiber or hair that a rape did not occur...[111]

Specifically, the court ruled, the lack of forensic hair or fiber evidence from the couch did not make the defense version either more or less probable. Because this evidence could have been present under either the defense or the prosecution version of the case, the fact that it was absent was deemed no more helpful to one side than it was to the other.[112]

VII. Conclusion

There are a number of very advanced fiber-related methods being investigated that will soon be presented to American and European courts for consideration. Raman spectroscopy,[113] advanced work on the specificity of fiber dyes,[114] and chemical imaging of fibers[115] are three examples. Given the fiber information resources discussed above, there is ample opportunity to keep abreast of the developments in this extremely important forensic discipline.

Endnotes

1. Report prepared by Prof. James Robertson, National General Manager, Prof. Claude Roux, Director, Centre for Forensic Science, University of Technology, Forensic and Technical Australian Federal Police, *Forensic Examination of Fibres, A Review*: 2001 to 2004, at 70. — The Interpol 14th Annual Forensic Science Symposium Review, Lyon, France November 2004. The extensive 585-page literature review summary and bibliography may be downloaded from the Interpol site, under Forensics, at http:\\www.interpol.org.

2. Major textile magazines and some relevant books were also consulted to provide useful background. The final report is a collation of information received from these various sources.

3. The two major groups are the European Fibres Group (EFG) of the European Network of Forensic Science Institutes (ENFSI) and the Fiber subgroup of the Scientific Working Group for Materials Analysis (SWGMAT) led by the FBI. See, Wiggins, K.G. The European Fibres Group (EFG) 1993–2002: *Understanding and Improving the Evidential Value of Fibres. Analytical and Bioanlytical Chemistry,* 2003 376, 1172–1177, outlining the history of the European Fibres Group and its aims and achievements since its formation in 1993. The Fibre Report also recommended perusal of several Fibre Working Group meetings: Proceedings of the 9th European Fibres Group meeting, Vantaa, Finland, 2001; Proceedings of the 10th European Fibres Group meeting, Rosny-sous-bois, France, 2002; and the Proceedings of the 11th European Fibres Group meeting, Istanbul, Turkey, 2003.

4. See, European Fibres Group: *Manual of Best Practice for the Forensic Examination of Fibres*, 2001, Winner, ENFSI Working Groups Award 2003. See, http://www.enfsi.org/fame/fiberswg/document_view. *The Fibre Report* authors emphasized the critical need for promoting information exchange in the critical areas of standardization, training, and research and development.

5. See, Wiggins, K.G. Forensic Textile Fiber Examination Across the USA and Europe, *J. For Sci* 2001, 46, 1303-1308; Grieve, M.C., Wiggins, K.G. Fibers Under Fire: Suggestions for Improving Their Use to Provide Forensic Evidence. *J. For. Sci.* 2001, 46, 835-843.

6. This is a common method used by forensic hair analysts in the United States.

7. *Interpol Fibre Report,* Supra N. 1 at 72.

8. The growing interest for Raman spectroscopy in the fiber arena prompted the European Fibres Group to create a Raman sub-group and to support the largest collaborative study undertaken on the topic. One promising new technology whose applications go well beyond the forensic examination of

fibres is Chemical Imaging. This technology combines molecular spectroscopy and digital imaging. This combination provides information on morphology, composition, structure and concentration from one analysis. *Interpol Fibre Report,* supra n. 1 at 73.

9. *Interpol Fibre Report* at 75.

10. See, Cantrell, S., Roux, C., Maynard, P., Robertson, J. A Textile Fibre Survey as an Aid to the Interpretation of Fibre Evidence in the Sydney Region. Forensic Science International 2001, 123, 48–53; Cresswell, S.L., Cunningham, D., Nic Daeid, N. Textile Survey of Cinema Seats in Glasgow. Forensic Science International 2003. 136(1), 117.

11. Ibid.

12. See, e.g., http://www.enfsi.org/; http://www.eurotexx.com/; http://www.fashion-links.de/; http://www.fashionseek.net/; http://www.techexchange.com/; http://www.texdata.com/; http://www.texi.org/; http://www.textile.fr/; http://www.textileweb.com/; http://www.textileworld.it/; http://www.textilexpert.com/. A simple search under fibers, cotton, wool, synthetic fibers, etc., will turn up a wealth of inter-linked data sources. Also see, the European Network of Forensic Science Institutes listing of Expert Working Groups on Digital Imaging; DNA Drugs; European Document Experts; European Fibres Group; European Paint & Glass Working Group; European Fingerprints Working Group; European Network of Forensic Handwriting Experts; Forensic Information Technology Working Group; Forensic Speech & Audio Analysis; Forensic International Network for Explosives Investigation; Scene of Crime; Road Accident Analysis Expert Working Group; Fire and Explosion Investigation Working Group; Marks [fingermarks, lip prints, etc.] Working Group; Firearms Working Group.

13. Fiber Report at 79.

14. See, e.g., Richard Spencer: Significant Fiber Evidence Recovered from the Clothing of a Homicide Victim After Exposure to the Elements for Twenty-Nine Days, *Journal of the Forensic Science Society,* Vol. 39, No. 3, pp. 854–859.

15. An initial determination has to be made that the crime scene datum is indeed fiber as opposed to a human or nonhuman hair. See Chapter 2, Science and the Criminal Law, for an examination of *People v. Sutherland*, 155 Ill.2d 1, 610 N.E.2d 1 (1993), an important example of the uses of microscopic fiber, hair, and tire impression analysis, set out as a case study.

16. See, http://www.fbi.gov/programs/lab/fsc/backissu/april1999/houcktoc/htm.

17. See Chapter 8, Fingerprints, infra. for a detailed discussion of the Mayfield case.

18. Also see the new extensively revised *FBI Handbook of Forensic Services* available via the FBI Web site. See, http://www.fbi.gov/programs/lab/handbook/intro.htm.

19. See, generally, Saferstein: *Criminalistics: An Introduction to Forensic Science* (Prentice Hall, 6th ed., 1998), pages 221–239; 81–96; Giannelli and Imwinkelried: *Scientific Evidence,* 2d ed. (The Michie Company, 1993) pages 365–380

and 1998 Cumulative Supplement, pages 93–95; Fisher: *Techniques of Crime Scene Investigation* (CRC Press, 5th ed., 1993) pages 178–187; Geberth: *Practical Homicide Investigation* (CRC Press, 3rd ed., 1996) pages 517–519. There is growing international interest and work in the area of standardizing fiber investigation analysis. See Interpol Fiber discussion, supra.

20. As will be seen in the extensive discussion of the Wayne Williams case, while not generally available to police authorities or the public at large, these database collections are typically made available to forensic experts on a cooperative, case-by-case basis by the international fiber industry. There is also a very significant amount of information about the fiber and textile industries available through searches on the Dialog Information service.

21. See, Forensic Fiber Examination Guidelines, published by the Federal Bureau of Investigation Scientific Working Group on Materials Analysis (SWGMAT), supra, at page 3.

22. See the categorized listing of fiber types and trade names produced by the American Fiber Manufacturers Association, set forth in Saferstein: *Criminalistics*, supra, at pages 224–225. Also see, Forensic Fiber Examination Guidelines, published by the Federal Bureau of Investigation Scientific Working Group on Materials Analysis (SWGMAT), located on the FBI Web site at http://www.fbi.gov/.

23. See, e.g., *State v. Ritt*, 599 N.W.2d 802 (Minn. Sp. Ct. 1999), where defendant was convicted of two counts of first-degree murder, two counts of second-degree murder, one count of third-degree murder, and one count of first-degree arson. The case contains an excellent discussion of acrylic fibers in relation to a faked accidental fire resulting in the death of a 23-month-old victim at the hands of her mother,

24. 155 Ill.2d 1, 610 N.E.2d 1 (1993).

25. 162 N.C. App.231, 590 S.E. 2d 324 (North Carolina App. 2004).

26. Ibid. at *239. Also see, *People v. Roderick*, 2001 WL 1422348 (CA. App. 2001), a voluntary manslaughter case, where the court addressed the issue of whether the probative value of fiber evidence was substantially outweighed by prejudice. Rodrick argued that the fiber evidence had minimal or no relevance because the fibers studied were common fibers, the fibers studied had been contaminated by the time they were collected and also subject to contamination when they were being preserved as evidence, and because Rodrick and Carolyn lived together there were innocent explanations for the fibers to match. Those issues went to the weight of the fiber evidence, not its admissibility. The court determined that the fiber evidence was clearly relevant to the prosecution theory that Rodrick killed Carolyn, put her body in the trunk of his Mercedes, and drove to San Diego County, where he dumped the body.

27. *Fox v. State*, 266 Ga. App. 307, 596 S.E. 2d 773 (2004).

28. Ibid. at 310.

29. 2004 WL 1462649 (Tenn. Ct. Crim. App. 2004).

30. Ibid at *9.

31. See, Houck, *Statistics and Trace Evidence: The Tyranny of Numbers,* Forensic Science Communications (1999) available for download at http://www.fbi.gov/hq/lab/fsc/backissu/oct1999/houck.htm

32. 1998 WL 10267 (Alaska App. 1998).

33. Id. at *1.

34. Id. at *2.

35. Id. at *3.

36. See Deadman, Fiber Evidence and the Wayne Williams Trial, *FBI Law Enforcement Bulletin,* March and May, 1984, for an account by the agent involved. The dissenting judge in Williams strongly criticized Agent Deadman's testimony.

37. 251 Ga. 749, 312 S.E. 2d 40 (1984). The state introduced evidence of ten other alleged murders to aid in establishing appellant's identity as the perpetrator of the murders of victims Payne and Carter.

38. See *Williams v. State,* supra, at pages 759-771 for a detailed listing and description of the individual circumstances of each victim's discovery and attendant circumstances. Also see pages 773–783 for the court's profiles of each murder illustrating the similarities of the victims and their deaths, the logical connection of the homicides, and the evidence that Williams was the perpetrator of each. See text above.

39. *Williams v. State,* supra, at 759.

40. Id. at 772.

41. Williams at 760.

42. Williams at 760.

43. Deadman, a microanalyst, described the microscopes that could be used to compare fibers and were in the case at hand: a stereobinocular microscope, which can magnify a single fiber about seventy times, and which is used to visually compare fibers; a compound microscope, which can magnify a single fiber approximately 400 to 500 times, and which, like the stereobinocular microscope, is used to visually compare fibers; a comparison microscope, which can magnify two fibers side by side, and which is used to compare the microscopic and optical properties of the two fibers; a microspectrophotometer; a polarizing light microscope, which is used to examine the optical properties of fibers in a more discriminating fashion than that provided by a comparison microscope; and a fluorescence microscope, which is used to determine the type of light a fiber emits after it has been illuminated with a certain type of light. A scanning electron microscope was also used to a more limited degree by these three experts. Williams at 756.

44. *Williams v. State,* at 53, 757.

45. Williams at 761.

46. Williams, at 251 Ga. 749, 762.

47. Williams at 55, 763.

48. Williams at 764.

49. Williams at 59, 766.

50. Williams, at 60, 767.

51. Williams, at 61, 769.

52. Williams at 770. The state also attempted to link Porter with Williams through a bloodstain found on the rear car seat of Williams' 1970 station wagon. Forensic serologists from the Georgia Crime Laboratory examined a blood sample from Porter, and determined that his blood type was International Blood Group B and that his blood enzyme type was PGM-1, a combination, a serologist testified, which exists in approximately seven percent of the population. Another bloodstain found on the car seat was determined to be blood from International Blood Group B, with an enzyme type PGM-1, and a serologist testified that this bloodstain was not more than eight weeks old. Moreover, a serologist testified that Williams could not have left this bloodstain as his blood type was International Blood Group O. Williams at 312 S.E. 2d 40.

53. Williams, at 312 S.E. 2d 40, 63. Deadman attributed this paleness of the two fibers to exposure to river water, basing his opinion on an experiment wherein the state had taken fibers from Williams' bedspread and placed them in water from both the Chattahoochee River and South River; the water had bleached the fibers, causing their color to fade.

54. Williams at 772, 773.

55. In April, 1981, the task force staked out bridges over rivers in the metropolitan Atlanta area in an attempt to apprehend whoever was responsible for throwing bodies into rivers. On the morning of May 22, a loud splash was heard, which, according to officers present, sounded like the sound of a human body hitting the water below the bridge. No lights had been observed up to that point, nor had the characteristic noise of the expansion joint been heard. There was testimony that the vehicular traffic was light at that hour of the day, and that a period of at least ten minutes elapsed between the time the last car was seen to cross the bridge and the sound of the splash. Shortly after the splash, a car's lights appeared on the bridge directly above where the splash had occurred, and were seen to start moving slowly toward the Fulton end of the bridge. Officers followed the car, stopped it, and determined that it was driven by defendant Wayne Williams. See, Williams at 791.

56. Williams, at 823.

57. Williams at 758.

58. This fact, critical to the state's "uniqueness" argument, stressed by Justice Smith in his dissenting opinion, was never conclusively established and was questionable in light of testimony (based on Wellman sales records) that

Wellman fiber was sold to a number of Georgia and southeastern manufacturers during the period in question. Williams, at 98, 824.

59. Williams at 98.

60. Williams at 73. Also see, *Stewart v. State*, 246 Ga. 70, 75, 268 S.E.2d 906 (1980); *Wisdom v. State*, 234 Ga. 650, 655, 217 S.E.2d 244 (1975).

61. Williams at 824. Historically, statistical evidence has not been a prerequisite to the admission of matching samples. Expert testimony about matching carpet fibers has been admitted in the absence of statistical evidence about the probability of the match. *State v. Koedatich*, 112 N.J. 225, 548 A.2d 939 (1988); *State v. Hollander*, 201 N.J.Super. 453, 467–68, 493 A.2d 563 (App.Div.1985). In Koedatich, a capital case, the State presented evidence of matching fibers from the defendant's automobile carpet and seat covers. In Koedatich the defense attacked the weight of the evidence by showing that manufacturers produced hundreds of thousands of yards of such fibers in a given year. Id. at 245, 548 A.2d 939. The court upheld the admission of the evidence of the matching fibers, observing that the quantity of the fibers went to the weight, not the admissibility of the evidence.

62. Williams, at 92, 815.

63. Williams at 814.

64. Williams at 91, 814.

65. See, e.g., Dateline, NBC, Tuesday, June 2, 1998 segment "The Wrong Man?" discussing interesting facts about the death of several of the victims that allegedly distort the unity of the forensic evidence presented at the 1984 trial and the nagging doubts of some of the key detectives involved in the investigation.

66. In fact, since the beginning of 1997, there have been literally hundreds of cases that have discussed, or much more often, accepted with little or no discussion, evidence based on forensic fiber analysis. Also see the *Interpol Fibre Report* (2004) and discussion, supra.

67. 173 Ill.2d 167, 670 N.E.2d 721 (1996).

68. Id. at 176.

69. Id. at 178. Also see, *Commonwealth v. McEnany*, 667 A.2d 1143 (Superior Ct. Penn. 1995), a 1995 Pennsylvania case, where defendant was convicted of second-degree murder, burglary, robbery, and conspiracy. Eighty-two year old Kathryn Bishop was found dead on the floor of her residence, having been stomped to death sometime between 9:00 p.m. and 11:30 p.m. on March 3, 1993. Paint chips were found on Mrs. Bishop's hands, and black tee-shirt fibers were on her face, neck, and clothing. The deceased's kitchen door window had been smashed, her basement window had been opened, and scuff marks were found on her clothes dryer located under the basement window. As the investigation continued, Trooper Stansfield obtained search warrants for McEnany's van and residence and took the clothes worn by appellant on the date of the murder. Chemist Lee Ann Grayson testified that

fibers found on Mrs. Bishop's body matched those of the tee-shirt appellant wore on the day of the murder.

70. *Strickland v. Washington*, 466 U.S. 668, 104 S.Ct. 2052, 80 L.Ed.2d 674 (1984).

71. 311 F. 3d 1288 (11th Circuit Ct. App. 2002).

72. Ibid. at 1293–1294.

73. Ibid. at 1304.

74. 2004 WL 362360 (Ala. App. 2004).

75. Ibid. at *14.

76. *Strickland v. United States*, 104 S. Ct. 2052 (1984).

77. 231 Ga.App. 793, 499 S.E.2d 642 (Ga. Ct. App. 1998).

78. Id. at 794.

79. Id. at 647.

80. See, Bresee, R.R., Evaluation of Textile Fiber Evidence: A Review, 32 (2) *J. Forens. Sci* (1987) at 510. (Fiber transfer, persistence after transfer, evidence collection, and fiber analysis); Robertson, J., Olaniyan, D.; Effect of Garment Cleaning on the Recovery and Redistribution of Transferred Fibers, 31 (1) *J. Forens. Sci* (1986) at 73.80 880 So.2d 768 (Fl. App 2004), Robertson, J., Kidd, C.B.M., The Transfer of Textile Fibres During Simulated Contact, *Journal of the Forensic Science Society*, Vol. 22 (1982), pp.301-308; Robertson, J., Kidd, C.B.M., and Parkinson, M.P. The Persistence of Textile Transferred During Simulated Fibre Contact, Journal of the Forensic Science Society, Vol. 22, (1982), at pp.353-360.; Scott, H.G., The Persistence of Fibers Transferred During Contact of Automobile Carpets and Clothing Fabrics, *Journal of the Canadian Society of Forensic Science*, Vol. 18 (1985), at pp. 185-199; Grieve, M.C,, Dunlop, J., Haddock, P.S., Transfer Experiments with Acrylic Fibers, *Forensic Science International*, Vol. 40 (1989), at pp. 267-277.

81. 880 So.2d 768 (Fl. App 2004).

82. Several witnesses contradicted Barfield's tale that he was an unwitting passenger. At least four people testified that they saw only one person in the cab of the truck, and several of them described a man who looked like Barfield. The witness who first arrived at the wreck saw only one man leave the cab.

83. 2004 WL 944479 (Ca. Ct. App. 2004).

84. Ibid. at *13.

85. 698 So.2d 151 (Ct. Crim. App. Ala. 1995). Also see Ex Parte Jack Harrison Trawick, 698 So.2d 162 (1997), addressing death penalty aspects of this case.

86. 909 P.2d 236 (Ut. Sp. Ct. 1995).

87. In addition, blood of the victim's type, found in 18 percent of the population and semen of defendant's type, found in 2 percent of the population, were found on the back seat of his car. A criminologist assigned to the serology DNA section of the State Criminal Forensics Laboratory testified to a DNA

match. He stated that the blood in the vehicle matched the victim's and was inconsistent with defendant's. He concluded that the random probability of the match was, by conservative estimates, about one in 14,000.

88. 975 S.W. 2d 269 (Tenn. 1998).

89. 264 Kan. 593, 957 P.2d 416 (Kan. 1998).

90. A police examiner made a fracture comparison of the duct tape from the shed and the tape on Jodi's body. The examiner testified that the torn end of the duct tape around Jodi's head matched the torn end of the roll of duct tape from the shed. Another end of the duct tape from the body matched an end of the duct tape that was found with hairs in it in the Chevette. There were two ends that did not match. Tire prints near where the body was found were not made by any of Higgenbotham's cars.

91. Id. at 420.

92. Higginbotham, at 600.

93. 591 N.W.2d 451 (Minn.Sp. Ct. 1999).

94. According to police, Bell was a reputed prostitute who frequented the Broadway Avenue area of Minneapolis. The autopsy revealed that Bell had ingested cocaine within a few hours before her death. Police investigators also observed that Bell's upper torso and vaginal areas were covered with mud. Police Sergeant Robert Krebs testified that the mud "appear[ed] to be packed, not just a matter of something [sic] had flowed over the body." Dr. Morey discovered mud inside Bell's vaginal vault as well, but found no other evidence of vaginal injury or any indication of sperm or seminal fluid inside Bell's vaginal vault. Dr. Morey declined to rule out the possibility of sexual assault, however, stating that the decomposition of Bell's body and her submersion in water could have masked evidence of such an assault. Id. at 455.

95. On June 3, 1996, the body of Deborah Lavoie was found approximately one and one-half blocks from where Bell's body had been discovered. On June 19, 1996, the body of Avis Warfield was found approximately one-half mile from Theodore Wirth Park. Both bodies had been burned with gasoline. On July 20, 1996, the body of Keooudorn Phothisane, a male transvestite, was discovered in Theodore Wirth Park within one and one-half blocks of where Bell's body had been found. Although Phothisane's body was also burned, police determined that he had been bludgeoned to death. Several juveniles claimed to have seen an African-American man running from the scene where Phothisane's body was found. The juvenile witnesses provided a composite sketch of the man to police. Profit is an African-American.

96. Profit, at 456. This case also contains an extensive discussion of the admissibility of other crimes, evidence and the value of a confession by a friend who had access to the car where the ligature related fibers were discovered.

97. 726 A.2d 1196 (Del.Sup. Ct. 1999).

98. Id. at 1200.

99. Id. at 1209.

100. Eaton argued that Detective Johnson seized his boots without sufficient probable cause to arrest him. The court concluded that while a very close issue factually, they need not decide the issue because Eaton's boots were admissible under the exigent circumstances exception to the search warrant requirement.

101. 999 WL 771070 (Ohio App. 7 Dist.).

102. Id. at *9.

103. Young, at *14. The forensic scientist testified that while some of the bloodstains on the concrete chunk could have come from a thirteen-foot fall, the blood spatters on a tree stump located near Heidi's body could not have been created by Heidi's impact with the concrete after the fall and that two impacts by a blunt force were made to an already exposed blood source on Heidi. Those impacts occurred more than thirty inches above the ground level where the tree stump was located.

104. 738 A.2d 254 (D.C. 1999).

105. Id. at *1.

106. 161 N.J. 515, 737 A.2d 55 (1999).

107. Id. at 544, 70. The autopsy found, among other things, petechial hemorrhages in both eyes, a common indicator of death by strangulation, and a ligature mark on the neck that was consistent with the leather belt found in defendant's room. More than thirty hairs found near defendant's bed, on a dishcloth, on the carpet, and in the black felt cloth had the same physical and microscopic qualities as Megan's. There were four head hairs on Megan's blouse that were consistent with defendant's hair and inconsistent with Cifelli's and Jenin's. A pubic hair on Megan's blouse compared favorably to defendant's. The forensic chemist examining fluid evidence found blood on defendant's bedsheets, the black belt, swabs taken from defendant's bedroom door, oral and anal swabs taken from the victim, and on her blouse and earring.

108. See discussion of the Locard Principle in Chapter 2.

109. 743 So.2d 1171 (Ohio App. 2 Dist. 1999).

110. At trial, defendant's defense was that he and the victim had consensual sex, defendant having testified that the two had intercourse. Here, however, in his post-conviction petition, his position was that he did not have intercourse with Canton, and did not penetrate or ejaculate. However, court observed, DNA results had eliminated and belied such a claim.

111. Goney, at *8.

112. Id.

113. *Journal of Forensic Sciences.* Submitted in 2004; Thomas, J., Doble, P., Roux, C., Robertson, J., Chemometrics and Raman Spectral Data from Dyed Cotton Fibres. Proceedings of the 17th International Symposium on the Forensic Sciences (Australian & New Zealand Forensic Science Society Symposium),

Wellington, 2004. (See *Interpol Fibre Report* at 73 et seq. for a discussion of the imaging research)

114. See, Tuinman, A.A., Lewis, L.A., Lewis, S.A. Sr. Trace-Fiber Color Discrimination by Electrospray Ionization Mass Spectrometry: A Tool for the Analysis of Dyes Extracted from Submillimeter Nylon Fibers, *Analytical Chemistry*, 2003, 75, 2753–2760; Huang, M., Yinon, J., Sigman, M.E. Forensic Identification of Dyes Extracted from Textile Fibers by Liquid Chromatography Mass Spectrometry (LC-MS), *Journal of Forensic Sciences*, 2004, 49(2), 238-249. (See *Interpol Fibre Report* at 73 et seq. for a discussion of the imaging research)

115. See, Payne, G., Reedy, B., Lennard, C., Exline, D., Roux, C. Evaluation of the CI Trace for Fibre Analysis, Proceedings of the 17th International Symposium on the Forensic Sciences (Australian & New Zealand Forensic Science Society Symposium), Wellington, 2004; Tuinman, A.A., Lewis, L.A., Lewis, S.A., Sr., Trace-Fiber Color Discrimination by Electrospray Ionization Mass Spectrometry: A Tool for the Analysis of Dyes Extracted from Submillimeter Nylon Fibers, *Analytical Chemistry*, 2003, 75, 2753–2760. (Discussed in *Interpol Fibre Report*, supra, at 73.)

Ballistics and Tool Marks

5

...(T)his left-handed twist bullet, No. III, was fired by a Colt .32. Was it fired by this Colt .32? Some one of the learned counsel for the defendant has said that it is coming to a pretty pass when the microscope is used to convict a man of murder. I say heaven speed the day when proof in any important case is dependant upon the magnifying glass and the scientist and is less dependent upon the untrained witness without the microscope. Those things can't be wrong in the hands of a skilled user of a microscope or a magnifying glass...

Massachusetts v. Sacco and Vanzetti:
Closing Argument by the Commonwealth

I. Introduction

Microscopic comparisons of firearms evidence have changed little since the development of the ballistic comparison microscope over 70 years ago. The Sacco and Vanzetti case, tried in 1921, where the defendants, known and very vocal anarchists, were accused of murder during a robbery, is perhaps the most famous of the early uses of ballistics in American Law. It was then, and is now, considered a definitive proof of a suspect's involvement in a crime if a particular weapon used can be traced to the defendant:

> ...I say to you on this vital matter of the No. III bullet...Take the three Winchester bullets that were fired by Captain Van Amburgh at Lowell and take the seven United States Bullets that were fired

> by Mr. Burns at Lowell, and, lastly, take the barrel itself which we
> will unhitch for you, and determine the fact for yourself, for
> yourselves…Take the glass, gentlemen, and examine them for
> yourselves. If you choose, take the word of nobody in that regard.
> Take the exhibits yourselves. Can there be a fairer test that I ask
> you to submit yourselves to?[1]

The preceding selection from the closing argument in the famous Sacco and Vanzetti case, tried in 1921, illustrates the longstanding belief in the certainty of ballistic matches by comparing projectile striations on bullets fired from a weapon linked to the defendant with one connected with the crime scene.[2] Since the pioneering efforts of ballistics expert Calvin Goddard in the 1920s up to present times, properly examined and supported ballistics analyses, along with fingerprint evidence, has been considered virtually unassailable.

The 14th Interpol Forensic Science Symposium Literature Review (2004), discussed in earlier chapters, has a very extensive section on Forensic Ballistics.[3] This extensive report reviews and comments on the ballistics literature in two broad areas:

Firearms identification: Homemade firearms; nonlethal weapons; ammunition reference collection; Interior, exterior and terminal ballistics; equipment and techniques; ballistic databases two-dimensional (2D) automated comparison systems; three-dimensional (3D) systems; crime-scene reconstruction equipment; professionalism; education law relating to firearms; expert witness testimony.

Firearms and chemistry: Compositions, classification, and interpretation methods and instrumentation; distribution of gunshot residue (GSR) particles in the surroundings of a shooting firearm and their sampling and persistence on different surfaces; proficiency tests for GSR analysis by SEM/EDX; detection and analysis of gunpowder (propellant) residues on suspects; estimation of shooting distance; chemical analysis for associating firearms and ammunition with gunshot entries; estimation of time since discharge; firearms and wound ballistics.

The Ballistics Report authors divided their textual analyses into four main issues: firearms, ammunition, equipment and techniques, and professionalism. The report covers advances in scientific methods applied to forensic issues (firearms ballistics, chemistry, and wound ballistics) reported since the 13th Interpol Forensic Science Symposium in October 2001. A literature review was conducted covering articles published in the principal forensic journals since 2001. The authors set out their primary research sources as:

- The FORS Forensic Bibliographic Database
- *Journal of AFTE* (Association of Firearms and Toolmark Examiners)
- *Journal of Forensic Sciences, Forensic Science International*
- Wound Ballistics Review
- *American Journal of Forensic Medicine and Pathology*
- *Science and Justice*, Forensic Science Society, at Harrogate, U.K.

The authors noted that the primary initial focus of the ballistics expert is the identification of the suspect firearm:

> The first stage involves classifying the firearm into firearm types: pistols, rifles, machine guns, etc. The next stage is to identify the subclass characteristics of these types, for example, identifying a semiautomatic gun with a Colt Browning Patent (CBP) mechanism such as a Colt 1911 pistol. The final stage involves the absolute identification (individual characteristics) between a specific firearm and bullets and cartridge cases. The origin of these characteristics stems from the manufacturing processes and maintenance of the firearms.

In the field of identifying firearms, the mechanical mechanisms, which take part in the firing process, are known and innovations are rare. However, the expert must be familiar with the different firearms, so that when these firearms or their products (bullets or cartridges) arrive at the lab, identifying their source is possible.[4]

One-third of the papers published since 2001 were on this complex topic, covering case reports and technical notes as to unique identifying characteristics of firearms and their relative value. Other studies involve different methods to calculate the minimum number of identification marks and their values in that process of positive comparison.[5]

The report stressed the continuing obligation to update the ammunition types and literature in their reference collection. Review of these articles focuses on new and unique types of ammunition, relevant to caliber data, bullet weights, ballistic coefficients, gunpowder composition, shelf life, and storage conditions.

The report examined all relevant literature[6] in the three traditional categories of Interior, Exterior and Terminal Ballistics (motion of projectiles; projectile impact features), plus it reviewed articles that addressed the rapid improvement and creation establishment of ballistic databases to help the forensic scientists that aid law enforcement agencies to connect cartridges and bullets from various crime scenes as well as suspected firearms. A number of articles examined the growing literature that deals with the reconstruction of crime scenes. The use of computer-generated animation for such reconstructions has already come under court scrutiny where, for example, the attempt is made to track bullet flight paths for angle of shot to isolate a shooter.[7] The recent literature important to the subject — the training of ballistics experts — receives extended treatment, indicating this as a definite growth area in ballistics literature.

The report also focuses on the ever-present problem of gunshot residue (GSR) and the ongoing search for stable and predictable methods for use in the field.[8]

II. Ballistics and Forensic Evidence

As mentioned earlier, most of the forensic sciences are observational disciplines supported by modern microscopy. Also, other than for DNA settings, databases regarding population match probabilities of a laboratory "match" testified to by experts are lacking. This absence gives rise to considerable doubt about the ultimate value of any such conclusions, whether couched in terms of similarity, consistency, or lack of dissimilarities, etc. Nonetheless, judicial support for forensic sciences such as hair, fiber, soil, paint, and footwear and tire impressions is growing. This is especially the case in the area of ballistics regarding gun type and brand, and bullet and shell-casing identifications. Unlike the majority of the forensic sciences, experts may explain their matching findings in terms of certainty, and typically do so.[9]

While a majority of the forensic sciences do not rest upon any core scientific or mathematical principles, with the possible exception of hair analysis, considerable and increasing interest is being shown by those outside the criminal justice system in gathering very detailed information about many of the data compared by forensic scientists, because of the commercial value of patents. A tremendous amount of information, contained in readily accessible databases, is continually updated in the area of textile manufacture and sales, international footwear, weapons and ammunition, DNA research, glass and paint manufacture, geology and mineral identification, and many other commercially generated and maintained information sources.[10] The strong commercial interest in minor differences of their commercial products both for marketing and intellectual property protection purposes has and will continue to support the uses of forensic science attempts to match crime scene datum to a suspect.

The wider science of ballistics encompasses the study of three distinct areas: internal ballistics, external ballistics, and terminal ballistics.[11]

- Internal ballistics, the study of striations and other marks made to a projectile as it passes through the barrel of a firearm, called rifling (lands, grooves, striations, manufacturing defects, wear characteristics, caliber, gauge), which are what is actually referred to when studying the forensic discipline of ballistics
- External ballistics, the study of flight and angle of shot patterns (homicide, suicide, sniper, ricochet)
- Terminal ballistics, the study of the effect of the projectile on or in the target; wound analysis or wound ballistics[12]

What are the recurring issues that must be considered when addressing the subject of the investigative and evidentiary value of the science of ballistics? These issues can be divided into several categories:

1. Crime-scene recognition, collection, and preservation
   - Angles of the shots
   - Location of slugs
   - Location of wounds
   - Location of shell casings
   - Damaged glass, metal or wooden structures or surfaces
   - Fingerprints on shell casings
   - Physical locations of the participants
   - Visual fix on contact versus noncontact wounds
   - Preliminary identification of firearm type
   - Witness statements, ammunition, wounds
2. Firearm and ammunition identification
   - Twists
   - Lands and grooves
   - Caliber of weapon
   - Gauge
3. Matching crime-scene bullets to defendant's gun
   - Peculiarities of firearm types: calibers and gauges
   - Rifles
   - Handguns
   - Shotguns
   - Misc.: machine guns; zip guns; tear gas guns; commercial nailers
4. Laboratory examination by ballistics experts
   - Bullet matching: Certainty is routinely achieved here:
   - Class characteristics — manufacturer's general and proprietary features:
   - Accidental characteristics — match to defendant's gun via test firing and the examination of the manufacturer's tool and die flaws, wear patterns in rifling, bone striations in some rare cases

- Probability analyses: ballistics identifiers or minutiae that are not as certain as fingerprints, because fingerprint minutiae never change, whereas the rifling in any specific gun can change with use or even long-term storage due to rust or corrosion[13]
- Cartridge case matching (certainty is routinely achieved here also):
  - Breech face
  - Firing-pin impressions
  - Extractor marks
  - Chamber marks

5. Wound analyses (especially where slugs are smashed)[14]
   - Forensic pathology
6. Angle of shot or distance of shot
   - Distance between shooter and victim (suicide or homicide)
   - Who of several participants actually fired
   - Positions of victims and shooters
   - Shotgun dispersion pattern studies (See G and I Appendix)
7. Ricochet patterns
8. Gunshot residue detection (controversial)[15]
9. Excluding function (of all types of forensic science disciplines, including ballistics)

A modern and standard feature of the science of ballistics is the development of computer systems for the digitalization of striation and other markings on spent bullets and shell casings.[16] Deployed in 1992, DRUGFIRE has been refined, improved, and expanded through developments in the imaging technology currently utilized in cutting-edge digitalization processes in criminal justice systems worldwide.[17] Lena Klasen, of the Swedish National Laboratory of Forensic Science, has stated in a paper presented at Proceedings of the 12th Interpol Forensic Science Symposium (October 20–23, 1998)[18] that the main difference between evidential images and images captured at a crime scene is found between a direct information source and an indirect representation of an item of evidence. She cautions that the border between these two image types is somewhat difficult to define, a fact of increasing importance to lawyers whose cases involve the validity of imaging processes' factual conclusion linking a suspect to a crime scene:

The introduction of digital images rapidly changed our possibilities to deal with images, and thereby also the need of methods, software, and hardware. The human visual system, although superior on dealing with visual information, such as motion and dynamic changes, cannot properly distinguish small quantitative visual differences in the same way as computer-aided methods. For example, we cannot resolve small geometrical differences of an object in an image, or small quantitative changes of the image resolution.

For this purpose we use computers as an aid and to complement the human visual system.[19]

The presentation of this important paper at the recent Interpol Forensic Science Symposium underscores the important future in store for the uses of digitalized imagery in the worldwide investigation, prosecution, and defense of crime.[20]

Electronic image associations made through the DRUGFIRE system, as with fingerprint identifications made through the Automated Fingerprint Identification System (AFIS), are still verified by traditional comparison microscopic examination of the firearms evidence by experienced technicians. DRUGFIRE is a screening tool to extend the capabilities of the examiner by facilitating the cross-referencing of thousands of stored images from across the country and informing the inquiring party of close associations. This system is in the process of being supplanted by NIBIN,[21] a newer system currently in use by the department of Alcohol, Tobacco, and Firearms.[22]

All probable associations made through the DRUGFIRE system are then, as before, verified by forensic firearms identification examiners using traditional, court-accepted comparison microscope techniques. The deployment of the FBI's DRUGFIRE system facilitated the opportunity for regional forensic laboratories to centrally store, search, and share forensic firearms data and imagery. With DRUGFIRE, digital images of these items are interchanged over high-speed cable or telephone lines, permitting different laboratories to remotely compare the data and thereby virtually eliminating jurisdictional, logistical, and chain-of-custody impediments.[23] There is considerable international interest in digitalized search systems for bullet and shell casing identification.[24]

Ballistics expertise encompasses, necessarily, the updating of material on the weapon manufacturing process and tooling, as these processes are the source of the striations used to match a found slug or casing to a weapon. Yet the authors of the Firearms Evidence section of the report of the Proceedings of the 12th Interpol Forensic Science Symposium found no articles in world forensic literature updating manufacturing techniques:

> No literature articles were found on research into new manufacturing techniques and tools for manufacturing firearms. This is nevertheless an important subject because it may provide information about the specific characteristics of a firearm. Given the number of publications in the expert field of firearms and ammunition, more research is carried out into the improvement of recording techniques and the statistical processing thereof than into the question of whether the striate indeed have characteristic qualities.[25]

The image processing advances discussed here are still closely allied with manufacturing profiles. Manufacturing technical reports and firing sequence data are still largely unavailable.[26]

III. Ballistics Experts: Qualifications

Qualifying an expert witness, in both general terms and as to any subspecialty, remains a key element in the use of any of the forensic sciences. It is no different in the field of ballistics. In some areas, such as wound analysis, testimony is often presented by forensic pathologists, who have the most precise, hands-on experience with the entrance and exit wound realities in a particular case. As noted in the Interpol 14th Forensic Science Symposium Review paper in 2004:

> The topic of wound ballistics or terminal ballistics can be divided into two main issues: shooting range and wound characteristics....
> The determination of the shooting range is of paramount importance in gunshot wound investigations; as a rule medical examiners estimate the shooting distance based on the morphological characteristics of the wound and its immediate tissues...

Much research has been conducted recently in the area of physico-chemical determination of shooting range, and various techniques, such as energy dispersive x-ray fluorescence spectrometry and nitrite residues, are advocated by prestigious police laboratories all over the world. The literature in wound morphology, trajectory, and the correlation between ammunition and lethality is extensive. Unusual entrance, trajectories, and exit wounds are described in detail, thus enhancing the awareness of the investigators to atypical postmortem findings as well as to new types of ammunitions and their wounding effects.[27]

In *Morgan v. State*,[28] defendant contended that the trial court erred in allowing a pathologist to provide expert testimony on ballistics. At trial, Dr. Hawley, a forensic pathologist, testified regarding the position that the defendant and the victim were in when the gun discharged.

Dr. Hawley testified that he determined that Wiley died of a gunshot wound to the head. The entrance wound was located on the left side of Wiley's head, and the gunshot tracked across Wiley's head from left to right before exiting the right side of Wiley's head. The nature of the wounds indicated to Dr. Hawley that the muzzle of the gun was against Wiley's head when it was discharged. Dr. Hawley also testified that he believed that defendant was shot through the hand, with the bullet entering the back of the hand and exiting through the outside edge of the hand.

Given the circumstances of the wounds and the fact that witnesses indicated that the shots were fired in rapid succession, Dr. Hawley gave his opinion as to the relative position of defendant and Wiley:

> [Prosecutor]: And for the shot which entered Mr. Wiley's skull, in your opinion what would be the relative positions of the bodies of Mr. Morgan and Mr. Wiley?

> [Dr. Hawley]: Well, the weapon is actually touching the skin of the side of the head on the left side which places, in your hypothetical presentation, the shooter's right hand at the top of the victim's left shoulder with the gun up against the left side of the victim's head.

> [Prosecutor]: How about the second or the additional shot when Mr. Morgan's injuries was (sic) sustained?

> [Dr. Hawley]: For the injury the shooter's left hand must be palm down, very close to the muzzle of the gun at the time the shot is fired and no more than a few inches from the barrel of the gun.[29]

(R. at 1035.)

The Indiana Supreme Court found that the trial court did not abuse its discretion by allowing Dr. Hawley to testify regarding the relative positions of defendant and Wiley at the time of the shooting. Dr. Hawley's conclusions were based on his expert analysis of the trajectory and location of the wounds. While providing a scenario or narrative would have pushed the limits of admissibility, it was within the trial court's discretion to allow Dr. Hawley, based on his examination, to offer an opinion of how the wounds were inflicted.

IV. Weapon Identification

There are no recent decisions questioning the scientific validity of the bases for firearms identification or projectile matching. Ballistics and fingerprints, at the present time, appear to be solidly accepted as being capable of providing assured match evidence.[30] Some questions still exist as to the validity of protocols for determining the presence of gunshot residue on the hands. Because ballistics is so widely accepted, this chapter provides a basic breakdown of the many cases that are still being decided annually with some aspect of ballistics as an important part of the case analysis. The lawyer must be as aware, if not more aware, of cases validating the increasingly diverse uses of ballistics disciplines, than initiating the occasional attack on the disciplines themselves.

Ballistics cases, like fingerprint and DNA cases, must be monitored on a regular basis to gain an understanding of the use of the disciplines by law enforcement. For example, this chapter discusses in detail recent decisions allowing testimony that unspent bullets found in defendant's home matched the bullets fired, due to a chemical analysis[31] of the lead content in the batch of bullets in the box in defendant's home.[32]

Most recently in the case of *United States v. Hicks*, a 2004 Fifth Circuit Court of Appeals ruling,[33] a court actually examined the reliability of ballistics as an acceptable scientific method under Daubert. The ballistics discussion arose in the course of defendant's trial for the shooting death of a police officer.

Hicks contended that the district court abused its discretion by admitting, over his pretrial and trial objections, the testimony of the government's ballistics expert, John Beene. Hicks asserted that Beene's testimony — concluding that the bullet casings in the field were fired from the .30–30 rifle found in Hicks' son's bedroom — should have been excluded under Fed.R.Evid. 702 because Beene was not qualified to render an expert opinion on shell-casing comparisons. Further, Hicks claimed that the government failed to demonstrate that the method Beene employed when comparing the casings met the criteria for reliability set forth in Daubert.[34]

Hicks argues that John Beene's shell-casing comparison technique did not meet the criteria for reliability set forth in Daubert for several reasons. First, he contended that Beene could not say: (1) if the technique had ever been empirically tested; (2) if the technique had been published in a peer-reviewed article; (3) if any studies have been performed to calculate the rate of error for the technique; and (4) if any standards exist for making shell-casing-to-firearm comparisons. Hicks also noted that Beene admitted that he had read articles and heard presentations critiquing shell casing comparisons precisely because no objective standards or criteria exist for making matches.

Hicks also argued that Beene's application of the casing comparison technique in this case was particularly unreliable because Beene could not remember (even when looking at his notes) how many marks he used to make the match, how wide or deep the markings were, and precisely where the marks were located on the casings. Additionally, Hicks emphasized that Beene admitted that he did not test-fire other .30–30 rifles to exclude markings that were not unique to the rifle found at Hicks' house. Finally, Hicks challenged Beene's qualifications, alleging that Beene was not qualified as an expert to testify that shell casings discovered at the crime scene were fired from the rifle found at Hicks' home.[35]

As for Hicks' challenge to Beene's qualifications as a ballistics expert, the court found more than ample evidence to permit the district court to find that he was a qualified ballistics expert. At the state-court Daubert hearing, Beene testified that he had a degree in chemistry, had received training in firearms comparisons testing from the FBI, and had done firearms examinations for over twenty years. At Hicks' trial in federal court, Beene repeated most of these claims, adding that he had performed more than a thousand cartridge-firearm comparisons in the course of his 28-year career with the Texas Department of Public Safety without a suggestion that any of his matches were incorrect. Based on Beene's training, 28 years of experience, and numerous prior cartridge comparisons, the district court did not abuse its discretion in allowing him to testify as an expert at trial.[36]

Turning to Hicks' attack on the reliability of Beene's methodology, the court observed that the matching of spent shell casings to the weapon that fired them has been a recognized method of ballistics for decades, pointing out that Beene had not pointed to a single case in its jurisdiction or that of any other circuit, suggesting that the methodology employed by Beene was unreliable.

Additionally, the court noted, standards controlling firearms comparison testing were recognized and used by the expert:

> As Beene testified at the state-court Daubert hearing, he followed well-accepted methods and scientific procedures in making his comparisons. He also testified in federal court that the Association of Firearm and Tool Mark Examiners produces literature about firearms comparison testing that he relied on and that is authoritative in the field of firearms and tool mark examination. Further buttressing the reliability of his methodology, Beene also testified at the state-court Daubert hearing that the error rate of firearms comparison testing is zero or near zero.

Based on the widespread acceptance of firearms comparison testing, the existence of standards governing such testing, and Beene's testimony about the negligible rate of error for comparison tests, the district court had sufficient evidence to find that Beene's methodology was reliable. Accordingly, the district court did not abuse its discretion by admitting his testimony.

In *Manning v. State*,[37] defendant was charged with the capital murder of Jon Steckler while engaged in the commission of a robbery. Manning argued that the state's ballistics expert's testimony that the projectiles taken from Tiffany Miller's body and found at the scene matched the projectiles taken from the tree at Manning's mother's house was beyond the scope of his expertise. A neighbor told police that Manning used to target practice with a gun into trees and cans around his mother's house. She noticed him shooting into a particular tree at his mother's house in the first part of December of 1992. Based on this statement to the sheriff, a search warrant was obtained for the mother's house. Investigators recovered .380 projectiles and slugs out of the tree described by the witness. The ballistics expert testified that the projectile found at the scene and the two projectiles taken from Tiffany Miller's body were fired from the same weapon as the projectiles taken from the tree into which Manning fired. The testimony objected to by the defendant follows:

> Q: That which has been marked state's for — in Evidence Number 37 which is a projectile found at the scene of these killings, and that which has been marked State's in Evidence 63 which are the two projectiles which have already been identified as being taken from the body of Tiffany Miller, they all three were fired from the exact same firearm, is that correct?
>
> A: That's correct.
>
> Q: To the exclusion of every other firearm in the world, is that correct?
>
> A: That's correct.[38]

The court noted that later in his testimony, the expert linked the projectiles taken from the victim to the projectiles taken from the tree in Manning's yard. Because there was no speculation in the course of the expert's testimony, in that he was sure that the projectiles taken from the victim and the projectiles taken from the tree came from the same gun, any issue regarding the degree of certainty of the match was deemed meritless.

In *State v. Andy*,[39] a manslaughter case, the court set out and approved typical ballistic findings in a case where the projectile is shattered and unable to be examined in its pristine form by comparison microscopy.

The bullet recovered from the victim was badly damaged and could not be matched to any particular weapon. However, it was identified by the state's firearm identification expert as more consistent with being fired from a .22-caliber gun and was inconsistent with having been fired from the only other weapon found at the scene, a .380 automatic. The coroner, Dr. Steven T. Hayne, also identified the fragment taken from Rabb's skull as consistent with a .22-caliber projectile.

David Yates, qualified as an expert in ballistics and firearms identification, testified that the fragment removed from Rabb's head was consistent with a .22-caliber bullet and that there was "no possibility whatsoever" that the fragment could have come from a .380-caliber bullet. Yates stated that the fragment could not be identified with any particular firearm. Yates pointed out that bullets, particularly those with small cartridges such as a .22, tend to fragment when they strike bone and that in general, .22-caliber bullets are harder than most other calibers to identify and compare.

The court noted that although the firearms examiner, David Yates, was unable to say that the fragmented bullet removed from the victim's skull (state's Exhibit # 6) was fired from the weapon (state's Exhibit # 1), as noted above, the evidence strongly supported a reasonable belief that it was.[40]

Some of the discrete areas where ballistics evidence is of central concern are, of course, clear-cut homicide cases, and issues respecting weapon type, brand, or caliber. Ballistics is typically of great import in suicide versus homicide inquiries, as is the related area of gunshot residue. There is also a close relationship in certain cases between ballistics and wound analysis to determine the relative positions between a shooter and victim or with surveying principles to determine the angle of shot in cases of snipers or drive-by shootings.

The introduction of a weapon not identified as used in a killing was approved in the case of *Smoote v. State*,[41] where defendant was convicted of murder, conspiracy to commit robbery, robbery, and being a habitual offender. Defendant alleged error, among other reasons, in permitting a ballistics expert to demonstrate to the jury how a shotgun would be loaded and prepared for firing.

According to the state, defendant and another man hatched a plan to rob a branch of the First America Bank. The next day, defendant borrowed a gold Buick Electra 224 from Robert Hartley, the murder victim in this case, and met his accomplice who was driving a blue station wagon. The two men drove to a residential area, parked the Buick, and drove to the bank together in the station wagon. The shotgun used in the murder was never recovered by the police and no connection was made between the shotgun used in the demonstration and either defendant or the victim. As such, defendant argues that there was no relevance to the shotgun demonstration. And even if marginally relevant, defendant contended the probative value of the demonstration was substantially outweighed by the danger of unfair prejudice or misleading the jury.[42]

The court rejected this argument, holding that at trial, the state made clear that it was not asserting that the shotgun was the one used in the murder or that it belonged or was in any way connected with defendant. While the court thought that the demonstration was, at best, of marginal relevance and marginal probative value, it was undisputed that the victim was killed by a shotgun blast. A demonstration of how such a weapon works, the court reasoned, might have been of some benefit to the jury in understanding the details of the killing. In any event, they did not see how the demonstration prejudiced the defendant or misled the jury. While the trial court would have been well within its discretion to exclude the demonstration, it was within its discretion to admit it.[43]

In *People v. Askew*,[44] the defendant was convicted of murder and armed robbery. The victim was shot in the course of an armed robbery attempt. One Bell, a neighbor of the defendant, called police after he saw defendant, who lived across the street in defendant's girlfriend's house, on the porch of that house with a shotgun and a pistol. The police discovered three guns, including a .22 pistol, all hidden under the cushions of a couch located in the alley between Bell's and defendant's girlfriend's home. Ballistic tests on both the .22 pistol and the bullet recovered from the robbery victim's body revealed that the bullet had the same class characteristics as the pistol, but it was uncertain whether the bullet had been fired from the pistol. After a hearing on defendant's motion *in limine*, the trial court ruled that there was an insufficient connection between the .22 pistol found in the alley to show that it was the murder weapon, or that it was ever in the possession of defendant. However, the trial judge ruled that the .22 pistol could be used for identification purposes, i.e., testimony that a similar gun was used to shoot the victim or was at one time in the possession of defendant.[45]

During closing argument the state emphasized the ballistics expert's testimony noting the consistencies present between the bullet recovered in the body and the .22 pistol, and reminded the jury of the testimony that defendant was seen with a gun very similar to the .22 only four days after the murder. Thereafter, the state drew the inference that the .22 pistol was the murder weapon defendant used to shoot the victim. Defendant argued that this inference was impermissible in light of the trial judge's earlier *in limine* ruling. The court concluded that the inference drawn by the state was reasonable and based on facts in evidence.

The appellate court noted that weapons were generally admissible when there was proof that they were sufficiently connected to the crime and that when there was evidence that the perpetrator possessed a weapon at the time of the offense, a similar weapon could be admitted into evidence even though not identified as the weapon used.[46] Moreover, a weapon need not be positively shown to have been used in committing the crime, and any doubt as to whether it was connected to the crime or to the defendant did not bar its admission, so long as a jury could find a connection:

Here, Juan was killed by a .22-caliber bullet; the lands, grooves, and twist of which were consistent with the .22 pistol introduced at trial. Just four days after Juan's death, Bell saw defendant with a pistol resembling a .22, and soon thereafter such a pistol, along with a sawed-off rifle and a shotgun, were found in the alley between defendant's girlfriend's home and Bell's home. Irma testified that Juan was searched by a man with a shotgun. Furthermore, Irma identified the .22 as being similar to a gun that defendant fired over her head. Based on this evidence, we conclude that a reasonable jury could have found that there was a connection between the .22 and defendant or Juan's murder — or both.[47]

As to the inference of such connection drawn by the prosecutor, the court concluded that the inference drawn by the state was reasonable and based on facts in evidence.

In a similar setting, a New York court condemned the misuse of this concept, especially in light of ballistic testimony favoring the accused. In *People v. Walters*,[48] defendant was convicted of attempted murder in the second degree, robbery in the first degree (three counts), robbery in the second degree, assault in the first degree, assault in the second degree, criminal possession of a weapon in the second degree, and criminal possession of a weapon in the third degree. The court ordered a reversal due to prosecutorial misconduct. Most egregious, the court stated, was the prosecutor's insinuation that the gun that had been recovered from the defendant two weeks after the crime in an unrelated arrest, may have been the gun that was used to shoot the victim. The prosecution had persisted with this implication despite his knowledge that the ballistics test performed by police conclusively established that the gun had not been used in the crime. The prosecutor's conduct in advocating a position that he knew to be false was an abrogation of his responsibility as a prosecutor.[49]

In *People v. Jackson*,[50] defendant was charged with aggravated battery with a firearm. The victim testified that at about 10:30 or 11 p.m. that night, he was walking back to the Carter residence when a Nissan Maxima pulled up beside him. He claimed he recognized the driver as Jackson. He testified that the driver asked him what he was up to, to which he responded "nothing much," and then the driver shot him. Jackson was arrested. A state policeman testified that he saw a .357-Magnum pistol on a nightstand in the bedroom where he arrested Jackson, who claimed that it belonged to a friend. The bullet had not been surgically removed from the shooting victim at the time of trial, so the caliber of the bullet was not established and no ballistics tests had connected the bullet to the pistol on Jackson's nightstand. Additionally, no witnesses ever identified the pistol as the weapon used to shoot the victims. Nonetheless, the pistol was admitted into evidence without objection.

The court here noted that the state did not offer any testimony to establish that the .357 Magnum found when Jackson was arrested was capable of producing an injury such as the one suffered by Rhodes or that it was similar to the weapon used to commit the crime. While questioning Rhodes, the state asked him about the lighting conditions, to establish that he clearly saw his shooter, but state never asked him to describe or identify the weapon used. As a matter of fact, the court observed, nowhere in the record is it established that Rhodes was shot with a handgun or pistol, as opposed to some other firearm.[51]

During the time this case had been pending on appeal, Rhodes was murdered in an unrelated incident. An autopsy was performed on Rhodes' body. The bullet from the shooting at issue in this appeal was removed, and it was conclusively established that the .357-Magnum pistol found on Jackson's nightstand and introduced into evidence was not the weapon used to shoot Rhodes. The state admitted these facts, but asserted that as a reviewing court, this court was not allowed to consider this new evidence. The court disagreed, stating this situation was one of those rare instances where the exercise of our original jurisdiction was proper. They concluded that the admission of the weapon, coupled with the emphasis placed upon it by the prosecution in its closing argument, resulted in clear prejudice to the defendant in light of the admitted fact that the weapon in question had absolutely no connection to the crime.[52]

In *Commonwealth v. Busch*,[53] a homicide case, the victims, Melvin Bonnett and Christopher Green, were shot and killed in the hallway of an apartment building where defendant also lived with his girlfriend in Brockton, Massachusetts on December 13, 1991. The defendant lived in the building with his girlfriend, India Noiles, and her two daughters. Bonnett also lived in the building. Six months after the murders, a tenant found two handguns under some bushes and turned them over to the police. One was a .32-caliber revolver, and the other was a .22-caliber revolver. There was a sufficient evidentiary basis to permit an inference by the jury that the two handguns admitted in evidence were the same handguns used by the defendant to commit the murders. The two handguns were of the same caliber as the handguns used to kill the victims. The four bullets recovered from the victims, and at the scene, were consistent with four bullets that could have been fired from the handguns. There was testimony that the rifling systems of the two handguns were similar to the handguns used in the murders.

Due to the "poor markings of the evidence," the police ballistics expert could not positively identify that the bullets recovered from the victims had been fired from these guns. However, both the bullet configurations and the "rifling" patterns were similar for the bullets recovered from the guns and those recovered from the victims. When shown the guns during her testimony, India Noiles stated that they looked exactly like the ones she saw in the possession of the defendant.

In *State v. Treadwell*,[54] a homicide case arose from a gang-related shooting outside a tavern. The bullets found in shooting victim Powell's car were analyzed and a ballistics report was issued which stated that, although the bullets found in a shooting victim's car could not be positively identified as coming from Treadwell's gun, the bullets were consistent with bullets fired from Treadwell's gun. The court ruled that although the physical evidence did not conclusively show that the bullets found in the car came from Treadwell's gun, it was far from correct to say that there was no physical proof of that fact. The ballistics report did state that:

> "Items AB, AE, AF, AG, and AH (bullets removed from Powell's car) were not positively identified to any firearm submitted." The report, however, also stated that "Examination of Items AB, AE, AF, AG, and AH revealed them to be consistent with damaged bullets fired through the barrel of a caliber 9MM Luger firearm having six lands and grooves with a right-hand twist."

Viewed in its totality, the ballistics report, rather than providing "no proof" that Treadwell's shots struck Powell's car, actually corroborated the other evidence supporting the state's case against Treadwell.

The court ruled, in *Commonwealth v. Spotz*,[55] that the state need not establish that a particular weapon was actually used in the commission of a crime for it to be introduced at trial. Rather, the Commonwealth need only show sufficient circumstances to justify an inference by the finder of fact that the particular weapon was likely to have been used in the commission of the crime charged. The admission of such evidence is a matter within the sound discretion of the trial court, and without an abuse of such discretion, the trial court's decision to admit the evidence must stand. A weapon found in the possession of the accused at the time of his arrest, although not identified as the weapon actually used in the crime on trial, is admissible where the circumstances justify an inference of the likelihood that the weapon was used in the crime.

V. Computer-Generated Animation of Crime Scenes

Recent cases have addressed the legitimacy of computer-generated animation to recreate crime scenes to locate the angle of shoot for purposes of identifying a shooter. This technology is also used to give visual rendition of bullet ricochets. Courts are open to this new technique as long as the film is a true and accurate rendition of the crime scene dynamics. More validation needs to be done before this expensive and foundation-heavy technology gains wide use and acceptance by the courts.[56]

In the leading Minnesota case of *State v. Stewart*,[57] defendant was convicted of two counts of first-degree murder and the lesser-included offense of second-degree murder, in the shooting of a bicyclist from a moving vehicle. The court found that a medical examiner's use of information other than autopsy findings as a basis for animated reconstruction of the murder was appropriate, where examiner testified that she was in contact with investigators, and that information she received included the types of facts relied on by medical examiners in forming an opinion on the point of fire and wound track. However, a computerized animation containing sequences demonstrating the shooting of the bicyclist from a moving vehicle was not entirely admissible in the murder trial

The court found that, though portions of the animated film accurately illustrated the witnesses' testimony — the point of fire, trajectory of bullet, and wound path were relevant to understanding the cause of the bicyclist's death — a portion of one sequence depicting events inside the car did not express or illustrate medical examiner's testimony. All such sequences contained depictions of defendant's face and eyes at the time of the shooting, and lacking any foundation in the case data, such depictions amounted to original evidence concerning defendant's intent, and intent was the most hotly disputed element in the trial.[58]

VI. Bullet Ricochet

In *People v. Vasquez*,[59] a jury convicted defendant Jesse Mario Vasquez of attempted murder and shooting from a motor vehicle. Defendant claimed that the bullet must have ricocheted because he fired into the sidewalk to frighten the victim who was threatening him. The forensic firearm examiner testified that a bullet shot into concrete may ricochet off concrete and strike another object depending on the angle and height from which the weapon was fired. But he indicated it was unlikely a bullet from a small-caliber weapon, like the one used in the present case, would have sufficient velocity to penetrate flesh after ricocheting off concrete.[60]

Ballistics expertise is often used to track the trajectory of a bullet (angle of shoot) in an attempt to isolate the shooter at a crime scene or to counter an argument about the presence of intent.

VII. Angle of Shoot

In *People v. Robertson*,[61] defendant was convicted of second degree murder and assault with infliction of great bodily injury, and of having personally used a firearm. Defendant told police that upon hearing a sound outside his home, he looked out and observed three or four men near his automobile, apparently engaged either in dismantling it or stealing it. Defendant recalled that the men looked at him in a threatening manner, and he was uncertain whether they would attempt to enter his residence. In his final statement to the police, defendant claimed that when he emerged from his residence, he held his gun at a 45-degree angle and fired two warning shots.

The physical evidence, however, indicated that three shots had been fired. A bullet hole discovered in the windshield of defendant's automobile and two other bullet holes found two feet from ground level in a vehicle that was parked across the street tended to disprove defendant's claim that he had held the gun at a 45-degree angle. A ballistics expert testified on behalf of defendant, stating that persons lacking experience in shooting firearms tend to shoot in a manner that causes them to strike objects below their intended target.

In *People v. Caldwell*,[62] a former police officer, employed as a crime scene technician at the time of the shooting, testified that after the shooting, he photographed and collected evidence from the deputy's patrol car. From his own observations and the use of a dowel and string, the technician testified that he tracked the paths of the two bullets, one that entered the vehicle just in front of the driver's side window near the spotlight and another that entered the vehicle through the metal frame behind the rear window, also on the driver's side. The photos of the vehicle depicting the bullet holes, fragments, and the dowel and string used by the technician were also admitted into evidence.

The court noted that the witness' testimony included only his observations about the entry locations of the bullets and the path they traveled inside the vehicle. Such observations, the court concluded, could just as easily have been made by the jury from the photographs. No special expertise is required to look at the hole made by the bullet and realize that it followed a straight-line path. Consequently, the court found no abuse of discretion in the trial court's ruling allowing this lay witness' opinion testimony.

Here, the witness did not conduct any experiments or attempt to reconstruct the incident. Rather, he testified about the location of the bullet holes and the paths of the bullets that were evident from the photographs without any additional explanation. Thus, the witness was not conveying information that required a specialized or scientific knowledge to understand.

In *Jones v. State*,[63] a homicide case, police officer Szafranski's car was the third in a series of police cars turning at the intersection of 6th and Davis Streets, when shots were fired. Officer Dyal, who was driving one of the two police cars immediately preceding Officer Szafranski's vehicle, testified that after he heard the first shot, he looked back and saw "flashes" from two more gunshots emanating from Jones' apartment building. Expert testimony revealed that Officer Szafranski was shot with a .30–.30-caliber Winchester Marlin rifle and two such rifles were found in defendant's apartment, each with one spent shell casing. His fingerprint was found on the breach area of one of the rifles.

While searching the downstairs, vacant apartment in defendant's building after the shooting, police found a fresh recoil mark on the sill of one of the windows and a ballistics expert testified that the bullet's trajectory was consistent with the bullet having been fired from the downstairs apartment. The expert also testified that the bullet entered the windshield of Officer Szafranski's car, around the area of the rearview mirror, traveling in an approximately horizontal plane. The court ruled that the physical evidence was consistent with the state's theory that Officer Szafranski was shot from the downstairs apartment.[64]

In *State v. Lyons*,[65] defendants Robert Lyons and Vincent Rossa were charged with robbery and several other crimes and their cases were consolidated. Lyons and Rossa committed two armed robberies of restaurants. After the report of the second robbery, police were dispatched to pursue the suspect vehicle. In the course of a lengthy pursuit, Lyons leaned out the passenger window and fired several shots from a shotgun toward the deputies. Lyons maintained that he fired his gun in the air just to frighten the deputies and to keep a distance between the two cars. One of Lyons' shots ricocheted off the suspect vehicle and hit one of the patrol cars, with Lyons maintaining that he accidentally discharged his gun in this instance.[66]

The state sought to introduce demonstrative evidence in the form of a videotape prepared by a ballistics expert demonstrating the effect of the shots fired towards the patrol cars' windshields. In attempting to duplicate the conditions of the shots fired, he obtained windshields from the same make and model as the patrol car, placed the windshields at the same angles, used the same type of shotgun and very same pistol, as well as the same type of ammunition. He also factored in the temperature and barometric pressure, and stated that they would have no appreciable difference in the demonstration. While none of the shots hit any of the windshields during the actual incident, the State offered the evidence for purposes of arguing defendant's intent to inflict and the potential for grievous bodily harm.

Here, the trial court determination that the demonstrative experiments were conducted in a reasonably similar manner and under substantially similar circumstances as the alleged crime was upheld on appeal. The court observed that the demonstration would assist the jury in its deliberations.[67]

Surveyor testimony and ballistics expertise were used to convict a gang member in the case of *People v. Torres*,[68] in which defendant was convicted of second-degree murder and aggravated discharge of a firearm, due to the shooting death of a bystander shot during a gang-related shoot-out. The victim was a janitor at a school across the street from the house where the defendant and others were exchanging fire with rival gang members. The janitor was looking out the second floor window and fatally struck by a stray bullet. A central issue in the case was the location of possible shooter given the angle of shot required to have hit the victim.

The police received a call that someone had been shot at Elgin Academy. Several officers responded to the Academy's Sears Hall, where they were directed upstairs to the second-floor cafeteria. There they found Earl Harris, a custodian, lying dead from a bullet wound to his head. Officer Michael Whitty traced the approximate trajectory of the bullet, and found small holes in the glass and screen of a window facing in the direction of 362 Franklin. He then notified the officers at the defendant's home of a probable connection between Harris' death and the shots fired at 362 Franklin. Surveyors were called, and they pinpointed the source trajectory as being within a small area immediately adjacent to the front porch at 362 Franklin, where witnesses had reported defendant Torres stood as he fired after the fleeing attackers.

At trial, forensic examiner Welty, employed by the Illinois State Police, testified that three of the bullets found at the school came from the same weapon that fired the fatal bullet, although he was unable to determine the same for a fourth slug because police had recovered only the inner core of the bullet, not the outer portion that would bear the unique markings of the gun that fired it. He further testified that casings found in a bucket on the defendant's porch also came from one weapon, but he was not sure whether that was the same weapon that fired the bullets found at the school. He also testified that the bullets and a clip found at the defendant's house were of the same sort as the spent bullets taken from the school and from the victim, and that the clip would fit either a 9-mm Baretta or a .380 automatic Browning.[69]

Michael Kreiser, also a forensic scientist employed by the Illinois State Police, testified that his study of the surveyors' documents and other physical evidence led him to the conclusion that the fatal bullet could only have been fired by someone standing within a narrow "window" of space immediately adjacent to the defendant's front porch. Eyewitnesses had established that only Torres and Soto had been positioned anywhere within that "window" during the shooting. However, eyewitness testimony established that defendant Soto was firing a shotgun and only defendant Torres was seen firing a handgun. Pursuant to Welty's and Kreiser's testimonies, the trial court determined that it was reasonable to conclude that Torres was the shooter:[70]

Four projectiles were recovered in and around Elgin Academy; three of them had been identified as coming from a .380 semiautomatic (gun). Four shell casings had been recovered at the scene from a .380 semiautomatic weapon.

One issue I have to deal with is * * * the missing gun theory. That
is, all the ballistics reports show that the guns that had been
recovered from the defendant's home, including the two pistols
and the .22 rifle, were not involved (in) shooting the projectiles
or the four casings. The state's theory was that basically the defendant hid the remaining gun.* * * Now, I have to take into
consideration several factors * * * and most importantly (sic) is
that a clip was recovered from the residence. The importance of
that clip is that it did not belong to any of the three weapons that
had been recovered. And that clip, in fact, the testimony showed
it did fit and function in a .380 Baretta (sic), not in the defendant's
pistol that was recovered from the room or the other guns. Now
that's significant and that's important. I also look at the fact that
the defendant would have had the time to hide that particular
weapon along with the fact that the four casings were hidden in
a bucket by the porch. No other casings were found in the front
yard where the shots were fired from. Therefore, my conclusion
is that the four shots fired by the defendant were shot at the fleeing
antagonists and they were fired toward the Elgin Academy.[71]

The appellate court, while recognizing the highly circumstantial nature
of the evidence, found that it was not able to conclude that no reasonable
trier of fact could have found that the defendant fired the shot that killed
Harris. Missing gun notwithstanding, it appeared that Torres met all of the
requisite criteria to have fired the fatal shot:

> … he was within the "window" of trajectory, he fired a .380-caliber
> handgun, and he fired in the direction of the academy. No other
> person met all three of these critical factors according to witness
> testimony and other evidence adduced at trial.[72]

The appeals court thus concluded that the state had proved the defendant
guilty beyond a reasonable doubt of second-degree murder.

In *Cammon v. State*,[73] defendants were convicted of felony-murder predicated on an aggravated assault at a nightclub. On the night of the homicide,
Cammon became involved in a fistfight with the deceased, Adrian Woods.
Later in the evening the defendant obtained a pistol and shot Woods who
was in a van carrying Woods and several others, and which pulled into Wood's
apartment complex. Cammon began shooting and the occupants of the van
returned fire. During the shootout, a Ms. Ellison was struck and killed by a
bullet as she stood in her living room. There was evidence that the bullet
that killed Ms. Ellison could have been fired from a Beretta pistol.[74]

Defendants argued trial error in allowing an officer who was not qualified as an expert in ballistics to give an opinion as to the trajectory of the bullet that killed the victim. The state argued that the opinion was based upon the officer's own extensive investigation of the homicide, and was clearly admissible over any objection to any lack of expertise in the field of ballistics. The ultimate issue, the court underlined, was not the bullet trajectory, but whether the defendants were guilty of an aggravated assault or not guilty by reason of self-defense:

> If the three codefendants were parties to an aggravated assault initiated against the occupants of the van, they all were guilty of felony murder regardless of who actually fired the shot which killed the victim. If, on the other hand, they were victims of an aggravated assault initiated by the occupants of the van, they all were not guilty by reason of self-defense even if one of them had shot the victim. The officer was not asked whether he believed that the three started the shoot-out or were justified in defending themselves against an aggravated assault begun by the occupants of the van. The officer was asked only if he had an opinion as to the path of the bullet, and his response to that inquiry was not inadmissible on the ground that it expressed his opinion, the ultimate issue in the case.

VIII. Bullet Matching

In cases of the clear application of striation matching after test firing of a gun connected to defendant, there is generally little or no discussion of ballistics issues. The cases of interest tend to focus on weapon identifications and linkage where no gun is available for comparison purposes. Several very recent cases deal with the relatively new ammunition matching issues in the context of trying to chemically match the lead content of bullets taken from a crime victim with unspent shells or ammunition otherwise connected to the defendant. These cases and the technology discussed therein are at the cutting edge in ballistics research and practice.

In *State v. Fulminante*,[75] defendant was found guilty of murder and sentenced to death. In September 1982, defendant lived in Phoenix with his wife, Mary, and his 11-year-old stepdaughter, Jeneane. On September 6, 1982, Mary checked into the hospital for surgery. Before leaving for the hospital, she told defendant she would leave him if he did not have a job by the time she fully recovered from her surgery. At two the next morning, defendant telephoned the Mesa Police Department to report Jeneane missing, and later that morning, when defendant brought Mary home from the hospital, he told her Jeneane had not come home the previous night. He said that when he realized Jeneane was missing, he first looked around the house, then around the neighborhood door to door, and then used his motorcycle to continue searching for her. When Mary questioned him on the details of his search, he admitted he had not gone door to door. At this point, Mary and defendant both went through the neighborhood looking for Jeneane. Sometime after returning to the house, after searching around the house, Mary discovered that defendant's pistol was missing. When the police visited their home on September 15, the Fulminantes reported the missing pistol.

On September 16, the child victim's body was found in a desert wash eleven miles from the Fulminantes' home. The body had two gunshot wounds to the head, a long, narrow cloth was wrapped loosely around her neck, her pants had been undone, and the waistband resting below her waist, while the elastic of her underpants was rolled under. Police later recovered a spent bullet from the ground near the place where her body was found. The autopsy determined that the child died of the gunshot wounds and gunpowder in the entry wounds suggested the shots had been fired at close range. In addition, lead fragments were recovered from Jeneane's brain. Police were unable to perform ballistics testing because defendant claimed he sold his guns while Mary was in the hospital. Police later discovered that defendant traded his rifle for eighty dollars in cash and a second barrel for his .357 Dan Wesson revolver. The extra barrel was also missing from the family home. Ballistics tests were able to determine that the wounds on Jeneane's body were made by either .357- or .38-caliber bullets. The wounds were most consistent with a .357, and a .357 was compatible with a .38. The police were able to recover a box of .357- and .38-caliber ammunition during a consensual search of the Fulminantes' house.[76]

According to the state, the ballistics evidence was consistent with guilt:

> Defendant possessed ammunition of the same caliber that probably killed Jeneane; lead retrieved from Jeneane's head was from the same batch of ammunition as the lead found in defendant's home; the projectile jacket recovered from the crime scene could have been fired from a .357 Dan Wesson; the projectile was fired from a dirty gun, and spent .357 cartridges retrieved from defendant's home indicated they were also fired from a dirty gun; and finally, the projectile jacket found at the scene and those retrieved from defendant's home indicated a similar manufacturer. Defendant had a gun and ammunition of the same type used to kill Jeneane and purchased an extra barrel for the gun the day Jeneane

disappeared. Both items were missing when police investigated, and defendant could not rationally explain their disappearance — strengthening an inference they might have been used to kill Jeneane.[77]

From the above-noted facts, the court found competent evidence from which the jury could have pieced together a web of suspicious circumstances tight enough that a reasonable person could conclude, beyond a reasonable doubt, that defendant was the perpetrator.[78]

Defendant argued that evidence comparing the lead fragments retrieved from Jeneane's head to the lead from the ammunition recovered from defendant's home should have been excluded because the probative value was substantially outweighed by the prejudicial impact and potential to mislead and confuse the jury. Defendant argued the fact that bullet fragments from Jeneane's head were of the same elemental composition as his ammunition was statistically irrelevant because there could have been as many as 40,000 boxes of such ammunition. The test for relevance, the court noted, was whether the offered evidence tends to make the existence of any fact in issue more or less probable. The court found that the lead comparison evidence here was probative in that it tended to demonstrate that defendant possessed ammunition consistent with that used to kill Jeneane. They did not see any prejudice that would substantially outweigh the probative value of the evidence to bar its admission.[79]

The issue of bullet or ammunition matching was raised again in *United States v. Davis*,[80] a bank robbery and armed violence case. The case centered around the armed robbery of three separate, federally insured financial institutions in Omaha, Nebraska, two of which occurred only minutes apart on January 29, 1994. The third took place on March 12, 1994. The defendant Cleophus Davis was arrested and charged with all three robberies. Shots were fired during two of the robberies. The gun was identified as a dark-colored, short-barreled gun.

An eyewitness and a bank teller provided the FBI with information sufficient for a rough sketch, and the defendant was eventually identified in a lineup.

When he was arrested, a partial box of .38-caliber wadcutter cartridges was found in a friend's car that defendant was driving. The .38-caliber wadcutter cartridges found in a box in the Nissan were later tested against the bullets found at the crime scenes and the crime scene bullets bore markings similar to each other, indicating that they were possibly fired by the same gun. The bullets from the box found in the Nissan were determined to be analytically indistinguishable from the bullets recovered at two of the bank robberies. A ballistics expert testified that such a finding was rare and that the bullets must have come from the same box or from another box that would have been made by the same company on the same day.[81]

The FBI tested the gun and found it to have a very worn, heavily leaded barrel, consistent with the markings on the bullets recovered from the crime scenes. A ballistics expert witness testified that it was possible that the bullets recovered from the two crime scenes where shots were fired were fired from that weapon. The court accepted as sufficiently probative and reliable the expert's testimony because it demonstrated a high probability that the bullets spent at the first robbery and the last robbery originated from the same box of cartridges.

The district court conducted a hearing to determine the admissibility of the scientific foundation supporting expert testimony proffered by the government on Inductively Coupled Plasma-Atomic Emission Spectrometry (IAP), a process used in this case to analyze and compare trace elements found in the bullet fragments. John Riley, special agent of the FBI, who specializes in the analysis of various materials for their elemental and trace elemental composition, was the government's witness. Riley had been doing this work for approximately 27 years, had a bachelor of science degree in chemistry and a master of science degree in forensic science, and had authored articles and lectured on this subject:

Agent Riley testified that IAP, an analysis that the FBI has been using for approximately 10 years, is a generally accepted scientific technique that has been subjected to testing, publication, and peer review, and the technique is the same no matter who performs it. Another procedure used to accomplish the same basic analysis is neuron activation analysis. The FBI has been using the neuron activation analysis since the mid-1960s but now favors IAP for trace elemental analysis because IAP is more sensitive. IAP can determine trace elements down to parts per million (.0000001%). The procedure determines which of five trace elements are present in the bullets to be compared. If the same elements are present in each, the procedure determines the percentage of each element present. If the same elements are present in the same amounts they are analytically indistinguishable.[82]

Agent Riley described at length the bullet manufacturing processes that supported his chemical analysis and linkage testimony as to defendant Davis:

> Mr. Riley testified that research had been conducted on the composition and comparison of bullets manufactured at the same plant on either the same or different days and at different plants. The research revealed that while 400,000 bullets could be produced at a factory in one day, the composition of those bullets will vary vastly unless they were manufactured side by side, because lead is a

heavy molten metal that cannot be mixed into a completely homogeneous mixture throughout; pockets of different elemental compositions will exist and additional lead of differing elemental compositions is periodically added to the cauldron throughout a day, changing the elemental composition of the bullets produced. Based on this research and the results of the trace elemental composition IAP analysis, the expert concluded that the bullets at issue were analytically indistinguishable from some of the bullets in the box of cartridges found in the Nissan, that they were generally similar to the remaining bullets in that box, and that there was a high correlation between the two bullets found at the crime scenes. He also concluded that these bullets must have been manufactured at the same Remington factory, must have come from the same batch of lead, must have been packaged on or about the same day, and could have come from the same box.[83]

Davis' counsel, during cross-examination of Riley, cited one paragraph from a book criticizing neuron activation analysis (inductively coupled plasma atomic emission spectroscopy, or IAP, was the analysis used here), because there was no way of knowing exactly how many bullets manufactured by the same company have this same elemental composition. Agent Riley admitted having no way of knowing how many other bullets Remington produced on the same day as these that also would have a composition that was analytically indistinguishable from the bullets tested here. Nonetheless, the court ruled that there was a sufficient scientific basis to admit the expert's testimony. Davis, the court observed, did not attempt to show that IAP was not a scientifically valid technique for determining the trace elemental composition of bullets, nor did he try to establish that Riley improperly utilized the technique.[84]

Another important case addressing the novel lead-matching issue where a gun is not available or the more traditional firing-match testimony is inconclusive, is *State v. Noel*,[85] where defendant was found guilty of murder, possession of a handgun without a permit, and possession of handgun with intent to use it unlawfully against another. The victim was a young man who was shot repeatedly on his front porch as he was returning to his home in the early evening. There was no known motive for the murder, nor was robbery involved. The shooting appeared random and senseless. Informant testimony led to the arrest of defendant. A bag containing 18 bullets was found in his locker, of which 9 were 9-millimeter bullets stamped with the manufacturer's name, Speers. The police had also recovered spent bullets and bullet casings at the crime scene, which were also stamped with the same manufacturer's name.

Charles Peters, a physical scientist with the materials analysis unit of the Federal Bureau of Investigation, examined 15 bullets, 4 collected at the crime scene, 2 recovered from the decedent's body, and the 9 Speer bullets found among defendant's belongings. The court characterized this complex testimony as follows:

> He analyzed the bullets using a process known as inductively coupled plasma atomic emission spectroscopy (IAP). IAP determines the proportions of six elements other than lead: copper, antimony, bismuth, arsenic, tin, and silver. The bullet manufacturer adds these elements to each batch of lead. From one batch to another, the proportions in bullets of the six elements vary. Thus, the chemical composition of a bullet from one batch may match that of another bullet from the same batch, but not the composition of a bullet from another batch.
>
> Peters divided the bullets into five compositional groups. Within each group, the bullets were of the same composition. Four of the five groups contained both a bullet from defendant's pouch and one recovered either from the crime scene or from the victim's body. For example, Group One included six bullets that were analytically indistinguishable: one bullet from the crime scene, one from the victim's body, and four from defendant's pouch. Group Four, which consisted of a solitary bullet found at the crime scene, did not match any other bullets. At trial, Peters testified that, in his experience and that of his unit, "bullets that come from the same box have the same composition of lead and bullets that come from different boxes … will have different compositions." He explained that the manufacturer fills a given box with bullets from a single batch of lead. Consequently, those bullets will possess the same chemical composition. Because mixing may occur during storage, however, bullets of different compositions may be found in the same box. Peters concluded that he would not expect random batches of lead to produce the match that existed among the subject bullets.[86]
>
> Before conducting his analysis, Peters testified that he had visited the Speer manufacturing plant in Lewiston, Idaho, to study the manufacturing processes. He limited his testimony on the manufacturing process to an explanation that each bullet was extruded from a billet, or seventy-pound cylinder of lead, each of which produces a number of billets. A billet yields approximately 4,300

bullets. Peters further noted that about five billion bullets were manufactured in the United States each year and at least fifty thousand bullets may have the same composition.[87]

The defendant argued in the appellate court that Peters failed to provide foundational evidence in the form of statistical probability evidence about the identical composition between the bullets recovered from the crime scene and the victim's body and those found in defendant's pouch. The appellate court agreed, concluding that Peters' testimony depended on the statistical probability that the two sets of bullets would have the same composition.

The New Jersey Supreme Court noted that the prosecutor's purpose in offering the testimony of Mr. Peters was to persuade the jury that the identical composition of the two sets of bullets significantly enhanced the strength of the link between defendant and the crime, that is, the link that had already been established by the identity of caliber and manufacturer. That was obvious from remarks made in his summation, by which the prosecutor sought to impart scientific certainty to an implied conclusiveness of that link, also attempting, the court noted, to bolster the argument with a patently improper character reference for witness Peters' credibility:

Finally, Mr. Charles Peters of the FBI. I realized that was some sophisticated testimony and I know I personally had trouble following it. But I hope the conclusions are what came clear.

It is a very precise, scientific process that has been used for, I believe, he said about, about 30 years to test these bullet leads and his testimony is critical to this case because it completely blows away the murder theory advanced by the defense that Malika and Lamar somehow engineered the murder.

Now do you think Mr. Peters was a liar? He's not a cop. He's not even an FBI agent. Charles Peters is a scientist and he looked like a scientist; didn't he? You could almost see him in a white lab coat. You could see him in math class in a high school in the back. He had all the answers.

He's a straight shooter. Did not testify beyond what the results of his examination were. Didn't try to make it out to be more than what it was, but it is something very critical in this case.

Basically what he told us was that an examination of bullets, whenever a manufacturer is going to run a line of bullets, they order a source of lead from a lead smelter.

I asked him if that was like a "batch." He said it was. The scientists like using the word "source." I think it is easier to conceive of as a batch of lead and he said that there are millions, literally millions of these batches of lead out in circulation. And from those millions of batches of lead out in circulation, there are billions of bullets produced each year.

The key, I submit to you, is not what Mr. Roberts said it is, not about the number of billets produced — the number of bullets produced, the key is the number of sources of lead; the number of batches. Millions of batches; each one unique like a snow flake; like a fingerprint.[88]

In initiating its analysis, the New Jersey Supreme Court noted that statistical evidence had not generally been a prerequisite to the admission of matching samples, noting, for example that in cases involving matching blood samples, statistical evidence of the probability of a match had not been required to establish a bloodstain as a link in the chain of evidence. Similarly, the court noted that expert testimony about matching soil and hair samples has been deemed admissible, with the weight of the evidence left to the jury. Finally, the court continued, expert testimony about matching carpet fibers had been admitted in the absence of statistical evidence about the probability of the match.[89] In the present case, the New Jersey Supreme Court observed, the expert's testimony established a match among the bullets found in defendant's belongings, at the crime scene, and in the victim's body. Defendant's contention that the large quantity of bullets produced by the manufacturer rendered the match among the bullets inconclusive went to the weight, not admissibility, as with the other observational forensic disciplines noted.

The jury in the present case, the court stated, received the guidance it needed to discharge its function. The expert explained the chemistry of lead analysis, why bullets of the same chemical composition generally came from the same box, and why a single box may contain several bullets of different compositions. The jury was left with the task of determining whether the bullets at issue came from the same box. The jury in the present case could evaluate the expert's testimony without recourse to mathematical calculations; like juries assessing samples of blood, soil, and fibers, it did not require statistical data to discharge its duties:

IAP is an accepted method of bullet lead analysis. The compositional match among the bullets increased the probability that the bullets in the victim came from the defendant. That evidence constituted a link in the prosecution's chain of evidence. The defense attempted to undermine that conclusion by cross-examining the expert, by showing that many bullets of the same composition had been manufactured, and by arguing an alternative conclusion to the jury. Consequently, we find that the trial court did not err in permitting Peters to testify about the similarity of the composition of the lead bullets.

We also conclude that Peters did not exceed the limits of his expertise in testifying about the manufacturing process. Peters testified that bullets of the same composition generally come from the same box, although a single box may contain bullets of several different compositions. He based his testimony on years of analyzing boxes of bullets and on a tour of the Speer plant. That tour may not qualify him as an expert on bullet manufacturing for all purposes. When combined with his substantial experience in analyzing bullets, however, the tour provided him with the "minimal technical training and knowledge essential to the expression of a reliable opinion." Although experts generally may not express opinions outside their areas of expertise, those areas may overlap, and in certain circumstances an expert in one area may be qualified to express an opinion in another. Here, Peters' testimony regarding the arrangement of bullets in a box provided an appropriate basis for the jury to evaluate the significance of the bullet matches.[90]

The dissenting judges saw the issue as whether Peters' testimony provided an adequate basis to support the conclusion that the bullets not only came from the same source of lead at the manufacturer but were sold from the same box. According to them, the issue was not whether Peters' testimony regarding the matches between the bullets was admissible, but whether too many bullets were in circulation to justify any real inference of guilt.

A second concern of the dissent, with reference to the "snowflake" remark in the state's closing, was that the prosecutor's summation elevated the testimony from "a bit of circumstantial evidence that adds to the state's case" to "scientific fact," led the jury to ignore the large number of bullets in circulation, and so prejudiced the jury that we must set aside its verdict. The Supreme Court of New Jersey observed that:

(E)xcessive statements from both sides are a regrettable fact of life in criminal trials. In such trials, an objection by counsel remains as the first line of defense. Although the prosecutor's statement may have been more temperate, it, particularly in the absence of an objection, does not justify upsetting the jury verdict. Given the realities of adversary proceedings, the prosecutor's remarks pass as fair comment.[91]

This IAP or IAC technology (inductively coupled plasma-atomic emission spectroscopy) is receiving increasing acceptance by the nation's courts, even though a considerable inferential leap of faith seems involved in the actual acceptance of its conclusion. Two very recent cases follow in detail, to aid the reader in comprehending this very high-tech theory of ballistics expertise.

IX. Bullet Lead Matching — ICP Methodology

In *Ragland v. Commonwealth*,[92] a murder case, the court addressed the admissibility of chemically analyzed lead bullet comparisons.

Trent DiGiuro, a student athlete at the University of Kentucky, was shot in the head and killed as he sat in a chair on the front porch of his residence at 570 Woodland Avenue, Lexington, Kentucky. DiGiuro was celebrating his 21st birthday with friends, some of whom were on the porch with him when he was killed. Although one eyewitness heard the shot, no one saw who fired it or from where it was fired. Fragments of the fatal bullet were recovered during the postmortem examination and a firearms expert concluded that the bullet most likely had been fired from a .243-caliber rifle with a four-grooves-and-lands, right-twist barrel pattern. Although numerous leads were followed and at least one suspect was identified, six years elapsed before anyone was charged with the murder. The police received a tip from defendant's girlfriend about his confession of the crime due to the victim having kept him out of a fraternity.

A search of several of defendant's residences turned up a .243-caliber Wetherby Vanguard rifle with 3 unspent .243-caliber bullets in the chamber and an ammunition box containing 17 unspent .243-caliber bullets. A label on the box indicated the Winchester Ammunition Company had manufactured the bullets on April 28, 1994.[93]

Kathleen Lundy, a forensic scientist employed by the FBI, subjected the 3 bullets found in the Wetherby Vanguard rifle, 16 of the 17 bullets found in the ammunition box, and the fragment of the bullet that killed DiGiuro to a comparative bullet lead analysis. She testified at trial that one of the bullets recovered from the rifle and nine of the bullets found in the ammunition box were "analytically indistinguishable" in metallurgical composition from the bullet that killed DiGiuro, a finding she described as "consistent with" the bullets having originated from the same source of molten lead. Markings on bullets test-fired from the .243 Wetherby Vanguard rifle found at one of the residences matched the markings on the murder bullet. Markings on bullets test-fired from three other .243 Wetherby Vanguard rifles manufactured during the same time period as the Ragland rifle did not match those found on the murder bullet.[94]

The ballistics expert who test-fired bullets from the .243 Wetherby Vanguard rifle found at 501 Capital Avenue testified that the markings found on the test bullets were similar to those found on the bullet fragment removed from DiGiuro's body. However, because of the degree of fragmentation of the murder bullet, the witness could not state conclusively that the Ragland rifle fired the murder bullet.[95]

Given the novelty of the bullet lead matching methodology, the court at defendant's request conducted an extensive Daubert hearing to determine the scientific reliability of this method as a basis for the expert's opinion. Because of its importance and the increasing utilization of lead bullet chemical matching[96] as an investigative tool by the FBI and more sophisticated state labs, a somewhat lengthy discussion of this hearing is warranted.

Defendant moved to suppress the expert opinion of Kathleen Lundy, an FBI forensic scientist, that the metallurgical composition of the .243-caliber bullet fragment removed from DiGiuro's body was analytically indistinguishable from one of the three bullets in the rifle found at 501 Capital Avenue and nine of the seventeen bullets in the ammunition box found at 1469 Old Lawrenceburg Road, a finding consistent with the bullets having originated from the same source, i.e., the same batch of molten lead. Defendant asserted that Lundy's conclusions in that regard were scientifically unreliable.

Lundy testified at the Daubert hearing that lead bullets were manufactured primarily from recycled automobile batteries. Most bullet manufacturers purchased their lead in bulk from secondary smelters (recyclers), who crush and melt the batteries, and then separate the lead to the extent possible from the other battery contents. The molten lead is then cooled and formed into 60-to-100-pound bricks or ingots, 70-to-125-pound cylindrical billets, or 1000-to-2000-pound blocks. Each ingot, billet, or block will inevitably contain traces of arsenic, antimony, tin, bismuth, copper, silver, or cadmium, elements that were contained in the batteries but did not separate from the lead during the recycling process. The bullet manufacturers only require that the percentages of these trace elements not exceed certain levels. The smelter tests each batch of molten lead as it is poured from its crucible and reports the percentages of impurities to the bullet manufacturer when the product is delivered.[97]

Lundy continued, addressing the processing of the lead at the bullet manufacturing plant. At the bullet manufacturing plant, she testified, the manufacturer inserts the lead into an extrusion press that forms it into a "bullet wire" having the diameter of the desired bullets. The wire is chopped into pieces that are then swaged into bullets. If the lead is purchased from the smelter in billet form, it can be inserted directly into the extrusion press. However, if it is purchased in ingot or block form, it must be remelted and reformed at the bullet manufacturing plant. When this occurs, the manufacturer will commonly add lead waste or scraps remaining from earlier extrusion, chopping, and swaging processes to the mix, thus changing the percentages of the impurities in that particular batch. Even if the manufacturer buys only billets, it will still remelt lead waste and scraps for reuse.

Because there was no way to know the exact source of the lead used in a particular bullet, i.e., whether it was melted by a secondary smelter, whether it was remelted from waste and scraps by the manufacturer, or whether each bullet in a box contains lead from the same melt, Lundy did not attempt to trace the origin of each bullet to its source. Instead, she used a machine that measures the percentages of trace elements by a methodology known as inductively coupled plasma-atomic emission spectroscopy, or ICP (also known as IAP). If the percentages of impurities in two bullets are the same, i.e., "analytically indistinguishable," that fact is "consistent with" the bullets having originated from the same batch of molten lead. As applied to this case, that finding constituted circumstantial evidence that the bullet that killed DiGiuro was manufactured at the same time as one of the bullets contained in the rifle found at 501 Capital Avenue and nine of the bullets contained in the ammunition box found at 1469 Old Lawrenceburg Road. From this circumstantial evidence, she continued, the jury could infer that the murder bullet, one of the bullets found in the rifle, and nine of the bullets found in the ammunition box were all purchased together and, thus, the murder bullet belonged to defendant.[98]

Contradicting this considerable inferential leap of faith, however, was the testimony of Paul Szabo, an employee of Winchester Ammunition. He stated that the ammunition box found at 1469 Old Lawrenceburg Road originally contained only 20 bullets. Three bullets were in the rifle and 17 bullets were in the ammunition box, making the murder bullet one bullet too many. Furthermore, as pointed out at trial, Winchester purchases its lead in billet form and, thus only remelts lead shavings and scraps at its manufacturing plant. The significance of that fact is that Winchester's furnace has only a 15,000-pound capacity whereas some smelters have crucibles with up to

200,000-pound capacities. Thus, literally millions more bullets could have the same "source" if they were last melted by a secondary smelter instead of by Winchester. However, the court noted, those facts affect only the weight of Lundy's evidence, not its scientific reliability.[99]

Defense expert William Tobin admitted that ICP was a scientifically accepted method of determining the percentages of trace elements in lead bullets; however, Tobin disagreed with Lundy's reasoning that a finding that any two bullets were analytically indistinguishable was "consistent with" their having the same source, i.e., being traceable to the same "last melt." The court observed that Lundy never opined that the analytically indistinguishable bullets did originate from the same source. Relying on data obtained from secondary smelters, Tobin described instances where the trace elements were not homogeneous, e.g., where the percentage of antimony would be different on one side of an ingot than on the other. In fact, the court noted:

> Lundy never claimed that the trace element percentages will always be homogeneous, i.e., the same throughout a particular batch of molten lead. Of course, if the trace element percentages in a particular batch are not homogeneous, bullets manufactured from that batch would not be analytically indistinguishable, thus would not be "consistent with" the two bullets having the same source even though they, in fact, did have the same source. That fact, of course, would redound to the benefit of the accused.[100]

> Defense expert Tobin also described "piggybacking," i.e., filling a mold with molten lead partially from one crucible and partially from another crucible. However, the court stated: *if that occurred and a homogeneous* mixture did not result, the bullets again would not be analytically indistinguishable, a result again redounding to the benefit of the accused. It is *only when the bullets are analytically indistinguishable that evidence from a comparison bullet lead analysis attains relevancy.*[101]

Finally, Tobin described several instances when manufacturers had reported identical percentages of impurities from two separate "pours." He did not speculate on the mathematical probabilities of such an occurrence. Again, the appeals court stated, Lundy did not testify that the bullets must have come from the same batch of molten lead but only that their metallurgical composition was consistent with having come from the same batch. Tobin's testimony tended only to prove that it was possible that the analytically indistinguishable bullets did not come from the same batch. The court observed that other jurisdictions have admitted similar evidence of comparative bullet lead analysis,[102] and that Lundy testified that the analysis had been subjected to peer review in a number of scientific journals. On this record, the court upheld the trial court's admission of the lead bullet comparison methodology:

> We conclude that there was substantial evidence to support the trial court's finding that the methodology used to determine the metallurgical composition of lead bullets and Lundy's reasoning that the fact that two or more bullets have an analytically indistinguishable metallurgical composition is consistent with their having come from the same source were both scientifically reliable. Whether Lundy's evidence would assist the trier of fact was a closer call, given that literally millions of bullets could come from the same source. Nevertheless, because that fact goes more to weight of the evidence than to its relevance, we conclude that the trial court did not abuse its discretion in determining that the evidence would assist the trier of fact in determining whether defendant fired the shot that killed DiGiuro.[103]

With considerable interest in the topic of bullet or ammunition matching, serious study is beginning in attempts to embrace or put to rest this most controversial methodology.[104]

X. Incompetence of Counsel

In *Boyd v. State*,[105] the defendant was convicted for intentionally murdering Evelyn Blackmon and Fred Blackmon during the course of a robbery and kidnapping. Accomplice Milstead testified at trial that Boyd took Milstead's gun and shot the victims. Among the claims made in a post-conviction petition were that his trial and appellate counsel were ineffective, in part for failing to aggressively attack the state's ballistic experts. Defendant maintained that it was essential that his attorneys impeached the credibility of the state's forensic experts, who gave evidence regarding which wounds were caused by which firearms, what kind of wounds the victims suffered, and how long after the infliction of the wounds they died. Boyd maintained that such testimony was most likely used to support the trial court's finding of heinous, atrocious, or cruel aggravating factor, justifying the death penalty, as well as to bolster the prosecutor's theory as to how the murders occurred. The court ruled that the testimony of a ballistics expert would not have resolved who pulled the trigger, and thus failed to see how a court financed ballistics expert could have impeached accomplice Milstead's testimony regarding who shot the victims.

In *Commonwealth v. Wallace*,[106] defendant was convicted of first-degree murder and was sentenced to death. Defendant appealed, arguing, among other grounds, on the basis of incompetency of counsel as regards the ballistics testimony admitted against him.

On August 17, 1979, Henry Brown and William Wallace, Jr. robbed Carl's Cleaners in Cannonsburg, Pennsylvania, in the course of which, defendant Wallace allegedly shot and killed the store owner and a 15-year-old employee, Tina Spalla. Wallace argued that his trial counsel was ineffective in failing to obtain an independent ballistics analysis of the bullet recovered from the body of Tina Spalla. At trial, the prosecution's theory was that Wallace had shot both victims with a .32-caliber handgun, and that while accomplice Henry Brown had carried a .38-caliber handgun, he had not fired at either victim. Brown's .38-caliber handgun was recovered and admitted as evidence at trial, but the .32-caliber murder weapon was never located.

State Trooper Daryl W. Mayfield, a ballistics expert for the State Police Crime Lab, examined the bullet slugs recovered from the victims' bodies and testified that they were all .32 caliber. However, Dr. Ernest Abernathy, the pathologist who performed the autopsies on the victims, testified that the bullet he removed from the body of Tina Spalla appeared to him, upon visual inspection, to be .38 caliber. Wallace argued that in light of Dr. Abernathy's testimony, and given the fact that Brown was carrying a .38-caliber weapon, his lawyer should have sought an independent ballistics analysis to definitively assess the caliber of the bullet that killed Tina Spalla.[107]

The court found this argument to be without merit, noting initially that no credible issue existed as to the slug's caliber. Dr. Abernathy was a pathologist who simply inspected the bullet visually and concluded that it was .38 caliber. Trooper Mayfield, on the other hand, was a State Police ballistics expert who performed a laboratory analysis of the bullet and determined that it was .32 caliber. In any event, the court concluded, it was clear that counsel's decision not to pursue an independent analysis was motivated by trial strategy, counsel being concerned that if a ballistics analysis establishing that the bullet was indeed a .32 caliber was performed, counsel would lose any reasonable doubt that could be created. The court concluded, defendant's incompetency of counsel's claim failed.

However, in the case of *Cravens v. State*,[108] counsel's failure to investigate the propriety of obtaining expert witnesses to testify regarding the distance from which shot was fired was considered unreasonable and fell below the customary skill and diligence of a reasonably competent attorney in murder prosecution. There, where defendant's entire defense rested upon the fact that the shot was fired from close distance, prosecutor's expert testified that the shot was made from six to eight feet distance, and counsel later admitted he thought that test-firing patterns and autopsy reports provided through discovery "meant nothing to the case. "

XI. Gunshot Residue

The 14th Interpol Forensic Science Symposium Firearms Literature Review in November of 2004 noted ongoing problems with the issue of reliable tests to determine the presence of gunshot residue (GSR):

> There is no consensus among the forensic laboratories regarding the number of particles needed to confirm the presence of GSR. The controversy among the experts on this question is still unresolved (personal communication, 8th Firearms Working Group meeting, Brugge, Belgium, September 2001). There is much more agreement regarding the wording of reports when a lab decided that there is a positive result. In such a case the statement:

> —The sample is consistent with the suspect having discharged a firearm, having been in the vicinity of a firearm when it was discharged, or having handled an item with GSR on it resembles the phrasing of most of the labs (2). In any case, it is very important to compare the GSR compositions found on a suspect to the GSR compositions of the spent cartridge cases (if found) at the scene of crime as well as to the GSR compositions in the suspected firearm (if apprehended). Sometimes the evidential value of such comparisons may be much higher than the degree of — uniqueness "of the GSR particles found on the suspect, for instance, if the GSR particles found on a suspect are consistent with the GSR in the spent cartridge cases of a rare ammunition."[109]

GSR continues to occupy the attention of modern courts.

In *Simmons v. State*,[110] defendant was convicted of murder. The Mississippi Supreme Court ruled that the probative value of expert testimony regarding the results of a gunshot residue test was not substantially outweighed by the danger of undue prejudice. This was so, because the expert never testified that the test established that the murder defendant had fired a weapon, but instead testified that characteristic particles were identified in the sample but that he could not say positively whether or not defendant had fired a weapon.

The cause of victim Wilkerson's death was a gunshot wound to the left side of her head. The recovered projectile entered the left cheek of Wilkerson's face, traveled through her skull and severed her spinal cord, causing her death.

John F. Dial, III, a firearms expert, identified the recovered projectile as being fired from a .38-caliber revolver-type pistol. Dr. Rodrigo Galvez, forensic pathologist, testified that the gunpowder soot or "tatooing" on the skin indicated that the shot was fired at very close range. Jackson Crime Scene Investigator Charles Taylor testified as to the evidence collected and documented at Wilkerson's apartment. Taylor testified at trial that he collected a gunshot residue (GSR) kit from defendant Simmons. Taylor explained that once collected, Simmons's GSR test was sent to the crime lab to be examined on a scanning electron microscope. The test results were mailed back to Taylor. While Taylor testified that the results came back positive, he also expressed his lack of confidence in GSR testing. Taylor testified that because you cannot tell whether a person actually fired a gun himself or whether he was only in the same area of someone else firing a gun, he did not place confidence in the GSR testing results.[111]

A GSR test was performed on Simmons, and the samples were sent to the state crime lab to determine if the samples contained gunshot residue. At trial, Whitehead, an employee of the Mississippi Crime Lab, was accepted as an expert by the court. Simmons did not question Whitehead's qualifications or his ability to follow the proper testing procedures generally accepted in the scientific community. Whitehead testified regarding the results of the GSR test conducted on samples taken from Simmons. Whitehead testified that the crime lab issues three types of reports after analyzing GSR tests: a positive report, which indicates that gunshot residue was positively identified, a negative report, which indicates no residue was found, or a characteristic report, which indicates there are particles present but they do not meet the strict definition of gunshot residue.

Whitehead's report regarding the Simmons' sample was a characteristic report. Defendant argued that Whitehead's testimony strongly and inaccurately suggested to the jury that the test results were positive for gunshot residue when in fact not all of the characteristics of residue were found. Simmons submitted that unless Whitehead could testify within a reasonable degree of scientific certainty that the test indicated gunshot residue on his hands any opinion rendered would be highly speculative and hypothetical.

When questioned by the state as to the GSR testing, Whitehead testified as follows:

> State: Did you find particles consistent with particles present in gunshot residue?
>
> Whitehead: Yes, sir, I did.
>
> State: And can you say that with a reasonable degree of scientific certainty that you found particles consistent with gunshot residue?

Whitehead: Yes, sir. There were particles present that were indicative of gunshot residue, but because they did not meet the strict definition of what gunshot residue is, they were not positively identified.

You can find particles that don't always — you know, they're not always round. They don't always contain — here could be antimony barium particles or lead antimony particles. I have no reason to believe it's anything else, but because it does not meet that strict definition of what gunshot residue is, it cannot be positively identified in our laboratory.

State: Now, so that we can be fair to everyone involved in this, would it be fair to say that you can neither rule in nor rule out Byron Simmons as a shooter of a firearm based on these tests?

Whitehead: I can never do that. All I can simply say is that person was either in the environment or not in the environment.

State: And can you say that he was nor wasn't in the area where a firearm was fired in this case?

Whitehead: No, sir.[112]

The State argued that the testimony was properly admitted, the results of the test were not speculative as to whether or not there were characteristics of gunshot residue, and that the test did not produce a negative result. Whitehead explained that while the particles could have contained the same elements of gunshot residue, the shape of the particles determines whether the findings will produce a positive or only characteristic result. If the proper shape is not found, despite the presence of gunshot residue, the test will determine that particles characteristic of gunshot residue were identified. That is exactly the situation Whitehead discovered when the samples taken from Simmons were tested.

The court, in rejecting defendant's argument, accepted the validity of the often-seen limbo-status testimony of forensic experts across the fields of the forensic sciences:

Whitehead testified that the test produced results characteristic of gunshot residue. The test results were not positive for gunshot residue based on the standards used by the crime lab, however, the test results were also not negative either. Whitehead further testified that the results of the test could not determine conclusively if someone fired a weapon, only that if they were in the "environment" of a discharged weapon...Whitehead never testified that the GSR test established that Simmons had fired a weapon. In fact, Whitehead only testified that characteristic particles were identified in the sample, but he could not say positively whether or not Simmons had fired a weapon. Whitehead explained to the jury how the test was interpreted. The trial court did not abuse its discretion in allowing the testimony from Whitehead to be admitted into evidence.[113]

Gunshot residue was recently addressed in the context of an ineffective counsel claim.

In *People v. Young*,[114] a 2004 Illinois case, defendant was convicted of first-degree murder. He pleaded self-defense. The shooting death arose out of an argument over money at a family barbecue. The defendant claimed ineffective assistance of counsel, arguing that his defense counsel failed to order a gunshot residue of the defendant's clothing or conduct adequate cross-examination of the State's expert scientific witnesses. The appellate court found that the performance of defense counsel was deficient, for purposes of defendant's ineffective assistance of counsel claim, where counsel did not object to misconduct of prosecutor that undermined defendant's right to a fair trial, admitted he lacked requisite experience to appropriately cross-examine prosecutor's experts, bolstered testimony of experts on cross-examination by not either refuting testimony or developing it in a way consistent with defendant's theories, and failed to order gunshot residue tests of the victim's clothing.

At trial, the state also called John Paulson, an employee of the forensic division of the Chicago Police Department, who worked for the department as an evidence technician forensic investigator. After taking numerous crime scene photographs and gathering shell casings, Paulson indicated that he administered the gunshot residue test to the hands of the victim. On cross-examination, Paulson reiterated what he found when he processed the crime scene. He was also asked to describe, step-by-step, the process of doing a gunshot residue test on a dead person's hands to determine the presence of lead, antimony, and barium.

The defense counsel admitted he was lacking in the expertise necessary to appropriately cross-examine Dr. Lifschultz, the pathologist, on his new and improved medical opinions as to the key issue of entrance and exit wounds.[115] Following the colloquy with the trial court about the change in testimony, Lifschultz was tendered to the trial court as an expert witness in forensic pathology. He testified to the autopsy process in general and the autopsy of Jeffrey Sturghill in particular. He found three through-and-through gunshot wounds, a small abrasion over the left eye, and a small abrasion on the back of the right ankle. Lifschultz found that the abrasions were consistent with a fall over the railing. He testified that he can tell the difference between entrance and exit wounds because of the tearing of the skin associated with exit wounds and the presence of specific abrasions of the tissue surrounding the entrance wounds. Lifschultz concluded that the wound at the side of the back was an entrance wound. The wound at the left side of the back was also an entrance wound.[116] The corresponding wound on the right side of the belly was an exit wound. There were also gunshot wounds to the left hip and lower right leg, the photographs of which were marked by the witnesses as to entrance and exit.

On cross-examination, Lifschultz was questioned as to how he could be so certain at trial as to which were entrance and exit wounds even though there were no such designations made at the time of the autopsy. At no point in the autopsy report did Lifschultz document which were entrance and which were exit wounds. He was then questioned as to the change in his opinions from the time they were originally made until 15 minutes prior to the testimony for which he was being cross-examined. Lifschultz claimed his new opinion was a refinement of his original opinion.[117]

The next state expert witness to testify was Scott Rochowicz, an employee of the Illinois State Police Forensic Science Center in Chicago, Illinois. He testified to the gunshot residue test, crucial on the issue of self-defense by defendant. He found elevated levels of barium, antimony, and lead on the decedent's hands. He found the levels to be inconclusive of gunshots because those levels were not as high as he would have expected, though he admitted he found levels that were elevated above the amounts normally found on the general population. He did not test the decedent's clothing for gunshot residue, even though he admitted there could have been residue there.

Defendant argued that the physical and scientific evidence corroborated his theory that the shooting was the result of self-defense. He pointed to the spent cartridge case found near victim Sturghill's body. That cartridge case was found not to be from the firearm used to shoot Sturghill. Young claims that the State offered little more than speculation for how that cartridge case got next to the body. According to Young, the scientific tests performed on Sturghill showed elevated levels of lead, antimony, and barium, all elements associated with the firing of guns. While the tests were deemed inconclusive, Young stressed that the levels of those elements were higher than the levels that would likely be found on the hands of an ordinary citizen who had not fired a gun.[118]

The court, in reversing defendant's conviction, emphasized prosecutorial error in asking whether he thought that the state's expert witness, among others, had lied:

In this case, the prosecutor asked defendant several times to comment on the state witnesses' veracity: "So the medical examiner lied when he said that this was an entrance wound?"; "So you can't think of any reason why he (Kenneth Simmons) would lie about what you did, can you? We expect our enemies to lie on us. It (sic) was your friend, wasn't he?" and "Can you think of any reason why she (Doanita Simmons) would lie?" Defendant answered that he did not know what the medical examiner said, that Kenneth and Doanita were his friends and he did not know of any reason why they would lie.

The prosecution's practice of asking a criminal defendant to comment on the veracity of other witnesses who have testified against him has consistently and repeatedly been condemned by this court because such questions intrude on the jury's function of determining the credibility of witnesses and serve to demean and ridicule the defendant. This practice has generally been deemed harmless error where evidence of defendant's guilt was overwhelming. Where the evidence in a case is closely balanced and the credibility of the witnesses is a crucial factor underlying the jury's determination of defendant's guilt or innocence, the error may not be harmless.[119]

Additionally, the court agreed with defendant's ineffective assistance argument in several instances:

...first from the failures of defense counsel to step up and object to the conduct of the prosecutor and also to the admission defense counsel made in *open court that he lacked the requisite expertise to appropriately cross-examine experts on their opinions. Though the trial court indicated that a continuance would be acceptable to give time to better prepare, Young's trial counsel indicated readiness. Admittedly, trial counsel was placed in a difficult situation when facing the defendant's competing interests of having a speedy trial with having effective representation at trial. Additionally, trial counsel's representation fell below the minimal Strickland level of effectiveness during cross-examination because he not only bolstered the testimony of the experts, but repeatedly referred to his inability to properly defend against those expert opinions. Trial counsel's only job was to explain ways the opinions of the expert were consistent with the theory of self-defense. If counsel is mounting a self-defense argument, effective representation would require either refuting opposition testimony or simply developing it in a way that is consistent with the defense theories being espoused. Additionally, though this is not necessarily a trial error, effective assistance in mounting a self-defense claim would dictate that counsel order gunshot residue tests of Sturghill's clothing if the clothing was still available, especially when the state seemed unable or unwilling to do so as part of its normal investigative process.*[120]

Ballistics related testimony is often linked with wound-analysis testimony by forensic pathologists to determine the relative location of shooter and victim by way of powder residue or stippling effects. Several recent examples follow. In a related matter, the tests utilized to determine gunshot residue on the hands or clothing of shooter or victim remain controversial. The article, Firearms Evidence, contained in the 1998 Interpol Forensic Science Symposium,[121] notes that the introduction of lead-free ammunition has had a noticeable impact on the testing for gunshot residue:

Recent contacts with ammunition showed that increasingly more manufacturers include lead-free ammunition in their assortment. The use of lead-free ammunition is steadily rising, but it has not yet resulted in an increasing number of publications in the field of investigation of lead-free gunshot residues.[122]

The 14th Interpol Forensic Science Symposium Ballistic Report addressed a number of articles about the complex and ongoing problem of the identification of gun-shot residue (GSR):

There is no consensus among the forensic laboratories regarding the number of particles needed to confirm the presence of GSR. The controversy among the experts on this question is still unresolved (*personal communication, 8th Firearms Working Group meeting, Brugge, Belgium, September 2001). There is much more agreement regarding the wording of reports when a lab decided that there is a positive result. In such a case the statement: — The sample is consistent with the suspect having discharged a firearm, having been in the vicinity of a firearm when it was discharged, or having handled an item with GSR on it* "resembles the phrasing of most of the labs (2). In any case, it is very important to compare the GSR compositions found on a suspect to the GSR compositions of the spent cartridge cases (if found) at the scene of crime as well as to the GSR compositions in the suspected firearm (if apprehended). Sometimes the evidential value of such comparisons may be much higher than the degree of — uniqueness" of the GSR particles found on the suspect, for instance, if the GSR particles found on a suspect are consistent with the GSR in the spent cartridge cases of a rare ammunition.[123]

XII. Suicide vs. Homicide

State v. Myszka[124] involved the murder of a woman whom police found dead in her bedroom as the result of a gunshot wound to her chest. A .32 Derringer pistol was removed from her left hand. The deceased was right-handed.

The state's ballistic firearm expert testified that he found no gunpowder residue on the shirt that the deceased wore at the time of her death. He further testified that he test-fired the gun and found that at 20 inches, gunpowder residue would be present on the garment, meaning that the gun had to be fired at a distance greater than 20 inches from the wound. Based on this, he concluded that this gunshot would have been inconsistent with the deceased shooting herself.

The medical examiner testified that it would be impossible for the gunshot wound on the deceased to have been self-inflicted, given the autopsy report on the deceased and the ballistics report. Dr. Bonita Peterson, who performed the autopsy, testified that, "with the left hand," a suicide "would" be "difficult and awkward" or "may not even be possible."[125]

The state's ballistic expert testified that because he found no gunpowder residue on the shirt the deceased was wearing at the time of her death, the gun had to have been fired at a distance greater than 20 inches from the wound. Dr. Peterson, who performed the autopsy, testified that the path of the bullet was at a very slight upward angle and at about a 20-degree angle to the left. She opined that it may not have been physically possible for the deceased to shoot herself with her left hand. She also testified that there was no sooting or tattooing in the deceased's gunshot wound, indicating that the gun was not close to and not in contact with the skin. Finally, the medical examiner testified that it would be impossible for the gunshot wound on the deceased to have been self-inflicted, because the ballistics report concluded that the gun had to have been fired more than 20 inches away and because of the wound track, angle, and characteristics reported by Dr. Peterson.[126] The court concluded that the killing was neither an accident nor a suicide, but a homicide:

> This is substantial evidence from which a jury could find that the death of the victim was not the result of an accident. Under the evidence at trial, a reasonable juror could find beyond a reasonable doubt that the appellant was guilty of second degree murder. The state provided ample evidence to prove the corpus delicti. The evidence showed the gunshot was not self-inflicted, and certainly not a natural event. Neither was any evidence offered to show that the gunshot was the result of an accident. This leaves one possibility: appellant shot the victim.[127]

Ballistics expertise, to a much lesser degree than firearms-related issues, involves the identification, class characteristics, and possible linking of a wide variety of tool marks observed and preserved at a crime scene.

XIII. Tool Marks

Tool-mark examination continues to be part of the forensic science corpus of disciplines used in criminal case investigations and trials. The idea encompasses striation marking made in wood, putty, and other media that must be forced to gain entry to property or, in rare cases, used to cause blunt trauma to an assault or homicide victim. It has been referred to as the breaking part of the breaking and entering common to a large number of crimes. Pry bars, screwdrivers, knives, pliers, crowbars, wire cutters, bolt cutters, and a host of other tools may leave striation marking in building media that can provide valuable trace evidence and possible identifications. Building materials, such as paint, brick, or glass also may attach to the tool and thereby provide a possibility of linkage.[128] Tool-mark matching is still far from confident, given the nature of the malleable medium that typically contains the mark. Nonetheless, recent decisions have had little difficulty accepting expert opinion based upon it.

In *People v. Genrich*,[129] defendant was convicted of use of explosives to commit a felony, third-degree assault, and two counts of extreme indifference homicide. The disputed evidence consisted of testimony from a BATF expert that three different sets of pliers recovered from defendant were used in making one or more of the bombs. According to this witness, one set of defendant's pliers was used to cut certain wire, the wire strippers were used to cut a different wire, and a third was used to fasten a cap to the pipe. The witness also testified that wires used in two of the bombs came from the same batch of wire.

Defendant, reciting the standard objections to nonscientific evidence, contended that the evidence was not based on a theory generally accepted in the scientific community, that no techniques in the examination were capable of producing reliable results, and that the prosecution's expert did not use tests that followed accepted scientific techniques. The prosecution offered to prove that tool-mark identification evidence had been accepted in a number of courts throughout the United States over an extended period of time and hence an evidentiary hearing was unnecessary.

Defendant noted that the BATF agent who served as the prosecution's expert did not have any post-high-school formal education, that no standard curriculum had been developed to train tool-mark examiners, and that no national certification program was available to confirm the knowledge and training of this type of expert. Defendant also pointed out that, unlike finger-print or ballistics testing, no data bank has been established relative to the various types of hand tools. In the instant case, defense counsel argued that the examination of only two consecutively manufactured tools was insufficient to support the expert's claim that every tool leaves a mark or marks different from every other tool.[130]

The court of appeal found no error in the trial court ruling, noting:

> ...that the record reflected that the basic premise for tool-mark analysis was that hand tools used either to cut or to clamp softer materials may leave a specific and essentially permanent type of mark on that material. The softer material is examined under a microscope that magnifies the marks to 80 times their original size. The handbook can then be examined to determine whether the marks were left by that specific tool.

According to this expert, no two tools make exactly the same mark on softer material either because of the manufacturing process or because of the subsequent use or misuse of the tool. In this regard, the witness stated that he had never encountered any research or other data indicating that any two hand tools of the same type can make the same mark.[131]

Legal research demonstrated that experts in the use and analysis of tools have traditionally and consistently been allowed to testify concerning the marks left by such instruments.[132] Hence, there was ample legal support for the trial court's conclusion that this type of evidence is accepted.

The court noted that neither a college degree nor formal training in an established curriculum was necessarily required before one may be considered an expert in a particular field. The absence of clear points of comparison or data banks relative to tool examination did not render the analysis inherently unreliable:

The critical factors are the marks, as magnified by the microscope, on the materials used in the bombs and similar test materials, and the examination of the cutting or clamping face of the tool itself... The expert's premise, that no two tools make exactly the same mark, is not challenged by any evidence in this record. Hence, the lack of a database and points of comparison does not render the opinion inadmissible.[133]

The court concluded that defendant's objections and arguments addressed the weight to be accorded the expert's opinion and that no pretrial evidentiary hearing was required.

The impact of modern forensics on the solution of old or cold files is demonstrated by a fascinating example in the case of State v. Parsons.[134] There, defendant was found guilty and sentenced for the 1981 murder of his wife,

Barbara Parsons. On the afternoon of February 11, 1981, Sherry Parsons discovered her mother's body lying at the foot of her parents' bed in their Norwalk home. Barbara Parsons had been beaten to death. The murder investigation quickly centered on appellant James Parsons, decedent's husband, when it was discovered that the Parsons were considering a divorce.

Norwalk police interviewed several persons associated with appellant including a mechanic who was employed at appellant's garage. The mechanic told police of an unusual statement appellant had made, where he announced that a "half-inch breaker bar" that had been missing from appellant's tool set had been left in a car he had sold to a friend two weeks earlier. Prosecutors labeled this statement as an attempt to establish an "alibi" for the murder weapon.

The detectives traced the car, recovered the bar and returned to Ohio, where it was examined. Criminalists, however, found no traces of blood or other material that might link the bar to the murder, and it was returned to Norwalk where it was stored in the police property room along with the bloodstained sheets, clothing, and other physical evidence taken from the crime scene. That evidence remained in storage for nearly a decade. During that time the case, although nominally still open, was not actively investigated by police.

In 1990, a new detective was assigned to review the case, who looked at the evidence collected in 1981, and believed that he saw a match of marks on the bloody sheets and the bar. The sheets and breaker bar were tested by the forensics experts at the Cuyahoga County Coroner's Office and the Ohio Bureau of Criminal Investigation (BCI). These experts testified that they found numerous impressions in blood on the sheets consistent with the breaker bar retrieved from Arizona in 1981. Importantly, the experts testified that none of the impressions were inconsistent with the breaker bar. The BCI expert testified that by chemically enhancing the bloodstains on the sheets, letters from the word "Craftsman" on the breaker bar could be seen and that the marks found in bloodstains on the nightgown Barbara Parsons was wearing matched "individuating" abnormalities unique to the breaker bar. This evidence gave clear support to the verdict against the husband:

> …from the ferocity of the attack on Barbara Parsons it can be reasonably inferred that whoever killed her intended to do so. The only real issue at trial was the identity of that actor. It was unquestioned that appellant owned a Craftsman half-inch breaker bar. There was expert forensic testimony that a specific Craftsman half-inch breaker bar left identifiable impressions in blood at the murder scene and that the shape and design of the bar was consistent with the wounds Barbara Parsons received. This specific

Craftsman breaker bar was found under the seat of a car appellant sold to Neil Burrass.[135]

At a bare minimum, the court concluded this was evidence by which reasonable minds could differ as to appellant's culpability.

In *State v. Hill*,[136] the defendant was convicted of aggravated murder. The coroner testified that the victim, defendant's mother, died as a result of ten stab wounds to her chest and back. Some were inflicted with "considerable force." One knife wound perforated the heart and nicked a lung; two others punctured a lung and broke ribs; and, another perforated the scapula or wing bone. No defensive-type wounds were evident. The victim, aged 61 years, had been partly paralyzed from a stroke. Defendant told detectives that around March 23 he had been driving in his mother's car and using cocaine, but denied any knowledge of his mother's death. Detectives talked with Jones and Vernon Hill, Hill's brother. Police further learned the defendant's mother never let either son drive her car without her being present. The police searched the victim's Oldsmobile and found a tire tool, two $20 bills, and two $1 bills in the trunk. One $1 bill was stained with type A blood, which was the victim's blood type. Microscopic examination of the tire tool revealed microscopic brass flakes matching the composition of a brass door protector on the victim's apartment door and the brass protector appeared to have "fresh jimmy marks." The black paint on that protector matched the painted tire tool.[137]

In *State v. Hayes*,[138] a 2002 Missouri case, the defendant was convicted of involuntary manslaughter and armed criminal action. The testimony of a forensic criminalist that the wounds on the defendant's forehead could have been self-inflicted was relevant to defendant's claim that he acted in self-defense after victim attacked him with a claw hammer. The state presented testimony that the victim was unarmed and struck defendant with his bare hands, that defendant retrieved a hammer from victim's work area after the shooting, and that defendant was not bleeding when witness first saw him after shooting.

The testimony of a criminalist with a specialty in toolmarks and wound analysis concluded that defendant's hammer wounds were self-inflicted. The witness Cayton had significant training and experience related to wounds caused to the human body by various objects, including hammers, and was a forensic criminalist who specialized in firearms and tool marks. Mr. Cayton testified that his expertise included examining tool marks on human beings, and that he was a member of the International Wound Ballistics Association, which studies wounds caused to the body by various objects. He further stated that he had studied the effects of various types of trauma to the body. Mr. Cayton testified that in the course of his work he had studied victims' wounds to compare with various objects that might have been used to inflict them.

He also testified that he had previously examined cases in which hammers had been used as weapons. The court readily approved his qualifications:

> Based upon the education and experience reflected in Mr. Cayton's curriculum vitae and his testimony, the trial court was well within its discretion to allow Mr. Cayton to testify about the nature of a hammer claw wound to the human body and to offer his opinion that the wounds on appellant's face were consistent with having been self-inflicted. Mr. Cayton's testimony involved his expert opinion as a criminalist and related to technical matters that exceed the ordinary experience of jurors. The trial court did not abuse its discretion in admitting that testimony.[139]

Mr. Cayton testified that appellant's facial injuries were consistent with having been caused by the claw hammer. He further testified that defendant had five different wounds from the hammer and that all of them were superficial and were caused by contact with only one of the two claws on the hammer. He also testified that the angle of the injuries indicated that they had come from defendant's right side and that the handle of the hammer would need to have been on the right of defendant. He testified that the wounds were consistent with defendant striking himself right-handed with the hammer; however, he acknowledged that the injuries were also consistent with someone else on defendant's right side having caused them.[140]

Totally unsupported tool-mark matching testimony was rejected in the 2003 Texas case of *Sexton v. State*,[141] where defendant was convicted of three counts of aggravated assault with a deadly weapon. On appeal, he argued the trial court erred in admitting the testimony of Ronald Crumley (a firearm and tool-mark expert with the Bexar County Forensic Science Center) that the nine-millimeter shell casings found at the scene were loaded into the same magazine as the live cartridges found in Sexton's bedroom, because the State failed to prove Crumley's testimony was reliable.

In its opening statement, the prosecution stated:

> Ronald Crumley, an expert forensic specialist, will testify and tell you that there is no doubt in his mind that the four shell casings found at the scene of the shooting ... and the 24 nine-millimeter live rounds found in this young man's bedroom were cycled through the exact same magazine. And that is how they got him, because without something else, even though they know he did it, they couldn't get him. So when they had that, they had the

defendant. He was in possession of bullets that went through the same exact magazine as the bullets that shot those kids that night and that is what the evidence is going to show you.[142]

Similarly, the state argued in closing:

You're left with this young man in possession of live shell casings of the exact same make, model, caliber as those found at the crime scene, you are left with live shell casings with the exact same tool markings on them as those found at the crime scene and you are looking at definitively, definitively, the bullets from the bedroom were cycled through the same magazine as the ones at the shooting.... And if that doesn't tend to connect somebody to a crime, I don't know what does. It does, and that is definitive.[143]

Because Crumley's testimony was unequivocal and because the state repeatedly emphasized its "definitive" nature, the court felt that it could not conclude that the error in admitting the challenged testimony was harmless. They accordingly reversed the trial court's judgment and remanded for a new trial.[144]

In *State v. Simerly*,[145] a 2004 Tennessee case, tool-mark expertise was accepted in a case about a prison murder involving homemade "shanks." A Tennessee Bureau of Investigation laboratory technician testified that he had been trained in the analysis of tool marks and that he had analyzed two of the shanks found in Northeast Correctional Center (NECC) following the victim's murder. He compared two shanks — the one from the defendant's cell and one of the other shanks recovered — with stab or gouge marks embedded in a fragment of the victim's skull, which had been provided by the medical examiner. The technician testified that the shank from the defendant's cell left impressions in a test surface made of lead that were very similar to the impressions found in the victim's bone fragment. The other shank tested made dissimilar marks.

XIV. Conclusion

The technology of gun manufacture has been fairly stable, allowing for considerable confidence by courts in ballistics testimony. This was noted in the Firearms Section of the 14th Interpol Forensic Science Review paper:

The main field of the ballistic expert's work is identifying firearms. The first stage involves classifying the firearm into firearm types: pistols, rifles, machine guns, etc. The next stage is to identify the subclass characteristics of these types, for example, identifying a semiautomatic gun with a CBP (Colt Browning Patent) mechanism such as Colt 1911 pistol. The final stage involves the absolute identification (individual characteristics) between a specific firearm and bullets and cartridge cases. The origin of these characteristics stems from the manufacturing processes and maintenance of the firearms.[146]

Approximately one-third of the papers in this literature scan describe identification issues. Many studies are case reports and technical notes regarding unique characteristics of firearms and their comparative value. Other studies involve different methods to calculate the minimum number of identification marks and their values in that process of positive comparison.

A ballistic expert's knowledge of technological developments regarding the production and manufacturing processes (such as lasers, CNC methods, and castings parts), as well as advances in material science (such as composite materials and polymers) is essential. The ability to identify and understand these new advancements is of critical importance to the firearms expert.

Endnotes

1. *Massachusetts v. Sacco and Vanzetti*: Closing Argument by the Commonwealth. Also see, Thorvald: *The Century of the Detective* (Harcourt, Brace and World, 1965) at 417 et. seq.; Starrs, Once More into the Breech: The Firearms Evidence In the Sacco and Vanzetti Case Revisited, 31 *J. Forensic Science* 630 (1986) [Part I]; 31 *J. Forensic Science* 1050 (1986) (Part II). See also, Frankfurter, The Case of Sacco and Vanzetti, *Atlantic Monthly* (March 1927).

2. See, James E. Hamby, The History of Firearm and Toolmark Identification, *Association of Firearm and Toolmark Examiners Journal*, 30th Anniversary edition, Vol. 31, No. 3 (Summer 1999), set out in full at http://www.firearmsID. com/A_historyoffirearmsID.htm. Also see, Thorvald: *The Century of the Detective* (Harcourt, Brace and World, 1965) at 417 et. seq.

3. 14th Interpol Forensic Science Symposium, Lyon, November 2004, *Firearms and Ballistics Report*, Prepared by: Gil Hocherman, M.Sc., Superintendent Arie Zeichner, Ph.D., Commander Tzipi Kahana, Ph.D., Superintendent. Approved by: Elazar (Azi) Zadok, Ph.D., Brig. General, DIFS Director Israel Police Investigation Department Division of Identification & Forensic Science (DIFS) National Police. Available for complimentary download at http://www.interpol.org/forensic.

4. *Interpol Firearms Report*, supra, at 50.

5. Id.

6. The 2004 *Interpol Firearms Report* has an extensive bibliography of 227 references from 2001to 2004, subdivided into the categories of Firearms-Ballistics (157), Firearms-Chemistry (44) and Firearms-Wound Ballistics (26).

7. See *State v. Stewart*, 643 N.W.2d 281 (Minn.2002). This is the leading case on this subject.

8. Citing Zeichner, A., Recent developments in methods of chemical analysis in investigations of firearm-related events. *Anal. Bional. Chem.* 2003;376:1178–1191; Romolo, S.R., Margot, P., Identification of gunshot residue: a critical review. *J. Forensic. Sci.* 2001; 119:195–211.

9. Ballistics and fingerprints are the only two of the forensic sciences where an opinion of a true or absolute match is allowed. Nonetheless, the recent spate of statutory post-conviction opportunities for new forensic testing does not appear to apply to ballistics testing. See, *People v. Pursley*, 792 N.E.2d 378 (Ill.App. 2003). (Statute allowing defendants to file a post-conviction motion for fingerprint or forensic DNA testing not available at trial did not apply to ballistics testing under Integrated Ballistics Identification Systems [IBIS], because the legislature had not broadened the scope of statute to include different forms of forensic testing, other than fingerprint and DNA testing. I. S.H.A. *725 ILCS 5/116-3.*)

10. The Dialog Information Services massive collection of bibliographic and full-text databases, accessible through Westlaw, provides a window for incredibly detailed information queries into the biotech, manufacturing, and chemical industries and research centers.

11. Generally, see, Saferstein: *Criminalistics: An Introduction to Forensic Science* (Prentice Hall, 6th ed., 1998, pp. 466–492; Giannelli and Imwinkelried: *Scientific Evidence* (The Michie Co., 2d ed., 1993), at pp. 374, and 375–408; Fischer: *Techniques of Crime Scene Investigation* (CRC Press, 5th ed., 1993), at 272-303; Geberth: *Practical Homicide Investigation: Tactics, Procedures, Techniques* (CRC Press, 3d ed., 1996) pp. 283–291, 513–517. Also see, Sprangers, Leuvan, Walinga, Beijer, and Dofferhoff, Firearms Evidence, *Proceedings of the 12th Interpol Forensic Science Symposium*, October 2–23, 1998 (The Forensic Sciences Foundation Press, 1998), pp136–151 for a very extensive international bibliography of literature published between July 1995 and May 1998.

12. Id.

13. See, Saferstein: *Criminalistics*, supra, at 466474; Giannelli and Imwinkelried, supra, at 378–382. For more recent general Internet-based discussions, see, *F.B.I. Handbook of Forensic Services: Firearms Examinations*, at http://www.fbi.gov/lab/handbook/examfire.htm. Also see, the excellent Web page maintained by Jeffrey Scott Doyle, a Kentucky State Police firearm and tool-mark examiner located at http://www.firearms ID.com. This is a first-rate example of the potential for forensic science on the Internet, containing large amounts of information and excellent graphics. Also see, the Firearm Image Library,

a large collection of images of weapons with basic descriptions of weapon configurations and ammunition, located at http://www.recguns.com.

14. See Giannelli & Imwinkelried, supra at 380. The authors of the recent interpol study of ballistics research note the recent publication of a large number of world studies on wound ballistics. See, Sprangers, Leuvan, Walinga, Beijer, and Dofferhoff, *Firearms Evidence, Proceedings of the 12th Interpol Forensic Science Symposium*, October 2–23, 1998 (The Forensic Sciences Foundation Press, 1998), at 138.

15. The historical types of gunshot residue test include: paraffin testing, Harrison-Gilroy Neutron Activator Analysis (NAA), ASV, SEM, and trace metal detection technique (TNDT) for metal traces. These tests attempt to determine if the defendant shot a gun or was present and if the shooting was a suicide or a homicide. See, Saferstein: *Criminalistics: An Introduction to Forensic Science*, supra, at 478; Giannelli and Imwinkelried, supra, at 394 et. seq.; *Proceedings of the 12th Interpol Forensic Science Symposium*, October 2–23, 1998, supra, at 136; Fisher: *Techniques of Crime Scene Investigation*, supra, at 167–168, 277280; Geberth: Practical Homicide Investigation, supra, at 199–201.

16. See, e.g., *State v. McLean*, 2004 WL 2185936 (Tenn. Crim. App. 2004) for an example of routine shell-casing analysis. In addition to striation analyses, the case notes that often, fingerprints on a casing can be rendered unusable due to heat.

17. Robert W. Sibert, DRUGFIRE: Revolutionizing Forensic Firearms Identification and Providing the Foundation for a National Firearms Identification Network, Federal Bureau of Investigation (April, 1996). Also see, definitions and Guidelines for the Use of Imaging Technologies in the Criminal Justice System, Scientific Working Group on Imaging Technologies (SWGIT), located on the FBI Web site at: http://www.fbi.gov/programs/lab/fsc/current/swgit1.htm. Also see, Sally A. Schehl, Firearms and Toolmarks in the FBI Laboratory (Part 2), *Forensic Science Communications*, April 2000; Volume 2, Number 2.

18. See, Lena Klasen, *Image Analysis, Proceedings of the 12th Interpol Forensic Science Symposium* (October 20–23, 1998) at 261. This is an excellent paper setting forth the history and current status of the equipment, software, and related topics in this technology of the 21st century criminal investigator. Also See, Braga, A.A., Pierce, G.L., *Linking crime guns: the impact of ballistics imaging technology on the productivity of the Boston Police Departments's Ballistics Unit, JFS*, Vol. 49, No. 4 (2004), pages 1–6:

Abstract by authors: Ballistics imaging technology has received national attention as a potent tool for moving the law enforcement response to violent gun criminals forward by linking multiple crime scenes to one firearm. This study examines the impact of ballistics imaging technology on the productivity of the Boston Police Department's Ballistics Unit. Using negative binomial regression models to analyze times series data on ballistics matches, we find that ballistics imaging technology was associated with a more than sixfold increase in the monthly number of ballistics matches made by the Boston Police Department's Ballistics Unit. Cost-effectiveness estimates and qualitative evidence also suggest that ballistics imaging technology allows law enforcement agencies to make hits that would not have been possible using traditional ballistics methods.

19. See, De-Kinder, J.; *Ballistic Fingerprinting Databases*; SCI-JUST; 2002; V42 (4); P197–203; Geradts, Z.; Bijhold, J.; *Content-Based Information Retrieval in Forensic Image Databases*; *J. Forensic Sci*; 2002; V47 (2); P285–292; Giverts, P.; Springer, E.; *IBIS and the 5.56 NATO Cartridge Case Fired from an M-16*, AFTE; 2003; V35 (2); P190–194; Argaman, U.; Shoshani, E.; Hocherman, G.; *Utilisation of the IBIS in Israel*, AFTE; 2001; V33 (3); P269–272; Francisco Javier Zanz, Nacional de Policia, Spain; IBIS in the Spanish Police 2000–2004, International forensic technology symposium, Rome, Italy, 4–5 May 2004; Miguel Oscar Aguilar, Mexico; *Integrating IBIS into the PGR laboratory workflow*; International Forensic Technology Symposium, Rome, Italy, 4–5 May 2004; Geradts, Z.J.; Bijhold, J.; Hermsen, R.; Murtagh, F.; *Image Matching Algorithms for Breech Face Marks and Firing Pins in a Database of Spent Cartridge Cases of Firearms*; Forensic-Sci-Int; 2001; V119 (1); June; P97–106.

20. See http://www.atf.gov/nibin/index.htm, for a complete profile of the National Integrated Ballistics Information Network (NIBIN) system and its relation to DRUGFIRE.

21. Ma, L., Song, J., Whitenton, E., Vorburger, T., Zhou, J., Zheng, A., *NIST bullet signature measurement system for RM (reference material) 8240 standard bullets*, JFS, Vol. 49, NO. 4, pages 1–11 (2004).

Abstract by authors: A bullet signature-measurement system based on a stylus instrument was developed at the National Institute of Standards and Technology (NIST) for the signature measurements of NIST RM (Reference Material) 8240 standard bullets. The standard bullets are developed as a reference standard for bullet signature measurements and are aimed to support the recently established NIBIN by the Bureau of Alcohol, Tobacco, and Firearms (ATF) and the Federal Bureau of Investigation (FBI).

22. Sibert, supra, note 9, at 2. DRUGFIRE's emphasis has been on the comparison of cartridge case imagery, rather than bullet imagery. Nevertheless, images of highly characteristic bullet striations can be stored in the DRUGFIRE system as supplemental images and compared. DRUGFIRE represents a major technological advancement in the discipline of forensic firearms identification. The same computer hardware that runs DRUGFIRE can be used to store an image database of firearm and ammunition exemplars from the FBI Laboratory's Reference Firearms Collection and Standard Ammunition File. This collection is the largest and most comprehensive in the world. Id.

23. See, e.g., Sprangers, Leuvan, Walinga, Beijer and Dofferhoff, *Firearms Evidence*, *Proceedings of the 12th Interpol Forensic Science Symposium*, October 2–23, 1998 (The Forensic Sciences Foundation Press, 1998), at 138. Also see, 2004 Ballistics Report, 14th Interpol Forensic Science Symposium Review

Paper, Firearms: A review, supra, at 47. For a broad discussion of imaging systems in the investigation of crime, see the 2004 Forensic Imaging Section of the 14th Symposium noted earlier.

24. Id.

25. For a complete listing of gun manufacturer Web sites, see, http://www. firearmscanada.com/gunmanufacturers.html.

26. Interpol Firearms Report, supra, n. 3, at 59. Also see the Association of Firearm and Toolmark Examiners (AFTE) Website. AFTE is the professional organization for those in the forensic ballistics field. This Website contains news, bulletins, and an important collection of links on the subjects of ammunition manufacturers and distributors, firearm manufacturers and distributors, forensic and ballistics links, and forensic and professional organizations and links to a wide variety of government agencies or offices, such as the ATF laboratory. This site may be accessed at www.afte.org/.

27. 755 N.E.2d 1070 (Sp. Ct. Ind. 2001).

28. Ibid. at 1077.

29. However, see In re Petition of Louis Vazquez, v. Howard Safir, 673 N.Y.S.2d 12 (N.Y.A.D. 1 Dept. 1998), where a proceeding was brought by police officer challenging his dismissal from police department, in that the officer, while off duty, discharged multiple rounds from a gun he owned, other than his service weapon, and thereafter failed to promptly report incident, and then made false and misleading statements concerning the incident. While ballistics evidence established that many of the shell casings found at the scene were fired from the gun in question, other ballistics evidence stated that there was no indication of discharge present in the bore of the gun in question. The testimony and reports of investigators concerning their interviews of witnesses either supporting or not inconsistent with petitioner's claim that he did not fire his gun, raised issues of weight of the evidence and credibility that were beyond judicial review in such proceedings.

30. Hicks, at 524.

31. See, State v. Fulminante, 193 Ariz. 485, 975 P.2d 75 (1999).

32. 389 F.3d 514 (5th Cir. Ct. App. 2004).

33. Daubert v. Merrell Dow Pharmaceuticals, Inc., 509 U.S. 579, 113 S.Ct. 2786, 125 L.Ed.2d 469 (1993).

34. Ibid. at 524.

35. Hicks, at 525.

36. 726 So.2d 1152 (Miss. Sp.Ct. 1998). (Overruled on polygraph issue)

37. Id. at 1181. The same level of acceptance of fingerprint identifications has resulted in modern cases increasingly discussing the failure to look for fingerprints by the police in areas where they would have been expected to be found, as inuring to the benefit of the defendant when challenging the state's crime scene investigation.

38. 793 So.2d 485 (La. App. 2001).

39. Ibid. at 490.

40. 708 N.E.2d 1 (Ind. Sp.Ct. 1999).

41. Id. at 3.

42. Id.

43. 273 Ill.App.3d 798, 652 N.E.2d 1045 (1st Dist. App. 1995).

44. Id.at 809.

45. See, *People v. Lee*, 242 Ill.App.3d 40, 42–43, 610 N.E.2d 727 (1993).

46. *People v. Askew* at 810.

47. 251 A.D.2d 433, 674 N.Y.S.2d 114 (1998).

48. Id.at 435.

49. 299 Ill.App.3d 323, 702 N.E.2d 590 (1998).

50. Id.at 593, 253.

51. Id. Also see, *Commonwealth v. Dennis*, 715 A.2d 404 (1998), where the commonwealth presented the testimony of three eyewitnesses, as well as evidence that defendant *had a gun of the type used* in the murder and clothing resembling that worn by the perpetrator. Although the murder weapon was never recovered, a ballistics expert testified that there was a ninety-nine percent (99%) chance that the bullet that killed the victim was fired from a Harrington and Richardson handgun.

52. 427 Mass. 26, 691 N.E.2d 218 (Sp. Ct 1998).

53. 577 N.W.2d 387 (1998).

54. 552 Pa. 499, 716 A.2d 580 (1998).

55. See *State v. Stewart*, 643 N.W.2d 281 (Minn 2002). This is the leading case on this subject. There are a growing number of law review and professional articles on this topic. See, e.g., Godden, Cartoon Criminals: The Unclear Future of Computer Animation in the Minnesota Criminal Courtroom — *State v. Stewart*, 30 *Wm. Mitchell L. Rev.* 355 (2003).

56. 643 N.W.2d 281(Minn. 2002).

57. Ibid. at 295. The Stewart case contains lengthy and valuable discussions of the many foundation factors required prerequisite to the attempt to introduce an animated film to provide a three-dimensional view of angle of shoot or other crime scene dynamic. It is well worth consulting on the recent important issue of computer-generated animation of crime scenes.

58. 2004 WL 249635 (Cal. App. 2004).

59. See also, *People v. Basden*, 264 Ill.App.3d 530 (Ill.App. 1994); *People v. Jefferson*, 260 Ill.App.3d 895 (Ill.App. 1 Dist. 1994) (Condition of bullets belied ricochet claims.).

60. 17 Cal. Rptr. 3d 604, 95 P. 3d 872 (2004).

61. 43 P.3d 663 (Colo. App. 2001) Also see, *United States v. Pierson*, 503 F.2d 173 (D.C.Cir.1974) (a layman, under certain circumstances, can look at a bullet hole in a wall and see whether it appears to come from one direction or another; no special expertise is required). Here, the witness did not conduct any experiments or attempt to reconstruct the incident. Rather, he testified about the location of the bullet holes and the paths of the bullets that were evident from the photographs without any additional explanation. Thus, the witness was not conveying information that required a specialized or scientific knowledge to understand.

62. 709 So.2d 512 (1998).

63. Id. at 516.

64. 91 Wash.App. 1019 (1998).

65. 1998 WL 293758, at *1.

66. Ibid. at *3.

67. 269 Ill.App.3d 339, 645 N.E.2d 1018(1995).

68. Id. at 345.

69. The defendant claimed that the weapon he fired was the one found by Officer Kaminski in his room. Prosecutors countered that the gun was found fully loaded and there was no opportunity for the defendant to have reloaded the weapon between the time of the shooting and when the officer found it. Consequently, prosecutors said, that gun could not have been the one the defendant fired. Rather, the prosecution opined, the "fatal" gun may have still been on the defendant's person when he brushed past the officer who searched his room, and he may have disposed of it outside during the commotion and milling about that went on after his room was searched, but prior to his arrest.

70. *Torres*, at 347, 1024.

71. *Torres*, at 348.

72. 269 Ga. 470, 500 S.E.2d 329 (1998).

73. Id.

74. 193 Ariz. 485, 975 P.2d 75 (1999).

75. Id. at 80, 490. In *Fulminante II*, the United States Supreme Court held that defendant's confession was coerced. The court found the admission prejudicial, in part, because both the trial court and the state recognized that a successful prosecution depended on the jury believing the two confessions. Absent the confessions, the court determined, it was unlikely that Fulminante would have been prosecuted at all, because the physical evidence from the scene and the other circumstantial evidence would have been insufficient to convict.

76. *Fulminante*, at 83, 493.

77. Id.

78. Id.

79. 103 F.3d 660 (8th Cir 1996).

80. Id. at 666.

81. Id. at 673.

82. Id. at 674.

83. Id.

84. 157 N.J. 141, 723 A.2d 602 (1999).

85. Id. at 145, 604.

86. IAP analysis of lead bullets is a process generally accepted by the scientific community and producing sufficiently reliable results to warrant the admission of expert testimony regarding the test and the test results. See, e.g., *Bryan v. Oklahoma*, 935 P.2d 338 (Okla.Crim.App.1997); *U.S. v. Davis*, 103 F.3d 660 (8th Cir.1996), cert. denied, — U.S. —, 117 S.Ct. 2424, 138 L.Ed.2d 187 (1997); *State v. Freeman*, 531 N.W.2d 190 (Minn.1995); *State v. Strain*, 885 P.2d 810 (Utah.Ct.App.1994); *State v. Grube*, 126 Idaho 377, 883 P.2d 1069 (1994), cert. denied, 514 U.S. 1098, 115 S.Ct. 1828, 131 L. Ed.2d 749 (1995); *People v. Johnson*, 114 Ill.2d 170, 102 Ill.Dec. 342, 499 N.E.2d 1355 (1986), cert. denied, 480 U.S. 951, 107 S.Ct. 1618, 94 L. Ed.2d 802, reh'g denied, 481 U.S. 1060, 107 S.Ct. 2205, 95 L. Ed.2d 860 (1987); *State v. Ware*, 338 N.W.2d 707 (Iowa 1983); *Jones v. State*, 425 N.E.2d 128 (Ind.1981) (Hunter, J. dissenting). See also Erwin S. Barbre, *Annotation, Admissibility of Evidence of Neutron Activation Analysis*, 50 A.L.R.3d 117 (1973) and supplemental service.

87. Id.at 162.

88. Id. at 604. See, *State v. Koedatich*, 112 N.J. 225, 548 A.2d 939 (1988); *State v. Hollander*, 201 N.J.Super. 453, 467–68, 493 A.2d 563 (App.Div.1985).

89. Id. at 150. See, *Hake v. Township of Manchester*, 98 N.J. 302, 316, 486 A.2d 836 (1985); *Landrigan v. Celotex Corp.*, 127 N.J. 404, 421–22, 605 A.2d 1079 (1992) (permitting epidemiologist to testify that asbestos can cause colon cancer); *Rubanick v. Witco Chemical Corp.*, 125 N.J. 421, 426, 452, 593 A.2d 733 (1991) (allowing biochemist to testify that PCBs can cause colon cancer).

90. Id. at 607, 152.

91. 2004 WL 2623926 (Sp. Ct. KY 2004).

92. Ibid. at *1.

93. Ibid. at *10.

94. There was evidence that 1,418 .243-caliber Wetherby Vanguard rifles were manufactured during the period 1986–2000. The police were able to locate three more of those rifles. Ballistics testing of those three rifles revealed that none could have fired the bullet that killed the victim. The court found that this evidence was relevant to dispel a possible claim that any .243-caliber Wetherby Vanguard rifle would have left the same markings on the murder bullet. Evidence demonstrating that other rifles of the same caliber manufactured by the same manufacturer caused different markings on test-fired bullets enhanced the relevancy of the evidence that markings on bullets test-

fired from the Ragland rifle were similar to the markings found on the murder bullet. In other words, it provided additional circumstantial evidence that the Ragland rifle fired the fatal shot.

95. *See, Robert D. Koons,*[1] *Ph.D. and Diana M. Grant,*[2] *Ph.D., Compositional Variation in Bullet Lead Manufacture, J Forensic Sci,* Sept. 2002, Vol. 47, No. 5 :

Abstract: The concentrations of antimony, copper, tin, arsenic, silver, bismuth, and cadmium in lead alloys produced by two smelters and one ammunition manufacturer were determined using inductively coupled plasma-atomic emission spectrometry. These element concentrations were used to measure the variations in composition of lead products that result from various processes involved in the manufacture of lead projectiles. In general, when a pot containing molten lead is used to cast a number of objects, these objects are similar, although not necessarily analytically indistinguishable in their elemental compositions. In each subsequent step in the processing of lead at the smelter and at the ammunition manufacturer, the size of an individual homogeneous melt of lead decreases as more distinct compositions are formed as a result of remelting and mixing of sources, including lead scrap. The ammunition manufacturer in this study produced at least 10 compositionally distinguishable groups of bullet wire in a 19.7-h period. The largest group could potentially be used to produce a maximum of 1.3 million compositionally indistinguishable 40 grain bullets.

96. Ragland at *10–11.

97. Ibid at *11.

98. Ragland at *12.

99. Id.

100. Id.

101. See, e.g., *United States v. Davis, 103 F.3d 660, 673-74 (8th Cir.1996); Commonwealth v. Daye, 411 Mass. 719, 587 N.E.2d 194, 207 (1992); State v. Noel, 157 N.J. 141, 723 A.2d 602, 605–06 (1999); State v. Krummacher, 269 Or. 125, 523 P.2d 1009, 1017 (1974).*

102. Ragland at 12. Also see, *Bramblett v. Commonwealth,* 257 Va. 263513 S.E.2d 400 (2001) [Murder of two adults and two children]. Forensic scientist analyzed the chemical composition of the bullets recovered. He testified that two of the bullets retrieved from the victims had the identical composition as a bullet found in the storage room. A cartridge found on steps in the home was "analytically indistinguishable" from a cartridge found in defendant's truck.

103. See, Koons, R.D., Grant, D.M., Compositional variation in bullet lead manufacture, 47 (5) J. Forens. Sci. (2002), at 950–958.

Abstract: The concentrations of antimony, copper, tin, arsenic, silver, bismuth, and cadmium in lead alloys produced by two smelters and one ammunition manufacturer were determined using inductively coupled plasma-atomic emission spectrometry. These element concentrations were used to measure the variations in composition of lead products that result from various processes involved in the manufacture of lead projectiles. In general, when a pot containing molten lead is used to cast a number of objects, these objects are similar, although not necessarily analytically indistinguishable in their elemental compositions. In each subsequent step in the processing of lead at the smelter and at the ammunition manufacturer, the size of an individual homogeneous melt of lead decreases as more distinct compositions are formed as a result of remelting and mixing of sources, including lead scrap. The ammunition manufacturer in this study produced at least 10 compositionally distinguishable groups of bullet wire in a 19.7-h period. The largest group could potentially be used to produce a maximum of 1.3 million compositionally indistinguishable 40 grain bullets.

104. 746 So.2d 364 (Ala.Crim.App.,1999).

105. 724 A.2d 916 (Sp.Ct.Penn. 1999).

106. Id. at 925.

107. 50 S.W.3d 290 (Mo.App. 2001).

108. 14th Interpol Forensic Science Symposium, Lyon, France, November 2004, Firearms and Ballistics Report, Prepared by: Gil Hocherman, M.Sc., Superintendent Arie Zeichner, Ph.D., Commander Tzipi Kahana, Ph.D., Superintendent. Approved by: Elazar (Azi) Zadok, Ph.D., Brig. General, DIFS Director Israel Police Investigation Department Division of Identification & Forensic Science (DIFS) National Police. Available for complimentary download at http://www.interpol.org/forensic.

109. 803 So. 2d 710 (Miss 2002).

110. Ibid. at *712.

111. Ibid. at *714.

112. Simmons at *714-715.

113. 347 Ill. App. 2d 909, 807 N.E. 2d 1125 (2004).

114. In spite of this, the court noted, defense counsel did not seek a continuance because he did not wish to break his four-term trial demand.

115. Young, at 915-916.

116. Young, at 1131, 290.

117. Defendant also argued that the gunshot wounds were consistent with the claim of self-defense. Dr. Lifschultz found that one of the bullets entered at the left side of Sturghill's back and exited at the right side of the belly, traveling at a downward angle. Young claims this is consistent with his testimony that he shot Sturghill as Sturghill started to turn back toward him. In light of all of the physical and scientific evidence, defendant claimed he was justified in shooting Sturghill.

118. Young at 929.

119. See, Sprangers, Leuvan, Walinga, Beijer and Dofferhoff, *Firearms Evidence, Proceedings of the 12th Interpol Forensic Science Symposium*, October 2–23, 1998 (The Forensic Sciences Foundation Press, 1998), pp. 136–137.

120. Id.

121. 14th Interpol Forensic Science Symposium, *Firearms Report*, at 54.

122. 963 S.W.2d 19 (Mo. App 1998).

123. Id. at 22.

124. Id.

125. Id. at 24.

126. See, Fisher: *Techniques of Crime Scene Investigation* (5th ed., CRC Press, 1993), at 173–178; Saferstein: *Criminalistics: an Introduction to Forensic Science* (Prentice Hall, 6th ed. 1998). Also see, Christophe Champod, Pierre A. Margot, *Fingermarks, Shoesole Impressions, Ear Impressions and Toolmarks, Proceedings of the 12th Interpol Forensic Science Symposium* (The Forensic Sciences Foundation Press, 1998), at 303, 313.

127. 928 P.2d 799 (Colo. Ct. App. 1996).

128. Id. at 801.

129. Id. at 802.

130. See, e.g., *State v. Baldwin*, 36 An. 1, 12 P. 318 (1886)(experienced carpenters permitted to testify that wood panel could have been cut by defendant's knife); See A. Moenssens & F. Inbau, *Scientific Evidence in Criminal Cases* s 4.24 (2d ed.1978). Also, this testimony has addressed a number of different types of tools. See *State v. Olsen*, 212 Or. 191, 317 P.2d 938 (1957)(hammers); *State v. Raines*, 29 N.C.App. 303, 224 S.E.2d 232 (1976)(crowbar); *State v. Wessling*, 260 Iowa 1244, 150 N.W.2d 301 (1967)(screwdriver); *State v. Churchill*, 231 An. 408, 646 P.2d 1049 (1982)(knives).

131. Genrich, at 802.

132. 1995 WL 29526 (Ohio App. 6 Dist.).

133. Id.at *8.

134. 73 Ohio St.3d 433, 653 N.E.2d 271(1995).

135. Id.at 275.

136. 88 S.W.3d 47 (Mo.App. W.D., 2002).

137. Ibid. at 63.

138. Hayes at 63. The court also rejected defendant's argument that Mr. Cayton's testimony regarding the nature of hammer-claw wounds on a human being and the angle at which the wounds would have needed to be inflicted clearly fell within the common experience of the jury:

Mr. Cayton opined that, based upon the nature of the injuries, the characteristics of the injuries from the hammer claws, and the angle at which the wounds were inflicted, appellant's injuries could have been self-inflicted. This testimony could have provided assistance to the jury in determining whether the decedent attacked appellant with the hammer.

139. 2003 WL 21800084 (Tex.App. 2003).

140. Sexton at *2.

141. Id.

142. But see, *People v. Draheim*, 2004 WL 385371 (Mich. App. 2004) where defendant was convicted of second-degree murder. The common feature of an earlier 1990 incident and the murder at issue were the use of flex cuffs. Here, flex cuffs bound the victim's wrists. A search of defendant's vehicle shortly after the earlier attempted kidnapping revealed that he had objects strongly resembling flex cuffs in his possession. There was evidence from three witnesses linking defendant with flex cuffs, including the testimony of two women who had been restrained by defendant with flex cuffs. Testimony from a Michigan State Police tool marks expert put defendant in possession of a flex cuff that was made "within a thousand" of the flex cuff found on the murder victim's body.

143. 2004 WL 443294 (Tenn. App. 2004).

144. Ibid. at *8.

145. 14th Interpol Forensic Science Symposium Review at 49–50.

Soil, Glass, and Paint

6

...The truth is, the Science of Nature has been already too long made only a work of the Brain and the Fancy: It is now high time that it should return to the plainess and soundness of Observations on material and obvious things...

Robert Hooke: Micrographia (1664)

I. Glass, Paint, and Soil in the Courtroom

Forensic science aims to provide both general and individual linking evidence for use in cases involving laboratory analysis of glass shards, paint, or soil connected to a crime scene. The microscopic examination of these items, found at many crime scenes, is, like others discussed so far, basically an observational discipline, but much more involved with chemical analyses than hair, fiber, or ballistics or tool-mark examinations.[1]

II. Glass Analysis

The subject of glass as forensic evidence typically involves crushed glass, glass shards or portions of a glass pane, present at the crime scene, as the result of an illegal entry or some type of violence causing the glass to disintegrate in some form. As with all of the forensic sciences, glass analysis can offer a wealth of class-characteristic as well as individual linkage evidence. Also as in the majority of the forensic sciences, this information is used to place the defendant at the crime scene or somewhere connected to it, so that the suspect can be charged and convicted.

The class characteristic data that may result from a close chemical and microscopic analysis includes determining the type of glass involved. What kind of glass is it? What is its source? What is there to compare to glass associated with defendant? Does the condition of the glass located at the scene indicate how or if a transfer of glass shards or spray could have been transferred to a suspect, such as shoes, clothing, or automobile carpeting?[2]

The many types of glass that may be generally identified with great precision are:

- Window glass
- Plate glass
- Safety glass
- Automobile window safety glass
- Automobile headlamp glass
- Tinted glass of all types
- Eye glasses glass (prescription, if big enough shards)
- Bottle glass
- Antique glass
- Architectural glass (shower stalls)
- Glass beads
- Pyrex and other cooking glass
- Clay, fired surfaces plates, dishes, etc.
- Crystal

Class characteristic information that can often be made with confidence includes the kind of glass it is; to a degree, the nature of the impacting projectile; the direction of impact (in or out); type of glass cutters; and comparisons for potential jigsaw matching of shards. Microscopic presence of glass is ubiquitous in modern urban life. Tiny glass particles are commonly found on shoe soles and clothing. Giannelli and Imwinkelried cite studies indicating that 67 of 100 men's suits examined at a dry cleaners contained glass fragments.[3] Given the extensive presence of glass particles picked up in our daily transit, it is especially important to be able to discriminate among the various types of glass products before any attempt is made to effect a suspect's link to a crime scene. The greatest amount of manufactured glass in the United States has a soda-lime base, and the nature of the glass components, visually and chemically, will differ with the proposed commercial or artistic use.[4]

As with all forensic sciences, a comparison is typically made of whatever there is to compare, of crime scene material and similar material associated with a suspect, to obtain a match. As noted throughout this book, a clear distinction must be continuously made between what forensic scientists see as a laboratory match and what the courts will allow to be said about any such finding. Here, as in the other forensic sciences, with the possible exception of fingerprints and DNA, the opinion, in court, must be couched in the language of consistent with, not dissimilar, etc.

Comparison of crime scene datum with that found to be associated with the suspect is the central idea of forensic evidence. Given the extraordinary length of the DNA testimony in the O. J. Simpson murder trial, remember that the sole purpose of the testimony was to get him at the crime scene. Like hair and fiber and ballistics and tool marks, we need to inquire initially as to what comparisons can be made here? Glass, paint, and soil can equally be broken down into component parts that may yield worthwhile comparisons going toward legally significant linkage testimony. Again, no definitive databases with which to determine the frequency of any stated "match" occurring in the general population exists, the same as in most other forensic disciplines. However, due to the considerable commercial attention to proprietary differences in the world glass industry and the consistent collection of glass data by the FBI progress is being made in that respect.[5]

Most commonly used comparison analyses utilize a combination of physical and chemical properties, such as refraction indices, dispersion staining, density, chemical components, mineral content, and color. As recently noted in:

> Recent advances in analytical capabilities for the trace element characterization of glass fragments have provided a high degree of discrimination between glass fragments that was previously not available with the physical property comparisons. There has been considerable interest in the probability of transfer of glass fragments and their retention on the clothing of a suspect of glass breaking.[6]

The increased cooperation with the glass industry and its significant proprietary databases, as with fiber, tire tracks, and shoe impressions, will enable rapid strides in the establishment of meaningful databases with which to engage in population percentage projection about proffered match opinions.[7]

The National Glass Association (NGA) Web site provides extensive information and education on the subjects of promoting safety and ethics in the flat glass and glass-related industries in the Americas. NGA publishes three magazines filled with very useful and current information, accessible from their Web site. The magazines are *Glass Magazine, Window and Door,* and *Auto Glass.*[8]

The scientific literature on the forensic utilization of glass technology is substantial and varied.[9]

III. Glass in the Courtroom

A typical use of forensic glass technology is seen in the 2004 Illinois case of *State v. Ceja*,[10] where the defendant was convicted of the first-degree murder of two individuals and unlawful possession of a motor vehicle. Because of its extensive discussion of the routine steps used in current forensic practice, it is described in detail here. The case involved a carjacking and crash that left significant glass debris on the carjacking and later crash site.

Defendant claimed that he was denied a fair trial because of the state's glass comparison evidence, which connected glass found in the defendant's shoe to glass from the automobile involved in the crime. First, he argued that the state's expert witness's opinion lacked a reasonable scientific basis for his opinion. The court noted that defendant did not object to the expert's testimony about the refractive index of the glass or the frequency of occurrence of the refractive index of glass. Instead, he argued that the expert should not have been allowed to testify that there was a "good probability" that the glass from the shoe came from the automobile.

The court found that defendant's argument on appeal that the state expert's opinion, based on a glass sample database, that there was a "good probability" that the glass from defendant's shoe came from the stolen vehicle, had no reasonably valid scientific basis, and should not have been allowed into evidence in prosecution for first-degree murder, was waived, where defendant neither objected to the testimony nor included the issue in his post-trial motion.

Alfred Luckas was a forensic scientist employed by the Du Page County sheriff's crime laboratory. He received a sample of tempered glass fragments from the broken window of the stolen Chevy Tahoe and a sample of tempered glass fragments recovered from the intersection of Grand and Oak Lawn Avenues. His analysis could not distinguish between the two samples. He determined that there was an "association" between the samples, meaning that they could have originated from the same source. Further, after referring to an Illinois State Police Crime Laboratory database of glass samples, Luckas opined that there was a "good probability of common origin" between the glass from the Tahoe window and the glass found at the intersection of Grand and Oak Lawn Avenues.[11]

Luckas also removed glass fragments from the shoes of defendant and Soto. Based on his analysis, Luckas concluded that the glass taken from those shoes and the glass from the Tahoe window "could have originated from the same source." Referring again to the Illinois State Police Crime Laboratory database, Luckas opined that there was a "good probability of common origin" between the glass from the Tahoe and the glass from the shoes of defendant and Soto.

Defendant challenges Luckas' opinion that there was a "good probability" that the glass fragment from defendant's shoe came from the broken window of the Tahoe.

Luckas explained that he analyzed four glass samples. One came from the broken window of the Tahoe; one came from the intersection of Grand and Oak Lawn Avenues. Luckas removed the other two samples from the shoes of defendant and Soto. Luckas compared the glass from defendant's shoe with glass from the Tahoe. Because the sample from defendant's shoe was so small — the size of a pinhead — Luckas was unable to make a visual comparison. Neither could he compare the two samples as to type, thickness, or density.

The only method of comparison available was the refractive index, which is a measure of how light passes through glass. To measure the refractive index of a piece of glass, it is ground up and placed on a microscopic slide. The slide is then placed inside an oven, which measures the refractive index of the glass at three different wavelengths of light. Using these measurements, an analyst can then compare the data from two glass samples to see if they are consistent. This means that the analyst can determine if the two samples either did not come from the same source, or they could have come from the same source. Regarding the samples from defendant's shoe and the Tahoe, the refractive index indicated an "association." In other words, the glass from the shoes of defendant and Soto "could have originated" from the Tahoe.[12]

Luckas then explained that there existed a means "to try and get a handle on what value to place [on] that association." According to Luckas, the Illinois State Police Crime Laboratory compiled a database containing 2087 glass samples "randomly collected through criminal investigations throughout the entire State of Illinois over approximately the past 20 years and that the glass analyst can compare that data to see how common, for instance, a glass sample is or how rare it was. Luckas further explained that a database finding falls in one of three ranges: "high probability of common origin," "good probability of common origin," or "common glass," i.e., there exists only the bare association. Referring to the database, Luckas found that the glass from defendant's shoe had a frequency of occurrence of 1 in 21 to 100, which was the middle range. Based on this finding, Luckas opined that there was a "good probability of common origin" between the glass from the Tahoe and the glass from the shoes of defendant and Soto.[13]

The Illinois Supreme Court noted that, before this court, defendant expressly does not challenge Luckas' testimony regarding the refractive index of the glass fragments. Also, defendant does not challenge Luckas' testimony regarding the "frequency of occurrence" of the refractive index of the glass from defendant's shoe in the database. Rather, defendant contends that Luckas' opinion, based on the database, that there was a "good probability" that the glass from defendant's shoe came from the Tahoe "had no reasonably valid scientific basis, and should not have been allowed into evidence."[14]

In the present case, the court determined that expert witness Luckas thoroughly explained the process by which he reached his ultimate opinion that there was a "good probability" that the glass from defendant's shoe came from the Tahoe. Also, the court noted, defendant presented his own expert to challenge Luckas' opinion. Thus, the jury was fully aware of any "infirmities" in the expert's opinion, and it was for the jury to determine his credibility.

Defendant further contends that the prosecutor, in closing argument, overstated Luckas' testimony. Defendant complains of the following three italicized statements:

> "What the glass does is it [sic] puts this defendant in the Tahoe where the broken glass is after the window is broken, and we know the window is broken at Grand and Oak Lawn, right, because that's where glass that also matches the Tahoe was found.

> *   *   *

> So the broken glass in the street matches the Tahoe. You know the Tahoe is at Grand and Oak Lawn, you know that's where the window broke. And the glass in the defendant's shoes puts him in the car right when the window breaks."

> *   *   *

> (T)he glass is one piece of evidence. One piece to consider. But it fits in, and it describes the defendant as being in the car because the glass from the Tahoe was in his shoes."[15]

Citing the earlier case of *People v. Linscott*,[16] which found prosecutorial misstatement of an expert's opinion, the court here likewise found that the prosecutor's earlier-quoted comments in this case overstated the evidence. However, the court ruled, the prosecutor's comments did not deprive defendant of a fair trial. Comments in closing argument must be considered in context of the entire closing argument of both the state and the defendant. The challenged remarks were only three brief statements contained in two paragraphs of the state's entire closing argument, which, transcribed, consisted of 32 record pages. Also, the court noted that the trial court instructed the jury to disregard statements made in closing argument not based on the evidence.

The 2004 Tennessee case of *State v. Graham*[17] provides an instructive look at the language used by forensic experts in explaining and expressing their opinions to a jury. Here, defendant was convicted of aggravated burglary, a Class C felony, and theft of property under $500, a Class A misdemeanor. On Monday, September 3, 2001, Sandra Stahr, the victim, returned home from a camping trip with her family to find her back door kicked in and two items missing: $250 in cash from her son's wallet and a caller ID box from her bedroom, and called the police. The defendant was dating the victim's cousin, Terri Bull, at the time, and on the previous Thursday had visited Bull as she babysat the victim's children in the home. When the police arrived, they found that several panels of glass around the handle in a French door at the back of the residence had been broken out and determined that the lock had been turned from the inside. Deputy Crim testified there was broken glass around the door, as well as in some large, dirty footprints leading toward the living room.[18]

After learning about the shattered glass on the floor mat of Bull's car, Detective Hailey sent the floor mat and samples of the glass from the victim's residence to the Tennessee Bureau of Investigation (TBI) Crime Laboratory in Nashville for analysis, as well as a pair of size 7 and 1/2 work boots he collected from the defendant on the fourth day following the burglary. The boots were the only shoes he collected from the defendant and appeared to have been cleaned. Special Agent Randall Nelson of the TBI Crime Laboratory in Nashville, who was accepted as an expert in the field of microanalysis, testified that the Rutherford County Sheriff's Department submitted the following items for analysis, a sample of glass from the victim's floor, a floor mat from which Agent Nelson recovered several large fragments of glass, and a pair of work boots.

> Agent Nelson testified he compared the glass from the victim's floor to the glass he recovered from the floor mat in terms of their respective method of manufacture, thickness, color, density, and refractive index. Because none of the tests he performed showed any inconsistencies between the samples, he concluded that the glass samples from the floor mat "were consistent with the samples that were taken from the victim's residence." He added, however, that the glass samples from the floor mat "could also be consistent with another source of glass with exactly those same optical and physical properties." Thus, he said, "there is that possibility that there is another source of glass out there with those identical properties." He did not find any glass on the pair of work boots submitted for analysis.[19]

The court noted that while Agent Nelson's opinion alone might be insufficient to support a conviction, the totality of the circumstantial evidence supported this conviction:

> Shattered glass found at the crime scene was consistent with pieces of shattered glass that Bull found on the floor mat of her automobile after she returned from a weekend trip, and when she had left her only spare set of keys with the defendant. There were no signs of forced entry into the vehicle. The vehicle had been parked crooked in the parking space and the steering wheel had been tilted down, both of which were things the defendant had done in the past. Bull knew the defendant to be a beer drinker. A Michelob Light beer bottle was lying on the ground beside the vehicle's driver's door when she inspected the vehicle on Monday afternoon, and a matching bottle cap was on the floorboard behind the driver's seat. Finally, the "born on" date and lot number of the bottle found beside Bull's vehicle indicated it had come off the same assembly line as the bottles in the victim's refrigerator, during the same fifteen-minute interval of production. None of these facts, alone, would be sufficient to establish the defendant's guilt of the offenses. Taken together, however, they were sufficient for a rational jury to find him guilty of aggravated burglary and theft under $500 beyond a reasonable doubt.[20]

The court concluded that the evidence was sufficient to support the defendant's convictions.

Many case reports address the forensic examination of glass, in one or more of the aspects just described. The transfer of glass fragments from the crime scene with something, typically items of clothing, is most prevalent.

In *People v. Dailey*,[21] the defendant was convicted of burglary. The Appellate Court held that evidence of tests on bits of glass found on defendant's sweatshirt, which were performed to establish defendant's presence at the scene of the crime, was properly admitted.

When the victims of the burglary were returning from a family outing, they noticed a car parked in front of their house, which was stipulated to be defendant's car. They opened the overhead garage doors, and as the wife walked into the garage, which was attached to the house, she noticed that the rear door of the garage was open. She closed and locked it, a wooden door with eight panes of glass in the middle. The 9-year-old son entered the house first and made some noise. There was a 75-watt bulb lit inside the house in the area of the door. The chain lock on the door had been broken.[22]

As the wife entered the house, she saw a man with a hooded blue sweat-shirt coming down the hall towards her. The man ran toward the rear door of the garage, found it locked, and proceeded to break the 4 center sections of glass, pulled the wooden frame out, and escaped. He was held by the husband when he returned to get his car and was arrested.

Three different samples of glass were tested. The first was made of samples of glass that had fallen on the floor in the garage, and these tests showed that the glass from the garage door was different from the glass found on the defendant's sweat shirt. On the day before the trial, the victim brought some more glass from the garage door to the state's attorney, and the second test resulted in testimony that there was a *high probability* that the sample from the glass on the sweatshirt and the sample brought in at that time were part and parcel of the same piece of glass. Four different panes were brought in for the second test — two were from panes broken by the burglar and two were not. They were unmarked.

Defendant presented the results of the third test, which allegedly determined that the glass fragments from the sweatshirt could not have originated from the immediate area of the glass taken from the defendant's storm door. The defendant argued that such tests were inconsistent and therefore threw grave doubt on the validity of the tests performed by the state's expert witness. The court rejected that argument, holding:

> However, these conclusions are truly not inconsistent, because as the trial judge noted there might have been glass on the defendant's sweatshirt from both the defendant's broken storm door and from the victim's garage door. The expert's testimony was that two samples of the glass had the same refractive indices and densities as did the matching samples and came from the same source.[23]

The defendant sought to keep this testimony out on the basis that it was irrelevant and that the tests came too late in the trial and thus were unfair to the defendant. The defendant had relied on the first test indicating no connection between the broken glass and the glass on the defendant's sweat-shirt. The defense contended that this all came as a surprise and that the results of the new tests were inadmissible.

The court ruled that in the absence of a showing in the record that the defendant either requested or was refused additional time in which to prepare his case, a reviewing court would not remand for a new trial on the grounds that the defendant did not have an adequate opportunity to prepare his defense. In the case at bar, the defendant did not accept the continuance offered by the court.

In *People v. Pruitt*,[24] defendant was convicted in Circuit Court, Winnebago County, of armed robbery. The issue of matching of glass fragments resulting from an automobile accident was involved here as in the Ceja case discussed earlier. The defendant allegedly robbed a Minit-Mart Grocery store in New Milford, Illinois. Two men armed with revolvers, and wearing gloves and disguised with false black beards, entered the grocery store and demanded money from the owner, who placed approximately $500 in a bag. The two men left with the money in a light-colored 1960 four-door Oldsmobile. Deputy Gene Burgess received a radio alert and spotted a car that fit the description of the car used in the robbery. Burgess pursued the Oldsmobile, when the driver ignored his police light, in his own car until the Oldsmobile collided with another car. Three men emerged from the Oldsmobile and attempted to escape on foot. Officer Burgess apprehended one of the men, Raymond Fuller, and other officers arrested the other two men, one of whom was the defendant here.

Detectives looked inside the 1960 Oldsmobile and observed a .38-caliber revolver with brown handles, and the bottom part of a beard or wig. Two guns were found nearby. A search of the car revealed the bag contained $354.90 in cash and $44.05 in checks identified by the proprietor as checks received by him in the store, a goatee-type beard and moustache, a false moustache, a pair of glasses with a rubber nose, three wigs, and a .38-caliber revolver.[25] The police combed out glass and paint particles from the defendant's hair using the defendant's comb.

Laboratory analysis of these things disclosed that the glass particles taken from the defendant's hair and clothing *matched* both *the safety glass* of the Oldsmobile and the glass particles taken from Fuller's hair. The paint particles taken from the defendant's person and clothing matched the paint from the car struck by the Oldsmobile. Also, fibers taken from the defendant's clothing matched the fibers of the false beard and moustache found in the Oldsmobile.[26] The court held that the various beards and disguises were properly admitted into evidence as they were connected to the defendant and the crime:

> The grocery store owner testified that the robbers wore beards. These beards were later found in the Oldsmobile which was identified by him as the getaway car. The defendant was linked to the getaway car by the automobile safety glass particles found in his hair.[27]

Additionally, the court observed, fibers found in the defendant's jacket pockets matched those in the beard found in the Oldsmobile.

In *People v. Colombo*,[28] a notorious Illinois murder case, defendants Patricia Colombo and her boyfriend Frank DeLucca were convicted in the Circuit Court, Cook County, of three counts of murder, conspiracy, and solicitation to murder. After several unsuccessful efforts to engage hired killers to murder Patricia's family, the two committed the murders themselves. Investigators discovered the bodies of Frank, Mary, and Michael Columbo. Frank Columbo, defendant Columbo's father, was found lying on his back in the living room, surrounded by broken glass with a torn and bloody lampshade nearby, and also had a two-inch slash across his throat. Mary Columbo, defendant Columbo's mother, was found lying on her back on the landing in front of the bathroom with a bullet wound on the ridge of her nose, right between her eyes, and a one-inch slash across her throat. Portions of a bloodied magazine and fake fern were lying next to her body, with broken glass and beads lying near her head. Michael Columbo, defendant Columbo's 13-year-old brother, was found lying on his back on his bedroom floor, and had what appeared to be a bullet wound on the left side and a second bullet wound on the back. In addition, there were 98 puncture wounds on Michael's neck and chest. A pair of bloodied scissors with crossed blades was found on Michael's desk and a marble-based bowling trophy, covered with blood, was lying next to Michael's body. In addition to the testimony regarding glass fragments, the jury heard evidence of blood typing and ballistics.[29]

Blair Schultz, a criminalist employed by the Illinois Bureau of Identification in the trace section, trained in glass analysis, testified as to her findings regarding twenty-eight exhibits she received from the crime scene, from a 1968 Buick that the defendants had rented around the time of the murders, and from Frank Columbo's 1972 Thunderbird and 1972 Oldsmobile. Fifteen of the twenty-eight items had glass in them. Schultz stated that there were three ways to analyze glass fragments: fit the pieces together; analyze the chemical properties and densities; or analyze the refractive index of the fragments.

By using the refraction method, Schultz concluded that two of the fragments, one from the broken lamp base found on Columbo's living-room floor and one found in the 1968 Buick, *had the same degree of tolerance and, thus, could have originated from the same source.* Schultz buttressed her opinion by noting that only five times in one thousand previous glass tolerance tests has glass with the identical degree of tolerance not been from the same source. On cross-examination, however, Schultz agreed that the matched glass fragment recovered from the Buick could have come from any of thousands of pieces of glass with the same optical properties as the lamp base.[30]

In *People v. White*,[31] the State filed a petition to revoke defendant's probation because he committed an aggravated battery by inflicting a cut with a broken bottle. After closing arguments, the trial court examined the cut on victim Jackson's arm and discussed the discrepancies between the witnesses' testimonies, concluding that the wound had been caused by either a knife or a piece of broken bottle:

> ...Now the court can take into account its own observations and experiences of life. Most broken bottles (are) round — if there is a flat part, it's on the bottom and normally when a bottle breaks it doesn't break in a perfectly straight line. Glass tends to break in a jagged fashion. The court notes the position of the wound. The wound is not on the palms. It's not on the heel of the palms. It's down two and a half to three inches down the wrist. One would think that if a man fell the likely thing to do would be to put your palms out and break the fall. That's not where the cut is. The cut is at a place further down the wrist. The nature of the cut — it's a straight cut. I described it earlier as about an inch and a half to about an inch to three quarters in length, not the type that one would think would be made with a round bottle. It doesn't add up. If it was made by a piece on the bottom I might expect a straighter cut but I would expect it to be more jagged. This is a fairly straight cut.[32]

The defendant argued that he was denied due process of law when the trial judge based his decision in part on the differences between glass and knife cuts, because this information was not in evidence. The appellate court agreed with the defendant, ruling that the ability to examine a cut and determine the instrument that made it was beyond the province of common knowledge. Accordingly, the trial judge erred in considering facts not in evidence in entering his judgment. Additionally, the court concluded, the trial judge *spent a significant part of his analysis of the evidence on the distinction between glass and knife cuts*. Given that fact and the overall weight of the evidence, they found the error to be grounds for a reversal.

Two different types of glass found on defendant's gloves were the key to a murder conviction, in the 1996 case of *Land v. State*.[33] Michael Jeffrey Land was convicted of the capital murder of Candace Brown, and sentenced to death.

The landlord observed that a window located near the rear entry to the house had been broken into, that the telephone wires to the house had been cut, and that the window on the driver's side of Brown's car had been shattered. When officers from the Birmingham Police Department arrived at Brown's residence, they established that all doors to the house were locked, that a storm window located near a rear entry to the house had been removed, and that several panes of the interior window behind that storm window had been cut and removed. One of the removed panes of glass, which was lying on the ground, contained a shoe imprint with a distinctive tread design bearing the lettering "USA." Brown's body was discovered by hikers in a rock quarry on Ruffner Mountain in Jefferson County. She had been shot once in the back of her head. The officers also found on a bulletin board a note with the name and telephone numbers of Michael Jeffrey Land and his mother, Gail M. Land. Police informed Land that they were investigating the disappearance of Brown, and he agreed to accompany them to the police station to answer some questions.

During the interrogation, Detective Fowler noticed that the tread design on the bottom of Land's tennis shoes appeared to match the print the officers had seen on the window glass at Brown's house. At the completion of Land's interview, Detective Fowler asked to see Land's shoes and, upon closer observation, noticed what appeared to be bloodstains. Land, in a second statement made after his first alibi based story was disproved, stated that he had told two men that the deceased was a good robbery target, and agreed to cut and remove a window for them from her house. Land said that after Brown was injured he became frightened and left the house and that he did not know what happened to her after that.

At trial, the state's expert testimony established that a pair of wire cutters found during the search of Land's car had made the cuts on the telephone wire leading into Brown's residence. The experts also testified that the two types of glass fragments found on a pair of gloves seized from Land's car were consistent with the glass in the shattered window of Brown's car and with the glass in the broken window near the rear entry of Brown's house, and that Land's tennis shoe sole had the same distinctive design as the shoe print found on a removed pane of glass at Brown's house.[34]

In *People v. Noascono*,[35] defendant was convicted of burglary, theft of property valued at less than $150, and possession of a controlled substance. Campbell's Drug Store in Marion, Illinois was burglarized on March 26, 1977, at approximately 3:30 a.m. Upon arrival, a police officer responding to an alarm found the front and rear glass doors broken, the cash drawer open, the change bin on the floor, and three pill containers on the counter near the rear door. Police collected samples of broken glass from the floor near the doors and separately packaged them. Leaving Detective Kobler and another officer at the scene, Officer Sprague returned to duty.

Police stopped defendant's car for an alleged brake light malfunction and noticed that he fit the description received earlier of the person running from the area of the drug store.

The state's forensic expert witness Smith, who worked in the mineralogy unit of the FBI laboratory in Washington, D.C., testified that he was trained in the examination of glass, soil, safe insulation, and other materials. He had received the defendant's clothing and picked out what appeared to be bits of glass, whereupon he examined them under a microscope and determined from their appearance that they were glass. Smith then performed light refraction and dispersion tests on the particles from defendant's shoes, socks, and clothing, and on samples from Campbell's Drug Store. He testified that the dispersion and refraction measurements of particles on the defendant's clothing *matched exactly the dispersion and refraction measurements of the samples* from Campbell's. Smith opined that the particles on defendant's clothing very probably came from the same source as the samples from Campbell's, but he could not say positively that they came from the same source. Smith testified that no chemical tests were performed to determine if the particles on defendant's clothing were glass or to determine the composition of these particles.[36]

In many cases, the simple breaking of glass, its location, or the presence of blood or fingerprints on a fragment, is the circumstantial key to identifying the dynamics of the crime scene, if not the actual perpetrator. In *Jensen v. State*,[37] a case where the glass evidence was central to the prosecution's theory, there was no chemical or microscopic testimony required. Here, the defendant was convicted of first-degree murder and the use of a handgun in commission of crime of violence. Theodore Daniels was murdered in his office in Woodlawn, Maryland. Dagmar E. Jensen, with whom Daniels had a business and romantic relationship, was arrested for the killing. The state hypothesized that the victim and defendant were at odds over his fidelity and his refusal tell her where he lived. The state argued that she broke into his office building, went to his office, and shot him.

Police officers came to the scene and attempted to gain entrance to the building via the second-floor back door and noticed that the pane of glass in the bottom window opening of the interior door had been broken. There were shards of glass lying on the floor both inside and outside the door and more glass on the exterior side of the door. There was also blood smeared on the interior and exterior of the door and on the broken glass. The blood smears suggested that someone had been cut by the broken glass. The blood smears were heavier on the exterior portion of the door and it seemed to the police, based on where the glass landed, that the glass was broken from the inside of the building while the storm door was closed.[38]

The broken window contained three to four inches of glass on the bottom left-hand side of the window frame. One of the responding officers described it as follows: "I observed that there was in the bottom left-hand corner a triangle shape of glass that still existed. The remainder had been cleanly knocked out and there were no glass splinters. The victim's body was found lying near his desk, with bloodstained clothing, a pair of bent eyeglasses, containing a shattered lens, lying immediately to Daniels's right, and a tennis ball, with signs of considerable damage, was further to the right of the eyeglasses The tennis ball, the police surmised, had been used as a "silencer" to muffle the sound of a gun as it was fired.

The court noted that this was a case with multiple strands of circumstantial evidence, including broken glass, all of which tied appellant to the murder:

> The state's evidence, if believed, showed that it is likely that the following transpired: (1) Sometime between 7:30 p.m. and 9:00 p.m. on the night of his death, Daniels let a visitor into his building, and then locked the front door; (2) Daniels next unlocked his office door and escorted the visitor into his office, where the visitor turned up the volume of the television to block out the noise; (3) the visitor shot Daniels and next proceeded to the rear door but could not unlock it because Daniels had the key to the dead-bolt lock; (4) the murderer kicked (or otherwise broke out) the window pane in the rear door; (5) as the glass was broken, most of the glass shards fell next to the closed storm door; (6) the murderer then crawled through the opening provided by the open window and, in doing so, was cut by glass shards still in the pane. The glass in the bottom window pane of the back door of Daniels's office building was intact at 7:30 p.m. at which time Daniels was still alive. Approximately an hour and a half later, the window was broken … it is reasonable to conclude that the person who broke the rear window pane was the person who killed Daniels. It is also reasonable to conclude that the person who broke the window did not possess a key to the building. Appellant's fingerprints were found on the interior side of the window panes to the rear entrance to the building. Her blood was found smeared on both sides of the rear wooden door. The glass in the rear door was mostly found on the exterior side of the dead-bolted door. From this it can be inferred that a person without a key broke out the pane to get out of the building. Going through an 11-inch high, 22-inch-wide window, thirty-eight inches off the ground at its lowest point, would take agility. Appellant was agile as demonstrated by the fact that she bragged that she could move her handcuffed hands from behind her back to her front. Even an agile person would likely be cut going through such a small opening. Appellant, by her own admission, was cut by the broken glass in the pane.[39]

In addition to this circumstantial evidence, the court noted that the jury had to weigh defendant's belated explanation for her fingerprints and blood being at the back door to Daniels's office, i.e., that she went to look for Daniels at his office even though she did not have a definite appointment with him and cut her hand on the already broken glass after receiving no response from Daniels.

The court determined that a rational jury might conclude that it was unlikely that she was cut reaching in to try to unlock the door because she admitted that the hall lights on the second floor were on; if there were glass shards there, it seems likely that she should have seen the glass and avoided injury if she had merely reached through the open window. Moreover, a rational jury could conclude that if she cut herself as she says she did, it would be unlikely that blood would be found afterwards smeared on both sides of the wooden door and on the glass pane.[40]

In *State v. Monroe*,[41] defendant was convicted of aggravated first-degree murder. On December 28, 1994, Michelle Smith arrived at work late, her face noticeably bruised and swollen. When asked what had happened, she became emotional and stated that the defendant Lloyd Monroe had hit and sexually assaulted her. Defendant was arrested after a supervisor at Smith's place of employment called police. Defendant was mistakenly released, and proceeded to stalk and murder Smith at her apartment. When Smith did not come to work on Monday, her supervisor called the police. The police found Smith's body in her apartment face down on a couch, clothed, and partially covered by a blanket. The cause of death was ligature strangulation. She had also suffered blunt trauma to her head prior to death.[42]

At trial, Helen Rae Griffin, a forensic scientist with the state patrol's crime lab, testified that four glass fragments taken from defendant's jacket matched the glass in Smith's bedroom window. She also testified that her examination determined that the window had been broken from the outside.

In response to defendant's challenge to her qualifications, Griffin testified that she had worked for six years as a forensic scientist at the state patrol crime lab; had worked previously for five and a half years in a similar capacity with the Royal Canadian Mounted Police; had received the standard training in glass examination from the state patrol, including training on the determination of the direction of force; and had been certified to perform casework in the field for approximately five and a half years. Although she had not received specific proficiency testing in directionality, she testified that the directionality analysis was straightforward.

> (I)t's the kind of examination where I couldn't explain why you're doing it to a lay person but I could show them how to do it within

an hour and have them fairly reliably be able to tell me which projectile was fired first and from which side of the glass.[43]

The court concluded that Griffin's on-the-job training and practical experience in this type of analysis was sufficient to qualify her as an expert. Thus the trial court did not err in admitting her testimony.

IV. Paint Analysis

A common instance of the utilization of forensic paint analysis is determining central facts in hit-and-run and vehicular homicide cases with respect to accident dynamics or simple identity of participating vehicles. It is also seen in burglary cases where paint residues are found on burglary tools or other devices used to gain entry to a residence or business establishment. The matching of automobile paints has risen to a highly sophisticated level across the world, again, due to the keen proprietary interest automobile and paint manufacturers have in the smallest differences among their commercial output from the competition.

However, forensic paint analyses involve different ultimate considerations. As noted in the FBI Forensic Paint Analysis and Comparison Guidelines:

> Forensic paint analyses and comparisons are typically distinguished by sample size that precludes the application of many standard industrial paint analysis procedures or protocols.[44]

The forensic paint examiner must be concerned with a number of non-commercial factors, such as case investigation requirements, crime scene collection and chain of evidence considerations, environmental factors, and a host of other factors that need be of concern toward the goal of supportable forensic evidence at trial.

> These factors require that the forensic paint examiner must choose test methods, sample preparation schemes, test sequence, and degree of sample alteration and consumption suitable to each specific case.[45]

> Forensic paint analysis encompasses considerable knowledge about automobile paint coating systems, as well as standard, repair and custom paint colors. Complex chemical analyses, such as pyrolysis gas chromatography, and a many other chemistry-related subjects' need to be understood. Color comparison is still central to forensic paint analyses. As noted by Saferstein:

...the criminalist need not be confined to comparisons alone. Crime laboratories can often provide valuable assistance in identifying the color, make, and model of an automobile by examining small quantities of paint recovered at an accident scene.[46]

The microscope remains a basic tool of the forensic paint analyst as with all other forensic scientists in all disciplines:

When one considers the thousands upon thousands of paint colors and shades that are known to exist, it is quite understandable why color, more than any other property, imparts paint with its most distinctive forensic characteristics. Questioned and known specimens are best compared side by side under a stereoscopic microscope for color, surface texture, and color layer sequence.[47]

The FBI-sponsored Forensic Paint Analysis and Comparison Guidelines available online are essential reading for any lawyer faced with a forensic paint issue. The Guidelines include discussion of terminology used in the field; practice summaries; collection, transport, and storage procedures; and detailed descriptions of physical match examinations. The chapter, Paint and Glass Evidence, in the Proceedings of the 12th Interpol Forensic Science Symposium, prepared by Ran Singh, Ph.D., should also be consulted for its discussion of techniques, such as infrared spectroscopy, chromatography, and UV/Vis spectroscopy, x-ray fluorescence and x-ray diffraction, and other techniques currently employed in forensic laboratories across the world. This valuable article also contains discussion of selected paint databases, books, and articles.[48]

The 14th Interpol Forensic Science Symposium Literature Review (2004), discussed in earlier chapters, has a very extensive review section on Paint and Glass.[49] The 2004 report covers significant advances in scientific methods applied to the forensic examination of paint and glass reported since the 13th Interpol Forensic Science Symposium in October 2001. A select body of sources was consulted for review:

Various resources were checked and relevant findings were imported into our literature database. After the three-year period, the most frequently cited periodicals in our collection are: Farbe & Lack, Journal of Analytical Chemistry, Journal of Analytical Atomic Spectrometry, Paint and Coatings Industry, JOT-Journal für Oberflächentechnik, Kunststoffe, Progress in Organic Coatings, Journal of Forensic Sciences, Nachrichten aus der Chemie, Spectroscopy Europe, GIT-Labor-Fachzeitschrift, Fresenius Journal of

Analytical Chemistry, Analytical and Bioanalytical Chemistry, Science & Justice, Problems of Forensic Sciences, LABO, Forensic Science International, The Analyst, Journal of Raman Spectroscopy, Glass Science Technology and Glass and Ceramics.[50]

The report authors estimate that more than a thousand literature entries were made in their paint and glass database during the period from January 2001 to March 2004. The report addresses the important distinguishing aspects of the raw materials present in any paint sample, which may aid in a preliminary match estimate for crime scene samples:

Additives, binders, extenders, and pigments are subjected to the continuous market change. Some interesting raw materials are presented in relevant trade journals dedicated to manufacturers of diverse paint products, such as the Paint and Coatings Industry or the European Coatings Journal.

Recommendable is the 2003 additives guide presented by the Paint Coatings Industry in glossary form presenting from A to Z the various additives in use in the paint and coatings industry.[51]

Recent pigment development discussions were found in the literature, *such as the use of colored alumina flakes, mica-based pigments, and in general the chemistry and physics of special-effect pigments and colorants.* Coating types, new color trends, plastics and polymers, art, and over 50 painting analysis and archaeological studies (ancient pigments, resins or binder types) are discussed.[52]

The report examines literature addressing general paint analysis and instrumental techniques such as: Color measurement and microspectroscopy (MSP), scanning electron microscope (SEM), atomic force microscope (AFM), and confocal microscopes (CM), cathodoluminescence (microscopy and spectroscopy for the analysis of minerals and materials), chromatography, PY-GC-MS (pyrolysis techniques for the characterization and discrimination of paint), spectroscopic methods infrared spectroscopy, Raman spectroscopy, x-ray spectroscopy, x-ray diffraction, and LA-ICP-MS (trace elemental analysis of automotive paints by laser ablation — inductively coupled plasma — mass spectrometry [LA-ICP-MS]).[53] The report also discusses the literature with respect to specific issues in paint investigation, new paint-related chemical databases, and new books published between 2001 and 2004.

In the area of forensic glass analysis, the report provides a review of recent articles addressing microscopic investigations, elemental analysis, SEM (the use of environmental scanning electron microscopes [ESEM] in forensic science), XRF (the classification and discrimination of glass fragments using nondestructive energy dispersive x-ray μ-fluorescence), interpretation/ICP-AES (the use of inductively coupled plasma-atomic emission spectrometry [ICP-AES] for glass investigations), ICP-MS/case (the assessment of the discriminating power of ICP-MS via the analysis of variance and pairwise comparisons), and LA-ICP-MS (comparing the discrimination potential of LA-ICP-MS methods with reported ICP-MS methods).

The report addresses the general literature on the forensic interpretation of glass evidence with respect to the significance of physical matches of fractured glass and the different kinds of fractures in flat glass, container glass, and automobile glass. It notes the literature referencing glass fractures caused by firearms and fires. Articles addressing the retention and persistence of glass fragments on clothing are also described.[54] A comprehensive list of Web sites relevant to the subjects of paint and glass is provided.[55]

Few criminal cases center in paint comparisons, when compared to the other forensic sciences discussed in this book. Nonetheless, the same components of *class characteristic* statements and *individual linkage statements* are the central features of this important forensic science discipline. The inferences put into the case by paint analysis-based testimony may be, as with all the forensic sciences, the weight tipping the jury's decision to one side or the other.

For example, in *People v. Mitchell*,[56] defendant was convicted of two counts of burglary. The court found it was proper to have admitted into evidence defendant's plastic Social Services card, which was bent and had streaks of paint on it, because the card was not introduced to show defendant's propensity to commit crimes, but rather was logically linked to one issue in the case — defendant's entry, without a key, into the complainants' hotel room. There was no paint-matching testimony of the paint on the card and that on the hotel room door.[57]

In *State v. Kandies*,[58] defendant was charged with murder. Sergeant Wilson's discovery of paint rather than blood in defendant's truck cab contradicted defendant's statement that he accidentally hit the victim Natalie with his truck and that she was bleeding when he put her in the truck. Sergeant Wilson testified that he examined the inside of defendant's truck and found some red dots in the cab to be red oxide primer (rather than blood). Sergeant Wilson testified that the spots in defendant's truck looked peculiar, so he sanded a spot with a knife and discovered it to be red oxide primer. He also testified that he held a part-time job doing car repair and body shop work. The court ruled that, based on his experience, it was likely that Sergeant Wilson could perceive the difference between blood and red oxide primer.[59]

The classic hit-and-run scenario was recently addressed in the important Illinois Supreme Court case of *People v. Digirolamo*,[60] where the defendant was convicted of failing to report accident resulting in person's death and of obstructing justice.[61] The detailed investigative, accident reconstruction, and forensic analyses merit extended examination for lawyers involved in such cases.

The victim, 72-year-old retiree William Pranaitis, arose in the early morning hours while it was still dark outside to take his routine morning walk. A local police officer discovered Pranaitis' dead body lying next to a telephone pole near the intersection of Blackjack Road and Lebanon Road at 6:36 a.m. that day. Detective Michael Ries of the Collinsville Police Department investigated the scene of the accident and found a flashlight lying in the center of Lebanon Road, near its intersection with Blackjack Road, a baseball hat, and eyeglasses three to four feet onto the grass. He also observed a bag containing cans, which the victim routinely collected on his walks, and a single set of tire tracks that entered the grassy area alongside Lebanon Road and then traveled approximately 50 to 60 feet before reentering Lebanon Road. Ries conjectured that these tracks, which were narrow in width, were made by two right-side tires of a small car or possibly a small truck.[62]

Officer David Schneider, an accident reconstruction specialist from the Collinsville Police Department, testified that he observed a "scrub" mark on the curb, made by the smear of rubber from a tire, and a 48-foot-long tire mark in the grass alongside Lebanon Road. Later, Schneider examined defendant's car and found scuff marks and a small dent to the edge of the rim of the right front tire, which he testified were *consistent with* the "scrub" mark found on the curb at the accident scene. He also observed the following damage to defendant's car: dirt in the right front wheel rim; a "broken out" windshield; dents on the right front quarter panel and in the right side pillar (the support from the hood to the roof); and a small, depression-type dent on the right side of the roof above the pillar.[63] Schneider concluded that a vehicle traveling east on Lebanon Road left the road at the point of the "scrub" mark and that the right front corner of the vehicle struck the victim from behind. The impact flipped the victim onto the hood, with his head striking the pillar on the right side, and then propelling him into the air to a resting point at the base of the telephone pole. Officer Schneider's opined that defendant's car *could have been* the one that struck Pranaitis because it displayed damage on the right side of the vehicle, which was *consistent with* the accident that killed the victim.[64]

The state experts testified as to the physical evidence. A forensic pathologist testified that the victim had extensive injuries, including large lacerations on the scalp and the back of his right leg in the knee area and a fracture to the left leg, which were consistent with his being struck by a motor vehicle while he was upright and moving. It was also determined that the victim's head injuries were consistent with his striking the dented right window-post area of defendant's car, although it was conceded on cross-examination that the window-post damage could have been caused by removal of the windshield from the car. While admitting that she could not say that defendant's car caused the victim's injuries, she nonetheless concluded that the car's damage was *consistent with the victim's injuries*.[65]

Blair Schultz, an Illinois State Police forensic chemist, compared a piece of standard laminated glass from defendant's windshield to a piece of glass from the victim's clothing and testified that the pieces had the same refractive index, which means that the two pieces of glass could have originated from the same source. Schultz testified that the likelihood of this match was one in five, meaning that one out of every five pieces of laminated glass would have the same refractive index.[66] However, Trace Chemist Cheryl Cherry testified that although she found several different colors of paint on the victim's clothing, the paint chips were not large enough to determine if it was automotive paint. There was also no match between the paint from defendant's car and the samples taken from the victim's clothing. She explained that when a person is thrown to the ground paint and debris will be picked up in his clothing. This result also occurs when a person is walking around.[67]

The court determined that the evidence was more than adequate to uphold defendant's conviction:

> Here, the circumstantial evidence against defendant showed that there was damage to the front passenger side of defendant's car that was consistent with William Pranaitis' injuries. There was also glass from defendant's car that was linked to the glass found on the victim's clothing. In addition, defendant admitted to being in an accident in an area near the scene of the accident killing the victim in this case. Following the accident, defendant appeared nervous and ultimately sought to replace the damaged windshield of his car. There was also evidence that defendant removed whitish-gray hair strands from his car's windshield. This circumstantial evidence, when viewed in the light most favorable to the prosecution, was sufficient for a rational trier of fact to conclude beyond a reasonable doubt that defendant's car struck and killed Pranaitis.[68]

Paint analyses are not restricted to automobile or injury settings, as may be exemplified by the case of *Commonwealth v. McEnany*,[69] where defendant was convicted of second-degree murder, burglary, and robbery. Eighty-two-year-old Kathryn Bishop was found dead on the floor of her residence. Testimony of a forensic pathologist established that Bishop had been stomped to death. Paint chips were discovered on the victim's hands, and black tee-shirt fibers were found on her face, neck, and clothing. The victim's kitchen door window had been smashed, her basement window had been opened, and scuff marks were found on her clothes dryer, which was located just below the basement window.

As the investigation continued, Trooper Stansfield obtained search warrants for appellant's van and residence and officers got possession of the clothes worn by appellant on the day of the murder. Expert examination of the clothing revealed paint chips in the pocket of his jacket, which a forensic paint analyst testified at trial were *consistent with* chips found on Bishop's hands. The chips found in defendant's jacket and on the victim's hands were also found to be *consistent with* the peeling paint around the broken basement window. Chemist Lee Ann Grayson testified that fibers found on Bishop's body matched those of the tee-shirt appellant wore on the day of the murder.[70]

The court found that the evidence was sufficient to place defendant and fellow chimney sweep at customer's residence at time of homicide and, therefore, supported convictions for second-degree murder of their elderly customer.

V. Soil Analysis

The 14th Interpol Forensic Science Symposium literature has a comprehensive Forensic Geology Review as part of the Review Papers report.[71] The authors emphasize that the most important development, in general terms, on the subject of forensic geology, was the meeting — Forensic Geoscience: Principles, Techniques, and Applications — held on March 3–4, 2003, at Burlington House of the Geological Society, in London:

> It was probably the first international meeting focused on only forensic geoscience to share knowledge and experiences. The two-day meeting was filled with a variety of topics, for example, basic techniques, researches, and applications to case works. Delegates were not only from forensic laboratories but also from academic fields and private companies. The study areas included broad fields: such as geology, microscopy, archaeology, botany, geography, and others.[72]

The report authors noted that soil transfer is often recognized on many substances in many cases, and the recovered soil evidence is examined and compared to control samples. Particle size and color are primary comparison factors. Many references are made to studies that utilize statistics, color analysis, particle size analysis, stable isotope ratios, and bulk chemistry. While significant improvement of traditional methods *was rather scarce* in the

2001–2004 review period, new analytical techniques were addressed in the literature. Standardless synchrotron radiation x-ray fluorescence (SR-XRF), the potential of stable isotopes in forensic soil analysis, metal extraction from soil, and road sediments using different strength reagents, were some of the techniques noted. Regardless of these recent suggestive techniques, the report concluded that microscopy was still the most important technique for forensic geological examination.

The report also included brief discussions of the literature addressing trace evidence originating in biological substances and organic matters. Comparisons of vegetation and pollen analysis[73] were noted as important subjects of ongoing study.[74]

Forensic examination of soil samples is common in many criminal cases, especially in instances of kidnapping by vehicle and disposing of bodies in rural or semirural areas or a wide variety of burial sites. Geological surveys, archeology, environmental concerns, oil and gas exploration, and the worldwide commercial interest in building materials originating in whole or part from mineral substances have generated much information that is available to those engaged in forensic soil analyses.

The definition of soil for forensic science purposes is necessarily broad. As observed by Saferstein:

> ...for forensic purposes, soil may be thought of as including any disintegrated surface material, both natural and artificial that lies on or near the Earth's surface.[75]

Such a necessarily broad net would encompass naturally occurring rocks, all manner of minerals, vegetation,[76] and animal matter.[77] The subject also comprises the recognition and analysis of a large number of commercial products, such as glass, paint chips, asphalt, brick fragments, cinders, ceramics, and other building materials that act as indicators of where all or part of a crime occurred.

Soil examinations can be relatively straightforward and conclusive:

> Most soils can be differentiated and distinguished by their gross appearance. A side-by-side visual comparison of the color and texture of soil specimens is easy to perform and provides a sensitive property for distinguishing soils that originate from different locations.[78]

As with glass, fiber, hair, and blood products, and finger, foot, or tire impressions, soil analysis can often impart important information linking a suspect to a crime scene. Also, as in all forensic science crime scene investigations, recognition, and collection issues are paramount.[79]

The broad nature of soil analysis, increasingly detailed, was noted at the Proceedings of the 2001 12th Interpol Forensic Science Symposium:[80]

> As one of the major components of airborne dust, soil particles can be frequently transferred by a suspect touching the dusty surface of structural forms, such as a door, a windowsill, etc. This (Forensic Geology Review) report therefore, includes not only soil materials, but also dust and other earth-related materials, such as plant chips, diatoms, pollen and spores, and concrete or brick fragments.[81]

In cases where unique items such as glass are embedded in both comparison samples, a comparison may be readily made. However, as noted in the same paper:

> The more difficult situations occur where there is a variation in components and composition among the samples from the same site. It requires extensive, tedious work, and patience … tedious long work and patience with a lot of examiner experience and statistical consideration.[82]

Examining soil and decayed matter from a landfill area would be a prime example of the above observations. The earlier-mentioned 2001 and 2004 symposium forensic literature review papers are well worth consulting for the comprehensive overview of this subject as well as the current world bibliography on soil analysis and related subjects.

It is incumbent on lawyers involved in the criminal justice system to become familiar with the key information points and players in the scientific field of soil analysis. Very few of the forensic sciences are or were ever created and developed for strictly forensic purposes. The keen commercial interest involved is typically the primary generator of detailed data sourcing. Soil analysis stems from and depends upon the sciences of geology as well as anthropology. There are several excellent books[83] and Web sites[84] recently available to get the investigator on his or her way in a soils-related criminal case. Several excellent case studies of soil-based kidnapping and homicide incidents are also available for study. Extensive articles on the murder investigation in the death of DEA agent Enrique Camarena and the kidnap and murder of Adolphe Coors provide both extremely instructive and interesting reading.[85]

VI. Soil and Cadaver Dogs

In *Clark v. State*,[86] defendant was convicted of second-degree murder. Defendant appealed, among other points, on the basis that the testimony of a cadaver dog's police handler was inadequate to establish expertise of cadaver dog and that an insufficient foundation was laid for the handling officers' testimony interpreting the actions of the cadaver dogs.

The court found that the testimony of cadaver dog's police handler with respect to training and ongoing certification of cadaver dogs was adequate to establish the expertise of a cadaver dog that alerted to site at which murder victim's body had been buried.[87] The dog had received 17 weeks of "utility training," covering article search, tracking, and controlled aggression; followed by additional training in location of cadavers, and had been certified as qualified cadaver dog annually by state police association and once every two years by North American Police Work Dog Association. During certification the dog never failed to find what was hidden, and never, in training, alerted on false holes.

The court found sufficient for dog-handling officers' testimony interpreting the actions of cadaver dogs at the site at which victim's body had at one time been buried, despite expert testimony at motion *in limine* that alert by a cadaver dog, without more, was "not enough by itself" to prove the presence or past presence of human remains to reasonable degree of scientific certainty. Here, the dogs' expertise was established by testimonies of their handlers and other circumstantial evidence indicated a prior clandestine burial at alert site; defendant had been seen with truck and shovel at alert site, and alert site matched spot marked on map in defendant's truck.

Defendant was accused of the murder of a child approximately 11 years earlier and of having dug up and moved the remains when police reopened the investigation. In January 1993, police were able to determine that a map found in defendant's car depicted the cemetery in Massachusetts that he had visited on October 31, 1992. On January 3, 1993, Sergeant Arthur Parker, of the Wellfleet, Massachusetts, Police Department, went to the cemetery and noticed that topsoil within the Clark family cemetery plot was "disturbed." The location of this disturbance corresponded closely to an asterisk on the map found in appellant's pickup truck. In addition, he noticed rust marks on a cemetery marker near the Clark family plot.[88]

Bruce Hall, an FBI expert knowledgeable in the field of soil comparisons, examined part of the undercarriage of appellant's truck (seized by police on November 6, 1992) and found that the soil consisted of the same essential minerals as the rust marks left on the cemetery marker. He also discovered that the disturbed soil area of the Clark family plot was the likely source of the dirt contained in the eyeglass case found in appellant's truck.[89]

Massachusetts State Trooper Kathleen Barrett, the handler of a cadaver dog named Dan, brought Dan to the Wellfleet cemetery on January 3, 1993. Cadaver dogs are trained to recognize the scents of blood, tissue, and decomposition of humans. On January 3, Trooper Barrett released Dan in the Wellfleet cemetery. Dan criss-crossed the cemetery, and then indicated an alert in the area of the soil disturbance, which was near a headstone marked "Clark." Barrett took Dan aside and waited while other officers transferred soil (from the place where Dan had alerted) onto a tarp. She then released Dan to search again. This time, Dan alerted on the soil lying on the tarp and not on the hole from which the soil had been excavated.

The second cadaver dog to search the Wellfleet cemetery was a canine named Panzer owned by the Rhode Island State Police. Panzer worked her way through the cemetery for 12 to 15 minutes, and then alerted on an area behind appellant's grandfather's grave, which was the same place where Dan had initially alerted. Panzer and her handler returned to the cemetery on a later date. The handler started Panzer from a different location, but the dog worked her way back to the same spot and alerted once more. The alert was "less intense," however, than it had been earlier.[90]

One of the state's theories in this case was that appellant, on Saturday, October 31, 1992 (Halloween), went to the Wellfleet cemetery where his father and grandfather were buried, dug up the corpse of Michelle Dorr and took it elsewhere. According to the state's theory, appellant took these actions because he realized at that point that the police were focusing on him as the person who had killed Michelle. In support of this theory, the state produced a witness who had seen appellant at the cemetery on October 31 and saw him pull his truck up next to the Clark family grave markers. There was a shovel in the back of the truck at that time. Additionally, the state produced evidence indicating that appellant's truck had struck one of the grave markers directly across the road from the Clark family cemetery plot. Moreover, according to the state's evidence, the ground near appellant's grandfather's grave had been disturbed between October 14, 1992, and January 3, 1993. The state's theory was that appellant was backing up, after removing the body, when he struck the grave marker.

As mentioned earlier, Trooper Kathleen Barrett of the Massachusetts State Police Department testified that, on January 3, 1993, her German Shepherd dog, Dan, alerted at the areas of disturbed soil in the Clark family plot. Trooper Matthew Zarrella of the Rhode Island State Police testified that his dog Panzer likewise alerted at the same spot in September 1995.

At trial, several questions asked by the prosecutor of Trooper Barrett and Trooper Zarrella were objected to by appellant's counsel. The trial judge overruled the objections, which appellant now contends was reversible error. The pertinent question asked of Trooper Barrett and her answer were:

Q: (Prosecutor): When the dog went to that particular spot (the area where the ground had been disturbed) and began to dig, what did that indicate to you as a trainer?....

A: It indicated to me that he (Dan) had located one of three things that he was trained to locate under those circumstances, which is human blood, human decomposition, and human tissue.

*   *   *

The objected-to questions addressed to Trooper Zarrella were quite similar, viz:

*573 Q (Prosecutor): ... (A)nd what did she [Panzer] do? How did she react?

A (Trooper Zarrella): She laid down.

Q: Okay. And what did that tell you?

A: She had discovered or detected the presence of human decomposition. She had detected the (sic) certain chemical byproducts that are present in human decomposition that we trained her to detect.[91]

Troopers Barrett and Zarrella both admitted that cadaver dogs make mistakes, as do their handlers.

At the hearing concerning the motion *in limine*, appellant presented the testimony of Dr. Ann Marie Mires, the Director of the Identification Unit of the Boston Medical Examiner's Office, who qualified as an expert in the field of forensic anthropology and the identification of human remains. Dr. Mires has experience using dogs to locate human remains in cemeteries. In light of modern embalming and burial practices, she believed a properly trained cadaver dog would be able to distinguish a legitimate grave from a clandestine one within a cemetery because during embalming all body fluids are drained from the corpse, whereas persons who bury corpses in clandestine graves usually do not remove body fluids.

According to Dr. Mires, there are only three tools available to locate clandestine burials of human bodies: Trained cadaver dogs, ground penetrating radar, and shovels. In Dr. Mires's opinion, the alert of a cadaver dog, standing alone, is not considered sufficient to show to a reasonable degree of scientific certainty that human remains are or were present at the location of the alert. After a cadaver dog alerts, digging or ground penetrating radar is used. But the fact that neither of these instruments reveals a body does not necessarily invalidate the cadaver dog's alert, because there is no chemical test yet devised that can confirm whether a body had once decomposed at a particular site. Dr. Mires testified that she was participating in the preliminary stages of scientific work to develop such a chemical test.[92]

Dr. Mires testified that the use of cadaver dogs "in trying to determine the existence or the one-time existence of human remains at a particular location is a concept that is widely accepted in the forensic anthropology and pathology fields." Despite this reliance, a dog can falsely alert because water flowing from the site of a human cadaver may cause the dogs to alert at a place removed from the spot where a body was buried, because the dog is fatigued, or because the handler misreads a dog's actions.

The court first addressed defendant's point that there was no showing of Dan's expertise. They noted Trooper Barrett's testimony in regard to Dan's rigorous 17-week training course and his excellent record in locating cadavers:

> We were called to a residence. A female had been missing from (her) home. (She had been missing) ... for quite some time. We came into the house, the dog immediately went to the cellar, started to dig, ... knocking things over...We later found that this is where the body had actually been stored. We went up into the master bedroom, ... (and Dan) alerted ... on the wall, standing on the wall, and then he went into a small crawl space, and I lost sight of him.

> And he tried to come back but he was falling (through) ... the insulation.... And he came back; he had a garbage bag in his mouth, and in the garbage bag was the victim's purse. And lab results indicated that there were body fluids....[93]

As additional examples of Dan's expertise, Trooper Barrett said that Dan had located seven bodies that were under water. Once he alerted on a body that was in a stone quarry, 157 feet below the water's surface. Dan had also been certified as a qualified cadaver dog once a year since 1991 by the New England State Police Association (NESPA). He had also been certified as a cadaver dog once every two years since 1991 by the North American Police Work Dog Association. During certification, Dan never failed to find what was hidden. Moreover, he never, in training, alerted on "false holes," which are dug in attempts to deceive the dogs.

The court accepted both Dan's and the handler's expertise and accepted the cadaver dog evidence:

> Based on all the above, we disagree with appellant's contention that the state failed to show Dan's expertise. It is true that Dr. Mires

testified at the motion in limine hearing that the fact that a cadaver dog alerted at a certain spot was "not enough by itself" to prove the presence (or presence at some time in the past) of human remains to a reasonable degree of scientific certainty. But here, the alert by Dan at the spot in the Clark family graveyard did not stand alone. Other circumstantial evidence pointed to the fact that there had been a clandestine burial at that spot, i.e., the fact that the Clark plot had been disturbed between October 14, 1992, and January 3, 1993; that appellant was present with his truck and shovel at the grave site on October 31, 1992; that a second cadaver dog alerted at the same spot two and one-half years after Dan's alert, and that the spot where the cadaver dogs alerted matched the spot, marked by an asterisk found on a map in appellant's truck on October 24, 1992. Under all these circumstances we believe that there was adequate foundation for the admission of the testimony regarding the officers' interpretations of the actions of Dan and Panzer.[94]

VII. Soil and Forensic Archeology

Few cases show soil analysis at the center of the investigation, but soil analysis often is an important part of the circumstantial physical evidence leading to acquittal or conviction. Several of these types of cases involve soil in the context of forensic archeology.

In *People v. Begley*,[95] defendant was convicted in the Superior Court, Shasta County, of conspiracy to injure an archeological object. In an attempt to apprehend looters of Native American artifacts, the United States Forest Service set up a sting operation in Shasta County where a Forest Service special agent opened a booth at a flea market and advertised as broker of Native American artifacts.

Defendant contacted Agent Price and informed Price that he had excavated a number of arrowhead projectile points, beads, obsidian chips, and other artifacts from a burial site. The agent eventually bought several arrowheads later examined by Dr. Eric Ritter, an archeologist for the Bureau of Land Management. Dr. Ritter testified that these items contained a teshoa flake, used by prehistoric Native Americans for cutting and scraping, a late prehistoric arrow point known as a Gunther barb, and obsidian chips, a form of volcanic glass. The items were consistent with those one would expect to find in archeological sites in Shasta County, including the Ono site.[96]

Defendant's residence was searched and officers seized trade beads, various midden-covered rocks, and documents and other materials suggesting defendant was in the business of fabricating Native American artifacts. Some of the items had characteristics consistent with recent removal from an archeological site. Midden was described by an archeologist as *a trash mound, that is composed of materials that have built up over time from cooking ovens and fires, house structures that have been built and either decomposed or have burnt, resulting in soil that is very dark colored and distinctive from surrounding soil.* Possession of such material suggested that defendant was also in the business of fabricating archeological treasures.[97]

In *People v. Davenport*,[98] defendant was convicted before the Superior Court, Orange County, of the vicious murder of a young woman with the special circumstance that the murder was intentional and involved infliction of torture. The defendant was sentenced to death.

Gayle Lingle, the victim, spent the evening of March 26, 1980, at the Sit 'N Bull Bar in Tustin. Between approximately midnight and 1 a.m., she and defendant left the bar. The victim's body was found the next morning lying in a large, uncultivated field south of the I-5 Freeway near Tustin. There were motorcycle tracks in the area.[99] The body bore signs of extreme cruelty and mutilation.

Bonnie Driver, a criminalist employed by the Orange County Sheriff's Department, testified that she had examined vegetable matter taken from defendant's motorcycle and compared it with vegetation taken from the area where the victim's body was found. Driver found the gross morphology of the plants in both samples to be *consistent with each other*.[100]

Forensic Microscopist Skip Palinek examined and compared the heavy mineral content of soil samples taken from defendant's bike with samples taken at the murder scene and testified that the samples were *generally consistent* with each other. In fact, he testified, one of the samples from the motorcycle contained sufficient similarity to the murder scene samples that he concluded they were *virtually indistinguishable*. Both of these witnesses admitted they had not compared the samples taken from defendant's bike with samples taken from other parts of Orange County. Dr. Stephen Dana, a geologist retained by defendant, examined the same soil samples and found similarities and differences in all of them, and based on his knowledge of the geology of the area, he opined that the samples could have come from anywhere in Orange County.[101]

In *State v. Lee*,[102] defendant was charged, along with a codefendant, with the second-degree murder of one Peter Weber. On April 21, 1997, a partially decomposed body was found in a wooded area in St. Bernard Parish. Dental records were used to positively identify the body as that of Peter Weber. Bruising and broken bones in the neck area indicated that the victim died of strangulation.

A North Lopez Street residence, defendant's former abode, was searched pursuant to a warrant and under the house the officers saw what appeared to be a shallow grave. Several articles were taken from both inside and underneath the house that were linked to the body of the victim. Analysis of soil samples indicated that the soil found in the soles of the victim's shoes was the same as that found underneath the house.

VII. Conclusion

Expertise in the areas of glass, paint, and soil is an ever-present feature of criminal trials at the beginning of the twenty-first century. Many easily accessible and authoritative information sources are available to the forensic litigator. This chapter has described several of the more important ones and a representative sample of relevant cases in each area. Given free access to the abstracts of the Journal of Forensic Science and the many Web sites noted here, keeping up in these fields is a very achievable goal for prosecutors, defense lawyers, and judges.

Endnotes

1. See, generally, Saferstein: *Criminalistics: An Introduction to Forensic Science* (Prentice Hall, 6th ed., 1998) at 97–126; Giannelli and Imwinkelried: *Scientific Evidence* (The Michie Company, 1993), Vol. 2, at §24–6; Ran B. Singh, *Paint and Glass Evidence, Proceedings of the 12th Interpol Forensic Science Symposium* (The Forensic Sciences Foundation Press, 1998) at 199; Yoshiteru Marumo and Ritsuko Sugita, *Soil Evidence, Proceedings of the 12th Interpol Forensic Science Symposium* (The Forensic Sciences Foundation Press, 1998) at 242; Geberth: *Practical Homicide Investigation* (CRC Press, 3rd ed. 1996) at 522; Fisher: *Techniques of Crime Scene Investigation* (CRC Press, 5th ed., 1993) at 195; *FBI Forensic Paint Analysis and Comparison Guidlines*, Scientific Working Group on Materials Analysis (SWGMAT), http://www.fbi.gov/programs/lab/fsc/current/painta.htm.

2. See, Hicks, T., Vanina, R., Margot, P., *Transfer and persistence of glass fragments on garments. Science and Justice* 1996; 36(2): 101–107.

3. Giannelli and Imwinkelried: *Scientific Evidence* (The Michie Company, 2d ed., 1993) at §24–6, Vol. 2, p.380.

4. Giannelli and Imwinkelried: *Scientific Evidence* (The Michie Company, 2d ed., 1993) at §24–6, Vol. 2, p.380. Also see, Saferstein, *Criminalistics: An Introduction to Forensic Science* (Prentice Hall, 6th ed., 1998), at 97 et. seq.

5. There is a small but growing 'third database' for glass and paint chips in the FBI laboratory regarding density and refraction indices. See, Max M. Houck, *Statistics and Trace Evidence: The Tyranny of Numbers, Forensic Science*

Communications, Vol. I, No.3, October 1999, http://www.fbi.gov/pro-grams/lab/fsc/ current/ houck.htm.

6. See, Ran B. Singh, the Proceedings of the 12th Interpol Forensic Science Symposium, at 209. Similar studies have been successfully conducted involving fiber transfers. See Robertson, J., Kidd, C.B.M., *The Transfer of Textile Fibres During Simulated Contact, Journal of the Forensic Science Society,* Vol. 22 (1982), pp.301–308; Robertson, J., Kidd, C.B.M., and Parkinson, M.P. *The Persistence of Textile Transferred During Simulated Fibre Contact, Journal of the Forensic Science Society,* Vol. 22, (1982), at pp.353–360.; Scott, H.G., *The Persistence of Fibers Transferred During Contact of Automobile Carpets and Clothing Fabrics, Journal of the Canadian Society of Forensic Science,* Vol. 18 (1985), at pp. 185–199; Grieve, M.C,, Dunlop, J., Haddock, P.S., *Transfer Experiments with Acrylic Fibers, Forensic Science International,* Vol. 40 (1989), at pp. 267–277.

7. A significant amount of information on the technical and compositional aspects of fiber, weapons manufacture, and glass and paint is available in the hundreds of full-text or bibliographic databases accessible on the Dialog Information Service through Lexis-Nexus or Westlaw.

8. See the NGA Web site at http://www.glass.org/. Also see Caddy: *Forensic Examination of Glass and Paint* (Taylor & Francis, 2001) for an excellent and comprehensive discussion of the forensic uses of glass and paint information.

9. See, e.g., Curran, J.M., Hicks, T.N., Buckleton, J.S.: *Forensic Interpretation of Glass Evidence* (CRC Press, 2000) (Baysesian approach to glass fragment analysis.) There are a number of comments and critiques of this approach. See, e.g., Commentary on: Bottrell, M.C., Webb, J.B., Review of: Forensic interpretation of glass evidence. *J. Forensic Sci* 2002; 47(4):926–7. Aitken, C.G.G., Taroni, F.. 2003; 48(3): 695; Commentary on: Bottrell, M.C., Webb, J.B., Review of: forensic interpretation of glass evidence. *J. Forensic Sci* 2002; 47(4) 926-7. Hicks, T.N., Buckleton, J.S., Curran, J.M., 2003; 48(3): 694; Review of: Forensic Interpretation of Glass Evidence. Bottrell MC, Webb JB. 2002; 47(4): 926–927; Interpretation of glass composition measurements: the effects of match criteria on discrimination capability. Koons, R.D., Buscaglia, J., *J. Forensic Sci* 2002; 47(3): 505–512.; Review of: Forensic examination of glass and paint. Houck, M.M., 2003; 48(2): 473. Also see, Glass-containing gunshot residue particles: a new type of highly characteristic particle. Collins, P., Coumbaros, J., Horsley, G., Lynch, B., Kirkbride, K.P., Skinner, W., Klass, G., 2003; 48(3): 538–552. Trends in explosive contamination. Oxley, J.C., Smith, J.L., Resende, E., Pearce, E., Chamberlain, T., 2003; 48(2): 334–342.

10. *State v. Ceja,* 204 Ill. 2d 332 (2004).

11. *State v. Ceja,* 204 Ill. 2d 332 (2004), at 342.

12. Ceja at 351-352.

13. Ceja at 351-352. Defendant presented his own expert, Dr. Ross Firestone, who challenged Luckas' opinion that there was a "good probability" that the glass from defendant's shoe came from the Tahoe. Firestone opined that there

was "nothing scientific" about referring a refractive index to a database to determine a frequency of occurrence.

14. The record showed that defendant neither objected to this testimony nor included the issue in his post-trial motion. Therefore, the court ruled, the issue was waived.

15. The court observed that because the record showed that defendant failed to object to these remarks at trial, and failed to raise the issue in his post-trial motion, the issue was waived.

16. *People v. Linscott*, 142 Ill.2d 22, 153 Ill.Dec. 249, 566 N.E.2d 1355 (1991). See Chapter 3, Hair Analysis, for a detailed discussion of the Linscott case.

17. 2004 WL 51821 (Tenn.Crim.App. 2004).

18. 2004 WL 51821 (Tenn.Crim.App. 2004), at *1.

19. 2004 WL 51821 (Tenn.Crim.App. 2004), at *4.

20. 2004 WL 51821 (Tenn.Crim.App. 2004), at *7.

21. 15 Ill.App.3d 214, 304 N.E.2d 156 (1973).

22. 15 Ill.App.3d 214, 304 N.E.2d 156 (1973), at 216.

23. 15 Ill.App.3d 214, 304 N.E.2d 156 (1973), at 217.

24. 16 Ill.App.3d 930, 307 N.E.2d 142 (1974).

25. 16 Ill.App.3d 930, 307 N.E.2d 142 (1974), at 147.

26. 16 Ill.App.3d 930, 307 N.E.2d 142 (1974), at 935.

27. 16 Ill.App.3d 930, 307 N.E.2d 142 (1974).

28. 118 Ill.App.3d 882, 455 N.E.2d 733 (1983).

29. Susan M. Twardosz, criminalist at the Illinois Bureau of Identification and specialist in the firearms and tool-mark section, testified that Officer Gonsowski gave her four complete bullets and a fragment of a fifth to identify. By using a comparison microscope, Twardosz identified the bullets and fragments as .32 caliber. Further, she identified the nonmutilated bullets as coming from the same weapon which, in her opinion, was a .32-caliber gun. She could not discern with certainty whether the projectiles were fired from a rifle, automatic, or revolver. In addition, Twardosz testified that her examination of four locks taken from the doors of the Columbo house revealed that nothing but a key had been used to open them. On cross-examination, however, Twardosz admitted that a lock could be opened with a shim device such as a credit card or thin-bladed knife and escape detection. Some of the locks taken from the Columbo house were equipped with an antishim device.

Michael Podlecki, criminalist employed by the Illinois Bureau of Identification, testified as to his examination of the hair standards found on Michael Columbo's tee shirt. Colombo at 752, 905.

30. *People v. Colombo*, at 905.

31. 183 Ill.App.3d 838, 539 N.E.2d 456 (1989).

32. 183 Ill.App.3d 838, 539 N.E.2d 456 (1989), at 840.

33. 678 So.2d 201 (Ala. Sp. Ct. 1996).

34. 678 So.2d 201 (Ala. Sp. Ct. 1996), at 230. Expert testimony also established that the bullet recovered from Ms. Brown's head had been fired from a .45-caliber handgun and that it matched a bullet test-fired from the .45-caliber handgun found in Land's car; and that a DNA profile of a semen stain found on Ms. Brown's blouse matched Land's known blood sample, and that only one in 20,620,000 white males would have those same DNA characteristics (Land is white).

35. 80 Ill.App.3d 921, 400 N.E.2d 720 (1980).

36. 80 Ill.App.3d 921, 400 N.E.2d 720 (1980), at 722. Also see, *McNish v. State*, 1999 WL 604436 (Tenn.Crim. App. 1999), where defendant was convicted of the murder of a seventy-year-old victim, Gladys Smith, who was brutally beaten about the head and face with a glass vase, the fragments of which were found in her apartment. Scientific tests of the blood found on appellant's trousers showed that it matched that of victim, Smith, and that it was not the blood of appellant. Some blood particles taken from his fingernails were found to be human blood, but it was in quantities too small to test. An analysis performed at the Tennessee Bureau of Investigation laboratories showed that a fragment of glass found inside the packaging material in which appellant's trousers had been transmitted matched the glass particles found on the rug and floor of Smith's apartment.

37. 127 Md.App. 103, 732 A.2d 319 (1999).

38. 127 Md.App. 103, 732 A.2d 319 (1999), at 323.

39. 127 Md.App. 103, 732 A.2d 319 (1999), at 328.

40. 127 Md.App. 103, 732 A.2d 319 (1999), at 330.

41. 1999 WL 211823 (Wash.App. Div. 1, 1999).

42. 1999 WL 211823 (Wash.App. Div. 1, 1999), at *1.

43. 1999 WL 211823 (Wash.App. Div. 1, 1999), at *7.

44. *Forensic Paint Analysis and Comparison Guidelines*, Scientific Working Group on Materials Analysis (SWGMAT), FBI Forensic Science Communications (January 1999), located at http://www.fbi.gov/programs/lab/fsc/current/painta. htm, at 1.0.

45. *Forensic Paint Analysis and Comparison Guidelines*, Scientific Working Group on Materials Analysis (SWGMAT), FBI Forensic Science Communications (January 1999), located at http://www.fbi.gov/programs/lab/fsc/current/painta. htm, at 1.1.

46. Saferstein: *Criminalistics: An Introduction to Forensic Science* (Prentice Hall, 6th ed. 1998), at 239.

47. Saferstein: *Criminalistics: An Introduction to Forensic Science* (Prentice Hall, 6th ed. 1998), at 241.

48. Ran B. Singh, *Paint and Glass Evidence, Proceedings of the 12th Interpol Foren-sic Science Symposium* (The Forensic Sciences Foundation Press, 1998) at 199–223.

49. 14th Interpol Forensic Science Symposium, Lyon, France, November 2004, *Paint and Glass Report,* prepared by Dr. Stefan Becker, Wolfgang Langer, Christine Wohlwend, Bundeskriminalamt Forensic Science Institute, Wiesbaden, Germany. Available for complimentary download at http://www.inter-pol.org/forensic.

50. To squeeze this huge quantum of information into a brief review is an extraor-dinarily difficult task and one cannot avoid admitting a small facet of sub-jectivism in this choice. The aim of this selective review is to highlight the most interesting contributions. 14th Interpol Forensic Science Symposium, Lyon, France, November 2004, *Paint and Glass Report,* prepared by Dr. Stefan Becker, Wolfgang Langer, Christine Wohlwend, Bundeskriminalamt Forensic Science Institute, Wiesbaden, Germany. Available for complimentary down-load at http://www.interpol.org/forensic, at 87.

51. 14th Interpol Forensic Science Symposium, Lyon, France, November 2004, *Paint and Glass Report,* prepared by Dr. Stefan Becker, Wolfgang Langer, Chris-tine Wohlwend, Bundeskriminalamt Forensic Science Institute, Wiesbaden, Germany. Available for complimentary download at http://www.interpol.org/forensic, at 87–88.

52. An extensive table is provided that lists the most commonly used techniques for the analysis of ancient pigments, binder, and resins with the relevant citations.

53. The report also provides a survey of articles appearing in publications that primarily appeal to forensic practitioners. To accomplish this objective, the report notes that the authors Brettell, Inman, Rudin, and Saferstein (2001), and Brettell, Rudin, and Saferstein (2003) have focused their attention on the following journals: *Journal of Forensic Sciences, Science and Justice, Forensic Science International, Journal of the Canadian Society of Forensic Science, Forensic Science Review, Analytical Toxicology, Electrophoresis, and BioTech-niques,* as well as *Chemical Abstracts Selects: Forensic Chem.* The first survey encompasses the period from January 1999 through December 2000 (Ref. 76). The second review encompasses the period from January 2001 through December 2002 (Ref. 77).

54. The report also contains a description of the many valuable features of inter-national scientific working groups such as Scientific Working Group of Mate-rials Analysis (SWGMAT) and ENFSI — European Glass Group (EGG) located at http://www.enfsi.org/.

55. See, e.g., http://www.glassonweb.com/, a very useful site about all aspects of glass; and http://www.paint.org/, for an excellent start for paint manufactur-ing data.

56. 224 A.D.2d 316, 637 N.Y.S.2d 733 (N.Y.A.D. 1 Dept. 1996).

57. 224 A.D.2d 316, 637 N.Y.S.2d 733 (N.Y.A.D. 1 Dept. 1996), at 734.

58. 342 N.C. 419, 467 S.E.2d 67 (N.C. Sp. Ct. 1996).

59. 342 N.C. 419, 467 S.E.2d 67 (N.C. Sp. Ct. 1996), at 444.

60. 179 Ill.2d 24, 688 N.E.2d 116 (1997).

61. In an important doctrinal ruling, the court held that the offense of failing to report an accident resulting in a person's death requires proof that accused driver had knowledge that he or she was involved in accident that involved another person. Accordingly the trial court's instruction that the state had to prove defendant's knowledge that he was involved in an accident, and omitting the requirement of a finding knowledge that another person was involved, constituted reversible error.

62. In an important doctrinal ruling, the court held that the offense of failing to report an accident resulting in a person's death requires proof that accused driver had knowledge that he or she was involved in accident that involved another person. Accordingly the trial court's instruction that the state had to prove defendant's knowledge that he was involved in an accident, and omitting the requirement of a finding knowledge that another person was involved, constituted reversible error, at 119.

63. In an important doctrinal ruling, the court held that the offense of failing to report an accident resulting in a person's death requires proof that accused driver had knowledge that he or she was involved in accident that involved another person. Accordingly the trial court's instruction that the state had to prove defendant's knowledge that he was involved in an accident, and omitting the requirement of a finding knowledge that another person was involved, constituted reversible error, at 30. There was no blood on defendant's car.

64. *Digirolamo*, at 30.

65. Kenneth Knight, an expert in hair and fiber evidence, analyzed Pranaitis' clothing, samples of his hair, and debris removed from the windshield glass of defendant's car. In the debris from the windshield, Knight identified animal hair from a dog and human Caucasian hair, which was not suitable for comparison. After comparing a cotton fiber found in the debris with Pranaitis' clothing, he concluded that they did not match.

66. *Digirolamo*, at 32.

67. *Digirolamo*, at 32.

68. *Digirolamo*, at 44. Also see, *State v. Buterbaugh*, 1999 WL 717268 (Ohio App. 10 Dist., 1999), where defendant was convicted of two counts of involuntary manslaughter, growing out of a drag-racing automobile accident. An analysis of paint scrapings from the two Firebirds involved at the scene showed that the vehicles, one of which was defendant's, made contact leading to the death of passengers in a third vehicle.

69. 446 Pa.Super. 609, 667 A.2d 1143 (Pa. Sup. CT. 1995).

70. 446 Pa.Super. 609, 667 A.2d 1143 (Pa. Sup. CT. 1995), at 616–617.

71. See, 14th Interpol Forensic Science Symposium Forensic Geology Report, 2004, authored by Ritusko Sugita and Shinichi Suzuki of the National Research Institute of Police Science, Japan, located at http://interpol. org/forensic. This extensive 2001–2004 literature review is available for free downloading.

72. See, 14th Interpol Forensic Science Symposium Forensic Geology Report, 2004, authored by Ritusko Sugita and Shinichi Suzuki of the National Research Institute of Police Science, Japan, located at http://interpol. org/forensic. This extensive 2001–2004 literature review is available for free downloading, at 126.

73. See, e.g., Horswell, J., Cordiner, S.J., Maas, E.W., Martin, T.M., Sutherland, B.W., Speir, T.W., Nogales, B., Osborn, A.M., Title: Forensic comparison of soils by bacterial community NDA profiling, *J. Forens. Sci.* 46 (4) (2001), 947–949; Horrocks, M., Walsh, K.J., Pollen on grass clippings: putting the suspect at the scene of the crime, *J. Forens. Sci* 47(2) 2002, 350–353.

74. Saferstein: *Criminalistics: An Introduction to Forensic Science* (Prentice Hall, 6th ed., 1998), at 121.

75. The separate forensic discipline of Forensic Limnology (leaves and grasses) or Palynology (pollens) focuses on plant life as related to questions of place of a murder, the movements of bodies, and other location-based concerns in a wide variety of crimes. See, e.g., Bate, D.M., Anderson, G.J., Lee, R.D., *Forensic Botany: Trichome Evidence, J. Forensic Sciences* 1997; 42:380–386.

76. This is especially important in cases of poaching and other illegal hunting cases. See, U.S. Fish and Wildlife Service Web site at http://www.fws.gov/.

77. Saferstein, at 122.

78. See, Bruce Wayne Hall, *The Forensic Utility of Soil, FBI Law Enforcement Bulletin* (September 1993), at 16.

79. See, Yoshiteru Marumo and Ritsuko Sugita, *Soil Evidence, Proceedings of the 12th Interpol Forensic Science Symposium* (The Forensic Sciences Foundation Press, 1998) at 242–252. The extensive literature review paper along with the 2004 edition is available for complimentary download at http://www.inter-pol.org/forensic.

80. See, Yoshiteru Marumo and Ritsuko Sugita, *Soil Evidence, Proceedings of the 12th Interpol Forensic Science Symposium* (The Forensic Sciences Foundation Press, 1998), at 242. Also see, Saferstein, at 122.

81. See, Yoshiteru Marumo and Ritsuko Sugita, *Soil Evidence, Proceedings of the 12th Interpol Forensic Science Symposium* (The Forensic Sciences Foundation Press, 1998), at 242.

82. See, McPhee: *Annals of the Former World* (Farrar Strouse & Giroux, 1998). This volume collects John McPhee's majestic study of the geology of America, composed of *Basin and Range* (1981), *In Suspect Terrain* (1983), *Rising From the Plains* (1986), *Assembling California* (1993), and *Crossing the Craton*

(1998). A number of books on the geology of very specific areas of the United States may be located at travel stores as well as libraries. Also see the *Roadside Geology* series published by Mountain Press Publishing Company, which describes the geology of the major roads in a large number of individual states. These are extremely detailed and are currently available in inexpensive paperbacks. Current titles include New Mexico, Utah, Colorado, Arizona, Pennsylvania, California, and many others. These Roadside Geology series can be of great educational value in criminal investigations involving soil analyses.

83. See, e.g., the following Web sites for good information and valuable links: National Soil Information System (NASIS) at http://www.itc.nrcs.usda.gov/nasis; National Soil Survey Center, at http://www.statlab.iastate.edu/soils/nsdaf; Soils Explorer, at http://www.itc.nrcs.usda.gov/soils_explorer/soils_ex.htm. See, e.g., Soil Science Society of America (http://www.soils.org/); The Soil Science Education Home Page (http://ltpwww.gsfc.nasa.gov/globe/); Soil Science Society of America Journal (http://soil.scijournals.org/; Soil Science Research (Lippincott, Williams and Wilkins); Canadian Journal of Soil Science (http://pubs. nrc-cnrc.gc.ca/aic-journals/cjss.html).

84. See, John McPhee, *The Gravel Page, The New Yorker* 71:46 (29 January 1996), 44ff.

Abstract: Presents cases that have been solved through forensic geology. Murder of Adolphe Coors III by Walter Osborne; Unmanned balloons launched by the Japanese during the Second World War; Death of a Drug Enforcement Administration agent. An excellent introduction to the uses of geology and soil analysis in the investigation of crime. Also see, John McPhee Homepage, http://www.johnmcphee.com/. His book, *Annals of the Former World,* is a terrific read and great geology sourcebook. See, McPhee: *Annals of the Former World* (Farrar, Straus and Giroux, 2000). Also see, Michael Malone, *The Enrique Camarena Case: A Forensic Nightmare*, FBI Law Enforcement Bulletin (September 1989).

85. 140 Md. App. 540, 781 A.2d 913 (Md. App. 2001).

86. See, Andrew J. Rebmann, Marcia Koenig, Edward David, Marcella H. Sorg: *Cadaver Dog Handbook: Forensic Training and Tactics for the Recovery of Human Remains*, (CRC Press 2000).

87. 140 Md. App. at 540, 553.

88. 140 Md. App. at 540, 553.

89. 140 Md. App. at 553–554.

90. 140 Md. App., at 572–573.

91. 140 Md. App., at 574.

92. *Clark v. State*, at 574–75.

93. *Clark v. State*, at 578.

94. 46 Cal.Rptr.2d 279 (Cal. Ct. App. 1995).

95. 46 Cal.Rptr.2d 279 (Cal. Ct. App. 1995), at 282.

96. 46 Cal.Rptr.2d 279 (Cal. Ct. App. 1995), at 283.

97. 11 Cal.4th 1171, 906 P.2d 1068, 47 Cal.Rptr.2d 800 (1996).

98. Jack Leonard, the production manager for the International Sport and Rally Division of Dunlop Tire Company, testified that the tracks of the rear tire at the crime scene had the same highly unique and distinctive characteristics as the rear tire of the motorcycle. See, Chapter 7, Footprint and Tire Impressions.

99. Jack Leonard, the production manager for the International Sport and Rally Division of Dunlop Tire Company, testified that the tracks of the rear tire at the crime scene had the same highly unique and distinctive characteristics as the rear tire of the motorcycle. See, Chapter 7, Footprint and Tire Impressions, at 1189.

100. Jack Leonard, the production manager for the International Sport and Rally Division of Dunlop Tire Company, testified that the tracks of the rear tire at the crime scene had the same highly unique and distinctive characteristics as the rear tire of the motorcycle. See, Chapter 7, Footprint and Tire Impressions, at 1190.

101. 1999 WL 1078733 (La.App. 4 Cir.1999).

102. Also, a piece of green carpet taken from the house matched the carpet in which the body was wrapped and police found pieces of cord and two knives under the house. Inside the house, the officers observed a red substance on the wall and a stain on the floor (pages unavailable).

Footprints, Tire Impressions, and Bite Marks

7

There is no branch of detective science which is so important and so much neglected as the art of tracing footsteps. Happily, I have always laid great stress upon it, and much practice has made it second nature to me. I saw the heavy footmarks of the constables, but I saw also the track of the two men who had first passed through the garden. It was easy to tell that they had been before the others, because in places their marks had been entirely obliterated by the others coming upon the top of them. In this way my second link was formed, which told me that the nocturnal visitors were two in number, one remarkable for his height (as I calculated from the length of his stride), and the other fashionably dressed, to judge from the small and elegant impression left by his boots.

Sherlock Holmes to Doctor Watson
Arthur Conan Doyle: A Study in Scarlet (1887)

I. Introduction

Footprints, tire prints, and bite marks are, as all crime scene datum, examined and preserved through some aspect of imaging technology, whether film, videotape, forensic photography, or some new imaging products. These are central subjects for police, prosecutors and defense counsel, and judges. The quality and quantity of much crime scene material is determined by the skilled use of such technologies. It is incumbent on lawyers in the criminal law field to keep current in the rapidly developing area of digital imaging. Fortunately, highly trained experts are constantly monitoring these developments, and their findings are readily accessible.

The 14th Interpol Forensic Science Symposium[1] has a literature review section devoted to the expanding topic of forensic imaging that reviews the significant forensic literature from 2001–2004, in four basic areas:

- Imaging technology, which captures images and video from analog and digital media, filtering and sorting large amounts of images and video, coding and decoding data, detection of manipulation, image authentication, and identification of cameras and systems as tools used for production.
- Crime scene photography, laser scanning, photogrammetry, 3D modeling, which includes crime-scene recording, using combinations of wide-view and close-up photography and laser scanning, panorama views, three-dimensional (3D) modeling of crime scenes, 3D models as tools for interpretation of questioned video recordings of subjects, e.g., shooting incidents, car accidents or explosions, scenario testing using 3D models of the crime scene, human bodies with wound channels, virtual stringing of bloodstain patterns, etc.
- Biometric identification, using biometric systems based on finger scans, facial photographs, and iris scans, where the demand for extremely large databases of finger scans and new insights from the development of DNA evidence has led to a new interest for the process of fingerprint capturing and identification.
- Pattern recognition and forensic image databases, which comprises systems development and demonstration for storage and retrieval of images captured from evidence, such as shoeprints, cartridges, tablets, and tool marks.[2]

The Forensic Imaging Report tracks the work and plans of international working groups in the subject areas, including European group ENFSIDIWG (methods and techniques); the U.S. groups SWGIT (guidelines and best practice manuals); and LEVA (training on video processing); and the Australian group EESAG (proficiency tests for video and audio processing).[3]

II. Foot Impressions in the Courtroom

The case reports each year contain many instances of the use of foot impression evidence, in a wide variety of settings, including both two-dimensional (2D) and 3D impressions, whether it is footprints in dust, plaster, blood, glass panes, paper, carpeting, oils, or other petroleum products, or impressions in soil, mud, or snow. With each, preservation issues are paramount. Crime scene photography and casting techniques are central to footwear impression cases.

Like the other forensic disciplines, footwear impression science offers valuable class characteristic and individual or linking information. Here, as with ballistics and tool-mark cases, manufacturing technology and machine tooling are highly important. Significant and growing knowledge is contained in books,[4] articles,[5] and Web sites,[6] with respect to the manufacture and styles of footwear of all kinds, ranging from sandals and moccasins to athletic shoes and expensive dress shoes. In addition to a routine search of the *Journal of Forensic Science* (available at http://www.aafs.org) you can consult the enormous and varied Medline citation search service provided by the National Center for Biotechnology Information (NCBI), located at http://www.ncbi.nlm.nih.gov/ (Medline searches).[7]

The World Wide Web of the Internet provides an enormous amount of information on footwear and tire retailers, manufacturers, conferences, etc. For example, a simple search using the Yahoo search engine for footwear will bring up links to numerous sites in the areas of accessories, athletic shoes, boots, brand names, children's shoes, clogs, custom-made shoes, manufacturer directories, retailers, and trade associations. Each of these sites, in turn, will lead to numerous other useful sites for lawyers beginning research on a footwear-related issue. Likewise, a Yahoo search on tires can bring up links to areas of brand names, distributors, and wholesalers; importers and exporters; and manufacturers of automobiles, trucks, and motorcycles.

Before moving to the details of footwear or tire impression cases, let's revisit the justice-related concerns at the heart of the modern utilization of the offerings of the forensic sciences world.

As with the issue of fingerprints, important to investigators is an understanding of what surfaces or media could hold an impression. Footwear impressions can be two- or three-dimensional. In the latter, it is a medium that has the capability to sink down, allowing for a depth measurement along with length and width. Two-dimensional impressions refer to footwear impressions made in or on dust, glass, paper products, human skin, paint, blood, and oil or other petroleum products, such as paint. Impressions made in a three-dimensional medium include carpeting, dirt, mud, snow, drywall, and other media capable of depth when trod upon.[8]

Given the original quality and integrity of the impression, examiners can often determine such important class characteristics as shoe type, shape, brand, and size. As noted by William J. Bodziak, a footwear expert, all crime scenes should be approached with the expectation that they contain footwear impressions in some form, whether visible or latent. Investigators must be, according to Bodziak, aggressive in their search for such impressions.[9] Bodziak lists several areas deserving special attention: actual point of commission; the party's point of entry: the route to and through the crime scene; the exit point; and the area in and around other visible impressions.[10]

Many supportable assumptions can be made from class characteristic categories, such as a person's general height, weight, ambulatory difficulties, loads being carried, and whether the footwear is new, capable of retaining crime scene medium, such as soil, mud, plant life, construction materials, etc. The preservation of the impression is of great interest, given the normally transitory nature of footwear impression evidence. This is especially so in crime scenes, where human traffic is ubiquitous, even when efforts are made to limit personnel, equipment, or vehicles. Photography and casting method-ologies are the methods used to preserve impression evidence for laboratory testing and subsequent use at trial.

International interest in footwear impression evidence is growing,[11] and great strides in the effort to perfect computerized databases of footwear images have occurred.[12] In the crime scene investigative area of collection and preservation, lawyers need to know how the experts photograph, cast, or otherwise preserve an impression.

Consulting William Bodziak's treatise or one of many articles that address forensic photography can help the neophyte become familiar with these key preservation methodologies.[13] Forensic photography is central to most of the forensic sciences, including forensic pathology, fingerprints, forensic anthro-pology, and blood-spatter pattern analyses.[14] There are a number of very useful Web sites addressed to forensic photography issues.[15] The Federal Bureau of Investigation has just electronically published a paper entitled *Definitions and Guidelines For the Use of Imaging Technologies in the Criminal Justice System*,[16] prepared by the Scientific Working Group on Imaging Tech-nologies (SWGIT). These guidelines, as all FBI announcements in the area of forensic science, can expect to receive considerable respect in future court discussions of forensic photography issues.

Basic information regarding modern impression-casting techniques is also required of lawyers if they are to interact effectively with forensic scien-tists and criminalists in footwear and tire track settings.[17] The Bodziak and forensic science articles contain good references about the various procedures used to preserve an impression other than straight photography. Some of these include the use of electrostatic- or adhesive-lifting techniques and new casting mediums, such as Traxtone and Ceramass RC (ceramic gypsum), magnetic powders, chemical agents and cyanoacrylate fuming, and luminol for prints in blood.[18]

An excellent source for information on footwear impression cases, spe-cifically, the individual, linking characteristics essential to tying a suspect to a particular crime scene, can be obtained by examining some of the testimony given by Agent William Bodziak himself in the notorious O. J. Simpson homicide trial. The famous size 12 Bruno Magli shoeprint, the centerpiece of that expert testimony, bears brief examination here, prior to a discussion of more recent footwear- and tire-impression cases.

The efforts related by Agent Bodziak in the Simpson case were extraordinary, and do not represent the standard in such cases, especially with regard to foreign travel to inspect the machinery used to manufacture the shoe type and size involved. Forensic shoeprint examiners do not normally go as far as locating the machine on which the shoes were run. Also, if they do so in major profile cases like O. J. Simpson, their extraordinary efforts are as good as the photography used to memorialize the burr marks, striations, etc, because they obviously cannot haul the foreign machine to court. The testimony of Agent Bodziak, available for download from Westlaw, especially the foundation laid for the testimony, is very extensive and most instructive.[19] An excerpt here is an example of translating forensic theory to practical courtroom work.[20]

Agent Bodziak began his testimony by explaining the class and individual characteristics in forensic footwear impression analyses:

> A. One of the primary purposes of footwear comparison is ultimately to examine the footwear impressions from the crime scene, which is depicted here on the right side, (indicating), with shoes of suspect that might be obtained during the investigation... This comparison involves the class characteristics first of the shoe, that is, the physical shape and size, the design or pattern on the bottom of the shoe, which leaves its print in the impression, and then subsequently we will draw attention to its wear characteristics. Maybe the heel may begin to wear on the edge and other wear that might be evident and would change the pattern of the shoe.
>
> The fourth area of comparison, after the size, design and wear, would be things such as accidental characteristics, for example, a cut mark that would also show up in the impression and would be found on both the test impression and the known shoe. These cut marks or changes to the pattern of the shoe are what makes a shoe unique and would possibly enable, if there was an adequate number of these, the positive identification of this shoe having made the impression at the crime scene.[21]

Proceeding to an analysis of the crime scene datum in the Simpson case, Bodziak noted that that typical type of analysis was not done due to the fact that no shoe associated with the defendant was available to him. Continuing, he testified:

> Q. All right. Now, in cases that are submitted to you for analysis at the FBI, since 1973 when you've been working there, can you give us an estimate as to what percent, where they are submitted to you, they do not have shoes of a suspect?
>
> A. Approximately forty percent of the case work that is submitted to us initially does not have the shoes of the suspect. A few of those may be submitted later, after we provide them additional information.
>
> Q. And are there some(cases) where the shoes are never recovered?
>
> A. Absolutely, yes.
>
> Q. Now, in cases where the shoes are not recovered, is it, nevertheless, possible to do other kinds of analysis on the shoes?[22]
>
> A. Yes. The second and third portions of the chart draw attention to those kinds of requests we get in situations where we do not have the shoes of a suspect, and we are asked to provide the brand name and manufacturer of the shoe and we do this by accumulating in a reference collection, thousands of designs of shoes and searching a particular pattern from the crime scene print through that reference collection, and hopefully we will be able to determine the manufacturer and brand name of that shoe. After that, depending on the quality of the impression and the completeness of the impression at the crime scene, as well as the kind of manufacturer of the shoe in question, we may be asked to give either a general estimate of the size and that would be just through a linear measurement, or an actual specific sizing of the shoe by directly working with the manufacturer.
>
> Q. And what is the purpose of trying to gather information about how shoes are manufactured from the standpoint of a forensic shoe examiner?
>
> A. In some cases the purpose is because of the need to in a particular case that I might be working, but as a general training tool it is important to learn the various ways that shoes can be manufactured,

because there is quite a lot of differences between a direct-attach injection molded shoe or a cut shoe that is made of unvulcanized rubber or a composition molded shoe.

Q. Now, in cases where you do have the information as to who manufactured the shoe, what can you do?

A. In that case we can specifically size the shoe, if it has been made in certain manners. If it has been cut from a sheet of goods and then just glued to the bottom that is usually not possible with an absolutely 100-percent certainty, but if the shoe has been folded and the molds have been made with a hand-milled method, where the person is actually guiding the milling device and creating the molds through personal direction, as opposed to a computer method, each of those molds, both in different sizes, as well as molds that may be duplicated in the same sizing, each of those will come out slightly different. And those differences will manifest themselves in impressions at the crime scene and enable a direct comparison to eliminate the molds that did not make the shoe and identify the mold which did make the shoe.

Q. Now, during your involvement in this case, when you first became involved in the case, what type of analysis were you asked to perform?

A. Initially I was asked to determine what type of shoe, what brand or manufacturer, made the impressions that were located in blood on the Bundy sidewalk.

Q. And did you consult any reference collections of the sort that you mentioned previously in order to do that?

A. Yes, I did. I initially consulted the FBI's reference collection which involves thousands of impressions on computer and in photographs and catalogues, but I was unable to find that particular design.

Q. And how long has this reference collection been in existence?

A. Well, we have changed it over the years, but it was initially started in 1937 basically as a rubber heel file.

Q. Is it a computerized system?

A. Part of it is computerized, yes, sir.

Q. All right. You also were unable to locate the design in your reference catalogue?

A. That's correct.

Q. After you were unable to locate the design based upon your own resources, did you take some additional steps?

A. Yes, I did.

Q. What did you do?

A. In looking at the detail in the shoe impressions in the thirty photographs which I was submitted which were the impressions from the Bundy location, I observed that there were certain features about that shoe that strongly suggested that it was a high end — that is a very expensive Italian-brand shoe. So I looked through our written reference material and I identified approximately 75 to 80 manufacturers and importers of high-end Italian shoes and some South American shoes or Brazilian shoes, and I prepared a sketch and a — one of the photographs, a composite photograph — excuse me — a composite sketch and three photographs of heel impressions from the Bundy scene, along with a letter, and contacted those manufacturers and importers to see if they recognized or knew the origin of that particular design.

Q. Did you get any information back as a result of that?

A. Yes. On August 17th I received a reply from Mr. Peter Grueterich of the Bruno Magli Uma shoe store in New Jersey.

Q. And did he send you anything?

A. Yes. He sent me two shoes that were left over from a Bruno Magli distribution of his in 1991 and 1992. These were both right shoes. One was a size 9 and a half and one was a size 12. And I believe from looking at them they were probably samples that were just left over.[23]

Q. Now, in addition to the information that you sent out that you just told us about to these shoe manufacturers, did you send out any other inquiries to law enforcement agencies?

A. Yes. Also sending — I sent an inquiry to eight international laboratories which I knew had computerized reference collections, such as the FBI, and I sent them pictures of the sole of the shoe as well as the pictures from the crime scene, a couple pictures from the crime scene at Bundy, and asked them the same question, could they identify the brand name or manufacturer of this shoe.

Q. Were any of those countries with computerized systems similar to the FBI's able to provide you with any information?

A. Yes. Seven of them responded and said they did not have this shoe in their collection. The eighth one, the National Police Agency in Tokyo, Japan, responded and advised that they had a shoe that they had obtained from a merchant of this design that was distributed in Europe and was made in Italy.[24]

Q. Now, as a result of the information that you have just talked to us about, did you determine who the manufacturer was of the Bruno Magli shoe?

A. Yes. Well, if I could comment on the bottom of the shoe, which has the manufacturer's name on it?

Q. Sure.

A. The bottom of the shoe has design elements … which are repeated across the entire sole area, as well as the heel, and these design elements, which repeat after one another across the width and length of the shoe, are identical in size in both the heel and the sole, and they are surrounded by a perimeter, a little raised line, and then there is an outer perimeter which does not actually touch the surface of the ground, but which is a little bit raised but can touch it if there is enough weight or other factors. The same is true of the heel and the leading edge of the heel is curved and has the notch cut off of the medial side, the inner side. This is a reverse photograph so this is actually the left — an enlargement of the left shoe, and this would be the outside of the body and this would be the inside to the right as you look at it, (indicating).

And in the center arch area, also, is the name "Bruno Magli," that is B-r-u-n-o M-a-g-l-i, as well as the capital "M" for Bruno Magli, the logo in the middle of that, and at the very bottom in the shadow here, which is probably hard to see, is the words "made in Italy" and up in the top corner here is the word "Silga," S-i-l-g-a, which to answer your question, this is the manufacturer in Italy of this outsole.

Q. Okay. Now, is that common in the footwear industry that the company whose name goes on the shoe doesn't necessarily have their own factories that they own?

A. That is very common in the footwear industry, to have one company make the outsoles and sell those to another company that will then create the upper, which are attached and glued and stitched to the bottoms.[25]

Q. So what is the Bruno Magli company? If it is not a shoe factory, it is a what?

A. Well, it may also be a shoe factory, but they may — I don't know their full habits of purchasing, but with regard to this shoe, they had this mold made by Silga. For their shoes and these molds — these molded bottoms which were sent to another factory which is called 4c also in Italy, in the same area of Italy, and then the uppers were stitched and placed into the bottom and made and sold as a shoe.

Q. As to the manufacturer of the sole of the Bruno Magli shoe and also the upper, did you decide to visit the factories, these two factories?

A. Yes, I did.

Q. And before getting into that, did you have some training and experience specifically in shoe manufacturing?

A. Yes. Over the years, since the late seventies, I have been to approximately footwear manufacturers on approximately 25 occasions.

Q. And what is the purpose of trying to gather information about how shoes are manufactured from the standpoint of a forensic shoe examiner?

A. In some cases the purpose is because of the need to in a particular case that I might be working, but as a general training tool it is important to learn the various ways that shoes can be manufactured, because there is quite a lot of differences between a direct-attach injection molded shoe or a cut shoe that is made of unvulcanized rubber or a composition molded shoe.

Q. Okay. And are you able to use this information in your analysis in determining shoe size that left impressions at a crime scene?

A. Yes, sir.

Q. Now, is this something that you are routinely able to do based on that kind of information and other information?

A. Yes, sir.

Q. Now, in cases where you do have the information as to who manufactured the shoe, what can you do?

A. In that case, we can specifically size the shoe if it has been made in certain manners. If it has been cut from a sheet of goods and then just glued to the bottom, that is usually not possible with an absolutely 100 percent certainty, but if the shoe has been folded and the molds have been made with a hand-milled method, where the person is actually guiding the milling device and creating the molds through personal direction, as opposed to a computer method, each of those molds, both in different sizes, as well as molds that may be duplicated in the same sizing, each of those will come out slightly different. And those differences will manifest themselves in impressions at the crime scene and enable a direct comparison to eliminate the molds that did not make the shoe and identify the mold which did make the shoe.[26] Different runs with same mold can yield minute differences.

Q. So does that mean, sir, that if you have two molds that were created with the same template, that as a forensic shoeprint examiner you would be able to distinguish those two molds?

A. Yes, sir.

Q. And is that based upon the placement, the exact placement of the mold with respect to the perimeter of the shoe?

A. It is based on the fact that in the hand-milling process, as opposed to a process where you make duplicate molds from the beginning, or a computer process where the computer of course is going to do exactly the same thing every time with a CAD/CAM device, in the hand-milling process each of these patterns will result in a slightly different position each time.

Q. Okay. And are there some other factors that are — in addition to the ones that are on this chart — that also go into the issue of shoe size?

A. Yes. There is other factors. One that is very important is the personal preference for fit. Some people, for instance, if they are buying a soccer shoe, may prefer it to be very tight. If they are buying a dress shoe, they may prefer it to be loose so they don't have to go into that breaking-in. If the shoe is in very expensive leather shoe, they may know in a couple wears it will be very soft and pliable and very much to their foot and they may like that fit, so they may intentionally buy it a little snug, so there is a lot of factors involving personal preference that play into account.

Q. Okay. Would it be just fair to say, to summarize this issue of shoe sizing, that there are more factors that go into it than a lay person might imagine?

A. Absolutely.[27]

After an extensive discussion of the foundation for his "matching" of the Bundy shoeprint to a Bruno Magli, size 12, Agent Bodziak concluded:

Q. And with respect to the print on the right that says "Shoeprints FBI Q68" even though only a heel of that is visible, you were able to determine that was a 46 European sole?

A. Yes.

Q. How?

A. Because the heels, like the rest of the shoe, are distinctly different and so no other heel in the other sizes could have made that impression.

Q. Were you able to determine whether these shoeprints were made with a shoe that was manufactured on that precise mold that you saw at the Silga factory, the 46 mold?

A. Yes, it was — it had to have been made in that mold. There would be no other mold like it. So it was made — the shoes that made the impressions that I have addressed here, q107 and q68, were positively shoes that came from the Silga mold size 46.[28] (Extensive testimony followed: see total transcript.)

III. Footwear Cases

Each year a significant number of reported cases involve footwear-impression expert testimony. As noted above, it is fairly predictable that some such data will be present in virtually every crime scene involving the physical presence or movement of one or more persons. The value of any such impressions depends on its integrity and the preservation methods used by police and forensic technicians. In addition to class characteristic information, wear marks, embedded glass or stone, and cuts and gouges can provide individual characteristics unique to an individual. Differences and similarities vie for the attention of prosecuting and defense lawyers.

The visual comparison of shoe impressions for purposes of size estimations or comparisons by police officers in the course of active crime scene investigation has been readily approved by the nation's courts. The analogy to permissible areas of lay-person opinion is often seen. In 2004 alone, there were over 175 appellate cases discussing some aspects of footprint evidence. None, as with virtually all of the forensic sciences or observational disciplines, question the reliability of footwear-impression evidence. The cases run the typical gamut of footwear cases, involving tracking a suspect from footprints in mud, blood, or snow as well as more complex examinations of the topic from qualified footwear experts.[29] The discussions to follow focus on some of the more interesting cases.

IV. Expert vs. Nonexpert Opinion

In *Cooper v. Woodford*, a 2004 9th Circuit case,[30] defendant was convicted of first-degree murder and sentenced to death. Defendant claimed, in part, that the government committed a Brady violation by not disclosing exonerating information about a bloody shoeprint. The defendant was convicted of the first-degree murder after escaping from prison. The state obtained evidence that the prisoners only wore a certain type of shoe, specifically manufactured for prisons, and the bloody shoeprint at the crime scene matched this type of shoe. However, the state also had a sworn declaration from the prison warden stating that the defendant was given a different type of shoe because he was on the prison basketball team. The declaration was never disclosed to the defense.

The court found the failure to hand over the declaration was a *prima facie* violation of the Brady rule. The court believed the shoeprint evidence was most definitely exculpatory, because the bloody shoeprint could have been left only by a prisoner and because it was the main focal point of the investigation. In other words, the court found that the defendant would have likely been exonerated if the warden had testified about the shoeprint evidence. The court also believed that the defendant could not have obtained this information through due diligence. In the end, the court stayed the defendant's execution pending federal habeas corpus review of the shoeprint evidence and other matters.

In *People v. Maglaya*,[31] a 2003 California decision, the defendant was convicted of first-degree murder and escape from custody, and eventually sentenced to death. Defendant claimed that the trial court erred by allowing a nonexpert police officer to testify that shoeprints found at the crime scene were "similar" to the defendant's shoe pattern. Specifically, he objected to a motion *in limine* that allowed the expert to testify if he laid the proper foundation for the evidence. The court found that the police officer could be considered a lay witness because his opinion was "rationally based on (his) perception" and because it was "helpful to a clear understanding of his testimony."

Cooper v. Woodford,[32] a 2004 9th Circuit case, is another decision addressing quick visual identification. On June 2, 1983, Cooper escaped from the minimum security area of the California Institute for Men (CIM) where he was incarcerated. He broke into and hid in an empty house in Chino Hills, about two miles away. The Ryens lived next door, about 125 yards away from the house in which Cooper was hiding. During the night of June 4, 1983, the members of the Ryen household were viciously attacked. Doug and Peggy Ryen, the father and mother, were killed, as were their 10-year-old daughter, Jessica, and an 11-year-old houseguest, Chris Hughes. Doug and Peggy's 8-year-old son, Josh, was left for dead but survived. The bodies of Doug, Peggy, Jessica, and Chris, as well as the still-living Josh, were discovered the next day by Chris's father. All of the murder victims were killed by multiple chopping, cutting, and puncture wounds. Josh suffered the same type of wounds. Jessica was found clutching a substantial amount of fairly long blond or light brown hair in her hand.

Cooper was apprehended at the end of July 1983, and he was tried for capital murder in late 1984 and early 1985. After seven days of deliberation, the jury found Cooper guilty of death — eligible first-degree murder. After four additional days of deliberation, the jury sentenced Cooper to death.

Only two pieces of evidence at trial connected Cooper to the Ryen house. One was a bloody tennis shoeprint found on a sheet in Doug and Peggy's bedroom.[33] A company representative testified at trial that "Pro-Ked Dude" tennis shoes are manufactured by StrideRite solely for distribution in prisons and other institutions. They are not distributed to the general public. The sheet from the Ryens' bedroom was initially not thought to have any footprints. However, a bloody footprint was discovered on the sheet after it was taken to the lab and refolded in the manner it had been folded when the footprint was made.

William Baird, the Crime Laboratory Manager, testified that the shoeprint on the sheet matched two prints found in the other house, and that all of the prints had been made by a close-to-new "Pro-Ked Dude" shoe. Baird further testified that he had a close-to-new "Pro-Ked Dude" shoe of approximately the same size in his lab, previously obtained from another prison. He testified that this shoe allowed him to analyze the print on the sheet and determine that it had come from a prison-issued "Pro-Ked Dude" shoe.[34]

James Taylor, an inmate at CIM during the time Cooper was incarcerated, was a recreation attendant. Taylor testified at trial that he initially gave Cooper a pair of "P.F. Flyer" tennis shoes. He testified that Cooper, then imprisoned under the false name of David Trautman, exchanged his "P.F. Flyers" for a pair of black "Pro-Ked Dudes" a few days before he was transferred to the minimum security area. Cooper escaped from the prison soon after he was transferred to the minimum security area.

Cooper attaches to his application a sworn declaration of Midge Carroll, who was Warden of CIM at Chino while Cooper was incarcerated there. Warden Carroll's declaration stated that he learned that the shoes were not prison-manufactured or specially designed prison-issue shoes, but rather, common tennis shoes available to the general public through Sears and Roebuck and other such retail stores. The court found that the declaration of Warden Carroll made out a prima facie case of a Brady violation:

> The significance of Warden Carroll's communication would have been clear to San Bernardino Sheriff's Department investigators. Because of the testimony of Baird and Taylor, the state was able to tell a damaging story about the presence of a bloody "Pro-Ked Dude" footprint in the bedroom of the murder victims, a footprint only Cooper, an escaped prisoner, could have left. But if Warden

Carroll had been put on the stand and had been believed by the jury, the jury would have known that Cooper was almost certainly not wearing "Pro-Ked Dude" shoes.[35]

Petitioner thus made out prima facie case of Brady violation, and thus was entitled to file second or successive application for writ of *habeas corpus* in district court; statement by warden of prison from which petitioner had escaped cast doubt on accuracy of evidence linking petitioner to footprint left at murder scene, and information contained in statement was not available to petitioner at time of trial.

V. Barefoot Impression Evidence

Barefoot impressions, as opposed to footwear impressions, have received increased attention in the literature and several recent cases. The latest impetus for the efforts to raise recognition of barefoot impression expertise to that of shoeprint testimony has been the work of the Canadian Robert B. Kennedy, formerly of the Royal Canadian Mounted Police (RCMP).[36] While this discipline is a respected endeavor in Europe, it has not fared so well in American courts. A series of recent decisions have determined that this theory of identification has not yet met the Frye or Daubert standards for scientific evidence.

In *State v. Berry*, a 2001 North Carolina case,[37] the defendant was charged with first-degree rape and first-degree murder. Barefoot impression analysis, as performed by officer who had been conducting "barefoot research" since 1989, was found to be not sufficiently reliable at time of trial to allow admission of barefoot impression testimony as expert scientific testimony, given officer's own testimony, on cross-examination, that barefoot impressions were not a "positive means to identify somebody at present because my research is not finished to prove that." Authorities located a pair of gray socks and worn, size nine, Spaulding high-top tennis shoes (Spaulding shoes) near her body. Janet's shorts and belt soaked in blood lay next to her throat.

Before trial, Robert Kennedy (Kennedy), of the Royal Canadian Mounted Police (RCMP), compared the Spaulding shoes with two pairs of shoes known to belong to the defendant. Kennedy also examined "inked impressions" and photographs of the defendant's feet to determine if the Spaulding shoes were regularly worn by the defendant. At trial, the trial court accepted Kennedy as an expert "in physical comparisons with a specialist (sic) in barefoot comparisons."

Kennedy stated that he had been conducting "barefoot research" since 1989. Kennedy defined "barefoot research" as "the research into the uniqueness of bare feet found inside of shoes at crime scenes and mud or blood, to ensure that the bare foot is unique enough to do a comparison on." Kennedy also testified that he has "collected 10,000 (inked impressions of) feet, that is 5,000 people ... and still adding to the data base." Kennedy also testified that he had also collected and analyzed the shoes of soldiers in the Canadian Army. Kennedy stated that he had testified "for the past 28 years on physical comparisons ... hundreds of times." Kennedy added that he had testified about "barefoot comparison" "approximately 20 times." Kennedy had written and published articles and presented lectures on numerous occasions regarding barefoot analysis. Kennedy explained the "hypothesis" regarding "barefoot impression" analysis:

> (A) barefoot (is) unique to an individual. Research is not done yet so obviously we can't say they are (unique).... We don't believe at present that we can identify a barefoot impression until our research is done. The research is showing that the barefoot is unique to the individual but obviously my research is ongoing, so I can't do research to prove that and before it's done say 'yes,' we can.[38]

During redirect examination, the following exchange occurred:

State: Okay, you feel like your research indicates that — that eventually you will feel it's a positive means of identification?

Kennedy: I think it's definitely going in that direction.

State: You just can't say that at this point because your research is not complete?

Kennedy: Yeah, I wouldn't do a positive yet, no.

State: You said that some person could have left the same similarities in those shoes as the defendant if he had the same features as to the wear in the uppers of the shoe, the same features that you saw as to the wear in the soles of the shoe and also as to the wear pattern of the overall shoe. So it would take similarities in all of those for another person to have worn those shoes, such as the defendant, is that what you are saying?

Kennedy: That is correct, yes.

State: You believe, Sergeant Kennedy, from your research that the individual persons have individual characteristics as to their bare feet and as to the way they wear shoes and the way the shoes are worn?

Kennedy: Yes. We have done research on that particular area and they definitely have unique areas, unique patterns on the out sole of the shoe, unique patterns on the inside uppers and they leave very good unique features inside the insole.

At the conclusion of *voir dire*, the Court asked the following questions regarding Kennedy's credentials and barefoot comparison:

*201 The court: Let me ask you, Sergeant Kennedy, you are employed as a forensic crime scene analyst?

Kennedy: That is correct, yes.

The court: And you are a member of professional organizations that are involved with identifications and comparisons?

Kennedy: Correct, both in the international and local, Canadian.

The court: Among those organizations and professionals and experts in your field of forensic crime scene analysis, is barefoot comparison generally accepted?

Witness: Definitely, yes.

The court: And are the tests, data, methodology employed by you and used by you reasonably relied upon by other experts in your field?

Witness: Yes, they are. As a matter of fact, I have doctors of podiatry and anthropology adding to the collection of the database. The quicker we finish it, the quicker we get results, so they can use the database also in their expertise.

After this colloquy, the defendant objected to the admission of the testimony, and asked the trial court to make findings of fact. The trial court overruled the objection, and denied the request:

The court: Well, the objection is overruled. He is allowed as an expert. I am not required to make findings of fact. I am considering 109 [N.C.App.] 184, 189, however, notwithstanding I do find that there is scientific, technical, or other specialized knowledge that this witness has that will assist the trier of fact to understand the evidence and determine facts which may be in issue. Also, this witness is qualified as an expert by his knowledge, skill, experience, and training or education and may therefore testify and form an opinion, if appropriate.[39]

Kennedy then explained barefoot comparison analysis to the jury, telling them he examines the impressions left by the heel, the ball of the foot, and the upper portion of the shoes. Kennedy stated that after examining barefoot impressions in shoes, he can make one of four conclusions: *(1) the shoes were positively worn by the same person, (2) the shoes were positively not worn by the same person, (3) the shoes were "highly likely" worn by the same person, (4) the shoes were "likely" worn by the same person.* Kennedy stated that he has never made a positive identification.

In the case at hand, Kennedy found many *similarities in the impressions* left in the Spaulding shoes found at the crime scene, to other shoes known to belong to the defendant, and to the characteristics of defendant's bare feet. Based on his examinations, he concluded that it was "likely" that the Spaulding shoes found at the crime scene and the defendant's other shoes were regularly worn by the same person. Kennedy explained that he could only conclude it was "likely" that the shoes were regularly worn by the same person, because of a lack of clarity in the impressions, not because of any dissimilarities between the impressions. The court here rejected his opinion as inadequate science, but nonetheless as harmless error:

> Kennedy testified that he could only state that it was "likely" that the two sets of barefoot impressions from the shoes found at the crime scene and defendant's shoes were made by the same person. He explained to the jury that his research was not yet complete. He stated that, although there were similarities between the footprints, he could not make a positive identification. We hold that although barefoot impression analysis was not yet a reliable science at the time of trial, the admission of such testimony was harmless error.[40]

In *State v. Jones*,[41] defendant was convicted of murder, first-degree burglary, armed robbery, and criminal conspiracy and was sentenced to death. He appealed. The Supreme Court of South Carolina held that barefoot insole impression evidence was not scientifically reliable and was inadmissible. A single bootprint was found on the victim Pipkin's bloody kitchen floor. The "steel toe" boots that made the impression, as well as another pair of "high-top" boots, were found in the room rented at Brown's parents' home. Brown claimed appellant wore the "steel toe" boots connected to the crime, while he wore the pair of high-top boots also found in the room.

At trial, the state was permitted to introduce testimony that the " barefoot impressions" left on the "steel toe" boots' insoles were consistent with the boots having been worn by defendant. Defendant argued that "barefoot insole impression" evidence is not scientifically reliable, and further that SLED (State Law Enforcement Division) Agent Derrick who conducted the examination was not a qualified expert. In addition, he argued that even if there exists such a science, and even if Derrick were qualified, the prejudicial impact of the testimony outweighed its probative value. The court set out the basic idea behind barefoot impression evidence:

> The central thesis of "barefoot insole impression" evidence is that the primary wearer of footwear, over time, begins to leave an impression of the wearer's foot in the footwear's insole. Inked impressions of the suspected wearer's feet, photos of the suspected wearer's known insoles, and a standing cast of the suspected wearer's foot are compared to the impressions in the boots, both visually and by using calipers to compare distances between toes and other features among the various exhibits. A Canadian researcher (Kennedy), who testified for the State at trial, is currently conducting a study following RCMP troopers and their new boots throughout the training process. Kennedy has compared the insole impressions made in some 200 Canadian army boots with the feet of the wearers. He began research in the area in 1989 after earlier work done by Dr. Louise Robbins was discredited. Kennedy testified that different researchers use different methods in making these types of comparisons, but that he felt his method (the one used by Agent Derrick) was the best. He also testified that he has revised some of his statements, but none of his methods, based on comments received after publication of his peer-reviewed articles. Kennedy is hoping to establish that each human foot is unique, but at present the most that can be said is that a foot may be "consistent" with a barefoot impression.[42]

The state relied most heavily on Kennedy to establish that there was a science underlying "barefoot insole impressions." The court noted that while Kennedy testified that he had published several peer-reviewed articles, he also testified *that he was still in the process of collecting data in order to determine which standards were appropriate for comparison purposes. Further, he candidly acknowledged that earlier work in this area had been discredited.*
The court ruled that the evidence presented was insufficient to meet requirements that (1) the technique be published and peer-reviewed; (2) the method had been applied to this type evidence; and (3) the method was

consistent with recognized scientific laws and proceedings. In the court's opinion, *it is premature to accept that there exists a science of "barefoot insole impressions.*[43]

An additional issue arose as to the quality control procedures used to ensure reliability:

> Neither Agent Derrick nor anyone connected with SLED had ever done this type of test before. Further, Agent Derrick admittedly had not conducted the testing in conformity with SLED's quality control precautions. The director of the SLED laboratories testified that SLED requires a written protocol on all laboratory procedures, which must be "thoroughly tested to prove their scientific validity, accuracy, and repeatability." Here, there was no written protocol in existence when Agent Derrick conducted his testing, much less one which had been subjected to SLED's quality control policies.

> We find, therefore, that the trial judge erred in permitting expert testimony purporting to demonstrate that "barefoot insole impression" testing revealed appellant's foot to be consistent with the impression made by the primary wearer of the "steel toe" boot. The admission of this evidence mandates reversal of appellant's convictions.[44]

Footwear Impression for Indigent Defendant

In *People v. Lawson*,[45] defendant was convicted of first-degree murder and was sentenced to death. On July 28, 1989, between 7 and 8 a.m., the body of eight-year-old Terrance Jones (known as T.J.) was found lying face down approximately 15 or 16 feet inside a small, abandoned church in East St. Louis, Illinois. He had been stabbed several times in the back, chest, and arm, and his throat had been cut. He was clothed in a tee shirt with his underpants pulled down around the knee area and on only one leg.[46]

The interior of the small church was dusty, dirty, and in a state of complete deterioration. During the morning hours following the discovery of the body and before the arrival of the police at around noon, many people in the surrounding neighborhood entered the church and observed the body, defendant being among them. During the investigation, a police crime scene analyst observed several shoeprints in a substance that appeared to be dried blood. Subsequent forensic tests revealed the substance to be human blood consistent in type with the victim's. The bloody shoeprints were on two pieces of wooden paneling located immediately to one side of the body and bore the legend "Pro-Wing," a brand of gym shoe indisputably worn by many individuals in the immediately surrounding neighborhood. At the direction of the crime scene analyst, police looked for persons in the crowd wearing Pro-Wing gym shoes. Police saw no one in the crowd other than defendant wearing the Pro-Wing shoe and requested that he give them his shoes for purposes of elimination, which he did.[47]

David Peck, a forensic scientist, testified as the state's fingerprint and footwear analysis expert. Peck testified that he found 5 of 12 bloody shoeprint impressions on the two pieces of wooden paneling as identifiable to either defendant's right or left Pro-Wing gym shoe. Peck testified that the seven remaining shoeprint impressions could have been made by defendant's shoes. Peck also opined that the shoeprint impression found on the page from the allegedly pornographic magazine could also have been made by defendant's shoe. Peck testified that the additional shoeprint impression, in the white, chalky substance on the wooden paneling, could not have been made by defendant's shoes.[48]

Peck showed the jury photographic enlargements of the shoeprint impressions, which he relied on as exhibits. Peck then directed the jury's attention to a prepared chart pointing out eight different individual characteristics of the bloody shoeprint impressions on the boards. He then matched each shoeprint impression on the boards with photographic enlargements of defendant's Pro-Wing gym shoes. Peck stated that he could not determine when the bloody shoeprint impressions were made.

Defendant contended that the trial court erred in denying his motion for funds to obtain the services of a fingerprint and shoeprint expert. Defendant asserted that the denial of funds for such expertise denied him due process of law, effective assistance of counsel and the right to obtain witnesses for his defense.[49] The state acknowledged the possible constitutional and statutory dimensions of the claimed error,[50] but claimed that defendant, as required, failed to provide the trial court with the name of a specific expert and an estimate of the fees involved.

The court ruled that in analyzing the particular circumstances of each case, whether deciding statutory or constitutional issues, a standard had evolved that there must be some showing that the requested expert assistance was necessary in proving a crucial issue in the case and that the lack of funds for the expert would therefore prejudice defendant. The Illinois Supreme Court noted that the United States Supreme Court, in *Ake v. Oklahoma*,[51] held that when an indigent defendant shows that his sanity at the time of an offense is to be a significant factor at trial, the state must, at a minimum, assure access to a competent psychiatrist who can examine the defendant and assist in his defense.

Here, defense counsel had filed a Motion to Provide Funds for Experts and Investigative Assistance, which stated that defendant was indigent, was represented by appointed counsel, could not afford to pay for experts pending reimbursement by the county, and that defendant would need a fingerprint expert to examine and compare shoeprints and fingerprints found at the crime scene. The court here noted that the state's expert Peck directed the jury's attention to enlarged photographic exhibits of the bloody shoeprint impressions found on the wooden paneling and of the bottom of defendant's Pro-Wing gym shoes and described in considerable detail the manner in which he was able to identify the impressions:

> What I've done again is put eight numbers on here and drawn them to areas which contain either one or numerous individual characteristics on the unknown bloody footwear impression on the paneling and the test impression of the bottom of this shoe. Number one is a little nick in a circular area in the ball of the shoe area.

*   *   *

> Again, I can point out eight different areas in — for instance, number five on the heel area I circled an area, and they are basically two or three individual cuts or gouges within that small circular area there. What I also do when I'm comparing is * * * look microscopically or very close at each of these individual characteristics to make sure that the cut or gouge, the outlying contours are the same between the unknown and the known.

*   *   *

> Of course, you look closely you can see that the * * * the class characteristics are also the same. You have the small linear bars in the heel area with a type of rectangular squares in both the unknown and the known.

*   *   *

> So I was able to determine, by looking that the class, in other words, the type of pattern, is the same and the number of individual characteristics being the same, was able to positively say that the footwear impression — laid footwear impression on the paneling was positively made by the left shoe of People's Exhibit No. 5.[52]

Peck then demonstrated to the jury how he matched each individual shoeprint impression found on the paneling to each of defendant's shoes and that based on wear characteristics of the two pieces of wooden paneling, he was able to align the wood as it was aligned at the murder scene.

At the close of the state's case, the court noted, defendant renewed his motion, requesting funds to hire a shoeprint and fingerprint expert and the trial court again denied it. During closing arguments, the prosecutor stated that *(t)he most important evidence in this case is the scientific evidence which was presented to you and that (t)he single, strongest piece of evidence in this case, and it's a piece of evidence that you can't get around, is that piece of wood with defendant's fresh footprints in it.*

Considering that record before it, the Illinois Supreme Court ruled that there was no question that defendant's indigence was established or that the opinion of a shoeprint expert was necessary to proving a crucial issue in the case and that defendant was prejudiced without such assistance. The expert's opinion of the shoeprint evidence, as acknowledged by the prosecutor, was also the strongest evidence presented by the state because it was the only evidence capable of establishing defendant's actual presence at the scene at the time of the murder. The state's remaining evidence consisted of highly inconsistent eyewitness testimony and circumstantial witness testimony going only to motive and opportunity.[53]

Footwear-Impression Testimony

Another important and comprehensive case in the footwear area is another decision by the Illinois Supreme Court in *People v. Campbell*,[54] where the defendant was charged with residential burglary. The case warrants extended discussion here.

Jeffrey Miller testified that on the evening of March 9, 1989, when he returned home from work, he found the front door wide open, most of the lights inside the home on, the house in disarray, and there were wet, muddy footprints throughout the living room and kitchen. Bills, which he had placed on the kitchen table that morning, were scattered over the kitchen and living room floors. When Miller and his roommate left home, however, only a small lamp in the living room had been left burning. Miller noticed also that a television and VCR *370 were missing. He then summoned the police. At about 10:30 p.m., after police completed their investigation, Miller left the house and picked up Buchanan from work.[55] Miller testified that when he arrived there were wet, muddy prints on the linoleum kitchen floor and on the living room carpet.

During his investigation, police officer Provensale found an empty Illinois Bell Telephone bill envelope lying on the floor in the living room/dining room area and there was a shoeprint on the envelope. Provensale examined Miller's shoes, as well as those of the other investigating officers at the scene, and concluded that their shoes did not match the print on the envelope.

Officer Richard Fonck testified that on March 12, 1989, he was on duty as an evidence technician at the Joliet police station when he encountered defendant, who was at the station on an unrelated matter. Officer Fonck noticed that defendant was wearing tennis shoes, which when compared to a photograph taken by Provensale of the print on the telephone bill envelope, appeared similar in design. Fonck secured defendant's shoes, and forwarded them to the state crime laboratory for examination.[56]

A forensic scientist employed by the Illinois State Police Crime Laboratory, Walter Sherk, testified that he had been with the forensic bureau of the crime lab for about 14 years, working in the specific area of firearms, tool marks, and shoeprints. He further testified that he received a bachelor's degree in forensic science, had two years' on-the-job training in his field of expertise; had attended a Federal Bureau of Investigation course in shoeprint identification; and that he attended annual lectures and meetings regarding shoeprint identification. In his career, he had performed approximately 300 shoeprint comparisons and testified in approximately 15 cases on his shoeprint analyses.[57]

The expert testified that, for purposes of shoeprint analysis, class characteristics refer to the size and pattern of the shoe, and individual characteristics refer to such things as nicks, cuts, and scratches, which were picked up after the shoe has been worn over a period of time. In comparing shoeprints, a forensic shoe impression analyst looks for both types of characteristics. Here, he testified that the Illinois Bell envelope bore two separate shoe impressions made by what appeared to be dust or dirt. He performed a comparison of the Nike brand tennis shoes taken from defendant with the prints on the envelope, and on the basis of dissimilar patterns, he concluded that the smaller of the two prints on the envelope could not have been made by defendant's shoes.

The expert then made a "test print" from defendant's right shoe for comparison with the larger print on the envelope, by inking the sole of the shoe and stepping on white paper. The larger print showed two-thirds of the middle portion of a shoe. Based upon his comparison, Sherk found the shoe size and patterns consistent with defendant's shoe. In addition, he identified six matching individual class characteristics. From this analysis, he testified that he could positively identify defendant's right shoe as having made the larger shoeprint on the envelope.[58]

On cross-examination, he testified that there was no requisite number of characteristics necessary for identification, because each identification depended upon the uniqueness of the individual characteristics. Depending on what the marks look like, he continued, an identification could be made based on as little as two or three marks. He further testified that he could say neither where the envelope was when the print was made, nor when the print was made.

The expert observed that if a shoe is worn for some period of time after the shoeprint was placed on an exhibit, some change in the shoe's characteristics could occur. On cross-examination, the following exchange occurred:

Q. Defense attorney: Are there any dissimilar points in the shoe and in the print on the envelope?

A. There are points, yes. There are dissimilarities, obviously, that may not show up on the test print or the evidence.

*   *   *

Q. I'm saying did you find some dissimilar points, some things that were on the envelope that weren't on the shoe? *373

A. Well, there may be, but I didn't look for dissimilarities. I mean. It's granted that there are dissimilarities in the shoe. There are points that are not going to possibly match up. You're talking about the wear, after the shoe print was on the shoe. And there may be —

The court: * * * How can you know if a dissimilarity is wear or how can you know if a dissimilarity was there before or after the offense?

There are a number of factors that come into play. There could be dirt on the portion of the shoe that is not there when I have the shoe that was there at the time the shoe print was made.

The court: But how would you know that?

I don't know that, if there was or there wasn't.

Q. Would you presume that if there was a dissimilarity?

A. I would presume it could be that, or it could be the fact that the shoe was worn after the shoe impression was made, and therefore it changed.

*   *   *

If you have the correspondence of individual characteristics that are present on both, you have to assume the envelope was smaller because it was a smaller size shoe or just a smaller print because of the way it was on the envelope. He responded that it was just a smaller print; to distinguish it from the larger print on the envelope.

Q. So, you can't tell us here now whether there is any dissimilar things on the print on the envelope and the shoe print?

A. Well, again, I didn't mark and specifically identify any dissimilarities. There may well be some though.[59]

During cross-examination, the trial judge asked the expert whether he meant that the second print on the envelope was smaller because it was a smaller size shoe or just a smaller print because of the way it was on the envelope. He responded that it was just a smaller print, to distinguish it from the larger print on the envelope.

Initially, the court noted that research had not revealed any recent Illinois case that addressed whether shoeprint evidence, standing alone, was sufficient to convict. It is the case in both state and federal courts that forensic evidence alone, with the possible exceptions of ballistics and fingerprints, to be soon joined by DNA evidence, are insufficient to sustain a conviction.[60]

The court noted defendant's argument that the strength of the expert's opinion on the similarity between the shoe and the test print was subject to doubt because, unlike fingerprint, bite-mark or ballistics evidence, shoeprints lacked original uniqueness and that their characteristics change over a period of time, which should result in a general distrust of shoeprint evidence. The court refused to find shoeprint evidence unreliable, as a matter of law:

> We believe that where there are significant general and individual characteristics, such as would provide a basis for a positive identification, shoeprint evidence may be as reliable and as trustworthy as any other evidence. Indeed, our review of the relevant case law lends no support to defendant's argument that shoeprint evidence is "generally distrusted." We note that in Illinois, correspondence of footprints found at the scene of a crime with the sole of one accused of the crime has long been admissible as competent evidence in an attempt to identify the accused as the guilty person... It simply does not follow that because, as defendant concludes, shoeprint evidence lacks the "original uniqueness" of certain other types of demonstrative evidence, it is untrustworthy.[61]

The court — while acknowledging that "general problems" with the probative value of shoeprint evidence may arise in a particular case where an attempt is made at positive identification of an accused in the absence of sufficient unique, distinctive characteristics — found no "general problems" with shoeprint evidence such as would support a conclusion of unreliability as a matter of law.[62]

The court took note of the fact that most shoes today have been mass produced, and identical shoes may be sold to many people, and that new shoes generally differ very little from one to another. Therefore, pattern and other general characteristics, alone, would seldom be sufficient for identification purposes. However, the court recognized, when shoes are worn, even for a limited period of time, the soles begin to show peculiar signs of wear, nail marks, cuts, and other accidental markings. Consequently, shoeprints may offer sufficient individual, unique markings and characteristics upon which to base a positive identification.[63]

In this case, the court recalled, the expert testified not only to the general pattern and size of the shoe, but also to peculiar signs of wear, and thus, the evidence here did not suffer for lack of evidence of peculiarities.

Finally, the defendant argued that the time between the occurrence of the crime and the police seizure of his shoes, wherein the shoes had been worn, may have resulted in a coincidental accumulation of any so-called distinguishing features. The court rejected any such argument:

> We find it unlikely, as apparently did the trial court, that the six similar individual characteristics could all be the result of coincidence. Were there only one similar characteristic, we would be more inclined to accept this argument. However, we believe that even one individual characteristic, depending on the nature and uniqueness, could be enough for a valid comparison. Defendant urges another point on the issue of coincidence as it relates to the lack of evidence of dissimilarities. He states that the expert "ignored" dissimilarities, explaining that any dissimilarity would be attributable to wear upon or injury to the shoe occurring after the test print had been impressed. Defendant argues that if subsequent wear caused dissimilarities, it is reasonable that the same wear attributed to "coincidental" similarities. He further maintains that because the expert "ignored" the dissimilarities, the appellate court properly discounted his comparison.[64]

The court noted that in shoeprint comparison, the first step in the analysis was to note any fundamental differences between the shoe and the shoeprint.

A fundamental difference was one such as size, shape, or make that precludes any further comparison. Absent fundamental differences, points of similarity were located and recorded, and explainable dissimilarities were differences between the shoe and the shoeprint that may have resulted from dust or dirt.[65]

Defendant also attempted to analogize fingerprint evidence to shoeprint evidence by pointing out that fingerprint analysis depended upon similarities, and that a dissimilarity between a test print and a defendant's fingerprint defeated an identification. It would seem, defendant opined, that the same should be true for interpretation of the far less precise science of shoeprint impression analysis. The court also quickly rejected this argument, observing that fingerprints do not essentially change and no two fingerprints are the same. Shoeprints, on the other hand, as conceded by the defendant, do change. Therefore, while a dissimilarity in a fingerprint may not be subject to explanation, such was not the case with shoeprint evidence.[66]

Defendant also argued that a comparison consisting of only six individual characteristics was far too few upon which to base any credible match testimony. The court noted that there were revealed no cases that expressly state a requisite number of points of similarity for either shoeprint or fingerprint evidence. The court also noted that cases with varying numbers of points in fingerprints ranging from 4, 5, 10, and 20 had been approved.[67] In this case, the court concluded, the expert testified that the six individual characteristics were a sufficient number upon which to base a positive identification.[68]

Finally, defendant contended that in order to connect the defendant with the offense, as with fingerprint evidence, there must be proof that the shoeprint was made at the time the offense was committed. The court agreed, stating:

> (D)efendant is correct in his assertion that in order to sustain a conviction solely on fingerprint evidence, fingerprints corresponding to those of the defendant must have been found in the immediate vicinity of the crime under such circumstances as to establish beyond a reasonable doubt that they were impressed at the time the crime was committed... Further, we agree with defendant that the same time/placement requirement should exist for shoeprint evidence. However, in either case, the state is not required to seek out and negate every conceivable possibility that the print was impressed at some time other than during the commission of the offense. In some cases, evidence of the particular location of the fingerprint satisfies the time/placement requirement, as does the prosecution's proof of the chain of contact of the touched item, which would show that the item could have been touched only at the time of the crime... Additionally, attendant circumstances may well support an inference that the print was made at the time of the commission of the offense.[69]

Here, the court determined that there were sufficient attendant circumstances to support the inference that the shoeprint was made at the time the offense was committed, inasmuch as Miller testified that when he left the house for work, the Illinois Bell envelope was on the kitchen table. He gave no permission to anyone to enter the house during his absence and upon his returning home, the envelope was on the floor. The expert testified that the shoeprint on the Illinois Bell envelope shared sufficiently similar individual characteristics with shoes in the possession of the defendant for him to make a positive identification. This evidence, the court stated, while not conclusive on the issue of when the print was impressed, has some tendency to establish that the defendant was at the scene of the crime, and further that the impression was made at the time the offense was committed.[70]

In *People v. Robinson*,[71] another case dealing with foot impressions on paper products, defendant was convicted of a first-degree murder and an armed robbery committed while he was a prisoner at the Stateville Correctional Center. He was accused of murdering a fellow inmate and stealing his cigarettes. When Officer Jessie White came out of the commissary, she found the victim's body. It was subsequently determined that the victim died from a severe head injury due to blunt-force trauma. A partial shoe impression was found on a paper sack on the floor of the commissary.

Walter Sherk, an expert in footprint comparisons, testified that he compared the footwear impression on the paper sack with the boots recovered from the defendant and stated that while the boots recovered from the defendant were standard issue at the Department of Corrections, the impression was consistent with defendant's right boot. Defendant alleges that the prosecutor misstated the boot-impression testimony of the state's expert witnesses. Specifically, the defendant objected to a statement in the prosecution's closing that defendant's boot impression was found in the commissary. The prosecutor had said:

> The important thing about what Walter Sherk said (the state's expert in footprint comparisons) is the boot (imprint) is consistent with the boots that Wesley is wearing. But the most important thing Walter Sherk said is they're the same size boots as Wesley. So what we're saying is that Wesley is not eliminated by the boot impression.[72]

The court determined that the remarks in the present case did not have to substantially prejudice the defendant. This correct statement regarding the relevance of the boot impression effectively alleviated any harm that was done by the immediately following isolated boot-imprint statement to which the defendant complained.

VI. Footwear Trails

An example of expert William Bodziak's advice to trace the dynamics of the crime scene as a means of locating foot impressions, may be seen in the case of *State v. Washington*,[73] where defendant was convicted of simple burglary. Police received an anonymous call reporting that someone was coming in and out of the True Hope Church of God and Christ. The caller said that the man was dressed in a red jacket, blue jeans and a plaid shirt. When Deputy John Baptiste arrived on the scene, he saw a man in the field next to the church. After returning to the church with the defendant, a police officer entered the church and observed a piano with a footprint on it and testified that the burglar would have stood on the piano to remove the speaker that was tied to the ceiling. The officer compared the shoes that the defendant was wearing to the footprints and observed that they were a visual match.

Another deputy observed a footprint in the mud outside the church's kitchen window. She, too, saw the footprint on the top of the church's piano. When the officers brought the defendant back to the church after he was stopped, she compared the defendant's shoes with the prints and concluded that the impression in the ground and the one on the piano and another near the amplifier were all made by defendant's shoes.[74]

Many cases have been reported where mention is made of police having followed footprints or bootprints made in the snow to track a perpetrator.[75] Less common are cases where an attempt has been made to present linking evidence regarding an impression in snow that was either preserved, or more commonly, where police testify to a visual match between a snowprint and the defendant's footwear.[76] A number of articles have been published on the subject of the preservation of shoewear impressions made in snow.[77]

In the footwear area, as with all others, too often the admissibility of such evidence is effected without any serious challenge. Nonetheless it, like the other areas of forensics, carries very significant circumstantial weight in the midst of a variety of nonforensic evidence.

In *State v. Delucca*,[78] defendant was convicted of armed robbery, conspiracy to commit armed robbery, and weapons offenses. On December 20, 1995, at approximately 8:15 p.m., a car stopped near a gasoline station and an armed man exited the vehicle and walked into the food store and demanded money from the owner. The perpetrator beat the victim and fled. Police Officer Steven Gonzalez responded to a police dispatch and went to the crime scene. As Gonzalez headed in the direction where a witness reported the suspect in the street, he noticed footprints with a distinctive pattern in the snow. Gonzalez testified that there was about 12 inches of snow, and that the temperature was "possibly below zero" the night of the incident. He further testified that the footprints appeared "consistent" and described them as a "vibrum type sole, a particular, like a triangular like pattern of the wearer."[79]

The appellate court held that the trial judge did not err in allowing Officer Gonzalez to testify about footprints found in the snow, because a nonexpert may give an opinion on matters of common knowledge and observation. The testimony of a police officer regarding his observations of footprints in the snow and his conclusion that the footprints were similar to the prints left by defendant's boots is not a matter of expert opinion.[80]

VII. Indirect Proof of Footwear Impression

In *State v. Matney*,[81] defendant was convicted of first-degree murder, armed criminal action, and first-degree robbery. The bodies of Cecil Phillips and Ethel Phillips were discovered inside their house at Malden, Missouri, late in the afternoon of December 18, 1996. Mrs. Phillips had multiple stab and slash wounds to the head, neck, and upper part of her body. Mr. Phillips had multiple skull fractures and incisions to the neck. Evidence officers discovered blood smears and spatter on the wall and footwear impressions in bloodstains on the carpet near the feet of the victim. The footprints in the carpeting were photographed and sections of the carpeting with the bloodstained footprints removed. There was a bloodstained vacuum cleaner in the hallway.[82]

A police officer who participated in the search of defendant's residence testified that he seized an empty boot box from underneath a bed, but did not locate the boots that belonged with the box. The box was for "Brahma brand, Canyon Split, size 8 boots."

Andy Wagoner, a firearms and tool marks examiner at Southeast Missouri Regional Crime Laboratory, testified that he received the part of the carpet from the Phillips' house that had bloody footprints and compared the imprints on the carpeting with the tread on the soles of a pair of Brahma brand, Canyon Split, size 8 boots secured from a Wal-Mart store for that purpose. Mr. Wagoner testified as follows:

> Q. Okay. And what were your findings with respect to the comparisons that you made?
>
> A. The findings were that the lug design of the outer sole on the boots that were submitted produced a similar lug design as that on this carpet.
>
> Q. Now, would you be able — do you have any opinion as to a reasonable scientific certainty as to whether there are class comparisons that are a match?

A. Yes.

Q. And what is that opinion?

A. The class comparisons of the lug design as well as the measurement of the width are the same.[83]

Pamela Johnson, a criminalist employed by Southeast Missouri Regional Crime Laboratory, testified that she compared fingerprints of defendant to an unidentified fingerprint from the tags that were inside the boot box recovered from defendant's residence. She gave the opinion that "the latent print that was on the tag that was contained inside Item 18 (the boot box)" was made by the left index finger of defendant.

In *Miller v. State*,[84] defendant was convicted in the District Court, Oklahoma County, of first-degree murder and sentenced to death. Kent Dodd worked as the night auditor for the Central Plaza Hotel located in Oklahoma City. Dodd registered a guest at approximately 3:15 a.m. on September 17, 1994, and soon after he was attacked by an assailant who stabbed him repeatedly, beat him with hedge shears and a paint can, and poured muriatic acid on him and down his throat. Bloody footprints were found near the body of the victim. Defendant Miller had worked as a maintenance man at the Central Plaza Hotel for two weeks about a month before the murder and had known the victim under an alias, Jay Elkins.

All of the evidence against George Miller was circumstantial. Experts testified that Miller's sandals could have left the bloody footprints found at the scene, but could not be exclusively identified. A microscopic drop of blood found on Miller's sandal was consistent with Dodd's blood, but also could not be exclusively identified. Miller told police he was at home with his wife at the time of the murder. Photographs of the crime scene revealed what appeared to be finger writing in the blood on the floor and wall what could be the letter "J" and the word, "Jay." The court stated that while Miller correctly pointed out that no eyewitness, fingerprint, or hair evidence connected him to the crime and no blood evidence conclusively placed him at the crime scene, there was a substantial amount of circumstantial evidence against him.[85]

The state's shoeprint expert, FBI criminalist Sarah Wiersema, created an acetate overlay of a life-size imprint of the sole of Miller's sandal, state's Exhibit No. 96. During her testimony, she placed it over a life-size photograph of a bloody shoeprint found at the scene of the crime. The size and shape of the prints matched. The defense objected on the grounds that the overlay had not been provided to the defendant prior to trial. The trial court overruled the objection and admitted state's Exhibit No. 96 on the grounds that the state had provided the defense with the sandal, the state's photograph of the sandal's sole, and photographs of the bloody footprints left at the scene:

The court found the evidence sufficient to sustain the conviction:

Bloody footprints left at the scene could have been made by sandals owned by Miller. The state's expert carefully explained that while the size and "interlocking dog bone" pattern of the sole was "consistent" with the footprints found at the scene, Miller's sandal could not be identified conclusively as the source of the print, for no unique flaws in the sole of the sandal were present in the footprint. The expert explained blood is an imperfect medium for the forensic identification of footprints, for it fills in the very flaws used for exclusive identification.[86]

Consistency between the sole of Miller's sandal and the crime scene footprint was sufficient to meet the evidentiary standard of relevance.

VIII. Tire Impressions

Tire impression evidence obtained at a crime scene and compared to tires of a vehicle associated with the defendant are often key circumstantial evidence of guilt. The extensive tire tread evidence presented in the 2004 Cecil Sutherland murder case discussed in Chapter 2 may serve as a striking example. Several more examples of tire-tread matching in recent cases are described next, affirming the significant amount of tire tread information that is available for analysis.[87]

United States v. Johnson,[88] a 9th Circuit case, is a typical example of the routine acceptance of tire tread expertise. Defendants were convicted on 19 counts relating to drug conspiracy, including 5 counts relating to murder. The defendants were accused of multiple murders, but the evidence in question stemmed from the murder of an individual the defendants believed had stolen money from them. Defendants claimed, in part, that the trial court abused its discretion by admitting expert witness testimony comparing the tire tread impressions from the crime scene with the defendant's car. Specifically, the defendants claimed that the evidence was "prejudicial and inflammatory because millions of the particular tires that made the tread marks were in circulation and it was impossible to know when the tread marks had been left at the scene of the crime."

The court found the probative value of the tire tread impression evidence outweighed its prejudicial or inflammatory value. The court noted that there was other, collaborating evidence supporting the comparison, especially because a car matching the defendant's car was seen leaving the murder scene. In addition, the impression was taken right after the murder, the expert could identify the tires based on the impression, and the type of tire was not manufactured until 6 months before the murder. The court also considered the likely number of vehicles with that tire make. In sum, the court agreed with the trial court that the evidence had probative value, and it did not reverse its admission.[89]

In *Wilson v. Cockrell*,[90] a 2002 Texas N.D.Tex. case, defendant was convicted of murder and sentenced to death. The Court of Appeals ruled that the evidence supported the defendant's conviction. In regard to the tire impression evidence, the court noted that the defendant admitted to driving a vehicle with two different types of tires, "tires that matched the tire tracks on the victim's body" and had "a large amount of human hair on its undercarriage." An expert witness testified that he could not conclusively state that the hair belonged to the victim, but he did find that the hair was consistent with the victim and that fibers on the undercarriage matched fibers from inside the car. Another forensic expert also stated that the tire tracks on the victim's body were made by two different types of tires, and, while he also could not conclusively testify that the tires belonged to the defendant's car, one type of tire impression was very unique. Taken with the other evidence in the case, the court found that the faulty tire impression evidence was harmless error.

In the 2004 Nebraska murder case, *State v. Hernandez*,[91] the victim, Mindy Schrieber, was murdered during a robbery at her place of employment. The cause of death was multiple stab wounds, and she had additionally been driven over by a vehicle. In connection with the death, Hernandez and Luis Fernando-Granados, also known as Luis Vargas, were later charged and convicted for first degree murder and use of a deadly weapon to commit a felony. Based on a lead from a discovered phone number, Sgt. Mark Gentile went with another officer to the 31st and California Streets area and then to Hernandez' address, where they located a Ford Escort in a parking lot; the vehicle was registered to Hernandez. The officers compared photographs of tire tread taken from Schrieber's pants to the left front tire of the Escort. In an application for a search warrant, the officers averred that the Escort was blue and that the tire tread matched. The officers examined the vehicle's undercarriage and averred in the warrant application that it matched an imprint on Schrieber's pants. The officers also observed small, thick, tissue-type substances splattered on the undercarriage in the same general area as a red and brown substance. The officers believed the substances to be bodily fluids such as blood and body tissue.[92]

Tire tread impression analysis works on principles quite similar to shoe impression analyses, i.e., style, brand and class, and individual wear pattern and other use factors.[93] A respectable number of reported decisions address this mode of forensic identification.

In *People v. Sutherland*,[94] defendant was convicted of aggravated kidnapping, aggravated criminal sexual assault, and murder, and was sentenced to death. The case arose out of the brutal sexual assault and murder of a 10-year-old child. Among many other types of forensic evidence, the court admitted tire casts testimony.

Illinois State Police Forensic Scientist David Brundage examined the plaster casts of the tire print impressions made at the scene of the crime. He concluded, and testified at trial, that the tire impressions left at the scene were consistent in all class characteristics with only two models of tires manufactured in North America, the Cooper "Falls Persuader," and the Cooper "Dean Polaris."

Several months after the discovery of Amy's body, the police at Glacier National Park in Montana called Jefferson County Deputy Sheriff Michael Anthis regarding Cecil Sutherland's abandoned car, a 1977 Plymouth Fury. At the time of Amy's murder, Sutherland had been living in Dix, Illinois, in Jefferson County, on the county line between Dix and Kell. Deputy Anthis determined that the car in question had a Cooper "Falls Persuader" tire on the right front wheel. Deputy Anthis and David Brundage then traveled to Montana where they made an ink impression of the right front wheel of Sutherland's car.

After comparing the plaster casts of the tire impression at the scene with the inked impression of the tire from Sutherland's car, Brundage concluded that the tire impression at the scene corresponded with Sutherland's tire and could have been made by that tire. Brundage, however, could not positively exclude all other tires due to the lack of comparative individual characteristics, such as nicks, cuts, or gouges.[95]

Similarly, Mark Thomas, the manager of mold operations at the Cooper Tire Company, concluded that due to the "mal" wear similarity, Sutherland's tire could have made the impression found at the crime scene. Thomas compared the blueprints of Cooper tires with the plaster casts of the tire impressions and concluded that the "probability" was "pretty great" that a size P2175/B15 tire — the same size as Sutherland's Falls Persuader tire — had made the impression. He conceded, however, that there was a significant number of such tires on the road.[96]

In *People v. Davenport*,[97] defendant was convicted before the Superior Court, Orange County, of murder in the first degree with the special circumstance that the murder was intentional and involved infliction of torture. The jury fixed defendant's sentence at death

Gayle Lingle, the victim, spent the evening of March 26, 1980, at the Sit 'N Bull Bar in Tustin. Between approximately midnight and 1 a.m., she and defendant left the bar. The victim's body was found the next morning lying in a large, uncultivated field south of the I-5 Freeway near Tustin. The victim suffered extremely violent injuries prior to death at the hands of her attacker. There were motorcycle tracks in the area.

Defendant owned a "350 cc" Honda motorcycle, and his nickname was "Honda Dave." The prosecution produced three eyewitnesses who placed a motorcycle similar to one owned by defendant at the murder scene between 12:30 and 1:30 a.m. on March 27. Three expert witnesses testified to facts that connected defendant's motorcycle to the crime.

Jack Leonard, the production manager for the International Sport and Rally Division of Dunlop Tire Company, testified that the tracks of the rear tire at the crime scene had the same highly unique and distinctive characteristics as the rear tire of the motorcycle. Both were Dunlop-brand motorcycle tires, size 4.00-18 with a K-70 tread pattern, and both were characterized by a rare defect in a portion of the tread pattern known as the cross-slot. The degree of wear of defendant's tire was consistent with the tracks at the scene. The track of the front motorcycle tire at the scene showed a tread pattern that he recognized as a Bridgestone tire, similar to the front tire on defendant's motorcycle.[98]

IX. Bite-Mark Impressions

A relatively recent phenomenon in the general area of impression expertise is the forensic odontology specialty of bite marks. While it is still controversial, an increasing number of courts are accepting bite-mark testimony as a scientifically sound basis for attempts to link a suspect to a crime scene, typically in homicide and sexual assault settings.

Bite marks often accompany especially violent rape homicides. The context of bite-mark testimony fits a very recent case, a violent sexual assault and homicide involving the use of a retired FBI profiler of violent crimes, which leads into the next discussion. It is an opportunity to illustrate the common use of profiling expertise, and its limitations, in such cases.

In State v. Fortin,[99] a 2004 Supreme Court of New Jersey decision, 25-year-old Melissa Padilla failed to return home after a brief trip to the store. Soon thereafter, Padilla's body was found 500 feet from the motel where she and her family resided, inside one of four concrete 30-inch pipes, which lay on the path Padilla had taken to and from the store.

An autopsy was conducted the next day. Dr. Schuster determined that Padilla had suffered numerous injuries, including a broken nose and bruises to her face and chest; lacerations to her chin and left breast that were possibly bite marks, and other serious sexually related injuries.[100]

Dr. Lowell Levine, the state's forensic expert in odontology, compared photographs of the marks on Padilla's chin and breast to molds of Fortin's teeth. Levine concluded to a "high degree of probability" that Fortin made the bite marks found on Padilla's chest. Levine, however, conjectured that Fortin "could have" been responsible for the bite mark on Padilla's chin. Dr. Norman Sperber, the defense's forensic odontologist, stated that bite-mark comparison is an imprecise science, far less reliable than DNA analysis and identification through dental records. Sperber opined that the injuries to Padilla's breast and chin probably were not bite marks and, if they were, they could not be attributed to Fortin.

The state introduced Robert R. Hazelwood, a retired FBI agent and expert in violent sexual crimes, to catalogue the similarities between the crimes committed on an earlier occasion against a Trooper Gardner and Padilla. The purpose of Hazelwood's testimony was to show that the manner in which the two crimes were committed was so unique that only one person committed both crimes. That Fortin had sexually assaulted Trooper Gardner was not disputed.

At trial, Hazelwood focused on motive, modus operandi, and signs of ritual, finding unique similarities between the two crimes on all three grounds.

First, Hazelwood concluded that both crimes were motivated by anger. In support of that conclusion, Hazelwood cited the evidence that both Padilla and Gardner were severely beaten, both were bitten and manually strangled, and both suffered serious anal injuries. Second, Hazelwood found 17 similarities in the modus operandi of the two crimes. The similarities were: (1) both crimes were "high risk" for detection, (2) committed impulsively, (3) against female victims, (4) of the same age range (25–34); (5) both were crimes of opportunity against victims who crossed the offender's path, (6) adjacent to or on well-traveled roadways, (7) at night, (8) while the victims were alone, and (9) the attacks occurred at the same location as the initial confrontation; (10) both crimes involved the use of blunt force consistent with blows from fists, (11) without weapons, (12) that caused primarily facial trauma, and (13) broken noses; (14) in both crimes the victims were undressed from the waist down, (15) their undergarments were found inside their pants or shorts, (16) their shirts were left on but their bras removed, and (17) there was the absence of any fresh seminal fluid in or on their bodies. Hazelwood testified that he had never before seen all 17 of these characteristics present in any crime other than those committed against Padilla and Gardner.[101]

Finally, Hazelwood testified about ritualistic behaviors present in both crimes. He defined a ritual as a "repeated pattern of behavior" "comprised of those acts unnecessary to the commission of the crime" that "complement [ ] the underlying motivation of the crime." According to Hazelwood, rituals are "designed for one single purpose, psychosexual gratification." Hazelwood found "five ritualistic behaviors that were similar between the two crimes": (1) bite marks to the chins, (2) bite marks to the left breast, (3) injurious anal penetration, (4) facial battering, and (5) manual, frontal strangulation. Hazelwood concluded that he had not seen the same combination of ritualistic behaviors in his work over the course of his 30-year career. He also stated that he had never seen the particular combination of modus operandi and ritualistic behaviors "in any other crime and I've never heard of it and I've never read of it."[102]

Hazelwood never produced a database of cases from which he made his comparisons and derived his conclusions, as ordered by the Court of Appeals as a precondition to his testimony. Accordingly, defendant argued that the trial court should not have permitted Hazelwood to testify in light of his failure to comply with the Court's discovery order. Without the database, defendant argued that he was denied, in essence, his constitutional right to confront Hazelwood on the terms required by this Court and, therefore, his right to a fair trial.

The defense had requested a "comprehensive listing" of the 4,000 cases referred to in Hazelwood's motion testimony, including the names of the cases, their locations, copies of police reports, the evidence reviewed by Hazelwood, and copies of his interviews. The defense also requested a listing of the crime scenes Hazelwood had visited and any database he had relied on in formulating his opinion on the unique characteristics between the Gardner and Padilla crimes.

Hazelwood responded, through the prosecutor, that he neither had a list of the files of those cases that he had investigated during his years in law enforcement, nor access to them, and that "(n)o database, evidence or scientific studies were reviewed in forming (his) opinion." He professed to have "relied upon (his) experience, education and training in arriving at (his) opinion."

The prosecutor explained that Hazelwood's opinion would be "based on his life's work as a military policeman, FBI special agent, violent crime analyst, sex crimes specialist, behavioral scientist, author, consultant on violent sex crimes around the world and distinguished national and international lecture(r) on violent sex crimes." Defendant responded by moving for either the production of the database or the preclusion of Hazelwood's testimony.[103]

The court rejected the State's argument the defendant somehow had the burden of gathering such information itself:

> Defendant was not required, as suggested by the State, to assemble Hazelwood's database by researching his publications and tracking down all or some portion of the relevant 7,000 cases that he

investigated over the course of his law enforcement career. Surely, Hazelwood — an author of five books and scores of articles, a university adjunct faculty member, a frequent lecturer, a former FBI agent, and former member of the FBI Behavioral Science Unit — could have compiled some manner of database of cases on which he had based his conclusions. We cannot agree with the trial court that Hazelwood's reference to his experience, training, and education was a substitute for a "database of cases" or that the failure to provide such case information only went to the weight to be given to his opinion, rather than its admissibility.[104]

Hazelwood's testimony, although presented as the application of criminal investigative techniques, was couched in the aura of science, more particularly, behavioral science. He was permitted to testify to his understanding of the state of mind of the perpetrator, who he described as impulsive, motivated by anger, and driven by the need for "psychosexual gratification." A very thin line demarcated the boundary between linkage analysis, which this Court found not to have achieved an acceptable level of scientific reliability, and the uniqueness analysis that this Court permitted as a subject of expert testimony.[105]

The court decided that Hazelwood's database should have consisted of violent sexual assault cases that he had investigated, studied, or analyzed during his professional career, and the peculiar modus operandi and ritualistic characteristics of those crimes. Such a database, the court stated, would have provided some basis for verifying the frequency of sexual assaults in which perpetrators bite the faces or breasts of their victims, or manually strangle them, or engage in high-risk attacks, to name but a few of the characteristics Hazelwood found distinctive in this case. The court stressed that Hazelwood need not present a complete database of his total career:

If Hazelwood was correct about the unique combination of characteristics that the Gardner and Padilla assaults had in common, the database would have strengthened and validated his conclusions. The jury also was entitled to know if there were any flaws in his analysis.

We do not suggest that the database had to be comprised of all of the cases investigated, studied, or analyzed by Hazelwood, or even a majority of them. We understand that it might be overly burdensome or impossible to construct such a record if he were not keeping such records on a running basis and if he truly were denied access to the records by other law enforcement authorities. Hazelwood, however, holds himself out as an expert in this field and presumably has kept records for the purpose of conducting research, publishing articles and books, and presenting lectures. We believe that if he had the will to do so, he could provide some credible database for submission to the trial court.[106]

The database, at a minimum, the court ruled, must permit an acceptable basis for comparison, while not prepared on the present record to say what number of cases would constitute a sufficient database. That determination we leave to the trial court, which must conduct a hearing, to determine what number of cases could be reconfigured within reason and what number of case comparisons is necessary to give the opinion validity.

Accordingly, the court concluded that the trial court committed reversible error in permitting Hazelwood to testify absent the production of a reliable database.[107]

X. Bite Marks: Enhanced Imaging and Overlays

In *State v. Swinton*,[108] a 2004 Connecticut Supreme Court opinion, defendant was convicted of murder, where bite marks were present on the victim's body. The case contains an extensive discussion of computer-generated bite-mark images and the accompanying foundation requirements. The defendant claimed that the trial court improperly admitted into evidence computer-enhanced bite-mark photographs and computer-generated exhibits without a proper foundation. Specifically, the defendant challenged the admissibility of two separate, but related, pieces of evidence: photographs of a bite mark on the victim's body that were enhanced using a computer software program known as Lucis, and images of the defendant's teeth overlaid, or superimposed, upon photographs of the bite mark that were made through the use of Adobe Photoshop, another computer software program.[109]

The defendant contended that the state did not present foundation testimony on the adequacy of these two programs for the task of matching the defendant's dentition with the victim's bite mark because the computer-enhanced and computer-generated exhibits were introduced through experts with no more than an elementary familiarity with the programs. Therefore, the defendant argues, the admission of this evidence violated his constitutional right to confrontation. The state responded that the exhibits were merely photographic or illustrative evidence, not scientific evidence, and therefore did not require the testimony of a witness who could explain the inner workings of the equipment that produced it to provide an adequate foundation. The Court here concluded that the trial court properly admitted into evidence the computer enhanced photographs, but improperly admitted the superimposed images created by Adobe Photoshop.

At trial, the state presented several images of the bite marks that were computer enhancements of a photograph taken at the victim's autopsy. The enhancements were created through the use of a software program called Lucis. The state introduced the enhancements through Major Timothy Palmbach, overseer of the division of scientific services in the state department of public safety. Palmbach has a master's degree in forensic science, and extensive experience in the forensic field. Palmbach had obtained the original photographs for the purpose of enhancement from forensic odontologist Constantine Karazulas. Because the state police did not possess the equipment necessary to generate the digitally enhanced photographs, Palmbach produced the computer-enhanced photographs at Lucis' manufacturer's offices in New Britain, a company called Image Content Technologies. Palmbach explained that Lucis was developed in 1994 specifically for "scientific applications," but that experts had used it in forensic settings.[110]

During his testimony, Palmbach explained how the Lucis program works:

> Simply put, what the program will do is it allows us to see image detail that we normally couldn't see otherwise. How it effectively works is it takes advantage … of the fact that a normal photograph … has many layers of contrast in it Your average photograph is going to have around 255 layers of contrast in it. At best our eyes are only capable of perceiving 32 layers of contrast…. So the net result is our eyes see very, very little of actually what's present inside of the image itself. Now, what our eye tends to perceive as far as contrast differences are … the major contrast differences. We don't have the ability with our own eyes to see the minor contrast differences…. So what this program's intent is … to allow us to make a selection of a particular range of contrast…. And by … narrowing (the) band of contrast layers down, we increase the image detail. So we reduce the amount of layers that we're looking at. We're not getting rid of them. We're just saying we only want to look at some of these layers at a particular time…. (T)he result is the picture's got tremendous detail…. At times we end up creating too much detail. We'll get background noise. And it depends upon what it's on. And skin would be a good example. Because if you imagined … magnifying (and) looking at all the fine detail on your skin — the hairs, the pores, the wrinkles… it might actually be very noisy looking. So then … we'll tell the computer to … stop showing us quite so much detail.[111]

With the use of a laptop computer, Palmbach demonstrated to the jury exactly how the original bite-mark photograph had been enhanced. Palmbach testified several times that nothing was added to or removed from the photograph by the enhancement process. Palmbach described how he and Karazulas had "tested" the accuracy of Lucis' enhancement process by taking a photograph of a bite mark that Karazulas had produced on his own arm, enhancing that photograph, and then comparing the enhancement with the original photograph.

Although much of Palmbach's testimony concerned how the Lucis program worked, he was not qualified as an expert in computer programs, generally, or in Lucis specifically, nor was he qualified as a programmer. Palmbach testified that he was not aware of how the computer makes the distinction as to how many layers there are in an image, or what the algorithm is, or how the algorithm actually sorts the layers. Although he testified that error rates are a cause for concern within the scientific field, he had not seen any published error rates concerning the Lucis program. Additionally, Palmbach testified that Lucis did not create any artifacts in its enhancement process. Palmbach described an artifact as "an addition. It's an artificial component.... (D)uring the (enhancement) process, the process would create something and do something that was never there to begin with."[112]

The defendant objected to the admission of the enhanced photographs, arguing that Palmbach's testimony laid an inadequate foundation. The state argued that the Lucis-enhanced photographs were mere "reproductions" of the photograph of the bite mark, and that their admissibility therefore should be governed by the foundational standard for photographs. Under that standard, all that was required was that a photograph be introduced through a witness competent to verify it as a fair and accurate representation of what it depicts. The state further argued that the enhancements met this burden because the authenticity of the original photographs was never questioned and the testimony at trial was that the enhancements accurately reflected the content of the originals.

The Connecticut Supreme Court initially observed that there was some question as to whether what was at issue here was actually computer-generated evidence. Currently, the court noted, there was no universal definition of that term; many commentators, however, and some courts had divided computer-generated evidence into two distinct categories of evidence: *simulations and animations*.[113]

The court noted that the evidence at issue in the present case did not fall cleanly within either category, but they determined it to be more than the mere "enlargement of a photograph," as the state argued. Enlargement, the court observed, simply involves making the details of an image larger, whereas the enhancement process in the present case "reveals" parts of an image that previously were unviewable. Research revealed that, of the few cases that actually discuss the admission of computer-enhanced evidence, none explicitly qualified such evidence as "computer generated."[114] The court recognized that the appearance of computer-generated evidence in courts was becoming more common. Not only could the court anticipate what forms this evidence might take, but also common sense dictated that the line between one type of computer-generated evidence and another would not always be obvious:

> Therefore, because in the present case, we cannot be sure to what extent the difference between presenting evidence and creating evidence was blurred, we let caution guide our decision. We do not agree with the state's proposition that the enhanced photographs in the present case are like any other photographs admitted into evidence, and we determine that, to the extent that a computer was both the process and the tool used to enable the enhanced photographs to be admitted as evidence, we consider these exhibits, for the purposes of this analysis, to be computer generated. Although computer-enhanced photographs, and the like, have surfaced as evidence in recent cases, both in Connecticut and elsewhere, their admissibility apparently has not been challenged on a basic foundational issue such as in the present case... We note, however, that similar computer enhancement has been discussed in the context of other types of evidence. For example, images from videotapes have been enhanced for evidentiary purposes. Those jurisdictions addressing the issue of enhancement in the context of videotape have permitted such enhancements as evidence, and we find these cases instructive.[115]

The Court next addressed the admissibility of the exhibits created with Adobe Photoshop. Through forensic odontologist Karazulas, the state offered overlays, created with the use of Adobe Photoshop, which superimposed images of the defendant's dentition over photographs of the bite mark. Karazulas had extensive training and experience in the study of bite-mark identification, and was admitted as an expert in the field of forensic odontology. He testified that bite-mark identification was based upon the recognition of unique characteristics of the person whose teeth had left that mark. He further testified that different teeth leave varying marks; for example, incisors leave rectangular marks while cuspids leave pointed or triangular marks.

In the process of coming to the conclusion that the defendant was the biter, Karazulas employed a number of comparative techniques. First, he examined the molds made from the defendant's teeth and testified that, from these molds, he could discern several unique characteristics.[116] Next, Karazulas examined unenhanced photographs of the bite mark. Looking at these, Karazulas testified that he could tell by their orientation that the marks had been inflicted by someone standing directly in front of the victim and approaching her breast in a head-on position. By the shape, circumference, size and individual characteristics of the bite marks, he could tell that the marks above the nipple had been made by the upper jaw, or maxillary teeth and the marks under the nipple had been made by the mandibular teeth.

Karazulas then compared the models made of the defendant's teeth with the various photographs of the bite mark. He testified that any unique or identifiable characteristics of the defendant's dentition depicted in the models appeared to have a corresponding mark on the victim's breast, and likewise, that the markings on the breast of the victim contained a corresponding mark for every unique characteristic of the defendant's dentition.[117]

Karazulas testified that he finished by engaging in a series of steps that eventually led to the creation of the Adobe Photoshop overlays at issue in this case. First, he made a wax impression using the plaster molds taken of the defendant's teeth, then placed the upper and lower molds of the defendant's teeth onto a copy machine and printed out an image from these molds. Next, placing paper over that image, and holding it over a lighted surface, he manually traced out the biting edges of the teeth. That tracing was then photocopied onto a clear piece of acetate, producing a transparent overlay depicting the edges of the defendant's dentition.[118]

The defendant objected to the admission of these overlays for lack of foundation. [FN40] The state argued that a proper foundation had been laid because Karazulas could testify that the scanned photographs appearing in the overlays were fair and accurate renditions of the original photographs of the bite mark, and that the scanned tracings or scanned dental molds appearing in the overlays were fair and accurate renditions of original acetate tracings or original dental molds of the defendant's dentition and, therefore, through authentication of the component parts, or individual layers, of the exhibits, the overlays themselves were authenticated. In essence, the state argued that Karazulas' lack of knowledge about how the computer generated the evidence was irrelevant, reasoning that, because two pieces of reliable evidence had gone into the computer, what came out of the computer therefore necessarily had to be reliable.

Defendant argued that the reliability of what had come out of the computer was the issue, and referred to the issue at hand as a "black-box phenomenon," whereby the jury was being asked to trust the computer. The defendant further argued that, although two separate images that could be authenticated were "fed" into a computer, there was no way for Karazulas to authenticate independently the result of the two images being superimposed other than by saying that the resulting product was a fair and accurate representation of what "came out" of the computer. The defendant argued that the reliability of what had gone into the computer did not ensure that the evidence coming out of the computer was also reliable, and that a witness who had spent almost eight hours merely watching another person create the superimposition was "uniquely disqualified" to testify regarding the inner machinations of the computer that had produced the evidence.

The court found the Adobe testimony admissible under these circumstances:

> The relevant scope of inquiry in the present case is whether the defendant was given an adequate opportunity to cross-examine Karazulas concerning his identification of the defendant as the biter. To that end, we observe that Karazulas' conclusion that the defendant's dentition matched the bite mark on the victim's breast involved several admissible building blocks, including *834 molds of the defendant's teeth, a wax impression taken from the molds, acetate tracings of the biting edges of the defendant's teeth, and enhanced and unenhanced photographs of the bite mark. The defendant had the opportunity to cross-examine Karazulas freely regarding all of these exhibits and how they informed his conclusion. Any failure to take full advantage of such an opportunity does not render the improper admission of the Adobe Photoshop overlays, just one part of the evidentiary whole, a confrontation issue.... Moreover, we note that the defendant had his own expert use the Adobe Photoshop overlays to support his conclusion that the defendant was not the biter.
>
> We conclude that Karazulas' properly admitted testimony regarding exhibits other than those created using Adobe Photoshop goes a long way in rendering harmless the improperly admitted evidence.[119]

The court found that enhanced photographs and computer-generated overlays were demonstrative evidence rather than merely illustrative evidence and thus could not be admitted based on trial court opinion that they would assist the jury in understanding expert testimony, but rather required proper foundation. Controversy will continue over the question of whether actual bite marks are actually on a body, let alone the solidity of a dentition match.[120] Developments here will go hand in hand with the rapid developing of forensic imaging technology and research.[121]

Endnotes

1. *Forensic Imaging: A Review:* 2001 to 2004, prepared by Jurrien Bijhold, Zeno Geradts, Lena Klasen, 1 Netherlands Forensic Institute (NFI). 2 Swedish Defense Research Agency (FOI), available for complimentary download at http://www.interpol.org/forensic. See, Review Papers, 14th International Forensic Science Symposium, Interpol, Lyon, October 19–22, 2004), at 21–46, for a brief overview of an extensive bibliography of tire impressions, shoe-sole impression, and other shoewear related papers published since 2001. This is a comprehensive and excellent listing for the forensic scientist, pros-ecutors, and defense counsel. It was prepared by Christophe Champod and Pierre Margot, two of the world's foremost criminalists.

2. *Forensic Imaging Report,* supra, at 191–198. The report also contains an excel-lent bibliography on these topics.

3. *Forensic Imaging Report,* supra, at 198–205.

4. See, Bodziak: *Footwear Impression Evidence* (CRC Press, 1995); James and Nordby: *Forensic Science: An Introduction to Scientific and Investigative Tech-niques,* Chapter 18, Forensic Footwear Evidence, Chapter 19, Forensic Tire Impression and Tire Track Evidence (William Bodziak) (CRC Press, 2005).

   Also see, Saferstein: *Criminalistics: An Introduction to Forensic Science* (Prentice Hall, 6th ed., 1998) at 492–499; Fisher: *Techniques of Crime Scene Investigation* (CRC Press, 5th ed., 1993), at 90; Geberth: *Practical Homicide Investigation* (CRC Press, 3rd ed., 1996), at 524–532; Giannelli and Imwinkelried: *Scientific Evidence* (The Michie Company, 2d ed., 1993) at Vol. 2, Chapter 16.

5. See, Christophe Champod, Pierre Margot, *Fingermarks, Shoesole Impressions and Toolmarks, Proceedings of the 12th Interpol Forensic Science Symposium* (1998), at 303-331. Also see the bibliography at the end of that Interpol Report section.

6. See, e.g., Ernest Hamm's comprehensive bibliography of footwear impression literature available for download at Zeno's Forensic Site, http://www.forensic. to/hamm.html. Zeno's site is by far the most comprehensive Web site avail-able, loaded with important links and routinely updated. Also see, Recording, Enhancement and Recovery of Footwear Marks, a comprehensive overview of the subject, a class based upon the report to the National Conference for Scientific Support (1997), located at http://www.nfstc.org/footwear.htm.

7. Here is a recent sample of the forensic information available at this major research center:

   Naples, V.L., Miller, J.S., Making tracks: the forensic analysis of footprints and footwear impressions, Anat. Rec. B. New Anat. 2004 Jul; 279(1):9–15; Thali, M.J., Braun, M., Bruschweiler, W., Dirnhofer, R.; Matching tire tracks on the head using forensic photogrammetry; *Forensic Sci Int.* 2000 Sep 11;113 (1–3):281-7; Pretty, I.A., A Web-based survey of odontologist's opinions concerning bite-mark analyses.; *J. Forensic Sci.* 2003 Sep;48(5):1117–20; Kittelson, J.M., Kieser, J.A., Buckingham, D.M., Herbison, G.P., Weighing evidence: quantitative measures of the importance of bitemark evidence.

J. Forensic Odontostomatol. 2002 Dec;20 (2):31–7; Pretty, I.A., Sweet, D.; Anatomical location of bite marks and associated findings in 101 cases from the United States. *J. Forensic Sci.* 2000 Jul;45(4):812-4.

8. See, generally, Giannelli and Imwinkelried: *Scientific Evidence* (The Michie Company, 2d ed., 1993) at Vol. 2, p.479 et.seq. (Supplements) Also see, Recording, Enhancement, and Recovery of Footwear Marks, supra, at p4.

9. Bodziak: *Footwear Impression Evidence* 2d Ed. (CRC Press, 2000), at 16. William J. Bodziak's treatise is an essential volume in the library of all police and private investigators, prosecutors, defense lawyers, and forensic evidence teachers. It is deservedly the bible of footwear impression investigators and contains information in a wide variety of areas not easily accessible.

10. Bodziak: *Footwear Impression Evidence,* 2d Ed. (CRC Press, 2000), at 18–19.

11. See, Geradts, Z., Keijzer, J. *The image-database REBOZO for shoeprints with developments on automatic classification of shoe outsole designs, Forensic Science International* 1996; 82(1):21–31; Geradts, Z. and Bijhold, J. Overview of Pattern recognition and image processing in forensic science. Anil Aggrawal's Internet Journal of Forensic Medicine and Toxicology, 2000; Vol. 1, No. 2 (July to December 2000); Girod, A. *Computerized classification of the shoeprints of burglars, soles, Forensic Science International* 1996;82(1):59–65; Mikkonen, S., Suominen, V., Heinonen, P. *Use of footwear impressions in crime scene investigations assisted by computerized footwear collection system, Forensic Science International* 1996; 82(1):67–79; Tart, M. United Kingdom SICAR: shoeprint image coding and retrieval, *Forensic Science in Europe ENFSI Bulletin* 1996;30(5):24.

12. See, Bodziak, supra, Chapter 2, Photography of Footwear Impressions, at 25.

13. See the following texts for references of the importance of forensic photography in their various disciplines: DiMaio and DiMaio: *Forensic Pathology* (CRC Press, 1993); Pickering and Bachman: *The Use of Forensic Anthropology* (CRC Press, 1997); Fisher: *Techniques of Crime Scene Investigation* (CRC Press, 5th ed.1993); Geberth: *Practical Homicide Investigation* (CRC Press, 3rd ed. 1996); Stuart James Ed: *Scientific and Legal Applications of Bloodstain Pattern Interpretation* (CRC Press, 1999); Bevel and Gardner: *Bloodstain Pattern Analysis* (CRC Press, 1997).

14. See, e.g., the excellent Web site primer on crime scene photography entitled Forensic Photography for the Crime Scene Technician. This excellent site also contains a wealth of important links to governmental and commercial sites of interest to the crime scene photographer. This site is sponsored by the University of California at Riverside Police Department, and is located at http://www.police.ucr.edu. The photography course page is located at http://www.police.ucr.edu/fet-ol.html.

15. Located at http://www.fbi.gov/programs/lab/fsc/current/swgit1.htm.

16. A related casting issue occurs with increasing frequency in recent cases involving bite-mark testimony. See, Golden, G.S., Use of Alternative Light Source Illumination in Bite-Mark Photography, 1994;39(3): 815–823.

17. See, Bodziak, supra, at Chapter 3, Casting Three-Dimensional Footwear Impressions, and Chapter 4, Lifting Two-Dimensional Footwear Impressions. Also see, Christope Champod, Pierre Margot, Fingermarks, *Shoesole Impressions and Tool Marks, Proceedings of the 12th Interpol Forensic Science Symposium* (1998), at 311–312.

18. The O. J. Simpson criminal and civil cases trial transcripts are available for download on Westlaw at the OJ-TRANS and OJCIV-TRANS databases.

19. The complete testimony along with the full testimony of Dr. Henry Lee on crime scene analysis, Dr. Robin Cotton and Gary Sims on DNA, pathologists and crime scene technicians, not to mention the cross-examinations throughout the case, should be in the library of all lawyers interested in the realities of a forensic science-centered prosecution.

20. See, *The People of the State of California v. Orenthal James Simpson*, Official Transcript. Examination of William Bodziak, Docket-Number: BA097211, Superior Court, Los Angeles County, Monday, June 19, 1995, 9:05 a.m., Judge: Hon. Lance A. Ito, at p. 8.

21. See, *The People of the State of California v. Orenthal James Simpson*, Official Transcript. Examination of William Bodziak, Docket-Number: BA097211, Superior Court, Los Angeles County, Monday, June 19, 1995, 9:05 a.m., Judge: Hon. Lance A. Ito, at p. 8.

22. See, *The People of the State of California v. Orenthal James Simpson*, Official Transcript. Examination of William Bodziak, Docket-Number: BA097211, Superior Court, Los Angeles County, Monday, June 19, 1995, 9:05 a.m., Judge: Hon. Lance A. Ito, at 10.

23. Simpson, at 11.

24. See, *The People of the State of California v. Orenthal James Simpson*, Official Transcript. Examination of William Bodziak, Docket-Number: BA097211, Superior Court, Los Angeles County, Monday, June 19, 1995, 9:05 a.m., Judge: Hon. Lance A. Ito, at p.12.

25. See, *The People of the State of California v. Orenthal James Simpson*, Official Transcript. Examination of William Bodziak, Docket-Number: BA097211, Superior Court, Los Angeles County, Monday, June 19, 1995, 9:05 a.m., Judge: Hon. Lance A. Ito, at 13.

26. See, *The People of the State of California v. Orenthal James Simpson*, Official Transcript. Examination of William Bodziak, Docket-Number: BA097211, Superior Court, Los Angeles County, Monday, June 19, 1995, 9:05 a.m., Judge: Hon. Lance A. Ito, at 17.

27. See, *The People of the State of California v. Orenthal James Simpson*, Official Transcript. Examination of William Bodziak, Docket-Number: BA097211,

Superior Court, Los Angeles County, Monday, June 19, 1995, 9:05 a.m., Judge: Hon. Lance A. Ito, at 23–24.

28. See, e.g., *State v. Divers*, 2004 WL 2659127 (La.App. 2004) (Defendant's shoes that he was wearing at the time of his arrest were seized and later found to be compatible with the footprint in victim Vandervield's carport); *Bethany v. State*, WL 2608264 (Tex. App. 2004)(footprint in the bloody dirt and other footprints and marks on the ground, indicating a struggle had taken place, "like two bulls had been fighting"); *People vs Borden*, 2004 WL 2624875 (Mich.App.2004) (police traced defendant's footprints in the snow to a vacant garage where they found the AK-47 The path created by defendant's footprints did not cross any other path. The footprints matched the soles of defendant's shoes); *People v. Chatman*, 2004 WL 2580819 (Cal.App 2004) (police discovered footprints in the dirt behind victim's house and through the backyard to a fence. On the other side of the fence, the footprints led to two suitcases hidden near some trees. No other footprints were observed. The pattern on the soles of the shoes defendant was wearing when he was arrested was consistent with the pattern in the dirt. Defendant's shoes also appeared dusty); *People v. Chatfield*, 2004 WL 2538157 (Cal.App. 2004) (Footprints in the victim's back yard matched the shoes appellant was wearing when he was arrested); *People v. Lyons*, 2004 WL 2452017 (Mich.App. 2004) (despite defendant's theory that two other individuals robbed and murdered Drummond, only one set of footprints were detected leading away from and back towards the victim's crashed truck, even though those footprints were never positively identified as defendant's); *People v. Turner*, 34 Cal.4th 406, 99 P.3d 505 (2004) (police arrested defendant and Souza the next day by tracking their footprints from the location of the Claxtons' abandoned cars); *State v. Adams*, 2004 WL 2415940 (La.App. 2004) (defendant's left tennis shoe had the same class characteristics as the shoe that left a footprint at the crime scene).

29. 358 F.3d 1117 (U.S. Ct. App. 9th 2004).

30. 112 Cal. App. 4th 1604 (2003).

31. 358 F.3d 1117 (C.A.9 2004).

32. The other was a single spot of blood found on a wall in the hallway. There was testimony at trial about the print of a "Pro-Ked Dude" tennis shoe found on a sheet in the Ryens' bedroom, as to which the testimony of two witnesses, William Baird and James Taylor, was particularly important. The California Supreme Court specifically discussed and relied on the testimony of these two men in sustaining Cooper's conviction on direct appeal. *People v. Cooper, 53 Cal.3d 771, 797-98, 281 Cal.Rptr. 90, 809 P.2d 865 (1991).*

33. Cooper, at 1121.

34. Cooper at 1122.

35. See, e.g., Robert B. Kennedy; Irwin S. Pressman, Ph.D.; Sanping Chen, Ph.D.; Peter H. Petersen; and Ari E. Pressman, M.D., F.R.C.S., Statistical Analysis of Barefoot Impressions, *J. Forensic Sci.*, Jan. 2003, Vol. 48, No. 1, 55–63.

Abstract by Authors: Comparison of the shapes of barefoot impressions from an individual with footprints or shoes linked to a crime may be useful as a means of including or excluding that individual as possibly being at the scene of a crime. The question of the distinguishability of a person's barefoot print arises frequently. This study indicates that measurements taken from the outlines of inked footprint impressions show a great degree of variability between donors and a great degree of similarity for multiple impressions taken from the same donor.

36. 143 N.C. App. 187 (2001).

37. 143 N.C. App. 187 (2001), at 200.

38. 143 N.C. App. 187 (2001), at 200–201.

39. 143 N.C. App. 187 (2001), at 207.

40. 343 S. C. 562, 541 S.E. 2d 813 (Sp. Ct. S. Car. 813 (2001).

41. 343 S. C. 562, 541 S.E. 2d 813 (Sp. Ct. S. Car. 813 (2001), at 572–573.

42. 343 S. C. 562, 541 S.E. 2d 813 (Sp. Ct. S. Car. 813 (2001), at 573.

43. I343 S. C. 562, 541 S.E. 2d 813 (Sp. Ct. S. Car. 813 (2001), at 574.

44. 163 Ill.2d 187, 644 N.E.2d 1172 (1994).

45. 163 Ill.2d 187, 644 N.E.2d 1172 (1994), at 190. Forensic tests revealed no physical evidence of sexual assault, and no presence of seminal fluids. Although an autopsy was performed on the body, it was impossible for medical examiners to determine the time of the child's death.

46. 163 Ill.2d 187, 644 N.E.2d 1172 (1994), at 191.

47. I163 Ill.2d 187, 644 N.E.2d 1172 (1994), at 204.

48. 163 Ill.2d 187, 644 N.E.2d 1172 (1994), at 219.

49. Defendant cited in support, United States Supreme Court in *Ake v. Oklahoma*, 470 U.S. 68, 105 S.Ct. 1087, 84 L.Ed.2d 53 (1985) which held that an indigent defendant's right to fair opportunity to present a defense, partially grounded in Fourteenth Amendment due process, required psychiatric evaluation and assistance at state expense where defendant's mental condition was a significant factor at trial. Also see, *People v. Watson*, 36 Ill.2d 228, 221 N.E.2d 645 (1966) holding that defendant's right to summon witnesses in his behalf under section 8 of article II of the Illinois Constitution and Sixth Amendment of the United States Constitution required reasonable funds for expert assistance where expert opinion may have been crucial in the case.

50. 470 U.S. 68, 105 S.Ct. 1087, 84 L.Ed.2d 53 (1985).

51. 163 Ill.2d 187, 227.

52. 163 Ill.2d 187, at 229–230.

53. 146 Ill.2d 363, 586 N.E.2d 1261 (1992).

54. 146 Ill.2d 363, at 370.

55. 146 Ill.2d 363, at 371.

56. 146 Ill.2d 363.

57. 146 Ill. 2d at 372.

58. 146 Ill.2d 363, at 373.

59. See, e.g., *Carlton v. People* (1894), 150 Ill. 181, 187, 37 N.E. 244, where, quoting Wharton's Criminal Evidence s 796 (8th ed.), the court stated: "The evidence of the footprints and their correspondence with the defendant's feet was competent, and, though 'not by itself of any independent strength, is admissible with other proof as tending to make out a case.'" Also see *Gilbreath v. State*, 158 Tex.Crim. 616, 617, 259 S.W.2d 223, 224 (1953) ("ordinarily, identity of an accused may not be established alone by tracks"); see also *Ennox v. State* (1936), 130 Tex.Crim. 328, 94 S.W.2d 473.

60. 146 Ill.2d, at 376–377. Also see, e.g., *Schoolcraft v. People* (1886), 117 Ill. 271, 7 N.E. 649; *Carlton v. People*, 150 Ill. 181, 37 N.E. 244 (1894); *People v. Zammuto*, 280 Ill. 225, 117 N.E. 454 (1917); *People v. Hanson*, 31 Ill.2d 31, 198 N.E.2d 815 (1964); *People v. Diaz*, 169 Ill.App.3d 66, 119 Ill. Dec. 527, 522 N.E.2d 1386 (1964); *People v. Henne*, 165 Ill.App.3d 315, 116 Ill.Dec. 296, 518 N.E.2d 1276 (1988); *People v. Howard*, 130 Ill.App.3d 967, 86 Ill.Dec. 148, 474 N.E.2d 1345 (1985); *People v. Ricketts*, 109 Ill.App.3d 992, 65 Ill.Dec. 471, 441 N.E.2d 384 (1982); *People v. Lomas*, 92 Ill.App.3d 957, 48 Ill.Dec. 377, 416 N.E.2d 408 (1981); *People v. Robbins*, 21 Ill.App.3d 317, 315 N.E.2d 198 (1974); *People v. Kozlowski*, 95 Ill.App.2d 464, 238 N.E.2d 156 (1968).

61. 146 Ill.2d, at 378. But see the concerns expressed by Dean Wigmore, where, in concluding his discussion about the weakness of such evidence, states: "This is because the features usually taken as the basis of inference — size, depth, contour, etc. — may not be distinctive and fixed in type for every individual, but may apply, even in combination, to many individuals. Hence their probative significance is apt to be small. * * * No doubt a witness to identity of footmarks should be required to specify the features on which he bases his judgment of identity, and then the strength of the inference should depend on the degree of accurate detail to be ascribed to each feature and of the unique distinctiveness to be predicated of the total combination. Testimony not based on such data of appreciable significance should be given no weight." 2 J. Wigmore, *Evidence* s 415, at 488–89 (Chadbourn rev. ed. 1979).

62. 146 Ill.2d, at 379.

63. 146 Ill.2d at 382.

64. See, 43 Proof of Facts 2d s 7, at 237–38 (1985).

65. See *People v. Lomas*, 92 Ill.App.3d 957, 48 Ill.Dec. 377, 416 N.E.2d 408 (1981), where the trial court, in rendering its decision, made certain findings regarding dissimilarity of markings made by a right shoe. Specifically, the judge suggested that an elongated gouge that showed up in some test prints but in none of the original prints was of recent origin and may have been made after defendant's arrest.

66. See 36 Proof of Facts 2d s 4, at 298 (1983). Also see, *People v. Cheek*, 93 Ill.2d 82, 93, 66 Ill. Dec. 316, 442 N.E.2d 877 (1982), (10 fingerprint comparison points), and People Reno, 32 Ill.App.3d 754, 757, 336 N.E.2d 36 (1975) (fingerprint technician testified that he found 20 different points of identical comparison); *State v. Pinyatello*, 272 N.C. 312, 158 S.E.2d 596 (1968) (expert testified that he identified between 20 and 25 points that were built into the shoe, no points of dissimilarity, and 11 different identifying points or marks that were not built into the shoe heel); *Giacone v. State*, 124 Tex.Crim. 141, 62 S.W.2d 986 (1933) (21 points of similarity observed). Also see Chapter 8, Fingerprints, for a discussion of this issue.

67. 146 Ill. 2d at 385.

68. 146 Ill. 2d, at 386.

69. 146 Ill. 2d, at 388.

70. 157 Ill.2d 68, 623 N.E.2d 352(1993).

71. 157 Ill.2d, at 74.

72. 727 So.2d 673 (La.App. 1999).

73. At trial, Captain Merrill Boling of the Jefferson Parish Sheriff's Office Latent Print Division testified that he was unable to match the fingerprints taken at the scene to the defendant's, because the fingerprints from the scene did not contain enough points of identification for comparison.

74. Also see, *State v. Keith*, 79 Ohio St.3d 514, 684 N.E.2d 47 (1997), at a snow bank where a witness witnessed a getaway car slide, investigators made a cast of the tire tread and of the indentation in the snow bank made by the car's front license plate number — "043." The indentation from the license plate matched the last three numbers of a 1982 Oldsmobile Omega seized from Melanie Davison shortly after she visited appellant in jail, under the pseudonym of Sherry Brown, a few weeks after the murders.

75. See, *People v. Williams*, 2005 WL 839552 (Mich.App.2005) (one of the first officers at the scene followed fresh footprints in the snow and found two witnesses who had just given the shooter a ride); *State v. Simmons*, 2005 WL 729485 (Mo.App. S.D2005)(NO. 25941). (The victim also reported seeing footprints in the snow leading from his building to the one next door, which happened to be defendant's premises.) Also see, e.g., *Martin v. Commonwealth*, 1999 WL 10088 (Va.App.) (footprints, which appeared to be made from a "lug-soled" or "mountain climbing-type" boot or shoe, that led from the broken glass to the back of the cleaners and then to the back of K-mart, another store located in the shopping center similar to shoes of defendant); *Corliss v. Vermont*, 168 Vt. 333, 721 A.2d 438 (1999) (defendant's footprints *found in snow* near body of homicide victim.).

76. See, A New Improved Technique for Casting Impressions in Snow. Ojena, S.M., 1984;29(1): 322–325; Daulby, Frank, An Evaluation of Snow Casting Materials, Identification Canada, 10:1 (1987); Nause, Lawren, Casting Footwear

Impressions in Snow: *Snowprint-Wax v. Prill Sulphur*, R.C.M.P. Gazette (Cand.), 54:12 (1992); Wolfe, James R. and Beheim, Chris W., Dental Stone Casting of Snow Impressions, FBI International Symposium on FWTT Evidence (1994); Kenny, Raymond L., Identification of a Footwear Impression in the Snow, FBI International Symposium on FWTT Evidence (1994); Allen, J.W., Making Plaster Casts in Snow, *International Criminal Police Review*, No. 89 (1955); Hueske, Edward E., Photographing and Casting Footwear/ Tiretrack Impressions in Snow, *Journal of Forensic Identification*, 41:2, (1991); Warren, Gaylan, Snowprint — Wax Casting Material Information, *AFTE Journal*, 15:2 (1983). Also see, Bodziak: Footwear Impression Evidence (CRC Press, 1995), at 87 (Casting Footwear Impressions In Snow).

77. 325 N.J. Super 376, 739 A.2d 455 (1999).

78. 325 N.J. Super 376, 739 A.2d 455 (1999), at 383–384 The morning after the crime, the State Police conducted a search of the area near the store and recovered from a mailbox on Hamilton Road: a blue ski mask, two latex gloves, and a revolver. The revolver had two spent .38-caliber rounds and four live rounds in the chamber. Subsequent ballistics tests confirmed that the bullet recovered from the gas station window frame had been fired from this gun. Also, two hairs discovered on the ski mask were found to be consistent with hair removed from defendant. In addition, DNA markers extracted from saliva stains on the blue ski mask were consistent with markers found in defendant's blood.

79. Also see, *United States v. Wilderness*, 160 F.3d 1173 (7th Cir. Ct. app. 1998), where defendant was convicted of carjacking and of using a firearm during a crime of violence. Edward Dame of the Gary, Indiana, Police Department found the car and followed footprints in the snow to a house about a block and a half away. Another officer came in response to a call for assistance. The two found Wilderness asleep in the house. His shoes matched the footprints they had followed. No challenge was made to this testimony on appeal. See also, *State v. LaBrutto*, 114 N.J. 187, 197, 553 A.2d 335 (1989); *State v. Johnson*, 120 N.J. 263, 294–95, 576 A.2d 834 (1990); *State v. Harvey*, 121 N.J. 407, 427, 581 A.2d 483 (1990), cert. denied, 499 U.S. 931, 111 S.Ct. 1336, 113 L. Ed.2d 268 (1991); *Johnson v. State*, 59 N.J.L. 535, 543, 37 A. 949 (E. & A. 1896) (finding that a witness' testimony about a footprint's appearance "involved in no sense the knowledge of an expert....").

80. 979 S.W.2d 225 (Mo. Ct. App 1998).

81. 979 S.W.2d 225 (Mo. Ct. App 1998), at 230.

82. 979 S.W.2d 225 (Mo. Ct. App 1998).

83. 977 P.2d 1099 (Okla.Crim.App.).

84. 977 P.2d 1099 (Okla.Crim.App.), at 1104.

85. 977 P.2d 1099 (Okla.Crim.App.), at 1108. See the important Polymerase Chain Reaction (PCR) DNA discussion in this case in Chapter 10 DNA Analysis. PCR DNA testing conducted on Miller's right sandal revealed

human DNA consistent with that of the victim, Kent Dodd. The state's expert testified the DNA could not be used to conclusively identify Dodd as the donor. It could have come from 1 in 19 Caucasians, 1 in 16 African-Americans or 1 in 55 Hispanics. Miller argued that this evidence was not admissible.

86. See, http://home2.pi.be/volckery/Library_Tire_impressions.htm (partial bibliography); http://www.fbi.gov/hq/lab/handbook/intro14.htm (*FBI Handbook Shoeprint and Tire Tread Examinations*; The C.A.S.T. [Chesapeake Area Shoeprint and Tire track] Web site [http://members.aol.com/varfee/mastssite/index.html]; Bessman, C.W. and Schmeiser, A., Survey of Tire Tread Design and Tire Size as Mounted on Vehicles in Central Iowa. *Journal of Forensic Identification*, 2001. 51(6): 587-596

87. 219 F.3d 349 (Ct. App. 9th Cir. 2000).

88. 219 F.3d 349 (Ct. App. 9th Cir. 2000), at 358.

89. 2002 WL 32590134 (N.D.Tex. 2002).

90. Also see, *People v. Wheetley*, 2004 WL 2413862 (Mich.App. 2004) (Additional evidence adduced at trial included tire tread patterns found at the murder scene that matched two of the tires from defendant's car); *Davis v. Com.*, 147 S.W.3d 709 (Ky., 2004) (Tire expert William Bodziak testified that a tire track from the crime scene possibly matched the tires on Appellant's rental truck. While he objected to Bodziak's evidence, he did not do so on grounds that Bodziak's method of comparison was scientifically unreliable; he objected because Bodziak was unable to state with certainty that the tire track left at the scene was a unique match to the tire on the truck rented by Appellant. The court held that the failure to conduct a *Daubert* review does not amount to palpable error when it was not requested.)

91. See the ENFSI Working Group Marks car database, maintained by the Judicial Police in Ghent, Belgium, a system for searching the makes and models of cars based on the measurements of tire track widths. The Web site includes data on tires, track widths, wheelbases, and other specifications of 4500 vehicles sold in Europe from 1969 to date. See also the publication called *Tread Design*, referenced by tire tread analysts.

92. 155 Ill.2d 1, 610 N.E.2d 1 (1992).

93. 155 Ill.2d 1, 610 N.E.2d 1 (1992), at 9.

94. 155 Ill.2d 1, 610 N.E.2d 1 (1992). See the extensive discussion of the Sutherland case in Chapter 2, Science and the Criminal Law. The tire tread analysis was repeated in the summer 2004 retrial where Sutherland was reconvicted.

95. 11 Cal.4th 1171, 47 Cal.Rptr.2d 800 (1995).

96. 11 Cal.4th 1171, 47 Cal.Rptr.2d 800 (1995), at 1191.

97. 178 N.J. 540, 843 A.2d 974 (2004).

98. 178 N.J. 540, 843 A.2d 974 (2004), at 985.

99. 178 N.J. 540, 843 A.2d 974 (2004), at 988.

100. 178 N.J. 540, 843 A.2d 974 (2004).

101. Fortin at 585.

102. Fortin at 587, 1000.

103. Fortin at 587, 1000.

Rules of Evidence, contrary to the state's assertions, do provide the basis for the production of a database before an expert testifies. N.J.R.E. *705* states, "The expert may testify in terms of opinion or inference and give reasons therefor without prior disclosure of the underlying facts or data, unless the court requires otherwise. The expert may in any event be required to disclose the underlying facts or data on cross-examination." Id.

104. Fortin, at 589.

105. Fortin, at 590. See also, *Garrison v. State*, 2004 WL 2775484 (Okla.Crim.App., 2004), where defendant was convicted of murder. (Expert's opinion testimony that photograph taken of defendant's right forearm showed presence of a probable partial bite mark was relevant and admissible during guilt phase of capital murder prosecution; defendant claimed his brother had caused wound by striking him with an entrenching tool, but defendant had originally reported that his brother struck him on left arm, and sudden presence of a probable bite mark on defendant's right forearm eight days after victim disappeared circumstantially suggested defendant was concocting an alibi.)

106. 268 Conn. 781, 847 A.2d 921 (2004).

107. 268 Conn. 781, 847 A.2d 921 (2004), at 795.

108. 268 Conn. 781, 847 A.2d 921 (2004), at 799.

109. 268 Conn. 781, 847 A.2d 921 (2004), at 800.

110. Swinton, at 801.

111. "In *a simulation*, data is entered into a computer which is programmed to analyze the information and perform calculations by applying mathematical models, laws of physics and other scientific principles in order to draw conclusions and recreate an incident.... In contrast, *an animation* does not develop any opinions or perform any scientific calculations and, to the contrary, is nothing more than a graphic depiction or illustration of the previously formed opinion of an expert." (Citing *Commonwealth v. Serge*, 58 Pa. D. & C.4th 52, 68–69 (2001).

112. See, e.g., *United States v. Calderin-Rodriquez, 244 F.3d 977, 986 (8th Cir.2001)* (digitally enhanced sound recordings); *Nooner v. State, 322 Ark. 87, 103-104, 907 S.W.2d 677 (1995)* (digitally enhanced videotape), cert. denied, *517 U.S. 1143, 116 S.Ct. 1436, 134 L.Ed.2d 558 (1996)*; *Dolan v. State, 743 So.2d 544, 545–46 (Fla.App.1999)* (same); *English v. State, 205 Ga.App. 599, 599–600, 422 S.E.2d 924 (1992)* (same); *State v. Hayden, 90 Wash.App. 100, 103, 950 P.2d 1024 (1998)* (digitally enhanced fingerprint).

113. Swinton, at 940.

114. In the upper-left side of the mouth, the left upper cuspid was rotated instead of being flush to the other teeth, and the cuspid on the other side was also rotated.

The upper left central and lateral incisors also were tipped forward. On the lower jaw, Karazulas pointed out that there were spaces behind several teeth — on the lower left between the cuspid and bicuspid, on the lower right between the cuspid and the lateral incisor, and between the right cuspid and the first bicuspid. He further pointed out that, "(a)s you look at the arch, it slants up to the right. All the teeth move upward and to the right." Swinton, at 947.

115. Swinton, at 947.

116. Swinton, at 948.

117. Swinton, at 948.

118. Doctor Michael West's controversial photographic technique employing ultraviolet (UV) light to determine the existence and nature of bite marks has been the subject of a 2003 Pensylvania decision.

119. In *Kunco v. Attorney General of the Commonwealth of Pennsylvania.*

120. The court found that the trial court's admission of forensic odontologist Michael West's expert testimony regarding inculpatory bite-mark photograph obtained by way of allegedly controversial photographic technique employing UV light did not violate defendant's due process rights. Even if the expert later encountered ethical troubles in connection with other research projects and unrelated court cases, where another expert's testimony upheld challenged expert's findings, bite mark revealed by UV photograph closely matched with the bite mark recorded by earlier photograph, and there was independent proof of defendant's connection to bite mark found on victim's shoulder.

121. See, Review Papers, 14th International Forensic Science Symposium, Interpol, Lyon, France, October 19–22, 2004, Forensic Imaging Report, supra, at 191–198. The report also contains an excellent bibliography on these topics.

Fingerprints

> Although this may seem a paradox, all exact science is dominated
> by the idea of approximation.

Bertrand Russell[1]

I. Introduction

The world fascination with fingerprints and related topics remains unabated
in the year 2005. The 14th International Forensic Science Symposium, held
in Lyon, France, has in its 585-page Review Papers, an extensive discussion
of recent fingerprint (fingermark in Europe) literature in a wide variety of
subjects and an extensive bibliography. Subjects covered include:

- Friction ridge skin individualization processes in court challenges
- Fingermark detection and visualization (composition of fingermarks,
  physical and chemical detection techniques [powder, physical devel-
  oper, cyanoacrylate, DFO, and ninhydrin])
- Vacuum metal deposition (VMD)
- Blood-centered fingermarks
- Fingermark detection and DNA or biological fluid analysis
- Alternative light sources, photography, and digital chemical imaging

II. International Working Groups

Since the early 1990s, the FBI Laboratory has led the way in sponsoring
scientific working groups (SWG) to improve discipline practices in laboratory
testing and training, and to help build consensus with federal, state, and local

forensic law enforcement agencies. Currently, the FBI Laboratory sponsors eight SWGs:

- SWGDAM — DNA Analysis
- SWGDE — Digital Evidence
- SWGDOC — Questioned Documents
- SWGFAST — Latent Fingerprints
- SWGGUN — Firearms and Toolmarks
- SWGIBRA — Illicit Business Records
- SWGIT — Imaging Technologies
- SWGMAT — Materials Scientific Working Groups[2]

Each of these SWGs publishes ongoing suggested standards for individual and laboratory certification as well as standards for the actual implementation of fingerprint technology at the working case level.

SWGFAST has recently prepared a list of topics with the intent of encouraging research in the following areas:

1. Vision Requirements for Latent Print Examiners
2. Perceptual Conditions Affecting an Individual's Aptitude for Latent Print Examinations
3. Comprehensive Review of Latent Print Training
4. Comparison of Fingerprint Powders
5. Determination of the Sequence of Friction Ridge Impression Deposition on Printed Documents
6. Development of Latent Prints on Human Skin
7. Use of Digital Image Enhancement
8. Sufficiency for Exclusion
9. Recovery of Latent Prints in the Processing of Clandestine Laboratories
10. Nondestructive Detection and Analysis of Latent Print Residue[3]

The Scientific Working Group on Friction Ridge Analysis Study and Technology (SWGFAST) documents are officially published in the *Journal of Forensic Identification*.[4] The documents are also available for downloading at the official SWGFAST Web site. See, http://www.swgfast.org/.

Several important documents that involve fingerprint technology should be of special interest to lawyers involved in criminal trials. All are available for download at the SWGFAST site; some are listed here:

- Position Statement Regarding Competency Testing of Noncertified Examiners
- Friction Ridge Automation Training Guidelines

- Friction Ridge Digital Imaging Guidelines (8/8/02 Version1.0)
- Friction Ridge Examination Methodology for Latent Print Examiners (8/22/02 Version 1.01)
- Guidelines for Latent Print Proficiency Testing Programs (9/11/03 Version 1.0)
- Guidelines for Professional Conduct (8/9/01 Version 1.0)
- Minimum Qualifications for Latent Print Trainees (8/22/02 Version 2.1)
- Quality Assurance Guidelines for Latent Print Examiners (8/22/02 Version 2.11)
- Standards for Conclusions (9/11/03 Version 1.0)
- Training to Competency for Latent Print Examiners (8/22/02 Version 2.1)
- Validation of Research and Technology (8/8/02 Version 1.0)
- Glossary — Consolidated (9/9/03 Version 1.0)

As noted throughout this volume, international working groups are working to achieve a set of international standards for use in forensic laboratory and investigative efforts. The Interpol Forensic Science Symposium noted all of the listed references its various literature review subreports. In addition to the Interpol and FBI working group Web sites, many other informative Web sites exist for examination in the fingerprint area, including lists of identification points required in various nations.[5]

The importance and fascination with fingerprint technology is reflected in the publication of new books on the subject. Several new books have been published since the first edition of this book, including two that should be in the forensic library of prosecutors, defense counsel, and judges. The first volume is by Christophe Champod, Chris J. Lennard, Pierre Margot, and Milutin Stoilovic, and is called: *Fingerprints and Other Ridge Skin Impressions* (CRC Press 2004). The book contains comprehensive discussions of most topics of concern to those with fingerprint cases, including friction ridge skin, the friction ridge identification process, chemistry, light and photography, fingerprint detection techniques, issues related to the exploitation of fingerprint evidence, and appendices covering statistical data for general fingerprint patterns, fingerprint detection sequences, preparation and application of reagents, and an extensive list of references.

The second volume is *Advances in Fingerprint Technology*, Second Edition, by Henry C. Lee (Editor), R. E. Gaensslen (Editor) (CRC Press 2001), containing ten chapters by some of the nation's top fingerprint experts on all aspects of fingerprint work and technology.[6] This fully updated Second Edition covers major developments in latent fingerprint processing, including physical, chemical, instrumental, and combination techniques. Written by a renowned group of leading forensic identification and criminalistic experts, this valuable work presents exciting progress in fingerprint technology. New in this edition are latent fingerprint chemistry, techniques directed at lipid-soluble components, more succinct treatment of AFIS, and new procedures that apply nanocrystal technology to latent fingerprint development.

The *Fingermarks Review* report prepared by Christophe Champod and Pierre A. Margot, for the 14th Interpol International Forensic Science Symposium, held at Lyon, France in 2004[7] noted the erroneous identification of two individuals in the last several years, resulting in increased scrutiny of the fingerprint identification system. The first case involved Stephan Cowans,[8] who has recently been exonerated by DNA analysis of a murder, the conviction having been based on erroneous fingerprint identification. The second case is that of Brandon Mayfield, who was wrongly associated by means of fingerprint to a latent mark revealed by the Spanish National Police on a plastic bag containing detonators recovered from the stolen van associated with the Madrid bombings. Three experts from the FBI and an independent court-appointed expert all identified Brandon Mayfield as the donor of the mark. Mayfield, an Oregon-based lawyer, came to the attention of the FBI once one of the latent marks sent by the Spanish authorities through Interpol gave a hit against his name on the FBI IAFIS. Brandon Mayfield was arrested and remained in custody for a few weeks until the Spanish fingerprint experts, who immediately had raised issues with this identification, finally identified the mark with the finger of an Algerian suspect. The FBI made official excuses and launched a full and transparent review of its operating procedures.[9]

There are a number of standard forensic science texts available with excellent introductions to the forensic discipline of fingerprint impression recognition, retrieval, and identification processes.[10] International interest in fingerprint impression evidence is growing and new publications are appearing that need to be in the library of any law firm or governmental unit addressing fingerprint theory, collection procedures, or the utilization of digital impression technology.[11] An increasing number of Web sites also contain valuable introductory and specialized fingerprint impression information[12] that should be regularly consulted for updates. Also, the rapid addition of new sites in the forensic science and law and science areas makes it imperative for lawyers to regularly consult the available Internet sites.

III. Fingerprints: American Experience

American courts accepted fingerprint identification evidence long before there was an FBI laboratory or any hint of computerized fingerprint image retrieval systems. Fingerprint identification methods were briefly preceded by the famous Bertillon system introduced by the Paris police in 1882. The

Bertillon method involved the recording and subsequent matching of scrupulous measurements of bodily structures, such as height, length, and width of head, fingers, feet, etc., from the recorded data and current suspects. This system was briefly utilized in America to identify military deserters in the early 1890s.[13] The first attempt to formalize a system for using the ridge characteristics of fingers is generally recognized as that of Sir William Herschel in the Indian state of Bengal in 1877 to check forgeries. In 1892 Francis Galton published the famous book *Finger Prints*, setting forth a statistical basis for supporting a friction ridge identification systems. Since its publication, it has remained in the literature as one of the formulistic bases for the modern science of fingerprint identification. Its system of classification of finger skin patterns labeled arches, loops, and whorls still serves today as a basis for modern fingerprint systems.

Dean Wigmore noted the growing importance of fingerprint evidence in the 1913 second edition of his famous treatise, *The Principles of Judicial Proof*.[14] Interestingly, the third edition, published in 1937, changed the title to *The Science of Judicial Proof*,[15] with a substantial increase in coverage of what would be considered today as forensic evidence. This is a still valuable and extensive treatise on proof of fact. Throughout all editions, the book is subtitled, "As Given by Logic, Psychology, and General Experience and Illustrated in Judicial Trials." It contains not only numerous and generous quotations from a host of classic texts on philosophy, psychology, logic, and law, but selections from the transcripts of famous trials from the 17th century to the Knapp Trial from 1830. It is centered in the idea that at the ground level of a trial, the scholastic delineation of the rules of civil and criminal liability theory and the rules of evidence[16] await the presentation of fact and inferences, which drive the daily operation of the American justice system.

In the 1913 edition, in the section entitled Circumstantial Evidence, Proof of Identity, Wigmore provides two selections, an excerpt entitled Finger-Print Identification, from a 1911 book entitled *Science and the Criminal* by Ainsworth Mitchell, and the full text of the famous fingerprint case of *People v. Jennings*,[17] decided by the Illinois Supreme Court in 1911. Mitchell notes that the work of Galton, set forth at the end of the 19th century, set the standard for estimating the match capability of fingerprints:

...(E)ven after making allowance for ambiguities and for possible alterations caused by accident or disease, a complete, or nearly complete, agreement between two prints of one finger and infinitely more so between two or more fingers, afforded evidence, which did not stand in need of corroboration, that the prints were derived from the fingers of one and the same person.[18]

The first major criminal case recognizing the scientific, and hence, legal viability of fingerprint evidence was the case of *People v. Jennings*,[19] decided by the Illinois Supreme Court in 1911. This case is described in detail, to illustrate the court's thoughts on this new and apparently definitive method of identification.

The defendant Thomas Jennings was convicted of the murder of a Mr. Hiller, the owner of a home that he had illegally entered. At the head of the stairs, near the door leading to a daughter's room, a gaslight was kept burning at night. Shortly after 2 o'clock on Monday morning of September 19, 1910, Mrs. Hiller was awakened and noticed that this light was out. She called her husband's attention to the fact and he went in his nightclothes to the head of the stairway, where he encountered an intruder, with whom he grappled. In the struggle both fell to the foot of the stairway, where Hiller was shot twice, dying in a few moments.

The house had recently been painted, and the back porch, which was the last part done, was completed on the Saturday preceding the shooting. Entrance to the house had been gained by the murderer through a rear window of the kitchen, from which he had first removed the window screen. Near the window was a porch, on the railing of which a person entering the window could support himself. On the railing in the fresh paint was the imprint of four fingers of someone's left hand. This railing was removed in the early morning after the murder by officers from the identification bureau of the Chicago police force and enlarged photographs were made of the prints. Jennings, who had been arrested after several eyewitnesses[20] identified him, when returned to the penitentiary for the violation of his parole, in March, 1910, had a print of his fingers taken and another print was taken after this arrest. These impressions were likewise enlarged for the purpose of comparison with the enlarged photographs of the prints on the railing.

Defendant argued that the evidence as to the comparison of photographs of the fingermarks on the railing with the enlarged fingerprints of him was improperly admitted. No questions were raised as to the accuracy of the photographic exhibits, the method of identifying the photographs, the taking of the fingerprints, or the correctness of the enlargements. However, defendant argued that fingerprint comparison evidence was not admissible under the common-law rules of evidence, and because there was no statute authorizing it the court should have refused to permit its introduction.

The court noted that as of 1913 there were no reported cases or state statutes addressing the admissibility of this class of evidence, although such evidence had recently been accepted in England.[21] The Illinois Supreme Court noted that while the courts of this country did not appear to have passed on the question, standard authorities on scientific subjects did discuss the use of fingerprints as a system of identification, and had concluded that experience had shown it to be reliable.[22] These authorities, the court observed, found this system of identification to be of very ancient origin, having been used in Egypt when the impression of the monarch's thumb was used as his sign manual and that it had been used in the courts of India for many years. More recently, its use had become very general by the police departments of the large cities of this country and Europe. The court was particularly impressed with the apparent great success of the system in England, where it had been used since 1891 in thousands of cases without error. The court also noted that this success had resulted in the sending of an investigating commission from the United States, upon whose favorable report a bureau was established by the United States government in several departments.[23]

The court began its analysis of the Jennings case by reviewing the proffered qualifications of the four fingerprint witnesses employed by the prosecution. William M. Evans testified that he began the study of the subject in 1904; had been connected with the bureau of identification of the Chicago Police Department in work of this character for about a year; had personally studied between 4000 and 5000 fingerprints and had himself made about 2000; that the bureau of identification had some 25,000 different impressions classified; that he had examined the exhibits in question, and on the forefinger he found 14 points of identity, and on the second finger 11 points; that in his judgment the fingerprints on the railing were made by the same person as those taken from the plaintiff in error's fingers by the identification bureau.

Edward Foster testified that he was Inspector of Dominion Police at Ottawa, Canada, connected with the bureau of identification; that he had a good deal to do with fingerprints for six years or more; that he had done fingerprint identification work in Vancouver and elsewhere in Canada; had studied the subject at Scotland Yard; that he began the study in St. Louis in 1904 under a Scotland Yard man and had taken about 2500 fingerprints; that he had studied the exhibits in question and found 14 points of resemblance on the forefinger; that the two sets of prints were made by the fingers of the same person

Mary E. Holland testified that she resided in Chicago and began investigation of fingerprint impressions in 1904, studied at Scotland Yard in 1908, and passed an examination on the subject, and started the first bureau of identification in this country for the United States government at Washington. She stated that her work at Scotland Yard involved a collection of over 100,000 prints. She also testified that she had examined the two sets of prints here and believed them to have been made by the fingers of the same person.

Finally, Michael P. Evans testified that he had been in the bureau of identification of the Chicago Police Department for 27 years; and that that bureau had been using the system of fingerprint impressions since January 1, 1905, while it also used the Bertillon system. He had studied the subject since 1905 or 1906 and had made between 6000 and 7000 fingerprints. He had been in charge of making the photographs of the prints on the railing, and in his judgment the various impressions were made by the fingers of the same person.[24]

The court noted that all of these witnesses testified at varying lengths as to the basis of the system and the various markings found on the human hand, stating that they were classified from the various forms of markings, including those known as arches, loops, whorls and deltas, the same as noted by Wigmore and Mitchell.

The court observed that when photographs were first sought to be admitted, it was seriously questioned whether pictures thus created could properly be introduced in evidence, but that method of proof, as well as by means of x-rays and the microscope, were now admitted without question.[25] The court found equal acceptability here:

> We are disposed to hold from the evidence of the four witnesses who testified, and from the writings we have referred to on this subject, that there is a scientific basis for the system of finger-print identification, and that the courts are justified in admitting this class of evidence; that this method of identification is in such general and common use that the courts cannot refuse to take judicial cognizance of it. Such evidence may or may not be of independent strength, but it is admissible, the same as other proof, as tending to make out a case. If inferences as to the identity of persons based on the voice, the appearance, or age are admissible, why does not this record justify the admission of this fingerprint testimony under common-law rules of evidence?[26]

After an examination of the rules as to when expert testimony is to be allowed, the court ruled that this category of expertise clearly qualified as an admissible area of expertise:

From the evidence in this record we are disposed to hold that the classification of fingerprint impressions and their method of identification is a science requiring study. While some of the reasons which guide an expert to his conclusions are such as may be weighed by any intelligent person with good eyesight from such exhibits as we have here in the record, after being pointed out to him by one versed in the study of fingerprints, the evidence in question does not come within the common experience of all men of common education in the ordinary walks of life, and therefore the court and jury were properly aided by witnesses of peculiar and special experience on this subject.[27]

The court also concluded that the four witnesses here were qualified to testify on the subject of fingerprint impression evidence.

It was further argued that some of the witnesses testified positively that the fingerprints represented by the photographs were made by a certain person whose fingerprint impressions had been photographed, enlarged, and introduced in evidence, when they should have been permitted to testify only that such was their opinion. The court noted that on questions of identity of persons and of handwriting it was common practice for witnesses to swear that they believed the person to be the same or the handwriting to be that of a particular individual, although they will not swear positively, and the degree of credit to be attached to the evidence was a question for the jury.

The FBI Identification Division was initiated in 1924, with the receipt of over 8,000,000 fingerprint files, mostly from the Leavenworth Penitentiary. Currently, the FBI collection contains well over 250 million sets of fingerprint records, composed of both criminal and civil prints. The civil file includes the prints of current government employees and applicants for federal jobs.

IV. Fingerprint Questions

Important fingerprint questions remain in the debate over the identification of a suspect. Set out below are several of the more important ones:

- Is fingerprint impressions analysis scientific with respect to the theoretical underpinnings of the discipline or because of its use of microscopy and other processes that aid its essentially observational nature?
- Should it make any difference if fingerprint-impressions analysis testimony is simply a combination of experience and modern microscopy? What else, from a forensic scientist's standpoint, is there to say about fingerprint impressions and its examination and the factual assumptions that follow? Is there more that can be found to give fingerprint impressions analysis as great or greater credibility than fingerprint impression, ballistics, tool marks, or DNA?

Issues that are standard fare for lawyers involved in crime scene investigations or, more often, the result of the work of others, normally include the following categories of inquiry:

- What surfaces can hold a print? Smooth, nonporous surfaces such as glass, painted or varnished surfaces, molded plastic surfaces, paper, cardboard, polyethelene-based products, vinyl, rubber, leathers, some metal surfaces, untreated wood products, waxed surfaces, and human skin.
- What is a fingerprint, palm print, or footprint? The capture on an accepting surface of several clusters of ridge characteristics, or "minutiae," present on the fingers of the human hand, as a result of natural oils and secretions of the human finger that leave an image of such minutiae on the surface at issue.

- What methods and chemicals are routinely used to recognize and preserve a print image for analysis? Flake powders such as silver latent print powder, varied fluorescence techniques such as ultraviolet illumination, iodine, ninhydrin, silver nitrate, small particle reagents, cyanoacrylate (super glue) fuming, and vacuum metal deposition (gold and zinc) are used to identify and maintain a print image for analysis.[28]

- What are the comparison points for attempting a fingerprint match? In comparing ridge characteristics (minutiae that include short ridges; dots; bifurcations; deltas; trifurcations; ridge endings), 150 "comparison points" are potentially available. Realistically, all prints are partial in the sense of always being less than 150. The courts in the United States generally only require 6–8 points, while other nations require 14 or more.[29]

The world fingerprint experts agreed in 1995 that there was no requisite number of comparison points to allow for positive identification of a suspect:

> The Ne'urim Declaration approved June 19, 1995, has been positively approved in the main fingerprint journals. No objections were raised for accepting that no scientific basis exists for requiring that a predetermined, minimum number of friction-ridge features must be present in two impressions to establish a positive identification.[30]

Some jurisdictions, such as Australia, are moving to a nonnumerical method of expressing sufficient criteria for a match statement.[31]

The SWGFAST guidelines issuing from that FBI-sponsored group are receiving increased attention. The focus for the immediate future appears to be on a uniformly accepted minimum qualifications guideline; training to competence guidelines; and quality assurance guidelines, as a basis for ongoing confidence in international fingerprint identification. Current thinking is that accomplishing these goals will help instill continued confidence, while the debate over numerical or nonnumerical "ridgeology" comparison methods continues.[32]

- What about AFIS, the Automated Fingerprint Identification System?
- Does it provide the eventual match using computer technology?[33]

The AFIS system does not provide match identification that is a basis for a fingerprint expert's identification testimony. This testimony is still the result of close visual examination of ridge characteristics by the expert and the expert's experience. The fingerprint identification testimony is an inference as with all of the other forensic opinions delivered daily in courts around the globe. AFIS has the amazing capability of searching through millions of digitalized images of prints originally provided by ink cards; or, more recently by initial digitalized recordings, and kicking out the ten closest "matches" in the collection. These matches then must undergo close examination by experienced fingerprint examiners. AFIS makes possible what was an impossible task of comparing millions of images from all over the country and narrowing down the candidates. If nine of the selections seem totally unrelated, but the tenth is the victim's estranged husband, the value of AFIS systems is evident. AFIS systems are being utilized worldwide. The FBI IAFIS, the Integrated Automated Fingerprint Identification System, is intended to greatly assist local authorities by speeding up the digitalization of inked cards as well as integrating criminal record data with the imprint data, and providing for increased speed and accuracy in doing AFIS searches.[34]

- What about current statistics and "population" databases for ruling out other suspects on something other than the match by an experienced fingerprint examiner?

V. Fingerprint Foundations

No databases of current information are available about fingerprints for use in statistical projection to determine the existence in the general population of an identical match.

The assumption has always been that the theoretical basis for fingerprint identification, established by Galton and his successors, internally provides the assurance of uniqueness to the identification. Dr. Saferstein, in his text *Criminalistics: An Introduction to Forensic Science*, cites three basic principles or assumptions that have historically supported this position.

1. To date, after almost a century of fingerprint experience, no two fingers have ever been found to possess identical ridge characteristics.
2. A fingerprint will remain unchanged during a person's lifetime.
3. Fingerprints have general ridge characteristics that permit them to be systematically classified and examined with great efficiency and efficacy.[35]

There were over 1200 reported decisions addressing, in part, fingerprint evidence in a wide variety of criminal prosecutions. None of them even came close to finding fingerprints lacking scientific reliability or general acceptance in the forensic community. That subject was laid to rest in a series of cases decided in 2002–2003 which are discussed next. The current issues regarding fingerprint evidence rise from a spectacular miscalculation by three of the FBI's top fingerprint analysts, who incorrectly identified the prints of an American lawyer resident in Oregon as belonging to one of the terrorists involved in the train bombings in Spain. Spanish forensic teams quickly identified an Algerian man as the origin of the prints.

VI. Fingerprints: Daubert Challenges

Challenges to the scientific reliability of fingerprint expertise have always been raised and usually fail. Such challenges are primarily directed toward the current judicial posture of allowing fingerprint expert opinion to identify a match of crime scene prints to a defendant as a certainty, rather than a more common *consistent-in-all-respects* statement for the majority of the forensic sciences. The only other forensic science graced with such finality is ballistics bullet matches from comparative firings of a gun associated with defendant and crime scene bullets or shell casings.[36] Several recent decisions support the traditional position.

In *United States v. Plaza*,[37] a federal case decided in 2002, defendants on trial for drug and murder charges moved to bar testimony on latent fingerprint identification evidence, claiming that latent fingerprint identification evidence did not meet the federal Daubert standard. The court concluded that latent fingerprint identification, as a science, met the Daubert factors but that every case was subject to tests for accuracy and reliability. A fingerprint examiner testified that "latent print and the rolled print (have) traditionally been … mainstays" of fingerprint identification, and reviewed the process and qualifications needed for fingerprint identification, including the proficiency test conducted. After a lengthy discussion of the history and methods of fingerprint identification, the court concluded that the current standards, combined with consistent court oversight, were sufficient to ensure that both types of fingerprinting met the Daubert factors.

In *United States v. Havvard*,[38] relying on a National Institute of Justice (NIJ) solicitation (March 2000), the defendant claimed that the assumption that all fingerprints are unique was an unproven premise because there were no objective standards for each examiner's comparison. The defendant took a statement in the article, saying the NIJ's goal was "to provide greater scientific foundation for forensic friction-ridge (fingerprint) identification," to mean that the science was not currently reliable. He also cited a *Collaborative Testing (CT) Service Report* (1995) suggesting a higher error rate for fingerprinting than cited at trial. The defendant then introduced several cases he believed undermined the reliability of fingerprinting, and he claimed that the court required him to disprove the reliability of fingerprinting, rather than making the state prove the reliability of fingerprinting.

First, the court did not consider the NIJ and CT articles because they were not part of the lower court record. The court noted that the *CT Service Report* was available prior to the Daubert hearing and could have been used to cross-examine the fingerprint expert witness. Second, the court found that the defendant had misconstrued the precedent cases and the Daubert hearing. In each case, the court found that the other courts had "contrast(ed) the rejected technique with latent print identification and specifically credit(ed) the greater reliability of fingerprint evidence," meaning that they had actually bolstered the credibility of fingerprinting. In addition, the court believed that the general acceptance of fingerprinting meant that the defendant needed to demonstrate its unreliability at the Daubert hearing. Ultimately, the court agreed with the lower court that "fingerprinting techniques have been tested in the adversarial system, that individual results are routinely subjected to peer review for verification, and that the probability for error is exceptionally low," thus accepting the reliability of fingerprint evidence.[39]

In *United States v. Crisp*,[40] a 4th Circuit decision, defendant claimed that his conviction was not valid because the fingerprint and handwriting analyses did not meet the Daubert standard. He contended that the premises underlying fingerprinting evidence had not been adequately tested, fingerprint examiners operate without a uniform threshold of certainty required for a positive identification, and fingerprint evidence had not achieved general acceptance in the relevant scientific community. After a lengthy discussion of the Daubert standard, the court concluded that fingerprint analysis was a reliable science. First, the court reviewed the history of fingerprinting and concluded that it had most definitely been "adequately tested." Second, the court found that fingerprint examiners use a valid method of "points and characteristics" in identifications and that they meet testing and proficiency requirements. Third and last, the court found that the defendant presented no evidence that would have negated the court's general acceptance of fingerprint evidence. The court also noted that, even if the fingerprint evidence was "shaky," the defendant had ample opportunity to invalidate it with direct examination, cross-examination, and jury instructions.

In *United States v. George*,[41] a 2004 7th Circuit decision, defendants were convicted in the United States District Court for the Northern District of Illinois of uttering and possessing counterfeited securities, bank fraud, and money laundering. The court held that expert testimony of an FBI fingerprint examiner was clearly admissible.

Defendant Mustapha's first argument was that the expert testimony of Kim DeCarla Smith, an FBI fingerprint examiner, should have been excluded. Mustapha argued that the district court erred when it relied on the 7th

Circuit's recent holding in *United States v. Havvard*, 260 F.3d 597 (7th Cir.2001) to admit Smith's expert testimony. In Havvard the court had closely examined fingerprint analysis techniques in light of Daubert and Federal Rule of Evidence 702 and concluded that such analysis was admissible.

Defendant Mustapha's concerns were twofold: first, he did not believe that the fingerprint analysis technique was able to be effectively tested, and second, he argued that Havvard incorrectly applied the Daubert test by relying only on the "general acceptance" prong. These arguments, the court ruled, easily answered. In Havvard we considered that fingerprint analysis was generally accepted, had a low rate of error, and could be objectively tested:[42]

> *This was more than sufficient ground to find it admissible under the Daubert test, and did not rely solely on one prong as Mustapha asserts. Additionally, in vacating its first opinion, the Eastern District of Pennsylvania noted that FBI fingerprint analysis had methods to control the techniques operation that were not purely subjective. Of particular note, and in answer to Mustapha's complaint that fingerprint analysis cannot be objectively tested, the Llera Plaza II court noted that the FBI annually tests its fingerprint examiners with sets of prints, the sources of which are known to the testers, but unknown to the test-takers. Hence, while an actual print taken in the field cannot be objectively tested, we are satisfied that the method in general can be subjected to objective testing to determine its reliability in application. For these reasons, we feel comfortable that Havvard correctly decided the issue of fingerprint analysis admissibility.[43]*

In regard to Mustapha's second argument, that the prints in his case were unreliable because they were partial rather than complete prints, the court found that the district court did not abuse its discretion:

> *Having found fingerprint analysis to be reliable, the issue as to whether particular prints can be connected to a particular defendant goes to the weight and credibility of the evidence. These are issues best left to the finder of fact, not an appellate court. Further, the issue that Mustapha is concerned about — the probability that the partial prints might be misattributed to him — was thoroughly covered in the cross-examination of Smith. (Br. for Defendant-Appellant Ola Mustapha at 20. Hence, the jury was functioning with a proper warning regarding the value of the fingerprint evidence. The district court did not abuse its discretion in allowing Smith to testify.[44]*

In *State v. Quintana*,[45] a 2004 Utah Supreme Court case, the defendant contended that, where fingerprint identification is the only evidence supporting conviction, the State must offer additional evidence establishing that he left the prints at the time of the crime. The court ruled fingerprint identification was not novel scientific evidence for which trial court had to make a preliminary finding of its reliability. A single fingerprint that defendant had left on a lacquer box in the victim's home was sufficient to support convictions for burglary and theft.

The Utah Supreme Court noted that it had previously rejected this argument, "We treat fingerprint evidence like any other piece of evidence whether or not there is additional evidence." The jury therefore could have properly concluded that the single fingerprint found on a lacquer box in the victims' home belonged to Quintana and that the fingerprint was left at the time the home was burglarized.[46]

Justice Thorne, dissenting, neatly expressed the argument against judicial acceptance of the finality of fingerprint-matching expert opinion:

> Unfortunately, our societal acceptance of the infallibility of examiners' opinions appears to be misplaced. Failure on any level clearly shows that examiner opinion is not infallible. Such fallibility, in light of society's trust in forensic certainty, opens our courts to a great risk of misidentification, and after examining the standards used to determine an examiner's proficiency, it is a risk that we should have understood long ago, and should never have allowed without certain precautions. Specifically, we should instruct our juries that although there may be a scientific basis to believe that fingerprints are unique, there is no similar basis to believe that examiners are infallible. In the absence of any nationally accepted credentialing process, the jury may be in the best position to determine whether a purported fingerprint expert properly determined that a latent fingerprint, left at the scene of a crime, matches a defendant's fingerprint.
>
> Until there is a nationally adopted certification system — ensuring examiner proficiency — and a nationally adopted minimum standard for matching latent fingerprints to known samples — minimizing the risk of misidentification — courts should ensure that juries are instructed that examiner testimony is informed opinion, but not fact.[47]

Regardless of the differences of opinion about the evidentiary strength of a single fingerprint, most jurisdictions hold that a single print is sufficient to get a warrant. This position is exemplified by the case of King v. State,[48] where the defendant was convicted of six counts of burglary. A law office was burglarized and the police uncovered fingerprints on a piece of glass, which had been broken to gain entry into the office. It was determined that the defendant matched the fingerprints in question. The police then obtained an arrest warrant for the defendant, based on this fingerprint evidence only. The defendant argued that the trial court erred when it determined that the fingerprint match alone was sufficient to support the arrest warrant. The court disagreed and found that under the circumstances of this case fingerprint evidence alone "constituted probable cause for the issuance of the arrest warrant." The court reasoned that in prior cases where convictions were obtained "based primarily on fingerprint evidence, Arkansas courts have upheld or overturned the conviction depending on the circumstances of the case." In addition, the court reasoned that "probable cause does not require the quantum of proof necessary to support a conviction."[49]

VII. Fingerprints: Digital Print Machines

The scientific reliability of digital fingerprint machinery was addressed by the 2002 4th Circuit decision in *United States v. Patterson*,[50] where the defendant was in possession of cocaine base with the intent to distribute. Defendant argued that the court erred by admitting into evidence the testimony of a deputy describing how the machine that took the defendant's fingerprints worked, as well as the actual fingerprint image produced by the machine. The court disagreed and found that if there was any error, it was harmless.

Subsequent to the defendant's arrest, a sheriff's deputy used a Digital Biometrics Tenprinter to produce an image of Patterson's fingerprints. At the defendant's trial, the deputy's testified that "this device is sort of like a laser scanner. The easiest way I could say, to give you a general idea about it, would be like going to the supermarket … where they scan your bar code for prices, it's similar to that. It reads — it actually picks up the ridges on your fingers." The deputy further acknowledged that this testimony was based on what he had been told by others; although he used the Tenprinter every day and had processed at least a thousand people with it, he did not know how it worked. Furthermore, the accuracy of fingerprints recorded by the Tenprinter had neither been confirmed nor challenged by any person whose prints the deputy had processed. An expert also testified that one of the prints on the Tenprinter image matched a print recovered from a bag containing cocaine base that the police discovered during their investigation of Patterson.[51]

While the court reasoned that the "deputy's lack of knowledge about the mechanism within the Tenprinter and the accuracy of the fingerprint images it produced undercut the probative value of his testimony," these weaknesses were exposed by defense counsel during cross, so the "jury was not misled into accepting testimony that the deputy was not qualified to offer." The court further reasoned that the actual fingerprint image produced by the machine was properly authenticated. The court framed the question as "whether the government offered sufficient evidence to demonstrate that the Tenprinter image reliably depicted Patterson's fingerprints," and to answer this question the court looked to the cases involving photographic evidence.

The court found that although there was no testimony from a witness who had "examined Patterson's fingers and could verify that they were actually rendered on the Tenprinter image," and the deputy's "lack of expertise rendered his testimony insufficient to prove the reliability of the device," an adequate foundation was established when it was testified that one of the fingerprint images matched a fingerprint found on the drug containers. The court reasoned that if the fingerprint match testimony was believed by the jury, it "provided compelling evidence that the Tenprinter reliably imaged Patterson's fingers; the alternative — that the machine generated an inaccurate fingerprint image that happened to be identical to a fingerprint recovered by a different person using a different process in a different location — is simply implausible."[52]

VIII. Fingerprints: Discovery of Automated Fingerprint System Printouts

The question of the discovery of crime lab AFIS printouts was raised in the case of *People v. Tims*,[53] a 2002 California decision. The defendant was convicted of burglary and residential robbery. At one of the homes, fingerprints were found on the inside of the window, which had been broken to gain entry. The fingerprints found at the crime scene were compared by two separate experts at the police crime lab, and were determined by them to match the defendant. On appeal, the defendant argued that the state had violated its obligation under Brady by failing to disclose a computer printout from the lab's Automated Latent Print system, which contained the first four matches in the system to the prints found at the scene. The defendant was the second best match on the list; however, neither he nor the first match had a very high "matching score."

The state responded that the lab does not normally keep these printouts, and it should not be considered a method of identification, but only a "filtering system." The state expert testified that an identification is only made by taking a sufficient match found by the system and comparing the actual fingerprints. The court found that the defendant's Brady claim must fail, because even if the printout had been turned over prior to the trial, it would not have had an effect on the outcome of the case. The court reasoned that the number one match by the system was excluded as a match for the fingerprints found at the scene, and neither the defendant nor the number one match received a high score on the printout. The court further reasoned that it is complete speculation that the victim would have actually identified the number one match in the photo array.[54]

IX. Fingerprints: Absence of Fingerprints

The longstanding acceptance of fingerprint evidence as being conclusive as to identification has, until very recently and unsuccessfully, resulted in a dearth of cases even approaching an attack on its claim to being scientifically sound. What has occurred, because of fingerprint identifications' tremendous esteem as an identifying process, are a series of cases addressing *whether the absence of fingerprints of the suspect when they would be expected to be there*, is entitled to any evidentiary value or the basis for a defense-oriented jury instruction.

It is a long-standing rule that the state's failure to collect and preserve potentially exculpatory evidence violates a defendant's due process rights only if the defendant demonstrates that the officers acted in bad faith.[55]

In *People v. Towns*,[56] a jury found defendant, Sherrell Towns, guilty of five counts of first-degree murder and sentenced him to death. The case arose out of the execution-style murder of five men in Madison, Illinois in a drug-related incident. Among other points, defendant claimed that his attorney should have presented the testimony of a forensic expert to dispute the state's fingerprint evidence. The trial testimony indicated that the state's expert, Garold Warner, and two of his associates concluded that there were 25 "points of agreement" between defendant's fingerprints and those found at the scene of the crimes. According to Warner, fingerprint examiners in the United States tend to use between 8 and 10 points of agreement before arriving at a conclusion. Based on that evidence, the court concluded that it could not be said that defense counsel's decision not to call an independent expert constituted ineffectiveness. The court observed that the failure may very well have been a matter of trial strategy to not call an expert — a withering crossexamination as to the points of agreement could only serve to reinforce the strength of the fingerprint identification in the eyes of the jury.[57]

The taking of fingerprints is a search for purposes of the Fourth Amendment to the Constitution of the United States of America.[58] In an interesting case involving two sets of prints taken from a defendant, where the first set was found to be improperly taken due to the defendant not being told that he need not supply prints, a court ruled that the use of both sets by an examiner did not prevent testimony on a match from the second set. In *Hooker v. State*,[59] defendant was convicted of murder in a trial based entirely on circumstantial evidence.

Around 5:30 a.m. on the morning of March 14, 1991, the sheriff's office responded to a call reporting a comatose man in a car, and upon arriving at the rural crime scene, a deputy discovered Walter Johnson's dead body behind the steering wheel of his vehicle. Investigators discovered that Johnson had been shot twice. Investigators searched Johnson's car and found three .25-caliber shell casings, a bag containing several unopened cans of Coors Light beer, and one opened, partially full can of Coors Light beer sitting on Johnson's dashboard.[60]

After questioning various people, investigators from the Sheriff's office were led to Charles C. Hooker, who, it was learned was a teacher at the middle school where Johnson had been principal. During the investigatory process, Hooker supplied the sheriff with several fingerprint cards. These prints were sent to the crime lab in Jackson, and ultimately the crime lab matched a latent print found on the half-full Coors Light beer can to Hooker.

Hooker argued that all fingerprint evidence should be suppressed as the "fruit of the poisonous tree,"[61] because the state did not prove that it informed Hooker prior to taking the first set of prints that he had the right to refuse the request that he give the police his prints. Hooker provided two sets of fingerprints to the sheriff, the first on March 19, 1991, and the second on March 28, 1991. The trial court did suppress the first set of prints, but refused to suppress the second set, ruling that Hooker had been properly informed at that time that he had the right to refuse to give his prints On appeal, Hooker argued that because the second set of prints were not "independently obtained," they too should be suppressed.

The court held that the second set of fingerprints was not gained by exploiting the alleged illegally seized first set of fingerprints, and thus the second set of fingerprints was admissible to identify defendant and not the "fruit of the poisonous tree." The first set of prints were, as claimed by defendant, taken without informing him that he had the right to refuse. The first set being found to be smudged, the state crime lab informed the sheriff they would need a second set, and the defendant, upon his return to provide the second set, was informed of his right to refuse the request for prints. This was so, even though the fingerprint examiner testified that when she affected her initial identification of defendant's thumbprint she had both set of prints before her and did not know whether she had used the first set of prints or the second, legally obtained, set, due to the fact that during trial she compared the second set of prints with the thumbprint obtained from the crime scene container and testified before the jury that it matched the defendant's.[62]

X. Time and Place Requirements

A number of jurisdictions require the state, if it wishes to rely solely or substantially on fingerprint evidence, to establish to some degree that the prints were made at a point contemporaneous with the commission of the crime. In *People v. Campbell*,[63] a 1992 Illinois Supreme Court decision, the court agreed with defendant that to sustain a conviction solely on fingerprint evidence, fingerprints corresponding to those of the defendant must have been found in the immediate vicinity of the crime under such circumstances as to establish beyond a reasonable doubt that they were impressed at the time the crime was committed.[64] The court also agreed with the defendant that the same time and placement requirements exist in many states for shoeprint evidence. However, in either case, the court explained, the state was not required to seek out and negate every conceivable possibility that the print was impressed at some time other than during the commission of the offense.

In some cases, the court noted, evidence of the particular location of the fingerprint might satisfy the time and placement requirement, as would the prosecution's proof of the chain of contact of the touched item, which could establish that the item could have been touched only at the time of the crime.[65] Additionally, the court observed, a wide variety of attending circumstances might support an inference that the print was made at the time of the commission of the offense.[66]

In *State v. Montgomery,*[67] defendant was convicted of first-degree murder, first-degree burglary, robbery with dangerous weapon, and attempted first-degree rape. At approximately 11:05 p.m., the victim's friends returned to the victim and discovered the body of Kimberly Piccolo lying on the floor next to her bed. When Piccolo's body was found, she was dressed in a sweatshirt, sweatpants which were inside out, and socks, but she was not wearing panties. The sofa on which Piccolo had been sitting when her roommates left had been moved out of place. The officers found a pair of panties lying on the sofa. A butcher knife was missing from the kitchen. Piccolo's eyeglasses were found on the coffee table. A fingerprint, which matched a print of defendant's left ring finger, was lifted from one of the lenses.

An autopsy showed that Piccolo had received nine stab wounds that were clustered in her chest, arm, back, and abdomen, and several defensive wounds on her hands. One stab wound went completely through her right hand. A fingerprint lifted from a lens of the victim's eyeglasses found in the apartment matched one of defendant's fingerprints.[68]

Defendant argued that the state failed to prove that the fingerprint found on the victim's eyeglasses was impressed at the time the crimes were committed. The court stated that regardless of the confidence attending fingerprint matching testimony, it is usually insufficient, alone, to sustain a conviction:

> *This court has considered the sufficiency of fingerprint evidence to identify defendant as the perpetrator in a number of cases. Where the state has relied solely on fingerprint evidence to establish that the defendant was the perpetrator of the crimes charged, this court has held that the defendant's motion to dismiss should have been granted.[69] On the other hand, where the state presented other evidence tending to show that the fingerprints could only have been impressed*

> *at the time the crimes were committed, this court has found that the*
> *case was properly taken to the jury.*[70]

The court concluded that testimony by a qualified expert that fingerprints found at the scene of the crime match the fingerprints of the accused, when accompanied by substantial evidence of circumstances from which the jury could find that the fingerprints could have been impressed only at the time the crime was committed, was sufficient to withstand a motion for dismissal and carry the case to the jury. The soundness of the rule lay in the fact that such evidence logically tends to show that the accused was indeed present and participated in the commission of the crime.

In the present case, the court ruled that the state submitted substantial evidence of circumstances from which the jury could find that defendant's fingerprints could have been impressed plastic at the time the crimes charged were committed:

> *The evidence showed that the victim was wearing her eyeglasses all*
> *day on the day the crimes charged were committed; was studying or*
> *reading most of that day; that she was reading when the group left*
> *at around 10:00 p.m. for a party, leaving her alone in the apartment.*
> *When the group left, the furniture was in order and the victim was*
> *sitting on the sofa with her eyeglasses on, reading the newspaper.*
> *When the group returned approximately an hour later, the apart-*
> *ment was in disarray, the victim's lifeless body was lying on the floor*
> *away from the sofa, which had been moved, and her eyeglasses were*
> *on the coffee table. No one else was in the apartment. Defendant's*
> *fingerprint was found on the inside lens of the victim's eyeglasses.*
> *This evidence, disclosing the circumstances under which the eyeglasses*
> *were found, when combined with other testimony placing defendant*
> *in the vicinity of the victim's apartment, constitutes substantial evi-*
> *dence from which the jury could find that defendant's fingerprints*
> *could have been impressed plastic on the lens between the hours of*
> *10:00 p.m. and 11:05 p.m. Because the evidence also showed that*
> *the crimes charged were committed during the same time period, the*
> *fingerprint evidence logically tends to show that defendant was*
> *present and participated in the commission of the crimes. Thus, we*
> *hold that the evidence was properly admitted and the trial court did*
> *not err in denying defendant's motion to dismiss for insufficiency of*
> *the evidence.*[71]

Defendant also argued that the portion of the state expert's testimony indicating that he had prepared his report with the aid of a previously prepared print card at the local jail was not prejudicial because he used the same card in cross-examination to challenge the accuracy of the expert's testimony.[72] This is a common problem faced by defendants with prior records.

Similar issues of contemporaneity were raised in *People v. Zizzo*,[73] where defendant was convicted of felony theft, arising from defendant's collusion with a bank employee to obtain and use false ATM cards.

The state's first witness, Carol Carl, testified that in May 1996, while updating her family's financial records, she discovered a series of unauthorized automatic teller machine (ATM) withdrawals from her account totaling over $62,000. The withdrawals were traced to the defendant.

In addition to bank employees and defendant's accomplice, the state called Dr. Jane Homeyer, executive director of the Northern Illinois Police Crime Laboratory. She testified that she performed a fingerprint analysis on the Daryl Simson ATM account file. She found two prints suitable for comparison, both of which matched defendant's. Homeyer noted, however, that her analysis could not establish either when or in what context the fingerprints had been left.

Defendant contended that because an innocent explanation was available for the discovery of her fingerprints on the Daryl Simson ATM file, those fingerprints could not be used to support her conviction. Defendant relied upon a 1991 case, *People vs. Gomez*,[74] in which the court had held that, to support a conviction, fingerprint evidence must satisfy both physical and temporal proximity criteria. The fingerprints must have been found in the immediate vicinity of the crime and under such circumstances that they could have been made only at the time the crime occurred.[75] Although the court did not dispute defendant's reading of Gomez, it stressed that the physical and temporal proximity criteria came into play only when a conviction was based solely upon circumstantial fingerprint evidence. Here, the court observed, discovery of defendant's fingerprints on the Daryl Simson ATM file was not the sole basis for defendant's conviction, as it was introduced to corroborate codefendant Carr's prior inconsistent statement. Accordingly, the jury properly could have considered the discovery of defendant's fingerprints on the Daryl Simson ATM file as evidence of defendant's guilt.

Contemporaneousness and proximity were also issues in *State v. Monzo*,[76] a 1998 Ohio decision. There, defendant was convicted of two counts of rape, one count of aggravated burglary, and one count of kidnapping. The victim had been assaulted in 1987, but the defendant was not identified until a fingerprint run under a newly installed AFIS system generated his card. Police found a knife beside the victim's bed, and her open wallet and purse in her bedroom, although she had left those items on the kitchen counter before going to bed, with the wallet inside the purse.

A fingerprint examiner testified that in 1987 he performed a preliminary examination of the fingerprint lifts from the victim's house, but had no known suspect to whom the lifts could be compared, so the prints were simply retained in the police file for future reference. Subsequently, the police put in place an AFIS system that subsequently generated defendant's prints several years later. The expert conducted a visual comparison of defendant's file fingerprints with the lifts from the basement door trim, and determined that these matched defendant's right-middle and ring finger. He later determined that the lift from the victim's wallet matched the right thumbprint of defendant. He testified that the lift from the wallet would be a relatively fresh print because dusting for prints on a porous surface would be effective in developing prints for perhaps only 15 days after the prints were made.[77]

A house painter, Donald Fraime, testified that shortly before the date of the 1987 attack, he painted the middle room in the victim's house, including new wood trim around the new basement door. A Columbus police officer testified that he worked for the crime scene search unit in October 1987, and collected fingerprints from the victim's house, dusting for and eventually lifting a total of 11 prints from the house. According to him, the most definitive print impressions were one lifted from the outside of the victim's wallet found in her bedroom, and one lifted from the doorframe of the door leading from the basement to the middle room. An FBI forensic and fingerprint expert found that these two prints were the most valuable for comparison purposes.

Comparing the lifts to the known fingerprints of defendant, he concluded that the single fingerprint lifted from the wallet was the right thumbprint of defendant, and the prints taken from the door trim were the right-middle and right-ring fingers of defendant. The agent testified that painting the door trim would have destroyed any fingerprints previously left there, so that the prints lifted from the door trim could not predate the last time the trim was painted, and that repeated handling would degrade or leave overlapping prints on an item. He saw no overlapping prints on the lift taken from the wallet, which was the victim's everyday wallet. It was pointed out that any print more than a few days old would have probably been obliterated or overlapped by her frequent handling of the wallet.[78]

As noted above, the uniform acceptance of the certainty and solidity of fingerprint evidence has resulted in claims by defendants that police failure to search for and to preserve such evidence where it could be reasonably expected to be present, denies them of due process by removing from consideration potentially exculpatory evidence. If the state fails to produce evidence that is reasonably available to it or fails to explain why it has not produced the evidence, a defendant is permitted to comment about the missing evidence in closing argument to the jury.

In *Eley v. State*,[79] a 1980 Maryland decision, defendant was convicted on charges arising out of a shooting and robbery. The state failed to produce fingerprint evidence against Eley and relied solely on eyewitness testimony for establishing his identification. In closing argument, defense counsel sought to argue that the state's failure to utilize the more reliable fingerprint identification, and its failure to explain why it did not produce such evidence, gave rise to an inference that Eley's fingerprints were not at the scene of the crime and, thus, he was not there. This court reversed stating, one can reasonably draw some adverse inference from the use of an inferior method when a superior (one) was readily available.[80]

The court held that possible relevant evidence not introduced, or its absence explained, could be used against the state.

This issue was again addressed in the case of *United States v. Hoffman*,[81] where defendants were convicted of narcotics offenses. The primary issue on appeal was whether a defense lawyer must lay some evidentiary foundation before arguing in closing that the jury should infer, based upon the absence of fingerprint evidence, that such evidence could have been obtained and would have been exculpatory. The court answered that question in the affirmative, and therefore affirmed the convictions.

On the afternoon of February 14, 1990, defendants Hoffman and Smithen went to Penn Station in New York City to catch an Amtrak train bound for Charlotte, North Carolina. While in the station, they attracted the attention of two Amtrak police officers, which eventually led to a search of a red duffel bag that Hoffman had identified as his. Inside, police observed a pair of tennis shoes with socks stuffed into them; closer examination revealed plastic bags containing cocaine base hidden inside the socks. They also found a spray deodorant can that proved to have a false bottom containing narcotics. At trial, the government's case consisted primarily of the testimony of the arresting officers, who recounted the events that occurred aboard the train. None of the government's witnesses made any mention of fingerprint evidence, and the attorneys representing Hoffman and Smithen did not cross-examine on that point.

During closing argument, Hoffman's counsel argued that the unknown passenger who had been seated next to Hoffman was actually a drug courier who left the narcotics under a pillow on his seat when he saw the officers enter the train in Washington. According to Hoffman's counsel, Detective Hanson had lied about finding the drugs in Hoffman's bag to be able to secure a conviction. Hoffman's attorney then raised the question of fingerprint evidence:

> If Officer Hanson had told you the truth in this case, wouldn't he after sending the drugs to the laboratory to be analyzed have sent them to be examined for fingerprints?

I mean I wouldn't be here making any argument at all if this bag containing cocaine had been examined by the police lab like they should have done.[82]

The government objected to this line of argument on the grounds that the record contained no evidence regarding whether the plastic bags containing the narcotics had been tested for fingerprints and, if so, what result was obtained. The district court sustained the objection and instructed the jury to disregard the comments about the lack of fingerprint evidence.

The court ruled that defense attorneys must be permitted to argue all reasonable inferences from the facts in the record, including the negative inferences that may arise when a party fails to call an important witness at trial, or to produce relevant documents or other evidence, where it is shown that a party such as police had some special ability to produce such witness or other evidence. However, the court continued, it was equally well-established that counsel may not premise arguments on evidence that has not been admitted. In this case, the only "evidence" on the fingerprint issue was purely negative — i.e., the fact that the government did not introduce any fingerprint evidence at all. As the government conceded here, the absence of such evidence was a relevant "fact" that properly could have been argued to the jury. Hence, it would not have been improper for defense counsel to point out to the jury that the government had not presented any evidence concerning fingerprints.

Here, the court noted:

Hoffman's attorney attempted to go far beyond merely pointing out the lack of fingerprint evidence and arguing that its absence weakened the government's case. Rather, his argument was that because the government had not produced fingerprint evidence, the jury should infer that: (1) the police did not attempt to obtain fingerprints from the plastic bags containing the narcotics; (2) this failure violated standard police procedures; and (3) the fingerprint evidence, if obtained, would have been favorable to Hoffman. Defense counsel further asserted that these three inferences supported the additional inference that Officer Hanson's trial testimony was false… By making these assertions, Hoffman's attorney moved from arguing fair inferences from the record to arguing the existence of facts not in the record — viz., that the police did not look for fingerprints, that fingerprints could have been obtained from the plastic bags containing the narcotics and that standard police procedure required fingerprint analysis.[83]

Because neither defense counsel had laid any evidentiary foundation for such claims, by, for example, asking one of the officers on cross-examination whether the plastic bags were or could have been tested for fingerprints, and whether standard procedure required such testing — Hoffman's closing argument in that regard was improper. The court ruled that the Eley case was distinguishable because the defense lawyer's argument in that case was limited to the contention that the absence of fingerprint evidence weakened the prosecution's case against his client — an argument that the government conceded in Hoffman.[84]

In *People v. Mafias*,[85] defendant was convicted in a bench trial of possession of controlled substance with intent to deliver and unlawful use of a weapon by a felon. At trial, Chicago Police Officer Thomas Horton testified that on February 5, 1996, he saw the defendant enter the apartment building, a multiple-unit building containing a security door that led to a common entry to front and rear apartments. After obtaining a search warrant the officers, with a key recovered from defendant, opened the security door to the common entrance, entered the building, and secured the apartment. The officers noticed that a bedroom door next to the kitchen was locked with a padlock and using a fourth key from defendant's set of keys, the officers unlocked the bedroom door. The officers then searched the bedroom and found, underneath a pile of clothes next to two dressers, 3_-kilograms of cocaine.

During their search of the apartment, the officers found no evidence that defendant resided there, nor did they find any fingerprints of defendant within the apartment. Defendant was then arrested. The trial court found defendant guilty of possession with intent to deliver and unlawful use of a weapon by a felon. In its ruling, the trial court emphasized that defendant had keys not only to the apartment but to the padlock on the bedroom door, where the drugs and guns were found, and no evidence indicated that anyone else had a key to the bedroom padlock, supporting the possession charge.[86]

The appeals court noted that to sustain a charge of unlawful possession of a controlled substance, the state is obligated to prove knowledge of the possession of the substance and that the narcotics were in the immediate and exclusive control of defendant. For both charges, possession may be actual or constructive. Here, the court found that the evidence was insufficient to prove defendant guilty beyond a reasonable doubt. The state relied heavily on the testimony of Officer Horton and the keys recovered from defendant. The state argued that the fact that the keys were on a single ring demonstrated defendant's guilt on a constructive possession basis. Here, the court ruled, there was no corroborating evidence, such as defendant's fingerprints in the apartment, offered to link the defendant with the narcotics and weapons, other than the testimony of Officer Horton. No utility bills in defendant's name were discovered in the apartment, no fingerprint evidence was offered, and the record indicates that others had access to the apartment. The prosecution has the burden to prove that defendant was responsible for the presence of the narcotics. The court concluded that these facts, combined with defendant's testimony, which was corroborated, cast doubt on defendant's knowledge of the possession of the contraband and cast doubt on defendant's immediate and exclusive control of the contraband.[87]

This chapter concludes with the analysis of two recent decisions addressing the general acceptability of lip print and ear print impression testimony. Given the novelty of both approaches, they are examined in detail.

XI. Lip Marks

The Review Papers note that a summary of recent lip-mark studies by Ball, *The Current Status of Lip Prints and Their Use for Identification,* has been published.[88] Research is seen as definitely needed in all basic areas, legal as well as scientific.

Judicial examination of the general acceptability of lip print identification testimony may be seen in a 1999 Illinois appellate decision involving lip prints allegedly left on duct tape in a homicide case. In *People v. Davis,*[89] defendant was convicted of first-degree murder while attempting to commit armed robbery, attempted armed robbery, and armed violence.

On December 18, 1993, Patrick "Pall Mall" Furgeson (Pall Mall) was shot and killed at the Burnham Mill (the Mill) apartment complex in Elgin. According to the forensic pathologist who performed the autopsy, Dr. Joseph Cogan, Pall Mall died as a result of a gunshot wound to the abdomen from a 12-gauge shotgun fired at close range.

Elgin Police Officer Michael Gough testified that he arrived at the Mill at 6:45 p.m. on December 18, 1993, to gather evidence. He found a shotgun leaning in a bush with the stock sawed off and one spent 12-gauge shotgun shell in the magazine. Around the side of the building, he also found a pair of black nylon hose, a pair of work gloves, and a roll of duct tape. Because the ground was wet but the items were dry, Gough concluded that the items were recently placed there.

Leanne Gray, an Illinois State Police lab forensic scientist specializing in latent print examination, testified as an expert in impression evidence. Gray testified that she had found an upper- and lower-lip print on the first six to eight inches of the duct tape's sticky side and photographed the impression to preserve it. She testified that lip prints, like fingerprints and other impression evidence, are unique and can be used to positively identify someone. Gray further testified that she took standards of defendant's lips, using the sticky side of duct tape and lipstick on paper. She performed a side-by-side comparison of the standards and the photograph for about a month and a half, focusing on the lower part of the lower lip, and could not determine whether defendant made the impression found on the tape. She the mailed the photograph and standards to Steven McKasson of the Southern Illinois Forensic Science Lab in Carbondale, Illinois. On January 3, 1995, she traveled to Carbondale, where she conducted additional comparisons with McKasson and concluded that the lip print was made by defendant.

McKasson, a document examiner for the Illinois State Police, was qualified as an expert after testifying in *voir dire* outside the presence of the jury. He testified that lip prints are unique and that lip-print comparison is an accepted form of identification. After comparing the lip prints, McKasson found at least 13 points of similarity between a standard and the photograph. He admitted that part of the latent print on the duct tape was not suitable for comparison. McKasson concluded that the person who gave the standards left the duct tape print.

Defendant argued that the trial court erred in admitting the lip print evidence and the testimony of the state's experts, Gray and McKasson, contending that the trial court was required to conduct a Frye hearing before admitting the lip-print identification because it was novel scientific evidence. While agreeing that a Frye hearing is typically required to determine the general acceptability of novel scientific evidence, the court observed that the attorneys had an opportunity to question the state's witnesses outside the presence of the jury during *voir dire*. The first witness, Gray, was an experienced latent print examiner with 10 years' experience, which adequately established her qualifications to discuss the matter of lip-print impressions. The court then noted her support for this relatively rare form of impression evidence:

> *Although this was the first time she was asked to conduct a lip print comparison, she completed over 100,000 latent print examinations, has been qualified as an expert in the area of fingerprint or impression evidence over 35 times, and she has given talks and in-house training on latent print evidence Gray testified that lip-print comparison is not a new form of identification but it is seldom used because lip prints are not readily available. Although this print is the only case of which she is aware in Illinois in the past 10 years, the methodology of lip print comparison is very similar to fingerprint comparison. She testified that lip-print comparison is a known and accepted form of scientific comparison. The methods used in her comparisons are accepted within the forensic science community, regardless of whether the comparison is a lip print or fingerprint. She*

*opined, in accord with the Federal Bureau of Investigation (FBI) and
Illinois State Police, that lip prints, like fingerprints, are unique and
a positive means of identification.*[90]

The state's other witness was Stephen McKasson, a document examiner
and training coordinator for the Illinois State Police, where he had been
employed in the area of forensic science for 25 years, 18 of those years with
the Illinois State Police. While employed by the United States Postal Inspection Service, he performed thousands of fingerprint examinations each year.
He stated that he had previously compared lip prints in other cases. Regarding
lip-print impression technology, the court noted that:

*According to McKasson, the basis for identification of impression
evidence is that everything is unique if looked at in sufficient detail,
and if two things are sufficiently similar, they must have come from
the same source. He testified that lip print comparison is an accepted
method of scientific identification in the forensic science community
because it appears in the field literature. He is unaware of any dissent
in the field regarding the methodology used to make a positive identification of a lip print.*[91]

After each witness testified, the trial court had held that the state met its
burden to qualify the witnesses as experts, while admitting that this was a
"unique comparison," in that lip prints have not gone into evidence "too
often" in the history of the court system. Nonetheless, the court found that
the witnesses were qualified as experts based on the scientific procedures
followed and the witnesses' experience.

The appellate court agreed, while recognizing the rarity of such testimony:

The question of the admissibility of lip print identification is a
matter of first impression in Illinois. Thus, because lip-print identification is novel scientific evidence and has yet to be accepted in
a court proceeding, the trial court was required to hold a Frye
hearing. A Frye hearing determines the admissibility of novel
scientific evidence based on whether the scientific principle on
which it rests has gained general acceptance in the relevant scientific community. As the experts testified, the scientific principle
upon which lip print identification rests is the same as fingerprints
and other impression evidence, i.e., that lip prints are unique and
that by employing a side-by-side comparison of a known standard
to a latent print, an expert will be able to positively identify whether the lips in the standard made the latent print. ...The experts

also testified that lip-print identification was generally accepted within the forensic science community. They testified that the FBI and the Illinois State Police consider lip prints as means of positive identification, that the technique has been around since 1950, that articles have been written about the subject, and that they did not know of any dissent inside the forensic science community on their methodology or whether lip prints were positive identification.[92]

In reviewing the witnesses' uncontroverted testimony, it was apparent that the trial judge considered the necessary facts to make a Frye determination during the voir dire questioning and that defendant failed to demonstrate any abuse of discretion.[93]

XII. Ear Impressions

The acceptance of ear impressions is a very long way off in the United States and is looked at with some skepticism in Europe. The 14th Interpol Forensic Science Symposium literature review of Crime Scene marks (foot and shoe-wear, fingerprints, tire impressions, tool marks) says with reference to ear marks:

> In our opinion, the field of ear-mark identification is at its infancy and would benefit from a structured program of research. Abbas and Rutty published a useful guide to Web-based material on earprints and concluded also that despite the availability of numerous Web sites about the uses of the human ear in forensic science, the true value of the ear in the process of forensic identification is still in its embryonic stages ... Ear mark to earprint comparison relies at the moment more on individual experience and judgment than on a structured body of research undertaken following strict scientific guidelines. The recognition process is highly subjective and takes advantage of the extraordinary power of the human eye-brain combination.[94]

The Review Papers note that the field of earprint identification is currently being researched through an initiative under the umbrella of the European community.

Following is an extensive analysis of a 1999 decision rejecting the admissibility of forensic ear impression identification testimony. The decision merits detailed study because it provides one of the relatively rare instances of an in-depth analysis of the methodology of a proffered forensic discipline, let alone an outright rejection, based on a lengthy Frye-Daubert discussion. Understand that European forensic specialists have not rejected earprint expertise, but on the contrary, continue to write about it and include its discussion in international forensic conferences.

As stated earlier, there has been, until the advent of DNA, a judicial readiness to accept the methodological bases of virtually all of the forensic sciences. The contemporary examination of RFLP, PCR, PCR STR, and mtDNA has also demonstrated a very rapid acceptance of these complex DNA technologies. The ear-print case, *State v. Kunze*,[95] was preceded by one unreported 1985 Florida trial court decision that rejected an earlier claim for the legitimacy of earprint impression identification testimony.

In the Florida trial court decision in *State v. Polite*,[96] an extensive analysis was made by the judge in the process of refusing to accept earprint identification as a recognized subspecialty in the field of forensic anthropology and impression evidence. In excluding the ear-print evidence as scientifically inadequate, the Florida trial judge stated:

> The state's witness claims to have made a positive identification of the defendant by comparing a latent ear-print found at the crime scene with a known ear-print of the defendant. This appears to be a case of first impression not only in Florida but also in the United States. There is almost no literature on ear-print identification and certainly no case law on this issue of ear-print identification to guide the court. The state has offered two witnesses as "experts" to support the admissibility of the ear-print identification. The court finds that one of the state's witnesses, Alfred V. Iannarelli, is not to be recognized as an expert by the court in determining the admissibility of this evidence.

> The court notes that there were no true scientific tests performed in making the ear-print identification. This identification was performed strictly as a comparison test between a known earprint and a latent ear-print. The state bases its data on the alleged uniqueness of ears between individuals to establish the reliability of the results of this type of identification. Forensic anthropologists recognize the possible uniqueness of an individual's ears but not as a means of identification.

> The testimony presented to the court suggests that there is a significant difference between comparing actual ears and photographs of ears and the comparing of ear prints to each other. Ear prints are impressions of an ear. The evidence shows that the ear

is a three dimensional object and is malleable. There are no friction ridges as in fingerprints. Different pressures may cause different results with the same ear or different ears to have similar ear prints. Furthermore, there are no studies concerning the comparisons of ear prints to establish their reliability and validity as a means of identification. The reliability and validity of the results of comparisons of ear prints are not recognized or accepted among scientists. There appears to be no science, as in odontology, existing at this time which makes the comparison of ear prints possible due to the alleged uniqueness of an individual's ear characteristics. Furthermore, the comparison techniques used in this case are not sufficiently established to be deemed reliable. The comparison of ear prints has not passed from the stage of experimentation and uncertainty to that of reasonable demonstrability.[97]

In *State v. Kunze,*[98] decided 15 years later, in November of 1999, the situation had not improved as regards the acceptability of ear impressions as a legitimate tool in the identification of the perpetrators of a crime. In Kunze, defendant was convicted of aggravated murder. The Court of Appeals held that the state did not establish that latent earprint identification was generally accepted in the forensic science community, as required for admissibility under Frye test.

In the early morning hours of December 16, 1994, an intruder entered the home of James McCann, who was asleep in the master bedroom. His son Tyler, age 13, was asleep in another bedroom. The intruder bludgeoned McCann in the head with a blunt object, killing him, and also bludgeoned Tyler in the head, resulting in a fractured skull.

The police were immediately interested in Kunze, who had been married to one Diana James from 1976 to April 1994. Four days before the intruder entered McCann's home, James told Kunze that she and McCann were planning to be married. She testified that Kunze was upset by the news.

George Millar, a fingerprint technician with the Washington State Crime Laboratory, processed the home for evidence. He discovered a partial latent earprint on the hallway-side surface of McCann's bedroom door. He "dusted" the print by applying black fingerprint powder with a fiberglass brush. He "lifted" the print by applying palm-print tape first to the door and then to a palm-print card. The resulting print showed the antitragus and portions of the tragus, helix, helix rim, and antihelix. Michael Grubb, a criminologist with the Washington State Crime Laboratory, compared the latent print from McCann's bedroom door with photos of the left side of Kunze's face. He concluded that the latent print "could have been made by Dave Kunze."

He also thought that "(i)t may be possible to obtain additional information by comparing the (latent print) to exemplar impressions."[99]

Millar and Grubb met with Kunze to obtain earprint exemplars. The court recited the steps taken by them, noting that neither had taken an earprint exemplar before, although each had practiced on laboratory staff in preparation for meeting with Kunze:

> *For each of the seven exemplars they took, they had Kunze put hand lotion on his ear and press the ear against a glass surface with a different degree of pressure ("light," "medium," or "hard"). They then dusted the glass with fingerprint powder and used palm-print tape to transfer the resulting impression onto a transparent plastic overlay. The reason Millar and Grubb took multiple exemplars is that they were consciously trying to produce one that would match (i.e., "duplicate") the latent print from McCann's door. They knew that earprints of the same ear vary according to the angle and rotation of the head, and also according to the degree of pressure with which the head is pressed against the receiving surface. They did not know the angle and rotation of the head that made the latent print, or the degree of pressure with which that head had been pressed against McCann's door. Hoping to compensate for these difficulties, they told Kunze to use a different degree of pressure each time ("light," "medium," or "hard"), and they looked at the latent print as they worked.[100]*

Grubb, the one who testified, concluded that David Kunze was a likely source for the earprint and cheekprint that were lifted from the outside of the bedroom door at the homicide scene. Grubb testified to his extensive qualifications as a criminalist. He had been working as a criminalist for more than 20 years, was currently the manager of the state crime lab's Seattle office, although he had never before dealt with earprints, he specialized in firearm and tool-mark identification, and had analyzed "impression evidence" of other kinds. The court recited his basis for providing an earprint opinion.

He admitted that he had not seen any data or studies on earprints, or on how often an ear having the general shape of the questioned print in this case appeared in the general human population. He had used transparent overlays to compare the latent and the exemplars in this case, and stressed that the use of overlays was a generally accepted method of making comparisons. When he compared the latent print with the exemplars taken from Kunze, he admitted accentuating the exemplars taken with "a lighter amount of pressure," because those "more closely approximated ... the impression from the crime scene." He opined that latent earprint identification was generally accepted in the scientific community, reasoning that "the earprint is just another form of impression evidence," and that other impression evidence was readily accepted in the scientific community.[101]

Cor Van der Lugt, the primary European proponent of ear print methodology, testified to extensive qualifications as a police evidence technician in the Netherlands. He had been a Dutch police officer since 1971 and a crime scene officer since 1979, had trained other crime scene officers for many years, and had written "a lot of letters all around the world to people who did something with earprints." He admitted that he had not gotten much response to his inquiries. He testified that he had adopted methods used by one Professor Lunga of Germany, who had investigated what parts of the ear look alike between parents and their children. He also testified to have relied on methods used by a Mr. Hirschi of Switzerland, who had investigated the relation of the height of defining of an earprint and the body length of the offender. He testified that he had received over 600 cases for comparative analysis and had made identification to his own satisfaction in "somewhere between 200 and 250 cases."

On the basis of "somewhere between 100 and 200 prints," he had concluded that pressure distortion is not a problem that prevents one from making identification or a comparison between ears, even though you must "get the same pressure on the ear as the ear that was found on the scene of a crime." He opined that the solution was merely to take several exemplars under different degrees of pressure, then "pick the one that comes closest" to the latent print.

He had been to court in six earprint cases, all in Holland, and the judges in those cases had not been concerned about his methodology; indeed, they had accepted that an identification of an individual can be made by his earprint. The witness did not present or refer to any published literature stating that earprint identification was generally accepted in the scientific community, but testified, nonetheless, as follows:

> Q: Do you have an opinion as to whether ... the uniqueness of the human ear as a basis for personal identification is a notion that is generally accepted in the Netherlands *983 and elsewhere among those engaged in forensic identification?
>
> A: It is accepted, yes.[102]

Alfred V. Iannarelli testified to his extensive qualifications as a law enforcement officer. He had worked as a deputy sheriff in Alameda County, California for 30 years, as the chief of campus police at California State University at Hayward, and in several other law enforcement positions and had worked as a consultant on ear identification. He stated he became interested in ears in 1948, and over the next 14 years classified perhaps 7000 ears from photographs (but not from latent prints). In 1964, he published a book describing his system, which he called "earology" or the "science of ear identification." In 1989, he stated, he published a second edition through a different publisher.[103] He admitted that he had been prohibited from testifying in a 1985 Florida case on the ground that his system of ear identification was not generally accepted in the scientific community,[104] but had testified without objection in a 1984 California murder case.

He stated that he did not know of any published scientific studies that confirmed his theory that individuals can be identified using earprints, nor did he assert that his system was generally accepted in the scientific community:

Q: Are you aware of any scientific research at all that would confirm your theory that ears are so unique that individuals can be positively identified by comparing known ear prints with latent ear impressions?

A: Ear photographs, not ear prints. Counsel, this is relatively a new science.

Dr. Ellis Kerley testified to extensive qualifications as a physical anthropologist. He had a doctorate in anthropology from the University of Michigan and was a professor of long standing in that subject. He had taught the anatomy of the human ear and had been President of the American Academy of Forensic Sciences, and President and First Diplomate of the American Board of Forensic Anthropology. He had worked on prominent cases such as the assassination of President John F. Kennedy. He testified that while the human ear was probably different for each person, he had no information indicating whether one ear could be differentiated from another by observing the ear's gross external anatomy. He did not consider Mr. Iannarelli's work scientific, but rather, simply narrative, not reported in a scientific manner, and not subjected to any statistical analysis. He also rejected Van der Lugt's approach of applying pressure until you could make the exemplar prints look about the same as the latent print in issue, concluding, "we don't do that in science ... (b)ecause we're not trying to make them look alike."

He also stated that earprint identification had not been presented in general scientific sessions or publications, and that he was not aware of any scientific research or authoritative literature concerning earprint identification. It was his opinion that earprint identification had not achieved "general acceptance" in the forensic science community.[105]

Professor Andre Moenssens testified to extensive qualifications as a fingerprint examiner and law professor.[106] Professor Moenssens testified in part:

Q: (D)o you have an opinion whether or not earprint identification is generally accepted as reliable in the forensic science community?

A: (T)he forensic sciences … do not recognize as a separate discipline the identification of ear impressions. There are some people in the forensic science community, the broader forensic science community, who feel that it can be done. But if we are talking about a general acceptance by scientists, there is no such general acceptance.

Q: Is there any evidence that earprint identification has ever been tested by scientific methodology?

A: To my knowledge, it has not been.

Q: Or adequately subjected to scientific peer review?

A: If by peer review, you mean inquiry and verification and studies to confirm or deny the existence of the underlying premise, that is, ear uniqueness, to my knowledge that has not been done.

* * *

Q: With respect to earprint identification, has it ever been shown that results can be reliably obtained in terms of an acceptable rate of error?

A: To my knowledge, there has been no investigation in the possible rate of error that comparisons between known and unknown ear samples might produce.[107]

While he agreed that one earprint could always be compared with another, he noted that "(t)he question is whether that comparison means anything." He testified that he did not know of any generally accepted methods for recording ear characteristics or determining the significance of a "match."

George Bonebrake, a latent fingerprint examiner, testified that he worked for the FBI from 1941 to 1978, that during his last three years with the FBI, he was in charge of its latent print section, supervising 100 examiners and 65 support people, and was currently in private practice. He testified that he never identified anyone based on earprints, and to his knowledge no one else at the FBI had either:

> Q: Is there anything in the materials that you have read that indicates earprint identification has been generally accepted in the forensic science community?
>
> A: No, sir.
>
> Q: What is your impression of the state of earprint identification at this point in forensic science history?
>
> A: That there have been a few cases of individuals making earprint comparisons and identifications, but I'm not aware of any study or research that would indicate to me the uniqueness of earprints when it comes to the comparison of (known) earprint impressions … with the latent earprint impressions; that's based on class characteristics.

*   *   *

> Q: Does the literature indicate that there are problems in attempting to obtain earprint exemplars?
>
> A: Especially when it comes to pressure, yes, sir.

*   *   *

> Q: Have you ever seen any authoritative text published in any discipline of forensic science that's gone on record claiming that earprint identification is generally accepted in the forensic science community?
>
> A: No, sir.[108]

Tommy Moorefield testified that he was a fingerprint specialist with the FBI in Washington, D.C., had worked for the FBI for 36 years as of December 1996; had conducted advanced latent fingerprint courses throughout the United States; instructed new agents on collecting and preserving evidence; and worked on both the Waco tragedy and the TWA Flight 800 disaster. He testified that he was not "real sure" that earprint identification was generally accepted in the community of forensic scientists, and was not aware of the FBI collecting any data on ear prints.[109]

William Stokes testified that he was a special agent and chief of all photographic operations for the FBI in Washington, D.C. and had identified individuals from photographs of their ears, but not from latent ear prints. He stated that he had no knowledge of whether latent ear-print identification was generally accepted by the scientific community.[110]

Ralph Turbyfill testified that he is the long-time chief latent fingerprint examiner for the Arkansas State Crime Laboratory and was able to identify a person from an earprint in one case, because of hair follicles that were peculiarly located. He had, however, tried unsuccessfully to identify people from earprints in two other cases. He did not believe that ear-print identification was generally accepted in the forensic science community, and he did not know of any publication or treatise that asserted that it was so accepted.[111]

Gary Siebenthal testified that he had been an officer with the Peoria, Illinois, Police Department for 23 years and a crime scene technician and though he had identified a defendant from an ear print on one occasion, he did not know of anyone who had proclaimed that ear-print identification was generally accepted as reliable in the forensic science community. He also did not know of any scientific research on reliable techniques for making earprints or dealing with pressure distortions in any such attempts.[112]

Ernest Hamm testified that he had been a crime laboratory analyst-supervisor in Jacksonville, Florida, for approximately 16 years and had made earprint identification in one case. He testified that he had been able to do that because the defendant had a very peculiar mark in the lobe area of the ear. Although he personally believed that earprints could be identified, he knew of nothing to indicate that earprint identification was generally accepted in the forensic science community.[113]

At the end of this extensive Frye hearing, the trial court nevertheless concluded that the principle known as individualization through the use of transparent overlays, applied to the comparison of the latent impression in the present case with the known standards of the defendant, and was based upon principles and methods that were sufficiently established to have gained general acceptance in the relevant scientific community, and as such was admissible.

At the ensuing trial, the state called Grubb and Van der Lugt, but not Iannarelli, to compare the latent print to the exemplars and to render an opinion as to the results of the comparison of defendant's ear print and that lifted from the home of the victim.

Grubb testified that the latent print showed "the antihelix, the interior portion of the ear; the helix rim, that is the top of the rim of the ear; tragus and antitragus, two portions of the ear down below;" that he had compared those anatomical features using transparencies; and that he had found "very good correspondence of those features." He opined, to a reasonable degree of scientific certainty, that "Mr. Kunze's left ear and cheek [were] the likely source of this [ear print] impression at the [crime] scene."

Van der Lugt testified that he also compared the latent earprint and the exemplars by using transparencies and found "a few parts that correspond completely," but also some "differences." He believed that the differences were insignificant, because investigators would never find a 100% fit and that any dissimilarities were caused "by pressure distortion." Although he conceded that no study had ever been published in the world that could tell the jury how much correspondence was actually required to declare a match, he nevertheless testified:

Q: Mr. Van der Lugt, as a result of your comparison of the Grubb standards and your independent comparison of your own standards with the crime scene tracing earprint that was taken in this case, do you have an opinion as to the probability that the defendant's left ear is the source of the latent impression which was left at the scene of the crime in this case?

A: I do have an opinion, yes.

Q: What is your opinion, then?

A: I think it's probable that it's the defendant's ear is the one that was found on the scene.

* * *

Q: *(H)ow confident are you of the opinion that you just expressed?*

A: *I'm 100 percent confident with that opinion.*[114]

Kunze was convicted of aggravated murder, burglary, and robbery. He was sentenced to life without possibility of parole on the murder conviction, and to standard range sentences on the other convictions.

The court of appeals ruled that the main issue was the scientific acceptability of ear imprint testimony: This appeal timely followed.

The main question on appeal was whether Grubb and Van der Lugt could properly opine, based on the similarities and differences that they observed in the overlays, that Kunze was the likely or probable maker of the latent print. Kunze said they could not, because they were relying on scientific, technical or specialized knowledge not generally accepted in the relevant scientific, technical, or specialized community. The state said they could, either because they were not relying on scientific, technical, or specialized knowledge, or because they were relying on scientific, technical or specialized knowledge that was generally accepted in the relevant scientific, technical, or specialized community.[115]

The court noted that a forensic scientist must make clear the difference between individualizing and class characteristics when opining about the maker of a latent print. On the basis of class characteristics alone, a forensic scientist could say that a suspect "cannot be excluded" as the maker of a latent print, that the suspect "could have made" a latent print, or that a latent print was "consistent with" exemplars. However, the court continued, on the basis of individualizing characteristics — and only on the basis of individualizing characteristics — a forensic scientist was allowed to opine that a suspect made or probably made a latent print.

Here, the court observed, Grubb and Van der Lugt claimed that Kunze probably made the latent print taken from McCann's door, and therefore were necessarily claiming that they had found, and were relying on, at least one individualizing characteristic. However, the court emphasized, both Grubb and Van der Lugt lacked personal knowledge of any individualizing characteristic:

> They could not have observed an individualizing characteristic like a scar, tear, mole, or abnormal hair follicle, because the overlays did not show any such feature. They were able to observe the antitragus, tragus, helix, helix rim, and antihelix, insofar as shown in the latent print, but each of those features was a class characteristic, not an individualizing one. They were able to observe the relationship between the antitragus, tragus, helix, helix rim, and antihelix, insofar as it was shown in the latent print, but a lay person using common knowledge would have had no idea whether such relationship was an individualizing characteristic; to conclude that it was, Grubb and Van der Lugt necessarily had to be employing scientific, technical, or specialized knowledge. We turn, then, to whether that knowledge was generally accepted in the relevant community.[116]

In this case, the court observed, 12 long-time members of the forensic science community stated or implied that latent earprint identification was not generally accepted in the forensic science community. Criminalist Grubb's assertion of general acceptance was not based on solid ground:

> He reasoned, essentially, that latent earprints are a form of impression evidence; that other forms of impression evidence are generally accepted in the forensic science community; and thus that latent

earprints must be generally accepted in the forensic science commu-nity. [FN86] We reject his premise that latent earprints automatically have the same degree of acceptance and reliability as fingerprints, toolmarks, ballistics, handwriting, and other diverse forms of im-pression evidence.[117]

The court concluded that the trial court erred by allowing Grubb and Van der Lugt to testify.

Endnotes

1. W. H. Auden and L. Kronenberger, *The Viking Book of Aphorisms* (New York, 1966).
2. SWGFAST documents are officially published in the *Journal of Forensic Iden-tification*. http://www.swgfast.org/
3. SWGFAST documents are officially published in the *Journal of Forensic Iden-tification*. http://www.swgfast.org/
4. See, International Assoc. for Identification, at http://www.theiai.org/publications/jfi.htm.
5. See, the European Fingerprint Standards page, setting out the identification points required in foreign nations in the fingerprint identification area. The listing of 31 countries shows a range from a high of 14–16 points (Gibraltar, Cyprus and Italy) to an average of from 10–12 points (Austria, Belgium, Czech Republic, Denmark, Ireland, Finland, France, Germany, Greece, Hun-gary, Malta, Netherlands, Poland, Romania, Slovenia, Spain, Sweden, Turkey, and Ukraine), to countries having "no set standard" (Latvia, Luxembourg, Monaco, Norway, Slovakia, Switzerland, and the United Kingdom). In the United States, the FBI recommends a 12-point standard but allows for wide variation. See Latent Fingerprint site, located at http://www.latent-prints.com/id_criteria.htm [European Points Chart]. Also see, The Fingerprint Soci-ety site] http://www.fpsociety.org.uk/.
6. Also see, e.g., Simon A. Cole: *Suspect Identities: A History of Fingerprinting and Criminal Identification* (Harvard University Press, 2001) for an interesting history and critique of fingerprint theory and technology.
7. This entire Review, a 550-page document, is available for downloading in PDF format at http://www.interpol.int/Public/Forensic/.
8. The reversal occurred two days after prosecutors vowed to retry Stephan Cowans for shooting Officer Gregory Gallagher, even though newly analyzed DNA evidence showed that Cowans was not the shooter. *Boston Globe*, 01/01/2004.
9. See, 14th Interpol Forensic Science Symposium, Review Paper at 12–13. Also see, *U.S. seeks review of fingerprint techniques*, Flynn McRoberts and Steve

Mills, *Chicago Tribune*, Feb. 21, 2005. There have been over 200 articles and reporting services updates during 2004 and early 2005 on the general subject of fingerprints. Most rehash the Daubert issue or address various DOJ, Immigration, Department of Transportation, or Homeland Security fingerprint requirements.

10. See, e.g., *Criminalistics: An Introduction to Forensic Science* (Prentice Hall, 6th ed., 1998) at 437; Giannelli and Imwinkelried: *Scientific Evidence* (The Michie Company, 2d ed., 1993), Vol. 2, at Chapter 16, p. 479; Geberth: *Practical Homicide Investigation* (CRC Press, 3d ed., 1996), at 524 et seq.; Fisher: *Techniques of Crime Scene Investigation* (CRC Press, 5th ed., 1993) at 90 et seq. Also see, Lee and Gaensslen: *Advances in Fingerprint Technology* (CRC Press, 1994).

11. See, Almog, J., Springer, E. (ed.), *Proceedings of the International Symposium on Fingerprint Detection and Identification* (Ne'urim, Israel, June 26-30, 1995, Hemed Press, Jerusalem, Israel) [Contact Israeli National Police, Investigations Department, Division of Identification and Forensic Sciences, Jerusalem, Israel]. Also see, Christopher Champed, Pierre Margot, *Fingermarks, Shoesole Impressions, Ear Impressions and Toolmarks, Proceedings of the 12th Interpol Forensic Science Symposium* (1998), at 303-331.

12. See, the Home Page for the FBI supported forensic sciences working groups, located at http://www.for-swg.org/home.htm, particularly here, the page for SWGFAST, the Scientific Working Group on Friction Ridge Analysis and SWGDE, the page for the Scientific Working Group for Digital Evidence. Also see, Scientific Working Group on Imaging Technologies (SWGIT), Definitions and Guidelines for the Use of Imaging Technologies in the Criminal Justice System, located at http://www.fbi.gov/programs/lab/fsc/current/swigit1. htm. The SWGFAST site contains a current listing of minimum latent print examiner's qualifications guidelines, training to competency guidelines, and quality assurance guidelines for such examiners. These materials are located at http://onin.com/twgfast/twgfast.html.

13. Galton: *Finger Prints* (MacMillan and Company Ltd. (1892).

14. Wigmore: *The Principles of Judicial Proof* (Little, Brown, and Company, 1913).

15. Wigmore: *The Science of Judicial Proof* (Little, Brown, and Company, 1937).

16. Dean Wigmore's 10 volume treatise, *Wigmore On Evidence*, remains the greatest scholarship on that subject that we possess.

17. 252 Ill. 543, 96 N.E. 1077 (1911).

18. Wigmore: *The Principles of Judicial Proof* (Little, Brown and Company, 1913) [quoting C. Ainsworth Mitchell: *Science and the Criminal* (1911)] at 79-83.

19. 252 Ill. 534, 96 N.E. 1077 (1911).

20. The defendant challenged the admissibility of eyewitness testimony per se, a claim that has returned with gusto as we close out this century.

21. *In re* Castleton's Case, 3 Crim. App. 74 (1909).

22. 252 Ill. 534, 547. The court cited 10 Ency. Britannica (11th Ed.) 376; 5 Nelson's Ency. 28, Gross's Crim. Investigation (Adams' Transl.) 277; *Fuld's Police Administration*, 342, and *Osborn's Questioned Documents*, 479.

23. 252 Ill. 534, 547.

24. 252 Ill., at 548.

25. Citing, *Wharton on Crim. Evidence* *549 (8th Ed.) § 544; 1 *Wigmore on Evidence*, § 795; *Rogers on Expert Testimony* (2d Ed.) § 140; *Jones on Evidence* (2d Ed.) § 581.

26. Jennings, at 549. The court noted the general rule that whatever tends to prove any material fact is relevant and competent. They also observed that testimony as to footprints has frequently been held admissible. See, *Wharton on Crim. Evidence* (8th Ed.) § 796; 1 *Wigmore on Evidence*, § 413; *State v. Fuller*, 34 Mont. 12, 85 Pac. 369, 8 L. R. A. (N. S.) 762, 9 *Am. & Eng. Ann. Cas.* 648, and note.

27. Jennings at 549.

28. See, Almog, J., Springer, E. (ed.), *Proceedings of the International Symposium on Fingerprint Detection and Identification* (Ne'urim, Israel, June 26-30, 1995, Hemed Press, Jerusalem, Israel), for a comprehensive series of articles on the detection and enhancement of latent prints by specialized lighting techniques, short wave UV reflection photography, superglue, vacuum methodologies, DMAC (dimethylaminocinnamaldehyde), PDMAC, amino acid reagents, reflected ultraviolet imaging systems, ninhydrin, black powder, iodine, and alpha-naphtoflavone. There are also recent studies of obtaining latent prints from human skis, plastic bags, and cartridge cases.

29. See, Saferstein: *Criminalistics: An Introduction to Forensic Science* (Prentice Hall, 6th ed., 1998), at 440-448; Giannelli and Imwinkelried: *Scientific Evidence* (The Michie Company, 2d ed., 1993), at 503-510, Fisher: *Techniques of Crime Scene Investigation* (CRC Press, 5th ed., 1993), at 99-118. Also see, *F.B.I. Handbook of Forensic Sciences*: Latent Print examinations, located on the F.B.I. Web site, at http://www.fbi.gov/programs/lab/labhome.htm.

30. Christopher Champed, Pierre Margot, Fingermarks, supra, *Proceedings of the 12th Interpol Forensic Science Symposium* (1998), at 304.

31. Christopher Champed, Pierre Margot, Fingermarks, supra, *Proceedings of the 12th Interpol Forensic Science Symposium* (1998), at 305. Also see, Evett, I.W., Williams, R.L., *A Review of the Sixteen Points Fingerprint Standard in England and Wales*, Proceedings of the International Symposium on Fingerprint Detection and Identification (1995).

32. Christopher Champed, Pierre Margot, Fingermarks, supra, *Proceedings of the 12th Interpol Forensic Science Symposium* (1998), at 305.

33. See, Peterson, *The Status of AFIS Systems Worldwide: Issues of Organization, Performance and Impact*, Proceedings of the International Symposium on Fingerprint Detection and Identification (1995). Also see Dr. Peterson's description of this conference in Peterson, J., Israel Fingerprint Conference Draws

22 Countries, Crime and Justice International, located at http://www.acsp.uic.edu/oic/pubs/cji/110505.htm.

34. The five key IAFIS services are: Ten-print Based Identification Services; latent fingerprint services; subject search and criminal history services; document and image services; and remote search services. IAFIS will consist of three integrated segments: Identification Tasking and Networking (ITN); Interstate Identification Index (III); and Automated Fingerprint Identification System (AFIS). See, *NCIC 2000, Linking It All Together, Fingerprint Matching Subsystem (FMS) (1997) and Fingerprint Identification and Related Information Services* (1997), both of which may located through a search on the FBI home page, located at http://www.fbi.gov.

35. See, Saferstein: *Criminalistics: An Introduction to Forensic Science* (Prentice Hall, 6th ed. 1998), at 440–446.

36. See Chapter 5, Ballistics and Tool Marks, supra.

37. 188 F. Supp. 2d 549 (2002).

38. 260 F.3d 597(2001).

39. 260 F.3d 597(2001), at 601. Also see *United States v. Turner,* (285 F.3d 909)(2002): Defendants claimed that the trial court erred by not conducting a Daubert hearing on the merits of fingerprinting, specifically the science underlying it and the methods used by the detectives in the case. According to the trial court, "(fingerprint evidence had) always been upheld as reliable and appropriate" and "any problems with it…(could) be raised in cross-examination of the government's witnesses." The court found that the trial court did not abuse its discretion by denying the Daubert hearing. It believed that fingerprint evidence, like DNA, is one of the most acceptable forensic sciences and that cross-examination was sufficient for refuting the methods used in this case.

40. 324 F.3d 261 (2003). Also see, In *United States v. King.*

41. 256 F.3d 774 (7th Cir. App. Apr. 2004), defendant argued that the trial court erred by denying him a fingerprint expert witness. Specifically, he contended that the expert would have shown that his fingerprints were not on the drugs and that the lack of fingerprints would have established his innocence. The state countered that the claim was frivolous because of the other, overwhelming evidence in the case.

The court agreed with the state that the claim was frivolous. "(The defendant)," according to the court, "did not have a plausible defense that would have made a fingerprint analysis necessary." The other evidence in the case included police surveillance of the drug sale, and the state had "already financed two separate expert analyses of the audio tapes to bolster an earlier theory that (the defendant) had sold the drugs but had been entrapped." In sum, the court believed the defendant was not entitled to a fingerprint analysis because, even if his fingerprints were not found, the analysis would have proven nothing.

42. 363 F.3d 666 (7th Cir 2004).

43. The court stressed that Mustapha supported his arguments with the Eastern District of Pennsylvania's short-lived opinion in *United States v. Llera Plaza,* 179 F.Supp.2d 492 (E.D.Pa.2002) (*"Llera Plaza I "*) vacated by, *673*United States v. Llera Plaza,* 188 F.Supp.2d 549, 566 (E.D.Pa.2002) (*"Llera Plaza II "*).

44. 363 F. 3d at 673.

45. 363 F. 3d at 674.

46. 103 P.3d 168, 512 Utah Adv. Rep. 47 (2004).

47. See generally, Jessica M. Sombat, Note, Latent Justice: Daubert's Impact on the Evaluation of Fingerprint Identification Testimony, *70 Fordham L.Rev. 2819 (2002)*; Jennifer L. Mnookin, Fingerprint Evidence in an Age of DNA Profiling, *67 Brook. L.Rev. 13, 21 (2001)* ("(E)ven if palm marks [and finger-prints] are different, it does not necessarily mean that experts can identify these differences with a high degree of accuracy."); Tara Marie La Morte, Comment, Sleeping Gatekeepers: *United States v. Llera Plaza* and the Unre-liability of Forensic Fingerprinting Evidence Under Daubert, *14 Alb. L.J. Sci. & Tech. 171, 208-09 (2003)* (highlighting studies that show the extraordinary value that jurors place on forensic evidence such as fingerprint examiner testimony. In essence, we have adopted a cultural assumption that a gov-ernment representative's assertion that a defendant's fingerprint was found at a crime scene is an infallible fact, and not merely the examiner's opinion. See Jennifer L. Mnookin, Fingerprint Evidence in an Age of DNA Profiling, *67 Brook. L.Rev. 13, 28 (2001)* ("From its earliest uses as legal evidence, fingerprint identification was generally presented in the language of certainty, rather than in the language of opinion."). As a consequence, fingerprint evidence is often all that is needed to convict a defendant, even in the absence of any other evidence of guilt.

48. Quintana, at **15.

49. 75 Ark. App. 405, 58 S.W.3d 875 (2001).

50. 75 Ark. App. 405, 58 S.W.3d 875 (2001), at 408.

51. 277 F.3d 709 (4th Cir. 2002).

52. 277 F.3d 709 (4th Cir. 2002), at 713.

53. 277 F.3d 709 (4th Cir. 2002), at 713-714.

54. . 2002 WL 202477 (Cal. App. 2002.

55. Ibid. at *11.

56. *Arizona v. Youngblood,* 488 U.S. 51, 58, 109 S. Ct. 333, 337–38, 102 L.Ed.2d 281 (1988); *Miller v. Vasquez,* 868 F.2d 1116, 1120 (9th Cir.1989), cert. denied, 499 U.S. 963, 111 S.Ct. 1591, 113 L.Ed.2d 654 (1991).

57. 174 Ill.2d 453, 675 N.E.2d 614 (1996).

58. 174 Ill.2d 453, 675 N.E.2d 614 (1996), at 468.

59. *Davis v. Mississippi,* 394 U.S. 721, 724, 89 S.Ct. 1394, 22 L.Ed.2d 676 (1969).

60. 716 So.2d 1104 (Miss. Sp. Ct. 1998).

61. 716 So.2d 1104 (Miss. Sp. Ct. 1998) at 1108.

62. *Wong Sun v. United States*, 371 U.S. 471, 83 S.Ct. 407, 9 L.Ed.2d 441 (1963), at 1113. During a break in the trial, examiner Morgan was allowed to compare the second set of prints with the latent print removed from the Coors Light beer can. At trial, and before the jury, Morgan testified that the thumbprint matched the known thumbprint of Hooker.

63. 146 Ill.2d 363, 586 N.E.2d 1261 (1992).

64. 146 Ill.2d 363, 586 N.E.2d 1261 (1992), at 387. Also see, *People v. Rhodes*, 85 Ill.2d 241, 422 N.E.2d 605 (1981); *People v. Gomez*, 215 Ill.App.3d 208, 574 N.E.2d 822 (1991).

65. See, *People v. Donahue*, 50 Ill.App.3d 392, 394, 365 N.E.2d 710 (1977).

66. *People v. Campbell*, supra, at 1272. Also see *People v. Taylor*, 32 Ill.2d 165, 204 N.E.2d 734 (1965) (defendant's fingerprints on the inside of a window sash in the apartment of a rape and burglary victim was sufficient evidence to establish guilt, since the presence of defendant's prints were unexplained); *People v. Reno*, 32 Ill.App.3d 754, 336 N.E.2d 36 (1975), the unexplained presence of defendant's thumbprint on a package of cigarettes found in a purse that had been stolen from the residence of murder, standing alone, was sufficient evidence to support conviction of murder).

67. 341 N.C. 553, 461 S.E.2d 732 (1995).

68. 341 N.C. 553, 461 S.E.2d 732 (1995), at 561.

69. See, e.g., *State v. Bass*, 303 N.C. 267, 278 S.E.2d 209 (1981) (where the only evidence tending to show that the defendant was ever at the scene of the crime was four of defendant's fingerprints found on the frame of a window screen on the victim's home, the state produced no evidence tending to show when they were put there, and the defendant offered evidence that he was on the premises at an earlier date); *State v. Scott*, 296 N.C. 519, 251 S.E.2d 414 (1979) (where the only evidence tending to show that defendant was ever in the victim's home was a thumbprint found on a metal box in the den on the day of the murder, and the niece of the deceased testified that during the week, she had no opportunity to observe who came to the house on business or to visit with her uncle); *State v. Smith*, 274 N.C. 159, 161 S.E.2d 449 (1968) (where the State had no evidence tending to show that the fingerprint of the defendant found on the victim's wallet could only have been impressed at the time the money was allegedly stolen from her wallet); *State v. Minton*, 228 N.C. 518, 46 S.E.2d 296 (1948) (where the defendant's fingerprint was found on broken glass from the front door of a store that had been unlawfully entered, and the defendant was lawfully in the store on the day the crime was committed).

70. See, e.g., *State v. Irick*, 291 N.C. 480, 231 S.E.2d 833 (1977) (where the defendant's fingerprint was found on the windowsill of the victim's house,

the defendant was apprehended near the scene of the crime, and other evidence tied defendant to the break-in); *State v. Miller*, 289 N.C. 1, 220 S.E.2d 572 (1975) (where the state's evidence established that the defendant's right thumbprint was found on the lock at the scene of the crime, no other fingerprints were found at the scene, and the defendant falsely stated to the police that he had never been in the building that was broken into); *State v. Jackson*, 284 N.C. 321, **737 200 S.E.2d 626 (1973) (where the State's evidence showed that the defendant's fingerprint *563 was lifted from the lower sash of the window inside the kitchen of the apartment occupied by the victim, the victim identified the defendant's voice, and nothing appeared in the record to show that the defendant had ever been in the apartment occupied by the victim prior to the morning of the crimes charged); *State v. Foster*, 282 N.C. 189, 192 S.E.2d 320 (1972) (where the victims testified that they did not know the defendant and had never given him permission to enter their home and the defendant testified he had never been in their home, and the evidence showed that the flower pot where the defendant's fingerprints were found had been frequently washed); *State v. Tew*, 234 N.C. 612, 68 S.E.2d 291 (1951) (where the defendant's fingerprints were found at the scene of the crime and the testimony of the owner and operator of the service station tended to show that she had not seen the defendant before the date of the crime); *State v. Reid*, 230 N.C. 561, 53 S.E.2d 849 (where the defendant was never lawfully in the apartment of the victim, and the defendant's fingerprint was present on the inside of the window sill in the sleeping quarters of the victim), cert. denied, 338 U.S. 876, 70 S. Ct. 138, 94 L.Ed. 537 (1949).

71. *State v. Montgomery*, at 564.

72. *State v. Montgomery*, at 564 at 565.

73. 301 Ill.App.3d 481, 703 N.E.2d 546 (1998).

74. 215 Ill.App.3d 208, 158 Ill.Dec. 709, 574 N.E.2d 822 (1991).

75. Gomez, 215 Ill.App.3d at 216, 158 Ill.Dec. 709, 574 N.E.2d 822.

76. 1998 WL 66942 (Ohio App.).

77. 1998 WL 66942 (Ohio App.), at *3.

78. 1998 WL 66942 (Ohio App.), at *4.

79. *Eley v. State*, 288 Md. 548, 555–56, 419 A.2d 384, 388 (1980).

80. Eley, 288 Md. at 555, 419 A.2d at 388 (quoting *People v. Carter*, 73 Ill.App.3d 406, 410, 29 Ill.Dec. 631, 392 N.E.2d 188, 192) (1979) (second alteration in original).

81. 964 F.2d 21 (Dist Col. Ct App. 1992).

82. 964 F.2d 21 (Dist Col. Ct App. 1992), at 24.

83. 964 F.2d 21 (Dist Col. Ct App. 1992), at 25.

84. See *Patterson v. State*, 356 Md. 677, 741 A.2d 1119 (Md. 1999), where defendant was convicted of possession of cocaine with intent to distribute and various driving offenses. The appellate court ruled on defendant's claim that

the trial court erred in refusing to give his requested "missing evidence" instruction. The court concluded that a party generally is not entitled to a missing evidence instruction, and affirmed the conviction. This is an excellent case that provides a very comprehensive analysis of the current status of the "missing evidence" issue, especially relating a defendant's right to a "missing evidence" jury instruction.

85. 299 Ill.App.3d 480, 701 N.E.2d 212 (1998).

86. 299 Ill.App.3d 480, 701 N.E.2d 212 (1998), at 482.

87. 299 Ill.App.3d 480, 701 N.E.2d 212 (1998), at 488.

88. See, Ball, J., The Current Status of Lip Prints and Their Use for Identification. *Journal of Forensic Odonto-Stomatology*, 2002. 20(2): 43-46.

89. 304 Ill.App.3d 427, 710 N.E.2d 1251(1999).

90. 304 Ill.App.3d 427, 710 N.E.2d 1251(1999), at 436.

91. 304 Ill.App.3d 427, 710 N.E.2d 1251(1999).

92. 304 Ill.App.3d 427, 710 N.E.2d 1251(1999), at 437.

93. Also see, *Smallwood v. State*, 907 P. 2d 217 (Ct. Crim. App. Okla. 1995) (Cups located in the living room and bedroom showed bloody lip prints, suggesting the victim had been conscious enough to drink from containers before finally being bludgeoned to death.)

94. Interpol 14th Forensic Science Symposium Literature Review, at 22-23. *The field of earprint identification is currently being researched through an important initiative under the umbrella of the European community (www.fearid.com). It is considered a welcome initiative that led to the publication of a review, and exploratory study on the intra- and inter-individual variability of ear marks has been proposed.*

95. 97 Wash.App. 832 988 P.2d 977 (1999).

96. No. 84-525 (14th Judicial Circuit, Fla. Jun. 10, 1985). This case is noted and referenced in *State v. Kunze*, 97 Wash.App. 832 988 P.2d 977 (1999), discussed in detail below.

97. Clerk's Papers at 1073–74. This case did not result in a published appellate opinion.

98. 97 Wash.App. 832, 988 P.2d 977 (1999).

99. 97 Wash.App. 832, 988 P.2d 977 (1999), at 981.

100. 97 Wash.App. 832, 988 P.2d 977 (1999). After Millar and Grubb took the exemplars, they were asked to compare them to the latent print. Millar declined because his laboratory supervisor thought that earprint identification was "out of the expertise of the (crime lab's) latent unit."

101. 97 Wash.App. 832, 988 P.2d 977 (1999), at 982–983.

102. 97 Wash.App. 832, 988 P.2d 977 (1999), at 983.

103. 97 Wash.App. 832, 988 P.2d 977 (1999), at 984. The court noted the 1989 edition of Iannarelli's book was introduced along with his oral testimony.

Titled *Ear Identification*, it was published by the Paramont Publishing Company of Fremont, California, and the court observed, contained no bibliography or other indicia of scientific verification or acceptability.

104. See *State v. Polite*, supra.

105. *Kunze* at 984.

106. Professor Moenssens is coauthor of the leading text, Moenssens, Starrs, Henderson & Inbau: *Scientific Evidence in Civil and Criminal Cases* (Foundation Press, 4th ed. 1995), still the leading law school casebook and treatise on scientific evidence.]

107. *Kunze*, at 984–985.

108. *Kunze*, at 984–985.

109. *Kunze*, at 986.

110. *Kunze* at 895.

111. *Kunze*, at 985.

112. *Kunze*, at 986

113. *Kunze*, at 986

114. *Kunze*, at 987.

115. *Kunze*, at 977–978.

116. *Kunze*, at 989.

117. *Kunze*, at 989.

Blood-Spatter Analysis

9

ANTONY

If you have tears, prepare to shed them now,
You do all know this mantle; I remember
The first time Caesar put it on;
Twas on a summer's evening, in his tent,
That day he overcame the Nervii;
Look, in this place ran Cassius' dagger through;
See what a rent the envious Casca made;
Through this the well-beloved Brutus stabbed;
And as he plucked his cursed steel away,
Mark how the blood of Caesar followed it,
As rushing out of doors...

Shakespeare: Julius Caesar, Act 3, Scene 2

I. Introduction

Arterial spurting, expired blood, flight paths, misting, wave casting, blood
dripping, satellite patterns, low, medium, and high velocity deposits, back
spatter, wipes, swipes, angular deposits, and off patterns, are just some of the
body of terms[1] utilized in the very telling discipline of bloodstain pattern

analysis. This strictly observation-based forensic tool is a highly specialized crime scene procedure that is combined with the equally important skills involved in forensic photography.[2] It is commonly used in homicide and suicide settings to determine the sequence of events, the distance of shooter to victim, self-defense, mental states such as intent, and a number of important crime scene dynamics that can be of inestimable use to both prosecutors and defense counsel.[3]

Luminol and phenolphthalein are used as presumptive tests in the field to identify potential blood stains. However, the two tests can generate false positive reactions.[4] The tests can react to metal surfaces, cleansers containing iron-based substances, horseradish, and rust. Neither test can distinguish between animal blood and human blood, and they cannot determine how long the substance has been at the scene. When a positive reaction occurs, a criminalist must do a confirmatory test to conclusively determine that the test sample is human blood. For these reasons, courts have been very wary of accepting the scientific validity of blood findings. It is important, however, to realize that luminol and phenolphthalein have been and continue to be routinely used by police as investigative tools and as a basis for obtaining a search warrant. There is a noticeable movement towards acceptance of these chemical tests as presumptive proof of the presence of human blood at a crime scene. Luminol analyses are often used in conjunction with blood-spatter pattern analysis, central to many crime scene reconstruction efforts.[5]

The International Association of Bloodstain Pattern Analysts (IABPA) Web site is an excellent resource to keep current as to the activities of blood-spatter analysts throughout the world. The IABPA is an organization of forensic experts specializing in the field of bloodstain pattern analysis. The official site provides the following simple definition of blood spatter work:

> Violent crimes can result in bloodshed. When liquid blood is acted upon by physical forces, bloodstains and bloodstain patterns may be deposited on various surfaces, including the clothing of the individuals present at the crime scene. These bloodstain patterns can yield valuable information concerning the events which lead to their creation when examined by a qualified analyst. The information gained can then be used for the reconstruction of the incident and the evaluation of the statements of the witnesses and the crime participants.[6]

During the past 14 years, the FBI Laboratory has organized and sponsored scientific working groups, whose goal is to establish professional forums in which federal, state, and local government experts, together with academic and commercial scientists, can address practical issues arising in the various forensic disciplines. As a result of this effort the Scientific Working Group on Bloodstain Pattern Analysis (SWGSTAIN) was established.[7] In addition to the IABPA Web site[8] there are several excellent information resources maintained by various police departments.[9]

II. Blood Spatter: Presumptive Tests for Blood

Courts since the late 19th century have been willing to accept testimony from both lay and expert witnesses that they observed what appeared to be human blood. The modern case law has also focused on the scientific reliability of luminol and other presumptive tests for blood. Testimony as to the simple presence or absence of blood can have a dramatic circumstantial effect on a case, and be the subject of sophisticated bloodstain pattern analyses.

This issue was revisited in a 1998 murder case, *Ayers v. State*,[10] an Arkansas Supreme Court decision, where defendant was convicted of a capital murder. Sometime between 12:00 midnight, February 24, 1995, and 1:00 a.m., February 25, 1995, in the parking lot of the Whisperwood Apartments on Baseline Road in Little Rock, appellant Antonio Ayers and William Hall were involved in an argument. As the argument intensified, Ayers drew a gun and shot Hall once in the chest and once in the back, as Hall tried to run away. Hall continued running from Ayers, but Ayers caught up with Hall and began kicking him and beating him until Hall was left lying on the parking lot. Ayers then left but returned in Hall's vehicle and drove over Hall's body. Ayers then fled the scene in Hall's vehicle, leaving Hall for dead.[11]

At trial, the state presented evidence showing that after appellant shot the victim he got into Hall's vehicle and drove over him. During the state's direct examination of Annette Tracy, a Little Rock Police Department crime-scene specialist, Tracy described an exhibit as a photograph of the underside of Hall's vehicle with what appeared to her to be possible blood on the oil pan. The state then moved to admit the photograph. Defendant objected to the admission of the exhibit, claiming that it was not relevant and was unduly prejudicial because Tracy had described only "possible blood." The state responded that subsequent evidence would establish that samples collected from the underside of the car were identified as human blood of the victim's blood type. On that basis, the trial court admitted the photograph.

At trial, Scott Sherill, a forensic serologist with the State Crime Lab, testified that the substance shown in State's Exhibit 25 was indeed human blood but that he was unable to determine the blood type. Defendant relied on *Brenk v. State*,[12] a 1993 Arkansas opinion, and the court here noted that the Brenk case confronted the issue of whether evidence of luminol testing should be allowed in light of the fact that luminol does not distinguish between certain metals, vegetable matter, human blood, or animal blood. There the court had held that evidence about the use of luminol would not be admissible unless additional tests showed that the substance tested was human blood related to the alleged crime. Brenk clearly did not apply to the facts of the instant case because luminol was not used and because serological testing showed that the substance found underneath Hall's car was, in fact, human blood.[13]

In the instant case, the state having presented unchallenged evidence that appellant drove over Hall in Hall's vehicle after shooting him, the court found that the state proved that Hall had, in fact, been underneath the car, where the blood was found, at a time when he was bleeding profusely from newly inflicted gunshot wounds. This, the court found, presented very convincing circumstantial evidence connecting the blood found underneath the victim's vehicle with this crime.[14]

In *State v. Canaan*,[15] a 1998 Kansas Supreme Court case involving presumptive tests for the presence of blood, defendant was convicted of premeditated murder, aggravated robbery, and aggravated burglary. Sometime in the morning hours of October 20, 1994, Michael Kirkpatrick was murdered. The evening before, he was observed at a bar with Canaan. During the investigation, neighbor of the deceased, one Jerry Staley, informed police that defendant had been at the victim's house the evening before and had been driving a maroon Oldsmobile. Because the victim had been with Canaan, police went to defendant's home to ask what he knew of the homicide. The officers observed a maroon Oldsmobile at Canaan's home.

Defendant was soon after injured in a crash following a high-speed car chase while attempting to evade arrest. During the investigation, the police requested John Wilson of the Regional Crime Lab to conduct luminol tests. Wilson tested Canaan's Oldsmobile and house. During the course of the investigation, John Wilson also performed a luminol test on the Oldsmobile Canaan was driving the night of the murder, which indicated the possible presence of blood on the left corner of the driver's seat and door panel. An additional luminol test of Canaan's home showed the presence of bloody footprints on the front porch and step and down the main hallway into the master bedroom. The footprints turned at the edge of the bed as if someone turned and sat down on the bed. The luminol also reacted when it was placed on a watch found in a bedroom. Further presumptive tests validated the reaction to blood on the Oldsmobile seat.[16]

Canaan then filed a motion asserting that the luminol testing failed to meet general acceptability requirements of Frye, but the trial court found that luminol testing had achieved widespread acceptance, was not really novel or new, and, once the state laid its foundation for use in the instant case, no Frye hearing was warranted.

At trial, Canaan renewed his objection to the introduction of luminol evidence, asserting luminol is only a presumptive test for blood. In other words, it may indicate the presence of blood, but also reacts similarly with other materials, including common household cleansers. The district court ruled that the fact the luminol test was a presumptive test goes only to the weight, rather than the admissibility, of the evidence. On appeal, Canaan argued the district judge should have conducted a Frye hearing because Kansas had never determined the reliability of luminol evidence.[17] Additionally, Canaan argued there was no evidence that state expert John Wilson was qualified to testify as an expert in the field of luminol testing techniques or as to the validity and reliability of the exact techniques he used in this case.

At trial, John Wilson testified that he had been the chief chemist at the Regional Crime Lab in Kansas City since 1978, where he supervised other chemists, analyzed various categories of trace evidence (such as blood) and went to crime scenes when requested. He also taught two crime scene classes a year for local law enforcement in Kansas and Missouri to train people how to conduct a proper crime scene investigation. He had also earned a degree in biology and chemistry and had worked at the Johnson County Crime Lab two years prior to becoming the chief chemist for the Regional Crime Lab. He had also attended a number of seminars on blood analysis presented by the FBI, American Association of Forensic Science and others. His total forensic chemistry career had spanned 23 years.[18]

Wilson started as a forensic chemist at the Kansas City, Missouri police lab in 1973 and had been involved in forensic chemistry for approximately 23 years; had attended a number of classes and various seminars with the American Academy of Forensic Science (an association of forensic scientists); also attended a number of seminars at the FBI academy in Quantico, Virginia, and classes on blood analysis at the University of California. Wilson further testified that he had received training in luminol testing. He had completed a number of classes at the FBI academy, including a crime scene investigation course, and had attended various seminars with the American Academy of Forensic Scientists and the Midwest Association of Forensic Scientists.[19] The court accepted expert Wilson's careful description of the process of presumptive blood testing using luminol:

> Wilson testified that luminol testing has been used by forensic scientists for about 60 years. It has been available for approximately 80 years and scientific papers on luminol were published in the 1920s. He testified that he had conducted luminol testing hundreds of times and has testified as an expert witness in other criminal cases over the years regarding the results of luminol testing.... Wilson explained how luminol testing works: luminol is a

chemical that reacts with blood and undergoes a chemical reaction that gives off light (chemiluminescence). When blood and luminol come into contact, it essentially causes a very faint blue glow that one can see in the dark. Luminol testing works by placing a luminol reagent in very small concentrations in a sodium hydroxide water solution and then placing it in a spray mister, which creates a very fine mist. The forensic chemist makes the area as dark as possible because the actual spraying needs to occur in total darkness. The forensic chemist then begins spraying the very fine mist in the area to be searched for bloodstains. If blood is present, a chemical reaction causes a blue glow. The chemiluminescence of the blood and luminol mixture occurs if it is dark enough and there is enough blood present. Luminol testing is extremely sensitive, depending on what one is looking for and what surface is being sprayed. It is sensitive to 1:1,000,000 to 1:10,000,000 parts per million.[20]

Responding to defendant's claims of the reaction of luminol to a number of common nonblood substances, Wilson testified that luminol is actually fairly specific for blood and that there are few things other than blood that cause it to react. Forensic scientists, he continued, use it on a regular basis as an investigative tool to locate crime scenes that have been cleaned and are able on occasion to reconstruct what occurred at the crime scene, such as the sequence of events, where the blood was, perhaps how it was cleaned up, and maybe even tracks made by footprints that have blood on them. Luminol could reveal tire tracks, shoe prints, and hand prints that were made in blood. The duration of the luminescent results of a positive test before fading would vary from a few seconds to several minutes, and ideally, it would last long enough to photograph.[21]

The time it remains luminescent depends upon the material the blood is on and how the spray that is being used affects it. In his years of experience, Wilson has had occasion to have positive luminol results for footprints 20 to 50 times. There was one occasion where he was able to follow a person outdoors across a public park for over a quarter of a mile. Wilson stated that the luminol test is generally accepted as a presumptive test for blood in the scientific community of forensic science and is recognized as reliable within the scientific community of forensic scientists.

The court in Canaan ruled that only when there was a doubt as to the scientific reliability of evidence must the state prove its reliability and acceptance of the science, and held that luminol testing was universally accepted. The trial court did require the state to lay a foundation as to Wilson's qualifications to administer the test, and a review of Wilson's testimony shows he was clearly qualified to administer the luminol tests and that the underlying science was reliable and accepted.[22]

Luminol also withstood challenge in the recent case of State v. Maynard,[23] where defendant was convicted of second-degree murder and armed criminal action. The Court of Appeals also held that a testifying police detective was qualified as expert witness in Luminol testing.

Wendell Maynard lived with his girlfriend, Rewa Walker, in Kansas City, Missouri. Walker spent the evening of March 10, 1993, with Lashawn Hollingshed, Maynard's cousin. According to Hollingshed, Walker called Maynard from a pay phone between 10:00 to 11:00 p.m. to tell him that she was on her way home and that she loved him. Walker's body was found over a year later. She had been murdered. Maynard was charged with first-degree murder and armed criminal action.

Detective Owings found blood droplets on a living room mirror and similar specimen scrapings on the fish tank in the living room. The detective noticed visible blood splatters on the living room walls, ceiling, and door molding and noticed a large bloodstain on a carpet remnant. Owings found a steamer carpet cleaner on defendant's porch that had blood in its internal chamber; a checkered comforter with blood on it in the dining room; a table in the kitchen with blood on it and two pieces of a gold-colored chain, a gold-colored lion pendant and a broken gold-colored ring in the bedroom, all with blood on them.[24]

Police performed Luminol tests on the stairs leading up to the front door of defendant's apartment, the dining room carpet, and the trunk of the deceased's automobile. The tests displayed a blue glowing color, which is a positive indication of blood. Frank Booth, a forensic chemist with the Regional Crime Lab, also testified that the positive tests indicated the presence of blood. Booth agreed, however, that the presence of rust, dust particles, or some cleaning agents could also cause a positive response.[25]

The police determined that the 24-inch bloodstain on the carpet remnant was consistent with having resulted from a gunshot wound to the head. While the blood splatters found throughout the house were not consistent with gunshot wounds, they could have been caused by two persons fighting or by moving a bloody object around. The bloodstains on the stairway leading up to Maynard's apartment were likely caused by someone's dragging a bloody object up or down the stairs. The bloodstains in the trunk of Walker's Saab were likely caused by a large bloody object being placed in the trunk. The examination of a pair of coveralls showed that they contained blood stains on the left hip area, and across the lap area, the back left shoulder and the right sleeve.[26]

The court ruled that Detective Owings was sufficiently qualified to testify as an expert about Luminol testing, because he had received training at the

Regional Crime Lab from the Chief Chemist, John Wilson, with respect to Luminol tests at crime scenes, and had conducted Luminol tests on multiple occasions.[27]

The extensive nature of the modern crime scene investigation and prosecution becomes apparent each year as defense counsel raise an increased number and variety of challenges to the claims of modern forensic science. Recent cases in a wide range of crimes, but especially in homicide and sexual assault charges, serve as indicators of the complexity of modern crime scenes and the extensive knowledge of forensic matters for which lawyers are responsible. A single crime scene can involve many forensic science and concomitant legal issues.

Considerable attention focused on this subject in the recent O. J. Simpson and the Lyle and Eric Menendez murder prosecutions.[28]

Blood-transfer mechanisms, blood sequencing, and whether the nose or mouth was involved in expired blood and blood spatters are the stock in trade of analysts in this area. Photography and string arrangements tracking the type, shape, extent, and direction of blood material, whether large or microscopic, can reprise the fatal event with an impressive degree of accuracy. As evidenced in the second Menendez prosecution, a clear reconstruction of just how a crime occurred can eliminate any number of defense arguments based on accident, recklessness, or sudden panic by illustration, cold calculation, or the minimal amount of premeditation required to convict.[29] For example, *arterial gushing* produces characteristic bloodstain patterns on a surface as a result of blood exiting under pressure from a breached artery; medium velocity impact spatter is produced when an object, such as a baseball bat, strikes a bloody object, such as a victim's head, at a velocity of approximately 25 feet per second; and high velocity impact spatter occurs when the velocity of the impact is at least 100 feet per second. This phenomenon is typically associated with gunshot wounds.

A pioneering study in this century was made by MacDonnell and Bialousz, *Flight Characteristics and Stain Patterns of Human Blood*, National Institute of Law Enforcement and Criminal Justice of the Department of Justice (1969), although important judicial acceptance came as long ago as 1922.[30] There are now several excellent texts, bibliographies, Web sites,[31] and training courses that address all aspects of this important forensic discipline.[32] The presence or absence of blood in and around a crime scene has been discussed in cases since the beginning of the nation, although the type of discussion concerning bloodstain pattern analysis is a phenomenon of the last quarter of this century.

In *People v. Davis*,[33] decided by the Michigan Supreme Court, the defendant was convicted of murder in the first degree, growing out of the killing of one Earl Zang. Zang was found on the sidewalk near the corner of Fort and Sixth streets, in the city of Detroit, about 5 o'clock in the morning of March 7, 1921. His death was caused by two knife wounds; one in the side, and the other in the neck. Defendant was one of the deceased's companions earlier in the evening and was eventually charged with his murder.

Dr. John E. Clarke, a county chemist, examined spots of blood on defendant's coat. He explained the difference in appearance when the blood was dropped on a garment and when it "squirted from a bleeding artery." He was then asked:

> Q. Can you say that the blood was dropped on, or was squirted on, * * * as by a bleeding artery? * * *
>
> A. My opinion is it was spread on.
>
> Q. Sprayed?
>
> A. Squirted.

This testimony was accepted without challenge to or discussion by the court.[34]

The initial step is to identify the presence of blood at various points in the crime scene. Luminol has been used by police for years as an investigative tool to accomplish this. It has been subject to debate as to the utility of such identifications as forensic evidence because of its tendency to indicate false positives results. Luminol and phenolphthalein are used as presumptive tests in the field to identify potential bloodstains. As noted, these two tests can generate false positive reactions. The tests can react to metal surfaces, cleansers containing iron-based substances, horseradish, and rust. Neither test can distinguish between animal blood and human blood and they cannot determine how long the substance has been at the scene. When a positive reaction occurs, a criminalist must do a confirmatory test to conclusively determine that the test sample is human blood. The potential for luminol destroying important markers needed for certain blood analyses was also cited as a concern in the early part of this decade.[35] Researchers continue to examine the effect of luminol type products to effect later attempts at extracting DNA.[36] The FBI has published an important paper entitled Critical Revision of Presumptive Tests for Bloodstains, which address this necessary step in the use of bloodstain pattern analysis testimony.[37] Luminol findings are routinely accepted.[38]

III. Blood Spatter in the Courtroom

There are almost 100 reported cases each year discussing some aspect of bloodstain or blood pattern expertise. It is a compelling common sense crime scene discipline, easily understood by court, counsel, and juries. This forensic discipline has rarely been seriously challenged on reliability or general acceptability bases. A representative sampling of typical blood pattern or blood spatter cases follows.

The constant presence of blood spatter and patterning in violent assaults and murders is illustrated in *People v. Mendez*,[39] a 2005 California case. Defendant Edward Mendez was convicted of the voluntary manslaughter of one Michael Gilligan. His codefendants at trial, Michael Davies and Robert Wright, were also convicted as a result of the killing. Dr. Rulon, a forensic pathologist, concluded that the cause of death was multiple sharp and blunt force injuries and the injury to the neck. From the blood evidence, it appeared that the neck wound was inflicted while the victim was on the ground. In all likelihood, he was lifted up, his throat was cut, and he was put back down on the floor.[40]

Several areas of blood were found in the apartment. There was blood from *arterial spurting* on the coffee table. There was *blood spatter* on the coffee table, the wall by the victim's head and the kitchen floor. This blood belonged to the victim. *Blood drops* appeared on the brass strip at the threshold of the front door. This blood belonged to Wright. Also, *bloodstains* were found on the left arm of the couch and another bloodstain on the back of the couch. The stain on the back of the couch was darker in color and appeared older. The stain on the arm of the couch was from Davies; the stain on the back of the couch was from Wright. A piece of skin found on the broken glass window came from Davies. The blood on the kitchen floor had shoe impressions; the impressions matched Davies' shoe.[41]

On the evening of February 28, 2001, officers went to the park. They talked to Davies and defendant. They came to the police station and their clothes were seized. Davies had a laceration on his hand and scratches on his neck and hands. There was a blood smear on the left leg of his jeans. Defendant had an abrasion on his right cheek.[42]

The two small blood spots on defendant's jacket came from the victim. There was blood on Davies's boot, sweatshirt, jeans, and socks. The stains on Davies' jeans matched his type. The human bloodstains on Davies' shoes and socks appeared to have been washed.

IV. Blood Spatter: Expert Qualifications

While qualifications vary, courts are very willing to qualify experts on seemingly minimum bases. A recent example is *State v. DeVolt*,[43] a 2004 Arizona Supreme Court decision that provides a good example of how the court will qualify someone as a blood-spatter analysis expert with very little consideration — even a Supreme Court in a very important death penalty case.

Defendant was convicted of two counts of first-degree murder and several other property crimes. He was sentenced to the death penalty and appealed.

Defendant claimed, in part, that a police detective was not qualified as an expert witness in blood-splatter analysis and, therefore, he should not have testified regarding the blood splatter found at the crime scene. The detective testified that "there appeared to be spots of blood around the perimeter — inside the perimeter of the garage, and it was in such a fashion as to suggest that somebody had walked around something there. Presumably, walked around a car in the garage."

The court found that the detective qualified as a blood-spatter analysis expert because he had attended crime scene management classes, a homicide investigation class, and watched two training videos on blood-spatter analysis as part of his advanced officer training. "While this training is not extensive," the court said, "it is significantly more extensive than the average person has received and is sufficient to allow the testimony to be heard by the jury."[44] The court, therefore, allowed the testimony to stand.

In *Holmes v. State*,[45] a 2004 Texas aggravated assault case, defendant claimed that the blood spatter analysis should not have been admitted because the expert witness' only qualification was a 40-hour blood-spatter analysis school and that the state did not establish the validity of the scientific techniques in blood-spatter analysis.

In regard to qualification, the court found that the expert witness, a police officer, had received adequate training to testify about blood splatter. Specifically, he had spent several hours studying weapons and blood velocities, patterns, and sources at the police academy. The court found this case was similar to another case where it decided there was "no abuse of discretion in qualifying a witness as an expert in blood-spatter analysis where the witness had received more than 60 hours of training, had read a book on the subject, and contended that the methods used were of the type relied on by experts in the field."[46]

In regard to the foundation, the court found that, in sum, blood splatter analysis was an acceptable investigative tool. The court believed that there was no reason to find that blood-spatter analysis was invalid because there had been several cases establishing its validity while there were no cases demonstrating its invalidity. "None of (the relevant) courts held," according to the court, "that, after an extensive hearing, blood-spatter analysis was unreliable. The courts either avoided the question or had nothing in the record before them to make a determination."[47]

In *State v. Roman Nose*,[48] a 2003 Minnesota case, defendant was convicted of first-degree murder while committing or attempting to commit criminal sexual conduct. Defendant claimed, in part, that the state improperly told the jury that it could infer the "spots of blood all over (the defendant's) shirt" proved that he killed the victim. Specifically, he contended that only an expert witness could interpret a blood-spatter analysis. The court found that the state was not conducting a blood-spatter analysis in order to prove the position of the victim's body. The court believed that the state was merely refuting the defendant's claim that "he had merely wiped his hands on his shirt." According to the court, "The average juror, through experience and common sense and without expert testimony, could determine that the presence of spots of blood on the shirt is not consistent with (the defendant's) testimony that he wiped his bloody hands on his shirt." Therefore, the court found that the state's comments did not amount to expert testimony.[49]

The qualifications of a forensic pathologist to give an opinion based upon blow-back theory was addressed in the case of *Commonwealth v. Begley*,[50] where defendant was convicted of kidnapping and first-degree murder and was sentenced to death. Defendant argued, among other bases, that the trial court erred in allowing the Commonwealth to present expert testimony regarding "blow-back" theory through a serologist.

The court ruled that it was not an abuse of discretion for the trial court to allow the Commonwealth to present expert testimony regarding the blow-back theory, even though the serologist was unable to scientifically establish the source of the blood found on defendant's glove or the shotgun that defendant had borrowed. Testimony regarding the blow-back theory provided the jury with a potential scientific explanation for the presence of blood on both the outside of defendant's left-hand glove and on the inside of the barrel of the shotgun, in support of the theory that defendant murdered victim by shooting her in the head with a shotgun at close range. The court ruled that given the physician's practical experience as a forensic pathologist and her educational experiences, including the class she attended on blood splatter, the physician, who testified in first-degree murder prosecution, had a reasonable pretension to specialized knowledge on the blow-back theory, even though she was not a ballistics expert.[51]

At trial, Forensic Pathologist Dr. Funke, Ballistics Expert Corporal Baltimore, and Serologist Lee Ann Grayson all testified in relatively general terms about the blow-back theory, which Corporal Baltimore explained during trial, is "often referred to as a phenomena of blood or flesh or tissue coming back towards the muzzle of a firearm — a discharged firearm after a person or an animal in some cases has been shot...." As the theory relates to the instant case, Ms. Grayson testified that due to the small amounts of blood she found present on defendant's glove and Tom March's shotgun, she could not scientifically identify the source of the blood on either item. Defendant argued that this testimony regarding the blow-back theory was irrelevant and misleading because the source of the blood found on his glove and on the inside of Tom March's shotgun could not be scientifically identified. The court quickly rejected this position:

Appellant's argument fails, however, because the testimony of Dr. Funke, Corporal Baltimore, and Ms. Grayson regarding the blow-back theory provided the jury with a potential scientific explanation for the presence of blood on both the outside of appellant's left-hand glove and on the inside of the barrel of Tom March's shotgun. Moreover, if the jury accepted the blow-back theory, this theory would strongly support the Commonwealth's position that appellant murdered Erica Miller by shooting her in the head with Tom March's shotgun at close range. If anything, Ms. Grayson's inability to scientifically establish the source of the blood found on the glove and the shotgun would affect the weight to be given to the expert testimony on the blow-back theory, not its admissibility. Thus, the trial court did not abuse its discretion by allowing the Commonwealth to present expert testimony on the blow-back theory.[52]

Defendant also argued that the trial court abused its discretion by permitting Dr. Funke to testify as an expert on the blow-back theory because she is a forensic pathologist and not a ballistics expert. The court found the pathologist to be adequately qualified:

Dr. Funke testified that she is a medical doctor, that she is board certified in the areas of anatomic, clinical, and forensic pathology, that she has conducted more than 1000 autopsies, and that she has been employed as a forensic pathologist since 1993. She further testified that in 1996, she attended a five-day class conducted by Herb McDonald, a recognized expert on blood spatter analysis. In addition, Dr. Funke testified that her training and practical experience conducting autopsies on homicide and suicide victims, including her observations of the homicide or suicide weapons and the victims' clothing, provided her with specialized knowledge about what happens to body fluids when they are subjected to a great amount of force.[53]

Defendant also additionally alleges that trial counsel was ineffective for failing to cross-examine Serologist Grayson about her training and experience as an expert in blood stain patterns because she had only testified as an expert on one prior occasion. The court also found this argument meritless:

Ms. Grayson testified that she was employed in the Serology Unit of the Pennsylvania State Police Crime Laboratory and that she had completed five courses, including one advanced course in bloodstain analysis. She further testified that although *298 she had only testified once before as an expert in the area of bloodstain analysis, she had testified as an expert in the area of serology approximately 35 times. Despite the fact that Ms. Grayson had only testified on one prior occasion as a blood stain expert, the court qualified Ms. Grayson as an expert in blood-stain and splatter analysis based on her other indisputable qualifications, including her practical experiences as a serologist and her extensive training in blood stain analysis. [FN30] Furthermore, because Ms. Grayson readily admitted before the jury that she had only testified once before as a bloodstain expert, the jury was aware of this information even though defense counsel did not cross-examine Ms. Grayson about it. Thus, the jury was free to consider this information in weighing Ms. Grayson's testimony. Given these circumstances, appellant's claim that defense counsel was ineffective for failing to cross-examine Ms. Grayson about this information fails.[54]

In *State v. Ordway,*[55] the court set out the basic profile of an acceptable presentation of forensic bloodstain pattern analysis. Here the defendant proffered an insanity defense to charges of first-degree murder and theft in the deaths of his parents and the theft of their automobile. A jury found him guilty of two counts of second-degree murder and one count of felony theft.

Betty and Clarence Ordway lived approximately a mile west of Stockton, Kansas. On Saturday evening, November 20, 1993, in response to a call from the Ordways' nieces, a sheriff's officer went to the Ordway house. Investigation disclosed drag marks leading to the garage where the officer found Clarence Ordway's body wrapped in bedding and partially concealed behind some garbage cans. The body of Mrs. Ordway was found several days later in the trunk of their stolen car. A search revealed blood spatters, sometimes combined with what appeared to be tissue or fat, in a number of different locations in the home. Betty Ordway also died as a result of shotgun wounds in her right chest and one entry wound in her back, which caused damage to her lungs, heart, liver, ribs, vertebrae, and aorta. In addition to the shotgun wounds, the pathologist found bruises, lacerations, abrasions, and fractures caused by impact with a blunt object.[56]

Ordway contended that the trial court, among other trial errors, abused its discretion in admitting the blood-spatter testimony of Kelley Robbins, an expert witness for the state. The core of the objection at trial was the state's failure to show that an adequate procedure for blood-spatter analysis was followed by the witness, because she was neither qualified to testify as an expert in blood-spatter identification nor had laid a sufficient foundation to show that she conducted the blood spatter testing in conformity with the generally accepted standards in the scientific field. The trial court was satisfied with the expert's qualifications and proffered methodology.

Out of the hearing of the jury, Robbins described blood-spatter analysis and explained its uses:

> Bloodstain pattern analysis is the evaluation of the size, shape and distribution of patterns that are identified in blood. The purpose is to possibly identify the activities that took place to deposit the blood, and also possibly to identify the location of the individual during the bloodshed...The first step involved is identifying basic patterns. By identifying patterns I can then draw conclusions as far as what type of activity took place to create those patterns. Those are recognizable patterns and they are reproducible patterns.[57]

The witness proceeded to display some pattern standards, linking each with its source. She exhibited and discussed examples of patterns created by blood dripping from a wound, blood being pumped from an artery, a bloody item coming into contact with a nonbloody item, blood spattered by the force of a bullet, and blood cast off a swinging object. She elucidated the procedure for finding the point of origin for the blood by noting the direction stains point and measuring the width and length of stains. She also explained that faint and trace stains could be detected by spraying them with Luminol, a chemical that emits light in reacting with blood. At the time of trial, Robbins had been a forensic scientist in the Biology Unit of the KBI Crime Laboratory for more than nine years, had satisfactorily demonstrated proficiency in blood spatter analysis after taking a 40-hour class on the technique, and later attended a three-day refresher course. Her primary duties were in blood-stain pattern analysis, and her educational background included a graduate degree combining administration of justice, investigation, and chemistry. The court noted that Robbins was nationally certified as a medical laboratory technician, had been regional vice-president of the International Association for Blood Stain Pattern Analysts, and had been an assistant instructor in blood-stain pattern analysis. The court concluded that she was a qualified expert whose testimony established that the tests were reliable and were accepted by the scientific community.[58]

In *Eason v. United States*,[59] defendant was convicted of second-degree murder of his fiancée while armed and possession of a firearm while committing a violent or dangerous crime. Eason argued on appeal that the trial court erred in admitting expert testimony on blood spatter from individuals not qualified in the field of blood-spatter analysis.

Detective Thomas Campbell of the Metropolitan Police Department Homicide Branch arrived at Eason's apartment and found Lenear "in a supine position on her back with her legs bent underneath her." Lenear had been shot in the left temple. Campbell observed a small tack hammer near the body, and a Browning automatic .22 with a sawed-off barrel was found in a backpack behind a door in the apartment. At trial Eason testified that he and Lenear had been fighting, that Lenear had swung a hammer at him, which he knocked out of her hand, and that she had retrieved a gun out of the closet. Eason testified that he attempted to take the gun out of her hands and during the course of the struggle the gun discharged.

Detective Campbell testified that based on his observations of the position of the body, the blood spatter, and other things on the scene, he concluded that Lenear was kneeling when she was shot. Dr. Silvia Comparini, the medical examiner who performed the autopsy, also testified that based on examining the wound and photographs from the crime scene, she concluded that Lenear was most likely kneeling. Eason argued that the trial court erred in finding Campbell qualified as a blood spatter expert and in allowing Dr. Comparini to give a blood spatter opinion, because she was only qualified as a forensic pathologist.

The trial court had concluded that Campbell could testify in this trial as an expert in the area of the appearance and recognition of blood splatter, the transfer of blood, and his conclusions in regard to the positioning of the decedent at the time the blood spatter and transfer that he sees has occurred. Campbell was a member of the Metropolitan Police Department for 16 years including 4 years as a homicide detective, and had attended both investigator's school and homicide school, where he learned to analyze the position of victims and any blood at homicide scenes, which included specific instruction and experiments regarding blood spatter. Campbell had worked with more experienced detectives analyzing blood spatter, and he had analyzed it himself at innumerable crime scenes.[60] The court noted that blood spatter referred to blood that is ejected from the body after force has been applied. Blood transfer or smudge occurred when something came into contact with blood and smeared it on a surface. For example, a hand that touched spatter and then smeared it across a surface makes a mark on a wholly new surface, creating a *blood transfer or smudge*.

The court found his opinion amply supported by his expertise when combined with the case facts here:

> When Campbell testified that in his opinion the victim was kneeling when she was shot, he stated that his opinion was based on the position of the body and that in relationship with the blood spatter. Campbell previously testified that he found the victim

"lying in a supine position on her back with her legs bent underneath her." He also testified as to the location of the blood spatter
on her body including the underside of her foot which led him to
believe that at the time of the shooting her feet were not flat on
the floor. Finally Campbell testified that he saw no blood spatter
on the upper part of the door.[61]

*The court noted that Detective Campbell did not attempt to engage in
sophisticated blood-spatter analysis involving more complicated calculations or
experiments, rather, his testimony concerned only the location of spatter and
transfers, the direction of the drip, and his opinion as to the position of the body
based both on the spatter and his visual observations of the victim at the scene.*[62]

The court allowed Dr. Comparini's testimony that in her opinion the
victim was most likely kneeling because her head had to be at a lower level
when the gun was fired. Comparini based her opinion on photographs of
the victim on the scene, where she noted that there were blood spatters on
the lower portion of the door. She pointed out how the blood dripped onto
the body consistent with the victim kneeling. She further testified that in
performing her autopsy she observed a muzzle imprint and soot at the site
of the wound indicating the muzzle of the gun was right against the skin.
Comparini also discussed the trajectory of the bullet once inside the victim's
head.

The trial court allowed this testimony after Comparini's qualifications had
been reviewed. She had been a deputy medical examiner for 10 years, had
studied and practiced anatomic and clinical pathology and serology, and
had conducted at least 2000 autopsies involving gunshot wounds and witnessed another 12,000 autopsies. Based on her experience the court could
not find the trial judge erroneously exercised its discretion in allowing her
to testify as to the position of the victim at the time of the gunshot.

V. Blood Spatter: Crime Scene Dynamics

In *State v. Perkins*,[63] defendant was charged with murder. In the late evening
hours of January 19, 1997, Lillian Perkins left the apartment of a friend and
drove, in her cab, to her apartment, where the decedent's husband, Robert
Perkins, attacked her with a hammer. After striking Lillian's head at least 15
times with the hammer, defendant put on a long-sleeved sweatshirt, shirt, and
coat to cover the blood spattered on his tee shirt. After returning to the apartment with his son, defendant allegedly faked an exhibition of shock and grief.

The state presented evidence of Perkins's guilt, including expert testimony regarding the blood spattered on Perkins's tee shirt and jeans. The expert

testified that the blood spatters on Perkins's tee shirt and jeans appeared to be the result of a casting-off motion of the object used to strike the victim, such as a motion used by hitting someone with a hammer, and that such evidence was consistent with the trauma injuries suffered by the victim.[64]

In *State v. Fleming*,[65] defendant was convicted of first-degree murder and sentenced to death.

Defendant entered the home of the victim and assaulted him with a blunt object. Based upon the blood-spatter marks found at the crime scene, Anthony Jernigan, a special agent with the State Bureau of Investigation (SBI) and a crime-scene specialist, testified regarding the dynamics of the assault. He concluded that the assault began in the victim's den and that the victim moved from the middle of the loveseat to the north end of the loveseat. While the assault continued, the victim moved from the den, to the kitchen, and finally to the main hallway. Based upon an examination of the level of the blood-spatter marks, the victim rose and fell approximately six different times as his assailant hit him on the head.[66]

The court determined that this blood-spatter analysis testimony established that the victim's assailant entered the victim's house and repeatedly hit the victim on the head as the victim tried to escape, leaving a trail of blood-spatter marks leading from the den, into the kitchen, and down the main hallway. Then the assailant manually strangled the victim while the victim unsuccessfully attempted to defend himself. Defendant's watch and a shoe impression that identically matched defendant's shoe were also found at the crime scene. While the watch and the shoe impression were not discovered until three days after the scene was initially examined, they were present in photographs taken at the initial examination. This evidence supported a reasonable inference that defendant was the perpetrator of the murder.[67]

Another case centered on the location or position of a body when shot, is the important 1997 Texas decision *in Ex parte* Freda S. Mowbray also known as Susie Mowbray,[68] where defendant was convicted of murder. She subsequently petitioned for *habeas corpus*, alleging she was denied due process by the state's knowing failure to disclose a blood spatter expert's report supporting the defendant's position that the victim committed suicide.

The deceased was shot in bed at night. The only occupants of the room in which the shooting occurred were the deceased and defendant. The defense theory was that she and the deceased were lying in bed with a pillow barrier between them when she saw the deceased's elbow point upward. When she reached to touch it, the gun went off. She made a taped statement about the shooting, and the tape was admitted into evidence. Witnesses to the defendant's statements recalled that she indicated that she had used her left hand to reach toward the deceased. The state, however, introduced a crime lab supervisor's analysis of defendant's nightgown showing traces of lead or gunshot residue on the lower right sleeve. That witness, Steve Robertson, conducted tests with the gun found at the scene and opined that the residue was consistent with someone firing that gun.

Estella Mauricio, who was dispatched to the Mowbray residence just after the shooting, testified that she found the deceased, still alive and shot through the head, lying on his left side and covered all the way up to his shoulder. The bullet had entered the right side of his head, exited to the left, and wounded his left hand, which was under his head with a pillow between his head and left hand. The right hand was lying across his chest under the covers. There was no blood or brain matter on the right hand and she did not ever see his hand being washed at home or at the hospital. Dr. Dahm, the pathologist, testified that if the deceased had shot himself, his right hand would have been covered with blood and brain matter. He found no such blood or brain matter on the deceased's right fingers, hand, or forearm. Dahm testified it would have been impossible for the deceased to have shot himself and the hand to be clean, and concluded that the death was a murder.[69]

Additionally, two blood spatter experts testified. Sergeant Dusty Hesskew of the Austin Police Department testified on behalf of the state, and Captain Tom Bevel of the Oklahoma City Police Department testified on behalf of defendant. Generally, blood spatter experts inspect the physical evidence to determine the injuries suffered and their location with respect to the other physical evidence. In the instant case, both experts examined defendant's nightgown for "high-velocity impact (blood)staining," which commonly occurs within a short distance from a contact gunshot wound. Hesskew testified that he identified and measured, through "luminol testing," high-velocity impact bloodstains on defendant's nightgown, which were invisible to the naked eye. Hesskew concluded the cause of death in the instant case was probably homicide. Bevel testified that his examination of the physical evidence led him to conclude the deceased could have died in the manner in which defendant testified, i.e., suicide.[70]

The *habeas* judge heard a third blood spatter expert, Herbert Leon Mac-Donell, the director of an independent forensic laboratory in Corning, New York, who is viewed as the preeminent authority on the science of blood spatters.

MacDonell was retained to review the photographs and physical evidence in the instant case by the Cameron County District Attorney's office approximately seven months prior to trial. MacDonell's examination of defendant's nightgown revealed no bloodstains either visible to the naked eye or under a microscope, and concluded that it was very unlikely that defendant's nightgown was in close proximity to the victim's gunshot wound at the time of his shooting, or it was protected from spatter in some manner if it were. After reviewing the crime scene, the physical evidence and the photographs, Mac-Donell's expert opinion was that it was more probable than not that the deceased died from a suicide rather than a homicide.[71] At the prosecutor's request, MacDonell prepared and mailed to the Cameron County District Attorney a written report of his findings approximately two weeks before trial.

MacDonell took issue with Hesskew's use of luminol to measure blood spattering. Noting that while Luminol is a substance that can react with blood that is invisible to the naked eye, it was not accepted as a positive test for blood. Luminol testing, he continued, was merely presumptive because luminol reacts with substances other than blood. In MacDonell's opinion, the luminescence from a luminol reaction could not accurately be measured. He stated:

> I think it would truly be an exercise in futility. I don't think you can put any reliability on it — I certainly wouldn't — and I've seen luminol sprayed many times. I've never heard of anyone trying to measure it, count it, other than saying there appears to be a dozen or more.... You could do it, but the validity of your conclusion would be highly suspect in my opinion. In MacDonell's view, Hesskew did not understand the chemistry behind luminol testing.[72]

Hesskew had testified he was retained by the Cameron County District Attorney's office as a blood-spatter expert and closely examined defendant's nightgown at the Department of Public Safety laboratory prior to the time it was shown to MacDonell. Hesskew stated that he was present when the nightgown was treated with luminol, and counted 48 small stain areas around the stomach and chest of the nightgown that appeared consistent with high-velocity stains. He even put on a similar nightgown and fired test shots into a cardiopulmonary resuscitation (CPR) dummy's head filled with blood in an attempt to duplicate the staining he observed through the luminol testing. Although Hesskew could not remember how he was able to duplicate the bloodstaining, in his expert opinion, defendant, wearing her nightgown, could not have been lying beside her husband at the time of his death. Thus, Hesskew's testimony contradicted defendant's defensive theory.

Expert Hesskew admitted that his testimony included several assumptions that involved more than his own test results, most important of which was that someone tested the invisible stains and determined them to be human blood. At the hearing on the instant *habeas* application, Hesskew conceded his trial testimony was not scientifically valid because no such confirmation was ever made. In other words, he conceded that his ultimate opinion that the victim died as a result of a homicide, and that defendant's statements were impossible, had no scientific basis.

Captain Tom Bevel, defense expert, testified that it was impossible to measure high-velocity impact blood spatter in the manner utilized by Hesskew. He, like Hesskew, only performed presumptive tests on defendant's nightgown because Hesskew had informed him that the Department of Public Safety laboratory confirmed human blood on defendant's nightgown. Because his trial testimony was based upon this erroneous premise, Bevel concluded:

> ...with the inability to determine that ... is blood that is there, especially because we are talking about blood that is only invisible to the unaided eye, I don't think you can really say anything.[73]

Bevel believed the failure to conduct confirmation tests undermined his examination and earlier testimony, and agreed with Hesskew that their trial testimony was not scientifically valid.

Steve Robertson, a chemist in the Texas Department of Public Safety (DPS) crime laboratory, testified that he examined defendant's nightgown and was present on three different occasions when the nightgown was sprayed with luminol. The nightgown was also sprayed with three chemicals to determine the presence of lead residue and treated with heat and chemicals to determine the presence of gunshot residue. His examination of the nightgown revealed very small red stains, visible to the naked eye, lead residue, and a yellowish stain. Robertson conducted two confirmatory tests on the red stains to determine if they were human blood. Both tests resulted in *negative* results. Robertson testified that, if the stains were blood, the tests for the gunshot residue could have destroyed the protein in the blood and would cause a negative reaction. Further, the chemicals sprayed on the nightgown could have diffused or dissolved the red stains to the extent they were undetectable without a microscope.

Prosecutors claim that they forwarded a copy of Dr. MacDonnell's reports to defendant's trial counsel ten days to two weeks prior to trial, but did not contact MacDonald to testify. A defense trial review expert also voted against calling MacDonnell out of concern that he might change his mind about his opinion in favor of the defense.

The *habeas* judge found that there was a rationale for both murder and suicide and that the rationale for suicide was, at least, equally persuasive, the deceased having vowed to kill himself. He had attempted suicide at least twice prior to his death, on one occasion of which he had shot himself. The court ruled that since the linchpin of the state's case was the high-velocity impact spatter (HVIS) allegedly found on the front of defendant's gown, if there, she could not have been prone in the bed at the time the shot was fired, and was thus lying.

Under these facts, the *habeas* judge determined the state violated defendant's due process right to a fair trial by suppressing evidence favorable to the defendant. The appeals court here held that the *habeas* judge's factual determinations were supported by the record and, therefore, would be accepted by it. Accordingly, the court ruled that defendant's due process rights were violated, and she was entitled to relief, and her conviction was set aside.[74]

In *State v. Gattis*,[75] defendant Robert Allen Gattis was convicted of first-degree murder and sentenced to death for the homicide of Shirley Y. Slay, shot when she opened the door of her apartment. Gattis argued to the Delaware Supreme Court that a forensic scientist would, if given the opportunity, testify that the prosecution's theory of the case was physically impossible. Based on these assertions, the Supreme Court remanded the case, directing the court to hold an evidentiary hearing if Gattis' expert produced an affidavit to the effect that the state's theory of the homicide was impossible. Mr. Stuart James submitted an affidavit stating that, based upon the evidence he had reviewed, the state's version of the events leading to Shirley Slay's death was "not plausible" to a reasonable degree of scientific certainty. He also stated that opinions on forensic matters are rarely formulated in empirical terms such as "impossible."

James offered expert opinions on three fact questions: (1) the distance the door to Slay's apartment was open when the fatal shot was fired; (2) the significance of certain bloodstain evidence, known as high-velocity back spatter; and (3) Gattis' opportunity to see Slay and enter the apartment. These questions of fact, the court noted, were highly relevant to the legal issue of intention, and, ultimately, to the question presently before the court, which was whether trial counsel was ineffective for not calling a witness such as James to testify on Gattis' behalf. The Court addressed several key fact questions: the distance the door was open; when the shot was fired; what was indicated by the high-velocity back spatter; could Gattis see the victim before shooting her, and whether he ever fully entered the apartment.

Conflicting evidence was gathered on the question of the distance the door was open when Slay was shot. The evidence showed that by the time the victim's position on the floor was marked, six people had come and gone from the apartment. When asked about this evidence, Dr. Galicano Inguito, M.D., the medical examiner, stated that Slay probably fell where she stood. However, he could not tell where the victim and the shooter stood when the shot was fired because (1) the victim may have been moving away from the shooter to protect herself, and (2) a reflex may have allowed her to move or shift her position even after she was shot if she did not die instantaneously.

He also stated that, based on the bloodstains around Slay's head, her head may have been moved as much as 7 inches after the murder by either para-medics or other witnesses.

High-velocity back spatter was found on Slay's telephone receiver but not on the door, the adjacent closet wall, or the floor near the door. Expert James in his affidavit concluded that the back spatter on the phone receiver indicated that the receiver was within a few feet of Slay when she was shot, and, in fact, the state and the defense agreed that Slay was on the phone when she was shot. James also concluded that the lack of back spatter on the door or wall indicated that Slay had probably not been standing near the door when she was shot. The court found that defendant's argument that he was denied due process by not having been able to avail himself of expert James' opinion, and court ruled that it actually supported the state, not him:

> It appears to the court that if James had testified at trial, this portion of his testimony would have allowed the prosecution to argue that Gattis' testimony was contradicted by the forensics and inconsistent with the opinion of his own expert, as follows. James relied on the lack of blood spatter on the door or adjacent wall to show that Slay was probably not standing near the door when the gun discharged. However, the medical examiner testified that the stippling and soot on Slay's skin showed that the gun was fired at a distance of 4 to 18 inches. If, as Gattis testified, he was standing outside the door and, consistent with the forensics, Slay was within 18 inches of the gun (and hence even closer to the door which was between them if Gattis was outside the door), the chances are greatly increased that the door and/or wall would have shown blood spatter, which typically travels no more than 2 to 3 feet.[76]

Expert James was also not able to resolve the question of Gattis' position when the gun discharged, and acknowledged that it was possible that Gattis got all the way into Slay's apartment. Thus, the court concluded, the crux of James' testimony was that Gattis' version was more plausible than the state's, but that he could not say that the state's version was impossible. Viewing these opinions in light of the other testimonial and physical evidence, the court concluded that James' testimony would not have altered the result of the trial.

In *State v. Laws*,[77] defendant was convicted in the Superior Court, Durham County (North Carolina), of first-degree murder. Earl Handsome died on June 27, 1993, as a result of multiple stab wounds to his chest and back. After interviewing potential witnesses at the scene, police were directed to defendant, who subsequently confessed to the murder.

The defendant, in his confession, stated that on the night of the murder, he was walking home when the victim drove up and started a conversation, whereupon defendant went to the victim's apartment and drank vodka and smoked marijuana with the victim. According to the defendant, the victim made several sexual advances toward him, and after trying unsuccessfully to stop him, the defendant grabbed a nearby knife and stabbed the victim in the neck. The defendant stated that he ran for the door and tried to open it, but the victim pushed it, at which point defendant grabbed a ceramic vase and hit the victim twice, knocking him to the ground. When the victim started to get back up, the defendant ran to the kitchen, got another knife and started stabbing the victim again. When that knife broke off inside the victim, the defendant got a pair of scissors and continued stabbing him.

Dr. Deborah Radisch, a forensic pathologist, performed an autopsy on the victim, which revealed several blunt-force injuries on the scalp and at least 18 stab wounds to the victim's chest and back. The blunt-force injuries consisted of numerous abrasions and lacerations and a fracture of the bones at the base of the skull, of a type and number to cause a loss of consciousness for a short period of time. Dr. Radisch opined that the victim died from a loss of blood due to severe damage to his lungs and heart caused by multiple stab wounds to the chest.

Della Owens-McKinnon, a certified to bloodstain pattern analyst, testified that her examination found that most of the bloodstains were found in the bedroom, with "overcast patterns" on the bedroom wall over the bed. She testified that this type of bloodstain pattern occurs when blood is being thrown off the tip of an object as it is being swung back and forth. She also testified to finding "back patterns" on the bedroom wall, which occurs as an object is being released or pulled out of the body. The bedroom stains reflected the infliction of a minimum of three or four blows in the area of the bed. She also observed "impact patterns" at the entrance to the bedroom, which indicated to her that two or three blows were inflicted at that location. She also found a trail of dripping blood and bloody handprints along the hallway leading to large "transfer patterns" and smudges on the front door, indicative of someone attempting to leave the apartment. Finally, she testified as to impact spatters on the front door, which indicated to her the infliction of a minimum of two to three blows at that location.[78]

The court concluded that when viewed in the light most favorable to the state, the evidence shows three clear indicators of premeditation and deliberation, i.e., the defendant dealt lethal blows to the victim after he had been felled, the killing was done in a brutal manner, and the victim suffered an excessive number of wounds.

Defendant's actions after the attack were also indicative of premeditation and deliberation, inasmuch as defendant did not seek help or medical assistance for the victim and did not call the police. After this brutal killing of the victim, the defendant stole the victim's jewelry and car and exchanged them for cash to buy drugs. This evidence belied any spontaneous action in response to an attempted sexual assault and implies a clear-headed decision to kill for a purpose.[79]

In *State v. Baston*,[80] defendant was convicted of aggravated robbery and capital aggravated murder and, after a penalty hearing, was sentenced to death.

Chong Mah, a retail merchant in Toledo, was found dead by his wife in a rear storage room. He had been shot once through the head. Police found a single .45-caliber hollow-point slug behind the wall paneling in the room where the victim was found. An autopsy disclosed that he had been shot in the back of the head at a range of two to three inches. Further investigation led police to the defendant.

Among other issues, Baston argued that three evidentiary rulings by the trial court deprived him of his constitutional rights. First, he argued that the trial court erred in allowing Dr. Diane Scala-Barnett, a deputy coroner in Lucas County, to provide expert testimony regarding (1) the distance from gunshot to wound; (2) blood spatter, pooling, droplet, and transfer patterns; and (3) cause of death. Baston argued that she was not qualified as an expert.[81]

The court noted that since 1985, Dr. Scala-Barnett had been a forensic pathologist and a deputy coroner whose responsibilities include attending scene investigations and performing medical-legal autopsies to determine the cause and manner of death. She was board certified in both pathology and forensic pathology. The court stressed the fact that while the state never formally tendered Dr. Scala-Barnett as an expert regarding the distance between the gun's muzzle and the wound, during the course of questioning to qualify her as an expert, defense counsel never objected or challenged her qualifications to testify, thus waiving any objection now. The court ruled that her experience as a deputy coroner and her board certifications in pathology and forensic pathology qualified her to testify regarding the cause of death and the distance between the gun's muzzle and the victim's head at the time the gun was fired.

The court noted that while defense counsel did object to Dr. Scala-Barnett's testimony as not being expert in blood spatter, and the trial court sustained the objection, when the witness returned to the subject of blood spatter, counsel did not object. Dr. Scala-Barnett then testified how the blood spatter evidence led her and the police criminologist Detective Chad Culpert to discover the spent slug behind the paneling. The court also observed that her testimony was similar to that of Detective Culpert, whose qualifications were not questioned. Furthermore, the court concluded, the testimony concerning blood spatter was helpful to an understanding of how the victim was shot and ended up in a supine position, but it was not crucial to any issue in dispute in this case. Assuming the admission of this evidence was error, it was harmless beyond a reasonable doubt.[82]

In *State v. Jacques*,[83] defendant was convicted of attempting to commit murder and carrying a pistol without a permit. Deborah Messina, a state criminalist, testified about blood found on the gunsight on a gun seized from the defendant, and on the defendant's jeans. She testified that a bloodstain pattern made up of 24 high-velocity blood spatters on the lower-right front of the jeans was consistent with a gunshot. Additionally, she continued, blood spattering from an entrance wound, also referred to as back spatter, sprays backward toward the weapon and the individual holding the weapon. Blood spatter would travel approximately three to four feet from an entrance wound.[84]

A case examining the dynamics of a blood trail at a crime scene is *Mills v. Commonwealth*,[85] where defendant was convicted of murder, first-degree burglary, and first-degree robbery and was sentenced to death. On August 30, 1995, Arthur L. Phipps was stabbed to death. Phipps' son-in-law, Terry Sutherland, discovered Phipps' body. On the day of the murder, Sutherland twice went to Phipps' house. On the first occasion, he left Phipps alive and in good spirits. Upon arriving the second time, he discovered a trail of blood leading up the front steps. He followed the trail of blood through the house. Sutherland found puddles of blood in the living room, and more blood in Phipps' bedroom and bathroom. He followed the blood trail to the kitchen where he found a pair of pants lying on the floor. Unable to locate Phipps inside the house, Sutherland went back outside where he found Phipps' body. While securing the crime scene, State Trooper Clyde Wells discovered a trail of blood leading away from Phipps's body. Wells and another police officer followed the blood trail to the front of a house rented from Phipps by Mills. Wells saw blood on the exterior walls of the house, on the front door, and a trail of blood crossing the front porch, which led to a window.[86]

A videotape of the crime scene was introduced with the testimony of Detective Partin. During the playing of the videotape, Partin commented on the images being displayed. Additionally, the videotape shows images of the victim. There was no objection to the playing of the videotape, nor was there any objection to Partin's commentary. Prior to the playing of the videotape, the following exchange between Partin and the Commonwealth's Attorney (CA) occurred:

CA: During your state police training, have you been trained in the science of understanding blood patterns?

Partin: Yes, sir.

CA: In doing so, are blood spatters part of the training?

Partin: Yes, sir.

CA: Explain to the jury what that is.

Partin: Blood-spatter training is when you look at the pattern of blood on an object and being able to see how that pattern may have gotten there. For instance, in a lot of stabbing cases, for instance, if someone is stabbing someone the stabber would bring the knife back this way; blood would be in like a streak, a dotted streak. That's called "cast off." Anther type of spatters would be like swabs of hair — hair type imprints against ... walls, that type of thing. Blood drops would be able to tell ... whether this was a drop coming straight down or (were) drops coming from a moving object.[87]

Defendant argued that this testimony was insufficient to establish Partin's qualifications as an expert witness in blood-spatter evidence.

Initially, the court noted that defense counsel did not object to Partin's qualifications as an expert witness and that while the trial court did not expressly recognize Partin as an expert witness, it did so impliedly by allowing Partin to testify concerning blood spatter evidence. The court ruled that while it believed that Partin was qualified to render expert testimony on blood spatter evidence, even assuming that defendant was correct, any error was harmless:

Partin referred to blood-spatter evidence only once during the narrative of the videotape. Referring to blood spots seen on a wall in a particular room, Partin concluded that Phipps was attacked in this room with a knife. This conclusion was based on his interpretation of the blood spots, which he characterized as being "cast off." There was no dispute that Phipps was stabbed repeatedly. Given all the other evidence linking Mills to the murder and to the house, testimony that Phipps was stabbed with a knife in a particular room could hardly have been prejudicial to Mills' case.[88]

The rest of Partin's testimony in connection with the narration of the videotape, the court concluded, did not rely on any blood spatter expertise, but was based on Partin's own personal observations and perceptions of the crime scene, which was proper lay testimony. The court observed that, with the exception of the brief reference to blood spatter evidence outlined above, Partin's testimony as to the location of where the attacks occurred was rationally based on his perceptions of the crime scene, e.g., the pooling and the amount of blood evidenced on the videotape.[89]

An interesting point of evidence law in relation to the admissibility of forensic reports prepared by nontestifying experts is seen in *State v. Tomah*,[90] where defendant was convicted of murder and robbery. Defendant's blood spatter expert, after submitting a report supporting defendant's position that he simply observed his codefendant beat the deceased, refused to appear to testify. Because it was a written statement made outside of the courtroom prior to trial that Tomah sought to offer in evidence to prove the truth of its contents, and to support its conclusion that the blood spatter patterns illustrate that Tomah did not participate in the beating, Dr. Miller's report fell within the definition of hearsay. The court rejected his argument that such reports were admissible under the business record exception to the hearsay rule:

> Forensic expert reports are the antitheses of the business records meant to be addressed by Rule 803(6). They are advocacy reports, expressly prepared for litigation to support one party to the litigation. Although the preparation of such a record is in the course of the expert's business of advocacy support, the preparation is not routine and the record is not of the type that is contemplated by the business records exception to the hearsay rule set out in Rule 803(6). Indeed, that it is prepared in anticipation of litigation is a common reason for a finding that a report lacks trustworthiness... The trustworthiness and reliability of the report is not free from doubt.[91]

Here the court noted Dr. Miller was an expert hired by Tomah. She prepared the report, as an advocate, specifically for the purpose of its use at Tomah's trial. She had not viewed the blood-spattered pants on which she based her report, but relied instead on photographs and statements made by Tomah and codefendant Chesnel. Moreover, Dr. Miller, who was the authenticating witness for the report, refused to appear at Tomah's trial at the appointed time.

In *State v. McClendon*,[92] defendant was convicted of manslaughter with a firearm. The victim, who was defendant's roommate, was fatally shot while standing near the door of their apartment, defendant testifying that he was asleep on the couch when he heard a loud noise. He awoke to find the victim standing in the doorway, clutching her side and saying she had been shot. There were no eyewitnesses to the shooting. Despite a search of the surrounding area, no weapon capable of shooting the fatal bullet was ever found. The testimony of the state's blood spatter expert allowed for the possibility that the shots came from outside the room where defendant was sleeping, and the testimony of a neighbor explicitly disclaimed observation for the entire period of time in question. Under these circumstances, the court ruled, defendant's motion for judgment of acquittal should have been granted.

In *State v. East*,[93] defendant was convicted of two counts of first-degree murder and sentenced to death, for the dual murder of his aunt and uncle after a dispute about money.

Defendant objected to the qualifications of one Agent Tulley. The record showed that Agent Tulley had extensive training and experience in crime-scene collection and processing, and had earned a bachelor's degree in criminology, during which she took a crime-lab class, and had a master's degree in criminal justice. She also had numerous hours of training in crime-scene collection and processing at the State Bureau of Investigation (SBI), specialized in forensic crime-scene collection and processing at the SBI, and had testified as a crime-scene specialist in over 75 cases.

In *People v. Bolin*,[94] defendant was convicted of two counts of first-degree murder and sentenced to death. When sheriff's deputies went to defendant's cabin, they found one Huffstuttler's body lying near a truck, and the body of one Mincy was in the creek bed in a fetal position. Both had several fatal gunshot wounds, and Huffstuttler had been shot with both a revolver and a rifle. Over defense objection, the trial court admitted into evidence three photographs of Mincy's body, which criminalist Greg Laskowski used to illustrate his testimony about blood spatters and drips found at the crime scene. Using the photographs of the crime scene, he testified regarding the various positions of Mincy's and Huffstuttler's bodies when they were shot. Based on blood spatters and drips depicted in the photos, he indicated one shot was to Mincy's body while in a "fetal-like" position on its left side; as to the other, his body was in a vertical position. He also concluded Mincy "was moving at a relatively rapid pace" after being initially wounded. With respect to Huffstuttler, he determined that for several shots the body was prone and not moving.

Blood-spatter testimony is often encountered in cases centered in the question of whether a death was the result of homicide or suicide. Blood spatter is also commonly used in the death-penalty aspects of cases to demonstrate the attribution of viciousness, or extreme cruelty or heinousness.

Blood-spatter or bloodstain pattern analyses will always be a staple of crime scene analysis in homicide cases. It is perhaps the least "scientific" but the most telling of the body of forensic disciplines commonly used in crime scene analysis. Knowledge of this important member of the forensic sciences is of central importance to prosecutors, defense counsel, and judges.

The IABPA Newsletters from June 2000–December of 2004 are available at the IABPA Site, at www.iabpa.org.

Endnotes

1. See Stuart James, *Bloodstain Atlas and Terminology, Scientific and Legal Applications of Bloodstain Pattern Interpretation* (CRC Press, 1999), at 177. [Bloodstain Atlas and Terminology].

2. See, Training in Crime Scene Photography and Crime Scene Investigation, a very useful site that has numerous links to photography sites. It is located at http://www.staggspublishing.com/training.html. Also see, Bevel and Gardner: *Bloodstain Pattern Analysis* (CRC Press, 1997); Stuart James (ed.) *Scientific and Legal Applications of Bloodstain Pattern Interpretation* (CRC Press, 1999), at 289 [Stop-Motion Photography Techniques].

3. See, Bloodstain Pattern Analysis Tutorial, by William G. Eckert and Stuart H. James, at www.bloodspatter.com/BPATutorial.htm

4. See, *Rivera v. State*, 2005 WL 16193, Tex.App, 2005, (false positives when luminol reacts with ammonia). See, generally, How Luminol Works, http://people.howstuffworks.com/luminol.htm (Simple introduction to luminol with photos.) Also see, *Effects Of Luminol On The Subsequent Analysis Of Bloodstains*, Laux, Dale L., *Journal Of Forensic Sciences* 36:5. (9/91). p1512–1520, 1991; *Recording Luminol Luminescence In Its Context Using A Film Overlay Method*, Niebauer, Joseph C.; Booth, Jack B., Jr.; Brewer, B. Lee, *Journal Of Forensic Identification* 40:5. (9-10/90). p278–278, 1990; *Fill Flash Color Photography to Photograph Luminol Bloodstain Patterns*, Gimeno, Fred E., *Journal Of Forensic Identification* 39:5. (9/10/89). p305–306, 1989

5. See, Wonder, Anita Y., *Blood Dynamics*, (Academic Press, 2001); Tom Bevel and Ross M. Gardner, *Bloodstain Pattern Analysis: With an Introduction to Crime Scene Reconstruction* (CRC Press, 2nd edition, 2001). Also see, Bevel and Gardner: Bloodstain Pattern Analysis (CRC Press, 1997); James (Ed.): *Scientific and Legal Applications of Bloodstain Pattern Interpretation* (CRC Press, 1999).

6. The Scientific Working Group on Bloodstain Pattern Analysis (hereinafter referred to as SWGSTAIN) serves as a professional forum in which bloodstain pattern analysis (BPA) practitioners, and practitioners from related fields, can share, discuss, and evaluate methods, techniques, protocols, quality assurance, education, and research relating to BPA.

7. The IABPA Web site provides a suggested terminology list, including: angle of impact, arterial spurting (or gushing) pattern, back spatter — blood directed back towards the source of energy or force that caused the spatter; bloodstains, bubble rings, cast-off patterns, directionality; — The directionality of a bloodstain or pattern that indicates the direction the blood was traveling when it impacted the target surface; directionality of a blood drop's flight, directionality angle, direction of flight — The trajectory of a blood drop, draw-back effect, drip pattern, expired blood, flight path, flow pattern, forward spatter, high-velocity impact spatter (HVIS), impact pattern,

impact site, low-velocity impact spatter (LVIS), medium-velocity impact spatter (MVIS), misting, parent drop, passive drop (bleeding), point (area) of convergence, point (area) of origin, projected blood pattern, ricochet, satellite spatter, perimeter stain, spatter, spine, swipe pattern, target, transfer/contact pattern, void (an absence of strains in an otherwise continuous bloodstain pattern) wave cast-off, wipe pattern.

8. The Brazoria County, Texas, Sheriff's Department Criminal Identification Division (Crime Scene Unit contains well-written and up-to-date bloodstain pattern tutorials and are well worth examining. See, http://www.brazoria-county.com/sheriff/id/blood/).

9. 334 Ark. 258, 975 S.W.2d 88 (1998).

10. 334 Ark. 258, 975 S.W.2d 88 (1998), at 264.

11. 311 Ark. 579, 847 S.W.2d 1.

12. Ayers, supra n.91 at 266.

13. The court noted that the tests appellant now complained of had been in existence for many years, were a routine part of criminal investigations, and were frequently admitted. In each of those cases, the evidence of blood identity, i.e., animal or human and blood typing, was introduced without challenge based upon its novelty or reliability.

14. 265 Kan. 835, 964 P.2d 681(Kan. 1998).

15. 265 Kan. 835, 964 P.2d 681(Kan. 1998) at 686.

16. It is important to realize that Canaan's observation is true for most jurisdictions and could apply equally to post-Daubert continuing acceptance of hair, fiber, footprint, and a host of other "widely accepted" forensic sciences.

17. 964 P.2d at 692.

18. Supra, n. 96 at 693.

19. Supra, n. 96 at 851.

20. Canaan, at 964, P.2d at 693.

21. Canaan, at 964, P.2d at 693.

22. 954 S.W.2d 624 (Mo. Ct. App. 1997).

23. 954 S.W.2d 624 (Mo. Ct. App. 1997), at 628.

24. The police performed DNA tests on the bloodstains in the carpet, the coveralls, and the carpet cleaner. Utilizing a genetic profile from blood samples obtained from Walker's parents, it was determined that only 64 out of 100 million couples could have produced the kind of genetic profile found in the bloodstains. Additionally, the genetic profile found in the bloodstains would occur only twice in a population of 100 million.

25. Supra, n. 125 at 629. Walker's skeletal remains were found over one year after her disappearance. Walker's skull was covered with a pair of shorts and a striped Unitog rental work shirt bearing the name "Wendell" and the numbers

"8223760004." The shirt and shorts that covered Walker's skull were wrapped with duct tape. Four projectiles were within the duct tape. Information obtained from Unitog established that the shirt had been rented by Maynard. Maynard admitted the shirt was his but stated that he had two to three weeks' worth of these shirts and did not realize one was missing. An examination of the skull showed multiple fractures of the left temporal and parietal areas and a gunshot wound in the left temporal region. Michael Edward Berkland, Deputy Medical Examiner from the Jackson County Medical Examiner's office, testified that Walker died from multiple gunshot wounds to the head. Berkland testified that the spatter of blood found in the apartment carpet remnant was consistent with multiple gunshot wounds to the head. Id.

26. Also see *State v. Stenson*, 132 Wash.2d 668, 940 P.2d 1239 (1997), where defendant was convicted of the first-degree premeditated murder of his wife and his business partner. The pants the defendant was wearing at the time of the murders was an important piece of evidence. There were stains on the right leg and smaller stains on the left leg of the pants. The stains were visually identified as blood by the forensic scientist whose specialty was crime scene reconstruction and the interpretation of bloodstain patterns. The stains all reacted positively upon application of phenolphthalein (phenol), which is a catalytic color test that is a presumptive test for blood. The court accepted the reliability of Luminol as a presumptive test for the presence of human blood. The appeals court ruled that the trial court correctly admitted the results of the phenol testing, which were supported by the forensic scientist's testimony that the stains on the pants looked like blood by visual inspection and under a microscope. So long as a jury is clearly told that the phenol test is only a presumptive test and may indicate a substance other than human blood, it is admissible.

However, see, *State v. Fukusaku*, 85 Hawaii 462, 946 P.2d 32 (1997), where the trial court excluded expert testimony on the luminol and phenolphthalein test results, ruling that, because of the limitations of the tests, the presumption of the presence of blood was relevant only to the extent that it could be supported by confirmatory tests. Moreover, the trial court ruled that, without confirmatory tests, the prejudicial effect of the evidence was not outweighed by its probative value. Inasmuch as confirmatory tests were not conducted, the trial court excluded the evidence.

27. See the extensive testimony of famed criminalist Dr. Henry C. Lee in the O. J. Simpson criminal case regarding blood spatter analysis. Dr. Lee provides extensive information about both general and specialized aspects of bloodstain pattern analysis. This is an excellent introduction to the subject as well as a model for laying a solid foundation for expert witness testimony. See, *People v. Simpson*, Official Transcript, Examination of Henry C. Lee, Docket Number BA097211, Superior Court, Los Angeles, Tuesday, August 22, 1995. Also see a wide variety of blood pattern analysis testimony available in the O. J. Simpson Civil Case, *Rufo v. Simpson*, Docket Number SC031947, Superior Court, Los Angeles. Another interesting source for actual blood spatter

testimony is the second trial of Lyle and Erik Menendez, in *People v. Menendez*, Docket Number BA068880, Superior Court of Los Angeles. These transcripts are available for searching and download on the Westlaw database, Legal News, Highlights and Notable Trials.

28. Menendez Case, supra.

29. See the discussion of *People v. Davis*, 217 Mich. 661, 187 N.W. 390 (1922), infra.

30. See, *Collection and Preservation of Blood Evidence*, by George Schiro of the Louisiana State Police Crime Laboratory, an excellent overview that addresses blood recognition and collection issues, located at http://police2.ucr.edu/evidenc3.htm.

31. See treatises listed above. Also see, Herbert L. MacDonell, *Crime Scene Evidence — Blood Spatters and Smears and Other Physical Evidence*, 1 Quinnipiac Health L.J. 33 (1996) for a brief overview of the subject by one of its most eminent practitioners. Dr. MacDonell provides a very extensive bibliography on the subject, as an appendix to the article. A 40-hour course in bloodstain pattern analysis is offered by the Midwest Association of Forensic Scientists, under the auspices of the Minnesota Criminal Apprehension Bureau Crime Lab.

32. 217 Mich. 661, 187 N.W. 390 (1922).

33. Also see *People v. Planagan*, 65 Cal. App.2d 371, 150 P.2d 927 (1944) where extensive blood-spatter evidence was also not challenged or discussed by the California Supreme Court. Defendant's conviction was upheld in large part due to the introduction of a substantial interview, over several days, between the defendant and a state forensic chemist about blood spots on defendant's leather jacket. This case is a fascinating example of the total lack of investigatory rights by suspects in that early WW II era.

34. Laux, D.L., *Effects of Luminol on the Subsequent Analysis of Bloodstains*, Journal of Forensic Sciences, Vol. 36, No. 5, Sept. 1991, pp. 1512–1520.; Grispino, R.R.J., *The Effects of Luminol on the Serological Analysis of Dried Bloodstains*, Crime Laboratory Digest, Vol. 17, No.1, Jan. 1990, pp.13–23.

35. See, e.g., Budowle, B., Leggitt, J.L., Defenbaugh, D.A., Keys, K.M., Malkiewicz, S.F., The presumptive reagent fluorescein for detection of dilute bloodstains and subsequent STR typing of recovered DNA, 45 *J. Forensic Sci.* (5) (2000, at 090–1092); Kent, E.J., Elliot, D.A., Miskelly, G.M., Inhibition of bleach-induced luminol chemiluminescence, 48 *J. Forensic Sci.* (1) (2003), at 64-67; Frégeau, C.J., Germain, O., Fourney, R.M., Fingerprint enhancement revisited and the effects of blood enhancement chemicals on subsequent Profiler Plus™ fluorescent short tandem repeat DNA analysis of fresh and aged bloody fingerprints, 45 *J. Forensic Sci.* (2) (2000), at 354–379.

36. Ponce, A.C. and Pascual, F.A.V., Critical Revision of Presumptive Tests for Bloodstains (1999), located at http://www.fbi.gov/programs/lab/fsc/backissu/july1999/ponce.htm. The authors are members of the Department of Legal

Medicine at the College of Medicine and Odontology of the University of Valencia, Valencia, Spain. Also see, Bylaws of the Scientific Working Group on Bloodstain Pattern Analysis (SWGSTAIN), available at http://www.fbi.gov/hq/lab/ fsc/backissu/july2002/swgstain.htm.

37. See, most recently, Admissibility of results of presumptive tests indicating presence of blood on object, 82 ALR5TH 67. Also see, *Risher v. State*, 2005 WL 374606 (Ark. 2005) (appellant did not establish a prima facie case…for funding for the testing of luminol, glass, and fibers.); *State v. Kimbrough*, 2005 WL 292419 (Tenn.Crim.App.2005) (a Luminol test revealed the presence of blood in the appellant's vehicle).

38. 2005 WL 100779 (Cal.App. 2005).

39. Fingerprint evidence was obtained from Gilligan's apartment. Defendant's fingerprint was on a pie dish in the apartment. Two fingerprints of Wright were on the inside of the glass bedroom door. Davies' prints were found on a glass cup, a white bowl, a pizza box, and on Gilligan's glasses. There were other prints in the apartment that did not match any of the defendant's.

40. 2005 WL 100779 (Cal.App. 2005), at *3.

41. 2005 WL 100779 (Cal.App. 2005), at *4.

42. 84 P.3d 456 (Ariz. Sp. Ct. 2004).

43. 84 P.3d 456 (Ariz. Sp. Ct. 2004), at 475.

44. 135 S.W.3d 178 (Tex.App. 2004).

45. 135 S.W.3d 178 (Tex.App. 2004), at 182.

46. I135 S.W.3d 178 (Tex.App. 2004), at 195.

47. 667 N.W.2d 386 (Minn. Sp. Ct. 2003).

48. 667 N.W.2d 386 (Minn. Sp. Ct. 2003), at 403. Also see, *Smith v. Commonwealth*, 265 Va. 250 (Va. Sp. Ct. 2003). ("In accordance with other jurisdictions," the court said, "we adhere to the view that this form of scientific analysis can form a basis for admissible proof upon an appropriate foundation.")

49. 566 Pa. 239, 780 A. 2d 605 (Penn. Sp. Ct 2001).

50. 566 Pa. 239, 780 A. 2d 605 (Penn. Sp. Ct 2001), at 266.

51. 566 Pa. 239, 780 A. 2d 605 (Penn. Sp. Ct 2001).

52. 566 Pa. 239, 780 A. 2d 605 (Penn. Sp. Ct 2001), at 266–267.

53. 566 Pa. 239, 780 A. 2d 605 (Penn. Sp. Ct 2001), at 298.

54. 261 Kan. 776, 934 P.2d 94 (1997).

55. 261 Kan. 776, 934 P.2d 94 (1997), at 97.

56. 261 Kan. 776, 934 P.2d 94 (1997), at 800.

57. 261 Kan. 776, 934 P.2d 94 (1997), at 809.

58. 687 A.2d 922 (D.C. Ct. App. 1996).

59. 687 A.2d 922 (D.C. Ct. App. 1996), at 925. See generally, Maj. Samuel J. Robb, *A Trial Attorney's Primer on Blood Spatter Analysis, The Army Lawyer* 36, 38

(August 1988) (defining blood-spatter terminology). Also see, Cathleen C. Herasimchuk, *A Practical Guide to the Admissibility of Novel Expert Evidence in Criminal Trials under Federal Rule 702*, 22 *St. Mary's L.J.* 181, 246 (1990) (noting blood-spatter analysis has recently become an accepted area for expert witness testimony and that "[w]hile the scientific theory and techniques employed in blood-spatter analysis depend upon a subjective interpretation, the testimony deals with evidence that is inherently understandable"). Cf. 3 C. Wecht, *Forensic Sciences*, ss 37.03[c] — [f], 37.04–09 (1996) (suggesting formal scientific training may be necessary for blood-spatter analysis involving calculations of velocity, volume and trajectory, and geometric determinations).

60. 687 A.2d 922 (D.C. Ct. App. 1996).

61. 687 A. 2d at 926.

62. 1999 WL 334974 (Ohio App. 1 Dist.).

63. 1999 WL 334974 (Ohio App. 1 Dist.), at *6-7.

64. 350 N.C. 109, 512 S.E.2d 720 (1999).

65. 350 N.C. 109, 512 S.E.2d 720 (1999), at 118.

66. 350 N.C. 109, 512 S.E.2d 720 (1999), at 120.

67. 943 S.W.2d 461 (Ct. Cr. App. Tex. 1997).

68. 943 S.W.2d 461 (Ct. Cr. App. Tex. 1997), at 462.

69. 943 S.W.2d 461 (Ct. Cr. App. Tex. 1997), at 463.

70. 943 S.W.2d 461 (Ct. Cr. App. Tex. 1997).

71. 943 S.W.2d 461 (Ct. Cr. App. Tex. 1997).

72. 943 S.W.2d 461 (Ct. Cr. App. Tex. 1997).

73. 934 S.W.2d 461, 466.

74. 697 A.2d 1174 (Del.Sup. Ct. 1997).

75. 697 A.2d 1174 (Del.Sup. Ct. 1997), at 1186.

76. 481 S.E.2d 641(N.C. Sp. Ct. 1997).

77. 481 S.E.2d 641(N.C. Sp. Ct. 1997), at 643.

78. 481 S.E.2d 641(N.C. Sp. Ct. 1997), at 646.

79. 85 Ohio St.3d 418, 709 N.E.2d 128 (1999).

80. 85 Ohio St.3d 418, 709 N.E.2d 128 (1999), at 130.

81. 85 Ohio St.3d 418, 709 N.E.2d 128 (1999), at 423–4.

82. 53 Conn.App. 507, 733 A.2d 242 (1999).

83. 53 Conn.App. 507, 733 A.2d 242 (1999), at 519. Also see, *De La Cruz v. Johnson* 134 F.3d 299 (5th Cir. (Tex.) 1998) where Jose De La Cruz was convicted of stabbing Domingo Rosas to death. Blood spatters on De La Cruz' pants indicated that the wearer had forcefully stabbed a seated victim. The deceased victim was paralyzed and confined to a chair; *U.S. v. Veal*, 153 F.3d 1233 (11th Cir. [Fla.] 1998) where defendant claimed noninvolvement in a

murder involving a total of four assailants. Blood spatter analysis evidence was used to demonstrate that the defendant struck the victim multiple times using medium-to-high force and the victim's blood spatter on walls in the corner of the room above the bed were consistent with the assailant having been in the immediate vicinity of a direct impact of the victim's head while the victim was in an upright position in the corner of the room.

84. 996 S.W.2d 473 (Sp. Ct. Kentucky 1999).

85. 996 S.W.2d 473 (Sp. Ct. Kentucky 1999), at 479.

86. 996 S.W.2d 473 (Sp. Ct. Kentucky 1999), at 487.

87. 996 S.W.2d 473 (Sp. Ct. Kentucky 1999)

88. Also see, *State v. Fleming*, 350 N.C. 109, 512 S.E.2d 720 (1999) (Blood-spatter testimony admissible to show the victim's progress through the house to escape and that the victim rose and fell six different times while being struck on the head. This blood spatter testimony was relevant to the applicability of the atrocious and cruelty death penalty factors.); *Sturgeon v. State*, 719 N.E. 2d 1173 (Sp. Ct. Indiana 1999) (Blood found on top of table and blood spatters on a wall calendar, admissible proof of a beating and stabbing in that room.); *State v. Pilot*, 595 N.W.2d 511 (Sp. Ct. Minn. 1999), where defendant was convicted of attempted first-degree murder, attempted first-degree murder while committing criminal sexual assault, and first-degree criminal sexual assault. Analysis of blood spatter patterns performed on the defendant's jacket and jeans was consistent with the blood spatter patterns at the H.T. crime scene — an impact spatter from an object striking a source of blood and the blood then projecting off from that source onto the jeans. The blood spatter pattern on the jacket was a hair swipe, a pattern created when bloody hair strikes a surface.

89. 736 A.2d 1047 (Sp. Ct. Maine 1999).

90. 736 A.2d 1047 (Sp. Ct. Maine 1999), at 1051.

91. 707 So.2d 800 (Ct App. Fla. 1998).

92. 481 S.E.2d 652 (Sp. Ct. N.C. 1997).

93. 956 P.2d 374, 75 Cal.Rptr.2d 412 (Calif. Sp. Ct. 1998).

94. See, e.g., *Zakrzewski v. State*, 717 So. 2d 488 (Fla. Sp. Ct. 1998) (Zakrzewski was charged with the first-degree murder of his wife, Sylvia, and his two children, Edward, age seven, and Anna, age five. The blood spatter expert testified that the only conclusion that could be drawn from the positioning of Anna's blood in the bathroom was that Anna was forced to kneel over the ledge of the bathtub — in execution-style fashion — before Zakrzewski delivered the deadly blows. Zakrzewski pled guilty to all three charges, and the case proceeded to the penalty phase.)

DNA Analysis 10

> It has been pointed out already that no knowledge of probabilities,
> less in degree than certainty, helps us to know what conclusions
> are true, and that there is no direct relation between the truth of
> a proposition and its probability. Probability begins and ends with
> probability.
>
> **John Maynard Keynes,**
> **The Applicability of Probability to Conduct**

I. Introduction

The history of the legal acceptance of DNA technology as a method to aid
in the identification of one or more participants in a crime has been a rapid
and relatively noncontroversial one. The judicial acceptance of various DNA
technologies, up to and including mitochondrial DNA, has been even more
rapid, to the point where judicial discussions of the scientific reliability of
DNA testimony have become centered in lengthy discussions of earlier DNA
cases rather than DNA technology itself.[1] The DNA-related progression of
judicial acceptance of DNA technology has advanced from blood typing and
enzyme matching to approval of DNA laboratory-testing methodologies categorized as RFLP, PCR, STR, Random Amplification of Polymorphic DNA
(RAPD), and mitochondrial DNA testing.[2]

To clarify increasingly multifaceted trial discovery requirements, several
state supreme courts have drafted very detailed discovery provisions for DNA
in criminal cases that reflect the complexity of trial lawyers' technical information needs.[3] These specialized DNA discovery provisions will experience
numerous revisions as DNA technology develops. The current Illinois
Supreme Court Rule may serve as an early example:

Illinois Supreme Court Rule 417. DNA Evidence (2001)

ILCS S. Ct. Rule 417:

(a) Statement of Purpose. This rule is promulgated to produce uniformly sufficient information to allow a proper, well-informed determination of the admissibility of DNA evidence and to insure that such evidence is presented competently and intelligibly. The rule is designed to provide a minimum standard for compliance concerning DNA evidence, and is not intended to limit the production and discovery of material information.

(b) Obligation to Produce. In all felony prosecutions, post-trial and post-conviction proceedings, the proponent of the DNA evidence, whether prosecution or defense, shall provide or otherwise make available to the adverse party all relevant materials, including, but not limited to, the following:

(i) Copies of the case file including all reports, memoranda, notes, phone logs, contamination records, and data relating to the testing performed in the case.

(ii) Copies of any autoradiographs, lumigraphs, DQ Alpha Polymarker strips, PCR gel photographs and electropherogams, tabular data, electronic files and other data needed for full evaluation of DNA profiles produced and an opportunity to examine the originals, if requested.

(iii) Copies of any records reflecting compliance with quality-control guidelines or standards employed during the testing process utilized in the case.

(iv) Copies of DNA laboratory procedure manuals, DNA testing protocols, DNA quality-assurance guidelines or standards, and DNA validation studies.

(v) Proficiency testing results, proof of continuing professional education, current curriculum vitae and job description for examiners, or analysts and technicians involved in the testing and analysis of DNA evidence in the case.

(vi) Reports explaining any discrepancies in the testing, observed defects, or laboratory errors in the particular case, as well as the reasons for those and the effects thereof.

(vii) Copies of all chain-of-custody documents for each item of evidence subjected to DNA testing.

(viii) A statement by the testing laboratory setting forth the method used to calculate the statistical probabilities in the case.

(ix) Copies of the allele frequencies or database for each locus examined.

(x) A list of all commercial or in-house software programs used in the DNA testing, including the name of the software program, manufacturer, and version used in the case.

(xi) Copies of all DNA laboratory audits relating to the laboratory performing the particular tests.

II. DNA Research Resources

What do courts, prosecutors, defense counsel and others interested in the place of DNA technology and identification claims in the criminal justice system need to know as we begin the 21st century?[4] The DNA story in this regard is a very short one when compared to the long history of Anglo-American criminal trials. The first appellate court validations of DNA-matching testimony were not even seen until 1988, in the decision by a Florida appeals court in the case of *Andrews v. Florida*,[5] where the court accepted DNA print-identification evidence linking defendant to a sexual assault. During the 18 years since that decision, American courts have rapidly examined and accepted the standard DNA testing methods of RFLP, PCR, PCR STR, and the product method of conducting DNA statistical analyses. We have also seen judicial acceptance of a variety of very specific laboratory procedures and related issues, such as the general acceptability of commercially produced DNA kits. The courts are also quickly moving toward a general acceptance of the heretofore-challenged mitochondrial DNA identification technology.

There are now a respectable number of authoritative texts,[6] articles, and Web sites addressing basic and specialized DNA subjects. There is also a rapidly developing international consensus among DNA laboratories regarding standards for laboratories and DNA technicians, as a result of major support from the FBI for working groups and conferences addressing these issues across the world, especially in Europe, through the vehicle of Interpol.[7]

In November 2004, at Lyon, France, Interpol sponsored the 14th International Forensic Science Symposium. The literature reviews in each of the major areas of forensic science were published in its Review Papers, which can be downloaded free at http://www.interpol.int/Public/Forensic/IFSS/ meeting14/abstracts.asp. An important part of this document is the Individual

Identification Evidence section, entitled: Recent Progress in Forensic DNA Profiling: A Review: 2001 to 2004, prepared by Dr. Peter Gill of the U.K. Forensic Science Services.

This extensive literature review focused upon the major advances in DNA profiling technology during the period 2001 through 2004 and is subdivided into several of the central categories of interest to those actively working in the DNA field:

- Mixture interpretation using expert systems
- Mitochondrial DNA
- Low copy number STR DNA profiling and its relationship to contamination
- Population genetics and the relationship to correction factors of match probabilities
- Y-chromosome markers
- Autosomal single nucleotide polymorphisms (SNPs) and other new DNA methods
- The forensic application of STRs in relation to national DNA database
- Recent steps taken by the Forensic Science Service to minimize the danger of DNA sample contamination

In addition to brief but excellent comments on the more important literature in these fields, Dr. Gill provides a bibliography of 57 studies in these areas published in the *Journal of Forensic Science, Forensic Science International,* and other focused DNA-related scientific journals.[8] Dr. Gill concluded his study by noting that:

> There has been significant progress during the past three years in the field of forensic DNA typing. The interpretation of STR profiles can be automated using expert systems; furthermore, interpretation of complex mixtures and low copy number has been enhanced. The development of Y-chromosome technology has led to the introduction of new commercial kits. Promising advances have been made in the area of SNP-typing and associated lab-on-a-chip technologies, although clearly this has not yet come of age in forensic terms.[9]

III. DNA: International Standards

Since the first edition of this book, international interest in DNA has increased even more with the FBI and international forensics groups seeking to establish uniform standards for the identification, collection, testing, and use DNA evidence in courts of law.

An Interpol-sponsored international DNA Users' Conference is organized every two years at the General Secretariat in Lyon, by the Interpol DNA Unit and its advisory team, the Interpol DNA Monitoring Expert Group. The aims of this conference are to *introduce best practice models* in Member States and widespread application of contemporary DNA usage in criminal investigations. Topics to date have included DNA profiling; DNA Databases; From the Scene of Crime; Quality Assurance and Training; DNA Evidence; Promoting DNA; and Use of DNA in Criminal Proceedings.[10]

New books focusing on DNA technology continue to be published. To learn about new DNA books, consult any of three Web sites on a regular basis: Academic Press,[11] ForensicNetBase,[12] and Amazon Books.[13] These three Web sites, especially ForensicNetBase, thoroughly cover the field in the area of forensic science.[14]

Increasing numbers of DNA studies continue to appear in the scientific literature. In early 2005, a series of articles focused on various aspects of STR DNA technologies was published in the *Journal of Forensic Science*, continuing the STR trend exhibited by the more than 200 articles that addressed STR DNA issues in the 2004 *Journal* volumes. Very recent articles describe case studies in the area of mitochondrial DNA and the new area of canine DNA.[15] The greatest number of important DNA articles is published by the prestigious *Journal of Forensic Science*. Most law-school libraries contain the full set of past and recent editions of the *Journal* for study. You may also search through the entire index of articles, with abstracts going back to 1981, by visiting the Web site of the American Academy of Forensic Sciences (AAFS), located at AAFS.org. A membership allows users to download the full text of most recent articles in PDF format. Many more law review articles and practice journals now address some of the important legal issues surrounding DNA as an investigative and evidentiary tool in American courts.[16]

IV. DNA: Questions for Lawyers

This rapid development and proliferation of information about the latest advances in the location, testing, and statistical validation of laboratory matches and their ultimate use in the courtroom burdens the litigator in attempting to stay current. However, regardless of the latest research, litigators must, in each case, it ensure they have considered and answered a series of basic questions:

- What is DNA, in both a theoretical, and, most importantly, a physiological sense?
- What is it that gives DNA laboratory and statistical identification models their great and growing authority?

- Why is there no ability to make a positive statement of identity rather than a "negative" response, utilizing extremely high numbers, in estimating the chances of any such "match" appearing in the general population being considered?
- How and where can DNA reside at a crime scene?
  - Blood
  - Semen
  - Hair pulp
  - Saliva
  - Tissue and cells
  - Hair shafts (mtDNA)
  - Bones and teeth (mtDNA)
  - Fingerprints
- What are the contemporary and prospective views on crime-scene DNA collection, storage, and transportation procedures? The FBI is issuing a number of proposed standards that will invariably be adopted by courts. The FBI Handbook of Forensic Services is available on the Internet and is a steady source of information in regard to both data collection standards and FBI laboratory procedures.[17] The FBI Web site, in particular the Forensic Communications section, should be consulted on a regular basis.
- What does the concept of DNA laboratory testing mean in regard to:
  - The actual physical manipulation of the subject crime scene material?
  - The preparation of the material for a laboratory "matching" procedure?
- What are the visual results of any such procedure and what do they mean?
- What is being compared preparatory to a proffered laboratory "match" opinion?
- How many markers, loci, etc., are there that can be compared? If a "match" opinion is based on less than all, how many and why? The FBI is currently utilizing a 13-STR-loci match working standard.
- What test methodology is being used and how does it differ in physical and procedural terms?
- What are the significant differences among restriction fragment length polymorphism (RFLP), PCR, PCR STR, mitochondrial, or nonhuman DNA tests, such as RAPD for plant comparison?
- Why is one test used over another? Are some tests better than others in certain settings? Why?

- How much of a match is any DNA laboratory "match" conclusion? Is it any less tentative than hair, fiber, footprints, ballistics, or any of the other conclusions reached by forensic scientists?
- What is involved in a discussion of population statistics, *the second half* of a DNA identification effort? What does it mean to testify to a laboratory DNA profile match if it cannot be determined what the frequency is of the appearance of such a profile in the general population? What is the current thinking about the appropriate ways to obtain an answer to this question? It is not possible to answer such a question in instances of the other forensic sciences, and has never been required. Is such an analysis always required in DNA cases? Why? In instances where such queries are made, what databases containing a body of previously tested DNA profiles are used?
- Who or what categories of individuals are in any such collections? Do racial or ethnic differences matter here?
- What is the FBI CODIS DNA profiles database and how does it work?[18]
- What is mitochondrial DNA? How do its processes differ from the more familiar and judicially approved methods of RFLP and variants of PCR technology, especially with regard to databases? Why was mtDNA downplayed for so long? Why is it receiving rapid judicial approval as we enter the early days of the 21st century?
- What about nonhuman DNA-matching technologies, such as for dog, cat, deer, whale, or plant DNA? How will these fare in the new century? How do DNA analyses in animals or differ from that of humans or from each other's DNA that might exclude them from judicial approval at this time? Are those technologies any less able to provide solid circumstantial proof of presence at a crime scene than RFLP, PCR, or even mitochondrial DNA investigations?

V. DNA Methodologies: RFLP

RFLP, which until recently was the most widely used DNA analysis technique, refers to restriction fragment length polymorphism. Many competent texts are available for lawyers to acquaint themselves with the technical aspect of DNA testing and RFLP testing in particular. An excellent overview is an early appellate case about DNA testing that is the lengthy Maryland Court of Appeal's decision in the case of *State v. Armstead*.[19] Following are descriptions of several important decisions involving RFLP DNA testing and population-statistics projections under the product rule model, and more extensive discussions of cases addressing PCR, PCR STR, mitochondrial, and nonhuman DNA methodologies.

In *People v. Miller*,[20] defendant was convicted of first-degree murder.

In September of 1993, the nude bodies of three women, Marcia Logue, Helen Dorrance, and Sandra Csesznegi, were found in rural Peoria County. The body of Marcia Logue was found in a drainage ditch in the 500 block of South Cameron Lane on September 18, with a pillow case stuck in her mouth. The body of Helen Dorrance was found 50 feet from Logue's body on the same date. The body of Sandra Csesznegi was found in a drainage ditch near Christ Church Road on September 26. Csesznegi's body was in a state of advanced decomposition. All three women were known prostitutes in the Peoria area.

On September 29, 1993, at approximately 11:30 p.m., Detectives Rabe and Pyatt of the Peoria Police Department and Detective Hawkins of the Peoria County Sheriff's Department went to the defendant's Peoria apartment to question him about crimes in the Peoria area. The search of defendant's apartment revealed two robes, female underwear, a broken miniblind rod, and a brown and white cloth covered with what appeared to be dried blood. The police also recovered pillows and a mattress from defendant's bedroom. These items had reddish-brown stains. Blood spatters were also found on a wall of the bedroom and the bed's headboard. A later search revealed a glove, a throw rug, and more women's underwear. During the second search, the police collected hair and fibers.[21]

The state's DNA expert, William Frank, testified that seminal fluid recovered from Logue matched that of defendant. Such a match would occur in 7% of the Caucasian population. Blood recovered from underneath Logue's fingernails also matched that of defendant and such a match could be expected in 1 in 465 million Caucasians. Bloodstains from a magazine, mattress, pillow, and towel found in the defendant's apartment and from the seat of Faggott's car matched that of Logue. Such matches would occur in 1 in 1.1 trillion Caucasians. Further, blood found on a napkin and a pillow taken from the defendant's apartment matched Dorrance's DNA profile, with such a match occurring in 1 in 466 billion Caucasians. Another bloodstain on one of defendant's pillows matched the DNA profile of Csesznegi with such a match occurring in 1 in 1 billion Caucasians. On cross-examination, Frank conceded that there were only five billion people in the world.

Defendant argued that the trial court erred in qualifying Frank to testify about the general acceptance and reliability of deoxyribonucleic-acid (DNA) evidence and in admitting the DNA evidence at his trial. The trial court held a pretrial hearing on the state's motion to admit DNA evidence. Frank was the only individual to testify at the hearing on behalf of the state. The defendant chose not to present any witnesses or evidence, notwithstanding that he had been provided the time and funds to secure an expert. After hearing testimony on Frank's background and training, the trial court qualified him as an expert. Frank then testified regarding the restriction fragment length polymorphism (RFLP) method of testing DNA and the manner in which DNA matches are calculated, including the manner in which such calculations are made at the Illinois State Police Bureau of Forensic Sciences, where Frank is employed. Frank testified that the techniques used by his laboratory in calculating DNA matches and their frequency in a population were similar to those used by the FBI. After hearing Frank's testimony, the trial court held that based on prior precedent in Illinois (FN1), the DNA procedures outlined in Frank's testimony were generally accepted in the particular scientific field and such testimony and DNA calculations would be allowed at defendant's trial.[22]

The court in addressing defendant's arguments gave a brief account of DNA profiling:

DNA is the genetic code that is found in the cells of the human body. A DNA molecule is composed of more than three billion "base pairs" of four different chemicals: adenine, thymine, cytosine, and guanine. The particular pattern *185 of these base pairs dictates an individual's genetic characteristics. Most of a DNA molecule is the same from person to person. DNA profiling focuses on those parts of the DNA molecule where there is a significant variation of a base-pair pattern. The areas of significant variation are referred to as "polymorphic," and base-pair patterns in polymorphic areas are called "alleles." There are approximately 3 million distinguishable polymorphic sites between individuals. Although an examination of all of these polymorphic sites is not currently feasible, an examination of a small number of polymorphic sites can establish a DNA profile, which can be compared to that from another DNA sample.[23]

RFLP was the laboratory methodology used to achieve a match here and testified to by expert witness Frank. The court made the following observations in accepting this technique:

> Restriction fragment length polymorphism is a six-step process which allows an analyst to physically see the results of a DNA profile in the form of bands. Because the length of polymorphic DNA fragments differs between individuals, individuals also tend to have different positioning of the bands on DNA prints, called an autoradiograph or autorad. An analyst makes a visual comparison of DNA band patterns to determine whether known and unknown DNA samples came from the same source, whether the samples did not come from the same source, or whether the comparison was inconclusive. If an unknown DNA sample has not been excluded from a comparison, a computerized measurement program is used to compare the lengths of the DNA fragments.

If the DNA band patterns fall within a certain range, the samples are declared a match.

For a match to be meaningful, a statistical analysis is required. The statistical analysis determines the frequency in which a match would occur in a database population. In this case, Frank used the fixed-bin method of determining the frequency of an occurrence. The process of binning is a way of counting or grouping bands and determining the frequency of the bands. The Hardy-Weinberg Equilibrium is used to determine the frequency of a particular band combination. Stated simplistically, the frequency of one band is multiplied by the frequency of a second, and so on. The product from this calculation is then multiplied by two to account for an individual inheriting one strand of DNA from his mother and one strand from his father. This result constitutes the statistical frequency of a match within a certain population. This process of binning and determining the frequency is also known as the product rule.[24]

The court, in the instant case, held that expert Frank was clearly qualified to explain and give an opinion regarding a *match* based upon RFLP and product rule methodology. The court noted that he had a bachelor's degree in chemistry and biology; was working toward his master's degree in biology, his thesis being on DNA extraction methods; and that he had taken several genetics courses and attended seminars and classes on DNA methods at both the FBI and private laboratories. In addition, he had been certified by the American Board of Criminalistics and had been subject to periodic testing on DNA issues.[25]

With respect to the RFLP and product rule methodology used by Frank as the basis of his opinion, the court ruled that the trial court did not abuse its discretion in relying on the cases that supported the use of the RFLP technique and the product rule. In addition to several Illinois appellate decisions accepting this method,[26] the court noted that Frank testified that the procedures he used were the same as those used by the FBI. The court also observed that the majority of courts deciding the issue of the admissibility of evidence on the six-step RFLP process had found such evidence to be admissible under several standards of admissibility, including Frye and Daubert.[27] There was little question that the RFLP technique itself was generally accepted in the relevant scientific community.

In *Thomas v. State*,[28] a capital murder appeal, the court, noting continuing affirmative findings in previous cases, concluded, under the facts of the case, that the product rule technique used to arrive at the DNA-population-frequency statistical evidence in this case was reliable under Daubert. Expert Brewer testified:

> Q. Are the statistical methods used in your laboratory to calculate an estimate of the significance of a DNA match generally accepted in the relevant scientific community?

> A. Yes. The standard statistical procedures that we use are routinely used in medical and research laboratories as well as forensic laboratories. The 1996 report from the National Research Council specifically endorsed these measures.[29]

The court noted that while expert Brewer did not use the precise term "product rule," by his testimony that he used the "standard statistical procedures" endorsed by the 1996 report of the National Research Council (hereinafter NRC), along with his cursory description of the method, it concluded that he indeed used the product rule.[30]

Thomas did not dispute the reliability of the application of the product rule in the context of DNA forensic analysis; indeed, he recognized in his brief that the product rule was the only valid method of computing the frequency of DNA patterns. The court also noted that the product rule's reliability had been recognized by a significant number of jurisdictions.[31]

The Thomas case also contains a detailed analysis of the potential chain-of-custody issues rising from the increased use and importance of DNA crime-scene collecting procedures and laboratory testing. Here, again, the issues raised through an alleged violation of the plain-error rule.

The court recognized that the increasing volume of DNA testing has considerably added to the importance of proper handling procedures. In regard to chain-of-custody requirements for critical DNA evidence, the court noted the following statement from the NRC Report:

> Even the strongest evidence will be worthless — or worse, might possibly lead to a false conviction — if the evidence sample did not originate in connection with the crime. Given the great individuating potential of DNA evidence and the relative ease with which it can be mishandled or manipulated by the careless or the unscrupulous, the integrity of the chain of custody is of paramount importance.[32]

More and more decisions address DNA-related chain-of-custody issues, as defense arguments challenging DNA laboratory testing and population projections continue to fall on deaf ears.

VI. PCR DNA Methodologies

The PCR, or polymerase chain reaction, method involves the copying or amplification of a short section of a strand of DNA. PCR allows tests to be performed on very small quantities of genetic material. In this method, the DNA is extracted from a sample of cellular material, such as blood or sperm cells. Then, depending on which genetic markers are being tested for, a particular location or set of locations on the strand of DNA is isolated and copied over and over until a sufficient quantity exists for testing.[33] Unlike the RFLP procedure, which is a much more accurate test used to establish a statistical match, the PCR technique is generally used as an exculpatory tool to "exclude certain individuals as possible contributors to a particular sample."[34] PCR can also be used on a much smaller sample obtained from a crime scene and may replicate samples to allow for multiple testing opportunities. The PCR method harnesses cellular enzymes to replicate portions of the DNA so that a sufficient number of copies of the DNA can be obtained to perform testing.[35]

The 12th Interpol Forensic Science Symposium Literature Review, published in 2001, noted that most laboratories were concentrating on DNA evidence as the main form of biological evidence. The author of the paper on DNA evidence, D. J. Werrett, concluded:

> The trend is now firmly established toward PCR STR-based technology and, in particular, to multiplexing. There appears to be widespread agreement as to the best choice of STRs and future opportunity for worldwide collaboration on STRs that are being added to current systems.[36]

The ability of PCR testing to reach results in cases where the amount of testable material is small or partially degraded, can be illustrated by a brief summary of a 1999 Illinois Supreme Court decision. In *People v. Davis*,[37] defendant was convicted of first-degree murder, aggravated criminal sexual assault, aggravated kidnapping, robbery, and concealment of homicidal death, and was given the death penalty. The state's evidence showed that, on Monday, August 21, 1995, Laurie Gwinn was reported missing after she failed to arrive at her job with the county health department. The next day, sometime after 11 a.m., Gwinn's dead body was found floating in the Hennepin Canal north of Annawan, Illinois. She was nude and was missing several pieces of expensive jewelry that she always wore.[38]

A vaginal swab taken during Gwinn's autopsy contained seminal material and sperm cells. Kristin Boster, a forensic scientist and expert in deoxyribonucleic-acid (DNA) analysis, testified that she isolated the DNA taken from the swab and determined it to be too degraded for a restriction fragment length polymorphism (RFLP) analysis. Elizabeth Benzinger, a molecular biologist and also an expert in DNA analysis, agreed that there was insufficient DNA to perform an RFLP analysis. She explained that the DNA was degraded because the murderer had placed Gwinn's body in the canal. Benzinger therefore analyzed the DNA using the polymerase chain reaction (PCR) technique. She compared the DNA taken from the swab to samples taken from defendant, James Linsley, who was a close acquaintance of the victim, and the victim. Benzinger concluded that Linsley could not have contributed to the vaginal swab. Benzinger could not, however, exclude defendant as the source of the semen on the swab. According to Benzinger, the percentage of the United States population that could have contributed the DNA recovered from the swab was 2.6% of white persons and 3.6% of black persons.[39]

A combination of DNA laboratory methods was successfully used to convict the defendant in *People v. Buss*,[40] a 1999 Illinois Supreme Court decision involving a particularly gruesome murder of a child. Defendant was convicted of six counts of first-degree murder, three counts of aggravated kidnapping, and one count of aggravated unlawful restraint, and was sentenced to death. Defendant was accused of luring a young male victim from a popular Kankakee River dockside park and brutally murdering him.

Deputy Scott Swearengen testified that he and another deputy were searching the hunting areas of the Kankakee State Park during the early morning hours of August 15. In a clearing at the end of a path leading from the parking area of Hunting Area 7, they found the body of a small child in a shallow grave under a sheet of plywood. Forensic evidence presented by the state established that the body was that of Christopher Meyer and that he had died from multiple stab wounds prior to sunset on August 7.

Other forensic evidence connected defendant to Christopher's murder. Experts testified to forensically important similarities between hairs, soil, and footprint data taken from the area where the body was found and items seized from defendant's possessions.[41]

Forensic scientists from the Illinois State Bureau of Forensic Sciences testified that there was human blood on the dent puller found in the trunk of defendant's car, that blood was found on the carpet from the trunk, and that a stain of human blood had soaked through the carpet. There was also human blood on a box found at the gravesite, as well as on the boots defendant had placed in a motel dumpster, although the test to determine whether the blood on the boots was human was not positive.

The court here accepted, without discussion, the testimony of William Frank, the DNA Research Coordinator for the Illinois State Police Forensic Sciences Command and an expert in forensic DNA (deoxyribonucleic acid) analysis. Frank testified that he analyzed DNA extracted from an inhaler prescribed for Christopher, from the carpet from the trunk of defendant's car, from a piece of Christopher's right femur, and from a bloodstained box found at the gravesite:

> Frank used two methods of DNA analysis: PCR and RFLP. Each of these methods is used to identify particular characteristics of a given sample of DNA. Those characteristics are referred to as the "profile" of that DNA. Because each method of analysis, PCR and RFLP, identifies different characteristics, two different profiles are obtained by subjecting a sample of DNA to both types of analysis…Frank used the PCR method to analyze DNA found on the inhaler, carpet, femur, and box. The PCR profile of the DNA from each of these items was the same. Frank calculated that this particular DNA profile could be found in one out of 19,000 Caucasian individuals.
>
> Using the RFLP method, which is more discriminating, Frank compared the DNA in blood samples from Christopher's parents and defendant to the DNA in blood found on the box and carpet. (Because the amount of DNA extracted from Christopher's inhaler and femur was insufficient for the RFLP method of analysis, Frank used DNA from Christopher's parents to determine whether the blood from the box and carpet belonged to Christopher.) By comparing the DNA profiles he obtained, Frank determined that the blood on the box and the carpet came from a child of Mika Moulton and James Meyer, Sr., Christopher's father. Frank calculated that the chance of two Caucasian parents producing a child with the same RFLP DNA profile as the DNA found on the carpet and box was one out of 3.8 million.[42]

After preparing both a PCR and an RFLP profile for the DNA found on the box and carpet, associated with defendant's vehicle, Frank proceeded to estimate the frequency of DNA with both of these profiles in the population, concluding that a person with such DNA would occur in the Caucasian population only 1 out of 419 million times.

VII. STR DNA Methodologies

In *People v. Allen*,[43] defendant was convicted of special circumstances murder and forcible rape. The state offered the results of laboratory DNA testing by the short tandem repeats (STR) method on a semen stain from the crime scene. The court ruled that this was competent evidence of general acceptance of testing in the scientific community.

Paul Colman, a senior criminalist for the Los Angeles County Sheriff's Crime Laboratory, conducted a DNA analysis on the semen stain. He typed six genetic loci by the RFLP testing process and found that two of those loci matched Allen's DNA sample. Colman concluded the DNA from the semen stain could have come from Allen, and calculated that the odds of a randomly selected African-American having the same two loci combination would be 6200 to 1.[44]

Testimony on these same samples was also provided by Dr. Charlotte Word, a microbiologist and the deputy director of the prominent Cellmark Labs. Cellmark performed PCR testing, a method used when there is only a limited supply of DNA available for testing. Cellmark used three different kinds of PCR testing: DQ-alpha (which tests a single genetic marker), poly-marker (which tests five genetic markers), and STRs (which test three genetic markers). The testing included a total of nine genetic markers when the results of all three tests were combined. Dr. Word put the random match probability as determined by the DQ-alpha and polymarker testing at 1 in 1,700 African-Americans. She concluded from these results that defendant could not be excluded as the source of the semen. Word specifically testified that the STR results had not excluded Allen as a source of the semen. Based on a combination of these results, Dr. Word testified she had concluded that Allen was the source of the semen stain, "within a reasonable degree of scientific certainty."

Allen argued that the trial court erred by (1) finding that STR testing was generally accepted in the scientific community, and (2) by admitting STR testing results while excluding the corresponding statistical probability evidence. The court rejected defendant's arguments, noting that two out-of-state cases had approved STR testing.[45]

The court noted that in the 1997 case of *Commonwealth v. Rosier*,[46] the Supreme Court of Massachusetts had affirmed a trial court's finding that STR testing was scientifically reliable. The Rosier case was quoted as follows:

> The defendant's appellate counsel appears to suggest that STR testing is unreliable because it is too new. No specific scientific or forensic evidence or literature is offered to support that sugges-tion. The judge heard testimony that, in 1991, several years before the STR kit became commercially available, Cellmark, working under contract to the United States Government, used STR testing to identify the remains of soldiers killed in Operation Desert Storm, and that, by the time of the hearing, Cellmark had per-formed STR analysis in approximately fifty cases and had been permitted to testify as to its test results in at least five cases. While we have not been directed to any decisional law approving STR

testing, an authoritative scientific study, the 1996 report of the National Research Council entitled, The Evaluation of Forensic DNA Evidence (1996 NRC Report), has concluded that STR testing is "coming into wide use," that "STR loci appear to be particularly appropriate for forensic use," and that "STRs can take their place along with variable number of tandem repeats (VNTRs) as forensic tools." The latter comment appears to recognize that STR testing is similar in principle to the RFLP (or VNTR) method, which has been found to be reliable. Based on the evidence before him and his careful analysis of the subject, the judge properly concluded that the methodology underlying the PCR-based tests in this case, including the STR testing, was scientifically valid and relevant to a fact at trial.[47]

The Allen court also noted that in 1998, in *State v. Jackson*,[48] the Supreme Court of Nebraska affirmed a trial court's finding that the prosecution had shown STR testing was generally accepted by the relevant scientific community, emphasizing that a director of the University of Nebraska Medical Center laboratory had testified that PCR STR testing was generally accepted in the scientific community. The expert had testified that this method had "been around several years now, and there is nothing unique about PCR STR versus any PCR."[49] The Jackson court concluded that based on this evidence, we can only conclude that the trial court was correct in determining that the PCR STR DNA test used in the instant case was generally accepted within the scientific community.

Finally, in response to Allen's argument that there was no evidence that STR testing had been validated by the time it was utilized in this case, the court stated that the issue was not when a new scientific technique is validated, but whether it is or is not valid, which was why the results generated by a scientific test once considered valid can be challenged by evidence the test has since been invalidated.[50]

Considerable effort is currently being expended to achieve uniform standards for PCR testing in the European Community. The major umbrella organization in coordinating this work is Standardization of DNA Profiling Techniques in the European Union (STADNAP).[51] The organization summarizes its research plan and goals on its Web site:

Project Summary

DNA profiling has become a standard technique in criminal investigations, because results can be obtained from any source of biological material provided it contains nucleated cells with genomic DNA. Due to the rapid progress in the field during the last ten years, parallel developments of methods and typing systems have been made in the laboratories involved in forensic DNA profiling. This has resulted in heterogeneity of typing procedures and genetic systems used for forensic casework within the European Union. However, intercomparison of DNA typing results becomes not only desirable, but absolutely necessary within Europe as mobile serial offenders will not be detected by DNA profiling unless methods are standardized.

On the basis of current cooperative efforts with 20 other European partners, STADNAP fosters the following series of goals:

Based on cooperative structures that have been already established independently among the network partners, the objectives of the STADNAP network are to:

1. Define criteria for the selection of forensic typing systems based on the PCR technique suitable for European standardization
2. Evaluate PCR systems for forensic stain typing
3. Exchange and compare methods for the harmonization of typing protocols
4. Carry out exercises for intercomparison of forensic typing results
5. Recommend reference PCR typing systems for European standardization
6. Exchange data for compilation of reference frequency databases for the European populations[52]

VIII. DNA Mixture Cases

In *State v. Mason*,[53] defendant was convicted of the murder of a coworker Hartanto Santoso in a violent encounter. Police found a great deal of blood on the interior and exterior of Santoso's car. While all of the blood on the exterior and most of the blood on the interior matched victim Santoso's genetic profile, samples from the driver's seat contained a mixture of blood belonging to Santoso and another source. During its case in chief, the state called Dr. Edward Blake, a forensic scientist specializing in DNA, to testify about his findings after analyzing the mixed DNA sample.

Blake testified that the chances that Mason was not a source of the sample were one in 14 trillion. In response, defense counsel sought to introduce the testimony of neurogeneticist Dr. Randall Libby. The state interviewed Libby the night before he was to testify. During that interview, Libby disputed Blake's method of interpreting the sample, discussed the difficulties associated with interpreting mixed DNA samples and the inadequacies of Dr. Blake's method of interpretation, and stated that 30 percent to 80 percent of the population cannot be excluded from a mixed DNA sample. According to the state, Libby also stated that he was unable to provide names of scientists or published papers to support his view and that his opinion was based only on his 25 years of experience as a geneticist. Based on this interview and citing *Frye v. United States*, the state moved *in limine* to exclude that portion of Libby's testimony that states that at least 30 percent of the population cannot be ruled out as possible sources of the DNA mixture.[54]

During that hearing, Libby provided a treatise to support his opinions and named several scientists who shared his interpretation. The court found that the defense presented no scientific authority supporting Libby's specific conclusion that 30 percent to 80 percent of the general population cannot be excluded when interpreting blood mixtures. The court noted that if Libby's statistic was true, there would be no use in interpreting mixed DNA samples at all, as such samples would be worthless. And if mixed DNA samples were worthless, there would be some authority saying so, but the court found none. Therefore, the court excluded Libby's testimony, but only that portion where he opined that at least 30 percent of the population cannot be excluded from mixed DNA samples.[55]

The appellate court found that the court did not refuse to admit Libby's opinion that mixed DNA samples are difficult to interpret, nor did it take issue with Libby's preferred statistical calculation method. It simply wanted scientific confirmation of Libby's "30% to 80%" statistic, and the defense presented none. The trial court did not err by refusing to admit this small portion of Libby's testimony.[56]

The phenomenon of DNA mixture interpretation has yet to be fully explored in recent case law. It has been observed in the literature by the author of the DNA report in the Review Papers of the 14th Interpol Forensic Science Symposium.[57] Several recent decisions have touched upon the DNA mixtures issue.

In *State v. Gapen*,[58] a 2004 Ohio case, defendant was convicted of 12 counts of aggravated murder, breaking detention, aggravated murder, and aggravated robbery. Defendant was sentenced to death.

Larry James Gapen was distraught over the recent dissolution of his marriage to Martha Madewell. Around 1:00 a.m. on September 18, 2000, Gapen entered Madewell's home in Dayton. Gapen found Madewell and Nathan Marshall, a former husband of Madewell, lying on a couch. Gapen killed them by repeatedly striking them with a maul. Gapen then went upstairs and struck 13-year-old Jesica Young with the maul as she slept in her bed. Jesica later died of her injuries.

Gapen was convicted of the aggravated murders of Madewell, Marshall, and Jesica and was sentenced to death for Jesica's murder. To establish Gapen's guilt, the state introduced Gapen's statements to the police, DNA evidence that Gapen's sperm was found on Madewell's right leg, abdomen, and rectum, testimony from two children in the house at the time of the murders, and evidence that Madewell's purse was found in Gapen's car at the time of his arrest. In response to police questions, Gapen explained his reasons for attacking Young, admitted bringing the maul and work gloves from his house to the murder scene, and provided other details about the murders.

At trial, David Smith, a serologist and DNA analyst, testified that DNA testing of blood samples from the maul murder weapon showed a "mixture." However, a major component of the mixture was blood "consistent with that of Jesica Young." Additionally, DNA testing of a blood sample from the external portion of the left-handed work glove "was a mixture. The major component was consistent with that of Martha Madewell." However, "Jesica Young could not be excluded as a contributor to the minor component." DNA testing of the left glove liner "was a mixture again. Larry Gapen could not be excluded as a possible donor to this mixture." Finally, DNA testing of the right glove indicated that Madewell or Young could be contributors.

Smith also testified that DNA testing of a rectal sample taken from Madewell was a "mixture," but the major component was from Larry Gapen. Microscopic analysis of a swab sample obtained from Madewell's right leg revealed the presence of sperm. Additionally, both chemical and microscopic analysis of swab samples obtained from Madewell's abdomen showed the presence of sperm. DNA testing of the sperm showed that "the DNA profile obtained from the right leg and the abdomen were consistent with that of Larry Gapen."[59]

Mixtures were again part of the prosecution DNA evidence in *State v. Holmes*,[60] a 2004 South Carolina case. Defendant was convicted of murder, first-degree criminal sexual conduct, first-degree burglary, and robbery, and sentenced to death.

The court ruled that evidence of third party's guilt did not raise reasonable inference as to defendant's innocence and thus was inadmissible at trial for capital murder and other crimes. There was forensic evidence that included defendant's palm print on the inside of a door of victim's house, fibers from the victim's bed, and a nightgown that matched fibers from defendant's clothing and underwear. There was also mixed DNA in defendant's underwear that matched both defendant and victim, and victim's bloodstains on defendant's shirt. Appellant's underwear contained a mixture of DNA from two individuals, and 99.99% of the population other than appellant and the victim were excluded as contributors to that mixture; and (6) appellant's tank top was found to contain a mixture of appellant's blood and the victim's blood.[61]

IX. Mitochondrial DNA: MtDNA

The most recent DNA testing methodology seeking court approval is mitochondrial DNA (mtDNA). The FBI has actively developed this technology and is currently publishing important papers about it on the FBI Web site.[62] A series of recent cases have been handed down establishing the general scientific acceptability and scientific reliability of identification opinions by forensic scientists based on mitochondrial DNA methodologies.[63] States are beginning to pass legislation[64] that provides for automatic acceptance of the reliability of standard DNA methodologies, which will no doubt aid in the current efforts by the FBI to have a quick judicial acceptance of mtDNA.[65] Several excellent mtDNA laboratories have developed and are publishing their case results.[66]

The Interpol Forensic Science Symposium DNA profiling review established the focus of mtDNA examinations:

> To report mtDNA results, the aim of an mtDNA analysis is to provide evidence to support one or two alternative propositions:
>
> 1) The contention that the evidential sample (Q) originated from the suspect (the donor of K) or a maternally linked relative;
>
> or
>
> 2) The contention that the evidential sample (Q) originates from the suspect's sample (K) or originate from different individuals (of different maternal lineage).
>
> The sequence is reported as a haplotype. Currently most laboratories use the counting method to estimate evidential strength. This means that the result is compared to a database size (n) where the number of matching sequences is reported.
>
> If two samples (K and Q) do not match, this does not necessarily mean that they do not have the same origin. There are hotspots within the mtDNA genome where mutations are more common.[67]

A series of very recent cases have validated the use of mtDNA technologies in American courts.[68] Human hair, teeth, and bones provide the raw material for mtDNA analyses. The leading case is *State v. Pappas*,[69] analyzed at length in Chapter 3, Hair Analysis.

Another excellent case on the validity and protocols for mtDNA is *United States v. Beverly*,[70] a well-written and comprehensive 2004 Sixth Circuit Court of Appeals decision. In this case, Noah Beverly, Douglas A. Turns, and Johnny P. Crockett were indicted for multiple bank robberies. Beverly appealed the introduction of mtDNA evidence against him at trial, arguing that the evidence was not scientifically reliable. The Circuit Court of Appeals found that the district court did not abuse its discretion in admitting expert testimony that less than 1% of the population would be expected to have the mtDNA pattern of hair found at the crime scene, even though mtDNA was not as precise an identifier as nuclear DNA, where any issues going to conduct of tests were fully developed and subject to cross-examination, testing in instant case was sufficiently reliable, and that the mathematical basis for evidentiary power of mtDNA evidence was carefully explained.[71]

Beverly argued that mtDNA testing was not scientifically reliable because the laboratory that did the testing in this case was not certified by an external agency, the procedures used by the laboratory "sometimes yielded results that were contaminated," and the particular tests done in this case were contaminated. In addition, Beverly argued that even if the mtDNA evidence is determined to be sufficiently reliable, its probative value is substantially outweighed by its prejudicial effect. In this part of his argument, Beverly focused on the statistical analysis presented, which he claimed to have artificially enhanced the probative value of the mtDNA evidence. According to Beverly, Dr. Melton, the government's expert, should have been allowed to testify only that Beverly could not be excluded as the source of the sample in question.[72]

The court, as in the Pappas case, provided a very useful overview concerning mtDNA analysis:

> Generally speaking, every cell contains two types of DNA: nuclear DNA, which is found in the nucleus of the cell, and mitochondrial DNA, which is found outside of the nucleus in the mitochondrion. The use of nuclear DNA analysis as a forensic tool has been found to be scientifically reliable by the scientific community for more than a decade. The use of mtDNA analysis is also on the rise, and it has been used extensively for some time in FBI labs, as well as state and private crime labs. This technique, which generally looks at the differences between people's mitochondrial DNA, has some advantages over nuclear DNA analysis in certain situations. For example, while any given cell contains only one nucleus, there are a vast number of mitochondria. As a result, there is a significantly greater amount of mtDNA in a cell from which a sample can be extracted by a lab technician, as compared to nuclear DNA. Thus, this technique was very useful for minute samples or ancient and degraded samples.[73]

The court took note of the fact that mitochondrial DNA could be obtained from some sources that nuclear DNA cannot, for example, mtDNA can be found in shafts of hair, which do not have a nucleus, but do have plenty of mitochondria, whereas nuclear DNA can only be retrieved from the living root of the hair where the nucleus resides.[74] On the other hand, the court also noted, mtDNA is not as precise an identifier as nuclear DNA. In the case of nuclear DNA, half is inherited from the mother and half from the father, and each individual, with the exception of identical twins, almost certainly has a unique profile. MtDNA, by contrast, is inherited only from the mother and thus all maternal relatives will share the same mtDNA profile, unless a mutation has occurred. Because it is not possible to achieve the extremely high level of certainty of identity provided by nuclear DNA, mtDNA typing has been said to be a test of exclusion, rather than one of identification.[75] The entire mtDNA sequence, about 16,000 base pairs, is considerably shorter than nuclear DNA, which has approximately 3 billion pairs.[76]

In its decision here, the court first addressed and dismissed the defendant's argument that the lack of external certification of the mtDNA expert's laboratory disqualified her opinion:

> This point was raised in the pretrial hearing, and, although there is no legal requirement that Dr. Melton's lab be so certified, the district court did question Dr. Melton on this point. Laboratories doing DNA forensic work are accredited through the American Society of Crime Laboratory Directors. However, Dr. Melton's lab, having been actively engaged in case work for only about 11 months at the time of the trial, was not yet able to apply for the accreditation, but was expected to go through the process the following spring. Furthermore, Dr. Melton's own credentials are considerable. Not only has she been working with mtDNA since 1991, she has a Ph.D. from Pennsylvania State University in genetics; her thesis investigated mitochondrial DNA as it would apply to forensic applications. In addition, Dr. Melton has published a significant amount of work in this field.[77]

Beverly further argued that Dr. Melton's procedures would sometimes yield results that were contaminated, and that furthermore, the sample analyzed in this particular case was contaminated. However, the court noted, Dr. Melton was confident that no contamination of the sample itself had occurred. The reagent blank in the test of the sample itself did not show any indication of contamination, in contrast to a separate reagent blank, used in a different test tube, which was a control in the experiment. Therefore, the actual data relied upon in this case, obtained from the sequencing machine, did not indicate any presence of a contaminant.

As to the defendant's argument that the probative value of the evidence would be substantially outweighed by prejudice, the court noted that the district court carefully considered during the pretrial hearing the question of whether the relevance of this evidence outweighed its probative value:

In particular, Beverly argued that the jury would associate mitochondrial DNA analysis with nuclear DNA analysis and give it the same value, in terms of its ability to "fingerprint" a suspect. The district court, however, decided that this issue was more appropriately dealt with through a vigorous cross-examination, and that was exactly what occurred at trial. Moreover, the court noted the important probative value that this evidence added to the trial.

Finally, the court separately considered the scientific reliability of the statistical analysis offered by the government, concluding that:

> The predictive effect of the statistical analysis is based upon a formula which is apparently recognized in the scientific community and used in a variety of scientific contexts, and it has been used specifically here in the analysis of mitochondrial DNA results. The court concludes that it's an accepted and reliable estimate of probability, and in this case, it led to results, interpreted results, which substantially increase the probability that the hair sample is the hair of the defendant in this case.[78]

Based on the record compiled in the district court's careful and extensive hearing on this issue, the court found no abuse of discretion in admitting the mtDNA testing results. The mathematical basis for the evidentiary power of the mtDNA evidence was carefully explained, and was not more prejudicial than probative:[79]

It was made clear to the jury that this type of evidence could not identify individuals with the precision of conventional DNA analysis. Nevertheless, any particular mtDNA pattern is sufficiently rare, especially when there is no contention that the real culprit might have been a matrilineal relative of the defendant, that it certainly meets the standard for probative evidence: "any tendency to make the existence of any fact that is of consequence to the determination of the action more probable or less probable than it would be without the evidence."[80]

Finally, *Wagner v. State*,[81] a 2005 Maryland decision, addressed the important issue of the phenomenon of heteroplasmy in MtDNA cases.

On February 15, 1994, Daniel and Wilda Davis were found dead in their home on West Wilson Boulevard in Hagerstown. The victims had been bound at their wrists and ankles and had been stabbed multiple times in the chest and back. On February 16, 1994, the victim's neighbor, Phyllis Carpenter, informed the police that during the morning of February 15, 1994, she discovered a work glove along the curb on a street near her home and had placed it on her back porch, intending to throw it away. Upon learning of the murders, however, she contacted the police.[82] Defendant was convicted of two counts of first-degree premeditated murder and one count of felony murder.

The Court of Special Appeals held that mitochondrial DNA evidence was sufficiently reliable and that the mere potential for contamination of mitochondrial DNA testing of hair found on a glove found near the murder scene affected the weight of evidence, not its admissibility. The court found that heteroplasmy, in which an individual could have more than one exact type of mitochondrial DNA, did not render mitochondrial DNA evidence indicating that defendant was the contributor of hair found on a glove near the murder scene unreliable. There was no evidence of heteroplasmy in the instant case, in that defendant's known mtDNA sequence had the same pattern and sequence as that found in the hair, and even if heteroplasmy existed, it would have created false exclusion of the defendant as the contributor of the sample, and not inclusion.

Prior to trial, defense counsel filed several motions to exclude the mtDNA evidence garnered from the examination of the glove. At the conclusion of the hearings on those motions, Judge Wright delivered an oral opinion that included the following findings and conclusions:

> Science evolves. Certainty and perfection are elusive. Even in this testing procedure of mitochondrial DNA, it is not a perfect identification process. We know that the final result of mitochondrial-DNA typing analysis is that a defendant is either excluded as a possible contributor of the genetic material, or defendant is included within a class of possible contributors. So there is uncertainty as to inclusion, because it is inclusion within a possible, a class of possible contributors.[83]

> The court observed that mtDNA analysis can be used on material without a nucleus, such as a bone sample or a piece of hair without a root segment.[84] It can also be used on unknown samples degraded by environmental factors or time. MtDNA was also more likely to survive in a dead cell than is nuclear DNA.[85]

During the motions hearings, state DNA Expert Dr. Stewart testified that mtDNA evidence has been entered into evidence at trial a total of approximately 50 times, in 25 states. He also submitted numerous peer review articles that demonstrate the general acceptance of mtDNA evidence, none of which rejected mtDNA analysis as unreliable. Even the defense's expert, Dr. Jeffrey Boore, did not controvert the proposition that the process of mtDNA extraction, amplification, and sequencing is generally accepted as reliable.[86]

At trial, Dr. Stewart testified that all of the sites in the mtDNA obtained from the hair on the glove matched the sites from appellant's mtDNA.

The profile from (appellant), his mitochondrial DNA profile did not have differences from the mitochondrial profile from the (hair found on the) glove at those positions. Therefore, appellant cannot be excluded as the source of that hair.[87] Most important, Dr. Stewart testified that, when he compared appellant's profile to the 5071 profiles in the FBI's database at the time, he found 11 individuals in the profile that had the same mtDNA profile. He also testified that all of the sites in the mtDNA obtained from the hair on the glove matched the sites from appellant's mtDNA.

In regard to defendant's arguments relative to an increased danger of contamination in mtDNA analyses, Dr. Stewart testified that, based on published literature on the subject, as well as on his own experience, the danger of laboratory contamination did not render mtDNA testing unreliable. He explained that the FBI laboratory has a strict contamination abatement program in place within the laboratory. That program involves sterilization of space, using bleach solution, ultraviolet light, gloves, masks, and lab coats, and restriction of movement of personnel from one area to the other. All of these precautions would have been taken in the analysis of the specific mtDNA evidence at issue. The defense's expert, Dr. Jeffrey Boore, testified that the FBI's method of guarding against contamination was better able to detect lower levels of contamination than the method used by his own lab, and added that "it's admirable that they go to such lengths to validate that they have not contaminated their sample."[88]

Finally, defendant raised the existence of heteroplasmy as an argument for the unreliability of mtDNA testing. Dr. Stewart testified that the term heteroplasmy means that you have at least more than one exact type of mtDNA in the same individual. Heteroplasmy can present difficulties for forensic investigators because, if an mtDNA sample of the perpetrator differs by one base pair from the suspect's mtDNA sample, this difference may be interpreted as sufficient to "eliminate" the suspect.[89] In most instances, the presence of heteroplasmy makes data interpretation more complex,[90] but does not render the data nonfunctional.

More important, the court stressed, Dr. Stewart testified that there was no evidence of heteroplasmy in this case, meaning that appellant's known mtDNA sequence shared a common base at every position with the mtDNA sequence found in the hair, and had the same pattern at every position.

Dr. Stewart also disagreed that heteroplasmy rendered mtDNA testing unreliable, stating that the published literature on the subject "does not support that."

During the pretrial hearings, Dr. Bruce Budowle, senior scientist in the FBI's biological laboratory division and an expert in mtDNA analysis, also testified regarding heteroplasmy. According to Dr. Budowle, heteroplasmy exists in "the rarest of the circumstances. And, again the rarest of the circumstances, we're willing to accept there possibly could be false exclusion."

Judge Wright, in the trial court, found that the existence of heteroplasmy in some mtDNA did not render the evidence generally unreliable:

> The court, also, would find that the specific procedures that were used by the FBI laboratory to extract, amplify, and sequence, and consequently analyze the particular hairs in this case to identify characteristics of another's genetic material was certainly reliable.... So the question is, ... is the testing procedure generally reliable? And I say, Yes, because it is accepted ... in the scientific community. And was the testing procedure that's used in this case reliable? And I would say, Yes. The existence of contamination, the existence of heteroplasmy does not affect the reliability of the scientific procedure generally, or the procedure used in this particular case by the FBI laboratory, Dr. Stewart, and those under him.[91]

The appellate court agreed with that conclusion and upheld Wagner's conviction.

X. Nonhuman DNA

At the present time there are no reported decisions formally addressing the acceptability of dog or cat DNA matches in a criminal case, although several trial court convictions have recently been reported and are working themselves up the appeals process.[92] One decision exists as to the admissibility of plant DNA testing to place a defendant at a crime scene.[93] It is simply a matter of time for mammal and plant DNA identification methodologies to also be recognized as reliable,[94] especially because the amount of experience and solid scientific data in those areas is enormous and compelling.[95]

A recent article in the Journal of Forensic Science by Dr. Joy Halverson addresses the PCR aspects of canine DNA matching.[96] Dr. Halverson has testified in a number of murder cases in recent years, most recently in *People v. Sutherland*, discussed in detail in Chapter 2, where she linked a dog hair found on the body of the child victim to the defendant's black Labrador dog Babe.[97]

XI. DNA Related Cases: Post-Conviction Testing and Mandatory Submission of DNA

What are some of the likely legal issues surrounding DNA identifications in the early years of the 21st century? A listing of some of the most important cases is followed by discussions of selected cases where these issues arose:

- Post-conviction DNA testing opportunities for prisoners convicted in blood-centered cases where identity was a central issue
- The legality of DNA registration schemes for convicts, arrestees, or the general population, and the inclusion of any such DNA profiles into national or international databases
- The expanded utilization of nonhuman DNA profiling technologies
- Increasingly sophisticated DNA laboratory procedures that must pass muster under Frye and Daubert reliability criteria

XII. Post-Conviction DNA Testing

Given the importance of DNA testing and the release of almost 160 prisoners based upon it,[98] most states have enacted legislation providing an opportunity for post-conviction DNA testing upon motion. An examination of the Illinois statute and the first appellate decision to address it will be beneficial given the great likelihood of this issue being a major one as the first decade of the 21st century proceeds. The Illinois statute reads as follows:

5/116-3. Motion for fingerprint or forensic testing not available at trial regarding actual innocence

(a) A defendant may make a motion before the trial court that entered the judgment of conviction in his or her case for the performance of fingerprint or forensic DNA testing on evidence that was secured in relation to the trial which resulted in his or her conviction, but which was not subject to the testing which is now requested because the technology for the testing was not available at the time of trial. Reasonable notice of the motion shall be served upon the state.

(b) The defendant must present a prima facie case that includes both of the following facts:

(1) Identity was the issue in the trial which resulted in his or her conviction

(2) The evidence to be tested has been subject to a chain of custody sufficient to establish that it has not been substituted, tampered with, replaced, or altered in any material aspect

(c) The trial court shall allow the testing under reasonable conditions designed to protect the state's interests in the integrity of the evidence and the testing process upon a determination that:

(1) The result of the testing has the scientific potential to produce new, noncumulative evidence materially relevant to the defendant's assertion of actual innocence

(2) The testing requested employs a scientific method generally accepted within the relevant scientific community.[99]

As noted by Public Defender Gregory O'Reilly in his article on the new Illinois statute, Illinois' new law applies only to cases where identity was the issue at trial. Thus, as he points out, a rape case defended on the basis of consent conceivably would not meet this threshold, whereas a case involving a crime scene with DNA datum where defendant claimed a false identification would so qualify.[100]

As can be seen, the statute creates a two-part process by initially providing a mechanism for a post-trial motion wherein a convicted felon may petition the court for fingerprint or DNA testing of evidence collected before trial, but, importantly, only if any such test was not then obtainable at that earlier date. There is no deadline for filing. In the event that the motion is granted and the test results tend to exculpate the inmate, the inmate may file a petition for a new trial based on this forensic evidence. In deciding whether to grant a new trial, the court will apply the existing standard for cases involving newly discovered evidence, which raises interesting issues as to the circumstantial or direct character of DNA or fingerprint evidence.

The Illinois law authorizes DNA and fingerprint testing if the new test meets the Frye standard for evidence based upon methodologies generally accepted in the relevant scientific community. The general acceptance of the more accurate and accessible PCR and PCR STR, not to mention mitochondrial DNA testing in some instances, provides a good opportunity for helping to alleviate current concerns over the wrongful incarceration of many, especially death-row, inmates. As noted by O'Reilly:

Courts in most states are likely to recognize RFLP testing and should recognize PCR testing, although there are new methods of PCR testing that may be subject to dispute. In the future, courts may routinely recognize mitochondrial DNA testing, which has the ability to profile hair samples without the roots.[101]

The post-conviction statutes around the country vary greatly as to time limits, forensic sciences included, and the standards that must be met to receive forensic testing. It is a considerable leap of faith for most states to assume that inmates are educated about the latest developments in DNA testing and population projection theories to adequately respond to the strictures of most of these statutes. A dissenting judge in a Florida case on this issue put it well:

> Frankly, I think it is a very harsh reading of the two-year time limit in rule 3.850 to bar testing and perhaps relief from conviction under the circumstances of this case. Rule 3.850(b) bars relief in noncapital cases unless the facts on which the claim is predicated were unknown to the movant and could not have been ascertained by the exercise of due diligence. DNA testing is a recent, highly accurate, application of scientific principles unknown at the time of Dedge's trial. It is not well known to or understood by most lawyers and judges, I would wager, even in 1998. I think it unfair and unrealistic to expect an indigent, serving two life sentences in prison, to have had notice of the existence of PCR-based testing, and possible application to his case prior to 1995 when it was first discussed by a Florida court.[102]

Computerized fingerprint or shell-casing searches now provided by the FBI AFIS and CODIS systems should be equally available in an appropriate case. However, as noted above, the expense and prospect of questioning the finality of convictions will certainly be a force against the expansion of this, itself, nascent national effort to achieve what has been referred to as genetic justice.[103]

In addition to those concerns, there are the equally important issues revolving around the storage of crime-scene evidence for use in post-conviction proceedings. Practices vary greatly around the country as to how long and under what circumstances crime scene materials and laboratory samples are kept. New techniques in all of the forensic sciences, but especially regarding DNA, require a reassessment of such practices to prevent contamination and to otherwise support the intention of the host of post-conviction forensic-evidence testing statutes that we will undoubtedly see come onto the books in the next several years.

As noted by public defender O'Reilly:

> Under the Illinois and New York forensic testing laws, the petitioner must show that the evidence had been collected for trial

and had not been altered. Police, prosecutors, and clerks sometimes destroy old evidence for innocuous reasons such as space
limitations. Sometimes such evidence is mistakenly destroyed, and
it is possible that it could be intentionally destroyed. This could
leave a wrongfully convicted petitioner who seeks testing in such
a case without a remedy. Defense counsel should therefore ask the
court to order forensic evidence impounded after trial and to take
similar steps to make sure police, prosecutors, and court clerks
also do not destroy or alter old evidence.[104]

This issue of post-conviction DNA testing and the variance in statutes
or court rulings with respect to them, bears close watching by those involved
in the criminal justice system.

XIII. DNA Samples

Once given, a DNA sample remains in the system, available to police in other
cases, although the basis for any earlier voluntary submission needs to be
scrutinized. In *Pace v. State*,[105] a jury convicted Lyndon Fitzgerald Pace of
four counts of malice murder, four counts of felony murder, four counts of
rape, and two counts of aggravated sodomy. A DNA expert determined that
Pace's DNA profile matched the DNA profile taken from the sperm in the
McAfee, Martin, McLendon, and Britt murders. The expert testified that the
probability of a coincidental match of this DNA profile is one in 500 million
in the McAfee, Martin, and Britt cases, and one in 150 million in the McLendon
case.

The defendant, while under investigation for another murder, of one
Mary Hudson, had signed a consent form that states, in part: "I fully understand that these hair and bodily fluid samples are to be used against me in
a court of law and I am in agreement to give these hair samples for further
use in this particular investigation." The form further stated that Pace was a
suspect in a murder that occurred on September 17, 1992 and the "name of
the murder victim in this case is Mary Hudson." There was no mention of
the other four murders. The FBI and GBI crime labs were subsequently
unable to match Pace's DNA or hair to any evidence from the Hudson
murder, but were able to obtain matches with evidence from the McAfee,
McLendon, Martin, and Britt cases.[106]

Pace claimed that he did not voluntarily consent to the drawing of his
blood for use in the investigation of the four murders for which he was
convicted, and argued that the police thus exceeded the bounds of his consent
by using his blood for investigations of murders other than the Hudson

murder. However, the court observed, unlike an implied consent warning, the form does not limit the use of the blood or hair to only the Hudson murder investigation or to any particular purpose, and there is no evidence that Pace placed any limits on the scope of his consent.

The police were not required to explain to Pace that his blood or hair could be used in prosecutions involving other victims, or that he had a right to refuse consent...Further, like a fingerprint, DNA remains the same no matter how many times blood is drawn and tested and a DNA profile can be used to inculpate or exculpate suspects in other investigations without additional invasive procedures. It would not be reasonable to require law enforcement personnel to obtain additional consent or another search warrant every time a validly obtained DNA profile is used for comparison in another investigation.[107]

The rapid judicial acceptance of DNA identification technologies does not mean that all legal issues involving it are resolved. It must be remembered that DNA evidence, as powerful and definitive as it is characterized, is just evidence nonetheless. It is typically categorized as *circumstantial evidence*, like fingerprints, ballistics, hair, fiber, and the rest of the forensic evidence corpus, as opposed to *direct evidence* of the fact for which it is offered, normally presence and participation at a crime scene. This is an important conceptual difference, which may be belied in the eyes of juries by the reputation that DNA, like fingerprints, has gained over the past decade.

In *Thomas v. State*,[108] a capital murder appeal, the court addressed the important issue of whether DNA evidence is direct or circumstantial proof of the fact or facts for which it is offered to prove. At issue was defendant's assertion that he was entitled to a circumstantial evidence instruction about the state's DNA evidence.[109] The attorney general, without citing any authority, responded that Thomas's argument completely ignored very direct evidence presented by the state, such as DNA matching, DNA population statistics, and fingerprint evidence.[110]

The court observed that contrary to the attorney general's assertion, fingerprint evidence was still generally considered circumstantial evidence. This characterization applied equally well to DNA evidence. The court noted that a limited search of case law on the question of the nature of DNA evidence found more cases that refer to DNA evidence as circumstantial than as direct. Because there was some, albeit little, legal authority for the conclusion that DNA evidence was "noncircumstantial" or "direct" evidence, there was some validity to the position that any error in not instructing the jury on the "reasonable-hypothesis-of-innocence" instruction is not "plain," i.e., not "clear" or "obvious" under the law. Therefore, the plain error test was not satisfied.[111]

Because DNA is evidence, it must comport with all of the rules of evidence, including specialized chain-of-custody proffers,[112] and a host of non-scientific constitutional and evidence rules.[113]

The controversy about the legitimacy of DNA technology other than mtDNA has certainly abated and recent concern has begun to focus on the issue of mandating DNA samples by convicted felons, whether incarcerated in penal institutions or on parole or probation. The federal statute addressing the collection and use of DNA identification and providing funding for similar state programs is contained in 2 U.S.C.A. § 14135a, Collection and use of DNA identification, effective: October 30, 2004:

a) Collection of DNA samples

(1) From individuals in custody

The Director of the Bureau of Prisons shall collect a DNA sample from each individual in the custody of the Bureau of Prisons who is, or has been, convicted of a qualifying Federal offense (as determined under subsection [d] of this section) or a qualifying military offense, as determined under section 1565 of Title 10.

(2) From individuals on release, parole, or probation

The probation office responsible for the supervision under Federal law of an individual on probation, parole, or supervised release shall collect a DNA sample from each such individual who is, or has been, convicted of a qualifying Federal offense (as determined under subsection [d] of this section) or a qualifying military offense, as determined under section 1565 of Title 10.

(3) Individuals already in CODIS

For each individual described in paragraph (1) or (2), if the Combined DNA Index System (in this section referred to as CODIS) of the Federal Bureau of Investigation contains a DNA analysis with respect to that individual, or if a DNA sample has been collected from that individual under section 1565 of Title 10, the Director of the Bureau of Prisons or the probation office responsible (as applicable) may (but need not) collect a DNA sample from that individual.[114]

The statute also sets forth a series of collection procedures directing the Director of the Bureau of Prisons or the probation office responsible (as applicable) *to use or authorize the use of such means as are reasonably necessary to detain, restrain, and collect a DNA sample from an individual who refuses to cooperate in the collection of the sample.* An individual from whom the collection of a DNA sample is authorized under the subsection who fails to cooperate in the collection of that sample shall be guilty of a class A misdemeanor. The Director of the Bureau of Prisons or the probation office responsible (as applicable) must furnish each DNA sample collected under subsection (a) of this section to the Director of the Federal Bureau of Investigation, who shall carry out a DNA analysis on each such DNA sample and include the results in CODIS.[115]

The leading case discussing the constitutionality of this statute is *United States v. Kincade,*[116] a 9th Circuit Court of Appeals decision.

Defendant appealed after a federal district judge sentenced him to four months' imprisonment, and two years' supervised release, for violating the terms of his supervised release by refusing to submit a blood sample for DNA testing, pursuant to the DNA Analysis Backlog Elimination Act. On rehearing *en banc,* the Court of Appeals held that the requirement under the Act that certain federal offenders who were on parole, probation, or supervised release submit to compulsory DNA profiling, even in the absence of individualized suspicion that they had committed additional crimes, was reasonable and did not violate Fourth Amendment.

The court framed the issue as to whether it must decide if the Fourth Amendment permits compulsory DNA profiling of certain conditionally released federal offenders in the absence of individualized suspicion that they have committed additional crimes. The court noted that pursuant to the DNA Analysis Backlog Elimination Act of 2000, individuals who have been convicted of certain federal crimes and who are incarcerated, or on parole, probation, or supervised release, must provide federal authorities with "a tissue, fluid, or other bodily sample on which an analysis of that sample's DNA identification information could be performed.[117]

The court initially addressed the issue of the warrant requirement typically required for searches:

> Ordinarily, the reasonableness of a search depends on governmental compliance with the Warrant Clause, which requires authorities to demonstrate probable cause to a neutral magistrate and thereby convince magistrate to provide formal authorization to proceed with a search by issuance of a particularized warrant (citations omitted). However, the general rule of the Warrant Clause is not unyielding. Under a variety of conditions, law enforcement may execute a search without first complying with its dictates. For instance, police may execute warrantless searches incident to a lawful arrest: It is reasonable for authorities to search an arrestee

for weapons that might threaten their safety, or for evidence which might be destroyed. And even outside the context of a lawful arrest supported by probable cause, officers are likewise authorized to conduct a warrantless, protective pat-down of individuals they encounter in the field so long as their concerns are justified by reasonable suspicion of possible danger.

The court noted several general search regimens that were free from the usual warrant-and-probable cause requirements.

Though not necessarily mutually exclusive, three categories of *searches help organize the jurisprudence.* The first category was "exempted areas," including searches conducted at the border, in prisons, and at airports and entrances to government buildings. The second category was labeled "administrative" searches, which included inspections of closely-regulated businesses, and other routine regulatory investigations. The third category of suspicionless searches, the court noted, was referred to as "special needs," and also noted that in recent years, the Supreme Court has devoted increasing attention to the development of the accompanying analytical doctrine. For the most part, the court observed, these cases involved searches conducted for *important nonlaw enforcement purposes in contexts where adherence to the warrant-and-probable cause requirement would be impracticable.*[118]

The court recognized that a number of other circuits had addressed this issue:

> We are not the first court called upon to address this unresolved issue. Confronted with challenges to the federal DNA Act and its state law analogues, our sister circuits and peers in the states have divided in their analytical approaches — both before and after the Supreme Court's recent special needs decisions. On one hand, the Second, Seventh, and Tenth circuits, along with a variety of federal district courts and at least two state Supreme Courts, have upheld DNA collection statutes under a special needs analysis (though not always ruling out the possibility that the totality of the circumstances might validate the search absent some special need.)[119]

By contrast, the Fourth and Fifth circuits, a Seventh Circuit Judge, numerous federal district courts, and a variety of state courts have approved compulsory DNA profiling under a traditional assessment of reasonableness gauged by the totality of the circumstances.[120]

In the final analysis, the overwhelming public importance of the DNA database for the investigation and prosecution of crime required a finding in the government's favor:

In light of conditional releasees' substantially diminished expectations of privacy, the minimal intrusion occasioned by blood sampling, and the overwhelming societal interests so clearly furthered by the collection of DNA information from convicted offenders, we must conclude that compulsory DNA profiling of qualified federal offenders is reasonable under the totality of the circumstances. Therefore, we today realign ourselves with every other state and federal appellate court to have considered these issues — squarely holding that the DNA Act satisfies the requirements of the Fourth Amendment.[121]

Because compulsory DNA profiling conducted pursuant to the federal DNA Act would have occasioned no violation of Kincade's Fourth Amendment rights, the judgment and accompanying sentence of the district court were upheld.[122]

XIV. John Doe DNA Warrants

The important issue of the legality of John Doe warrants in sexual assault cases where the statute of limitations is about to expire, was raised in the 2005 Wisconsin case of State v. Davis.[123]

Lonnie C. Davis was found guilty of four counts of second-degree sexual assault, use of force. Davis claimed, among other points of error, that the trial court erred in finding that the complaint filed before the statute of limitations expired, which identified Davis only by a DNA profile, was sufficient.

A nurse examined the victim Kylesia, and secured as evidence the underwear she was wearing at the time of the assaults. Semen was obtained from the underwear and a DNA analysis was performed, using the RFLP technique. The DNA profile from the analysis was run through the convicted offender index of the Wisconsin DNA databank, but no match to the profile was found.

In 1997, Davis was convicted for sexually assaulting a different victim. He was sentenced to 105 years in prison and was required to provide a DNA sample. On August 30, 2000, shortly before the statute of limitations was due to expire in Kylesia's case, the state filed a criminal complaint and obtained an arrest warrant identifying the perpetrator of Kylesia's assaults as "John Doe" with the particular DNA profile identified from the semen in Kylesia's underwear. John Doe was charged with one count of forcible kidnapping and six counts of second-degree sexual assault.

In 1998 and 1999, the state crime lab began making the transition from the RFLP DNA technique to a new DNA technology known as PCR. Because RFLP profiles and PCR profiles are not comparable, the state began to reanalyze all of the evidentiary samples in its databank. When the DNA profile in this case was reanalyzed and the new PCR DNA profile was compared to those in the Wisconsin databank, it was determined that a match was found. The PCR DNA profile in this case matched that of convicted sex-offender Lonnie Davis.[124]

On April 24, 2002, pursuant to a search warrant, an oral swab was taken from Davis and DNA testing was conducted on that swab. A comparison between the DNA from the swab and the DNA from the semen in Kylesia's underwear was conducted. The conclusion was that the DNA from both matched and the only reasonable scientific explanation was that Davis was the source of the semen in Kylesia's underwear.

An amended complaint was filed substituting Davis for John Doe and the case proceeded to trial. Davis waived his right to a jury trial in exchange for the dismissal of the kidnapping charge and two counts of sexual assault. The case was tried to the court and defendant was convicted.

On September 4, 2002, the state filed an amended criminal complaint in this case identifying Davis as the John Doe whose DNA profile matched that of the DNA retrieved from the semen in the victim's underwear. In 1998, the state crime lab stopped performing the RFLP DNA analysis and converted to the DNA technology known as PCR. The two technologies were different; one could not compare an RFLP DNA profile to a PCR DNA profile. As a result, during 1998 and 1999, the state crime lab reanalyzed all evidentiary samples that had previously generated RFLP DNA profiles under the new PCR DNA technology, so that the profiles could be compared to the offender database.

When the sample in this case was reanalyzed producing a PCR DNA profile, it was compared to all of the convicted offender samples in the database, and a match was found. Davis' DNA profile matched that of the PCR DNA sample generated from the semen in the victim's underwear. Based on this information, the state obtained a search warrant to take an oral swab directly from Davis, who was incarcerated. The DNA results from this oral swab also matched that of the DNA sample generated from the semen in the victim's underwear. Based on this information, the amended complaint charged Davis with the kidnapping and sexual assaults by substituting his name for that of John Doe.[125]

Davis argued that because the original complaint identified the DNA profile using a different technology than the amended complaint that eventually led to his identification, he maintained that because the RFLP DNA profile identified in the complaint was not the profile used to identify him by name, the amended complaint does not relate back to a date preceding the expiration of the statute of limitations. The court dismissed this argument, holding:

The DNA was the same. Both the RFLP DNA profile and the PCR DNA profile contained Davis' DNA exclusively. His argument elevates form over substance. The state specifically identified Davis' DNA in a complaint before the statute of limitations expired. The fact that the type of DNA analysis technology changed does not somehow alter the accuracy of the identification. The person with the DNA in the original complaint was the same person with the DNA in the amended complaint — Davis. Thus, his claim that the analysis was different is of no consequence. His DNA did not change, but remained the same. Thus, it satisfied the reasonable certainty requirements for an arrest warrant and answered the "who is charged" question required for a sufficient complaint. (Id.) Thus, the trial court did not err in finding that the complaint was sufficient.

XV. The Future of DNA Testing

The National Institute of Justice, in the report, *The Future of Predictions of the Research and Development Working Group* (November 2000), set out its technology projections for 2010:

> Of course, the farther we peer into the future, the cloudier is our vision. Nevertheless, we expect that, although better procedures will undoubtedly have been developed, the 13 core STR loci will still be the standard currency. The reason is that changing systems is expensive and inefficient, and a system that is in place and working well is likely to be continued.

> There may be some transition to new technologies, mainly to supplement the standard STRs. SNPs will be widely used in medical and agricultural research, so there will be many opportunities to carry these over for forensic purposes. We therefore envisage additions to the STR loci for some casework.

> Within 10 years we expect portable, miniaturized instrumentation that will provide analysis at the crime scene with computer-linked remote analysis. This should permit rapid identification and, in particular, quick elimination of innocent suspects.

> By this time there should be a number of markers available that identify physical traits of the individual contributing the DNA. It should be possible, using this information, to narrow the search for a suspect, with consequent increases in the accuracy and efficiency of operation.

The full impact of DNA technology in the near future remains to be seen. It is rapidly becoming the centerpiece of the investigation and prosecution of crime worldwide.

Endnotes

1. See, e.g., *State v. Bowers*, 135 N.C.App. 682, 522 S.E.2d 332 (N.C.App., 1999), where the defendant was found guilty of first-degree burglary and statutory rape of a 14-year-old girl. Michael Budzynski, a DNA analyst, examined the blood samples and determined that the defendant's DNA could not be ruled out as being the same DNA found in the victim's panties and sweat pants. According to Mr. Budzynski, the probability of finding the same DNA profile in another person was at least 1 in 5.5 billion.

   The court ruled that none of the scientific methods employed by the expert was a new method where reliability was at issue. Therefore, any analysis of the DNA methods used, which were not even identified in the appeal, was not necessary. Indeed, the issue getting the most attention was what does "nighttime" mean? Because the pertinent element at issue was the nighttime element, the court focused, in the absence of a statutory definition on the common-law definition of *nighttime*, which defined it *as a condition when it is so dark that a man's face cannot be identified except by artificial light or moonlight.*

2. We are now becoming very familiar with quick DNA profile information through the use of computerized systems for rapid DNA profile matching via the NDIS and CODIS database systems.

3. See, e.g., Illinois Supreme Court Rule 417. DNA Evidence (2001) ILCS S. Ct. Rule 417.

4. It is essential that prosecutors and criminal defense lawyers consult *Champion*, the publication, and the Web site of the National Association of Defense Lawyers, located at http://www.nacdl.org. *Champion* magazine routinely publishes excellent articles by some of the top DNA experts in the country. As an example of the high quality of its offerings, see the two-part article on evaluating a DNA case by William C. Thompson, Simon Ford, Travis Doom, Michael Raymer, and Dan E. Krane.

   William C. Thompson; Simon Ford; Travis Doom; Michael Raymer, Dan E. Krane, Evaluating forensic DNA evidence: Essential elements of a competent defense review, *Champion* May 2003, at 24; William C. Thompson; Simon Ford; Travis E. Doom; Michael L. Raymer; Dan E. Krane, Evaluating Forensic DNA Evidence, Part 2, Champion.

   Champion April 2003, at 16; William C. Thompson; Simon Ford; Travis E. Doom; Michael L. Raymer; Dan E. Krane, *Evaluating Forensic DNA Evidence, Part 2*, May 2003, at 24. Also see, How the probability of a false positive affects the value of DNA evidence. Thompson, W.C., Taroni, F., Aitken, C.G.G. 2003; *J. Forensic Sci.* 48(1): 47-54 and the extensive commentaries on this article in the *J. Forensic Sci.* See, Commentary on: Thompson, W.C., Taroni, F., Aitken, C.G.G., *J. Forensic Sci.* 2003;48(1):47-54. Brenner, C.H., Inman, K. 2004;49(1): 1-2.; Authors' response. Thompson, W.C., Taroni, F., Aitken, C.G.G.. 2004;49(1): 1-2.; Authors' response. Thompson, W.C., Taroni, F., Aitken, C.G.G. 2003;48(5): 1202.; Commentary on: Thompson, W.C., Taroni, F., Aitken, C.G.G. How the probability of a false positive affects the value of DNA evidence. *J. Forensic Sci.* 2003 Jan;48(1):47-54. Clarke, G.W. 2003;48(5): 1201.; Commentary on: Thompson, W.C., Taroni, F., Aitken, C.G.G. How the probability of a false positive affects the value of DNA evidence. *J. Forensic Sci.* 2003;48(1):47-54. Cotton, R.W., Word, C.J. 2003;48(5): 1200.

5. 533 So. 2d 842 (Fla. Dist. Ct. App. 1988). See Giannelli and Imwinkelried: *Scientific Evidence* (The Michie Company, 2d ed., 1993), Vol. 2, at 26, for a good discussion of the early days of judicial acceptance of DNA technology.

6. See, generally, Saferstein: *Criminalistics: An Introduction to Forensic Science* (Prentice Hall, 6th ed., 1998), at 361 (Serology) and 403 (DNA); Robertson and Vignaux: *Interpreting Evidence: Evaluating Forensic Science in the Courtroom* (John Wiley & Sons, 1995); Eckert (ed): *Introduction to Forensic Sciences* (CRC Press, 2d ed., 19997); Giannelli and Imwinkelried, *Scientific Evidence* (The Michie Company, 2d ed., 1993), *The DNS Genetic Marker,* Vol. 2, at 1ans 1998 Cumulative Supplement, at 1.

7. Note: Revised Validation Guidelines, Scientific Working Group on DNA Analysis Methods (SWGDAM):

The validation section of the Guidelines for a Quality Assurance Program for DNA Analysis by the Technical Working Group on DNA Analysis Methods (*Crime Laboratory Digest* 1995:22(2):21–43) has been revised due to increased laboratory experience, the advent of new technologies, and the issuance of the Quality Assurance Standards for Forensic DNA Testing Laboratories by the Director of the FBI (*Forensic Science Communications,* available: *www.fbi.gov/hq/lab/fsc/backissu/july2000/codis2a.htm*). This document provides validation guidelines and definitions approved by SWGDAM on July 10, 2003.

8. See, 14th International Forensic Science Symposium, at 137–147.

9. 14th International Forensic Science Symposium at 144.

10. *Development projects were taking place in many parts of the world.

*The sharing of examples of good practice and case studies in various areas during the presentations were extremely enlightening and no doubt extremely useful. This session was an excellent opportunity to identify challenges and issues faced by the various countries and by Interpol.

See, http://books.elsevier.com/.

11. See, http://www.forensicnetbase.com/

12. See, http://www.amazon.com/

13. A very recent treatise has been published by John Butler, *Forensic DNA Typing: Biology, Technology, and Genetics behind STR Markers*, published in 2005 by Academic Press. The second edition of this book includes recent information on DNA typing systems, Y-chromosome material and mitochondrial DNA markers. Additional chapters address statistical genetic analysis of DNA data, and statistical analysis of short tandem repeat (STR) typing data.

14. See, e.g., Joy Halverson, D.V.M. and Christopher Basten, Ph.D., *A PCR Multiplex and Database for Forensic DNA Identification of Dogs*, 50 JFS (2) at 1 (2005); and Terry Melton, Ph.D.; Gloria Dimick, M.S.; Bonnie Higgins, M.S.; Lynn Lindstrom, B.S.; and Kimberlyn Nelson, Ph.D., *Forensic Mitochondrial DNA Analysis of 691 Casework Hairs*, 50 JFS (1) (2005).

15. See, e.g., 19-WTR Crim. Just. 54 Criminal Justice Winter, 2005 Department Mitochondrial DNA, Paul C. Giannelli; 89 *Cornell L. Rev.* 1305 *Cornell L. Rev.* September, 2004, Article *Ake V. Oklahoma*: The Right To Expert Assistance In A Post-Daubert, Post-DNA World, Paul C. Giannelli; September, 2004 *Prosecutor* July/August, 2004 Highlight from the Prosecutor, Forensic Palynology And Plant DNA: The Evidence That Sticks, Danielle M. Weiss; Mark Hansen, DNA Dragnet, 90 May *ABAJ* 38 (2004); 71 *U. Chi. L. Rev.* 587 *U. Chi. L. Rev.* Spring 2004 Comment Habeas, Section 1983, And Post-Conviction Access To DNA Evidence.

16. The current *Handbook* may be downloaded at http://www.fbi.gov/hq/lab/handbook/forensics.pdf.

17. See the FBI CODIS home page at http://www.fbi.gov/hq/lab/codis/index1.htm.

18. 342 Md. 38, 673 A. 2d 221 (1996).

19. 173 Ill.2d 167, 670 N.E.2d 721 (1996).

20. 173 Ill.2d 167, 670 N.E.2d 721 (1996), at 176.

21. Miller, at 670 N.E.2d 721, 730.

22. See *State v. Anderson*, 118 N.M. 284, 881 P.2d 29 (1994), *Springfield v. State*, 860 P.2d 435 (Wyo.1993), or *United States v. Jakobetz*, 955 F.2d 786 (2d Cir.1992), for a more extensive discussion of this topic.

23. Miller, at 173 Ill. 2d 185-186.

24. Miller, at 187.

25. See, *People v. Stremmel*, 258 Ill.App.3d 93, 197 Ill.Dec. 177, 630 N.E.2d 1301 (1994); *People v. Watson*, 257 Ill.App.3d 915, 196 Ill.Dec. 89, 629 N.E.2d 634 (1994); *People v. Mehlberg*, 249 Ill.App.3d 499, 188 Ill.Dec. 598, 618 N.E.2d 1168 (1993); *People v. Miles*, 217 Ill.App.3d 393, 160 Ill.Dec. 347, 577 N.E.2d 477 (1991); *People v. Lipscomb*, 215 Ill.App.3d 413, 158 Ill.Dec. 952, 574 N.E.2d 1345 (1991). All of these cases agree that the theory underlying DNA profiling and the RFLP matching technique is generally accepted in the relevant scientific community.

26. See, e.g., *Harmon v. State*, 908 P.2d 434, 440 (Alaska App.1995); *Taylor v. State*, 889 P.2d 319, 333 (Okla.Crim.App.1995); *State v. Cauthron*, 120

Wash.2d 879, 896–97, 846 P.2d 502, 511 (1993) (citing 15 cases that support general acceptance of RFLP testing); *United States v. Porter*, 618 A.2d 629, 636 (D.C.App.1992).

27. See, discussion of the earlier Thomas case with respect to the issue of the circumstantial evidence nature of DNA evidence.

28. The National Research Council (the NRC) has generated several primary sources cited almost universally in judicial decisions assessing DNA forensic analysis and the associated statistics. The NRC is a private, nonprofit society of distinguished scholars that is administered by the National Academy of Sciences, the National Academy of Engineering, and the Institute of Medicine. The NRC formed the Committee on DNA Technology in Forensic Science to study the use of DNA analysis for forensic purposes, resulting in the issuance of a report in 1992. See, Committee on DNA Technology In Forensic Science, National Research Council, DNA Technology in Forensic Science (1992); see generally, *State v. Marcus*, 294 N.J.Super. 267, 683 A.2d 221, 227 n. 6 (1996). A new committee was subsequently formed to study recent developments in the field, which also issued a frequently cited report. See National Research Council, *The Evaluation of Forensic DNA Evidence* 63 (1996); see generally, R. Stephen Kramer, *Comment, Admissibility of DNA Statistical Data: A Proliferation of Misconceptions*, 30 Cal.W.L.Rev. 145, 147 and n. 17 (Fall, 1993) (noting that courts have traditionally deferred to pronouncements from the National Academy of Sciences) (citing Rorie Sherman, DNA Unraveling, Nat'l L.J. 1, 30 (Feb. 1, 1993); *Commonwealth v. Blasioli*, 552 Pa. 149, 713 A.2d 1117, 1119–20 n. 3 (Pa.1998).

29. Id. at *46. The 1996 NCR Report — National Research Council, The Evaluation of Forensic DNA Evidence (1996) — states that, "[i]n general, the calculation of a profile frequency should be made with the product rule." Id. at 5. See also, 2 Paul C. Giannelli and Edward J. Imwinkelried, *Scientific Evidence* § 18–4, p. 12 (Supp.1998) ("With some modifications for special situations, the 1996 report endorses the use of the traditional product rule to compute the random match probability.").

30. See *Watts v. State*, 733 So.2d 214, 226 (Miss.1999) (citing court opinions from 14 states for its observation that "courts which have considered the admissibility of statistical evidence based on the product rule have determined that the challenges to its use have been sufficiently resolved" and its finding that "the product rule has been accepted in the scientific community and found to be a reliable method of calculating population frequency data"); *State v. Kinder*, 942 S.W.2d 313, 327 (Mo.1996), cert. denied, 522 U.S. 854, 118 S.Ct. 149, 139 L.Ed.2d 95 ("the overwhelming majority of recent cases in other jurisdictions ... approve the use of the product rule"); *State v. Loftus*, 573 N.W.2d 167, 174 (S.D.1997) ("an overwhelming amount of scientific commentary and legal authority exist" resolving any earlier dispute concerning DNA statistical evidence, and the "product rule method ... is now generally accepted in the relevant scientific community;" *People v. Chandler*, 211

Mich.App. 604, 536 N.W.2d 799, 803 (1995), cert. denied, 453 Mich. 883, 554 N.W.2d 12 (1996)); See, for example, the following cases finding the product rule evidence admissible under the *Daubert* test: *United States v. Chischilly*, 30 F.3d 1144, 1153 (9th Cir.1994), cert. denied, 513 U.S. 1132 (1995); *State v. Loftus*, 573 N.W.2d 167 (S.D.1997). Also see, the following cases relying, in part, on the 1996 NRC Report in upholding use of the product rule: *State v. Marshall*, 193 Ariz. 547, 975 P.2d 137, 141 (Ariz.App.1998) (quoting *State v. Johnson*, 186 Ariz. 329, 922 P.2d 294, 299 (Ariz.1996)) ("Endorsement by the NRC 'is strong evidence of general acceptance within the relevant scientific community.'"); *Clark v. State*, 679 So.2d 321, 321 (Fla.App.1996) ("product rule calculations are appropriate as a matter of scientific fact and law"); *State v. Kinder*, 942 S.W.2d 313, 327 (Mo.1996), cert. denied, 522 U.S. 854, 118 S.Ct. 149, 139 L.Ed.2d 95 (1997); *State v. Freeman*, 253 Neb. 385, 571 N.W.2d 276, 293 (Neb.1997); *State v. Copeland*, 130 Wash.2d 244, 922 P.2d 1304, 1319–20 and n. 6 (Wash.1996).

31. National Research Council, *The Evaluation of Forensic DNA Evidence* 25 (1996) (hereinafter "1996 NRC Report"). [FN13] See also, *State v. Morel*, 676 A.2d 1347, 1356 (R.I.1996) ("[I]n the preservation and testing of DNA evidence, careful attention and proper handling of the crime sample by police and scientists are crucial in defending chain-of-custody issues and in ensuring that laboratory mislabeling and inadvertent contamination have not occurred; *Reference Manual on Scientific Evidence*, at 293 [(Federal Judicial Center 1994)]."); Sally E. Renskers, *Comment, Trial by Certainty: Implications of Genetic "DNA Fingerprints,"* 39 Em.L.J. 309, 316-17 (1990).

32. The PCR technique involves three basic phases: "First, a fragment of DNA is extracted from a sample of evidence. Second, during the amplification phase, millions of copies of the fragment are created by mixing the sample with enzymes, chemicals, and primers. Third, the finished product is tested for comparison with a known DNA sample from a victim or suspect." See *U.S. v. Hicks*, 103 F.3d 837 (9th Cir.1996).

33. See, *Dedge v. State*, 723 So.2d 322 (Fla. Ct. App. 1998).

34. 1 Modern Scientific Evidence, "Forensic Identification," § 16-3.0 at 679 (1997).

35. Werrett, D.J., *DNA Evidence*, Proceedings of the 12th Interpol Forensic Science Symposium (1998), at 61. See the excellent bibliography of current references associated with this article.

36. 185 Ill.2d 317, 706 N.E.2d 473(1999).

37. Dr. Violette Hnilica, the forensic pathologist who performed the autopsy, testified that the body was decomposing and swollen. Hnilica used dental records to make a positive identification of the body as Gwinn. She also identified injuries to the body including torn skin on the right side of the mouth and cheek; "broken back" fingernails; bruises on the upper abdomen, shoulders, and right side of the head; hemorrhages and tissue compression in the neck; a blunt-force injury to the scalp; and bruises in the vagina. Hnilica

stated that the cause of death was strangulation and blunt-force injuries, and that the victim's injuries were consistent with sexual assault.

38. 185 Ill.2d 317, 706 N.E.2d 473(1999), at 477.

39. 187 Ill.2d 144, 718 N.E.2d 1 (1999).

40. Dr. Edward Pavlik, an expert in forensic odontology, testified that he was asked to assist in identifying the body recovered in Hunting Area 7. Based on the development of the teeth in the body and a comparison of these teeth to photographs of Christopher's teeth before his death, Pavlik determined that the body belonged to Christopher. Dr. Larry Blum, an expert in forensic pathology, testified that he performed the autopsy of Christopher's body. The body was unclothed and showed signs of decomposition. Blum found a contusion to Christopher's jaw and 52 stab wounds and cuts on the body, primarily to the chest, abdomen, and back. In Blum's opinion, the stab and slash wounds were made by a sharp, single-edged knife that was relatively long and narrow. This knife could have been a filet knife. There was also evidence that this type of knife had been used to cut Christopher's genital area; his external genitalia were missing. None of Christopher's wounds, including one stab wound to his heart and 12 to his lungs, was sufficient to cause immediate death. Blum opined that the cause of death was multiple stab wounds. Al Haskell, a forensic entomologist, explained that certain insects are attracted to human remains, sometimes within seconds of death, and lay their eggs in these remains. Based on the stage of development of the insects found in a corpse, a precise estimation of the time of death may be obtained. Haskell analyzed the insects recovered from Christopher's body, as well as the environmental conditions to which the body had been subjected. He concluded that the time of death was most likely sometime before sunset on August 7. 187 Ill.2d 144, 718 N.E.2d 1 (1999), at 168–169.

41. 187 Ill.2d 144, 718 N.E.2d 1 (1999), at 170–171.

42. 72 Cal.App.4th 1093, 85 Cal.Rptr.2d 655 (Cal. Ct. App. 1999).

43. 72 Cal.App.4th 1093, 85 Cal.Rptr.2d 655 (Cal. Ct. App. 1999), at 1097.

44. "(O)nce a trial court has admitted evidence based upon a new scientific technique, and that decision is affirmed on appeal by a published appellate decision, the precedent so established may control subsequent trials, at least until new evidence is presented reflecting a change in the attitude of the scientific community." (*People v. Kelly*, 17 Cal.3d at p. 32, 130 *Cal.Rptr.* 144, 549 P.2d 1240.(1976). Also see, *People v. Morganti*, 43 Cal.App.4th at p. 666, 50 Cal.Rptr.2d 837 [1996] [pointing out that although PCR evidence had not been found admissible in any published California case, "courts in other jurisdictions have concluded that PCR analysis of DQ alpha is generally accepted as reliable in the scientific community"].)

45. 425 Mass. 807, 685 N.E.2d 739 (1997).

46. *Commonwealth v. Rosier,* supra, 685 N.E.2d at p. 743. Id. at 1100.

47. 255 Neb. 68, 582 N.W.2d 317 (1998).

48. Jackson, at 325.

49. Allen at 1101. See, *People v. Smith*, 215 Cal.App.3d 19, 25, 263 *Cal.Rptr.* 678 (1989) (In determining whether particular technique is generally accepted, a defendant is not foreclosed from showing new information which may question the continuing reliability of the test in question or to show a change in the consensus within the scientific community concerning the scientific technique.)

50. See STADNAP home page at http://www.stadnap.uni-mainz.de/.

51. 215 Cal.App.3d 19, 25, 263 *Cal.Rptr.* 678 (1989). *Technology transfer will be carried out and exchange of personnel will be encouraged within the framework of the EU fellowship programmes.*

52. 110 P. 3d 245 (Wash. Ct. App. 2005).

53. 110 P. 3d 245 (Wash. Ct. App. 2005), at para. 35-37.

54. In his appellate brief, Mason argued that had Dr. Libby been allowed to testify, he would have explained the flaws in Dr. Blake's overinflated claim that Mr. Mason was the contributor to the DNA in the car to these extreme odds. Dr. Libby would have cautioned the jury against accepting this testimony, and explained how many scientists prefer to calculate the likelihood of DNA in a mixture belonging to a certain source. Instead of 14 trillion to one, Dr. Libby calculated the odds to be one in 121,951 for the black population and one in 833,333 for the Caucasian population. 110 P. 3d 245 (Wash. Ct. App. 2005), at para. 36–38.

55. 110 P. 3d 245 (Wash. Ct. App. 2005), at para. 39.

56. The original method of DNA mixture interpretation was proposed by Evett et al. (2). Several years ago, a theory to interpret mixed DNA profiles that included a consideration of peak area using the method of least squares was proposed by Gill et al. (3). This method of mixture interpretation was not widely adopted because of the complexity of the associated calculations. Currently, most reporting officers take account of peak area in an intuitive way based upon their experience and judgment. A formalized approach has been written into a computer program package called PENDULUM (4). This program uses a least-squares method to estimate the preamplification mixture proportion for two potential contributors. It then calculates the heterozygous balance for all of the potential sets of genotypes. A list of — possible genotyes is generated using a set of heuristic rules. External to the program the candidate genotypes may then be used to formulate likelihood ratios that are based on alternative casework propositions. *Interpol DNA Review,* supra, at 138.

57. 104 Ohio St.3d 358, 819 N.E.2d 1047 (2004)

58. 104 Ohio St.3d 358, 819 N.E.2d 1047 (2004), at 363.

59. 361 S.C. 333, 605 S.E. 2d 19 (Sp. Ct. S.C. 2004)

60. 361 S.C. 333, 605 S.E. 2d 19 (Sp. Ct. S.C. 2004), at 343. Also see, *People v. Perez Poye'* 2005 WL 1022174 (Cal. App. 2005); (Additional expert testimony established that defendant was a possible contributor of the DNA mixture

found on both ski masks used in a residential robbery); *LaPointe v. State*, 2005 WL 995371 (Texas 2005) (DNA testing revealed that victim and her boyfriend could not be excluded as contributors to a mixture of DNA found on the water bottle collected from defendant's apartment.); *State v. Jones*, 109 P.3d 1158 (Kan. 2005.) (Mary Koch, a forensic scientist with the KBI, examined the evidence to determine whether it matched victim Paddock's or Jones' DNA. Paddock's DNA was found throughout the room and its contents. A mixture of DNA was found on fingernail scrapings, the black jeans, the trash can, and a black coat. The major portion of those mixtures was consistent with her DNA. The minor portion of the DNA from the trash can was consistent with Jones' DNA. The minor portions of the DNA from the jeans and the fingernail scrapings were consistent with Jones' DNA, but were fairly common DNA mixtures. The minor portion of the DNA found on the coat was insufficient for comparison.)

61. See, Alice R. Isenberg and Jodi M. Moore, *Mitochondrial DNA Analysis at the FBI Laboratory*, Forensic Science Communications, Vol. I, No. 2, July 1999, located at http://www.fbi.gov/programs/lab/fsc/current/dnalist.htm, covering background, a six-step analysis procedure, interpretation guidelines, population database, and reporting statistics. This will undoubtedly be a major supportive document for the use of mitochondrial DNA identifications in criminal trials.

62. The 14th Interpol Forensic Science Symposium, *DNA Report*, at 138–139 provides a brief discussion of recent MtDNA work in Europe.

63. For example, Tennessee has a statute governing the admissibility of DNA, which provides, in part, as follows:

(a) As used in this section, unless the context otherwise requires, "DNA analysis" means the process through which deoxyribonucleic acid (DNA) in a human biological specimen is analyzed and compared with DNA from another biological specimen for identification purposes.

(b)(1) In any civil or criminal trial, hearing, or proceeding, the results of DNA analysis, as defined in subsection (a), are admissible in evidence without antecedent expert testimony that DNA analysis provides a trustworthy and reliable method of identifying characteristics in an individual's genetic material upon a showing that the offered testimony meets the standards of admissibility set forth in the Tennessee Rules of Evidence.

(2) Nothing in this section shall be construed as prohibiting any party in a civil or criminal trial from offering proof that DNA analysis does not provide a trustworthy and reliable method of identifying characteristics in an individual's genetic material, nor shall it prohibit a party from cross-examining the other party's expert as to the lack of trustworthiness and reliability of such analysis.

Tenn.Code Ann. § 24-7-117

64. In *State v. Scott*, 1999 WL 547460 (Tenn.Crim.App.), involving mtDNA analysis of a hair identified as defendant's in a sexual assault case, defendant

complained the terms of the statute authorized the admission of novel scientific evidence such as mtDNA without a showing that the evidence was reliable. Defendant argued that the mitochondrial technique was not even developed until June, 1996, and that his case was only the fourth in the country in which this type of evidence had been admitted. The defendant unsuccessfully argued that the portion of the DNA statute that provided that the evidence was admissible "upon a showing that the … testimony meets the standards of admissibility set forth in the Tennessee Rules of Evidence" requires that the state show the evidence is scientifically reliable.

65. See the Mitotyping Technologies Web site at http://www.mitotyping.com/mitotyping/site/default.asp.

66. Supra, n. 63 at 139.

67. See Chapter 3, Hair Analysis, for a discussion of the use of mitochondrial DNA in contemporary forensic lab examination of hair shafts.

68. 256 Conn. 854, 776 A. 2d 1091 (2001).

69. 369 F. 3d 516 (U.S. Ct. App. 6th Cir 2004).

70. Beverly, at 523.

71. Beverly, at 528.

72. Beverly, at 528, at 529.

73. *United States v. Coleman*, at 966.

74. *United States v. Beverly*, at 530.

75. Also see, *People v. Mason*, 2004 WL 2951972 (Ct. App. Mich 2004): Dr. Terry Melton, the president and CEO of Mitotyping Technologies, a company that specializes in mitochondrial DNA (mtDNA) testing, testified that defendant's mtDNA profile matched that of the foreign hair found on the decedent's body and that 99.93% of the population of North America would not match this profile.

76. Beverly at 530–531.

77. Beverly at 531. See, Erica Beecher-Monas, *The Heuristics of Intellectual Due Process: A Primer for Triers of Science*, 75 N.Y.U.L.Rev. 1563, 1655 n. 535 (2000).

78. *Fed.R.Evid. 401*. "The statistical evidence at trial showed that, at most, less than 1% of the population would be expected to have this mtDNA pattern. Even an article critical of mtDNA stated the most frequent pattern applies in no more than 3% of the population. It would be unlikely to find a match between Beverly's hair and the hair of a random individual. The testimony was that, with a high degree of confidence, less than 1% of the population could be expected to have the same pattern as that of the hair recovered from the bank robbery site, and that Beverly did have the same pattern, and thus could not be excluded as the source of the hair. Finding Beverly's mtDNA at the crime scene is essentially equivalent to finding that the last two digits of a license plate of a car owned by defendant matched the last two numbers of

a license plate of a getaway car. It would be some evidence — not conclusive, but certainly admissible. We find the same here." Beverly at 531.

79. 160 Md.App. 531, 864 A.2d 1037 (Md. App. 2005).

80. State's evidence regarding chain-of-custody of glove found near murder scene indicated there was reasonable probability that glove, which contained hair sample placing defendant at scene, was in same condition when scientifically tested as it was when discovered by witness, in trial for murder.

81. Wagner at 1044.

82. Citing *United States v. Coleman*, 202 F.Supp.2d 962, 965 (E.D.Mo.2002).

83. Citing *People v. Holtzer*, 255 Mich.App. 478, 660 N.W.2d 405, 408 (2003).

84. During the motions hearings, Dr. Stewart testified that mtDNA evidence has been entered into evidence at trial a total of approximately 50 times, in 25 states. He also submitted numerous peer review articles that demonstrate the general acceptance of mtDNA evidence, none of which rejected mtDNA analysis as unreliable. Even the defense's expert, Dr. Jeffrey Boore, did not controvert the proposition that the process of mtDNA extraction, amplification, and sequencing is generally accepted as reliable.

85. Wagner at 1048.

86. Wagner at 1048.

87. See, Charles A. Linch, B.S., Davis A. Whiting, M.D. & Mitchell M. Holland, Ph.D., *Human Hair Histogenesis for the Mitochondrial DNA Forensic Scientist*, 46 J. Forensic Sci. 844, 850 (July 2001).

88. See, Alice R. Isenberg, *The FBI Law Enforcement Bulletin*: Forensic mitochondrial DNA analysis: A different crime-solving tool, p. 3–4, August 2002. For more information on heteroplasmy, see M.M. Holland & T.J. Parsons, Mitochondrial DNA Sequence Analysis — Validation and Use for Forensic Casework, 11 Forensic Science Review 22, 23–25 (1999) ("Heteroplasmy has the potential to both complicate and strengthen forensic identify testing, and must be taken into account.").

89. Wagner, at 1051.

90. *The Toronto Globe and Mail* reports the matching of the blood of a dog, killed along with his owner in a six-year-old murder case. Experts testified that blood on the defendant's shirt matched both that of the human victim and also that of his pet dog Chico. Experts testified to an 8 billion to 1 match with the dog's DNA. See 10/02/1999 GlobeMail; A10.

A similar finding was testified to in the case of a double murder in Seattle. Experts testified to a match of the victim's dog's blood, which had also been shot, to blood from the defendants' jackets. PE AgGen matched bloodstains on the two defendants' jackets and testified to a 1 in 350 million match.

In New York, a man was convicted of murder based in part on the hair from defendant's cat, which had been found on a jacket discarded at the crime scene near the body of the homicide victim. Experts at the National Cancer Institute in Frederick, Maryland, who had been studying cat DNA for years, testified to a 1 in 45 million match between defendant's cat and the jacket he had thrown away at the crime scene dump site. See, *Source News and Reports*, April 24, 1997.

In Canon Lake, Texas, investigators have used DNA testing to identify a dog believed to have mauled a 77-year-old woman. Http://www.reporternews. com/texas/dogdna0515.html.

91. See, *State v. Bogan*, 183 Ariz. 506, 905 P.2d 515 (1995) (results of randomly amplified polymorphic DNA [RAPD] testing of seed pods from paloverde trees were admissible and expert testimony declaring "match" between paloverde seed pods found in defendant's truck and paloverde tree growing at crime scene was admissible).

92. See, George Sensabaugh and D.H. Kaye, *Non-human DNA Evidence*, 38 *Jurimetrics J.* 1 (1998) for an extensive discussion of this general issue.

93. See the following Web sites that address varying aspects of important animal DNA issues. These sites are important for obtaining nonhuman DNA in cases of mammals:

Wildlife Forensic DNA Lab, http://www.trentu.ca/academic/forensic/labservices. html.

Breaking the Canine Genetic Code, http://www.canismajor.com/dog/gencode. html.

The Dog Genome Project, http://www.mendel.berkeley.edu/dog.html.

Also see, Korpelainen, H., Virtanen, V., DNA fingerprinting of mosses, 48 JFS (4) (2003).

Abstract: Our study introduces the use of DNA fingerprinting of clonal plants in combination with phylogenetic and vegetation studies as a prospective forensic tool in criminal investigations. In this homicide case, the bryophyte species found on the suspects were identified as *Brachythecium albicans*, *Calliergonella lindbergii*, and *Ceratodon purpureus*. Colonies of all three species occurred at the crime site. DNA fingerprinting analyses were conducted for *B. albicans* and *C. lindbergii*, which were expected to reproduce mainly clonally, unlike *C. purpureus*, and included samples found on the suspects and samples collected from the crime site and other locations. It was concluded that *B. albicans* found on the suspects was likely to originate from the crime scene and that the sample of *C. lindbergii* may also have originated from the same site.

94. *Joy Halverson,*[1] *D.V.M and Christopher Basten,*[2] *Ph.D.,* A PCR Multiplex and Database for Forensic DNA Identication of Dogs, 50 *J. Forensic Sci.* (2) 207 (2005)

95. Also see, *People v. Slover*, 339 Ill.App.3d 1086 (Ill.App. 4th 2003). In this case, involving the release of trial exhibits for scientific testing during an appeal, the state established in its motion that Dr. Joy Halverson indicated she was

capable of performing and willing to perform DNA testing on animal hairs from defense exhibits and cat hairs from Mary Slover's former residence. The state alleged the testing would advance the interests of justice in the pending juvenile case and the determination of whether the parental rights of Mary and Michael, Jr., should be terminated. Specifically, the state alleged the evidence could point to Mary's connection with the Karen Slover murder or its concealment. Defendants, on the other hand, argued at the hearing that destructive testing would be prejudicial in the event of a retrial. However, the state noted the evidence was not large enough for a jury to assess, unlike a "big coat" or "bloody knife." Also, the state indicated the conclusions made after scientific testing could benefit the defense.

In its decision, the trial court found "good cause" for the scientific testing. The court also required as a condition of the scientific testing that a photograph be taken of any exhibits of sufficient quality to identify them.

96. See, The Innocence Project site, at http://www.innocenceproject.org/.

97. 725 ILCS 5/116-3 (Appv'd 07/14/99). New York, the only state with a similar law, limits the type of post-trial forensic testing to DNA.

98. 81 Judicature 114 (1997).)

99. I81 Judicature 114 (1997), at 116.

100. See, Dissent, *Dedge v. State*, 723 So.2d 322, 324.(Fla. Ct. App. 1998).

101. Charles M. Strom, *Genetic Justice: A Lawyer's Guide to the Science of DNA Testing*, 87 Ill. B.J. 18 (1999).

102. O'Reilly, 81 Judicature, at 116.

103. 1999 WL 1087018 (Ga. 1999).

104. 1999 WL 1087018 (Ga. 1999), at *2.

105. 1999 WL 1087018 (Ga. 1999), at *3.

106. 24 So.2d 1 Ala.Crim.App., 1999.

107. 824 So.2d 1 (Ala.Crim.App., 1999).

108. Here, DNA extracted from vaginal fluid recovered from the victim's body and from Thomas' blood were compared to determine whether he could have been the source of the semen present in the victim's body. The DNA profiles from the vaginal fluid matched the DNA profiles from Thomas' blood. Statistically, the probability of finding an unrelated individual at random from the population who would match the particular DNA of the semen recovered from the victim's body was approximately 1 in 323,533,000 whites and 1 in 322,149,000 African-Americans.

109. 1999 WL 1087018 (Ga. 1999), at *26.

110. For cases characterizing DNA evidence as circumstantial, see, for example, *People v. Groves*, 854 P.2d 1310, 1315 (Colo.App.1992); *Greenway v. State*, 207 Ga.App. 511, 428 S.E.2d 415, 416 (1993); *People v. Stremmel*, 258 Ill.App.3d 93, 630 N.E.2d 1301, 1307, 197 Ill.Dec. 177 (1994); *State v. Spaeth*, 552 N.W.2d 187, 192-93 (Minn.1996); *Parker v. State*, 606 So.2d 1132, 1140-41

(Miss.1992). See also 1 Edward J. Imwinkelried et al., *Courtroom Criminal Evidence* § 308 (3d ed.1998) (noting that "many types of circumstantial evidence such as DNA tests are highly reliable"). Also see, *State v. Mosely*, 338 N.C. 1, 449 S.E.2d 412, 433 (1994), cert. denied, 514 U.S. 1091, 115 S.Ct. 1815, 131 L.Ed.2d 738 (1995), for a case reference to a DNA match as direct evidence.

111. In specific regard to chain-of-custody requirements for critical DNA evidence, the National Research Council observed:

Even the strongest evidence will be worthless — or worse, might possibly lead to a false conviction — if the evidence sample did not originate in connection with the crime. Given the great individuating potential of DNA evidence and the relative ease with which it can be mishandled or manipulated by the careless or the unscrupulous, the integrity of the chain-of-custody is of paramount importance.

National Research Council, The Evaluation of Forensic DNA Evidence 25 (1996).

Also see, *State v. Morel*, 676 A.2d 1347, 1356 (R.I. 1996) ("[I]n the preservation and testing of DNA evidence, careful attention and proper handling of the crime sample by police and scientists are crucial in defending chain-of-custody issues and in ensuring that laboratory mislabeling and inadvertent contamination have not occurred. Reference Manual on Scientific Evidence, at 293 [(Federal Judicial Center 1994)]."); Sally E. Renskers, *Comment, Trial by Certainty: Implications of Genetic "DNA Fingerprints,"* 39 Em.L.J. 309, 316–17 (1990).

112. See, 1 Edward J. Imwinkelried et al., *Courtroom Criminal Evidence* § 503, pp. 134–37 (3d ed.1998).

113. 2 U.S.C.A. § 14135a. Collection and use of DNA identification, effective: October 30, 2004.

114. In this section:

(1) The term "DNA sample" means a tissue, fluid, or other bodily sample of an individual on which a DNA analysis can be carried out.

(2) The term "DNA analysis" means analysis of the deoxyribonucleic acid (DNA) identification information in a bodily sample.

(d) Qualifying Federal offenses

The offenses that shall be treated for purposes of this section as qualifying Federal offenses are the following offenses, as determined by the Attorney General:

(1) Any felony.

(2) Any offense under chapter 109A of Title 18.

(3) Any crime of violence (as that term is defined in *section 16 of Title 18*).

(4) Any attempt or conspiracy to commit any of the offenses in paragraphs (1) through (3).

115. 379 F. 3d 813 (9th Cir 2004).

116. Kincaide at 817. The court also noted that with passage of the PATRIOT Act, *Pub.L. No. 107-56, ß 503, 115 Stat. 272*, 364 (2001), acts of terrorism (as defined in *18 U.S.C. 2332b(g)(5)(B)*) and additional crimes of violence (as defined in *18 U.S.C. ß 16*) have been added to the ranks of qualifying federal offenses. *See 42 U.S.C. ß 14135a(d)(2)*.

117. Citing, See, *Illinois v. Lidster*, 540 U.S. 419, 124 S.Ct. 885, 157 L.Ed.2d 843 (2004) (upholding a highway checkpoint designed to enable police to question citizens about a recent crime); *Bd. of Educ. v. Earls*, 536 U.S. 822, 122 S.Ct. 2559, 153 L.Ed.2d 735 (2002) (upholding a program that subjected all students participating in extracurricular activities to submit to random, suspicionless drug testing); *Ferguson v. City of Charleston*, 532 U.S. 67, 121 S.Ct. 1281, 149 L.Ed.2d 205 (2001) (invalidating a public hospital's nonconsensual drug testing of maternity patients); *Edmond*, 531 U.S. at 48, 121 S.Ct. 447 (invalidating a roadside checkpoint designed to discover and interdict illegal drugs); *Vernonia Sch. Dist. 47J v. Acton*, 515 U.S. 646, 115 S.Ct. 2386, 132 L.Ed.2d 564 (1995) (upholding a program subjecting student athletes to random, suspicionless drug testing); *see also, Nat'l Treasury Employees Union v. Von Raab*, 489 U.S. 656, 109 S.Ct. 1384, 103 L.Ed.2d 685 (1989) (upholding suspicionless drug testing of certain U.S. Customs officials); *Skinner*, 489 U.S. at 634, 109 S.Ct. 1402 (upholding compulsory blood and urine tests of railroad employees involved in certain train accidents); *Griffin*, 483 U.S. at 879–80, 107 S.Ct. 3164 (upholding a warrant-less search of a probationer's residence).

118. *See Green*, 354 F.3d at 680–81 (Easterbrook, J., concurring); *Groceman v. U.S. Dept. of Justice*, 354 F.3d 411, 413–14 (5th Cir.2004) (per curiam); *Velasquez v. Woods*, 329 F.3d 420, 421 (5th Cir.2003) (per curiam); *Jones v. Murray*, 962 F.2d 302, 306–07 (4th Cir.1992); *Nicholas v. Goord*, 2004 WL 1432533, *2-*6 (S.D.N.Y. Jun 24, 2004); *United States v. Stegman*, 295 F.Supp.2d 542, 548–50 (D.Md.2003); *Padgett v. Ferrero*, 294 F.Supp.2d 1338, 1343–44 (N.D.Ga.2003); *United States v. Meier*, No. CR97-72HA, 2002 U.S. Dist. LEXIS 25755 (D.Or.2002); *United States v. Lujan*, No. CR98-480-02HA, 2002 U.S. Dist. LEXIS 25754 (D.Or.2002); *Shelton v. Gudmanson*, 934 F.Supp. 1048 (W.D.Wis.1996); *Kruger v. Erickson*, 875 F.Supp. 583 (D.Minn.1995); *Vanderlinden v. Kansas*, 874 F.Supp. 1210 (D.Kan.1995); *Sanders v. Coman*, 864 F.Supp. 496 (E.D.N.C.1994); *Ryncarz v. Eikenberry*, 824 F.Supp. 1493 (E.D.Wash.1993); *Landry v. Attorney General*, 429 Mass. 336, 343-48, 709 N.E.2d 1085 (1999); *Gaines v. State*, 116 Nev. 359, 998 P.2d 166, 171-73 (2000); *Johnson v. Commonwealth*, 259 Va. 654, 529 S.E.2d 769, 779 (2000); *Doles v. State*, 994 P.2d 315, 317-20 (Wyo.1999); *In re Maricopa County Juvenile Action*, 187 Ariz. 419, 930 P.2d 496, 500-01 (1996); *People v. Adams*, 115 Cal.App.4th 243, 9 Cal.Rptr.3d 170, 180-84 (2004); *L.S. v. State*, 805 So.2d 1004, 1006–07 (2001); *People v. Calahan*, 272 Ill.App.3d 293, 208 Ill.Dec. 532, 649 N.E.2d 588, 591-92 (1995); *Cooper v. Gammon*, 943 S.W.2d 699, 704-05 (Mo.Ct.App.1997); *Surge*, 94 P.3d 345, 2004 WL 1551561, *7 (Wash.Ct.App. July 12, 2004).

119. Kincaid at 839.

120. Also see, *United States v. Sczubelek*, 2005 WL 638158 (3rd Cir. Ct. App. 2005) (The court concluded that under Fourth Amendment reasonableness standard for analyzing the constitutionality of government searches and seizures, the collection of DNA samples from individuals on supervised release is constitutional. The government's interest in building a DNA database for identification purposes, similar to its interest in maintaining fingerprint records, outweighed the minimal intrusion into a criminal offender's diminished expectation of privacy.)

For similar results in a case involving a California state statute, see, *People v. Meinz*, 2005 WL 67092 (Ca Ct. App. 2005).

121. 2005 WL 524900 (Ct. App. WI 2005).

122. 2005 WL 524900 (Ct. App. WI 2005), at para. 6–7.

123. 2005 WL 524900 (Ct. App. WI 2005), at para. 7–8.

124. 2005 WL 524900 (Ct. App. WI 2005), at para. 34. Also see, See, Comment: Meeting the Statute or Beating It: Using "John Doe" Indictments Based on DNA to Meet the Statute of Limitations, Meredith A. Bieber, 150 *U.Pa.L. Rev.* 1079 (2002); Note: Using DNA Profiles To Obtain "John Doe" Arrest Warrants And Indictments, Frank B. Ulmer, 58 *Wash.&Lee L.Rev.* 1585 (2001).

125. See, http://www.ojp.usdoj.gov/nij/pubs-sum/183697.htm.

Forensic Anthropology and Entomology

Full fathom five thy father lies,
Of his bones are coral made;
Those are pearls that were his eyes:
Nothing of him that doth fade
But doth suffer a sea change
Into something rich and strange.

Shakespeare, The Tempest, Act I, Sc. 2.

I. Introduction

This chapter addresses the significant contributions made to the criminal justice system by the academic disciplines of anthropology and entomology. The theory and methods developed by scholars in these two fields have provided consistent and ongoing aid in the identification of the remains of homicide victims and in narrowing the range of time-of-death determinations.[1] The analysis of human remains to reveal our cultural antecedents can also reveal much about the identity or general profiles of unidentified remains. The close study of the universe of insect species can be narrowed to species that consistently accompany the deterioration of the human body and provide investigative timelines of often decisive value to the state and defendant alike. The principles and practice of these two academic subjects are used in the fields of forensic anthropology and forensic entomology on a regular basis in the investigation and trial of criminal cases.

II. Forensic Anthropology

As in the anticipated use of any forensic discipline, lawyers need to be aware of many discrete aspects of forensic anthropology. The basic question of just what forensic anthropology can or cannot do as an aid to criminal investigation must be ascertained.[2] This is especially important with forensic disciplines such as forensic anthropology and forensic entomology, which are both academic, university-based, sciences where the forensic aspects are not the major focus or *raison d'etre* for its study. There is much to know in these two fields that have little to do with the identification of human remains or estimating a time of death.

How does a forensic anthropologist differ from a university anthropologist not associated with criminal investigations? Is the fact that prominent practitioners in this field are typically university professors of any real consequence? It is important to understand that here, as in all other forensic sciences or disciplines, opinion statements come in the same *class or individualistic* forms. Some central, basic investigative questions that may be readily answered by forensic anthropologists examining human skeletal remains follow:

Is it a bone at all, as opposed to plastics or tree roots? Is it a human as opposed to animal bone? What bones are there from a total of 100% of the human skeletal structure and why those if less than the total? Are missing bones the result of animal scavengers or human agency? Are the bones of more than one person present? If so, is there any indication of the length of time all of such bones have been there? What is the sex? What is the age range? What is the left- or right-handed status? What is the general type of build? What are the distinguishing dental traits? Does there appear to be a history of bone injuries? Is there any indication of disease processes? Finally, can experts pinpoint the racial characteristics of the person as claimed by forensic hair analysts?[3]

A relatively new field utilized by investigators that is a staple of anthropological research is that of cranial and facial reconstruction techniques used to identify an individual from a skull.[4] Given the massive deaths in contemporary wars, forensic anthropology has once again been challenged to aid in the identification of war crimes.[5]

A number of excellent scholarly[6] and popular books[7] and articles devoted to the study of various levels and subdisciplines in the field of forensic anthropology are available to make interesting reading or required examination for lawyers increasingly involved in the use of forensic anthropological techniques, in the investigation and prosecution of a homicide. Excellent and comprehensive Web sites devoted to anthropology proper and to the field of forensic anthropology are also appearing with regularity.[8]

III. Forensic Anthropology Cases

The primary uses of anthropology in the investigation of crime has been in the identification and number of individuals associated with unidentified human remains. Given the prestigious pedigree of anthropology and the rigorous schooling and field work associated with this discipline, there are few cases addressing any significant qualification issues with respect to academic anthropologists. However, as new techniques or theories emerge in the academy, foundational issues will follow the professors to the courtroom.

In *Commonwealth v. Baker*, a 2003 Massachusetts case,[9] defendant was convicted of the first-degree murder of his seven-month old son. The Commonwealth's theory at trial was that the defendant fatally injured his child Dymitris by smashing his head into the wall (or walls) of the apartment.

Prior to trial, the defendant's trial counsel had sought, and received, funds for the purpose of retaining a mechanical engineer to conduct an independent examination of the wall and assess the validity of the Commonwealth's anticipated theory of the wall as the murder weapon. The order for those funds, however, was rescinded by a judge (not the trial judge), over objection, during a hearing on the defendant's motion to continue the case to allow his experts sufficient time to make their findings and conclusions. The judge's rescission order came after the prosecutor stated to the judge that the Commonwealth had "no intention of specifying that the baby's head was smashed against a wall."[10]

As a result of the rescission of the order for funds, the defendant's trial counsel proceeded to trial without the assistance of any expert. He stated in his affidavit that he was surprised at trial when the Commonwealth actually presented evidence and argument with respect to the wall.[11]

An expert for the Commonwealth, Dr. Ann Marie Mires, a forensic anthropologist and the director of the Human Identification Unit at the Medical Examiner's Office, compared the size of a plaster replica of Dymitris' skull with the indentations in the wallboard from the living room and hallway. Dr. Mires opined that the size and shape of the indentations were consistent with the dimensions of Dymitris' head. Dr. Mires illustrated to the jury, using a doll as a model, that the indentations in the wallboard were consistent with having been "impacted" by the left side of Dymitris' head.

The use of models, such as the doll, generally lay in the sound discretion of the judge. Here, however, the doll that was used in the examination of the expert was, by all accounts, of dimensions much smaller than those of Dymitris and, thus, had the potential to mislead the jury. The defendant's trial lawyer, therefore, was on firm ground when he objected to the use of the doll, because its dimensions did not approximate those of Dymitris, thus giving the jury an inaccurate impression. The questionable use of the doll by the prosecutor served to strengthen the court's conclusion that the trial was unfair.

The Commonwealth also introduced the single hair found in the indentation in the hallway wall. Although the jury knew, from the defendant's trial counsel's vigorous questioning of the Commonwealth's forensic chemist, that the hair had not been determined to be from Dymitris' head, the prosecutor strongly suggested otherwise in her closing comments to the jury:

> Ladies and gentlemen, this wall has the defendant's signature all over it. There is the first punch in the middle and there's the overlaying impression that Doctor Mires spoke of, the overlaying indentation consistent with the size, the shape, the dimensions of Baby Dymitris' head, this wall that held the tiny hair, the human hair that was imbedded in the plaster, this wall that right underneath there was fresh plaster in the carpet.[12]

The court noted that the single hair was the only physical evidence used by the Commonwealth to link Dymitris to the indentations in the wallboard. The reports and affidavit submitted in support of the defendant's motion for a new trial indicated that, had the defendant's trial counsel retained an expert to examine the hair:

- A microscopic examination of the hair (which would not have consumed the hair) would have had the defendant's trial counsel retained an expert to examine the hair.
- A microscopic examination of the hair (which would not have consumed the hair) would have revealed that its likely source was not a human head at all, but a human limb.
- Mitochondrial DNA analysis would have determined that the hair had not belonged to Dymitris.[13]

Dr. Peter R. DeForest, a forensic crime scene reconstructionist, and Dr. Terry Melton, a DNA specialist, participated in the investigation. Dr. DeForest examined the impressions of the indentations in the walls of the living room and hallway and the plaster skull replica of Dymitris head used by the Commonwealth at trial and concluded that, contrary to the testimony of Dr. Mires, there was no evidence either wall had been "impacted" by Dymitris' head. Also, after examining the single hair found in the wall under a microscope, Dr. DeForest said "it was more likely that the hair was a limb hair from the defendant than a head hair from [Dymitris]." Dr. Melton conducted mitochondrial DNA testing on the hair and concluded that the hair did not belong to Dymitris.

The court concluded that the defendant was entitled to a new trial, where the prosecution's pretrial position was that the prosecution would not present evidence at trial that the size and shape of the indentations in the wallboard of the defendant's apartment were consistent with the dimensions of his son's head, but prosecution did present such evidence at trial, and defense counsel, after learning that prosecution would present such evidence, did not request a continuance so that defendant could once again seek funds for an expert's thorough evaluation of the wallboard evidence.

The court also ruled that defendant's trial counsel was ineffective where trial counsel made no attempt to determine the accuracy of the findings and conclusions of Commonwealth's forensic, medical, or scientific experts regarding the single hair found in the indentation in the wallboard in defendant's apartment, which prosecutors asserted during closing arguments was a hair from the son's head, and counsel made no attempt to determine whether other available tests might have excluded the child as the source of hair or what risks those tests entailed.[14]

In the 2003 Louisiana decision in *State v. Wright*,[15] the defendant was convicted of second-degree murder of young woman. In April 1998, Rosalind Greenhouse, a 17-year-old female, was reported missing. Two years later, human remains found under a house were believed to be hers. DNA testing supported this assumption, although it was not conclusive. Rosalind was last seen entering an apartment where Mr. Wright resided. Defendant alleged that the state failed to establish that the victim was Rosalind Greenhouse, thus failing in their basic duty to establish the *corpus delecti*.

The court initially noted that independent proof necessary to satisfy *corpus delecti* may be either direct or circumstantial and does not have to go to every element of the offense; it need only establish the commission of a criminal act:

Mr. Wright claimed the state failed to establish *corpus delecti*. In other words, the state's only proof that Rosalind died from a criminal act was Mr. Wright's own uncorroborated confessions. However, the independent proof necessary to satisfy *corpus delecti* may be either direct or circumstantial and does not have to go to every element of the offense; it need only establish the commission of a criminal act.[16] Here, however, the court observed, all of the forensic evidence pointed to Rosalind Greenhouse.

Dr. Pat Wojtkiewicz, qualified as an expert in the field of DNA analysis, testified that his lab tested a tooth, an arm bone, and a reference sample Rosalind's mother provided. The latter was used to determine, through mitochondrial DNA, whether the bones could belong to a maternal relative of Mrs. Greenhouse. Mitochondrial DNA is not highly individual between persons; rather, as Dr. Wojtkiewicz testified:

It's only passed from the mother to the children. And this is primarily the type of DNA that's used to type skeletal remains or bones from ancient sites and so forth.... And its type is used for skeletal remains because it's a longer-lasting and more numerous a quality of that DNA. So typically, when we do skeletal remains, we'll do mitochondria DNA typing.[17]

Dr. Wojtkiewicz explained that the type of mitochondrial DNA samples examined in the present case has not been found in Caucasian, Hispanic, Asian or Native Americans.

Dr. John Verano, qualified as an expert in forensic anthropology, examined the remains found in the present case and concluded that the skeletal remains were consistent with an African-American female, approximately 16 to 20 years of age. According to Rosalind's mother, Rosalind's teeth were in perfect condition when she disappeared. This is consistent with Dr. Verano's testimony that he did not observe any cavities or fillings in the skull. He noted that none of the human bones showed carnivorous damage and that the head was partially mummified, both of which were indications that the body was not placed under the house right away. When asked if the death of the person to whom the skeletal remains belonged could have been accidental, Dr. Verano stated:

> I guess what I would say is that the circumstances under which the remains were found are highly suspicious and what I would say is that in my opinion it would be highly unlikely that someone died accidentally or committed suicide and ended up under that house without human aging. And my argument comes from the fact that that skull shows so much dry tissue that in my opinion it must have been kept somewhere protected from flies, protected from carnivores.

Dr. Verano further stated that he saw "human factors in manipulation of the body."

The use of cranial reconstruction combined with photographic overlays was the key to a murder victim's identification in *State v. Nyhuis*,[18] a 1995 capital murder case. Photographs provided by defendant and photographs obtained from his missing wife's immigration file were sent, along with photographs of two other missing females, to a forensic pathologist for overlay comparison with the skull. The pathologist determined that the skull was compatible only with the photographs of his wife.

A forensic anthropologist who specialized in identifying skeletal remains of unknown victims made a facial reconstruction from the skull. The anthropologist provided the Missouri State Highway Patrol with a photograph of the facial reconstruction. He also gave them an estimation of the victim's age, height, and weight, and informed them that the victim was an Asian female. After the Highway Patrol published the photograph, it received a phone call stating that the photograph resembled defendant's wife, Bunchee Nyhuis.

The state offered the skeletal remains to illustrate the wounds and to demonstrate how the victim was identified. The cause of death, the nature of the victim's wound, and the identity of the victim were all at issue. The skull and bones helped to illuminate these issues and were thus probative. The appellate court ruled that the trial court did not abuse its discretion in admitting the skeletal remains.[19]

In *State v. Bondurant*,[20] defendant was convicted of murder and arson. An excavation revealed burned human cranial fragments mixed with charcoal and burned soil. Dr. Bass, a forensic anthropologist, found seven cranial bone fragments that were large enough to make positive identifications. While the other bone fragments were too small to positively identify the area of the skull they came from, he was certain that they were human skull fragments. From studying the larger fragments, Dr. Bass testified that the bones appeared to have been broken before being burned, and that the irregular broken edges suggested that blunt trauma had occurred. He was more than 50% certain that some force had been applied to the skull before it was burned. Moreover, based on the thickness of six larger fragments that could be measured, Dr. Bass was 75% certain that the bones were from a human male, and he was 90% certain that the bones had been there one to 15 years. Id. at 7.

On occasion, human remains are subject to examination by forensic anthropologists long after death or burial has occurred, and nonetheless yielded dispositive information as to the existence of criminal agency. In *State v. Delgros*,[21] defendant was convicted of a double murder. On January 3, 1978, a fire broke out at the residence of appellant and Donald D. Morris, her husband. They lived in a mobile home with Christopher Styles, John Styles, and Edward Bridge, appellant's children from two previous marriages. Donald Morris and Christopher Styles were found dead, and the other two children were seriously burned, but they ultimately recovered from their injuries. Appellant did not suffer any injuries. After the blaze, questions were raised concerning the cause of the fire, but the County Coroner determined that because both bodies had been severely burned as a result of the fire, the deaths were accidental. The file was reopened in 1993.

Another witness noted that when he had viewed the bodies in the morgue, Morris appeared to be missing an ear. Even though the body had been severely burned, he noted the charred remnants of one ear but not the other.

Edward Bridge, Sr., who had a lengthy criminal record and who was confined to prison in Pennsylvania stemming from a rape conviction, was contacted by police and stated that he had witnessed defendant strike Morris on the head, knocking him to the floor. According to Bridge, she then obtained a knife, stabbed Morris four or five times, poured some liquid by the furnace, and then set fire to the trailer.[22]

On the basis of this information, the bodies of the decedents were exhumed. The state of Ohio contacted Summit County Coroner, Dr. Samuel Cox, and Dr. Douglas Owsley, a forensic anthropologist employed by the Smithsonian Institute, who conducted independent examinations of the remains. They both concluded that Morris had sustained multiple stab wounds to the back prior to the fire. Owsley examined the body and presented testimony using the actual bones during his presentation. However, at the conclusion of state's case, the prosecutor requested that the court admit the slides in evidence in place of the actual bones. After hearing the objection, and conducting an *in camera* inspection of the slides and the witness' proposed testimony, the court allowed the substitution. The court ruled that the substitution was appropriate, holding that the slides would be a better substitution than the actual bones themselves.[23]

On occasion, the use of statistics is combined with the tools of forensic anthropology to establish or assist in the identification of human remains. In *State v. Klindt*,[24] the defendant was convicted of murdering his wife and using a chainsaw to dismember the body. Joyce Klindt disappeared from her Davenport, Iowa, home on March 18, 1983, and on April 16, 1983, fishermen found a female torso lodged against a bank of the Mississippi River. The torso had been severed just above the navel and just below the hips. A pathologist testified that a mechanical saw, probably a chain saw, had been used to cut up the body. The state was faced with the task of identifying the torso as that of defendant's wife Joyce.

A statistician testified that the torso found in the river was more likely to be that of Joyce Klindt than any other person who had been reported missing in the area. Investigating officers had developed a list of all the white females who had been reported missing in a four-state area around Davenport as of April 16, 1983, the date the torso was discovered. This list, originally containing data on 17 women, was narrowed by eliminating those who had obvious identifying characteristics such as scars. Four missing women remained on the list, including Joyce Klindt.

Dr. Russell Lenth testified that, as a statistical analyst, he takes data or facts that are known and attempts to determine what is likely to be true by applying the mathematical laws of probability. He testified that he was furnished with data on the torso, including race, sex, age range, and blood type. He also considered the fact that the torso had borne a child, had had an episiotomy (a surgical procedure in connection with childbirth), and that it had not been surgically sterilized. Evidence showed Joyce Klindt fell within all of these categories. From other sources, Lenth obtained information concerning some of these conditions with respect to the other three missing women and determined the frequency of certain of these conditions among the general female population. Based upon the likelihood of the concurrence of those factors among the missing women, Lenth testified that the probabilities were over 99% that the torso was Joyce Klindt's rather than any of the other three. The court concluded that the statistical evidence utilized to identify the body was properly admitted.

IV. Racial or Ethnic Identification

Pinpointing the race of the individual's remains is instrumental in aiding identification in certain cases, but is still a controversial subject.[25] As noted by Pickering and Bachman in their recent treatise, *The Use of Forensic Anthropology*:

> It is important to recognize that of all the major biological variables, this one (determining race) is perhaps the most difficult and easiest to misidentify. For this reason, your consulting anthropologist may not always be able to determine the race.[26]

In *Pipkin v. State*,[27] defendant was convicted of murder. Defendant argued that his trial counsel was ineffective for failing to challenge the qualifications of witness Emily Craig, proffered by the state to testify as an expert on the race of the human remains recovered from the river. Her preliminary testimony demonstrated that she was a doctoral student studying under Dr. William Bass at the University of Tennessee in forensic anthropology, had a master's degree from the Medical College of Georgia and was slated to receive her doctoral degree in approximately five months. Her specialty in forensic anthropology was in the knee and shoulder, an area in which she had extensive training from working at the Houston Orthopaedic Clinic for 15 years.

Craig explained that she had spent the last three years researching a method to determine a person's race by measuring the end of the femur and the angle in the knee joint. In addition to being the topic of her dissertation, she had also written an article on that subject that had been accepted for publication. She stated that this area was not a new field of study, but rather a new method. Using this method, she testified that the human remains in this case were of a white or Caucasian person.[28] On cross-examination, Craig stated that she believed her methods had been generally accepted by the forensic science community. The conviction was affirmed.

V. Individual Identifications

In *Robedeaux v. State*,[29] defendant was convicted of first-degree murder, and was sentenced to death in a case where a woman had been beaten and dismembered. An examination of the skull and comparison to x-rays of the decedent were performed by Dr. Larry Balding, Medical Examiner's Office, and the famous anthropologist, Dr. Clyde Snow. The conclusion reached was that the skull was that of the decedent. They also examined the leg found at Deep Fork River and were of the opinion that the leg was that of the decedent. Examining the arm and attached hand found at Coon Creek, the doctors opined that it too belonged to the decedent. Dr. Balding testified that there was no way, from the three body parts, to determine the cause of death, but because of the evidence of dismemberment of the body, he believed it to be a homicide.[30]

In *State v. Cross*,[31] defendant was convicted of the murder of one Sharon Elise George. In 1991 hunters found a human skull, later identified as that of the victim, who had disappeared in 1982. State witness Joseph Norman testified that he met the defendant, who lived next door to his mother, in 1981 at which time defendant expressed jealousy of the victim, who was her ex-husband's girlfriend. She eventually solicited him to arrange for the murder of the victim, which was accomplished. The victim's ex-husband identified a picture of the victim, who had a chipped tooth and was wearing a brown belt with white lacing.

Dr. William Bass testified that he was a professor and director of the Forensic Anthropology Center at The University of Tennessee, where he worked as a member of the medical examiner's staff identifying skeletal remains. The Tennessee Bureau of Identification contacted him to identify remains of a teenage white female with chipped teeth. He said that the body was clothed when buried and that he found a black belt edged with white stitching around the waist. He stated that after taking a bitewing x-ray, he identified the remains as those of Sharon Elise George. He said that x-rays of the remains revealed a fracture to the back of the skull. He stated that this skull fracture could have resulted from the victim's being hit with a large, flat rock. He said that he found lead pieces, which were most likely shotgun pellets, in the vertebrae. He stated that the fragmented cervical bones in the upper body indicated that the victim had been shot with a shotgun.[32]

VI. Forensic Anthropology: Photography

The use of forensic photography is a staple of crime scene investigation and of most of the forensic sciences routinely used in criminal prosecutions. The use of such photography is normally limited to visual support for the laboratory or field examination opinion proffered at trial. However, on occasion forensic anthropologists are asked to examine photographs of a suspect's face or other body part to effect an identification of such person as the perpetrator of a crime.

In *United States v. Dorsey*,[33] defendant was convicted of bank robbery arising out of two robberies of two institutions allegedly robbed by defendant. In both cases surveillance photos were available. The FBI showed a bank clerk a photo array containing photographs of Dorsey and five other black males. Initially, she was unable to decide which of two of the six photographs portrayed the robber, at which point Special Agent Lane Betts asked her if viewing the bank surveillance photographs would refresh her recollection. After indicating that it would, bank clerk Habersack identified Dorsey as the man who robbed her. On the same day, the photo spread was also shown to Keeley, another eyewitness, who, after viewing the surveillance pictures, also identified Dorsey as the man who robbed the Signet Bank. At trial, both victim tellers made positive in-court identifications of Dorsey as the man who robbed them. The jury was shown both the photo arrays shown to the tellers, and numerous surveillance photographs depicting each of the two robberies in progress.

At trial, Dorsey presented a defense of mistaken identity, and in support of that defense, Dorsey sought to introduce the testimony of two forensic anthropologists who would testify that Dorsey was not the individual depicted in the Bank of Baltimore surveillance photographs. He argued that the district court committed reversible error by excluding the testimony of these two defense witnesses. Spencer Jay Turkel and James Vandigriff Taylor, both forensic anthropologists, were hired to compare the surveillance photographs of the bank robberies to recent photographs of Dorsey and photographs of the boots that were seized from Dorsey's house. Their report concluded that the person depicted in the Bank of Baltimore surveillance videos was not Dorsey. The district court ruled to exclude the evidence, stating:

> I am not so sure this is a recognized science such as a forensic chemist, or forensic scientist who does fingerprints, who does chemical analyses, who does handwriting; they are recognized. I think ... what we are doing here is comparing, is comparing some photographs. What we are really asking this expert to do is to tell the jury not to believe the witnesses in this case, because the witnesses in this case have already made their identification of the same evidence. They have said I looked at the photographs at the bank and I have been able to ID these photographs that belong

to Mr. Dorsey. And I think that becomes clearly a jury function as to whether they are or are not. They believe them, why should we need an expert to say that they are wrong? I don't believe an expert can usurp the jury function in that regard.... I don't believe that I would need it. He said he would conclude with a reasonable degree of scientific certainty. I don't even believe that is enough.[34]

The appeals court ruled that it was clear that the testimony to be presented by the two forensic anthropologists in the instant case did not plainly satisfy the first prong of Daubert — that is, that the evidence to be presented by the experts amounted to scientific knowledge.

However, the use of photographs by experts in forensic anthropology was accepted in the Supreme Court of Illinois' 1988 decision in *People v. Hebel*,[35] where defendant was convicted of aggravated criminal sexual assault and aggravated criminal sexual abuse. The defendant was accused of molesting and taking illicit nude photographs of overnight guests of his minor daughter. He was arrested after a photograph development store called police.

Defendant argued that his conviction should be reversed because the only substantive evidence against him was a photograph. The photograph in question (People's Exhibit No. 15) was found in a search of defendant's home. It shows a hand spreading apart a minor female's sex organ. The victim's parents identified her as the female in the photograph, based on identifying marks.

The victim's father testified that to his knowledge his daughter spent the night at the Hebel residence only once in the summer of 1984. He stated that the victim has identifying moles, freckles, or brown spots on her right buttock and on her right thigh. He identified People's Exhibits Nos. 5 and 6 as photographs of his daughter asleep in a bed, People's Exhibits Nos. 12, 13, and 14, as photographs of her buttocks and vagina, and People's Exhibit No. 15 as a photograph showing a hand opening her "vaginal cavity." Number 17 was an enlargement of No. 15.[36]

Gerald Richards, an FBI agent specializing in forensic photography, testified as an expert witness in the area of forensic photography. Richards did a side-by-side comparison of People's Exhibit No. 15 with known photographs, looking for folds or creases of the hand, scars, marks, and general characteristics. He found a number of fairly unique characteristics in common; however, he was "not able to positively identify both hands to the exclusion of all other people in the world." Richards did find numerous characteristic that "strongly suggest" the hands in the photographs are the same hand. He did not observe any differences that would suggest they are not the same hand. He said the hands in the photographs appeared to be those of a male.

Ellis Kerley, a professor of physical anthropology with the University of Maryland, testified that he specialized in forensic anthropology and, after questioning by the attorneys, he was declared an expert in that field. He compared the questioned photographs with the known photographs and photocopied one of the known photographs to mark for comparative purposes. People's Exhibit No. 26 is a marked photocopy *15 of People's Exhibit No. 22K illustrating points of comparison in red ink. Kerley found no points indicating dissimilarity. He found 22 points of similarity. In his opinion, the hand in People's Exhibit No. 22K is the same hand depicted in People's Exhibit No. 17. Kerley admitted it was "possible" that the hands in the known and questioned photographs are not the same hand.[37]

The court accepted the expert testimony as a solid basis for the identification of the hand in the photograph as belonging to the defendant:

> Based upon the foregoing evidence, we believe defendant was clearly proved guilty beyond a reasonable doubt. Expert testimony that defendant's hand is depicted in the relevant photographs is convincing. We see the similarities noted by the experts. Moreover, when the strong circumstantial evidence is considered, proof that it is defendant's hand in the picture is overwhelming. The photograph was found hidden in defendant's house. Apparently, he was the only adult male that had access to the victim while she was asleep. He had taken photographs of the victim nude earlier in the day.[38]

The importance of forensic anthropology to the investigation and prosecution of crime continues to be recognized. This has become especially and unfortunately a means of identification of victims and the prosecution of genocide in the wars and massacres of our new century.[39]

VII. Cultural Anthropology

Cultural anthropology, the study of religious and cultural beliefs, customs, and folkways in numerous cultures and world subcultures, has recently been utilized in criminal cases as a guide to determining behavior or the outlines of certain cultural aspects tangential to a prosecution. Cultural and social anthropology are growing fields and there is much to learn about the cultures of recent immigrants or religious converts that is increasingly appearing in the criminal justice system.[40]

In *People v. Jones*,[41] where defendant was convicted of first-degree murder for the beating death of his wife, the court held that his trial counsel was not ineffective for failing to call an amir or sheik or other expert to testify regarding defendant's Islamic faith and its sanction of wife-beating.

> We seriously doubt that anyone knowledgeable on Islamic teach-ings would have proved helpful to this defense. Had such an expert been found, had he explained the righteousness of defendant's conduct, or merely explained how defendant may have believed that his actions conformed to religious teachings, the expert would not have changed the outcome. The sovereign State of Illinois has a longstanding rule *692 of law that prohibits the engaged-in conduct. This society will not abide defendant's actions regardless of the religious beliefs that may have motivated them. If a religion sanctions conduct that can form the basis for murder, and a prac-titioner engages in such conduct and kills someone, that practi-tioner need be prepared to speak to God from prison.[42]

In *State v. Haque*,[43] defendant was convicted of murder and assault with a dangerous weapon. The Maine Supreme Court ruled that a psychiatrist's testimony that defendant was in a "blind rage" when he killed victim embraced an ultimate issue and was properly excluded, and that the testi-mony of a cultural anthropologist was properly excluded as irrelevant.

In January 1991, Haque left his home in Raniganj, India, to attend college in Lewiston. Soon after his arrival, Haque was befriended by Lori Taylor, a fellow student, who was married and living with her husband and daughter. The two began a romantic relationship, which led to an engagement. Prob-lems between the two led to relationship counseling. Shortly after Taylor called the relationship off, Haque stabbed her to death with a kitchen knife.

At trial, the defense argued that Haque did not form the requisite *mens rea* to be guilty of murder and that he was guilty of manslaughter, rather than murder, because he acted while under the influence of extreme anger brought about by adequate provocation. The theory supporting the defense was that Haque's traditional Muslim Indian upbringing, immigrant experi-ence, and psychological condition strongly influenced his perception of his relationship with Taylor and, eventually, the way he reacted to Taylor's ter-mination of the relationship.

The court noted the testimony of Dr. Bloom, the defense medical expert, who stated that defendant suffered from major depression and attention def-icit disorder. Bloom placed special emphasis on Haque's response to Taylor's statement that they were just too different, which according to Bloom, Haque interpreted as meaning that she saw him as being racially inferior to her. Bloom testified that as a result of the statement, Haque was in "a state of blind rage and it was in that state of mind" that he acted. The trial court excluded any testimony that Haque went into a rage.

The court also excluded all testimony by the defense expert, Dr. Caughey, a cultural anthropologist with an interest in psychological anthropology, who had conducted research into the experience of immigrants to the United States and how people manage multiple cultural traditions:

> During voir dire, Caughey discussed the various factors that affect an individual's transition between two different cultures and how those factors were relevant to Haque's experience in the United States. Caughey also discussed gender relationships in traditional Muslim India and how an understanding of that topic would help explain Haque's relationship with Taylor. According to Caughey, in traditional Muslim India there is no dating and relationships are expected to last for life. Caughey testified that given Haque's traditional Muslim upbringing, the "on-again-off-again quality" of his relationship with Taylor "must have been ... extremely difficult to manage."[44]

Haque contended that the trial court erred in excluding Caughey's testimony on cultural transitions because the testimony would have assisted the jury in determining whether Haque had the requisite state of mind to be guilty of murder. The court recognized that a cultural anthropologist or other expert in cultural norms may very well possess specialized knowledge that can assist the trier of fact in setting requiring in depth knowledge of foreign cultures and the impact of living in a new country.[45] However, the court stated, any such testimony must be relevant. Here, the expert's testimony had nothing to do with the important issue of the defendant's mental state:

> Dr. Caughey qualified as an expert in cultural anthropology, but was not qualified to, and did not, offer testimony as to Haque's state of mind. Although cultural differences may be relevant to a defendant's state of mind, Caughey's testimony was not relied on by Haque's psychiatric expert, Dr. Bloom. Moreover, Haque expressly disavowed any reliance on a cultural defense. Accordingly, the testimony of Dr. Caughey was irrelevant to any state of mind defense.[46]

The court concluded that the one area here where the testimony of the cultural anthropologist might be relevant would be the affirmative defense of adequate provocation, which might reduce murder to manslaughter, if the defendant demonstrates that he caused the death while under the influence of extreme anger or extreme fear brought about by adequate provocation.[47] Here, however, the court observed that the events that Haque contended provoked his extreme anger were Taylor's refusal to marry him, her desire to terminate their relationship, and her statement that "we are just too different." As mere words that ended a romantic relationship, they failed to so qualify.[48]

VIII. Forensic Entomology

Entomology is the study of insects, involving, among other topics, their biology, locations, mutations, and their control in relation to the world's environment. It is an extensive field with a worldwide network of university professors and commercial experts utilizing its findings in the areas of agriculture and other studies of natural phenomenon. Entomologists are involved in studying the reduction of harmful species of insects that destroy food, housing, plants, and clothing, or cause sickness in humans, livestock, and pets. Other entomologists study new methods to increase the growth and spread of insects that provide food (honey), pollinate crops, assist in destroying harmful insects, or are eaten as food by birds and fish.

More and more books[49] and Web sites[50] are available to the neophyte in learning about this important subject.[51]

Entomology is also a staple of the world of forensic sciences due to its significant contribution in resolving questions as to the time of death of victims or whether a death is the result of suicide or homicide. The arrival and departure of insects and their *indicia* have been proven to be accurate predictors of the relative time of death of a partially decomposed body. This primary use of this science and its value and general acceptance is consistently recognized in reported decisions. Given the centrality of time-of-death estimations in homicide cases where an alibi is claimed, it is no wonder that this context is so often the basis for judicial scrutiny. However, given the very nature of forensic entomological testimony, claims are bound to arise in regard to the gruesome nature of the photographs used to support the forensic entomologist's testimony.[52]

A recent example of the importance of entomology on time-of-death cases was presented in the notorious murder trial of David Westerfield for the murder of 7-year-old Danielle van Dam. The death was a crucial issue in the 2002 capital murder trial of her neighbor, David Westerfield. Westerfield, based on his entomologist expert's estimation of the time of death, proffered an alibi that he was alone on a camping trip. The victim was missing for 26 days before rescuers found her naked, badly decomposed body along a roadside. Prosecutors claim she was killed within the first couple days of her abduction. Westerfield's lawyers alleged that the state of her remains indicated that the defendant was already under police surveillance when she was killed and, therefore, he could not be the perpetrator. The defense called a pair of forensic entomologists who said insect evidence supported that theory. Prosecutors fought back with their own time-of-death experts. This case received extended attention from the media and spawned several Web sites tracking the entomological aspects of the testimony.

Court TV's extensive coverage of this trial, centered in time-of-death issues debated by rival forensic entomologists, can be viewed at http://www.courttv. com/trials/westerfield/. This Court TV special coverage in their Court TV Trial series is an excellent and fascinating look at the actual work of forensic entomologists on the crucial time of death issue. Coverage extends from investigation, trial, and sentencing. It is a unique opportunity to view testimony and photographs in this tragic case.[53]

Forensic entomologists David Faulkner, Dr. Neal Haskell, Dr. William C. Rodriguesz, III, Dr. Madison Lee Goff, and Dr. Robert Hall provided prosecution and defense testimony on the entomological bases for determining the time of the child's death, crucial to defendant Westerfield's alibi.[54]

IX. Entomology Cases

In *Seebeck v. State*,[55] defendant was convicted of felony murder and second-degree larceny. Examination of the area in front of the victim's house revealed that a struggle apparently had taken place there, because the victim's hat, bow tie, and camera were strewn about. Near the front door, the police found an area of matted-down grass on which there was a bloodstained brick, and from that area, there were drag marks along the right side of the house to the rear corner where the body was found. An autopsy revealed that the victim had suffered extensive injuries to the head, a fractured skull, a broken right arm, a dislocated wrist, four stab wounds in the back, and six fractured ribs. The cause of death was a depressed skull fracture with laceration of the brain, caused by an object such as the corner of a brick. There was considerable maggot activity on the victim's head and body.

Stephen Adams, an assistant medical examiner, went to the scene to investigate the circumstances of the victim's death. On the basis of his observations of the victim's body, the yard, and surrounding locations, Adams concluded that the victim had died two to four days before his body was discovered on June 24. Catherine Galvin, the acting chief medical examiner, who had performed the autopsy, examined photographs of the victim's body taken at the scene, inspected temperature records and viewed the actual scene.

She concluded that within reasonable medical probability, the time span between the victim's death and the delivery of his body to the medical examiner's office on June 24 was between two and four days. Wayne Lord, a forensic entomologist who had been consulted by the Office of the Chief Medical Examiner, concluded that the victim's death occurred sometime between the late afternoon of June 19 and the early afternoon of June 21.[56]

The defendant claimed in the trial court that there was newly discovered evidence regarding, generally, developments in the field of forensic entomology, and specifically, alleged changes in the opinion of expert Lord, who had testified as a witness for the state in the original trial. As the present trial court, "(t)he focus of (the petitioner's) claim as newly discovered evidence is that Lord's testimony at the (criminal) trial was crucial in establishing the time of death of (the victim) to be late morning or early afternoon of Friday, June 20, 1980, (that is, before the petitioner had left the Waterford area), but, since that testimony in 1986, he has given (an) opinion in subsequent homicide cases which differs entomologically" from the opinion expressed in that testimony.[57]

In support of this assertion, the defendant offered in evidence two depositions of Lord, taken on September 7, 1990, and on June 9, 1992, as well as two scientific papers through the testimony of William Kriniski. One of the papers was entitled *Nocturnal Oviposition Behavior of Blow Flies*, by Bernard Greenberg, published in 1990,[58] wherein Greenberg reports observing nocturnal oviposition, or laying of eggs, by blow flies. The trial court stated:

> Kriniski, Greenberg, and Lord, all entomologists, testified at the petitioner's criminal trial. Kriniski and Greenberg testified at the trial that in their opinion, from analysis of the stage of larvae on the (victim's) body, death could not have occurred before Saturday, June 21, 1980. Their opinions were based on their belief that nocturnal oviposition does occur. The (petitioner) did not offer (the testimony of Kriniski and the scientific papers introduced through him) simply to bolster Kriniski and Greenberg's opinion (expressed at the criminal trial) but (also to show that in Lord's deposition of June 9, 1992, he did not dispute Greenberg's observation of such nocturnal oviposition." Thus, the petitioner claimed that Lord's deposition response, when asked about Greenberg's study, constituted new evidence that Lord had now adopted Greenberg's opinion.[59]

The trial court found, however, that the petitioner's evidence did not indicate any material change in Lord's opinion.

The trial court had apparently found that Lord still disagreed with Greenberg, noting that, when asked about Greenberg's study at his deposition, Lord had commented, "if Greenberg said he saw oviposition at night, he believed it," and that Lord further testified that no other scientist had been able to duplicate such observations and that another prominent entomologist had found to the contrary. On the basis of those findings, the trial court concluded that the petitioner had failed to offer any new entomological evidence. Rather, in the court's view, insofar as the evidence indicated that the opinions of Lord, Greenberg, and Kriniski had not changed, the evidence was essentially the same as, and cumulative to, the evidence offered at the criminal trial.

In addition, the appeals court noted that the trial court had ruled that Lord's opinion given in 1986 was not, as claimed, crucial in establishing the time of death. After carefully reviewing the record regarding this issue, the appellate tribunal found nothing in the record to suggest that the trial court's findings and conclusions were incorrect and concluded that the trial court did not abuse its discretion in denying certification to appeal with respect to this issue.[60]

In *State v. Thibodeaux*,[61] defendant was convicted of first-degree murder. On Friday, July 19, 1996, the victim, 14-year-old Crystal Champagne, left her home at the Tanglewood apartments in Westwego at about 5:15 p.m. to walk a short distance to a nearby supermarket. Defendant was related to the Champagnes through his mother's previous marriage to Dawn's brother. Crystal was Defendant's step-cousin. After a search, Crystal's corpse was found on a concrete slab. She was naked, with her shirt and bra pulled up to her shoulders, revealing a red wire ligature wrapped around her neck. Her shorts and panties were pulled down around her ankles. Crystal's mother recalled that she had washed the clothes Crystal had on the previous morning before she took her home. Maggots and ants had invaded her body. Crystal's mother went and called the police, who arrived on the scene at 7:47 p.m.

Dr. Fraser MacKenzie of the Jefferson Parish coroner's office performed the autopsy on Crystal. He attributed the cause of death to asphyxiation by ligature strangulation.

Dr. Lamar Leek, professor of Entomology at Louisiana State University, testified as an expert in the field of forensic entomology. He examined the insect samples taken from Crystal's body and testified that flies will lay eggs on a carcass within a couple of hours, but will not lay eggs after dark. Therefore, he determined that the eggs were laid before nightfall on July 19, 1996, and calculated the age of the fly larvae (maggots) to be between 24–28 hours old at discovery.[62]

In *Commonwealth v. Auker*,[63] the court focused on the possible prejudice to defendants by the exhibition of maggots and other insects on the body of the deceased in conjunction with the testimony of forensic entomologists. In

Auker, defendant was convicted of first-degree murder and kidnapping, and received a death sentence. Robert Donald Auker was convicted for the murder and kidnapping of his former wife, Lori Ann Auker. The body was discovered on a hot day, June 12, 1989, by a young woman who was walking down a dirt road near the home of her grandparents. She smelled an odor, investigated, and saw a badly decomposed body clad in a jacket, jeans, and sneakers. She rushed back home and her family contacted the police. The pathologist, Dr. Mihalakis, testified that the cause of death was homicide, most likely as the result of between seven and ten knife stab wounds in the back and chest area.

Dr. Mihalakis further confirmed the approximate date of death through the use of an entomological expert, Dr. K.C. Kim, whose specialty was the classification and identification of insects and parasites of humans and animals. The court summarized Dr. Kim's testimony:

> Dr. Mihalakis collected samples of the various insects present on and within the corpse for analysis and Dr. Kim examined the insects. Dr. Kim testified that the presence and relative maturity of insects allowed him to estimate the approximate time of death He testified that different decomposition stages attract different types of insects. He also explained that ambient air temperature and physical site (open field, shaded locale, or aquatic area) also affect the rate of maturity of insects. In determining the approximate decomposition period, Dr. Kim utilized a climate report from the national weather service, description of the autopsy, and description of the scene where the corpse was discovered.[64]

Dr. Kim identified samples of the insects found on the victim. He was also shown autopsy photographs depicting a mass of insects on the body and in the body bag. Dr. Kim concluded that accounting for the average mean temperature during the time the corpse had been missing, the maturity of the various insects present and the stages of decomposition at which certain insects would be present, the body had been decaying 19–25 days.[65]

The corpse was identified as Lori Auker through dental records. Lori had been missing since May 24, 1989, and was last seen wearing clothing like that found on the corpse. Nineteen days had elapsed from the date of her disappearance until the discovery of her body on June 12, 1989. Defendant was connected to the crime by the May 24 film from an automated teller machine video camera and through strands of human and cat hair.[66]

Defendant alleged error in the exhibition to the jury of inflammatory photographs of the victim covered with insects. Both color and black-and-white photographs taken at the scene of discovery and at the autopsy were presented at trial. Seven black-and-white photographs of the body at the scene were presented to show the jury the unnatural position of the body in a secluded wooded area on a steep ravine and in a decomposing state. The autopsy photographs included color and black-and-white photographs. Thirteen color photographs of the stained, knifed clothing and one small color photograph of the insects in the body bag without the body were presented. Two black-and-white photographs of the insects on the body were also presented. The first black-and-white photograph was of a totally jeans-clad lower body from below the knees down to the sneakers. The other was of the body from the position of the sneakers so that the decomposition of the upper body was not clearly visible.[67]

The court found no error in the presentation of such photographs because they were necessary to support Dr. Kim's opinion on the implications of the presence and condition of the insects:

> The photographs of the body with insects were all black and white. They were presented to assist the jury in understanding Dr. Kim's scientific testimony about the presence of various insects and the use of entomology in determining the relative date of death of the victim.[68] As Dr. Kim testified, the approximate date of death could be determined by the presence of certain types of insects on the skeletal remains at that specific site and climate. Thus, the pictures helped the jury to understand and evaluate that testimony.

In addition to the necessity of the photographs to bolster Dr. Kim's opinion, the court noted that the trial court, prior to the presentation of the black-and-white photographic evidence, warned the jury of the nature of the photographs and limited the period of time for viewing them.

In *State v. Hart,*[69] defendant was convicted of aggravated murder and aggravated burglary, for purposely tying and leaving to starve to death a 90-year-old victim while committing or attempting to commit the offense of aggravated burglary. The case was reversed due to prosecutorial misconduct, in part, by displaying and focusing on disturbing evidence of the ravages of insect damage inflicted on Steffin's body over an extended period. Such evidence had been admitted only for limited purposes, and was inappropriately distorted as to its significance and reinforced by the use of photographs of the victim's corpse throughout the closing argument. While the time of death was an important fact in issue and was a proper subject of argument, the court ruled that the prosecutor's ploy, coming as it did immediately after urging the jury to contemplate a particularly horrid, lingering death, focused the jurors not on what the photographs proved, but on the feelings and emotions they evoked. The court ruled that while a prosecutor may use gruesome photos to illustrate essential elements of the crime to be proven, he may not use them to appeal to the jurors' emotions. The prosecutor's use of the photos, in this instance, the court concluded, further encouraged the jury to react emotionally and convict on matters not before the court.

Defendant argued that the trial court erred in admitting seven photographs into evidence. He claimed that the graphic photographic depictions of the decomposed and fly-ravaged body of Steffin were so gruesome, inflammatory, and repetitive as to influence the jury unfairly. The court ruled that the trial court properly admitted a number of photographs of the victim's body. The court also excluded at least six photographs of the corpse. Only four of the photographs assigned as error were admitted over objection. The photographs that were admitted were relevant, not cumulative, and were used to illustrate the coroner's testimony and the testimony of expert witness Stein.

X. Conclusion

The area of entomology is closely linked to the broader topic of forensic taphonomy, a related discipline that addresses the history of a body after death, including insect infestation. The leading text is Haglund, W.D. and Sorg, M.H., eds. Forensic Taphonomy: The Post-Mortem Fate of Human Remains (CRC Press, 1997). Also see, Haglund, W.D. and Sorg, M.H., eds. *Advances in Forensic Taphonomy: Method, Theory, and Archaeological Perspectives* (CRC Press, 2004).

Endnotes

1. See, Stewart H. James and John J. Nordby: *Forensic Science: An Introduction to Scientific and Investigative Techniques* (2d edition, CRC Press, 2005), Chapter 7, Marcella H. Sorg, Forensic Anthropology; Chapter 8, William D. Haglund, Forensic Taphonomy; Chapter 9, Gail S. Anderson. Forensic Entomology. This 2005 text has excellent overview articles, bibliographies, photographs and graphics.

2. See, Pickering and Bachman: *The Use of Forensic Anthropology* (CRC Press, 1997), at Chapter 3, What a Forensic Anthropologist Can and Cannot Do, p.15. Also see, Geberth: *Practical Homicide Investigation* (CRC Press, 3d ed., 1996), at 253; Fisher: *Techniques of Crime Scene Investigation* (CRC Press, 5th ed 1993), at 128. See also, Komar, D.A., Twenty-seven years of forensic anthropology casework in New Mexico, 48 *JFS* (3) (2003). A review of anthropological consult cases for the New Mexico Office of the Medical Investigator was conducted for the years 1974 through 2000. A total of 596 cases are summarized and information is presented on the sex and age of the individuals, season of recovery, depositional environment, body covering, time since death, perimortem trauma, postmortem animal activity, and skeletal element

recovery. Data presented in this study may prove useful in supporting expert witness testimony and generating future research models.

3. Pickering and Bachman, Chapter 5, Ten Key Questions, at 69.

4. See, Iscan, M.Y. and Kennedy, K.A.: *Reconstruction of Life From the Skeleton* (Alan R. Liss, New York 1989). Also see, Smith, S.L., Throckmorton, G.S., A New Technique for Three Dimensional Ultrasound Scanning of Facial Tissue, 49 *J. Forensic Sci.* (3) (2004). The authors report the development of an ultrasonic facial scanning technique that allows for the visualization of continuous contours without deforming surface tissues. Reliability of repeat measurements at landmarks is reported good, and individual tissues (skin, subcutaneous, muscle) can be distinguished. The authors conclude that the method is simple, reliable, less expensive and less time consuming than alternatives such as magnetic resonance imaging (MRI). It is applicable in both research and clinical contexts.

5. Pickering and Bachman: *The Use of Forensic Anthropology* (CRC Press, 1997). See their bibliography at pages 145-146.; Mehmet Yasar Iscan and Susan R. Loth, *The Scope of Forensic Anthropology,* Eckert (ed.): *Introduction to Forensic Sciences* (CRC Press, 2d ed., 1997); Geberth: *Practical Homicide Investigation* (CRC Press, 3rd ed., 1996), at 253; Reichs and Bass (eds.): *Forensic Osteology: Advances in the Identification of Human Remains* (Charles C. Thomas, 2d ed., 1998); *Human Skeletal Remains: Excavation, Analysis, Interpretation-Manuals of Archaeology Series No. 2* (Taraxacun, 2d ed., 1989); Burns: *The Forensic Anthropology Training Manual* (Prentice Hall, 1999); Haas, Buikstra, Ubelaker: Standards for Data Collection from Human Skeletal Remains: Proceedings of a Seminar at the Field Museum of Natural History (1994).

6. See, e.g., Smith: *Mostly Murder* (David McKay Company, 1959) [The famous autobiography of Sir Sydney Smith, relating his work as a forensic specialist in numerous prominent cases in Egypt and England during the early years of the 20th century.]; Maples and Browning: *Dead Men Do Tell Tales* (Doubleday, 1994); Manhein: *The Bone Lady: Life as a Forensic Anthropologist* (Louisiana State University Press, 1999); *Bone Voyage: A Journey in Forensic Anthropology* (University of New Mexico Press, 1998); Jackson and Fellenbaum: *The Bone Detectives: How Forensic Anthropologists Solve Crimes and Uncover Mysteries of the Dead* (Little, Brown & Co., 1996).

7. See, e.g., http://www.physanth.org/

The American Association of Physical Anthropologists

The AAPA is the world's leading professional organization for physical anthropologists. Formed by 83 charter members in 1930, the AAPA now has an international membership of over 1700. The Association's annual meetings draw more than a thousand scientists and students from all over the world.

American Journal of Physical Anthropology

http://www3.interscience.wiley.com/cgi-bin/jhome/28130

OSTEOINTERACTIVE:

http://medstat.med.utah.edu/kw/osteo/index2.html

[Human Osteology, Forensic Anthropology, Paleopathology, Histology] This important site also lists the sites and topics of upcoming conferences of interest to lawyers involved with forensic issues, such as the British Association for Human Identification (BAHID) http://www.bahid.org/; The Forensic Science Society, http://www.forensic-science-society.org/; International Association for Identification, http://www.theiai.org/; American Academy of Forensic Sciences, http://www.aafs.org. The site also lists the most recent articles published in leading jornals that focus on anthropological issues. See also, *Odontology and Anthropology Examinations, F.B.I. Handbook of Forensic Services* (1999), located at http://www.fbi.gov/programs/lab/handbook/examodon.htm.; American Board of Forensic Anthropology, located at http://www.csuchico.edu/anth/ABFA [AFBA Diplomate information and listing]; Universia di Pavia website, located at http://www.unipv.it/webbio/homepag1.htm [excellent and very extensive links to world anthropology and related sites].

8. 440 Mass. 519, 800 N.E.2d 267 (2003).

9. The prosecutor made this assertion, without any prompting, in response to the judge's question (directed at the defendant's trial counsel) whether a mechanical engineer was indeed necessary. The prosecutor also informed the judge that "[w]e are not retaining mechanical experts in this area," and "[w]e are not alleging that the wall is the murder weapon in this case. There are all sorts of holes in the apartment. One of them could or could not be consistent with the shape of the baby's head. But that's not the key to this case by any means." Ibid. at 525.

10. In his findings and order denying the defendant's motion for a new trial, the judge expressly rejected that portion of the defendant's trial counsel's affidavit in which he claimed surprise. The judge determined that the defendant's representation was not in any way ineffective or incompetent and characterized the defendant's trial counsel's performance as "effective as it could be."

11. Baker, at 528.

12. Baker at 800 N.E.2d 267, 276.

13. Baker at 800 N.E.2d 267, 276.

14. 839 So.2d 1112 (La.App 2003).

15. 839 So.2d 1112 (La.App 2003), at 1118.

16. Wright at 1117.

17. 906 S.W.2d 405 (Missouri Ct. App. 1995).

18. 906 S.W.2d 405 (Missouri Ct. App. 1995), at 408.

19. 1998 WL 120291 (Tenn.Crim.App. 1998).

20. 104 Ohio App.3d 531, 662 N.E.2d 858 (1995).

21. 104 Ohio App.3d 531, 662 N.E.2d 858 (1995), at 533.

22. 104 Ohio App.3d 531, 662 N.E.2d 858 (1995), at 533, at 536. Also see, *Armstrong v. State*, 958 S.W.2d 278 (Ct. Appeals, Amarillo, Texas 1997) where there was extensive testimony by forensic anthropologists as to whether the victim was stabbed with a knife. Two of these witnesses, Drs. Harold Gill-King and Randall Frost, testified for the State. The other, Dr. Steven A. Symes, testified for the defense. Doctor Gill-King is an expert in anthropology and forensic pathology and director of the Laboratory for Human Identification and Forensic Anthropology at the University of North Texas Health Science Center. Doctor Frost is a forensic pathologist with the Lubbock County Medical Examiner's Office. Doctor Symes is a forensic anthropologist and is an instructor at the University of Tennessee Medical School and is an Assistant Director of the Regional Forensic Center in Memphis, Tennessee.

23. 389 N.W.2d 670 (Sp. Ct. Iowa 1986).

24. See, Buck, T.J., A proposed method for the identification of race in sub-adult skeletons: a geometric morphometric analysis of mandibular morphology, 49 JFS (6) (2004).

    Abstract: The identification of biological race (ancestry) in skeletal material is an important aspect of forensic investigations. Results showed significant morphological differences between the samples and obtained cross-validation results of over 70% accuracy in identification of unknown individuals using the complete mandible. It is suggested that these techniques could provide a method for the identification of race in sub-adult individuals.

25. See, Pickering and Bachman: The Use of Forensic Anthropology (CRC Press, 1997), at 80.

26. 1997 WL 749441 (Tenn.Crim.App. 1997) [Not officially reported].

27. See, See, Rebecca Tsosie, Privileging Claims to the Past: Ancient Human Remains and Contemporary Cultural Values, 31 *Arizona St.L.J.* 583 (1999); C. Loring Brace, Region Does Not Mean "Race" — Reality Versus Convention in Forensic Anthropology, 40 *J. Forensic Sci.* 171 (1995).

28. 866 P.2d 417 (Ct. Crim. App. Ok. 1994).

29. 866 P.2d 417 (Ct. Crim. App. Ok. 1994), at 428-429.

30. 1999 WL 1076958 (Tenn.Crim.App.).

31. 1999 WL 1076958 (Tenn.Crim.App.) at *5.

32. 45 F.3d 809 (4th Cir. Ct. App. 1995).

33. 45 F.3d 809 (4th Cir. Ct. App. 1995), at 812.

34. 174 Ill.App.3d 1, 527 N.E.2d 1362 (1988).

35. 174 Ill.App.3d 1, 527 N.E.2d 1362 (1988), at 1375.

36. 174 Ill.App.3d 1, 527 N.E.2d 1362 (1988), at 1376.

37. 174 Ill.App.3d 1, 527 N.E.2d 1362 (1988), at 31.

38. See, Steadman, D.W., Haglund, W.D., The scope of anthropological contributions to human rights investigations, 50 JFS(1) (2004). This paper exam-

ines the participation of anthropologists in international human rights investigations between 1990 and 1999 by surveying four of the most active organizations, including the Argentine Forensic Anthropology Team, the Guatemalan Forensic Anthropology Foundation, Physicians for Human Rights, and the U.N.-sponsored International Criminal Tribunal for the former Yugoslavia.

39. See, Cultural Anthropology, the website for the *Journal for the Society for Cultural Anthropology,* located at http://bernard.pitzer.edu/~cultanth, and the Social/Cultural Anthropology Internet Guide, located at http://www.ualberta.ca/~slis/guides/canthro/anthro.htm, for information on and links to this extensive field of anthropology.

40. 297 Ill.App.3d 688, 697 N.E.2d 457 (1998).

41. 297 Ill.App.3d 688, 697 N.E.2d 457 (1998), at 692-693.

42. 726 A.2d 205 (1999).

43. 726 A.2d 205 (1999), at 208.

44. See, e.g., *Dang Vang v. Vang Xiong X. Toyed,* 944 F.2d 476, 481 (9th Cir.1991) (upholding decision in civil trial to allow epidemiologist to testify about women in the Hmong culture); *People v. Aphaylath,* 68 N.Y.2d 945, 510 N.Y.S.2d 83, 502 N.E.2d 998, 999 (1986) (reversing order excluding expert testimony on the stress encountered by Laotian refugees).

45. 944 F.2d 476, 481 (9th Cir.1991), at 209. Also see *State v. Girmay,* 139 N.H. 292, 652 A.2d 150, 152 (1994) (testimony of expert in Ethiopian culture not relied on by defendant's psychiatric expert in murder case involving Ethiopian defendant was irrelevant and properly excluded); *People v. Poddar,* 26 Cal.App.3d 438, 103 Cal.Rptr. 84, 88 (1972), reversed on other grounds, 10 Cal.3d 750, 111 Cal.Rptr. 910, 518 P.2d 342 (1974) (testimony relating to defendant's culture properly excluded as to issue of diminished capacity).

46. In this context, it should be noted that states vary considerably as to what categories of stress producing incidents may be considered under the idea of "adequate provocation."

47. Also see, *State v. Tenerelli,* 598 N.W.2d 668 (Minn. Sp. Ct. 1999), where defendant was convicted of assault, and ordered to pay restitution for the costs of a Hmong healing ceremony performed for his victim. The victim, Txawj Xiong, filed a victim impact statement and a request for restitution, including those relating to a traditional Hmong ceremony known as Hu Plig, which involves the sacrifice of live animals to heal the soul of someone who has been physically and emotionally harmed. After reviewing the testimony of the victim and a defense expert in Hmong religious ceremonies and the costs typically associated with them, the court concluded that the trial court was within its discretion in ordering restitution for the costs of Txawj Xiong's Hu Plig ceremony.

48. See, e.g., Haskell and Cates: *Entomology and Death, a Procedural Guide* (Forensic Entomology Associates (Spiral edition 1990); Haglund and Sorg

(eds): *Forensic Taphonomu: The Postmortem Fate of Human Remains* (CRC Press, 1996); Smith, K.G.V: *A Manual of Forensic Entomology* (Comstock Publishing Associates, Cornell Univ. Press, Ithaca, NY, 1986).; Geberth: *Practical Homicide Investigation* (CRC Press, 3d ed., 1996)[Chapter 9, Estimating Time of Death]; Fisher: *Techniques of Crime Scene Investigation* (CRC Press, 5th ed. 1993), at 439; Saferstein: *Criminalistics: An Introduction to Forensic Science* (Prentice Hall, 6th ed. 1998), at 22.

49. Forensic Entomology Pages, International site, is an extensive site covering world entomology sites, bibliographies, basic texts, and much more. This important site is located at http://www.uio.no/~mostarke/forens_ent/forensic _entomology.html; XXI International Congress of Entomology, located at http://www.embrapa.br/ice/central.htm; MSU Entomology on the WWW, containing a searchable database of over 700 articles, faculty publications, and important links, is located at http://www.ent.msu.edu/dept/; Iowa State University's Entomology Index of Internet Resources, a very comprehensive links to virtually every entomological area of interest, located at http://www.ent.iastate.edu/list; Colorado State University Entomology Page, containing conference meeting schedules, recent literature sites, links, and a picture gallery, may be located at http://www.colostate.edu/Depts/Entomology/ ent.html; American Board of Forensic Entomology, which contains texts on general background, history, case studies, and useful references to professional standards and membership, is located at http://web.missouri.edu/cafnr/entomology/ index.html.

50. See, e.g., Smithsonian National Museum of Natural History Entomology Department, http://entomology.si.edu/; Forensic Entomology Pages, International, http://folk.uio.no/mostarke/forens_ent/forensic_entomology.html [Good source for other entomological resources on this site. Also see, The World-Wide Web Virtual Library: Entomology (BioSciences), http://www. metla.fi/info/vlib/Forestry/Topic/Entomology/; American Board of Forensic Entomology, esp., Case Histories of the Use of Insects In Investigations [Wayne D. Lord, FBI], http://www.research.missouri. edu/entomology/, Iowa State Entomology Index Of Internet Resources, http://www.ent.iastate.edu/ list/ [Extensive coverage of a wide variety of insects].

51. See, e.g., *Amjur Homicide* § 422, Gruesomeness As Affecting Admissibility (2004).

52. Additional websites provide a variety of information about the case. A good one is maintained by Vance Holmes at http://www.vanceholmes.com/court/ trial_westerfield.html. Also see, http://folk.uio.no/mostarke/forens_ent/ bugsontrial.shtml, for additional transcript information.

53. Also see, *People v. Milka*, 211 Ill.2d 150, 810 N.E.2d 33 (Ill.. Sp. Ct 2004), where the defendant was convicted of felony murder predicated on predatory criminal sexual assault of an 11-year-old girl. Forensic entomologists testified as expert witnesses on behalf of both the State and defendant. Based on an examination **38 ***385 of maggot larvae and eggs collected during the

autopsy, the State's expert concluded that the colonization of maggots found on the body occurred on May 9, 1997, during the hottest part of the day, or between 12 and 4 p.m. Death preceded the colonization. Defendant's expert concluded that the colonization could have occurred as late as May 12, 1997.

54. 246 Conn. 514, 717 A.2d 1161 (1998).

55. 246 Conn. 514, 717 A.2d 1161 (1998), at 656-59, 557 A.2d 93.

56. 246 Conn. 514, 717 A.2d 1161 (1998).

57. B. Greenberg, *Nocturnal Oviposition Behavior of Blow Flies*, 27 J. Med. Entomol. 797, 808 (1990).

58. B. Greenberg, *Nocturnal Oviposition Behavior of Blow Flies*, 27 J. Med. Entomol. 797, 808 (1990), at 1173.

59. Also see, *People v. Reynolds*, 257 Ill.App.3d 792, 629 N.E.2d 559 (1994), where defendant, who claimed an alibi, was convicted of first-degree murder for the killing of his mother, Lealer Reynolds. Defendant's case consisted solely of the expert testimony of Dr. Bernard Greenberg, who was a consultant in the field of forensic entomology and had been studying maggots for 40 years. Based on his experience and a photograph of a maggot taken from the victim's body, Dr. Greenberg opined that the time of death was 1 p.m. on June 2, 1989, at which time defendant claimed an alibi.

60. 1999 WL 694726 (La.).

61. Also see, *Commonwealth v. Copenhefer*, 719 A.2d 242 (Pa. 1998), where a Commonwealth entomologist testified as to the victim's time of death. The defendant's expert gave conflicting testimony. Trial counsel eventually agreed to the Commonwealth's estimate because the defendant had an alibi for that time, therefore trial counsel was not unreasonable in basing the alibi argument on the Commonwealth's time of death.

62. 545 Pa. 521, 681 A.2d 1305 (1996).

63. 545 Pa. 521, 681 A.2d 1305 (1996), at 1311.

64. 545 Pa. 521, 681 A.2d 1305 (1996), at 533.

65. Human hairs later found in the Celebrity's upper door seal and from the door jamb were similar to those of Lori Auker. Hairs presumably on Lori's body from Lori's cats were found in the trunk and on appellant's Velcro splint.

66. 545 Pa. 521, 681 A.2d 1305 (1996), at 545.

67. 545 Pa. 521, 681 A.2d 1305 (1996), at 546.

68. 94 Ohio App.3d 665, 641 N.E.2d 755 (1994).

69. 94 Ohio App.3d 665, 641 N.E.2d 755 (1994), at 764. Also see, *Coe v. Bell*, 161 F.3d 320 (6th Cir. 1998), where defendant was convicted of a rape and murder. The court ruled that the entomological evidence that defendant now marshaled (refuting the prosecution's asserted time of death based on the extent of insect infestation on Medlin's corpse) did not seem to have been such an obvious or common part of a defense in the time and place of Coe's trial that counsel was ineffective for neglecting it.

Epilogue

12

And indeed, most of the Law Books extant, if not all, (setting aside the Reports) are nothing else but Collections out of others. This I speak, not in Derogation of them, in the least; for as tis equally, if not more laborious, for tis full as glorious, judicially to cull Authentick Cases out of the Volumes of the Law (where so many are no Law) and rightfully place them in a particular Treatise, as tis to report the Judgements and resolutions from the Mouth of the Court... Than which Benefit I know not whether any Man can ever imagine another, either to Lawyers more grateful, or to the Commonwealth more profitable, or for the Illustration of Divine Honor more fit. For with the least Labour, a small Price, and little Time, they present you with those Resolutions and Judgements which lie scattered in the Voluminous Books of the Law; which would otherwise cost much Time, Pains, and Charges to find out.

Giles Duncombe: Trials Per Pais, or the Law of England Concerning Juries by Nisi Prius (1725)

This book has attempted to set out the general framework of the ongoing use of forensic evidence in the criminal justice system. Forensic evidence, simply stated, is a body of factual material generated by a large body of forensic sciences to serve as evidence in criminal prosecutions. Due to the scientific bases of the processes used to generate any such testimony by forensic experts, each of the forensic sciences must continue to justify the basis for any class or individual-characteristic linkage testimony proffered in a case. As evidenced by the recent rejection of earprint evidence and the ready acceptance of lip-print testimony, discussed in Chapter 8, the challenge to the claims of the forensic sciences continues unabated.

The areas of forensic science addressed here at length — hair, fiber, ballistics, and tool marks, soil, glass and paint, footwear and tire impressions, fingerprints, blood spatter, DNA, and forensic anthropology and entomology — are the staple fare of appellate tribunals in state and federal courts.

For that reason, and because of the concomitant importance of them in the daily work of the players in the criminal justice system, they have been chosen for extended coverage.

The goal of this present volume has been to provide a comprehensive, but not unwieldy, single volume, setting out the general lines of the judicial perspective on the use of forensic science in American courts. The number of appellate decisions, not to mention statutory measures addressing the forensic sciences analyzed here, will yield an equal or increased volume of new decisions that will need to be found, analyzed, and classified.

The cases discussed have primarily served to acquaint the reader with the ongoing practice of forensic science and forensic evidence in American courts. The number of cases actually denying the scientific reliability or general acceptance are few and far between. Working lawyers and students will benefit by the numerous examples of the forensic evidence processes.

The author recognizes that an equal amount of attention could be given to vast areas of highly specialized areas of forensic science, such as forensic pathology, forensic toxicology, or forensic odontology. Also left out are lengthy studies of the development of laser technology, image-digitalization processes, voice-analysis technology, handwriting and computer-generated document analysis, and many subjects that will be the main concern of the future. Entire areas of what are often referred to as the *soft sciences* have also been omitted.

Many of these essential disciplines, such as forensic psychiatry, forensic psychology, serial-killer profiling techniques, witness-credibility assessment expertise, coerced confessions expertise, and a number of other mind-science disciplines, merit focus. Those chosen here are hard-science-based, if grounded nonetheless in probability assessments in the end. Future editions of this book will address more of these essential subjects.

Using the information provided in the individual chapters of this book, hopefully, the reader will be equipped to begin efficient, practical work in the fascinating world of forensic science and forensic evidence.

Index